Table of Contents

1. Introduction
S. W. Nunnally
1

2. Earthmoving Materials and Operations
S. W. Nunnally
11

3. Excavating and Lifting
S. W. Nunnally
25

4. Loading and Hauling
S. W. Nunnally
49

5. Compacting and Finishing
S. W. Nunnally
77

6. Rock Excavation
S. W. Nunnally
95

7. Production of Aggregate, Concrete, and Asphalt Mixes
S. W. Nunnally
113

8. Paving and Surface Treatments
S. W. Nunnally
131

9. Compressed Air and Water Systems
S. W. Nunnally
143

10. Foundations
S. W. Nunnally
161

11. Wood Construction
S. W. Nunnally
183

12. Concrete Construction
S. W. Nunnally
213

13. Concrete Form Design
S. W. Nunnally
237

14. Masonry Construction
S. W. Nunnally

255

15. Steel Construction
S. W. Nunnally

275

16. Planning and Scheduling
S. W. Nunnally

289

17. Construction Economics
S. W. Nunnally

311

18. Contract Construction
S. W. Nunnally

325

19. Construction Safety and Health and Equipment Maintenance
S. W. Nunnally

333

20. Improving Productivity and Performance
S. W. Nunnally

343

Index

359

Pearson New International Edition

Construction Methods and Management
Stephens W. Nunnally
Eighth Edition

PEARSON®

Pearson Education Limited
Edinburgh Gate
Harlow
Essex CM20 2JE
England and Associated Companies throughout the world

Visit us on the World Wide Web at: www.pearsoned.co.uk

© Pearson Education Limited 2014

ISBN 10: 1-292-03935-3
ISBN 13: 978-1-292-03935-0

British Library Cataloguing-in-Publication Data
A catalogue record for this book is available from the British Library

Printed in the United Kingdom

INTRODUCTION

1 THE CONSTRUCTION INDUSTRY

The construction industry (including design, new and renovation construction, and the manufacture and supply of building materials and equipment) is one of the largest industries in the United States, historically accounting for about 10% of the nation's gross national product and employing some 10 million workers (references 2 and 3). Annual U.S. new construction volume has exceeded $800 billion in recent years. Because construction is an exciting, dynamic process which often provides high income for workers and contractors, it is an appealing career opportunity. However, the seasonal and sporadic nature of construction work often serves to significantly reduce the annual income of many workers. In addition, construction contracting is a very competitive business with a high rate of bankruptcy.

It is widely recognized that construction as a discipline is a combination of art and science. While understanding the technical aspects of construction is extremely important, it is also essential that construction professionals have knowledge of the business and management aspects of the profession. Close observation and participation in actual construction projects are very valuable in obtaining an understanding of the construction process as well. Thus, the author encourages those who are studying construction in an academic environment to take every opportunity to observe and participate in actual construction activities. An understanding of the topics presented in the following chapters will provide a foundation in the methods and management of construction.

While construction has traditionally been a very conservative industry, the increasing rate of technological development and growing international competition in the industry are serving to accelerate the development of new construction methods, equipment, materials, and management techniques. As a result, coming years will see an increasing need for innovative and professionally competent construction professionals.

Construction Contractors

Companies and individuals engaged in the business of construction are commonly referred to as *construction contractors* (or simply *contractors*) because they operate under a contract arrangement with the owner. Construction contractors may be classified as general contractors or specialty contractors. *General contractors* engage in a wide range of construction activities and execute most major construction projects. When they enter into a contract with an owner to provide complete construction services, they are called *prime contractors*. *Specialty contractors* limit their activities to one or more construction specialties, such as electrical work, plumbing, heating and ventilating, or earthmoving. Specialty contractors are often employed by a prime contractor to accomplish some specific phase of a construction project. Since the specialty contractors are operating under subcontracts between themselves and the prime contractor, the specialty contractors are referred to as *subcontractors*. Thus, the terms *subcontractor* and *prime contractor* are defined by the contract arrangement involved, not by the work classification of the contractors themselves. Thus, a specialty contractor employed by an owner to carry out a particular project might employ a general contractor to execute some phase of the project. In this situation, the specialty contractor becomes the prime contractor for the project and the general contractor becomes a subcontractor.

While the number of construction contractors in the United States has been estimated to exceed 800,000, some 60% of these firms employ three or fewer workers. Contractors employing 100 or more workers make up less than 1% of the nation's construction firms but account for about 30% of the value of work performed. The trend in recent years has been for the large construction firms to capture an increasing share of the total U.S. construction market.

FIGURE 1. Construction of St. Louis Gateway Arch. (Copyright© American Institute of Steel Construction, Inc. Reprinted with permission. All rights reserved.)

Construction Industry Divisions

The major divisions of the construction industry consist of building construction (also called "vertical construction") and heavy construction (also called "horizontal construction"). The distribution of total U.S. construction volume for a representative year is illustrated in Figure 2. *Building construction* (Figure 3), as the name implies, involves the construction of buildings. This category may be subdivided into public and private, residential and nonresidential building construction. While building construction accounts for a majority of the total U.S. new construction market (see Figure 2), many of the largest and most spectacular projects fall in the heavy construction area. *Heavy construction* (Figure 4) includes highways, airports, railroads, bridges, canals, harbors, dams, and other major public works. Other specialty divisions of the construction industry sometimes used include industrial construction, process plant construction, marine construction, and utility construction.

FIGURE 2. Distribution of U.S. new construction volume. (Source: Bureau of the Census)

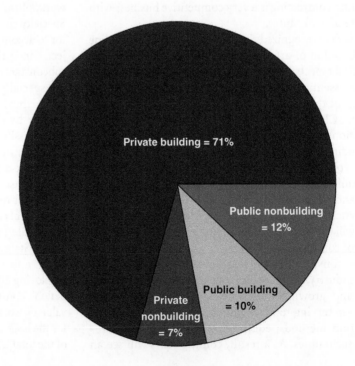

Private building = 71%

Public nonbuilding = 12%

Public building = 10%

Private nonbuilding = 7%

FIGURE 3. Modern building construction project.

FIGURE 4. Heavy construction project—Kennedy Space Center launch complex. (U.S. Air Force photograph)

2 THE CONSTRUCTION PROCESS

Project Development and Contract Procedures

The major steps in the construction contracting process include bid solicitation, bid preparation, bid submission, contract award, and contract administration. However, before the bidding process can take place, the owner must determine the requirements for the project and have the necessary plans, specifications, and other documents prepared. These activities make up the project development phase of construction. For major projects, steps in the project development process include the following:

- Recognizing the need for the project.
- Determining the technical and financial feasibility of the project.
- Preparing detailed plans, specifications, and cost estimates for the project.
- Obtaining approval from regulatory agencies. This involves ascertaining compliance with zoning regulations, building codes, and environmental and other regulations.

For small projects, many of these steps may be accomplished on a very informal basis. However, for large or complex projects this process may require years to complete.

How Construction Is Accomplished

The principal methods by which facilities are constructed are illustrated in Figures 5 to 9. These include the following:

- Construction employing an owner construction force.
- Owner management of construction.
- Construction by a general contractor.
- Construction using a design/build (turnkey) contract.
- Construction utilizing a construction management contract.

FIGURE 6. Owner-managed construction. [Either (a) or (b) or both may be employed.]

Many large industrial organizations, as well as a number of governmental agencies, possess their own construction forces. Although these forces are utilized primarily for performing repair, maintenance, and alteration work, they are often capable of undertaking new construction projects (Figure 5). More frequently, owners utilize their construction staffs to manage their new construction (Figure 6). The work may be carried out by workers hired directly by the owner (force account), by specialty contractors, or by a combination of these two methods.

Construction by a general contractor operating under a prime contract is probably the most common method of having a facility constructed (Figure 7). However, two newer methods of obtaining construction services are finding increasing use: design/build (or turnkey) construction and construction utilizing a construction management contract. Under the *design/build* or *turnkey* construction concept (Figure 8), an owner contracts with a firm to both design and build a facility meeting certain specified (usually, performance-oriented) requirements. Such contracts are frequently utilized by construction firms that specialize in a

FIGURE 5. Construction employing owner construction forces.

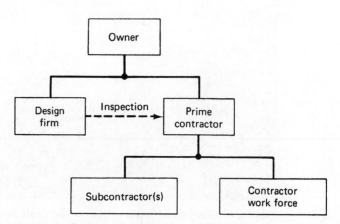

FIGURE 7. Construction by a general contractor.

FIGURE 8. Construction employing a design/build firm.

particular type of construction and possess standard designs which they modify to suit the owner's needs. Since the same organization is both designing and building the facility, coordination problems are minimized and construction can begin before completion of final design. (Under conventional construction procedures, it is also possible to begin construction before design has been completed. In this case, the construction contract is normally on a cost reimbursement basis. This type of construction is referred to as *fast-track* construction.) The major disadvantages of the design/build concept are the difficulty of obtaining competition between suppliers and the complexity of evaluating their proposals.

Construction of a facility utilizing a *construction management contract* (Figure 9) is also somewhat different from the conventional construction procedure. Under the usual arrangement, also known as Agency Construction Management, a professional *construction manager* (CM) acts as the owner's agent to direct both the design and construction of a facility. Three separate contracts are awarded

— Contractual relation

--- Management relation (owner's agent)

FIGURE 9. Construction utilizing a construction management contract.

by the owner for design, construction, and construction management of the project. This arrangement offers potential savings in both time and cost compared with conventional procedures, as a result of the close coordination between design and construction. However, opponents of the method point out that the CM typically assumes little or no financial responsibility for the project and that the cost of his/her services may outweigh any savings resulting from improved coordination between design and construction. There is another, less common form of construction management contract known as Guaranteed Maximum Price Construction Management. Under this arrangement, the CM guarantees that the project cost will not exceed a specified amount. Under this procedure, which entails a certain amount of contractor risk, the construction contract is also normally held by the CM.

3 CODES AND REGULATIONS

Projects constructed in most areas of the United States must comply with a number of governmental regulations. These include building codes, zoning regulations, environmental regulations, and contractor licensing laws, among others.

Building Codes

Building codes, which are concerned primarily with public safety, provide minimum design and construction standards for structural and fire safety. As the name implies, such codes apply only to the construction of buildings. In the United States, the Board of Fire Underwriters in 1905 published a *Recommended National Building Code,* which provided minimum standards for fire protection and structural safety. This code, later known as the *Basic/National Building Code,* published by the Building Officials and Code Administrators International, was the only nationally recognized building code for a number of years. Other major building codes later published include the *Uniform Building Code,* published by the International Conference of Building Officials, and the *Standard Building Code,* published by the Southern Building Code Congress International. In 1994 these three model code groups jointly formed the International Code Council (ICC) to publish a single set of model construction codes. Some of the International Codes since published include the *International Building Code* and the *International Residential Code* (which governs the construction of one- and two-family dwellings). A majority of the U.S. states and the District of Columbia have adopted these two building codes. The International Code Council has also published a number of other International Codes, including a plumbing code, a mechanical code, and an electrical code. However, most U.S. electrical construction is commonly governed by *NFPA 70: National Electrical Code,* published by the National Fire Protection Association under the auspices of the American National Standards Institute (ANSI).

Since the national model codes are purely advisory, a building code must be put into effect by local ordinance. While local building codes are usually based on the model codes, they often contain local modifications, which may be unnecessarily restrictive. Such restrictions, along with delays in updating local codes, result in increased building costs. Another problem associated with building codes at the local level is the quality of code administration. The lack of an adequate number of technically qualified building officials often leads to cursory inspections using a checklist approach and discourages contractors from utilizing new materials and procedures.

In most cases, a *building permit* must be obtained before construction of a building can begin. After a permit is issued, the local building department will inspect the project at designated points during construction. The scheduling of these inspections may pose problems for the contractor and often results in construction delays. When utilities are not available at the construction site, additional permits may be required for power plants, water wells, water treatment plants, sewage treatment plants or septic tanks, and similar facilities.

Zoning, Environmental, and Other Regulations

Although building codes apply only to building construction, many other regulations impact both building and heavy construction. Such regulations include zoning regulations, environmental regulations, safety regulations, labor laws, and others. Transportation construction (highways, bridges, airports, and ports) falls primarily under the jurisdiction of state transportation departments. These agencies are responsible for the design, construction, maintenance, and operation of transportation facilities. While much of the design and most construction is accomplished by private firms under contract to the state, the state transportation agency establishes design specifications, monitors design and construction, and operates and maintains the completed facilities.

Zoning regulations, which control land use, limit the size, type, and density of structures that may be erected at a particular location. Some typical zoning classifications include commercial, residential (with specified density), industrial, office, recreational, and agricultural. Zoning classifications are normally designated by a combination of letters and numbers. As an example, the R-4 zoning classification might represent residential housing with a maximum density of 4 units per acre. In order to construct a facility not conforming to the current zoning, it would be necessary to obtain a change in zoning or an administrative exception.

Environmental regulations protect the public and environment by controlling such factors as water usage, vehicular traffic, precipitation runoff, waste disposal, and preservation of beaches and wetlands. Large projects, such as new highways and airports, waste disposal facilities, major shopping centers, large industrial plants, large housing developments, and athletic centers, may require preparation and approval of an *Environmental Impact Statement* (EIS) describing and quantifying the effect the project will have on the environment. The preparation of an EIS is a complex, time-consuming, and expensive task which should be undertaken only with the assistance of a professional experienced in such matters. If municipal utility services are not available at the project site, additional permits may be required for water treatment plants, wells, sewage treatment, and similar facilities.

Safety regulations are designed to protect both construction workers and the public. In the United States, almost all industries, including construction, are governed by the Occupational Safety and Health Act of 1970 administered by the Occupational Safety and Health Administration (OSHA). However, states are permitted to adopt more stringent safety regulations if desired. Construction safety is discussed in more detail in Section 5.

The construction profession is also regulated by a number of governmental licensing and certification procedures. Communities having building departments usually require construction contractors to have their professional qualifications verified by licensing or certification. This may be done at the local level or by the state. State certification or licensing often requires satisfactory completion of a comprehensive written examination plus proof of financial capacity and verification of character. A business or occupational license is also normally required of all contractors. In addition, bonding is often required of construction contractors to further protect the public against financial loss.

4 STATE OF THE INDUSTRY
Construction Productivity

U.S. construction productivity (output per labor hour), which had shown an average annual increase of about 2% during the period after World War II until the mid-1960s, actually declined between 1965 and 1980. During the same period, inflation in construction costs rose even faster than inflation in the rest of the economy. However, indications are that construction productivity again increased substantially in the 1980s and 1990s (reference 1).

Concerned about the effects of declining construction industry productivity in the 1970s on the U.S. economy, the Business Roundtable (an organization made up of the chief executive officers of some 200 major U.S. corporations) sponsored a detailed study of the U.S. construction industry. Completed in 1982, the resulting Construction Industry Cost Effectiveness (CICE) study is probably the most comprehensive ever made of the U.S. construction industry. The study identified a number of construction industry problems and suggested improvements in the areas of project management, labor training and utilization, and governmental regulation (see references 5 and 8). It concluded that while much of the blame for industry problems should be shared by owners, contractors, labor, and government, many of the problems could be overcome by improved management of the construction effort by owners and contractors with the cooperation of the other parties. Conflicting productivity data for the period 1979 through 1998 makes it difficult to determine whether construction productivity has actually declined, remained constant, or increased since 1979 (reference 9).

Some techniques for improving construction productivity and performance are discussed in the following sections.

Reducing Construction Costs

Some of the best opportunities for construction cost savings occur in the design process even before construction begins. Some design factors that can reduce construction costs include the use of modular dimensions, grouping plumbing and other equipment to minimize piping and conduit runs, incorporating prefabricated components and assemblies, utilizing economical materials (eliminating "gold plating"), and employing new technology. Injecting constructability considerations into the design process is one of the advantages claimed for the use of the construction management contract arrangement.

Some ways in which productivity can be increased and costs minimized during construction include the following:

- Good work planning.
- Carefully selecting and training workers and managers.
- Efficiently scheduling labor, materials, and equipment.
- Properly organizing work.
- Using laborsaving techniques, such as prefabrication and preassembly.
- Minimizing rework through timely quality control.
- Preventing accidents through good safety procedures.

5 CONSTRUCTION MANAGEMENT

Elements of Construction Management

The term *construction management* may be confusing since it has several meanings. As explained earlier, it may refer to the contractual arrangement under which a firm supplies construction management services to an owner. However, in its more common use, it refers to the act of managing the construction process. The construction manager (CM), who may be a contractor, project manager, superintendent, or one of their representatives, manages the basic resources of construction. These resources include workers and subcontractors, equipment and construction plant, material, money (income, expenditure, and cash flow), and time. Skillful construction management results in project completion on time and within budget. Poor construction management practices, on the other hand, often result in one or more of the following:

- Project delays that increase labor and equipment cost and the cost of borrowed funds.
- High material costs caused by poor purchasing procedures, inefficient handling, and/or loss.
- Increased subcontractor cost and poor contractor–subcontractor relations.
- High insurance costs resulting from material and equipment loss or damage or a poor safety record.
- Low profit margin or a loss on construction volume.

Such poor management practices, if long continued, will inevitably lead to contractor failure.

While the principal objectives of every construction manager should be to complete the project on time and within budget, he or she has a number of other important responsibilities. These include safety, worker morale, public and professional relations, productivity improvement, innovation, and improvement of technology.

The scope of construction management is broad and includes such topics as construction contracts, construction methods and materials, production and cost estimating, progress and cost control, quality control, and safety. These are the problems to which the following portions of this book are addressed.

Quality Management

It has long been recognized that in all construction projects steps must be taken to ensure that the constructed project meets the requirements established by the designer in the project plans and specifications. More recently, the terms *quality management* (QM) and *quality assurance* (QA) have been adopted to include all aspects of producing and accepting a construction project which meets all required quality standards. Quality management includes such activities as specification development, process control, product acceptance, laboratory and technician certification, training, and communication. *Quality control* (QC), which is a part of the quality management process, is primarily concerned with the process control function. Since the contractor has the greatest control over the construction process, it has been found that quality control is most effective when performed by the contractor.

Regardless of the procedures established, the construction contractor is primarily responsible for construction quality. Quality assurance inspections and tests performed by an owner's representative or government agency provide little more than spot checks to verify that some particular aspect of the project meets minimum standards. Contractors should realize that the extra costs associated with rework are ultimately borne by the contractor, even on cost-type contracts. Poor quality control will result in the contractor gaining a reputation for poor work. The combined effect of increased cost and poor reputation often leads to construction company failure.

In recent years, there has been an increasing use of statistics-based methods for quality assurance, particularly in asphalt and concrete pavement construction (see reference 3). While the details of such procedures are beyond the scope of this book, the following is a brief explanation of some of the concepts involved.

Since the results of virtually all construction processes are products which vary over some statistical distribution, statistical methods can be used for the following purposes:

- Ensuring that all elements of the work have an equal chance of being included in test samples.
- Verifying that test samples taken by the contractor and by other parties come from the same population.
- Analyzing the variations in the test results of material and processes sampled.
- Establishing acceptable levels of variation in sample results.
- Developing a payment schedule which rewards or penalizes the contractor depending on the level of quality attained in the constructed product.

Safety and Health

Construction is inherently a dangerous process. Historically, the construction industry has had one of the highest accident rates among all industries. In the United States, concern over the frequency and extent of industrial accidents and health hazards led to the passage of the Occupational Safety and Health Act of 1970, which established specific safety and health requirements for virtually all industries, including construction. This act is administered by the Occupational Safety and Health Administration (OSHA). As a result, management concern has tended to focus on OSHA regulations and penalties. However, the financial impact of a poor safety record is often more serious than are OSHA penalties.

The following construction operations have been found to account for the majority of serious construction injuries:

- Concrete construction, especially construction of formwork, placing concrete into formwork, and failure of formwork during construction.
- The erection of prefabricated trusses, precast concrete elements, and structural steel.

- The construction and operation of temporary facilities including scaffolding, construction plants, lifts, and storage facilities.
- Working from elevated positions resulting in falls.
- Construction equipment operations.

Construction managers should give special attention to the control of the safety hazards described above.

In the area of worker health, the major environmental hazards likely to be encountered by construction workers consist of noise, dust, radiation, toxic materials, and extreme temperatures.

Organization for Construction

There are probably as many different forms of construction company organization as there are construction firms. However, Figure 10 presents an organization chart that reasonably represents a medium- to large-size general construction company.

Reasons for Construction Company Failure

Dun & Bradstreet and others have investigated the reasons for the high rate of bankruptcy in the construction industry. Some of the major factors they have identified include lack of capital, poor cost estimating, inadequate cost accounting, and lack of general management ability. All of these factors can be categorized as elements of poor management. Such studies indicate that at least 90% of all construction company failures can be attributed to inadequate management.

Use of Computers

The wide availability and low cost of personal computers have placed these powerful tools at the disposal of every construction professional. Construction applications of computers are almost unlimited. Examples of construction applications of personal computers are presented in the end-of-chapter problems.

Perhaps the most exciting development in the construction application of computers is the wide availability of the Internet (World Wide Web) with its almost unlimited resources, along with electronic mail (e-mail) services. Equipment manufacturers are increasingly engaging in electronic communications with dealers and dealers with contractors. Contractors exchange information and data among projects and between project sites and the home office. Manufacturers are also providing online parts catalogs, as well as service and repair bulletins to dealers. Equipment warranty service requests are also being electronically processed. While some manufacturers' information is available only to dealers and not to contractors,

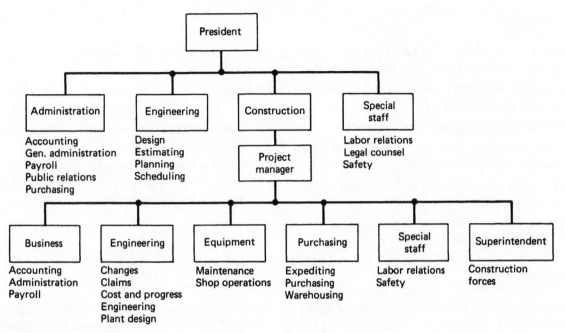

FIGURE 10. Representative construction company organization chart.

increasingly such data and services will become available to contractors. Electronic sales of new and used equipment and parts are also growing rapidly. In addition, much information of value to contractors is available on the Internet.

More traditional construction applications of computers include word processing, cost and time estimating, financial planning, planning and scheduling, project management, and equipment management, among others. With the increasing power and declining cost of computers, more powerful user-friendly construction software is becoming available almost daily.

6 CONSTRUCTION TRENDS AND PROSPECTS

Construction Trends

Some of the major trends noted in the construction industry in recent years include increasing international competition, rapid changes in technology, the wide availability of information via the Internet, increasing speed and ease of communication, and increasing governmental regulation of the industry, particularly in the areas of safety and environmental protection. As a result of these developments, the larger well-managed construction firms are capturing an increasing share of the total construction market.

These trends, along with the increasing use of computers for design and management, have created a growing demand for technically competent and innovative construction managers. With the increasing automation of construction equipment has come an increasing demand for highly skilled equipment operators and technicians.

Problems and Prospects

In recent years, industry problems of low productivity and high cost have served to reduce construction's share of the U.S. gross national product. This problem has been particularly acute in the building construction industry because the use of larger and more productive earthmoving equipment has served to keep earthmoving costs relatively stable.

Studies of international competition in design and construction have found that the U.S. share of the world's market has declined significantly since 1975. During this period, foreign construction firms greatly increased their share of the U.S. domestic construction market. Despite these trends, many observers are confident that the U.S. construction industry will, over time, regain its predominant position in the world construction market.

Although high costs have often served to limit the demand for construction, during times of high demand the U.S. construction industry has actually approached its maximum capacity. When the demand for construction again peaks, it is probable that new forms of construction organization and management as well as new construction methods will have to be developed to meet these demands. In any event, the U.S. construction industry will continue to provide many opportunities and rewards to the innovative, professionally competent, and conscientious construction professional.

In summary, the future of construction appears as dynamic as does its past. An abundance of problems, challenges, opportunities, and rewards wait for those who choose to enter the construction industry.

Problems

1. Describe the size of the U.S. construction industry and the distribution of contract value within the industry.

2. List and briefly explain three major characteristics of the U.S. construction industry.

3. Briefly explain the purpose of a building code.

4. Describe the principal methods by which construction of a facility may be accomplished.

5. Briefly explain the effect of construction productivity on the U.S. economy.

6. Are heavy (horizontal) construction projects more likely to be private or public projects? Explain.

7. What is construction quality control and whose responsibility is it?

8. Identify those construction operations which account for a majority of serious construction injuries.

9. What is an Environmental Impact Statement (EIS) and how is it prepared?

10. Describe three specific construction applications of a personal computer which you believe would be valuable to a construction professional.

References

1. Allmon, Eric, Carl T. Haas, John D. Borcherding, and Paul M. Goodrum. "U.S. Construction Labor Productivity Trends, 1970–1998," *ASCE Journal of Construction Engineering and Management*, vol. 126, no. 2 (2000), pp. 97–104.

2. Barry, S., ed. *U. S. Industry and Trade Outlook*. New York: DRI/McGraw-Hill, 2000.

3. Bernstein, H., and A. Lemer. *Solving the Innovation Puzzle: Challenges Facing the U.S. Design and Construction Industry*. Reston, VA: ASCE, 1996.

4. *Construction Dictionary*, 9th ed. Construction Dictionary, P.O. Box 6142, Phoenix, AZ 85005, 1996.

5. *Construction Industry Cost Effectiveness Project Report* (22 vols.). The Business Roundtable, Washington, D.C., 1980–1982.

6. *Construction Quality Management for Managers* (Publication No., FHWA-SA-94-044). U.S. Department of Transportation, Federal Highway Administration, Washington, D.C., 1993.

7. Frein, Joseph P. *Handbook of Construction Management and Organization*, 2nd ed. New York: Van Nostrand Reinhold, 1980.

8. *More Construction for the Money*. The Business Roundtable, Washington, D.C., 1983.

9. Rojas, Eddy M., and Peerapong Aramvareekul. "Is Construction Labor Productivity Really Declining?" *ASCE Journal of Construction Engineering and Management*, vol. 129, no. 1 (2003), pp. 41–6.

10. Stein, J. Stewart. *Construction Glossary*, 2nd ed. New York: Wiley, 1993.

EARTHMOVING MATERIALS AND OPERATIONS

EARTHMOVING MATERIALS
AND OPERATIONS

1 INTRODUCTION TO EARTHMOVING

The Earthmoving Process

Earthmoving is the process of moving soil or rock from one location to another and processing it so that it meets construction requirements of location, elevation, density, moisture content, and so on. Activities involved in this process include excavating, loading, hauling, placing (dumping and spreading), compacting, grading, and finishing. Efficient management of the earthmoving process requires accurate estimating of work quantities and job conditions, proper selection of equipment, and competent job management.

Equipment Selection

The choice of equipment to be used on a construction project has a major influence on the efficiency and profitability of the construction operation. Although there are a number of factors that should be considered in selecting equipment for a project, the most important criterion is the ability of the equipment to perform the required work. Among those items of equipment capable of performing the job, the principal criterion for selection should be maximizing the profit or return on the investment produced by the equipment. Usually, but not always, profit is maximized when the lowest cost per unit of production is achieved. Other factors that should be considered when selecting equipment for a project include possible future use of the equipment, its availability, the availability of parts and service, and the effect of equipment downtime on other construction equipment and operations.

After the equipment has been selected for a project, a plan must be developed to efficiently utilize the equipment.

The final phase of the process is, of course, competent job management to assure compliance with the operating plan and to make adjustments for unexpected conditions.

Production of Earthmoving Equipment

The basic relationship for estimating the production of all earthmoving equipment is as follows:

$$\text{Production} = \text{Volume per cycle} \times \text{Cycles per hour} \qquad (1)$$

The term *volume per cycle* should represent the average volume of material moved per equipment cycle. Thus the nominal capacity of the excavator or haul unit must be modified by an appropriate fill factor based on the type of material and equipment involved. The term *cycles per hour* must include any appropriate efficiency factors, so that it represents the number of cycles actually achieved (or expected to be achieved) per hour. In addition to this basic production relationship, specific procedures for estimating the production of major types of earthmoving equipment are presented in the chapters that follow.

The cost per unit of production may be calculated as follows:

$$\begin{array}{l} \text{Cost per unit} \\ \text{of production} \end{array} = \frac{\text{Equipment cost per hour}}{\text{Equipment production per hour}} \qquad (2)$$

There are two principal approaches to estimating job efficiency in determining the number of cycles per hour to be used in Equation 1. One method is to use the number of effective working minutes per hour to calculate the number of cycles achieved per hour. This is equivalent to using an efficiency factor equal to the number of working minutes per hour divided by 60. The other approach is to multiply the number of theoretical cycles per 60-min hour by a numerical efficiency factor. A table of efficiency factors based on a

12

Table 1. Job efficiency factors for earthmoving operations (From TM 5-331B, U.S. Department of the Army)

Job Conditions**	Management Conditions*			
	Excellent	Good	Fair	Poor
Excellent	0.84	0.81	0.76	0.70
Good	0.78	0.75	0.71	0.65
Fair	0.72	0.69	0.65	0.60
Poor	0.63	0.61	0.57	0.52

*Management conditions include the following:
  Skill, training, and motivation of workers.
  Selection, operation, and maintenance of equipment.
  Planning, job layout, supervision, and coordination of work.

**Job conditions are the physical conditions of a job that affect the production rate (not including the type of material involved). They include the following:
  Topography and work dimensions.
  Surface and weather conditions.
  Specification requirements for work methods or sequence.

combination of job conditions and management conditions is presented in Table 1. Both methods are illustrated in the example problems.

2 EARTHMOVING MATERIALS

Soil and Rock

Soil and rock are the materials that make up the crust of the earth and are, therefore, the materials of interest to the constructor. In the remainder of this chapter, we will consider those characteristics of soil and rock that affect their construction use, including their volume-change characteristics, methods of classification, and field identification.

General Soil Characteristics

Several terms relating to a soil's behavior in the construction environment should be understood. *Trafficability* is the ability of a soil to support the weight of vehicles under repeated traffic. In construction, trafficability controls the amount and type of traffic that can use unimproved access roads, as well as the operation of earthmoving equipment within the construction area. Trafficability is usually expressed qualitatively, although devices are available for quantitative measurement. Trafficability is primarily a function of soil type and moisture conditions. Drainage, stabilization of haul routes, or the use of low-ground-pressure construction equipment may be required when poor trafficability conditions exist. Soil drainage characteristics are important to trafficability and affect the ease with which soils may be dried out. *Loadability* is a measure of the difficulty in excavating and loading a soil. Loose granular soils are highly loadable, whereas compacted cohesive soils and rock have low loadability.

Unit soil weight is normally expressed in pounds per cubic yard or kilograms per cubic meter. Unit weight depends on soil type, moisture content, and degree of compaction. For a specific soil, there is a relationship between the soil's unit weight and its bearing capacity. Thus soil unit weight is commonly used as a measure of compaction. Soil unit weight is also a factor in determining the capacity of a haul unit.

In their natural state, all soils contain some moisture. The moisture content of a soil is expressed as a percentage that represents the weight of water in the soil divided by the dry weight of the soil:

$$\frac{\text{Moisture}}{\text{content (\%)}} = \frac{\text{Moist weight} - \text{Dry weight}}{\text{Dry weight}} \times 100 \qquad (3)$$

If, for example, a soil sample weighed 120 lb (54.4 kg) in the natural state and 100 lb (45.3 kg) after drying, the weight of water in the sample would be 20 lb (9.1 kg) and the soil moisture content would be 20%. Using Equation 3, this is calculated as follows:

$$\text{Moisture content} = \frac{120 - 100}{100} \times 100 = 20\%$$

$$\left[= \frac{54.4 - 45.3}{45.3} \times 100 = 20\% \right]$$

3 SOIL IDENTIFICATION AND CLASSIFICATION

Soil is considered to consist of five fundamental material types: gravel, sand, silt, clay, and organic material. *Gravel* is composed of individual particles larger than about $\frac{1}{4}$ in. (6 mm) in diameter but smaller than 3 in. (76 mm) in diameter. Rock particles larger than 3 in. (76 mm) in diameter are called *cobbles* or *boulders*. *Sand* is material smaller than gravel but larger than the No. 200 sieve opening (0.7 mm). *Silt* particles pass the No. 200 sieve but are larger than 0.002 mm. *Clay* is composed of particles less than 0.002 mm in diameter. *Organic soils* contain partially decomposed vegetable matter. *Peat* is a highly organic soil having a fibrous texture. It is normally readily identified by its dark color, odor, and spongy feel. It is generally considered unsuitable for any construction use.

Because a soil's characteristics are largely determined by the amount and type of each of the five basic materials present, these factors are used for the identification and classification procedures described in the remainder of this section.

Soil Classification Systems

Two principal soil classification systems are used for design and construction in the United States. These are the *Unified System* and the *AASHTO* [American Association of State Highway and Transportation Officials, formerly known as the American Association of State Highway Officials

(AASHO)] *System.* In both systems, soil particles 3 in. or larger in diameter are removed before performing classification tests.

The *liquid limit* (LL) of a soil is the water content (expressed in percentage of dry weight) at which the soil will just start to flow when subjected to a standard shaking test. The *plastic limit* (PL) of a soil is the moisture content in percent at which the soil just begins to crumble when rolled into a thread $\frac{1}{8}$ in. (0.3 cm) in diameter. The *plasticity index* (PI) is the numerical difference between the liquid and plastic limits and represents the range in moisture content over which the soil remains plastic.

The Unified System assigns a two-letter symbol to identify each soil type. Field classification procedures are given in Table 2. Soils that have less than 50% by weight passing the No. 200 sieve are further classified as *coarse-grained soils,* whereas soils that have more than 50% by weight passing the No. 200 sieve are *fine-grained soils.* Gradation curves for well graded and poorly graded sand and gravel are illustrated in Figure 1.

Under the AASHTO System, soils are classified as types A-1 through A-7, corresponding to their relative value as subgrade material. Classification procedures for the AASHTO System are given in Table 3.

Field Identification of Soil (Unified System)

When identifying soil in connection with construction operations, adequate time and laboratory facilities are frequently not available for complete soil classification. The use of the procedures described here together with Table 2 should permit a reasonably accurate soil classification to be made in a minimum of time.

All particles over 3 in. (76 mm) in diameter are first removed. The soil particles are then separated visually at the No. 200 sieve size: This corresponds to the smallest particles that can be seen by the naked eye. If more than 50% of the soil by weight is larger than the No. 200 sieve, it is a coarse-grained soil. The coarse particles are then divided into particles larger and smaller than $\frac{1}{4}$ in. (6 mm) in diameter. If over 50% of the coarse fraction (by weight) is larger than $\frac{1}{4}$ in. (6 mm) in diameter, the soil is classified as gravel; otherwise, it is sand. If less than 10% by weight of the total sample is smaller than the No. 200 sieve, the second letter is assigned based on grain size distribution. That is, it is either well graded (W) or poorly graded (P). If more than 10% of the sample is smaller than the No. 200 sieve, the second classification letter is based on the plasticity of the fines (L or H), as shown in the table.

Table 2. Unified system of soil classification—field identification

Coarse-Grained Soils (Less Than 50% Pass No. 200 Sieve)		Percent of Coarse Fraction Less Than $\frac{1}{4}$ in.	Percent of Sample Smaller Than No. 200 Sieve	
Symbol	Name			Comments
GW	Well-graded gravel	50 max.	< 10	Wide range of grain sizes with all intermediate sizes
GP	Poorly graded gravel	50 max.	< 10	Predominantly one size or some sizes missing
SW	Well-graded sand	51 min.	< 10	Wide range of grain sizes with all intermediate sizes
SP	Poorly graded sand	51 min.	< 10	Predominantly one size or some sizes missing
GM	Silty gravel	50 max.	≥ 10	Low-plasticity fines (see ML below)
GC	Clayey gravel	50 max.	≥ 10	Plastic fines (see CL below)
SM	Silty sand	51 min.	≥ 10	Low-plasticity fines (see ML below)
SC	Clayey sand	51 min.	≥ 10	Plastic fines (see CL below)

Tests on Fraction Passing No. 40 Sieve (Approx. $\frac{1}{64}$ in. or 0.4 mm)*

Fine-Grained Soils (50% or More Pass No. 200 Sieve)				
Symbol	Name	Dry Strength	Shaking	Other
ML	Low-plasticity silt	Low	Medium to quick	
CL	Low-plasticity clay	Low to medium	None to slow	
OL	Low-plasticity organic	Low to medium	Slow	Color and odor
MH	High-plasticity silt	Medium to high	None to slow	
CH	High-plasticity clay	High	None	
OH	High-plasticity organic	Medium to high	None to slow	Color and odor
Pt	Peat	Identified by dull brown to black color, odor, spongy feel, and fibrous texture		

*Laboratory classification based on liquid limit and plasticity index values.

FIGURE 1. Typical gradation curves for coarse-grained soils. (U.S. Army Engineer School)

15

Table 3. AASHTO system of soil classification (Courtesy of BOMAG Americas)

| | | | | | | | Group Number | | | | | |
| | A-1 | | A-2 | | | | | | | | | |
	A-1-a	A-1-b	A-2-4	A-2-5	A-2-6	A-2-7	A-3	A-4	A-5	A-6	A-7
Percent passing											
No. 10 sieve	50 max.										
No. 40 sieve	30 max.	50 max.					51 min.				
No. 200 sieve	15 max.	25 max.	35 max.	35 max.	35 max.	35 max.	10 max.	36 min.	36 min.	36 min.	36 min.
Fraction passing No. 40											
Liquid limit	6 max.	6 max.	40 max.	41 min.	40 max.	41 min.		40 max.	41 min.	40 max.	41 min.
Plasticity index			10 max.	10 max.	11 min.	11 min.		10 max.	10 max.	11 min.	11 min.
Typical material	Gravel and sand		Silty or clayey sand or gravel				Fine sand	Silt	Silt	Clay	Clay

If the sample is fine-grained (more than 50% by weight smaller than the No. 200 sieve), classification is based on dry strength and shaking tests of the material smaller than $1/64$ in. (0.4 mm) in diameter.

Dry Strength Test   Mold a sample into a ball about the size of a golf ball to the consistency of putty, adding water as needed. Allow the sample to dry completely. Attempt to break the sample using the thumb and forefinger of both hands. If the sample cannot be broken, the soil is highly plastic. If the sample breaks, attempt to powder it by rubbing it between the thumb and forefinger of one hand. If the sample is difficult to break and powder, it has medium

plasticity. Samples of low plasticity will break and powder easily.

Shaking Test   Form the material into a ball about $3/4$ in. (19 mm) in diameter, adding water until the sample does not stick to the fingers as it is molded. Put the sample in the palm of the hand and shake vigorously. Observe the speed with which water comes to the surface of the sample to produce a shiny surface. A rapid reaction indicates a nonplastic silt.

Construction Characteristics of Soils

Some important construction characteristics of soils as classified under the Unified System are summarized in Table 4.

Table 4. Construction characteristics of soils (Unified System)

Soil Type	Symbol	Drainage	Construction Workability	Suitability for Subgrade (No Frost Action)	Suitability for Surfacing
Well-graded gravel	GW	Excellent	Excellent	Good	Good
Poorly graded gravel	GP	Excellent	Good	Good to excellent	Poor
Silty gravel	GM	Poor to fair	Good	Good to excellent	Fair
Clayey gravel	GC	Poor	Good	Good	Excellent
Well-graded sand	SW	Excellent	Excellent	Good	Good
Poorly graded sand	SP	Excellent	Fair	Fair to good	Poor
Silty sand	SM	Poor to fair	Fair	Fair to good	Fair
Clayey sand	SC	Poor	Good	Poor to fair	Excellent
Low-plasticity silt	ML	Poor to fair	Fair	Poor to fair	Poor
Low-plasticity clay	CL	Poor	Fair to good	Poor to fair	Fair
Low-plasticity organic	OL	Poor	Fair	Poor	Poor
High-plasticity silt	MH	Poor to fair	Poor	Poor	Poor
High-plasticity clay	CH	Very poor	Poor	Poor to fair	Poor
High-plasticity organic	OH	Very poor	Poor	Very poor to poor	Poor
Peat	Pt	Poor to fair	Unsuitable	Unsuitable	Unsuitable

4 SOIL VOLUME-CHANGE CHARACTERISTICS

Soil Conditions

There are three principal conditions or states in which earthmoving material may exist: bank, loose, and compacted. The meanings of these terms are as follows:

- **Bank:** Material in its natural state before disturbance. Often referred to as "in-place" or "in situ." A unit volume is identified as a *bank cubic yard* (BCY) or a *bank cubic meter* (BCM).
- **Loose:** Material that has been excavated or loaded. A unit volume is identified as a *loose cubic yard* (LCY) or *loose cubic meter* (LCM).
- **Compacted:** Material after compaction. A unit volume is identified as a *compacted cubic yard* (CCY) or *compacted cubic meter* (CCM).

Swell

A soil increases in volume when it is excavated because the soil grains are loosened during excavation and air fills the void spaces created. As a result, a unit volume of soil in the bank condition will occupy more than one unit volume after excavation. This phenomenon is called *swell*. Swell may be calculated as follows:

$$\text{Swell (\%)} = \left(\frac{\text{Weight/bank volume}}{\text{Weight/loose volume}} - 1 \right) \times 100 \quad (4)$$

Example 1 Find the swell of a soil that weighs 2800 lb/cu yd (1661 kg/m^3) in its natural state and 2000 lb/cu yd (1186 kg/m^3) after excavation.

Solution

$$\text{Swell} = \left(\frac{2800}{2000} - 1 \right) \times 100 = 40\% \quad \text{(Eq 4)}$$

$$\left[= \left(\frac{1661}{1186} - 1 \right) \times 100 = 40\% \right]$$

That is, 1 bank cubic yard (meter) of material will expand to 1.4 loose cubic yards (meters) after excavation.

Shrinkage

When a soil is compacted, some of the air is forced out of the soil's void spaces. As a result, the soil will occupy less volume than it did under either the bank or loose conditions. This phenomenon, which is the reverse of the swell phenomenon, is called *shrinkage*. The value of shrinkage may be determined as follows:

$$\text{Shrinkage (\%)} = \left(1 - \frac{\dfrac{\text{Weight/}}{\text{bank volume}}}{\dfrac{\text{Weight/}}{\text{compacted volume}}} \right) \times 100 \quad (5)$$

Soil volume change caused by excavation and compaction is illustrated in Figure 2. Note that both swell and shrinkage are calculated from the bank (or natural) condition.

Example 2 Find the shrinkage of a soil that weighs 2800 lb/cu yd (1661 kg/m^3) in its natural state and 3500 lb/cu yd (2077 kg/m^3) after compaction.

Solution

$$\text{Shrinkage} = \left(1 - \frac{2800}{3500} \right) \times 100 = 20\% \quad \text{(Eq 5)}$$

$$\left[= \left(1 - \frac{1661}{2077} \right) \times 100 = 20\% \right]$$

Hence 1 bank cubic yard (meter) of material will shrink to 0.8 compacted cubic yard (meter) as a result of compaction.

Load and Shrinkage Factors

In performing earthmoving calculations, it is important to convert all material volumes to a common unit of measure. Although the bank cubic yard (or meter) is most commonly used for this purpose, any of the three volume units may be used. A *pay yard* (or meter) is the volume unit specified as the basis for payment in an earthmoving contract. It may be any of the three volume units.

Because haul unit and spoil bank volume are commonly expressed in loose measure, it is convenient to have a conversion factor to simplify the conversion of loose volume to bank volume. The factor used for this purpose is called a *load factor*. A soil's load factor may be calculated by use of

FIGURE 2. Typical soil volume change during earthmoving.

Table 5. Typical soil weight and volume change characteristics*

	Unit Weight [lb/cu yd (kg/m³)]			Swell (%)	Shrinkage (%)	Load Factor	Shrinkage Factor
	Loose	Bank	Compacted				
Clay	2310 (1370)	3000 (1780)	3750 (2225)	30	20	0.77	0.80
Common earth	2480 (1471)	3100 (1839)	3450 (2047)	25	10	0.80	0.90
Rock (blasted)	3060 (1815)	4600 (2729)	3550 (2106)	50	−30**	0.67	1.30**
Sand and gravel	2860 (1697)	3200 (1899)	3650 (2166)	12	12	0.89	0.88

*Exact values vary with grain size distribution, moisture, compaction, and other factors. Tests are required to determine exact values for a specific soil.
**Compacted rock is less dense than is in-place rock.

Equation 6 or 7. Loose volume is multiplied by the load factor to obtain bank volume.

$$\text{Load factor} = \frac{\text{Weight/loose unit volume}}{\text{Weight/bank unit volume}} \quad (6)$$

or

$$\text{Load factor} = \frac{1}{1 + \text{swell}} \quad (7)$$

A factor used for the conversion of bank volume to compacted volume is sometimes referred to as a *shrinkage factor*. The shrinkage factor may be calculated by use of Equation 8 or 9. Bank volume may be multiplied by the shrinkage factor to obtain compacted volume or compacted volume may be divided by the shrinkage factor to obtain bank volume.

$$\text{Shrinkage factor} = \frac{\text{Weight/bank unit volume}}{\text{Weight/compacted unit volume}} \quad (8)$$

or

$$\text{Shrinkage factor} = 1 - \text{shrinkage} \quad (9)$$

Example 3 A soil weighs 1960 lb/LCY (1163 kg/LCM), 2800 lb/BCY (1661 kg/BCM), and 3500 lb/CCY (2077 kg/CCM). (a) Find the load factor and shrinkage factor for the soil. (b) How many bank cubic yards (BCY) or meters (BCM) and compacted cubic yards (CCY) or meters (CCM) are contained in 1 million loose cubic yards (593,300 LCM) of this soil?

Solution

$$\text{(a) Load factor} = \frac{1960}{2800} = 0.70 \quad \text{(Eq 6)}$$

$$\left[= \frac{1163}{1661} = 0.70 \right]$$

$$\text{Shrinkage factor} = \frac{2800}{3500} = 0.80 \quad \text{(Eq 8)}$$

$$\left[= \frac{1661}{2077} = 0.80 \right]$$

(b) Bank volume = 1,000,000 × 0.70 = 700,000 BCY

[= 593,300 × 0.70 = 415,310 BCM]

Compacted volume = 700,000 × 0.80 = 560,000 CCY

= [415,310 × 0.80 = 332,248 CCM]

Typical values of unit weight, swell, shrinkage, load factor, and shrinkage factor for some common earthmoving materials are given in Table 5.

5 SPOIL BANKS

When planning and estimating earthwork, it is frequently necessary to determine the size of the pile of material that will be created by the material removed from the excavation. If the pile of material is long in relation to its width, it is referred to as a *spoil bank*. Spoil banks are characterized by a triangular cross section. If the material is dumped from a fixed position, a *spoil pile* is created which has a conical shape. To determine the dimensions of spoil banks or piles, it is first necessary to convert the volume of excavation from in-place conditions (BCY or BCM) to loose conditions (LCY or LCM). Bank or pile dimensions may then be calculated using Equations 10 to 13 if the soil's angle of repose is known.

A soil's *angle of repose* is the angle that the sides of a spoil bank or pile naturally form with the horizontal when the excavated soil is dumped onto the pile. The angle of repose (which represents the equilibrium position of the soil) varies with the soil's physical characteristics and its moisture content. Typical values of angle of repose for common soils are given in Table 6.

Table 6. Typical values of angle of repose of excavated soil

Material	Angle of Repose (deg)
Clay	35
Common earth, dry	32
Common earth, moist	37
Gravel	35
Sand, dry	25
Sand, moist	37

Triangular Spoil Bank

$$\text{Volume} = \text{Section area} \times \text{Length} \qquad (10)$$

$$B = \left(\frac{4V}{L \times \tan R}\right)^{\frac{1}{2}}$$

$$H = \frac{B \times \tan R}{2} \qquad (11)$$

where B = base width (ft or m)
H = pile height (ft or m)
L = pile length (ft or m)
R = angle of repose (deg)
V = pile volume (cu ft or m^3)

Conical Spoil Pile

$$\text{Volume} = \frac{1}{3} \times \text{Base area} \times \text{Height}$$

$$D = \left(\frac{7.64V}{\tan R}\right)^{\frac{1}{3}} \qquad (12)$$

$$H = \frac{D}{2} \times \tan R \qquad (13)$$

where D is the diameter of the pile base (ft or m).

Example 4 Find the base width and height of a triangular spoil bank containing 100 BCY (76.5 BCM) if the pile length is 30 ft (9.14 m), the soil's angle of repose is 37°, and its swell is 25%.

Solution

$$\text{Loose volume} = 27 \times 100 \times 1.25 = 3375 \text{ cu ft}$$
$$[\ = 76.5 \times 1.25 = 95.6 \text{ m}^3]$$

$$\text{Base width} = \left(\frac{4 \times 3375}{30 \times \tan 37°}\right)^{\frac{1}{2}} = 24.4 \text{ ft} \qquad (\text{Eq } 10)$$

$$\left[\ = \left(\frac{4 \times 95.6}{9.14 \times \tan 37°}\right)^{\frac{1}{2}} = 7.45 \text{ m}\right]$$

$$\text{Height} = \frac{24.4}{2} \times \tan 37° = 9.2 \text{ ft} \qquad (\text{Eq } 11)$$

$$\left[\ = \frac{7.45}{2} \times \tan 37° = 2.80 \text{ m}\right]$$

Example 5 Find the base diameter and height of a conical spoil pile that will contain 100 BCY (76.5 BCM) of excavation if the soil's angle of repose is 32° and its swell is 12%.

Solution

$$\text{Loose volume} = 27 \times 100 \times 1.12 = 3024 \text{ cu ft}$$
$$[\ = 76.5 \times 1.12 \times 85.7 \text{ m}^3]$$

$$\text{Base diameter} = \left(\frac{7.64 \times 3024}{\tan 32°}\right)^{\frac{1}{3}} = 33.3 \text{ ft} \qquad (\text{Eq } 12)$$

$$\left[\ = \left(\frac{7.64 \times 85.7}{\tan 32°}\right)^{\frac{1}{3}} = 10.16 \text{ m}\right]$$

$$\text{Height} = \frac{33.3}{2} \times \tan 32° = 10.4 \text{ ft} \qquad (\text{Eq } 13)$$

$$\left[\ = \frac{10.16}{2} \times \tan 32° = 3.17 \text{ m}\right]$$

6 ESTIMATING EARTHWORK VOLUME

When planning or estimating an earthmoving project, it is often necessary to estimate the volume of material to be excavated or placed as fill. The procedures to be followed can be divided into three principal categories: (1) pit excavations (small, relatively deep excavations such as those required for basements and foundations), (2) trench excavation for utility lines, and (3) excavating or grading relatively large areas. Procedures suggested for each of these three cases are described in the following sections.

The estimation of the earthwork volume involved in the construction of roads and airfields is customarily performed by the design engineer. The usual method is to calculate the cross-sectional area of cut or fill at regular intervals (such as *stations* [100 ft or 33 m]) along the centerline. The volume of cut or fill between stations is then calculated, accumulated, and plotted as a *mass diagram*. While the construction of a mass diagram is beyond the scope of this book, some construction uses of the mass diagram are described in Section 7.

When making earthwork volume calculations, keep in mind that cut volume is normally calculated in bank measure while the volume of compacted fill is calculated in compacted measure. Both cut and fill must be expressed in the same volume units before being added.

Pit Excavations

For these cases, simply multiply the horizontal area of excavation by the average depth of excavation (Equation 14).

$$\text{Volume} = \text{Horizontal area} \times \text{Average depth} \qquad (14)$$

To perform these calculations, first divide the horizontal area into a convenient set of rectangles, triangles, or circular segments. After the area of each segment has been calculated, the total area is found as the sum of the segment areas. The average depth is then calculated. For simple rectangular excavations, the average depth can be taken as simply the average of the four corner depths. For more complex areas, measure the depth at additional points along the perimeter of the excavation and average all depths.

Example 6 Estimate the volume of excavation required (bank measure) for the basement shown in Figure 3. Values shown at each corner are depths of excavation. All values are in feet (m).

FIGURE 3. Figure for Example 6.

Solution

$$\text{Area} = 25 \times 30 = 750 \text{ sq ft}$$

$$[= 7.63 \times 9.15 = 69.8 \text{ m}^2]$$

$$\text{Average depth} = \frac{6.0 + 8.2 + 7.6 + 5.8}{4} = 6.9 \text{ ft}$$

$$\left[= \frac{1.8 + 2.5 + 2.3 + 1.8}{4} = 2.1 \text{ m} \right]$$

$$\text{Volume} = \frac{750 \times 6.9}{27} = 191.7 \text{ BCY}$$

$$[= 69.8 \times 2.1 = 146.6 \text{ BCM}]$$

Trench Excavations

The volume of excavation required for a trench can be calculated as the product of the trench cross-sectional area and the linear distance along the trench line (Equation 15). For rectangular trench sections where the trench depth and width are relatively constant, trench volume can be found as simply the product of trench width, depth, and length. When trench sides are sloped and vary in width and/or depth, cross sections should be taken at frequent linear intervals and the volumes between locations computed. These volumes are then added to find total trench volume.

$$\text{Volume} = \text{Cross-sectional area} \times \text{Length} \qquad (15)$$

Example 7 Find the volume (bank measure) of excavation required for a trench 3 ft (0.92 m) wide, 6 ft (1.83 m) deep, and 500 ft (152 m) long. Assume that the trench sides will be approximately vertical.

Solution

$$\text{Cross-sectional area} = 3 \times 6 = 18 \text{ sq ft}$$

$$[= 0.92 \times 1.83 = 1.68 \text{ m}^2]$$

$$\text{Volume} = \frac{18 \times 500}{27} = 333 \text{ BCY}$$

$$[= 1.68 \times 152 = 255 \text{ BCM}]$$

Large Areas

To estimate the earthwork volume involved in large or complex areas, one method is to divide the area into a grid indicating the depth of excavation or fill at each grid intersection. Assign the depth at each corner or segment intersection a weight according to its location (number of segment lines intersecting at the point). Thus, interior points (intersection of four segments) are assigned a weight of four, exterior points at the intersection of two segments are assigned a weight of two, and corner points are assigned a weight of one. Average depth is then computed using Equation 16 and multiplied by the horizontal area to obtain the volume of excavation. Note, however, that this calculation yields the net volume of excavation for the area. Any balancing of cut and fill within the area is not identified in the result.

$$\frac{\text{Average}}{\text{depth}} = \frac{\text{Sum of products of depth} \times \text{Weight}}{\text{Sum of weights}} \qquad (16)$$

Example 8 Find the volume of excavation required for the area shown in Figure 4. The figure at each grid intersection represents the depth of cut at that location. Depths in parentheses represent meters.

Solution

$$\text{Corner points} = 6.0 + 3.4 + 2.0 + 4.0 = 15.4 \text{ ft}$$

$$[= 1.83 + 1.04 + 0.61 + 1.22 = 4.70 \text{ m}]$$

$$\begin{aligned}\text{Border points} = \ &5.8 + 5.2 + 4.6 + 3.0 + 2.8 + 3.0 \\ &+ 3.5 + 4.8 + 4.8 + 5.5 = 43.0 \text{ ft}\end{aligned}$$

$$\begin{aligned}[= \ &1.77 + 1.59 + 1.40 + 0.92 \\ &+ 0.85 + 0.92 + 1.07 + 1.46 \\ &+ 1.46 + 1.68 = 13.12 \text{ m}]\end{aligned}$$

$$\begin{aligned}\text{Interior points} = \ &5.0 + 4.6 + 4.2 \\ &+ 4.9 + 4.0 + 3.6 = 26.3 \text{ ft}\end{aligned}$$

$$\begin{aligned}[= \ &1.52 + 1.40 + 1.28 + 1.49 \\ &+ 1.22 + 1.10 = 8.01 \text{ m}]\end{aligned}$$

$$\text{Average depth} = \frac{15.4 + 2(43.0) + 4(26.3)}{48} = 4.30 \text{ ft}$$

$$\left[= \frac{4.70 + 2(13.12) + 4(8.01)}{48} = 1.31 \text{ m} \right]$$

$$\text{Area} = 300 \times 400 = 120,000 \text{ sq ft}$$

$$[= 91.4 \times 121.9 = 11,142 \text{ m}^2]$$

$$\text{Volume} = \frac{120,000 \times 4.30}{27} = 19,111 \text{ BCY}$$

$$[= 11,142 \times 1.31 = 14,596 \text{ BCM}]$$

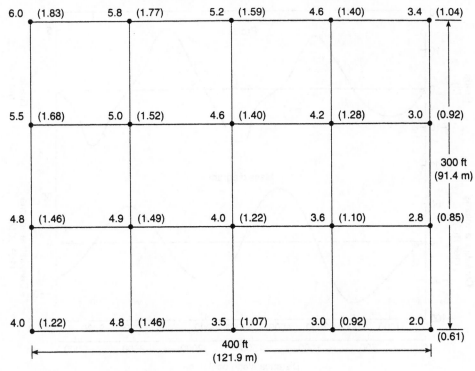

FIGURE 4. Figure for Example 8.

7 CONSTRUCTION USE OF THE MASS DIAGRAM

A *mass diagram* is a continuous curve representing the accumulated volume of earthwork plotted against the linear profile of a roadway or airfield. Mass diagrams are prepared by highway and airfield designers to assist in selecting an alignment which minimizes the earthwork required to construct the facility while meeting established limits of roadway grade and curvature. Since the mass diagram is intended as a design aid, it is not normally provided to contractors as part of a construction bid package. However, the mass diagram can provide very useful information to the construction manager, and it is usually available to the contractor upon request. A typical mass diagram and corresponding roadway profile are illustrated in Figure 5.

Characteristics of a Mass Diagram

Some of the principal characteristics of a mass diagram include the following:

- The vertical coordinate of the mass diagram corresponding to any location on the roadway profile represents the cumulative earthwork volume from the origin to that point.
- Within a cut, the curve rises from left to right.
- Within a fill, the curve falls from left to right.
- A peak on the curve represents a point where the earthwork changes from cut to fill.

- A valley (low point) on the curve represents a point where the earthwork changes from fill to cut.
- When a horizontal line intersects the curve at two or more points, the accumulated volumes at these points are equal. Thus, such a line represents a balance line on the diagram.

Using the Mass Diagram

Some of the information which a mass diagram can provide a construction manager includes the following:

- The length and direction of haul within a balanced section.
- The average length of haul for a balanced section.
- The location and amount of borrow (material hauled in from a borrow pit) and waste (material hauled away to a waste area) for the project.

The following explanation of methods for obtaining this information from a mass diagram will be illustrated using Figure 6.

1. For a balanced section (section 1 on the figure), project the end points of the section up to the profile (points A and B). These points identify the limits of the balanced section.
2. Locate point C on the profile corresponding to the lowest point of the mass diagram within section 1. This is the point at which the excavation changes from fill to cut. The areas of cut and fill can now be identified on the profile.
3. The direction of haul within a balanced section is always from cut to fill.

FIGURE 5. A mass diagram.

4. Repeat this process for sections 2, 3, and 4 as shown.

5. Since the mass diagram has a negative value from point D to the end, the ordinate at point E (−50,000 BCY or −38,230 BCM) represents the volume of material which must be brought in from a borrow pit to complete the roadway embankment.

6. The approximate average haul distance within a balanced section can be taken as the length of a horizontal line located midway between the balance line for the section and the peak or valley of the curve for the section. Thus, the length of the line F–G represents the average haul distance for section 1, which is 1800 ft or 549 m.

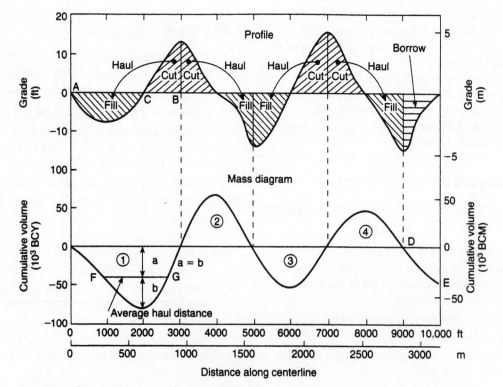

FIGURE 6. Construction use of a mass diagram.

Problems

1. Eliminating the four points on the right-hand side of Example 8 (depths of 3.4, 3.0, 2.8, and 2.0 ft), calculate the volume of excavation in bank measure.

2. A sample of gravel from a stockpile weighs 15 lb (6.80 kg). After oven drying, the sample weighs 14.2 lb (6.44 kg). Calculate the moisture content of the sample.

3. Find the size of a conical spoil bank created by the excavation of 500 BCY (382 BCM) of clay. The soil's swell is 30% and its angle of repose is 35°.

4. Use the profile and mass diagram of Figure 6 to find the following values:
   a. The total volume of (1) cut, (2) fill, (3) waste, and (4) borrow.
   b. The average length of haul for Section 2.

5. A soil weighs 2400 lb/cu yd (1089 kg/m^3) loose, 3050 lb/cu yd (1383 kg/m^3) in-place, and 3600 lb/cu yd (1633 kg/m^3) compacted. Find the swell and shrinkage of this soil.

6. Observations indicate that an excavator carries an average bucket load of 3.0 LCY (2.3 LCM) per cycle. The soil's load factor is 0.80. Cycle time averages 0.35 min. Job conditions are rated fair, and management conditions are rated as good. Estimate the hourly excavator production in bank measure.

7. A ditch having a cross-sectional area of 50 sq ft (4.6 m^2) is being excavated in common earth. The soil's angle of repose is 35° and its swell is 25%. Find the height and base width of the triangular spoil bank that will result from the excavation.

8. The hourly cost of a hydraulic shovel is $65 and of a truck is $35. If an equipment fleet consisting of one shovel and a fleet of six trucks achieve a production of 300 BCY (180 BCM), what is the unit cost of loading and hauling?

9. Using the AASHTO System, classify the soil whose test results are shown below:

   Passing No. 200 Sieve = 34%

   Liquid Limit = 30

   Plasticity Index = 8

10. Develop a computer program to determine the height and base width (ft or m) of the triangular spoil bank that will result from a rectangular trench excavation. Input should include the ditch width and average depth (or cross-sectional area) and length, or the bank volume of the excavation, as well as the soil's angle of repose (degrees) and swell (%). Solve Problem 7 using your program.

References

1. Ahlvin, Robert G., and Vernon A. Smoots. *Construction Guide for Soils and Foundations*, 2nd ed. New York: Wiley, 1988.

2. Bowles, Joseph E. *Engineering Properties of Soils and Their Measurements*, 4th ed. New York: McGraw-Hill, 1992.

3. *Caterpillar Performance Handbook*. Caterpillar Inc., Peoria, IL.

4. Hickerson, Thomas F. *Route Location & Design*, 5th ed. New York: McGraw-Hill, 1967.

5. Nunnally, S. W. *Managing Construction Equipment*, 2nd ed. Upper Saddle River, NJ: Prentice Hall, 2000.

6. *Production and Cost Estimating of Material Movement with Earthmoving Equipment*. Terex Corporation, Hudson, OH.

7. *Soil Mechanics*. Compaction America, Kewanee, IL.

8. *Soils Manual for Design of Asphalt Pavement Structures* (MS-10). The Asphalt Institute, Lexington, KY.

EXCAVATING AND LIFTING

From Chapter 3 of *Construction Methods and Management*, Eighth Edition. S. W. Nunnally. Copyright © 2011 by Pearson Education, Inc.
Published by Pearson Prentice Hall.

EXCAVATING AND LIFTING

1 INTRODUCTION

Excavating and Lifting Equipment

An *excavator* is defined as a power-driven digging machine. The major types of excavators used in earthmoving operations include hydraulic excavators and the members of the cable-operated crane-shovel family (shovels, draglines, hoes, and clamshells). Dozers, loaders, and scrapers can also serve as excavators. In this chapter, we focus on hydraulic excavators and the members of the crane-shovel family used for excavating and lifting operations.

Excavators and Crane Shovels

In 1836, William S. Otis developed a machine that mechanically duplicated the motion of a worker digging with a hand shovel. From this machine evolved a family of cable-operated construction machines known as the *crane shovel*. Members of this family include the shovel, backhoe, dragline, clamshell, mobile crane, and pile driver.

While *hydraulic excavators* (Figure 1) have largely replaced the cable-operated crane-shovel family, functionally similar hydraulic machines are available including the front shovel and backhoe. The advantages of hydraulic excavators over cable-operated machines are faster cycle time, higher bucket penetrating force, more precise digging, and easier operator control. Hydraulic telescoping-boom mobile cranes are also available. The major remaining cable-operated machines based on the original crane shovel are the dragline and the mobile lattice-boom crane.

Some of many attachments for the hydraulic excavator and their uses include the following:

Arms, extendible: Replaces the standard stick to provide extra reach.

Auger: Drills holes for poles, posts, soil sampling, and ground improvement.

Booms: Extended booms used for long-reach applications.

Breaker/hammer: Vibratory hammer used to break up concrete and rock.

Bucket, 4-in-1: Also called a multipurpose bucket or multisegment bucket. Such buckets are capable of performing as a clamshell, dozer, or scraper, as well as a conventional excavator bucket.

Bucket, articulating clam: A hydraulic clamshell bucket with full rotation.

Bucket, cemetery: Used for digging straight wall trenches.

Bucket, clamshell: Performs like the clamshell described in Section 5.

Bucket, ditch cleaning: Wide, shallow, and smooth-edged bucket; may be perforated for drainage.

Bucket, drop center: Used for trenching. The drop center excavates for pipe bedding while the sides excavate to the required trench width.

Bucket, general purpose: Standard excavator bucket.

Bucket, muck: Used for excavating mud and muck; usually perforated for drainage.

Bucket, pavement removal: A forked bucket used for removing and loading pavement slabs.

Bucket, ripper: The bucket sides and bottom are lined with ripper teeth to break up hard soil or soft rock.

Bucket, rock: A heavy-duty bucket designed for loading rock.

Bucket, sand: Has a flat bottom and tapered sides to reduce the chance of soil cave-in.

Bucket, side tilting: Can be tilted for grading slopes and for ditching.

FIGURE 1. Hydraulic excavator. (Courtesy of Volvo Construction Equipment North America, Inc.)

Compaction plate/tamper

Compaction wheel

Coupler, quick: Permits rapid exchange of attachments.

Cutter/processor: Power jaws primarily used for crushing concrete.

Drill, rock: Mounted on the end of the stick to drill blast holes.

Grapple: Equipped with tong-type arms for handling rock, logs, and other materials.

Pile driver/extractor: Used for driving and extracting piles.

Shear: Primarily used for processing scrap metal but also used for demolition.

Thumb, bucket: Attached to bucket to provide a hook capability. It can be retracted when not needed.

Excavators and crane shovels consist of three major assemblies: a carrier or mounting, a revolving superstructure containing the power and control units (also called the revolving deck or turntable), and a front-end assembly. Carriers available include crawler, truck, and wheel mountings, as shown in Figure 2. The crawler mounting provides excellent on-site mobility, and its low ground pressure enables it to operate in areas of low trafficability. Crawler mountings are widely used for drainage and trenching work as well as for rock excavation. Truck and wheel mountings provide greater mobility between job sites but are less stable than crawler mountings and require better surfaces over which to operate. Truck mountings use a modified truck chassis as a carrier and thus have separate stations for operating the carrier and the revolving superstructure. Wheel mountings, on the other hand, use a single operator's station to control both the carrier and the excavating mechanism. Truck mountings are capable of highway travel of 50 mi/h (80 km/h) or more, whereas wheel mountings are usually limited to 30 mi/h (48 km/h) or less.

In this chapter, we discuss the principles of operation, methods of employment, and techniques for estimating the production of shovels, backhoes, clamshells, and draglines. Cranes and their employment are also discussed.

Excavator Production

In order to estimate the production of an excavator using the Production = Volume per cycle × Cycles per hour equation, it is necessary to know the volume of material actually contained in one bucket load. The methods by which excavator bucket and dozer blade capacity are rated are given in

FIGURE 2. Crane-shovel mounting and revolving superstructure. (U.S. Department of the Army)

Table 1. *Plate line capacity* is the bucket volume contained within the bucket when following the outline of the bucket sides. *Struck capacity* is the bucket capacity when the load is struck off flush with the bucket sides. *Water line capacity* assumes a level of material flush with the lowest edge of the bucket (i.e., the material level corresponds to the water level that would result if the bucket were filled with water). *Heaped volume* is the maximum volume that can be placed in the bucket without spillage based on a specified angle of repose for the material in the bucket.

Since bucket ratings for the cable shovel, dragline, and cable backhoe are based on struck volume, it is often assumed that the heaping of the buckets will compensate for the swell of the soil. That is, a 5-cu-yd bucket would be assumed to actually hold 5 bank cu yd of material. A better estimate of the volume of material in one bucket load will be obtained if the nominal bucket volume is multiplied by a *bucket fill factor* or bucket efficiency factor. Suggested values of bucket fill factor for common soils are given in Table 2. The most accurate estimate of bucket load is obtained by multiplying the heaped bucket volume (loose measure) by the bucket fill factor. If desired, the bucket load may be converted to bank volume by multiplying its loose volume by the soil's load factor. This procedure is illustrated in Example 1.

Table 1. Bucket capacity rating methods

Machine	Rated Bucket Capacity
Backhoe and shovel	
Cable	Struck volume
Hydraulic	Heaped volume at 1:1 angle of repose
Clamshell	Plate line or water line volume
Dragline	90% of struck volume
Loader	Heaped volume at 2:1 angle of repose

Table 2. Bucket fill factors for excavators

Material	Bucket Fill Factor
Common earth, loam	0.80–1.10
Sand and gravel	0.90–1.00
Hard clay	0.65–0.95
Wet clay	0.50–0.90
Rock, well-blasted	0.70–0.90
Rock, poorly blasted	0.40–0.70

Example 1 Estimate the actual bucket load in bank cubic yards for a loader bucket whose heaped capacity is 5 cu yd (3.82 m^3). The soil's bucket fill factor is 0.90 and its load factor is 0.80.

Solution

Bucket load $= 5 \times 0.90 = 4.5 \text{ LCY} \times 0.80 = 3.6 \text{ BCY}$

$[= 3.82 \times 0.90 = 3.44 \text{ LCM} \times 0.80 = 2.75 \text{ BCM}]$

2 HYDRAULIC EXCAVATORS

Operation and Employment

The original and most common form of hydraulically powered excavator is the *hydraulic excavator* equipped with a hoe front end. This machine is also called a *hydraulic hoe* or *hydraulic excavator-backhoe*. A *backhoe* (or simply *hoe*) is an excavator designed primarily for excavation below grade. As the name implies, it digs by pulling the dipper back toward the machine. The backhoe shares the characteristics of positive digging action and precise lateral control with the shovel. Cable-operated backhoes exist but are largely being replaced by hydraulic models because of their superior speed

FIGURE 3. Components of a hydraulic excavator backhoe.

of operation and ease of control. Backhoe attachments are also available for loaders and tractors.

The components of a hydraulic excavator are illustrated in Figure 3. In this machine, the boom and dipper arms are raised and lowered by hydraulic cylinders. In addition, the dipper is pivoted at the end of the dipper arm so that a wrist-like action is provided. When the dipper is filled, the dipper is curled up to reduce spillage, and the boom is raised and swung to the unloading position. The load is then dumped by swinging the dipper up and away from the machine.

The backhoe is widely utilized for trenching work. In addition to excavating the trench, it can perform many other trenching functions, such as laying pipe bedding, placing pipe, pulling trench shields, and backfilling the trench. In trench excavation, the best measure of production is the length of trench excavated per unit of time. Therefore, a dipper width should be chosen which matches the required trench width as closely as possible. For this reason, dippers

are available in a wide range of sizes and widths. Side cutters are also available to increase the cutting width of dippers. Other suitable backhoe applications include excavating basements, cleaning roadside ditches, and grading embankments.

A special form of hydraulic excavator which utilizes a rigid telescoping boom in place of the boom and dipper arm of a conventional hydraulic backhoe is shown in Figure 4. Because of their telescoping boom and pivoting bucket, these machines are very versatile and capable of ditching, sloping, finishing, cleaning ditches, ripping, and demolishing as well as trenching.

The use of compact or "mini" excavating equipment is a growing trend in the construction equipment industry. Such equipment includes the skid steer loader and the compact loader described in Section 3 as well as hydraulically powered *mini-excavators*. The advantages of such equipment include compact size, hydraulic power, light weight, maneuverability, and versatility. A typical mini-excavator is

FIGURE 4. Telescoping-boom hydraulic excavator. (Courtesy of JLG Industries, Inc.)

FIGURE 5. Mini-excavator. (Courtesy of JCB Inc.)

illustrated in Figure 5. These machines are available in sizes from about 10 to 60 hp (7.5–45 kW) with digging depths from about 7 to 15 ft (2.1–4.6 m). Some machines are as narrow as 29 in. (0.74 m) making them very useful for excavating in confined spaces. The mini-excavator's ability to operate with a full 360° swing, its hydraulic power, and its low ground pressure have resulted in its replacing back-hoe/loaders in some applications. When equipped with dozer blade, they may also be employed in leveling, grading, backfilling, and general job cleanup.

Production Estimating

No production tables have been prepared for the hydraulic excavator. However, production may be estimated by using Equation 1 together with Tables 3 and 4, which have been prepared from manufacturers' data.

$$\text{Production (LCY/h)} = C \times S \times V \times B \times E \quad (1)$$

where C = cycles/h (Table 3)

S = swing-depth factor (Table 4)

V = heaped bucket volume (LCY or LCM)

B = bucket fill factor (Table 2)

E = job efficiency

Table 4. Swing-depth factor for backhoes

Depth of Cut (% of Maximum)	Angle of Swing (deg)					
	45	60	75	90	120	180
30	1.33	1.26	1.21	1.15	1.08	0.95
50	1.28	1.21	1.16	1.10	1.03	0.91
70	1.16	1.10	1.05	1.00	0.94	0.83
90	1.04	1.00	0.95	0.90	0.85	0.75

In trenching work, a fall-in factor should be applied to excavator production to account for the work required to clean out material that falls back into the trench from the trench walls. Normal excavator production should be multiplied by the appropriate value from Table 5 to obtain the effective trench production.

Example 2   Find the expected production in loose cubic yards (LCM) per hour of a small hydraulic excavator. Heaped bucket capacity is ¾ cu yd (0.57 m³). The material is sand and gravel with a bucket fill factor of 0.95. Job efficiency is 50 min/h. Average depth of cut is 14 ft (4.3 m). Maximum depth of cut is 20 ft (6.1 m) and average swing is 90.

Table 3. Standard cycles per hour for hydraulic excavators

Type of Material	Machine Size			
	Wheel Tractor	Small Excavator: 1 yd (0.76 m³) or Less	Medium Excavator: 1¼–2¼ yd (0.94–1.72 m³)	Large Excavator: Over 2½ yd (1.72 m³)
Soft (sand, gravel, loam)	170	250	200	150
Average (common earth, soft clay)	135	200	160	120
Hard (tough clay, rock)	110	160	130	100

Table 5. Adjustment factor for trench production

Type of Material	Adjustment Factor
Loose (sand, gravel, loam)	0.60–0.70
Average (common earth)	0.90–0.95
Firm (firm plastic soils)	0.95–1.00

Solution

$$\text{Cycle output} = 250 \text{ cycles}/60 \text{ min (Table 3)}$$
$$\text{Swing-depth factor} = 1.00 \text{ (Table 4)}$$
$$\text{Bucket volume} = 0.75 \text{ LCY (0.57 LCM)}$$
$$\text{Bucket fill factor} = 0.95$$
$$\text{Job efficiency} = 50/60 = 0.833$$
$$\text{Production} = 250 \times 1.00 \times 0.75 \times 0.95 \times 0.833$$
$$= 148 \text{ LCY/h}$$
$$[= 250 \times 1.00 \times 0.57 \times 0.95 \times 0.833$$
$$= 113 \text{ LCM/h}]$$

Job Management

In selecting the proper excavator for a project, consideration must be given to the maximum depth, working radius, and dumping height required. Check also for adequate clearance for the carrier, superstructure, and boom during operation.

Although the excavator will excavate fairly hard material, do not use the bucket as a sledge in attempting to fracture rock. Light blasting, ripping, or use of a power hammer may be necessary to loosen rock sufficiently for excavation. When lifting pipe into place, do not exceed load given in the manufacturer's safe capacity chart for the situation.

3 SHOVELS

Operation and Employment

The *hydraulic shovel* illustrated in Figure 6 is also called a *front shovel* or *hydraulic excavator-front shovel*. Its major components are identified in Figure 7. The hydraulic shovel digs with a combination of crowding force and breakout (or prying) force, as illustrated in Figure 8. Crowding force is generated by the stick cylinder and acts at the bucket edge on a tangent to the arc of the radius from point A. Breakout force is generated by the bucket cylinder and acts at the bucket edge on a tangent to the arc of the radius through point B. After the bucket has penetrated and filled with material, it is rolled up to reduce spillage during the swing cycle.

Both front-dump and bottom-dump buckets are available for hydraulic shovels. Bottom-dump buckets are more versatile, provide greater reach and dump clearance, and produce less spillage. However, they are heavier than front-dump buckets of equal capacity, resulting in a lower bucket capacity for equal bucket weight. Hence front-dump buckets usually have a slight production advantage. In addition, front-dump buckets cost less and require less maintenance.

Although the shovel has a limited ability to dig below track level, it is most efficient when digging above track level. Other excavators (such as the hydraulic excavator and dragline) are better suited than the shovel for excavating below ground level. Since the shovel starts its most efficient digging cycle at ground level, it can form its own roadway as it advances—an important advantage. The shovel is also able to shape the sides of its cut and to dress slopes when required. Material dug by the shovel can be loaded into haul units, dumped onto spoil banks, or side-cast into low areas.

FIGURE 6. Hydraulic shovel. (Courtesy of Kobelco Construction Machinery America LLC)

FIGURE 7. Components of a hydraulic shovel.

FIGURE 8. Digging action of a hydraulic shovel.

The shovel should have a vertical face to dig against for most effective digging. This surface, known as the *digging face*, is easily formed when excavating a bank or hillside. When the material to be excavated is located below ground level, the shovel must dig a ramp down into the material until a digging face of suitable height is created. This process is known as *ramping down*. Once a suitable digging face has been obtained, the cut is typically developed by using one of the two basic methods of attack (or a variation of these) illustrated in Figure 9. The frontal approach allows the most effective digging position of the shovel to be used, since the shovel can exert the greatest digging force in this position. This is an important consideration in digging hard materials. Trucks can be located on either or both sides of the shovel with a minimum swing, usually no greater than 90°. The parallel approach permits fast move-up of the shovel as the digging face advances, and it permits a good traffic flow for hauling units. This approach is often used for highway cuts and whenever space is limited.

Production Estimating

Production for hydraulic shovels may be estimated using Equation 2 together with Table 6, which has been prepared from manufacturers' data.

$$\genfrac{}{}{0pt}{}{\text{Production(LCY/h)}}{\text{or (LCM/h)}} = C \times S \times V \times B \times E \qquad (2)$$

where C = cycles/h (Table 6)
   S = swing factor (Table 6)
   V = heaped bucket volume (LCY or LCM)
   B = bucket fill factor (Table 2)
   E = job efficiency

Example 3   Find the expected production in loose cubic yards (LCM) per hour of a 3-yd (2.3-m³) hydraulic shovel equipped with a front-dump bucket. The material is common earth with a bucket fill factor of 1.0. The average angle of swing is 75° and job efficiency is 0.80.

FIGURE 9. Shovel approach methods.

Table 6. Standard cycles per hour for hydraulic shovels

Material	Machine Size					
	Small Under 5 yd (3.8 m³)		Medium 5–10 yd (3.8–7.6 m³)		Large Over 10 yd (7.6 m³)	
	Bottom Dump	Front Dump	Bottom Dump	Front Dump	Bottom Dump	Front Dump
Soft (sand, gravel, coal)	190	170	180	160	150	135
Average (common earth, soft clay, well-blasted rock)	170	150	160	145	145	130
Hard (tough clay, poorly blasted rock)	150	135	140	130	135	125

Adjustment for Swing Angle						
Angle of Swing (deg)						
	45	60	75	90	120	180
Adjustment factor	1.16	1.10	1.05	1.00	0.94	0.83

Solution

Standard cycles = 150/60 min (Table 6)

Swing factor = 1.05 (Table 6)

Bucket volume = 3.0 LCY (2.3 LCM³)

Bucket fill factor = 1.0

Job efficiency = 0.80

Production = 150 × 1.05 × 3.0 × 1.0 × 0.80

= 378 LCY/h

[= 150 × 1.05 × 2.3 × 1.0 × 0.80

= 290 LCM/h]

For cable-operated shovels, the Power Crane & Shovel Association (PCSA) Bureau of Construction Industry Manufacturers Association (CIMA) has developed production tables that are widely used by the construction industry.

Job Management

The two major factors controlling shovel production are the swing angle and lost time during the production cycle. Therefore, the angle of swing between digging and dumping positions should always be kept to a minimum. Haul units must be positioned to minimize the time lost as units enter and leave the loading position. When only a single loading position is available, the shovel operator should utilize the time between the departure of one haul unit and the arrival of the next to move up to the digging face and to smooth the excavation area. The floor of the cut should be kept smooth to provide an even footing for the shovel and to facilitate movement in the cut area. The shovel should be moved up frequently to keep it at an optimum distance from the working face. Keeping dipper teeth sharp will also increase production.

4 DRAGLINES

Operation and Employment

The *dragline* is a very versatile machine that has the longest reach for digging and dumping of any member of the crane-shovel family. It can dig from above machine level to significant depths in soft to medium-hard material. The components of a dragline are shown in Figure 10.

Bucket teeth and weight produce digging action as the drag cable pulls the bucket across the ground surface. Digging is also controlled by the position at which the drag chain is attached to the bucket (Figure 11). The higher the point of attachment, the greater the angle at which the bucket enters the soil. During hoisting and swinging, material is retained in the bucket by tension on the dump cable. When tension on the drag cable is released, tension is removed from the dump cable, allowing the bucket to dump. Buckets are available in a wide range of sizes and weights, solid and perforated. Also available are archless buckets which eliminate the front cross-member connecting the bucket sides to provide easier flow of material into and out of the bucket.

FIGURE 10. Components of a dragline.

FIGURE 11. Dragline bucket.

While the dragline is a very versatile excavator, it does not have the positive digging action or lateral control of the shovel. Hence the bucket may bounce or move sideways during hard digging. Also, more spillage must be expected in loading operations than would occur with a shovel. While a skilled dragline operator can overcome many of these limitations, the size of haul units used for dragline loading should be greater than that of those used with a similar-size shovel. The maximum bucket size to be used on a dragline depends on machine power, boom length, and material weight. Therefore, use the dragline capacity chart provided by the manufacturer instead of the machine's lifting capacity chart to determine maximum allowable bucket size.

Production Estimating

The Association of Equipment Manufacturers (formerly the CIMA), through its PCSA Bureau, has made studies of cable-operated dragline operations and has developed production tables that are widely used by the construction industry. Tables 7 to 9 are based on PCSA data. Note, however, that these tables are applicable only to diesel-powered, cable-operated draglines.

To estimate dragline production using the tables, determine the ideal output of the dragline for the machine size and material (Table 7), then adjust this figure by multiplying it by a swing-depth factor (Table 9) and a job efficiency factor, as shown in Equation 3. Notice the conditions applicable to Table 7 given in the table footnote.

$$\frac{\text{Expected}}{\text{production}} = \frac{\text{Ideal}}{\text{output}} \times \frac{\text{Swing-depth}}{\text{factor}} \times \text{Efficiency} \quad \textbf{(3)}$$

To use Table 9, it is first necessary to determine the optimum depth of cut for the machine and material involved from Table 8. Next, divide the actual depth of cut by the optimum depth and express the result as a percentage. The appropriate swing-depth factor is then obtained from Table 9, interpolating as necessary. The method of calculating expected hourly production is illustrated in Example 4.

Example 4   Determine the expected dragline production in loose cubic yards (LCM) per hour based on the following information:

Dragline size = 2 cu yd (1.53 m³)

Swing angle = 120°

Average depth of cut = 7.9 ft (2.4 m)

Material = common earth

Job efficiency = 50 min/h

Soil swell op = 25%

Table 7. Ideal dragline output—short boom [BCY/h (BCM/h)]*. (This is a modification of data published in *Technical Bulletin No. 4,* Power Crane and Shovel Association, Bureau of CIMA, 1968.)

Type of Material	\frac{3}{4} (0.57)	1 (0.75)	1\frac{1}{4} (0.94)	1\frac{1}{2} (1.13)	1\frac{3}{4} (1.32)	2 (1.53)	2\frac{1}{2} (1.87)	3 (2.29)	3\frac{1}{2} (2.62)	4 (3.06)	5 (3.82)
					Bucket Size [cu yd (m³)]						
Light moist clay or loam	130 (99)	160 (122)	195 (149)	220 (168)	245 (187)	265 (203)	305 (233)	350 (268)	390 (298)	465 (356)	540 (413)
Sand and gravel	125 (96)	155 (119)	185 (141)	210 (161)	235 (180)	255 (195)	295 (226)	340 (260)	380 (291)	455 (348)	530 (405)
Common earth	105 (80)	135 (103)	165 (126)	190 (145)	210 (161)	230 (176)	265 (203)	305 (233)	340 (260)	375 (287)	445 (340)
Tough clay	90 (69)	110 (84)	135 (103)	160 (122)	180 (138)	195 (149)	230 (176)	270 (206)	305 (233)	340 (260)	410 (313)
Wet, sticky clay	55 (42)	75 (57)	95 (73)	110 (84)	130 (99)	145 (111)	175 (134)	210 (161)	240 (183)	270 (206)	330 (252)

*Based on 100% efficiency, 90° swing, optimum depth of cut, material loaded into haul units at grade level.

Table 8. Optimum depth of cut for short boom. (This is a modification of data published in *Technical Bulletin No. 4,* Power Crane and Shovel Association, Bureau of CIMA, 1968.)

	Bucket Size [cu yd (m³)]										
Type of Material	$\frac{3}{4}$ (0.57)	**1** (0.75)	$1\frac{1}{4}$ (0.94)	$1\frac{1}{2}$ (1.13)	$1\frac{3}{4}$ (1.32)	**2** (1.53)	$2\frac{1}{2}$ (1.87)	**3** (2.29)	$3\frac{1}{2}$ (2.62)	**4** (3.06)	**5** (3.82)
Light moist clay, loam, sand, and gravel	6.0 (1.8)	6.6 (2.0)	7.0 (2.1)	7.4 (2.2)	7.7 (2.3)	8.0 (2.4)	8.5 (2.6)	9.0 (2.7)	9.5 (2.9)	10.0 (3.0)	11.0 (3.3)
Common earth	7.4 (2.3)	8.0 (2.4)	8.5 (2.6)	9.0 (2.7)	9.5 (2.9)	9.9 (3.0)	10.5 (3.2)	11.0 (3.3)	11.5 (3.5)	12.0 (3.7)	13.0 (4.0)
Wet, sticky clay	8.7 (2.7)	9.3 (2.8)	10.0 (3.0)	10.7 (3.2)	11.3 (3.4)	11.8 (3.6)	12.3 (3.7)	12.8 (3.9)	13.3 (4.1)	13.8 (4.2)	14.3 (4.4)

Table 9. Swing-depth factor for draglines. (This is a modification of data published in *Technical Bulletin No. 4,* Power Crane and Shovel Association, Bureau of CIMA, 1968.)

Depth of Cut (% of Optimum)	Angle of Swing (deg)							
	30	**45**	**60**	**75**	**90**	**120**	**150**	**180**
20	1.06	0.99	0.94	0.90	0.87	0.81	0.75	0.70
40	1.17	1.08	1.02	0.97	0.93	0.85	0.78	0.72
60	1.25	1.13	1.06	1.01	0.97	0.88	0.80	0.74
80	1.29	1.17	1.09	1.04	0.99	0.90	0.82	0.76
100	1.32	1.19	1.11	1.05	1.00	0.91	0.83	0.77
120	1.29	1.17	1.09	1.03	0.98	0.90	0.82	0.76
140	1.25	1.14	1.06	1.00	0.96	0.88	0.81	0.75
160	1.20	1.10	1.02	0.97	0.93	0.85	0.79	0.73
180	1.15	1.05	0.98	0.94	0.90	0.82	0.76	0.71
200	1.10	1.00	0.94	0.90	0.87	0.79	0.73	0.69

Solution

$$\text{Ideal output} = 230 \text{ BCY/h (176 BCM/h) (Table 7)}$$

Optimum depth of cut = 9.9 ft (3.0 m) (Table 8)

$$\frac{\text{Actual depth/}}{\text{optimum depth}} = 7.9/9.9 \times 100 = 80\%$$

$$[= 2.4/3.0 \times 100 = 80\%]$$

Swing-depth factor = 0.90 (Table 9)

Efficiency factor = 50/60 = 0.833

Volume change factor = 1 + 0.25 = 1.25

Estimated production = 230 × 0.90 × 0.833 × 1.25

= 216 LCY/h

[= 176 × 0.90 × 0.833 × 1.25

= 165 LCM/h]

Job Management

Trial operations may be necessary to select the boom length, boom angle, bucket size and weight, and the attachment position of the drag chain that yields maximum production.

As in shovel operation, maximum production is obtained with a minimum swing angle. In general, the lightest bucket capable of satisfactory digging should be used, since this increases the allowable bucket size and reduces cycle time. It has been found that the most efficient digging area is located within 15° forward and back of a vertical line through the boom point, as illustrated in Figure 12. Special bucket hitches are available which shorten the drag distance necessary to obtain a full bucket load. Deep cuts should be excavated in layers whose thickness is as close to the optimum depth of cut as possible.

5 CLAMSHELLS

When the crane shovel is equipped with a crane boom and clamshell bucket, it becomes an excavator known as a *clamshell.* The clamshell is capable of excavating to great depths but lacks the positive digging action and precise lateral control of the shovel and backhoe. Clamshells are commonly used for excavating vertical shafts and footings,

FIGURE 12. Most efficient digging area for a dragline.

unloading bulk materials from rail cars and ships, and moving bulk material from stockpiles to bins, hoppers, or haul units. The components of a cable-operated clamshell are identified in Figure 13. Clamshell attachments are also available for the hydraulic excavator.

A clamshell bucket is illustrated in Figure 14. Notice that the bucket halves are forced together by the action of the closing line against the sheaves. When the closing line is released, the counterweights cause the bucket halves to open as the bucket is held by the holding line. Bucket penetration depends on bucket weight assisted by the bucket teeth. Therefore, buckets are available in light, medium, and heavy weights, with and without teeth. Heavy buckets are suitable for digging medium soils. Medium buckets are used for general-purpose work, including the excavation of loose soils. Light buckets are used for handling bulk materials such as sand and gravel.

The orange peel bucket illustrated in Figure 15 is principally utilized for underwater excavation and for rock placement. Because of its circular shape, it is also well suited to excavating piers and shafts. It operates on the same principle as does the clamshell.

Production Estimating

No standard production tables are available for the clamshell. Thus, production estimation should be based on the use of the Equation Production = Volume per cycle × Cycles per hour. The procedure is illustrated in Example 5.

FIGURE 13. Components of a clamshell.

Example 5 Estimate the production in loose cubic yards per hour for a medium-weight clamshell excavating loose earth. Heaped bucket capacity is 1 cu yd (0.75 m³). The soil is common earth with a bucket fill factor of 0.95. Estimated cycle time is 40 s. Job efficiency is estimated at 50 min/h.

Solution

$$\text{Production} = \frac{3600}{40} \times 1 \times 0.95 \times \frac{50}{60} = 71 \text{ LCY/h}$$

$$B = \frac{3600}{40} \times 0.75 \times 0.95 \times \frac{50}{60} = 53 \text{ LCM/hR}$$

Job Management

The maximum allowable load (bucket weight plus soil weight) on a clamshell should be obtained from the manufacturer's clamshell loading chart for continuous operation. If a clamshell loading chart is not available, limit the load to 80% of the safe lifting capacity given by the crane capacity chart for rubber-tired equipment or 90% for crawler-mounted equipment. Since the machine load includes the weight of the bucket as well as its load, use of the lightest bucket capable of digging the material will enable a larger bucket to be used and will usually increase production. Tests may be necessary to determine the size of bucket that yields maximum production in a particular situation. Cycle time is reduced by organizing the job so that the dumping radius is the same as the digging radius. Keep the machine level to avoid swinging uphill or downhill. Nonlevel swinging is hard on the machine and usually increases cycle time.

6 TRENCHING AND TRENCHLESS TECHNOLOGY

The use of backhoes and other excavators for digging trenches was discussed earlier in this chapter. In addition, there is a growing demand for methods of installing utility systems below the ground with minimum open excavation. Some methods available for achieving this goal include specialized trenching machines and plows as well as trenchless technology (also called trenchless excavation).

FIGURE 14. Clamshell bucket.

Holding line

Closing line

Counterweights

FIGURE 15. Orange peel bucket. (Courtesy of ESCO Corporation)

Trenching Machines and Plows

Some of the types of trenching machines available include chain trenchers, ladder trenchers, and bucket wheel trenchers. Figure 16 shows a large chain trencher capable of digging 14- to 36-in.-(356- to 914-mm-)wide vertical-sided trenches to a depth of 10 ft (3.1 m). Ladder trenchers are similar to chain trenchers but are larger. They are capable of digging trenches up to 10 ft (3.1 m) wide and 25 ft (7.6 m) deep. Bucket wheel trenchers use a revolving bucket wheel to cut a trench up to 5 ft (1.5 m) wide and 9 ft (2.7 m) deep.

Plows can be used to cut a narrow trench and simultaneously insert a small diameter cable or pipeline in most soils. Vibratory plows such as those shown in Figure 17 deliver a more powerful cutting action than static plows and can be used to insert utility lines in hard soil or soft rock.

Trenchless Technology

While a number of different techniques are used in trenchless technology, the principal categories include pipe jacking, horizontal earth boring, and microtunneling.

The process of *pipe jacking* (Figure 18) involves forcing pipe horizontally through the soil. Working from a vertical shaft, a section of pipe is carefully aligned and advanced through the soil by hydraulic jacks braced against the shaft sides. As the pipe advances, spoil is removed through the

FIGURE 16. Chain trencher. (Copyright © Vermeer Manufacturing Company, All Rights Reserved)

FIGURE 17. Hydrostatic vibratory plow. (Copyright © Vermeer Manufacturing Company, All Rights Reserved)

FIGURE 18. Installing a utility line by pipe jacking.

inside of the pipe. After the pipe section has advanced far enough, the hydraulic rams are retracted and another section of pipe is placed into position for installation. The process often requires workers to enter the pipe during the pipe jacking operation.

In *horizontal earth boring*, a horizontal hole is created mechanically or hydraulically with the pipe to be installed serving as the casing for the hole. Some of the many installation methods used include auger boring, rod pushing (thrust boring), rotational compaction boring, impact piercing, horizontal directional drilling, and fluid boring. A track-mounted thrust boring machine with percussive hammer action is shown in Figure 19. Many of these technologies utilize lasers and television cameras for hole alignment and boring control. A number of types of detectors are available to locate the drill head and ensure that the desired alignment and depth are being maintained. The use of a pneumatic piercing tool to create a borehole for a utility line is illustrated in Figure 20. After the bore has been completed, several methods are available to place pipe into the borehole. In one method, pipe is pulled through the bore using the tool's air hose or a steel cable pulled by the air hose. Another method uses the piercing tool to push the pipe through the borehole. A third method uses a pipe pulling adapter attached to the piercing tool to advance the pipe at the same time as the piercing tool advances the bore.

Microtunneling or *utility tunneling* is similar to the conventional tunneling except for the tunnel size and use. Since the tunnels are used for utility systems rather than for vehicle passage, they are normally smaller than road or rail tunnels. They differ from other trenchless methods in their use of a conventional tunnel liner instead of using the pipe itself as a liner. Small moles are frequently used in creating such tunnels.

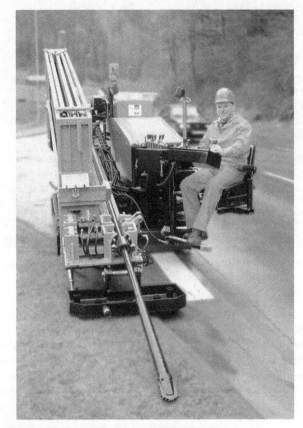

FIGURE 19. Thrust boring machine with percussive action. (Courtesy of TT Technologies, Inc.)

Vacuum Excavation Systems

Originally employed for cleaning out drainage systems and for removing waste from horizontal directional drilling operations, these machines (Figure 21) have become more

FIGURE 20. Installing a utility line by horizontal earth boring.

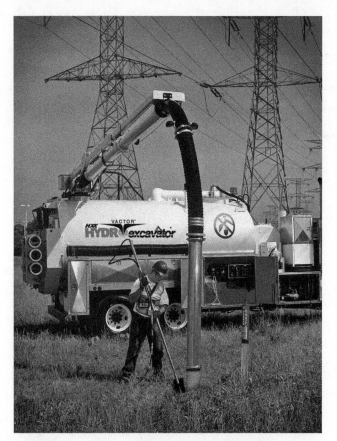

FIGURE 21. Vacuum excavator. (Photograph © Federal Signal Corporation. Used by permission. All rights reserved.)

and excavating near utility lines. By keeping the jet pressure sufficiently low, damage to utility lines can be avoided during excavation. This is not true of the conventional excavators previously discussed.

Repair and Rehabilitation of Pipelines

The repair and rehabilitation of existing pipelines without excavation is another form of trenchless technology. While a number of methods exist, most involve the relining of the existing pipeline or the bursting of the existing pipe while inserting a new pipe.

The relining of a pipeline is accomplished by pulling a new plastic pipe into the existing pipe or by inserting a liner into the existing pipe. When a new pipe is used to reline the pipe, the resulting pipe must be slightly smaller than the original pipe. Another relining technique involves pulling a folded liner into the existing pipe, expanding the liner, treating the liner with an epoxy, and curing it in place.

Pipe bursting (Figure 22) uses a high-powered hydraulic or pneumatic piercing tool equipped with a special bursting head to shatter the existing pipe and enlarge the opening. A new, often larger, pipe is then pulled into the opening by the piercing head.

7 CRANES

Cranes are primarily used for lifting, lowering, and transporting loads. They move loads horizontally by swinging or traveling. Most mobile cranes consist of a carrier and superstructure equipped with a boom and hook, as illustrated in Figure 23. The current trend toward the use of hydraulically operated equipment includes hydraulically powered telescoping-boom cranes. The mobile telescoping-boom

widely used as specialized excavators. Usually truck- or trailer-mounted, these machines utilize a high pressure jet of water or air to loosen soil which is then removed by the vacuum system. The major construction applications of these machines, in addition to supporting horizontal directional drilling operations, involve excavating small diameter holes

FIGURE 22. Schematic of pneumatic pipe bursting method. (Courtesy of Earth Tool Company LLC)

FIGURE 23. Components of a crane.

FIGURE 24. Large mobile hydraulic crane with telescoping boom. (Courtesy of Manitowoc)

crane shown in Figure 24 is capable of lifting loads to the top of a 24-story building.

The major factor controlling the load that may be safely lifted by a crane is its *operating radius* (horizontal distance from the center of rotation to the hook). For other than the horizontal jib tower cranes to be described later in this section, this is a function of boom length and boom angle above the horizontal. Some of the other factors influencing a crane's safe lifting capacity include the position of the boom in relation to the carrier, whether or not *outriggers* (beams that widen the effective base of a crane) are used, the amount of counterweight, and the condition of the supporting surface. Safety

regulations limit maximum crane load to a percentage of the *tipping load* (load that will cause the crane to actually begin to tip). Crane manufacturers provide charts, such as that shown in Figure 25, giving the safe load capacity of the machine under various conditions. Notice that hook blocks, slings, spreader bars, and other load-handling devices are considered part of the load and their weight must be included in the maximum safe load capacity calculation. Electronic load indicators are available that measure the actual load on the crane and provide a warning if the safe capacity is being exceeded.

A standard method of rating the capacity of mobile cranes has been adopted by the PCSA Bureau of the Association of Equipment Manufacturers (which incorporates the

RATED LIFTING CAPACITIES IN POUNDS
29 FT. - 95 FT. BOOM

ON OUTRIGGERS FULLY EXTENDED - 360°

Radius in Feet	#0001							
	Main Boom Length in Feet							
	29	40	50	60	70	80	90	95
10	60,000 (60.5)	50,100 (69.5)	46,950 (74.5)					
12	54,650 (56)	50,100 (66.5)	44,950 (72)	*38,850 (76)				
15	42,850 (47.5)	43,800 (61.5)	41,050 (68)	36,000 (72)	*29,450 (76)	*22,450 (76)		
20	30,700 (30)	31,650 (53)	32,100 (61.5)	29,500 (67)	27,400 (71)	22,450 (73.5)	*18,550 (76)	*15,500 (76)
25		24,050 (42.5)	24,500 (54.5)	24,800 (61.5)	23,100 (66.5)	19,250 (70)	16,500 (72.5)	15,300 (74)
30		18,800 (29)	19,250 (47)	19,550 (56)	19,600 (61.5)	16,850 (66)	14,400 (69)	13,200 (70.5)
35			15,550 (38)	15,850 (49.5)	16,000 (56.5)	14,850 (61.5)	12,700 (65.5)	11,500 (67.5)
40			12,800 (26)	12,950 (42.5)	13,000 (51.5)	13,050 (57.5)	11,000 (62)	10,000 (64)
45	See Note 16			10,450 (34.5)	10,500 (46)	10,550 (53)	9,630 (58.5)	9,060 (60.5)
50				8,610 (23.5)	8,630 (39.5)	8,670 (48)	8,720 (54.5)	7,990 (57)
55					7,170 (32)	7,200 (43)	7,250 (50)	7,100 (53)
60					6,000 (22)	6,030 (37)	6,100 (45.5)	6,110 (49)
65						5,080 (30)	5,120 (40.5)	5,150 (44.5)
70						4,270 (20.5)	4,330 (35)	4,350 (40)
75							3,650 (28.5)	3,700 (34.5)
80							3,100 (20)	3,100 (28)
85								2,600 (20)
Minimum boom angle (°) for indicated length (no load)								0
Maximum boom length (ft.) at 0° boom angle (no load)								95

NOTE: ( ) Boom angles are in degrees.
#LMI operating code. Refer to LMI manual for operating instructions.
*This capacity is based on maximum boom angle.

Lifting Capacities at Zero Degree Boom Angle On Outriggers Fully Extended - 360°								
Boom Angle	Main Boom Length in Feet							
	29	40	50	60	70	80	90	95.2
0 deg.	26,100 (22.8)	15,800 (33.8)	11,000 (43.8)	7,430 (53.8)	5,220 (63.8)	3,730 (73.8)	2,660 (83.8)	2,220 (89)

NOTE: ( ) Reference radii in feet.　　　　　A6-829-101755

FIGURE 25. Crane load capacity chart. (Courtesy of Manitowoc) former CIMA). Under this system, a nominal capacity rating is assigned which indicates the safe load capacity (with outriggers set) for a specified operating radius [usually 12 ft (3.6 m) in the direction of least stability]. The PCSA class number following the nominal rating consists of two number symbols. The first number indicates the operating radius for the nominal capacity. The second number gives the rated load in hundreds of pounds at a 40-ft (12.2-m) operating radius using a 50-ft (15.2-m) boom. Thus, the crane whose capacity chart is shown in Figure 25 has a nominal capacity of 22 tons (19.9 t) at a 10-ft (3-m) operating radius. Therefore, this crane should be able to safely lift a load of 22 tons (19.9 t) at a radius of 10 ft (3 m) and a load of 8000 lb (3629 kg) at an operating radius of 40 ft (12.2 m) with a 50-ft (15.2-m) boom. Both capacities require outriggers to be set and apply regardless of the position of the boom relative to the carrier.

Heavy Lift Cranes

Cranes intended for lifting very heavy loads are usually crawler-mounted lattice-boom models such as that shown in Figure 26. The crane shown has a maximum lifting capacity of 230 tons (209 t) and a maximum lifting height of 371.5 ft (113.3 m).

To lift even heavier loads, several cranes can be used together or the crane can be modified to allow the use of extra counterweight. When a modified counterweight is used, some method must be provided to support the counterweight when there is no load on the hook. One method of accomplishing this is to remove the crane from its mounting and support the counterweight and boom butt on a circular track called a ring mount. Such an arrangement is illustrated in Figure 27. Such an attachment for the crane shown in Figure 24 can boost the maximum capacity to 600 tons (544 t).

Tower Cranes

Another special type of crane is the *tower crane*, illustrated in Figure 28. The tower crane is widely used on building construction projects because of its wide operating radius and almost unlimited height capability. Major types of tower cranes include *horizontal jib* (or *saddle jib*) cranes, *luffing boom* cranes, and *articulated jib* cranes, as illustrated in Figure 29.

The majority of tower cranes are of the horizontal jib type shown in Figure 28. The terminology for this type of crane is illustrated in Figure 30. However, luffing boom (inclined boom) models have the ability to operate in areas of restricted horizontal clearance not suitable for horizontal jib cranes with their fixed jibs and counterweights.

FIGURE 26. Large crawler-mounted lattice-boom mobile crane. (Courtesy of Manitowoc)

Counterweight

Boom pivot

Ring track

FIGURE 27. Crane with ring attachment. (Courtesy of Manitowoc)

FIGURE 28. Tower crane on a building site. (Courtesy of Manitowoc)

Horizontal jib   Luffing boom   Articulated jib

FIGURE 29. Major types of tower cranes.

FIGURE 30. Terminology of a horizontal jib tower crane. (Courtesy of Manitowoc)

Articulated jib cranes are able to reposition their hinged jibs to convert excess hook reach into added hook height. Thus, such cranes can be operated in either the horizontal or luffed position.

Types of tower crane by method of mounting include static (fixed mount) tower cranes, rail-mounted tower cranes, mobile tower cranes, and climbing cranes. Climbing cranes are supported by completed building floors and are capable of raising themselves from floor to floor as the building is

erected. Most tower cranes incorporate self-raising masts. That is, they can raise themselves section by section until the mast or tower reaches the desired height. A typical procedure is as follows (refer to Figure 31). The crane lifts an additional tower section together with a monorail beam and trolley (a). The monorail beam is fastened to the crane's turntable base and the new section is trolleyed close to the tower. The turntable base is unbolted from the tower. The climbing frame's hydraulic cylinders lift the climbing frame and the

a.   b.   c.

FIGURE 31. Self-raising tower crane mast. (Courtesy of FMC Construction Equipment Group)

new section is inserted into the climbing frame using the monorail beam trolley (b). The climbing frame is then lowered and the new section is bolted to the tower and the turntable base (c).

As always, tower crane capacity depends on the operating radius, amount of counterweight, and the mounting used. The lifting capacity of a representative horizontal jib tower crane is shown in Table 10. The weight of the hook block has been incorporated into Table 10. However, the weight of all other load-handling devices must be included in the calculated weight of the load.

Job Management

A number of attachments besides the basic hook are available to assist the crane in performing construction tasks. Several of these attachments are illustrated in Figure 32. Among these attachments, concrete buckets, slings, special hooks, and load dropping tools (weights) are most often used in construction applications. The skull cracker (wrecking ball) is a heavy weight that is hoisted by the crane and then swung or allowed to drop free to perform like a huge sledge hammer. It is used to break up pavement and for demolition work. The simplest form of pile driver, a *drop hammer,* uses a similar action to drive piles. The hammer is hoisted and then dropped onto the pile cap to hammer the pile into the soil.

High-voltage lines present a major safety hazard to crane operations. U.S. Occupational Safety and Health Act (OSHA) regulations prohibit a crane or its load from approaching closer than 10 ft (3 m) to a high-voltage line

carrying 50 kV or less. An additional 0.4 in. (1 cm) must be added for each kilovolt over 50 kV. These safety clearances must be maintained unless the line is deenergized and visibly grounded at the work site or unless insulating barriers not attached to the crane are erected which physically prevent contact with the power line.

Crane accidents occur all too frequently in construction work, particularly when lifting near-capacity loads and when operating with long booms. In an effort to reduce U.S. crane accidents by ensuring that crane operators are fully qualified, a National Commission for the Certification of Crane Operators has been formed. The purpose of the commission is to establish and administer a nationwide program for the certification of crane operators. Some suggestions for safe crane operations include the following:

- Carefully set outriggers on firm supports.
- The crane base must be level. Safe crane capacity is reduced as much as 50% when the crane is out of level by only 3° and operating with a long boom at minimum radius.
- Use a communications system or hand signals when the crane operator cannot see the load at all times. Make sure that all workers involved in the operation know the hand signals to be used.
- Provide *tag lines* (restraining lines) when there is any danger caused by swinging loads.
- Ensure that crane operators are well trained and know the capability of their machines.
- Check safe-lifting capacity charts for the entire range of planned swing before starting a lift. Use a load indicator if possible.

Table 10. Maximum capacity vs. lift radius for a tower crane [pounds (kilograms)]

Lift Radius ft (m)	Boom Length (maximum hook radius)—ft (m)					
	260 (79.2)	230 (70.1)	200 (61.0)	170 (51.8)	140 (42.7)	110 (33.5)
110 (33.5)	21,564 (9781)	23,607 (10,708)	28,458 (12,908)	34,857 (15,811)	39,680 (18,000)	39,680 (18,000)
120 (36.6)	19,584 (8883)	21,465 (9737)	25,938 (11,765)	31,842 (14,444)	38,097 (17,281)	
130 (39.6)	17,802 (8075)	19,548 (8867)	23,652 (10,729)	29,124 (13,211)	34,920 (15,840)	
140 (42.7)	16,380 (7430)	18,018 (8173)	21,861 (9916)	26,982 (12,239)		
150 (45.7)	15,057 (6830)	16,596 (7528)	20,196 (9161)	24,984 (11,333)		
160 (48.8)	13,699 (6214)	15,143 (6869)	18,534 (8407)	24,705 (11,206)		
170 (51.8)	12,654 (5740)	14,012 (6356)	17,214 (7808)	23,037 (10,450)		
180 (54.9)	11,818 (5361)	13,119 (5951)	16,160 (7330)			
190 (57.9)	10,468 (4748)	11,666 (5292)	14,450 (6555)			
200 (61.0)	9700 (4400)	10,811 (4904)	12,440 (5643)			
210 (64.0)	9092 (4124)	10,156 (4607)				
220 (67.1)	8208 (3723)	9215 (4180)				
260 (79.2)	7334 (3327)					

Minimum lift radius = 12.0 ft (3.6 m)

FIGURE 32. Crane boom attachments. (Reproduced with permission from the Association of Equipment Manufacturers.)

Problems

1. A small hydraulic excavator will be used to dig a trench in hard clay (bucket fill factor = 0.80). The minimum trench size is 26 in. (0.66 m) wide by 5 ft (1.53 m) deep. The excavator bucket available is 30 in. (0.76 m) wide and has a heaped capacity of $\frac{3}{4}$ cu yd (0.57 m^3). The maximum digging depth of the excavator is 16 ft (4.9 m). The average swing angle is expected to be 85°. Estimate the hourly trench production in linear feet (meters) if job efficiency is 70%.

2. A 3-yd dragline is excavating and stockpiling sand and gravel. Average depth of cut is 5.4 ft (1.65 m), average swing angle is 75°, and job efficiency is 45 min/h. Estimate the dragline's hourly production in bank measure.

3. Estimate the time required to load 500 cu yd (382 m^3) of gravel from a stockpile into trucks using a clamshell having a heaped capacity of 0.75 cu yd (0.57 m^3). Estimated cycle time is 20 s. Job efficiency is estimated to be 50 min/h.

4. Estimate the actual bucket load in bank measure for a shovel bucket whose capacity is 3 yd (2.29 m^3). The shovel is excavating sand and gravel.

5. A 4 yd (3.06 m^3) (heaped) hydraulic shovel with a bottom-dump bucket is excavating tough clay. The swing angle is 150° and job efficiency is 50 min/h. Estimate the shovel's hourly production in bank measure.

6. The tower crane whose capacity chart is shown in Table 10 is equipped with a 265-ft (80.8-m) boom.

The crane is preparing to lift a load weighing 10,000 pounds (4536 kg). The weight of slings and the spreader bar to be used is 1200 pounds (544 kg). What is the maximum safe lift radius for this load?

7. A hydraulic excavator is excavating the basement for a large building. Heaped bucket capacity is 1.5 cu yd (1.15 m^3). The material is common earth with a bucket fill factor of 0.90. Job efficiency is equivalent to a 50-min hour. The machine's maximum depth of cut is 24 ft (7.3 m^3), and the average digging depth is 13 ft (4.0 m). The material is common earth with a bucket fill factor of 0.90. Job efficiency is equivalent to a 50-min hour. Average swing angle is 90°. Estimate the hourly production in loose measure.

8. What is the minimum clearance required by OSHA regulations between a crane and a 100-kV power line?

9. How can a contractor verify that the desired alignment and depth are being maintained while performing horizontal earth boring?

10. Develop a computer program to estimate the production of a hydraulic shovel based on Equation 2 and Table 6. Input should include rated shovel size, type of material, angle of swing, heaped bucket capacity, bucket fill factor, soil load factor, and job efficiency. Output should be in bank measure if the soil load factor is input; otherwise, it should be in loose measure.

References

1. *Caterpillar Performance Handbook*. Caterpillar Inc., Peoria, IL.

2. *Crane Safety on Construction Sites*. Reston, VA: ASCE, 1998.

3. *Deere Performance Handbook*. Deere & Company, Moline, IL.

4. *Hydraulic Excavators and Telescoping-boom Cranes*. PCSA Bureau of Association of Equipment Manufacturers, Milwaukee, IL.

5. Iseley, D. T., and R. Tanwani. *Trenchless Excavation Construction Methods and Equipment Manual*. Arlington, VA: National Utility Contractors Association, 1992.

6. Nunnally, S. W. *Managing Construction Equipment*, 2nd ed. Upper Saddle River, NJ: Prentice Hall, 2000.

7. *Operating Safety: Link-Belt Cranes and Excavators*. Link-Belt Construction Equipment Company, Lexington, KY.

8. *Production and Cost Estimating of Material Movement with Earthmoving Equipment*. Terex Corporation, Hudson, OH.

9. Shapiro, H. I., J. P. Shapiro, and L. K. Shapiro. *Cranes and Derricks*, 3rd ed. New York: McGraw-Hill, 2000.

LOADING AND HAULING

1 ESTIMATING EQUIPMENT TRAVEL TIME

In calculating the time required for a haul unit to make one complete cycle, it is customary to break the cycle down into fixed and variable components.

$$\text{Cycle time} = \text{Fixed time} + \text{Variable time} \quad (1)$$

Fixed time represents those components of cycle time other than travel time. It includes spot time (moving the unit into position to begin loading), load time, maneuver time, and dump time. Fixed time can usually be closely estimated for a particular type of operation.

Variable time represents the travel time required for a unit to haul material to the unloading site and return. As you would expect, travel time will depend on the vehicle's weight and power, the condition of the haul road, the grades encountered, and the altitude above sea level. This section presents methods for calculating a vehicle's resistance to movement, its maximum speed, and its travel time. Methods for estimating fixed times are given in Sections 2 to 5, which describe specific types of hauling equipment.

Rolling Resistance

To determine the maximum speed of a vehicle in a specific situation, it is necessary to determine the total resistance to movement of the vehicle. The resistance that a vehicle encounters in traveling over a surface is made up of two components, rolling resistance and grade resistance.

$$\text{Total resistance} = \text{Grade resistance} + \text{Rolling resistance} \quad (2)$$

Resistance may be expressed in either pounds per ton of vehicle weight (kilograms per metric ton) or in pounds (kilograms). To avoid confusion, the term *resistance factor* will be used in this chapter to denote resistance in lb/ton (kg/t). *Rolling*

resistance is primarily due to tire flexing and penetration of the travel surface. The rolling resistance factor for a rubber-tired vehicle equipped with conventional tires moving over a hard, smooth, level surface has been found to be about 40 lb/ton of vehicle weight (20 kg/t). For vehicles equipped with radial tires, the rolling resistance factor may be as low as 30 lb/ton (15 kg/t). It has been found that the rolling resistance factor increases about 30 lb/ton (15 kg/t) for each inch (2.5 cm) of tire penetration. This leads to the following equation for estimating rolling resistance factors:

$$\text{Rolling resistance factor (lb/ton)} = 40 + (30 \times \text{in. penetration}) \quad (3A)$$

$$\text{Rolling resistance factor (kg/t)} = 20 + (6 \times \text{cm penetration}) \quad (3B)$$

The rolling resistance in pounds (kilograms) may be found by multiplying the rolling resistance factor by the vehicle's weight in tons (metric tons). Table 1 provides typical values for the rolling resistance factor in construction situations.

Crawler tractors may be thought of as traveling over a road created by their own tracks. As a result, crawler tractors

Table 1. Typical values of rolling resistance factor

Type of Surface	Rolling Resistance Factor	
	lb/ton	kg/t
Concrete or asphalt	40 (30)*	20 (15)
Firm, smooth, flexing slightly under load	64 (52)	32 (26)
Rutted dirt roadway, 1–2 in. penetration	100	50
Soft, rutted dirt, 3–4 in. penetration	150	75
Loose sand or gravel	200	100
Soft, muddy, deeply rutted	300–400	150–200

* Values in parentheses are for radial tires.

From Chapter 4 of *Construction Methods and Management*, Eighth Edition. S. W. Nunnally. Copyright © 2011 by Pearson Education, Inc. Published by Pearson Prentice Hall. All rights reserved.

are usually considered to have no rolling resistance when calculating vehicle resistance and performance. Actually, of course, the rolling resistance of crawler tractors does vary somewhat between different surfaces. However, the standard method for rating crawler tractor power (drawbar horsepower) measures the power actually produced at the hitch when operating on a standard surface. Thus, the rolling resistance of the tractor over the standard surface has already been subtracted from the tractor's performance. Although a crawler tractor is considered to have no rolling resistance, when it tows a wheeled vehicle (such as a scraper or compactor) the rolling resistance of the towed vehicle must be considered in calculating the total resistance of the combination.

Grade Resistance

Grade resistance represents that component of vehicle weight which acts parallel to an inclined surface. When the vehicle is traveling up a grade, grade resistance is positive. When traveling downhill, grade resistance is negative. The exact value of grade resistance may be found by multiplying the vehicle's weight by the sine of the angle that the road surface makes with the horizontal. However, for the grades usually encountered in construction, it is sufficiently accurate to use the approximation of Equation 4. That is, a 1% grade (representing a rise of 1 unit in 100 units of horizontal distance) is considered to have a grade resistance equal to 1% of the vehicle's weight. This corresponds to a grade resistance factor of 20 lb/ton (10 kg/t) for each 1% of grade.

$$\frac{\text{Grade resistance}}{\text{factor (lb/ton)}} = 20 \times \text{grade (\%)} \quad \textbf{(4A)}$$

$$\text{Grade resistance factor (kg/t)} = 10 \times \text{grade (\%)} \quad \textbf{(4B)}$$

Grade resistance (lb or kg) may be calculated using Equation 5 or 6.

$$\frac{\text{Grade}}{\text{resistance (lb)}} = \frac{\text{Vehicle}}{\text{weight (tons)}} \times \frac{\text{Grade resistance}}{\text{factor (lb/ton)}} \quad \textbf{(5A)}$$

$$\frac{\text{Grade}}{\text{resistance (kg)}} = \frac{\text{Vehicle}}{\text{weight (t)}} \times \frac{\text{Grade resistance}}{\text{factor (kg/t)}} \quad \textbf{(5B)}$$

$$\frac{\text{Grade}}{\text{resistance (lb)}} = \text{Vehicle weight (lb)} \times \text{Grade} \quad \textbf{(6A)}$$

$$\frac{\text{Grade}}{\text{resistance (kg)}} = \text{Vehicle weight (kg)} \times \text{Grade} \quad \textbf{(6B)}$$

Effective Grade

The total resistance to movement of a vehicle (the sum of its rolling resistance and grade resistance) may be expressed in pounds or kilograms. However, a somewhat simpler method for expressing total resistance is to state it as a grade (%), which would have a grade resistance equivalent to the total resistance actually encountered. This method of expressing total resistance is referred to as *effective grade, equivalent grade,* or *percent total resistance* and is often used in manufacturers'

performance charts. Effective grade may be easily calculated by use of Equation 7.

$$\frac{\text{Effective}}{\text{grade (\%)}} = \frac{\text{Grade}}{(\%)} + \frac{\frac{\text{Rolling resistance}}{\text{factor (lb/ton)}}}{20} \quad \textbf{(7A)}$$

$$\frac{\text{Effective}}{\text{grade (\%)}} = \frac{\text{Grade}}{(\%)} + \frac{\frac{\text{Rolling resistance}}{\text{factor (kg/t)}}}{10} \quad \textbf{(7B)}$$

Example 1 A wheel tractor-scraper weighing 100 tons (91 t) is being operated on a haul road with a tire penetration of 2 in. (5 cm). What is the total resistance (lb and kg) and effective grade when (a) the scraper is ascending a slope of 5%; (b) the scraper is descending a slope of 5%?

Solution

$$\text{Rolling resistance factor} = 40 + (30 \times 2)$$
$$= 100 \text{ lb/ton} \quad \text{(Eq 3A)}$$
$$[= 20 + (6 \times 5) = 50 \text{ (kg/t)}]$$
$$\text{Rolling resistance} = 100 \text{ (lb/ton)}$$
$$\times 100 \text{ (tons)} = 10{,}000 \text{ lb}$$
$$[= 50 \text{ (kg/t)} \times 91 \text{ (t)} = 4550 \text{ kg}]$$
(a) $$\text{Grade resistance} = 100 \text{ (tons)} \times 2000 \text{ (lb/ton)}$$
$$\times 0.05 \quad \text{(Eq 6A)}$$
$$= 10{,}000 \text{ lb}$$
$$[= 91 \text{ (t)} \times 1000 \text{ (kg/t)}$$
$$\times 0.05 = 4550 \text{ kg}] \quad \text{(Eq 6B)}$$
$$\text{Total resistance} = 10{,}000 \text{ lb} + 10{,}000 \text{ lb}$$
$$= 20{,}000 \text{ lb} \quad \text{(Eq 2)}$$
$$[= 4550 \text{ kg} + 4550 \text{ kg} = 9100 \text{ kg}]$$
$$\text{Effective grade} = 5 + \frac{100}{20} = 10\% \quad \text{(Eq 7A)}$$
(b) $$\text{Grade resistance} = 100 \text{ (tons)} \times 2000 \text{ (lb/ton)}$$
$$\times (-0.05) \quad \text{(Eq 6A)}$$
$$= -10{,}000 \text{ lb}$$
$$[= 91 \text{ (t)} \times 1000 \text{ (kg/t)} \times (-0.05)$$
$$= -4550 \text{ kg}] \quad \text{(Eq 6B)}$$
$$\text{Total resistance} = -10{,}000 \text{ lb} + 10{,}000 \text{ lb} = 0 \text{ lb}$$
$$[= -4550 \text{ kg} + 4550 \text{ kg}$$
$$= 0 \text{ kg}] \quad \text{(Eq 2)}$$
$$\text{Effective grade} = -5 + \frac{100}{20} = 0\% \quad \text{(Eq 7A)}$$
$$\left[= -5 + \frac{50}{10} = 0\% \right] \quad \text{(Eq 7B)}$$

Example 2 A crawler tractor weighing 80,000 lb (36 t) is towing a rubber-tired scraper weighing 100,000 lb (45.5 t) up a grade of 4%. What is the total resistance (lb and kg) of the combination if the rolling resistance factor is 100 lb/ton (50 kg/t)?

Solution

$$\text{Rolling resistance} \atop \text{(neglect crawler)} = \frac{100{,}000 \text{ (lb)}}{2000 \text{ (lb/ton)}} \times \frac{100}{\text{(lb/ton)}} = 5000 \text{ lb}$$

$$[= 45.5 \text{ (t)} \times 50 \text{ (kg/t)} = 2275 \text{ kg}]$$

$$\text{Grade resistance} = 180{,}000 \times 0.04$$

$$= 7200 \text{ lb} \quad (\text{Eq } 6A)$$

$$[= 81.5 \times 1000 \text{ kg/t} \times 0.04$$

$$= 3260 \text{ kg}] \quad (\text{Eq } 6B)$$

$$\text{Total resistance} = 5000 + 7200 = 12{,}200 \text{ lb} \quad (\text{Eq } 2)$$

$$[= 2275 + 3260 = 5535 \text{ kg}]$$

Effect of Altitude

All internal combustion engines lose power as their elevation above sea level increases because of the decreased density of air at higher elevations. There is some variation in the performance of two-cycle and four-cycle naturally aspirated and turbocharged diesel engines. However, engine power decreases approximately 3% for each 1000 ft (305 m) increase in altitude above the maximum altitude at which full-rated power is delivered. Turbocharged engines are more efficient at higher altitude than are naturally aspirated engines and may deliver full-rated power up to an altitude of 10,000 ft (3050 m) or more.

Manufacturers use a *derating factor* to express percentage of reduction in rated vehicle power at various altitudes. Whenever possible, use the manufacturer's derating table for estimating vehicle performance. However, when derating tables are not available, the derating factor obtained by the use of Equation 8 is sufficiently accurate for estimating the performance of naturally aspirated engines.

$$\text{Derating factor (\%)} = 3 \times \left[\frac{\text{Altitude (ft)} - 3000^*}{1000} \right] \quad (8A)$$

$$\text{Derating factor (\%)} = \frac{\text{Altitude (m)} - 915^*}{102} \quad (8B)$$

The percentage of rated power available is, of course, 100 minus the derating factor. The use of derating factors in determining maximum vehicle power is illustrated in Example 3.

Effect of Traction

The power available to move a vehicle and its load is expressed as *rimpull* for wheel vehicles and *drawbar pull* for crawler tractors. Rimpull is the pull available at the rim of the driving wheels under rated conditions. Since it is assumed that no slippage of the tires on the rims will occur, this is also the power available at the surface of the tires. Drawbar pull is the power available at the hitch of a crawler tractor operating under standard conditions. Operation at increased altitude may reduce the maximum pull of a vehicle, as explained in the previous paragraph. Another factor

---

* Substitute maximum altitude for rated performance, if known.

limiting the usable power of a vehicle is the maximum traction that can be developed between the driving wheels or tracks and the road surface. Traction depends on the coefficient of traction and the weight on the drivers as expressed by Equation 9. This represents the maximum pull that a vehicle can develop, regardless of vehicle horsepower.

$$\text{Maximum} \atop \text{usable pull} = \text{Coefficient} \atop \text{of traction} \times \text{Weight on} \atop \text{drivers} \quad (9)$$

For crawler tractors and all-wheel-drive rubber-tired equipment, the weight on the drivers is the total vehicle weight. For other types of vehicles, consult the manufacturer's specifications to determine the weight on the drivers. Typical values of coefficient of traction for common surfaces are given in Table 2.

Example 3 A four-wheel-drive tractor weighs 44,000 lb (20,000 kg) and produces a maximum rimpull of 40,000 lb (18,160 kg) at sea level. The tractor is being operated at an altitude of 10,000 ft (3050 m) on wet earth. A pull of 22,000 lb (10,000 kg) is required to move the tractor and its load. Can the tractor perform under these conditions? Use Equation 8 to estimate altitude deration.

Solution

$$\text{Derating} \atop \text{factor} = 3 \times \left[\frac{10{,}000 - 3000}{1000} \right] = 21\% \quad (\text{Eq } 8A)$$

$$\left[= \frac{3050 - 915}{102} = 21\% \right] \quad (\text{Eq } 8B)$$

$$\text{Percent} \atop \text{rated power} \atop \text{available} = 100 - 21 = 79\%$$

$$\text{Maximum} \atop \text{available power} = 40{,}000 \times 0.79 = 31{,}600 \text{ lb}$$

$$[= 18{,}160 \times 0.79 = 14{,}346 \text{ kg}]$$

$$\text{Coefficient of} \atop \text{traction} = 0.45 \quad (\text{Table 2})$$

$$\text{Maximum} \atop \text{usable pull} = 0.45 \times 44{,}000 = 19{,}800 \text{ lb} \quad (\text{Eq } 9)$$

$$[= 0.45 \times 20{,}000 = 9000 \text{ kg}]$$

Table 2. Typical values of coefficient of traction

Type of Surface	Rubber Tires	Tracks
Concrete, dry	0.90	0.45
Concrete, wet	0.80	0.45
Earth or clay loam, dry	0.60	0.90
Earth or clay loam, wet	0.45	0.70
Gravel, loose	0.35	0.50
Quarry pit	0.65	0.55
Sand, dry, loose	0.25	0.30
Sand, wet	0.40	0.50
Snow, packed	0.20	0.25
Ice	0.10	0.15

Because the maximum pull as limited by traction is less than the required pull, the tractor *cannot perform under these conditions*. For the tractor to operate, it would be necessary to reduce the required pull (total resistance), increase the coefficient of traction, or increase the tractor's weight on the drivers.

Use of Performance and Retarder Curves

Crawler tractors may be equipped with direct-drive (manual gearshift) transmissions. The drawbar pull and travel speed of this type of transmission are determined by the gear selected. For other types of transmissions, manufacturers usually present the speed versus pull characteristics of their equipment in the form of performance and retarder charts. A *performance chart* indicates the maximum speed that a vehicle can maintain under rated conditions while overcoming a specified total resistance. A *retarder chart* indicates the maximum speed at which a vehicle can descend a slope when the total resistance is negative without using brakes. Retarder charts derive their name from the vehicle retarder, which is a hydraulic device used for controlling vehicle speed on a downgrade.

Figure 1 illustrates a relatively simple performance curve of the type often used for crawler tractors. Rimpull or drawbar pull is shown on the vertical scale and maximum vehicle speed on the horizontal scale. The procedure for using this type of curve is to first calculate the required pull or total resistance of the vehicle and its load (lb or kg). Then enter the chart on the vertical scale with the required pull and move horizontally until you intersect one or more gear performance curves. Drop vertically from the point of intersection to the horizontal scale. The value found represents the maximum speed that the vehicle can maintain while developing the specified pull. When the horizontal line of required pull intersects two or more curves for different gears, use the point of intersection farthest to the right, because this represents the maximum speed of the vehicle under the given conditions.

Example 4 Use the performance curve of Figure 1 to determine the maximum speed of the tractor when the required pull (total resistance) is 60,000 lb (27,240 kg).

Solution

Enter Figure 1 at a drawbar pull of 60,000 lb (27,240 kg) and move horizontally until you intersect the curves for first and second gears. Read the corresponding speeds of 1.0 mi/h (1.6 km/h) for second gear and 1.5 mi/h (2.4 km/h) for first gear. The maximum possible speed is therefore 1.5 mi/h (2.4 km/h) in first gear.

Figure 2 represents a more complex performance curve of the type frequently used by manufacturers of tractor-scrapers, trucks, and wagons. In addition to curves of speed versus pull, this type of chart provides a graphical method for calculating the required pull (total resistance). To use this type of curve, enter the top scale at the actual weight of the vehicle (empty or loaded as applicable). Drop vertically until you intersect the diagonal line corresponding to the percent total resistance (or effective grade), interpolating as necessary. From this point, move horizontally until you intersect one or more performance curves. From the point of intersection, drop vertically to find the maximum vehicle speed.

When altitude adjustment is required, the procedure is modified slightly. In this case, start with the gross weight on the top scale and drop vertically until you intersect the total resistance curve. Now, however, move horizontally all the way to the left scale to read the required pull corresponding to vehicle weight and effective grade. Next, divide the required pull by the quantity "1 − derating factor (expressed as a decimal)" to obtain an adjusted required pull. Now, from the adjusted value of required pull on the left scale move horizontally to intersect one or more gear curves and drop vertically to find the maximum vehicle speed. This procedure is equivalent to saying that when a vehicle produces only one-half of its rated power due to altitude effects, its maximum speed can be found from its standard

FIGURE 1. Typical crawler tractor performance curve.

FIGURE 2. Wheel scraper performance curve. (Reprinted Courtesy of Caterpillar Inc.)

performance curve by doubling the actual required pull. The procedure is illustrated in Example 5.

Example 5 Using the performance curve of Figure 2, determine the maximum speed of the vehicle if its gross weight is 150,000 lb (68,000 kg), the total resistance is 10%, and the altitude derating factor is 25%.

Solution

Start on the top scale with a weight of 150,000 lb (68,000 kg), drop vertically to intersect the 10% total grade line, and move horizontally to find a required pull of 15,000 lb (6800 kg) on the left scale. Divide 15,000 lb (6800 kg) by 0.75 (1 – derating factor) to obtain an adjusted required pull of 20,000 lb (9080 kg). Enter the left scale at 20,000 lb (9080 kg) and move horizontally to intersect the first, second, and third gear curves. Drop vertically from the point of intersection with the third gear curve to find a maximum speed of 6 mi/h (10 km/h).

Figure 3 illustrates a typical retarder curve. In this case, it is the retarder curve for the tractor-scraper whose performance curve is shown in Figure 2. The retarder curve is read

in a manner similar to the performance curve. Remember, however, that in this case the vertical scale represents *negative* total resistance. After finding the intersection of the vehicle weight with effective grade, move horizontally until you intersect the retarder curve. Drop vertically from this point to find the maximum speed at which the vehicle should be operated.

Estimating Travel Time

The maximum speed that a vehicle can maintain over a section of the haul route cannot be used for calculating travel time over the section, because it does not include vehicle acceleration and deceleration. One method for accounting for acceleration and deceleration is to multiply the maximum vehicle speed by an average speed factor from Table 3 to obtain an average vehicle speed for the section. Travel time for the section is then found by dividing the section length by the average vehicle speed. When a section of the haul route involves both starting from rest and coming to a stop, the average speed factor from the first column of Table 3 should be applied twice (i.e., use the square of the table value) for that section.

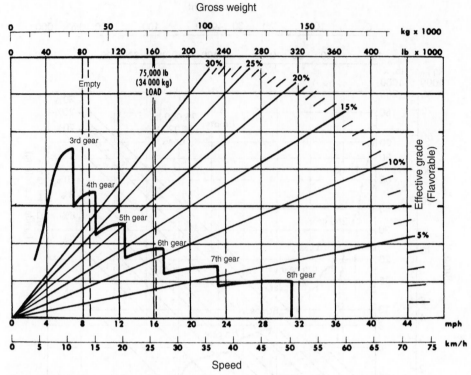

FIGURE 3. Wheel scraper retarder curve. (Reprinted Courtesy of Caterpillar Inc.)

Table 3. Average speed factors

Length of Haul Section		Starting from 0 or Coming to a Stop	Increasing Maximum Speed from Previous Section	Decreasing Maximum Speed from Previous Section
ft	m			
150	46	0.42	0.72	1.60
200	61	0.51	0.76	1.51
300	92	0.57	0.80	1.39
400	122	0.63	0.82	1.33
500	153	0.65	0.84	1.29
700	214	0.70	0.86	1.24
1000	305	0.74	0.89	1.19
2000	610	0.86	0.93	1.12
3000	915	0.90	0.95	1.08
4000	1220	0.93	0.96	1.05
5000	1525	0.95	0.97	1.04

A second method for estimating travel time over a section of haul route is to use the travel-time curves provided by some manufacturers. Separate travel-time curves are prepared for loaded (rated payload) and empty conditions, as shown in Figures 4 and 5. As you see, travel time for a section of the haul route may be read directly from the graph given section length and effective grade. However, travel-time curves cannot be used when the effective grade is negative. In this case, the average speed method must be used along with the vehicle retarder curve. To adjust for altitude deration when using travel-time curves, multiply the time

obtained from the curve by the quantity "1 + derating factor" to obtain the adjusted travel time.

The use of both the average speed and the travel-time curve method is illustrated in the example problems of this chapter.

2 DOZERS

Tractors and Dozers

A tractor equipped with a front-mounted earthmoving blade is known as a *dozer* or *bulldozer*. A dozer moves earth by lowering the blade and cutting until a full blade load of

FIGURE 4. Scraper travel time—loaded. (Reprinted Courtesy of Caterpillar Inc.)

material is obtained. It then pushes the material across the ground surface to the required location. The material is unloaded by pushing it over a cliff or into a hopper or by raising the blade to form a spoil pile.

Both rubber-tired (or wheel) dozers and crawler (or track) dozers are available. Because of their excellent traction and low ground pressure (typically 6–9 lb/sq in.; 41–62 kPa), crawler dozers (Figure 6) are well suited for use in rough terrain or areas of low trafficability. Low-ground-pressure models with extra-wide tracks are available having ground pressures as low as 3 lb/sq in. (21 kPa). Crawler dozers can operate on steeper side slopes and climb greater grades than can wheel dozers. Wheel dozers, on the other hand, operate at higher speed than do crawler dozers. Wheel dozers are also capable of operating on paved roads without damaging the surface. While the wheel tractor's dozing ability is limited somewhat by its lower traction and high ground pressure (25–35 lb/sq in.; 172–241 kPa), its high ground pressure makes it an effective soil compactor.

FIGURE 5. Scraper travel time—empty. (Reprinted Courtesy of Caterpillar Inc.)

FIGURE 6. Crawler tractor dozer. (Courtesy of New Holland Construction)

Either rubber-tired or crawler tractors may be equipped with attachments other than dozer blades. These include rakes used for gathering up brush and small fallen trees, and plows, rippers, and scarifiers, which are used to break up hard surfaces. Tractors are also used to tow many items of construction equipment, such as compactors, scrapers, and wagons. Towing applications are discussed in succeeding chapters.

Dozers may be equipped with direct-drive, power-shift, or hydrostatic transmissions. *Hydrostatic transmissions* utilize individual hydraulic motors to drive each track. Therefore, the speed of each track may be infinitely varied, forward or reverse. As a result, it is possible for a dozer equipped with a hydrostatic drive to turn in its own length by moving one track forward while the other track moves in reverse.

Recently, high-speed crawler dozers have been introduced as shown in Figure 7. This dozer is equipped with rubber tracks and an articulated frame permitting the dozer to travel on paved surfaces without damage. A GPS (Global Positioning System) receiver can be incorporated into the dozer control system to permit automatic control of excavating and finish grading. It has been estimated that such a machine can operate at up to twice the speed of a conventional crawler dozer when producing precision grades.

Another recent development in crawler dozer design is the electric drive crawler dozer. In this dozer, the dozer's diesel engine drives an electric generator which powers electric motors driving each track.

Dozer Blades

A number of types of dozer blades are available, and the four most common types are illustrated in Figure 8. The three types of adjustments that may be made to dozer blades are illustrated in Figure 9. Tilting the blade is useful for ditching and breaking up frozen or crusty soils. Pitching the blade forward reduces blade penetration and causes the loosened material to roll in front of the blade, whereas pitching the blade backward increases penetration. Angling the blade is helpful when sidehill cutting, ditching, and moving material laterally. All the blades shown in Figure 8 may be tilted except the cushion blade. However, only the angle blade may be angled.

The two indicators of potential dozer performance are based on the ratio of tractor power to blade size. These indicators are horsepower per foot of cutting edge and horsepower per loose cubic yard. A blade's *horsepower per foot of cutting edge* provides a measure of the blade's ability to penetrate hard soils. The *horsepower per loose cubic yard* rating provides an indication of the blade's ability to push material once the blade is loaded.

FIGURE 7. High-speed crawler dozer. (Courtesy of John Deere Construction & Forestry Company)

Straight blade

Angle blade

Universal blade

Cushion blade

FIGURE 8. Common types of dozer blades.

Tilting

Pitching

Angling

FIGURE 9. Dozer blade adjustment.

The wings on the universal blade (Figure 8) enable it to push a large volume of material over long distances. However, its low horsepower per foot of cutting edge and per cubic yard limit its ability to penetrate hard soils or to move heavy materials. The straight blade is considered the most versatile dozer blade. Its smaller size gives it good penetrating and load pushing ability. The ability of angle blades to angle approximately 25° to either side makes them very effective in sidehill cutting, ditching, and backfilling. They may also be used for rough grading and for moving material laterally. The cushion blade is reinforced and equipped with shock absorbers to enable it to push-load scrapers. It may also be used for cleanup of the loading or dumping areas and for general dozing when not push-loading scrapers. Other available types of dozer blades include light-material U-blades, special clearing blades, and ripdozer blades (blades equipped with ripper shanks on each end).

Estimating Dozer Production

The basic earthmoving production equation Production = Volume per cycle × Cycles per hour equation may be applied in estimating dozer production. This method requires an estimate of the average blade load and the dozer cycle time. There are several methods available for estimating average blade load, including the blade manufacturer's capacity rating, previous experience under similar conditions, and actual measurement of several typical loads. A suggested method for calculating blade volume by measuring blade load is as follows:

- Doze a full blade load, then lift the blade while moving forward on a level surface until an even pile is formed.
- Measure the width of the pile (W) perpendicular to the blade and in line with the inside of each track or wheel. Average the two measurements.
- Measure the height (H) of the pile in a similar manner.
- Measure the length of the pile parallel to the blade.
- Calculate blade volume using Equation 10.

$$\frac{\text{Blade load}}{(\text{LCY})} = 0.0139 \times H(\text{ft}) \times W(\text{ft}) \times L(\text{ft}) \qquad (10A)$$

$$\frac{\text{Blade load}}{(\text{LCM})} = 0.375 \times H(\text{m}) \times W(\text{m}) \times L(\text{m}) \qquad (10B)$$

Total dozer cycle time is the sum of its fixed cycle time and variable cycle time. *Fixed cycle time* represents the time required to maneuver, change gears, start loading, and dump. Table 4 may be used to estimate dozer fixed cycle time. *Variable cycle time* is the time required to doze and return. Since the haul distance is relatively short, a dozer usually returns in reverse gear. Table 5 provides typical operating speeds for dozing and return. Some manufacturers provide dozer production estimating charts for their equipment.

Table 4. Typical dozer fixed cycle times

Operating Conditions	Time (min)
Power-shift transmission	0.05
Direct-drive transmission	0.10
Hard digging	0.15

Table 5. Typical dozer operating speeds

Operating Conditions	Speeds
Dozing	
Hard materials, haul 100 ft (30 m) or less	1.5 mi/h (2.4 km/h)
Hard materials, haul over 100 ft (30 m)	2.0 mi/h (3.2 km/h)
Loose materials, haul 100 ft (30 m) or less	2.0 mi/h (3.2 km/h)
Loose materials, haul over 100 ft (30 m)	2.5 mi/h (4.0 km/h)
Return	
100 ft (30 m) or less	Maximum reverse speed in second range (power shift) or reverse speed in gear used for dozing (direct drive)
Over 100 ft (30 m)	Maximum reverse speed in third range (power shift) or highest reverse speed (direct drive)

Example 6 A power-shift crawler tractor has a rated blade capacity of 10 LCY (7.65 LCM). The dozer is excavating loose common earth and pushing it a distance of 200 ft (61 m). Maximum reverse speed in third range is 5 mi/h (8 km/h). Estimate the production of the dozer if job efficiency is 50 min/h.

Solution

$$\text{Fixed time} = 0.05 \text{ min} \quad (\text{Table 4})$$

$$\text{Dozing speed} = 2.5 \text{ mi/h } (4.0 \text{ km/h}) \quad (\text{Table 5})$$

$$\text{Dozing time} = \frac{200}{2.5 \times 88} = 0.91 \text{ min}$$

$$\left[= \frac{61}{4 \times 16.7} = 0.91 \text{ min} \right]$$

Note: 1 mi/h = 88 ft/min; 1 km/h = 16.7 m/min

$$\text{Return time} = \frac{200}{5 \times 88} = 0.45 \text{ min}$$

$$\left[= \frac{61}{8 \times 16.7} = 0.45 \text{ min} \right]$$

$$\text{Cycle time} = 0.05 + 0.91 + 0.45 = 1.41 \text{ min}$$

$$\text{Production} = 10 \times \frac{50}{1.41} = 355 \text{ LCY/h}$$

$$\left[= 7.65 \times \frac{50}{1.41} = 271 \text{ LCM/h} \right]$$

Job Management

Some techniques used to increase dozer production include downhill dozing, slot dozing, and blade-to-blade dozing. By taking advantage of the force of gravity, downhill dozing enables blade load to be increased or cycle time to be reduced compared to dozing on the level. Slot dozing utilizes a shallow trench (or slot) cut between the loading and dumping areas to increase the blade capacity that can be carried on each cycle. Under favorable conditions, slot dozing may increase dozer production as much as 50%. The slot dozing technique may be applied to the excavation of large cut areas by leaving uncut sections between slots. These uncut sections are removed after all other material has been excavated. Blade-to-blade dozing involves two dozers operating together with their blades almost touching. This technique results in a combined blade capacity considerably greater than that of two single blades. However, the technique is not efficient for use over short dozing distances because of the extra maneuvering time required. Mechanically coupled side-by-side (S × S) dozers equipped with a single large blade are available and are more productive than are blade-to-blade dozers.

Undercarriages (including track, rollers, idlers, and drive sprockets) are high wear items on all tracked equipment. They are also expensive to buy and maintain. Some operating suggestions for reducing undercarriage wear include the following:

- Make a daily equipment inspection with special attention to the undercarriage.

- Avoid spinning the track by reducing track speed until slippage is minimized.
- Don't operate the equipment at high speed, especially over rough ground or when operating in reverse.
- Use rubber track or rubber track pads when operating on concrete or other hard surfaces.
- During operation, minimize turns. Also, attempt to balance left and right turns and operation up- and down-slope. Alternate directions when it is necessary to traverse slopes.

3 LOADERS

A tractor equipped with a front-end bucket is called a *loader, front-end loader,* or *bucket loader.* Both wheel loaders (Figure 10) and track loaders (Figure 11) are available. Loaders are used for excavating soft to medium-hard material, loading hoppers and haul units, stockpiling material, backfilling ditches, and moving concrete and other construction materials.

Wheel loaders possess excellent job mobility and are capable of over-the-road movement between jobs at speeds of 25 mi/h or higher. While their ground pressure is relatively low and may be varied by the use of different-size tires and by changing inflation pressures, they do not have the all-terrain capability of track loaders. Most modern wheel loaders are *articulated.* That is, they are hinged between the front and rear axles to provide greater maneuverability.

FIGURE 10. Articulated wheel loader with articulated hauler. (Courtesy of Volvo Construction Equipment North America, Inc.)

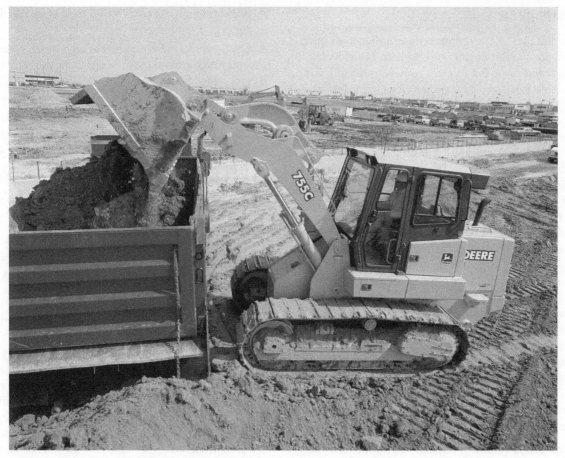

FIGURE 11. Track loader. (Courtesy of John Deere Construction & Forestry Company)

Track loaders are capable of overcoming steeper grades and side slopes than are wheel loaders. Their low ground pressure and high tractive effort enable them to operate in all but the lowest trafficability soils. However, because of their lower speed, their production is less than that of a wheel loader over longer haul distances.

Attachments available for the loader include augers, backhoes, crane booms, dozer and snow blades, and forklifts in addition to the conventional loader bucket. Some models of wheel loader are designed as a combination backhoe and loader. This piece of equipment, often called a *backhoe loader*, is illustrated in Figure 12.

Tool Carriers

Tool carriers are similar to wheel loaders but are more versatile because they are equipped with quick coupling devices to accommodate a wide range of attachments or tools. Some of the many attachments available include buckets, forks, blades, material handling arms, rotary brooms, asphalt cutters, hooks, augers, and hydraulic hammers.

Skid-Steer Loaders

A *skid-steer loader* (Figure 13) is a small wheel loader having rigid axles. It steers by braking the wheels or tracks on one side of the machine while applying power to the other side. A compact track loader is shown in Figure 14. These machines usually weigh less than 10,000 lb (4536 kg), have 17–115 hp (13–86 kW), and have lift capacities of 600–6300 lb (272–2858 kg). While rubber-tired machines predominate, track machines are also available for operating in muddy or loose soils and on steep slopes. In recent years, skid-steer loaders have become increasingly popular because of their small size, high productivity, and versatility. Like the tool carrier, they can accommodate a number of attachments in addition to the basic loader bucket. Some of the many available attachments include the following:

augers	buckets, dirt
brooms	buckets, utility
buckets, general-purpose	buckets, light-material
buckets, multipurpose	rakes
cold planers	stump grinders
forks	tillers
hammers	trenchers
landscape rake	vibratory compactors

FIGURE 12. Backhoe loader. (Courtesy of JCB Inc.)

Material Handlers

Cranes and wheel loaders are often used to move materials around a construction site. However, specialized machines called *material handlers* or *rough-terrain forklifts* have been developed for this purpose. The material handler shown in Figure 15 has a maximum lift capacity of 9000 lb (4082 kg) and a lift height of 40 ft (12 m). Other machines are available which have a maximum lift greater than 60 ft (18 m).

FIGURE 13. Skid-steer loader with backhoe attachment. (Courtesy of the Bobcat Company)

FIGURE 14. Compact track loader. (Courtesy of the Bobcat Company)

FIGURE 15. Material handler. (Courtesy of JLG Industries, Inc.)

Estimating Loader Production

Loader production may be estimated as the product of average bucket load multiplied by cycles per hour Production = Volume per cycle × Cycles per hour. Basic cycle time for a loader includes the time required for loading, dumping, making four reversals of direction, and traveling a minimum distance (15 ft or less for track loaders). Table 6 presents typical values of basic cycle time for wheel and track loaders. While manufacturers' performance curves should be used whenever possible, typical travel-time curves for wheel loaders are presented in Figure 16.

Federal Highway Administration (FHWA) studies have shown little variation in basic cycle time for wheel loaders up to a distance of 80 ft (25 m) between loading and dumping position. Therefore, travel time should not be added until one-way distance exceeds this distance.

Loader bucket capacity is rated in heaped (loose) volume. Bucket capacity should be adjusted by a bucket fill factor to obtain the best estimate of actual bucket volume.

Table 6. Basic loader cycle time

| Loading Conditions | Basic Cycle Time (min) | |
	Articulated Wheel Loader	Track Loader
Loose materials	0.35	0.30
Average material	0.50	0.35
Hard materials	0.65	0.45

Example 7 Estimate the hourly production in loose volume (LCY and LCM) of a $3^{1}/_{2}$-yd (2.68-m^3) wheel loader excavating sand and gravel (average material) from a pit and moving it to a stockpile. The average haul distance is 200 ft (61 m), the effective grade is 6%, the bucket fill factor is 1.00, and job efficiency is 50 min/h.

Solution

$$\text{Bucket volume} = 3.5 \times 1 = 3.5 \text{ LCY (2.68 LCM)}$$
$$\text{Basic cycle time} = 0.50 \text{ min} \quad \text{(Table 6)}$$
$$\text{Travel time} = 0.30 \text{ min} \quad \text{(Figure 14)}$$
$$\text{Cycle time} = 0.50 + 0.30 = 0.80 \text{ min}$$
$$\text{Production} = 3.5 \times \frac{50}{0.80} = 219 \text{ LCY/h}$$
$$\left[= 2.68 \times \frac{50}{0.80} = 168 \text{ LCM/h} \right]$$

Job Management

Some considerations involved in choosing a loader for a project have already been presented. Cutting of tires is a major problem when loading shot rock with a wheel loader. Type L-5 tires (rock, extra deep tread) should be used to increase tire life when loading rock. The pit must be kept well drained, because water acts as a lubricant to increase the cutting action of rock on rubber tires.

Because of tipping load limitations, the weight of the material being handled may limit the size of the bucket that may be used on a loader. In selection of a loader, consideration must also be given to the clearances required during loading

FIGURE 16. Travel time, wheel loader (haul + return).

One-way haul distance

*Effective grade

FIGURE 17. Multisegment loader bucket.

and dumping. Like excavators, optimum positioning of the loader and haul units will minimize loading, maneuver, and dump times. Multisegment buckets, also called 4-in-1 buckets and multipurpose buckets (Figure 17), are capable of performing as a clamshell, dozer, or scraper, as well as a conventional loader. Such buckets are often more effective than are conventional buckets in handling wet, sticky materials. Blasting or ripping hard materials before attempting to load them will often increase loader production in such materials.

4   SCRAPERS

Operation and Employment

Scrapers are capable of excavating, hauling, and dumping material over medium- to long-haul distances. However, only the elevating scraper and the pull-scraper are capable of

achieving high efficiency in loading without the assistance of a pusher tractor or another scraper. Loading procedures are discussed later in this section. The scraper excavates (or cuts) by lowering the front edge of its bowl into the soil. The bowl front edge is equipped with replaceable cutting blades, which may be straight, curved, or extended at the center (stinger arrangement). Both the stinger arrangement and curved blades provide better penetration than does a straight blade. However, straight blades are preferred for finish work.

Although there are a number of different types of scrapers, principal types include single-engine overhung (two-axle) scrapers, three-axle scrapers, twin-engine all-wheel-drive scrapers, elevating scrapers, auger scrapers, push-pull or twin-hitch scrapers, and pull-scrapers. *Two-axle* or *overhung scrapers* utilize a tractor having only one axle (Figure 18). Such an arrangement has a lower rolling resistance and greater maneuverability than does a *three-axle scraper* that is pulled by

FIGURE 18. Twin-engine all-wheel drive scraper. (Reprinted Courtesy of Caterpillar Inc.)

a conventional four-wheel tractor. However, the additional stability of the three-axle scraper permits higher operating speeds on long, relatively flat haul roads. *All-wheel-drive scrapers*, as the name implies, utilize drive wheels on both the tractor and the scraper. Normally, such units are equipped with twin engines. The additional power and drive wheels give these units greater tractive effort than that of conventional scrapers. *Elevating scrapers* (Figure 19) utilize a ladder-type elevator to assist in cutting and lifting material into the scraper bowl. Elevating scrapers are not designed to be push-loaded and may be damaged by pushing. *Auger scrapers* are self-loading scrapers that use a rotating auger (similar to a posthole auger) located in the center of the scraper bowl to help lift material into the bowl. *Push-pull* or *twin-hitch scrapers* (Figure 20) are all-wheel-drive scrapers equipped with coupling devices that enable two scrapers to assist each other in loading. Their operation is described later in this section.

Pull-scrapers (Figure 21) utilize one or more scraper pans towed by a tractor. One of the earliest types of scraper, these scrapers had largely fallen out of construction use but are now finding renewed construction application. When towed by a tractor having high-flotation tires, these units can operate under adverse soil conditions and are capable of loading without pusher assistance in sandy and sandy-clay soils. Such a combination has a lower initial price and lower operating cost than does a conventional scraper but can be even more productive on medium hauls in suitable soils. Pull-scrapers can also be connected in tandem as shown in Figure 22.

Estimating Scraper Production

Scraper cycle time is estimated as the sum of fixed cycle time and variable cycle time. Fixed cycle time in this case includes spot time, load time, and maneuver and dump times. Spot

FIGURE 19. Elevating scraper. (Reprinted Courtesy of Caterpillar Inc.)

FIGURE 20. Twin-hitch scraper loading. (Courtesy of CMI Terex Corporation)

FIGURE 21. Pull scraper. (Courtesy of John Deere & Company)

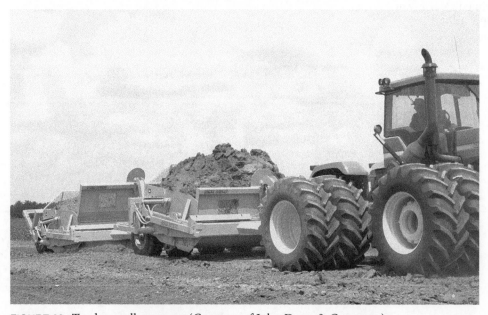

FIGURE 22. Tandem pull-scrapers. (Courtesy of John Deere & Company)

Table 7. Scraper fixed time (min)

	Spot Time		
Conditions	Single Pusher	Tandem Pusher	
Favorable	0.2	0.1	
Average	0.3	0.2	
Unfavorable	0.5	0.5	

	Load Time				
Conditions	Single Pusher	Tandem Pusher	Elevating Scraper	Auger	Push-Pull*
Favorable	0.5	0.4	0.8	0.7	0.7
Average	0.6	0.5	1.0	0.9	1.0
Unfavorable	1.0	0.9	1.5	1.3	1.4

	Maneuver and Dump Time	
Conditions	Single Engine	Twin Engine
Favorable	0.3	0.3
Average	0.7	0.6
Unfavorable	1.0	0.9

*Per pair of scrapers.

time represents the time required for a unit to position itself in the cut and begin loading, including any waiting for a pusher. Table 7 provides typical values of fixed cycle time for scrapers.

Variable cycle time, or travel time, includes haul time and return time. As usual, haul and return times are estimated by the use of travel-time curves or by using the average-speed method with performance and retarder curves. It is usually necessary to break a haul route up into sections having similar total resistance values. The total travel time required to traverse all sections is found as the sum of the section travel times.

In determining the payload per scraper cycle, it is necessary to check both the rated weight payload and the heaped volume capacity. The volume corresponding to the lesser of these two values will, of course, govern. The method of estimating production is illustrated in Examples 8 and 9.

Example 8 Estimate the production of a single-engine two-axle tractor scraper whose travel-time curves are shown in Figures 4 and 5 based on the following information:

Maximum heaped volume = 31 LCY (24 LCM)

Maximum payload = 75,000 lb (34,020 kg)

Material: Sandy clay, 3200 lb/BCY (1898 kg/BCM), 2650 lb/LCY (1571 kg/LCM), rolling resistance 100 lb/ton (50kg/t)

Job efficiency = 50min/h

Operating conditions = average

Single pusher

Haul route:

    Section 1. Level loading area

    Section 2. Down a 4% grade, 2000 ft (610 m)

    Section 3. Level dumping area

    Section 4. Up a 4% grade, 2000 ft (610 m)

    Section 5. Level turnaround, 600 ft (183 m)

Solution

Load per cycle:

Weight of heaped capacity = 31 × 2650 = 82,150 lb

$$[= 24 \times 1571 = 37{,}704 \text{ kg}]$$

Weight exceeds rated payload of 75,000 lb (34,020 kg); therefore, maximum capacity is

$$\text{Load} = \frac{75{,}000}{3200} = 23.4 \text{ BCY/load}$$

$$\left[= \frac{34{,}020}{1898} = 17.9 \text{ BCM/load} \right]$$

Effective grade:

$$\text{Haul} = -4.0 + \frac{100}{20} = +1\%$$

$$\left[= -4.0 + \frac{50}{10} = +1\% \right]$$

$$\text{Return} = 4.0 + \frac{100}{20} = +9\%$$

$$\left[= 4.0 + \frac{50}{10} = +9\% \right]$$

$$\text{Turnaround} = 0 + \frac{100}{20} = 5\%$$

$$\left[= 0 + \frac{50}{10} = +5\% \right]$$

Travel time:

$$\text{Section 2} = 1.02 \text{ min} \quad \text{(Figure 4)}$$
$$\text{Section 4} = 1.60 \text{ min} \quad \text{(Figure 5)}$$
$$\text{Section 5} = \underline{0.45 \text{ min}} \quad \text{(Figure 5)}$$
$$\text{Total} = 3.07 \text{ min}$$

Fixed cycle (Table 7):

$$\text{Load spot} = 0.3 \text{ min}$$
$$\text{Load} = 0.6 \text{ min}$$
$$\text{Maneuver and dump} = \underline{0.7 \text{ min}}$$
$$\text{Total} = 1.6 \text{ min}$$

$$\text{Total cycle time} = 3.07 + 1.6 \text{ min} = 4.67 \text{ min}$$

$$\text{Estimated production} = 23.4 \times \frac{50}{4.67} = 251 \text{ BCY/h}$$

$$\left[= 17.9 \times \frac{50}{4.67} = 192 \text{ BCM/h} \right]$$

Example 9 Solve the problem of Example 8 using the average-speed method and the performance curves of Figure 2.

Solution

$$\text{Payload} = 23.4 \text{ BCY (17.9 BCM) from Example 8}$$

Effective grades from Example 8:

$$\text{Haul} = +1.0\%$$
$$\text{Return} = +9.0\%$$
$$\text{Turnaround} = +5.0\%$$

Maximum speed (Figure 2):

$$\text{Haul} = 32 \text{ mi/h (52 km/h)}$$
$$\text{Return} = 16 \text{ mi/h (26 km/h)}$$
$$\text{Turnaround} = 28 \text{ mi/h (45 km/h)}$$

Average speed factor (Table 3):

$$\text{Haul} = 0.86 \times 0.86 = 0.74$$
$$\text{Return} = 0.86$$
$$\text{Turnaround} = 0.68$$

Average speed:

$$\text{Haul} = 32 \times 0.74 = 24 \text{ mi/h (38 km/h)}$$
$$\text{Return} = 16 \times 0.86 = 13 \text{ mi/h (22 km/h)}$$
$$\text{Turnaround} = 28 \times 0.68 = 19 \text{ mi/h (31 km/h)}$$

Travel time:

$$\text{Haul} = \frac{2000}{24 \times 88} = 0.95 \text{ min}$$

$$\left[= \frac{610}{38 \times 16.7} = 0.95 \text{ min} \right]$$

$$\text{Return} = \frac{2000}{13 \times 88} = 1.75 \text{ min}$$

$$\left[= \frac{610}{21 \times 16.7} = 1.75 \text{ min} \right]$$

$$\text{Turnaround} = \frac{600}{19 \times 88} = 0.36 \text{ min}$$

$$\left[= \frac{183}{31 \times 16.7} = 0.36 \text{ min} \right]$$

$$\text{Total} = 3.06 \text{ min}$$

$$\text{Fixed cycle} = 1.6 \text{ min} \quad \text{(Example 8)}$$

$$\text{Total cycle time} = 4.66 \text{ min}$$

$$\text{Estimated production} = 2.34 \times \frac{50}{4.66} = 251 \text{ BCY/h}$$

$$\left[= 17.9 \times \frac{50}{4.66} = 192 \text{ BCM/h} \right]$$

Note: The travel-time curves of Figures 4 and 5 assume acceleration from an initial velocity of 2.5 mi/h (4 km/h) upon leaving the cut and fill and deceleration to 2.5 mi/h (4 km/h) upon entering the cut and fill. The result of adding together the travel times for several sections will, because of an excessive allowance for acceleration and deceleration, yield a travel time greater than that obtained by the use of the average-speed method. The time estimate obtained by the use of the average-speed method should be more realistic.

Push-Loading

Except for elevating, pull-scrapers, and push-pull scrapers, wheel scrapers require the assistance of pusher tractors to obtain maximum production. The three basic methods of push-loading scrapers are illustrated in Figure 23. The back-track method is most commonly used since it permits all scrapers to load in the same general area. However, it is also the slowest of the three methods because of the additional pusher travel distance. Chain loading is suitable for a long, narrow cut area. Shuttle loading requires two separate fill areas for efficient operations.

A complete pusher cycle consists of maneuver time (while the pusher moves into position and engages the scraper), load time, boost time (during which the pusher assists in accelerating the scraper out of the cut), and return time. Tandem pushing involves the use of two pusher tractors operating one behind the other during loading and boosting. The use of tandem pushers reduces scraper load time and frequently results in obtaining larger scraper loads. The dual tractor described in Section 2 is a more efficient pusher than tandem tractors because the dual tractor is controlled by a single operator and no time is lost in coordination between two operators.

FIGURE 23. Methods of push-loading scrapers.

Optimum Load Time

In field studies performed by Caterpillar Inc., it was found that the scraper loading time which yielded maximum scraper production in a given situation was usually less than the loading time required to obtain the maximum scraper load. Caterpillar called the loading time which yielded maximum production the *optimum load time*. A simple method for determining the optimum load time is described below.

To determine the optimum load time, it is first necessary to plot the volume of scraper load versus loading time. To do this, the scraper must be loaded for controlled periods of time and weighed each time after loading. The load weight is then converted into scraper volume and plotted as a *load growth curve* (see Figure 24). As you recognize, the slope of the load growth curve at any loading time corresponds to the rate of loading at that time.

A simple graphical method for determining the optimum load time is illustrated in Figure 25. First, extend the horizontal axis of the load growth curve to the left of the origin. Next, locate a point (A) on this axis whose distance from the origin represents "total cycle time less loading time." Finally, draw a tangent to the load growth curve from Point A intersecting the curve at Point B. The loading time (C) corresponding to Point B is the optimum load time. To prove this, realize that the distance A–C represents total scraper cycle time and B–C represents the corresponding volume per cycle. The slope of the line A–B thus represents production (volume) per unit of time. When the slope of A–B is at a maximum, the scraper production per unit of time is maximized.

Calculating the Number of Pushers Required

The number of scrapers that can theoretically be handled by one pusher without a scraper having to wait for a pusher can be calculated by the use of Equation 11. The number of pushers required to fully service a given scraper fleet may then be determined from Equation 12. It is suggested that the result obtained from Equation 11 be rounded down to one decimal place for use in Equation 12. The result obtained from Equation 12 must be rounded up to the next whole number to ensure that scrapers do not have to wait for a pusher. Methods for estimating scraper cycle time have already been presented. Table 8 may be used for estimating pusher cycle time.

$$\text{Number of scrapers served} = \frac{\text{Scraper cycle time}}{\text{Pusher cycle time}} \quad (11)$$

$$\frac{\text{Number of}}{\text{pushers required}} = \frac{\text{Number of scrapers}}{\text{Number served by one pusher}} \quad (12)$$

When the number of pushers actually used is less than the number required to fully serve the scraper fleet, expected production is reduced to that obtained using Equation 13.

FIGURE 24. A load growth curve.

In performing this calculation, use the precise number of pushers required, not the integer value.

$$\text{Production} = \frac{\text{Number of pushers}}{\text{Required number}} \times \frac{\text{No. of}}{\text{scrapers}} \times \frac{\text{Production}}{\text{per scraper}} \quad (13)$$

Table 8. Typical pusher cycle time (min)

Loading Method	Single Pusher	Tandem Pusher
Back-track	1.5	1.4
Chain or shuttle	1.0	0.9

Example 10 The estimated cycle time for a wheel scraper is 6.5 min. Calculate the number of pushers required to serve a fleet of nine scrapers using single pushers. Determine the result for both backtrack and chain-loading methods.

Solution

Number of scrapers per pusher (Eq 11):

$$\text{Back-track} = \frac{6.5}{1.5} = 4.3$$

$$\text{Chain} = \frac{6.5}{1.0} = 6.5$$

FIGURE 25. Finding the optimum load time.

Number of pushers required (Eq 12):

$$\text{Back-track} = \frac{9}{4.3} = 2.1 = 3$$

$$\text{Chain} = \frac{9}{6.5} = 1.4 = 2$$

Example 11 Find the expected production of the scraper fleet of Example 10 if only one pusher is available and the chain-loading method is used. Expected production of a single scraper assuming adequate pusher support is 226 BCY/h (173 BCM/h).

Solution

Number of pushers required to fully serve fleet = 1.4

$$\text{Production} = \frac{1}{1.4} \times 9 \times 226 = 1453 \text{ BCY/h} \quad \text{(Eq 13)}$$

$$\left[= \frac{1}{1.4} \times 9 \times 173 = 1112 \text{ BCM/h} \right] \quad \text{(Eq 13)}$$

Push-Pull Loading

In *push-pull* or *twin-hitch* scraper loading, two all-wheel-drive scrapers assist each other to load without the use of pusher tractors. The scrapers are equipped with special push blocks and coupling devices, as shown in Figure 20. The sequence of loading operations is as follows:

1. The first scraper to arrive in the cut starts to self-load.
2. The second scraper arrives, makes contact, couples, and pushes the front scraper to assist it in loading.
3. When the front scraper is loaded, the operator raises its bowl. The second scraper then begins to load with the front scraper pulling to assist in loading.
4. The two scrapers uncouple and separate for the haul to the fill.

Although there are a number of advantages claimed for this method of loading, basically it offers the loading advantages of self-loading scrapers while retaining the hauling advantages of standard scrapers. No pusher tractor or its operator is required. There is no problem of pusher-scraper mismatch and no lost time due to pusher downtime. However, scrapers must operate in pairs so that if one scraper breaks down, its partner must be diverted to a different operation. Conditions favoring push-pull operations include long, straight hauls with relatively easy to load materials. An adequate number of spreading and compacting units must be available at the fill, since two scrapers dump almost simultaneously.

Job Management

The type of scraper that may be expected to yield the lowest cost per unit of production is a function of the total resistance and the haul distance, as shown in Figure 26. Elevating scrapers can use their self-loading ability effectively for short hauls. However, their additional weight puts them at a disadvantage on long hauls. Of the conventional scrapers, single-engine overhung units are best suited to medium distances on relatively flat haul roads where maneuverability is important and adequate pusher power is available. Three-axle units are faster on long hauls and uneven surfaces. All-wheel-drive tandem-powered units are favored for conditions of high total resistance at all but the shortest haul distances. Notice that push-pull or twin-hitch scrapers overlap the entire all-wheel-drive zone of Figure 26 and extend into the elevating and conventional zones.

Some techniques for maximizing scraper production include the following:

- Use downhill loading whenever possible to reduce the required pusher power and load time.
- Use chain or shuttle loading methods if possible.
- Use rippers or scarifiers to loosen hard soils before attempting to load.
- Have pushers give scrapers an adequate boost to accelerate units out of the cut.

FIGURE 26. Scraper application zones.

= push-pull zone

- Keep the cut in good condition by using pushers during their idle time or by employing other equipment. Provide adequate drainage in the cut to improve trafficability.
- Maintain the haul road in the best possible condition. Full-time use of a motor grader on the haul road will usually pay off in increased scraper production.
- Make the haul road wide enough to permit high-speed hauling without danger. One-way haul roads should be utilized whenever possible.
- Keep the fill surface smooth and compacted to minimize scraper time in the fill.
- Boost scrapers on the fill if spreading time is excessive.

Supervisors must carefully control operations in the cut, on the haul road, and in the fill to maximize production. Scrapers must be kept evenly spaced throughout their cycle to avoid interference between units. Scrapers that break down or cannot maintain their place in the cycle must be repaired promptly or replaced by standby units.

5 TRUCKS AND WAGONS
Operation and Employment

Because hauling (or the transportation of excavation) is a major earthmoving activity, there are many different types of hauling equipment available to the constructor. In addition to the dozer, loader, and scraper already described, hauling equipment includes trucks, wagons, conveyor belts, and trains. Most of the belt-type conveyors used in construction are portable units used for the movement of bulk construction materials within a small area or for placing concrete. However, conveyors are capable of moving earth and stone relatively long distances at high speed. Their ability to move earth for highway construction has been demonstrated in Great Britain. In the United States, they have been utilized on a number of large construction projects, such as dams. Their application is primarily limited by their large capital cost.

Conventional freight trains may be used to haul earth or rock over long distances when tracks are located near the excavation and fill areas. However, most construction applications involve narrow-gauge rail lines built in the construction area. This type of equipment is often used to remove the spoil from tunneling. Special rail cars are available for hauling plastic concrete. Although not usually thought of as a piece of earthmoving equipment, a dredge is capable of excavating soil and fractured rock and transporting it through pipelines in the form of a slurry.

Trucks and wagons are still the most common forms of construction hauling equipment. The heavy-duty rear-dump truck is most widely used because of its flexibility of use and the ability of highway models to move rapidly between job sites. There are a wide variety of types and sizes of dump truck available. Trucks may be powered by diesel or gasoline engines, have rear axle or all-wheel drive, have two or three axles, be equipped with standard or rock bodies, and so on. Trucks used for hauling on public highways are limited by transportation regulations in their maximum width, gross weight, and axle load. There is a growing trend toward the use of off-highway models that can be larger and heavier and carry payloads up to several hundred tons. Figure 27 shows

FIGURE 27. Forty-one-ton rear-dump truck. (Courtesy of Volvo Construction Equipment North America, Inc.)

FIGURE 28. All-wheel-drive articulated dump truck. (Courtesy of CMI Terex Corporation)

a 41-ton rear-dump truck being loaded by a shovel. The all-wheel-drive articulated dump truck illustrated in Figure 28 (also called an *articulated hauler*) is finding increasing usage because of its ability to carry large loads over low-trafficability soils.

Wagons are earthmoving trailers pulled by tractors or truck-tractors. They are sometimes referred to as pure haulers because they have many characteristics of tractor-scrapers, but they are designed for hauling only. They are available in bottom-dump, end-dump, and side-dump models. Bottom-dump models are often preferred for moving earth and crushed rock because of their ability to dump and spread while moving at a relatively high speed. Dump gates are available as either longitudinal flow gates or cross-flow gates. Longitudinal flow dumping is desirable for windrowing and stockpiling while cross-flow dumping permits better spreading of base materials and aggregates. Some wagons are capable of either cross-flow or longitudinal-flow spreading. Although wagons are independent pieces of equipment, some are especially designed to work with a particular make and model of tractor. A 70-ton, bottom-dump wagon equipped with two longitudinal-flow gates is shown in Figure 29.

FIGURE 29. Bottom-dump wagon. (Courtesy of CMI Terex Corporation)

Determining the Number of Haul Units Needed

The components of the truck or wagon cycle are similar to those of the scraper described in Section 4. Thus, total cycle time is the sum of the fixed time (spot, load, maneuver, and dump) and the variable time (haul and return). The fixed time elements of spot, maneuver, and dump may be estimated by the use of Table 9. Loading time, however, should be calculated by the use of Equation 14 or 15.

$$\text{Load time} = \frac{\text{Haul unit capacity}}{\text{Loader production at 100\% efficiency}} \quad (14)$$

$$\text{Load time} = \frac{\text{Number of}}{\text{bucket loads}} \times \text{Excavator cycle time} \quad (15)$$

The reason for using an excavator loading rate based on 100% excavator efficiency in Equation 14 is that excavators have been found to operate at or near-100% efficiency when actually loading. Thus, the use of the 100% efficiency loading rate is intended to ensure that an adequate number of trucks are provided so that the excavator will not have to wait for a truck. Either bank or loose measure may be used in Equation 14, but the same unit must be used in both numerator and denominator.

The number of trucks theoretically required to keep a loader fully occupied and thus obtain the full production of the loader may be calculated by the use of Equation 16. Although this method gives reasonable values for field use, it should be recognized that some instances of the loader waiting for haul units will occur in the field when this method is used. This is due to the fact that some variance in loader and hauler cycle time will occur in the real-world situation. More realistic results may be obtained by the use of computer simulation techniques or the mathematical technique known as queueing theory (see reference 5).

$$\frac{\text{Number of haulers}}{\text{required } (N)} = \frac{\text{Haul unit cycle time}}{\text{Load time}} \quad (16)$$

The result obtained from Equation 16 must be rounded up to the next integer. Using this method, the expected production of the loader/hauler system is the same as though the excavator were simply excavating and stockpiling. Reviewing the procedure, system output is assumed to equal

Table 9. Spot, maneuver, and dump time for trucks and wagons (min)

Conditions	Bottom Dump	Rear Dump
Favorable	1.1	0.5
Average	1.6	1.1
Unfavorable	2.0	2.5

normal loader output, including the usual job efficiency factor. However, the number of haul units required is calculated using 100% loader efficiency.

If more than the theoretically required number of trucks is supplied, no increase in system production will occur, because system output is limited to excavator output. However, if less than the required number of trucks is supplied, system output will be reduced, because the excavator will at times have to wait for a haul unit. The expected production in this situation may be calculated by the use of Equation 17. In performing this calculation, use the precise value of N, not its integer value.

$$\frac{\text{Expected}}{\substack{\text{production} \\ \text{(Number units} \\ \text{less than } N)}} = \frac{\substack{\text{Actual number} \\ \text{of units}}}{N} = \frac{\text{Excavator}}{\text{production}} \quad (17)$$

Example 12 Given the following information on a shovel/truck operation, (a) calculate the number of trucks theoretically required and the production of this combination; (b) calculate the expected production if two trucks are removed from the fleet.

$$\frac{\text{Shovel production}}{\text{at 100\% efficiency}} = 371 \text{ BCY/h (283 BCM/h)}$$

$$\text{Job efficiency} = 0.75$$

$$\text{Truck capacity} = 20 \text{ BCY (15.3 BCM)}$$

$$\frac{\text{Truck cycle time,}}{\text{excluding loading}} = 0.5\text{h}$$

Solution

$$\text{(a) Load time} = \frac{20}{371} = 0.054 \text{ h} \quad \text{(Eq 14)}$$

$$\left[= \frac{15.3}{283} = 0.054 \text{ h} \right]$$

$$\text{Truck cycle time} = 0.5 + 0.054 = 0.554 \text{ h}$$

$$\frac{\text{Number of}}{\text{trucks required}} = \frac{0.554}{0.054} = 10.3 = 11 \quad \text{(Eq 16)}$$

$$\text{Expected production} = 371 \times 0.75 = 278 \text{ BCY/h}$$

$$[= 283 \times 0.75 = 212 \text{ BCM/h}]$$

(b) With nine trucks available,

$$\frac{\text{Expected}}{\text{production}} = \frac{9}{10.3} \times 278 = 243 \text{ BCY/h} \quad \text{(Eq 17)}$$

$$\left[= \frac{9}{10.3} \times 212 = 186 \text{ BCM/h} \right]$$

Job Management

An important consideration in the selection of excavator/haul unit combinations is the effect of the size of the target that the haul unit presents to the excavator operator. If the target is too small, excessive spillage will result and excavator cycle time will be increased. Studies have found that the resulting loss of production may range from 10 to 20%. As a rule, haul units loaded by shovels, backhoes, and loaders should have a capacity of three to five times excavator bucket capacity. Because of their less precise control, clamshells and draglines require larger targets. A haul unit capacity of 5–10 times excavator bucket capacity is recommended for these excavators. Haul units that hold an integer number of bucket loads are also desirable. Using a partially filled bucket to top off a load is an inefficient operation.

Time lost in spotting haul units for loading is another major cause of inefficiency. As discussed under excavator operations, reducing the excavator swing angle between digging and loading will increase production. The use of two loading positions, one on each side of the excavator, will reduce the loss of excavator production during spotting. When haul units are required to back into loading position, bumpers or spotting logs will assist the haul unit operator in positioning his vehicle in the minimum amount of time.

Some other techniques for maximizing haul unit production include the following:

- If possible, stagger starting and quitting times so that haul units do not bunch up at the beginning and end of the shift.

- Do not overload haul units. Overload results in excessive repair and maintenance.
- Maintain haul roads in good condition to reduce travel time and minimize equipment wear.
- Develop an efficient traffic pattern for loading, hauling, and dumping.
- Roads must be wide enough to permit safe travel at maximum speeds.
- Provide standby units (about 20% of fleet size) to replace units that break down or fail to perform adequately.
- Do not permit speeding. It is a dangerous practice; it also results in excessive equipment wear and upsets the uniform spacing of units in the haul cycle.

In unit price earthmoving contracts, payment for movement of soil or rock from cut to fill that exceeds a specified distance is termed *overhaul*. Overhaul can be minimized by selection of an optimum design surface elevation (grade) and by use of borrow and waste areas at appropriate locations.

Problems

1. Using the data of Problem 7, calculate the expected production and unit cost of loading and hauling if the truck fleet consists of five trucks.

2. A scraper whose weight on the driving wheels is 36,000 lb (16,330 kg) has a gross weight of 64,000 lb (29,030 kg). If the road surface is wet earth having a rolling resistance factor of 120 lb/ton (60 kg/t), what is the maximum grade the scraper could ascend?

3. The tractor-scraper whose travel-time curves are shown in Figures 4 and 5 hauls its rated payload 4000 ft (1220 m) up a 5% grade from the cut to the fill and returns empty over the same route. The rolling resistance factor for the haul road is 120 lb/ton (60 kg/t). Estimate the scraper travel time.

4. A power-shift crawler tractor is excavating tough clay and pushing it a distance of 95 ft (29 m). Maximum reverse speeds are as follows: first range, 3 mi/h (4.8 km/h); second range, 5 mi/h (8.1 km/h); and third range, 8 mi/h (12.9 km/h). Rated blade capacity is 10 LCY (7.65 LCM). Estimate dozer production if the job efficiency factor is 0.83.

5. The load growth data for a scraper are given below. The scraper's total cycle time minus load time is 3.0 min. Find the scraper's optimum load time.

Load Time min	Average Load	
	BCY	BCM
0.2	11.4	8.37
0.4	18.7	14.3
0.6	22.7	17.4
0.8	24.8	19.0
1.0	26.1	20.0
1.2	26.8	20.5
1.4	27.2	20.8

6. How many hours should it take an articulated wheel loader equipped with a 4-yd (3.06-m^3) bucket to load 3000 cu yd (2294 m^3) of gravel from a stockpile into rail cars if the average haul distance is 300 ft (91.5 m) one way? The area is level with a rolling resistance factor of 120 lb/ton (60 kg/t). Job efficiency is estimated at 50 min/h.

7. A hydraulic shovel will be used to excavate sandy clay and load it into 12-BCY (9.2-BCM) dump trucks. The shovel's production at 100% efficiency is estimated to be 300 BCY/h (229 BCM/h), and job efficiency is 0.80.

Truck travel time is estimated to be 8.0 min, and truck fixed cycle time (excluding loading) is estimated to be 2.0 min. Equipment costs for the shovel and trucks are $40/h and $20/h, respectively.

a. How many trucks are theoretically required to obtain maximum production?

b. What is the expected production of the system in bank measure using this number of trucks?

c. What is the expected unit loading and hauling cost ($/BCY or $/BCM)?

8. A wheel tractor-scraper whose weight on the driving wheels is 38,720 lb (17,563 kg) has a gross weight of 70,400 lb (31,933 kg). If the road surface is dry earth having a rolling resistance factor of 100 lb/ton (50 kg/t), what is the maximum grade the scraper could ascend?

9. What is a pull-scraper? What advantages does it have over conventional scrapers?

10. Develop a computer program to calculate the number of pushers required to service a specified scraper fleet. Input should include scraper cycle time, method of push loading, and whether single or tandem pushers will be used. Using your program, verify the solution given in Example 10.

References

1. Bernard, D. A., T. R. Ferragut, and D. L. Neumann. *Production Efficiency Study on Large-Capacity, Rubber-Tired Front-End Loaders* (Report No. FHWA-RDDP-PC-520). U.S. Department of Transportation, Federal Highway Administration, Arlington, VA, 1973.

2. *Caterpillar Performance Handbook*. Caterpillar Inc., Peoria, IL.

3. Clemmens, J. P., and R. J. Dillman. *Production Efficiency Study on Rubber-Tired Scrapers* (Report No. FHWA-DP-PC-920). U.S. Department of Transportation, Arlington, VA, 1977.

4. *Deere Performance Handbook*. Deere & Company, Moline, IL.

5. *Euclid Hauler Handbook*. VME Americas, Inc., Cleveland, OH.

6. Nunnally, S. W. *Managing Construction Equipment*, 2nd ed. Upper Saddle River, NJ: Prentice Hall, 2000.

7. *Production and Cost Estimating of Material Movement with Earthmoving Equipment*. Terex Corporation, Hudson, OH.

COMPACTING AND FINISHING

1 PRINCIPLES OF COMPACTION

The Compaction Process

Compaction is the process of increasing the density of a soil by mechanically forcing the soil particles closer together, thereby expelling air from the void spaces in the soil. Compaction should not be confused with *consolidation,* which is an increase in soil density of a cohesive soil resulting from the expulsion of water from the soil's void spaces. Consolidation may require months or years to complete, whereas compaction is accomplished in a matter of hours.

Compaction has been employed for centuries to improve the engineering properties of soil. Improvements include increased bearing strength, reduced compressibility, improved volume-change characteristics, and reduced permeability. Although the compaction principles are the same, the equipment and methods employed for compaction in building construction are usually somewhat different from those employed in heavy and highway construction. Some of the building construction characteristics producing these differences include the limited differential settlement that can be tolerated by a building foundation, the necessity for working in confined areas close to structures, and the smaller quantity of earthwork involved.

The degree of compaction that may be achieved in a particular soil depends on the soil's physical and chemical properties, the soil's moisture content, the compaction method employed, the amount of compactive effort, and the thickness of the soil layer being compacted (lift thickness). The four basic compaction forces are static weight, manipulation (or kneading), impact, and vibration. Although all compactors utilize *static weight* to achieve compaction, most compactors combine this with one or more of the other compaction forces. For example, a plate vibrator combines static weight with vibration. *Manipulation* of soil under pressure to produce compaction is most effective in plastic soils. The forces involved in impact and vibration are similar except for their frequency. *Impact or tamping* involves blows delivered at low frequencies, usually about 10 cycles per second (Hz), and is most effective in plastic soils. *Vibration* involves higher frequencies, which may extend to 80 cycles per second (Hz) or more. Vibration is particularly effective in compaction of cohesionless soils such as sand and gravel. The selection and employment of compaction equipment is discussed in Section 2.

Optimum Moisture Content

Although soil moisture content is only one of the five factors influencing compaction results, it is a very important one. As a result, a standard laboratory test called a *Proctor test* has been developed to evaluate a soil's moisture-density relationship under a specified compaction effort. Actually, there are two Proctor tests which have been standardized by the American Society for Testing and Materials (ASTM) and the American Association of State Highway and Transportation Officials (AASHTO). These are the Standard Proctor Test (ASTM D 698, AASHTO T-99) and the Modified Proctor Test (ASTM D 1557, AASHTO T-180). Characteristics of these two tests are given in Table 1. Since the modified test was developed for use where high design loads are involved (such as airport runways), the compactive effort for the modified test is more than four times as great as for the standard test.

To determine the maximum density of a soil using Proctor test procedures, compaction tests are performed over a range of soil moisture contents. The results are then plotted as dry density versus moisture content as illustrated in Figure 1. The peak of each curve represents the maximum density obtained under the compactive effort supplied by the test. As you might expect, Figure 1 shows that the maximum density achieved under the greater compactive effort of the modified test is higher than the density achieved in the standard test. Note the line labeled

From Chapter 5 of *Construction Methods and Management,* Eighth Edition. S. W. Nunnally. Copyright © 2011 by Pearson Education, Inc. Published by Pearson Prentice Hall.

Table 1. Characteristics of Proctor compaction tests

Test Details	Standard	Modified
Diameter of mold		
in.	4	4
mm	102	102
Height of sample		
in.	5 cut to 4.59	5 cut to 4.59
mm	127 cut to 117	127 cut to 117
Number of layers	3	5
Blows per layer	25	25
Weight of hammer		
lb	5.5	10
kg	2.5	4.5
Diameter of hammer		
in.	2	2
mm	51	51
Height of hammer drop		
in.	12	18
mm	305	457
Volume of sample		
cu ft	$\frac{1}{30}$	$\frac{1}{30}$
l	0.94	0.94
Compactive effort		
ft-lb/cu ft	12,400	56,200
kJ/m^3	592	2693

"zero air voids" on Figure 1. This curve represents the density at which all air voids have been eliminated; that is, all void spaces are completely filled with water. Thus, it represents the maximum possible soil density for any specified water content. Actual density will always be somewhat less than the zero air voids density because it is virtually impossible to remove all air from the soil's void spaces.

The moisture content at which maximum dry density is achieved under a specific compaction effort is referred to as the *optimum moisture content of the soil*. Referring to Figure 1, we see that for the Standard Proctor Test the optimum moisture content for this soil is about 20% of the soil's dry weight. Notice, however, that the optimum moisture content for the modified test is only about 15%. This relationship is typical for most soils. That is, a soil's optimum moisture content decreases as the compactive effort is increased. If tests are run at several different levels of compactive effort, a line of optimum moisture contents may be drawn as shown in Figure 1 to illustrate the variation of optimum moisture with compactive effort. The effect of soil type on compaction test results is illustrated in Figure 2. While most soils display a similar characteristic shape, notice the rather flat curve obtained when compacting uniform fine sands (curve 5). The compaction curve for heavy clays (curve 7) is intermediate between that of uniform fine sands and those of the more typical soils.

The importance of soil moisture content to field compaction practice can be demonstrated using Figure 1. Suppose that specifications require a density of 100 lb/cu ft (1.6 g/cm^3) for this soil and that the compactive effort being used is equal to that of the Standard Proctor Test. From Figure 1 it can be seen that the required density may be achieved at any moisture content between 13 and 24%. However, a density of 105 lb/cu ft (1.68 g/cm^3) can only be achieved at a moisture content of 20%. Relationships among field and laboratory results for various soils, different types of equipment, and varying levels of compactive effort are discussed in Section 2.

FIGURE 1. Typical compaction test results.

FIGURE 2. Modified Proctor Test results for various soils. (Courtesy of Dr. Harvey E. Wahls)

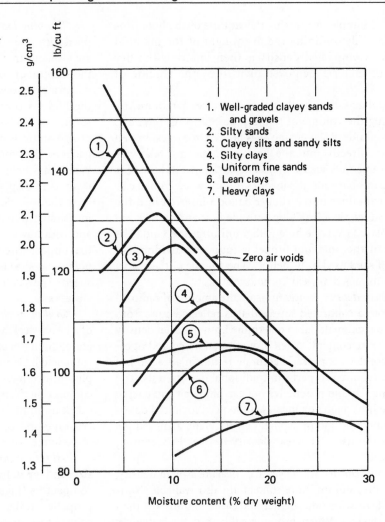

1. Well-graded clayey sands and gravels
2. Silty sands
3. Clayey silts and sandy silts
4. Silty clays
5. Uniform fine sands
6. Lean clays
7. Heavy clays

Zero air voids

Moisture content (% dry weight)

Compaction Specifications

Compaction specifications are intended to ensure that the compacted material provides the required engineering properties and a satisfactory level of uniformity. To ensure that the required engineering properties are provided, it is customary to prescribe the characteristics of the material to be used and a minimum dry density to be achieved. If the natural site material is to be compacted, only a minimum density requirement is needed. The Proctor test is widely used for expressing the minimum density requirement. That is, the specification will state that a certain percentage of Standard Proctor or Modified Proctor density must be obtained. For the soil of Figure 1, 100% of Standard Proctor density corresponds to a dry density of 105 lb/cu ft (1.68 g/cm^3). Thus, a specification requirement for 95% of Standard Proctor density corresponds to a minimum dry density of 99.8 lb/cu ft (1.60 g/cm^3).

Typical density requirements range from 90% of Standard Proctor to 100% of Modified Proctor. For example, 95% of Standard Proctor is often specified for embankments, dams, and backfills. A requirement of 90% of Modified Proctor might be used for the support of floor slabs. For the support of structures and for pavement base courses where high wheel loads are expected, requirements of 95–100% of Modified Proctor are commonly used.

A lack of uniformity in compaction may result in differential settlement of structures or may produce a bump or depression in pavements. Therefore, it is important that uniform compaction be obtained. Uniformity is commonly controlled by specifying a maximum variation of density between adjacent areas. Compaction specifications may range from performance specifications in which only a minimum dry density is prescribed to method specifications that prescribe the exact equipment and procedures to be used.

Measuring Field Density

To verify the adequacy of compaction, the density (soil or asphalt) actually obtained in the field must be measured and compared with the specified density. The methods available for performing in-place density tests include a number of traditional methods (liquid tests, sand tests, etc.), nuclear density gauges, nonnuclear density gauges, and equipment-mounted compaction measurement systems. All of the traditional test methods involve removing a material sample, measuring the volume of the hole produced, and determining the dry weight of the material removed. Compacted density is then found as the dry weight of material removed divided by the volume of the hole.

Liquid tests measure the volume of material removed by measuring the volume of liquid required to fill the hole. A viscous fluid such as engine oil is poured from a calibrated container directly into the hole when testing relatively impermeable soils such as clays and silts. A method used for more permeable materials involves forcing water from a calibrated container into a rubber balloon inserted into the hole. *Sand tests* involve filling both the hole and an inverted funnel placed over the hole with a uniform fine sand. The volume of the hole and funnel is found by dividing the weight of sand used by its density. The volume of the funnel is then subtracted to yield the hole volume.

Nuclear density devices measure the amount of radioactivity from a calibrated source that is reflected back from the compacted material to determine both material density and moisture content. When properly calibrated and operated, these devices produce accurate results in a fraction of the time required to perform traditional density tests. The increasing size and productivity of earthmoving and paving equipment have greatly increased the need for rapid determination of the soil or asphalt density being achieved. As a result, the use of nuclear density devices is becoming widespread.

Nonnuclear density gauges that measure asphalt density, temperature, and moisture content are also available. Nonnuclear devices are safer, lighter, and easier to transport than nuclear devices. When properly calibrated, such devices claim to be as accurate as nuclear devices.

Responding to the need for rapid measurement of compaction results, *equipment-mounted compaction measurement and control systems* are being offered by a number of compaction equipment manufacturers. In addition to measuring and recording the material density actually achieved, some systems control the energy being delivered by the compactor to avoid over- or undercompaction of the material. Some systems also record the temperature of the asphalt being compacted. Measurement systems which provide a continuous record of compaction results over the entire area covered by the roller are valuable for providing proof of the compaction actually achieved.

2 COMPACTION EQUIPMENT AND PROCEDURES

Types of Compaction Equipment

Principal types of compaction equipment include tamping foot rollers, grid or mesh rollers, vibratory compactors, smooth steel drum rollers, pneumatic rollers, segmented pad rollers, and tampers or rammers (see Figure 3).

Tamping foot rollers utilize a compaction drum equipped with a number of protruding feet. Tamping foot rollers are available in a variety of foot sizes and shapes, including the sheepsfoot roller. During initial compaction, roller feet penetrate the loose material and sink to the lower portion of the lifts. As compaction proceeds, the roller rises to the surface or "walks out" of the soil. All tamping foot rollers utilize static weight and manipulation to achieve compaction. Therefore, they are most effective on cohesive soils. While the sheepsfoot roller produces some impact force, it tends to displace and tear the soil as the feet enter and leave the soil. Newer types of tamping foot rollers utilize a foot designed to minimize displacement of soil during entry and withdrawal. These types of rollers more effectively utilize impact forces. High-speed tamping foot rollers may operate at speeds of 10 mi/h (16 km/h) or more. At these speeds they deliver impacts at a frequency approaching vibration.

Grid or *mesh rollers* utilize a compactor drum made up of a heavy steel mesh. Because of their design, they can operate at high speed without scattering the material being compacted. Compaction is due to static weight and impact plus limited manipulation. Grid rollers are most effective in compacting clean gravels and sands. They can also be used to break up lumps of cohesive soil. They are capable of both crushing and compacting soft rock (rock losing 20% or more in the Los Angeles Abrasion Test).

Vibratory compactors are available in a wide range of sizes and types. In size they range from small hand-operated compactors (Figure 4) through towed rollers to large self-propelled rollers (Figure 5). By type they include plate compactors, smooth drum rollers, and tamping foot rollers. Small walk-behind vibratory plate compactors and vibratory rollers are used primarily for compacting around structures and in other confined areas. Vibratory plate compactors are also available as attachments for hydraulic excavators. The towed and self-propelled units are utilized in general earthwork. Large self-propelled smooth drum vibratory rollers are often used for compacting bituminous bases and pavements. While vibratory compactors are most effective in compacting noncohesive soils, they may also be effective in compacting cohesive soils when operated at low frequency and high amplitude. Many vibratory compactors can be adjusted to vary both the frequency and amplitude of vibration.

Steel wheel or *smooth drum rollers* are used for compacting granular bases, asphaltic bases, and asphalt pavements. Types available include towed rollers and self-propelled rollers. Self-propelled rollers include three-wheel (two-axle) and two- and three-axle tandem rollers. The compactive force involved is primarily static weight.

Rubber-tired or *pneumatic rollers* are available as light- to medium-weight multitired rollers and heavy pneumatic rollers. Wobble-wheel rollers are multitired rollers with wheels mounted at an angle so that they appear to wobble as they travel. This imparts a kneading action to the soil. Heavy pneumatic rollers weighing up to

Smooth, steel wheel roller

Self-propelled vibrating roller

Small, multitired pneumatic roller

Heavy pneumatic roller

Self-propelled tamping foot roller

Self-propelled segmented
steel wheel roller

Towed sheepsfoot roller

Grid roller

FIGURE 3. Major types of compaction equipment. (Reprinted Courtesy of Caterpillar Inc.)

200 tons are used for dam construction, compaction of thick lifts, and proof rolling. Pneumatic rollers are effective on almost all types of soils but are least effective on clean sands and gravels.

Segmented pad rollers are somewhat similar to tamping foot rollers except that they utilize pads shaped as segments of a circle instead of feet on the roller drum. As a result, they produce less surface disturbance than do tamping foot rollers. Segmented pad rollers are effective on a wide range of soil types.

Rammers or *tampers* are small impact-type compactors which are primarily used for compaction in confined areas.

Some rammers, like the one shown in Figure 6, are classified as vibratory rammers because of their operating frequency.

Compaction in Confined Areas

The equipment available for compaction in confined areas such as trenches and around foundations includes small vibratory plate compactors (Figure 4), tampers or rammers (Figure 6), walk-behind static and vibratory rollers (Figure 7), and attachments for backhoes and hydraulic excavators.

FIGURE 4. Walk-behind vibratory plate compactor. (Courtesy of Wacker Corp.)

FIGURE 5. Vibratory tamping foot compactor. (Courtesy of BOMAG (USA))

FIGURE 6. Small vibratory rammer. (Courtesy of Wacker Corp.)

Compactors which mount on the boom of backhoes and excavators include compaction wheels and vibratory plate compactors. Such compactors are highly maneuverable and are especially useful for compacting the material in deep excavations such as trenches. Due to their long

reach, these compactors often eliminate the safety hazard involved in having a compactor operator down in the trench.

Compaction wheels (Figure 8) are small compactors similar in design to tamping foot rollers. They are normally mounted on the boom of backhoes or hydraulic excavators.

Vibratory plate attachments (Figure 9) are small vibratory plate compactors which are powered by the hydraulic system of the equipment to which they are attached.

Characteristics of typical compactors for confined areas are given in Table 2.

Selection of Compaction Equipment

The proper selection of compaction equipment is an important factor in obtaining the required soil density with a minimum expenditure of time and effort. The chart in Figure 10 provides a rough guide to the selection of compaction equipment based on soil type.

Compaction Operations

After selecting appropriate compaction equipment, a compaction plan must be developed. The major variables to be considered include soil moisture content, lift thickness, number of passes used, ground contact pressure, compactor weight, and compactor speed. For vibratory compactors, it is also necessary to consider the frequency and amplitude of vibration to be employed.

The general concepts of optimum moisture content as related to compaction effort and soil density have been discussed in Section 1. However, it must be recognized that the compactive effort delivered by a piece of compaction equipment will seldom be exactly the same as that of either the standard or modified compaction test. As a result, the field

FIGURE 7. Walk-behind vibratory roller with remote control. (Courtesy of Wacker Corp.)

optimum moisture content for a particular soil/compactor combination will seldom be the same as the laboratory optimum. This is illustrated by Figure 11, in which only one of the four compactors has a field optimum moisture content close to the laboratory optimum. For plastic soils it has been observed that the field optimum moisture content is close to the laboratory Standard Proctor optimum for pneumatic rollers. However, the field optimum is appreciably lower than laboratory optimum for tamping foot rollers. For nonplastic soils, the field optimum for all nonvibratory equipment appears to run about 80% of the laboratory Standard Proctor optimum. The vibratory compactor appears to be most effective in all types of soil when the field moisture is appreciably lower than laboratory optimum.

Lifts should be kept thin for most effective compaction. For all rollers, except vibratory rollers and heavy pneumatic rollers, a maximum lift thickness of 5–8 in. (15–20 cm) is suggested. Lift thicknesses of 12 in. (30 cm) or more may be satisfactory using heavy pneumatic rollers. However, precompaction with a light roller may be required to prevent rutting when heavy pneumatic rollers are used on thick lifts. The maximum lift thickness for effective vibratory compaction depends on the static weight of the compactor. Appropriate lift thicknesses for clean granular soils may range from 8 in. (20 cm) for a 1-ton compactor to 48 in. (122 cm) for a 15-ton (13.6 t) compactor. Heavy vibratory rollers have successfully compacted rock using lift thicknesses of 7 ft (2.1 m).

The compaction achieved by repeated passes of a compactor depends on the soil/compactor combination utilized. For some combinations (such as a tamping foot

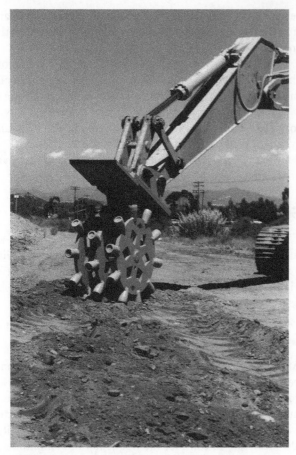

FIGURE 8. Compaction wheel mounted on hydraulic excavator. (Courtesy of American Compaction Equipment, Inc.)

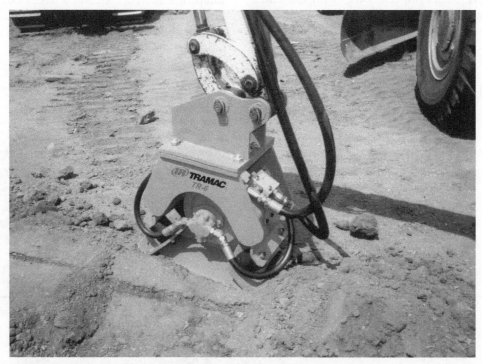

FIGURE 9. Vibratory plate compactor attachment for excavator. (Courtesy of Ingersoll-Rand Tramac)

Table 2. Compactors for confined areas

Type	Weight [lb(kg)]	Power [hp(kW)]	Frequency [vpm]	Force [lb(kN)]	Width [in.(cm)]
Rammer/tamper	108–235 (49–107)	3–5 (2–4)	550–700	1850–5900 (8.2–26.2)	4–16* (10–41)
Vibratory plate	99–1335 (45–606)	3–14 (2–10)	2580–6325	1320–15,000 (5.9–66.7)	12–32* (30–81)
Vibratory roller	1000–3400 (454–1542)	7–24 (5–32)	1800–4200	3400–16,000 (15.1–71.2)	4–43 (10–109)
Excavator Attachments					
Compaction wheel	600–5155 (272–2338)	NA	NA	NA	4–46 (10–117)
Vibratory compactor	825–2250 (374–1021)	NA	1700–2400	6400–22,000 (28.5–97.9)	19–35** (48–89)

*Extensions available.
**Narrow trench attachments available.

Material	Steel wheel	Pneumatic	Vibratory	Tamping foot	Grid
Rock	●	○	●	●	●
Gravel, clean or silty	●	◑	●	●	●
Gravel, clayey	●	◑	◑	●	◑
Sand, clean or silty	○	○	●	○	◑
Sand, clayey silt	○	◑	◑	●	○
Clay, sandy or silty	○	●	◑	●	○
Clay, heavy	○	●	◑	●	○

● Recommended
◑ Acceptable
○ Marginal

FIGURE 10. Compaction equipment selection guide.

FIGURE 11. Variation of optimum moisture content with roller type (from reference 6).

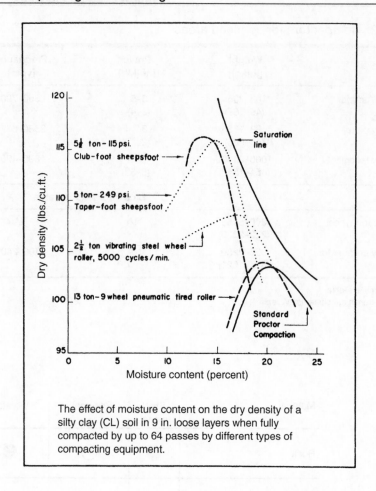

The effect of moisture content on the dry density of a silty clay (CL) soil in 9 in. loose layers when fully compacted by up to 64 passes by different types of compacting equipment.

roller compacting a clayey gravel), significant increases in density may continue to occur beyond 50 passes. However, as shown in Figure 12, the increase in density is relatively small after about 10 passes for most soil/compactor combinations.

Ground contact pressure may vary from 30 lb/sq in. (207 kPa) for a pneumatic roller to 300 lb/sq in. (2070 kPa) or more for a tamping foot roller. Within these ranges, it has been found that total roller weight has a much more pronounced effect on the compaction achieved than does

FIGURE 12. Typical effect of number of passes.

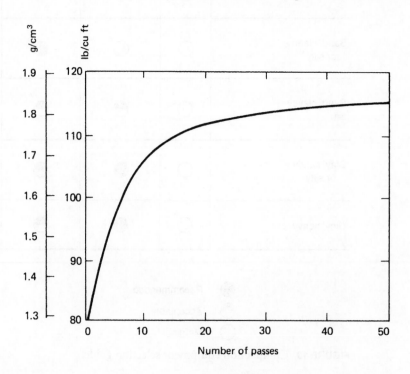

contact pressure. Thus, increasing the foot size on a tamping foot roller while maintaining a constant contact pressure will increase both the soil density and the surface area covered in one pass. Likewise, increasing the weight of a pneumatic roller at constant tire pressure will increase the effective depth of compaction. The use of excessive ground contact pressure will result in shearing and displacement of the soil being compacted.

If a tamping foot roller fails to "walk out" to within 1 in. (2.5 cm) of the surface after about five passes, it usually indicates that either the contact pressure or the soil moisture content is too high.

Tests have shown little relationship between compactor travel speed and the compaction achieved, except for vibratory compactors. In the case of vibratory equipment, travel speed (at a fixed operating frequency) determines the number of vibrations that each point on the ground surface will receive. Therefore, when using vibratory equipment, tests should be performed to determine the compactor speed that results in the highest compactor productivity. For conventional equipment, the highest possible speed should be utilized that does not result in excessive surface displacement.

For compaction wheels, typical lift thickness ranges from 24–48 in. (61–122 cm) for excavators to 18–30 in. (46–76 cm) for backhoes. Compaction to 90% relative density is usually achieved in five to six passes of the wheel. It is recommended that a minimum cover over pipe of 3 ft (91 cm) be maintained for excavators and 2 ft (61 cm) for backhoes.

Estimating Compactor Production

Equation 1 may be used to calculate compactor production based on compactor speed, lift thickness, and effective width of compaction. The accuracy of the result obtained will depend on the accuracy in estimating speed and lift thickness. Trial operations will usually be necessary to obtain accurate estimates of these factors. Typical compactor operating speeds are given in Table 3.

$$\text{Production (CCY/h)} = \frac{16.3 \times W \times S \times L \times E}{P} \quad (1A)$$

$$\text{Production (CCM/h)} = \frac{10 \times W \times S \times L \times E}{P} \quad (1B)$$

where P = number of passes required
W = width compacted per pass (ft or m)
S = compactor speed (mi/h or km/h)
L = compacted lift thickness (in. or cm)
E = job efficiency

The power required to tow rollers depends on the roller's total resistance (grade plus rolling resistance). The rolling

Table 3. Typical operating speed of compaction equipment

Compactor	Speed mi/h	km/h
Tamping foot, crawler-towed	3–5	5–8
Tamping foot, wheel-tractor-towed	5–10	8–16
High-speed tamping foot		
First two or three passes	3–5	5–8
Walking out	8–12	13–19
Final passes	10–14	16–23
Heavy pneumatic	3–5	5–8
Multitired pneumatic	5–15	8–24
Grid roller		
Crawler-towed	3–5	5–8
Wheel-tractor-towed	10–12	16–19
Segmented pad	5–15	8–24
Smooth wheel	2–4	3–6
Vibratory		
Plate	0.6–1.2	1–2
Roller	1–2	2–3

resistance of tamping foot rollers has been found to be approximately 450–500 lb/ton (225–250 kg/t).

Job Management

After applying the principles explained above, trial operations are usually required to determine the exact values of soil moisture content, lift thickness, compactor weight, and vibrator frequency and amplitude that yield maximum productivity while achieving the specified soil density. The use of a nuclear density device to measure the soil density actually being obtained during compaction is strongly recommended. Do not use boom-mounted compactors such as compaction wheels to trim trench walls, pull backfill into the trench, or to lift heavy objects.

Traffic planning and control is an important factor in compaction operations. Hauling equipment must be given the right-of-way without unduly interfering with compaction operations. The use of high-speed compaction equipment may be necessary to avoid conflicts between hauling and compacting equipment.

3 GROUND MODIFICATION

The process of giving natural soils enough abrasive resistance and shear strength to accommodate traffic or design loads is called *ground modification* or *soil stabilization*. Methods available include mechanical methods, hydraulic methods, reinforcement methods, and physiochemical

Table 4. Soil stabilization methods

Mechanical	Hydraulic	Reinforcement	Physiochemical
Compaction	Drainage	Confinement	Admixtures
Deep compaction	Preloading	Inclusions	Freezing
Vibroflotation	Electroosmosis	Minipiles	Grouting
		Soil nailing	Heating
		Stone columns	

methods. Some techniques falling under each of these categories are shown in Table 4.

Mechanical Methods

As you see, the compaction process discussed in the preceding sections of this chapter is a form of mechanical stabilization. Additional mechanical stabilization methods include dynamic or deep compaction and vibratory compaction.

Dynamic compaction, or *deep compaction,* involves dropping a heavy weight from a crane onto the ground surface to achieve soil densification. Typically, drop weights of 10–40 tons (9–36 t) are used with a drop height of 50–100 ft (15–30 m) to produce soil densification to a depth of about 30 ft (9 m). The horizontal spacing of drop points usually ranges from 7 to 25 ft (2–8 m).

Vibratory compaction, also called *vibroflotation* and *vibrocompaction,* is the process of densifying cohesionless soils by inserting a vibratory probe into the soil. After the probe is jetted and/or vibrated to the required depth, the vibrator is turned on and the device is slowly withdrawn while the soil is kept saturated. Clean, granular material is added from the surface as the soil around the probe densifies and subsides. The process is repeated in a pattern such that a column of densified soil is created under each footing or other load. The process is quite effective on granular soils having less than 15% fines and often allows bearing capacities up to 5 tons/sq ft (479 kPa) or more. In such cases, vibratory compaction will usually be less expensive than installing piles. However, the process can also be used in conjunction with pile foundations to increase pile capacity. A related technique for strengthening cohesive soils is called *vibratory replacement,* *vibro-replacement,* or *stone column* construction. The process is similar to vibratory compaction except that the fill added as the probe is withdrawn consists of crushed stone or gravel rather than sand. The resulting stone column is vibrated to increase its density and interaction with the surrounding soil. Stone column capacities of 10–40 tons (9–36 t) are typically developed.

Hydraulic Methods

Saturated cohesive soils are particularly difficult to densify since the soil grains cannot be forced closer together unless water is drained from the soil's void spaces (see Section 1).

Surcharging, or placing additional weight on the soil surface, has long been used to densify cohesive soils. However, this is a very-long-term process (months to years) unless natural soil drainage can be increased. *Sand columns* consisting of vertical drilled holes filled with sand have often been used for this purpose. A newer technique that provides faster drainage at lower cost involves forcing *wicks,* or plastic drain tubes, into the soil at intervals of a few feet. *Electroosmosis* employs electrical current to speed up the drainage of cohesive soils.

Reinforcement Methods

These include confinement, inclusions, minipiles, soil nailing, and stone columns. *Stone column* construction, also called *vibratory replacement* or *vibro-replacement,* is a technique for strengthening cohesive soils. The process, described just previously, is similar to vibratory compaction.

Physiochemical Methods

While soil stabilization technically includes all the techniques described above, in common construction usage the term *soil stabilization* refers to the improvement of the engineering properties of a soil by use of physical or chemical admixtures.

The principal physiochemical admixtures used for soil stabilization include granular materials, portland cement, lime, and asphalt. Table 5 lists these materials along with the applicable soil, typical percentage employed, and their curing time. Some considerations involved in the use of these

Table 5. Common stabilization materials

Material	Soil	Quantity (% by weight)	Curing Time
Granular admixtures	Various	Varies	None
Portland cement*	Gravel	3–4	24 h
	Sand	3–5	
	Silt/clayey silt	4–6	
	Clay	6–8	
Lime*			
Hydrated	Clayey gravel	2–4	7 days
	Silty clay	5–10	
	Clay	3–8	
Quicklime	Clayey gravel	2–3	4 h
	Silty clay	3–8	
	Clay	3–6	
Asphalt	Sand	5–7	
	Silty or clayey sand	6–10	1–3 days

*May be combined with fly ash.

admixtures are described below. In addition, it has been found that the addition of fly ash will generally increase the strength of stabilized soil. Also, the addition of 0.5–1.5% by weight of calcium chloride will increase the early strength of portland cement or lime stabilization.

Granular Admixtures Soil blending with granular material is often used to produce a well-graded mixture, without excessive fines, which is suitable for compaction.

Portland Cement The effectiveness of portland cement as an admixture diminishes rapidly as the soil's plasticity index exceeds 15. The soil-cement mixture may need to be placed in multiple lifts to obtain depths greater than about 8 in. (20 cm).

Lime The use of quicklime results in much faster strength gain than does hydrated lime. However, quicklime is hazardous to handle.

Asphalt Asphalt admixtures are generally not effective in soils having more than about 30% fines by weight or a plasticity index greater than about 10.

Some techniques for employing physiochemical admixtures include surface mixing, placing layers of admixture in embankments, and deep mixing methods. Some considerations in the use of these techniques include the following:

- **Surface mixing.** This is probably the most widely used procedure. While the usual depth of mixing is about 6–10 in. (15–25 cm), the mixing depth can go as high as 40 in. (1 m) with special mixing equipment.

- **Embankment layers.** One such field application successfully used 2-in. (5-cm) layers of quicklime confined by filter fabric separated by 28–48 in. (71–119 cm) of compacted cohesive soil.

- **Deep mixing methods.** These consist of several related techniques which provide in-place (*in situ*) soil treatment. A stabilizing admixture, usually cementitious, is blended into the soil using hollow rotating drill shafts equipped with cutting tools and mixing paddles or augers at the tip. Admixture materials may be in either wet (grout) or dry form. Mixing may occur using rotary action only or may be combined with jet action. Mixing action may take place only near the end of the tool or it may extend some distance along the tool when the shaft is equipped with multiple augers or paddles. An early application of deep mixing involved the *lime column* technique, in which lime is augered into a plastic soil to form a strengthened soil column which aids in transferring loads to deeper soils.

4 GRADING AND FINISHING

Grading is the process of bringing earthwork to the desired shape and elevation (or grade). *Finish grading,* or simply *finishing,* involves smoothing slopes, shaping ditches, and bringing the earthwork to the elevation required by the plans and specification. Finishing usually follows closely behind excavation, compaction, and grading. Finishing, in turn, is usually followed closely by seeding or sodding to control soil erosion. The piece of equipment most widely used for grading and finishing is the motor grader (Figure 13). Grade

FIGURE 13. Modern motor grader. (Courtesy of John Deere Construction & Forestry Company)

FIGURE 14. Typical roadway components.

trimmers and excavators are frequently used on large highway and airfield projects because their operating speed is greater than that of the motor grader.

In highway construction, the process of cutting down high spots and filling in low spots of each roadway layer is called *balancing*. *Trimming* is the process of bringing each roadway layer to its final grade. Typical tolerances allowed for final roadway grades are $\frac{1}{2}$ in./10 ft (1.25 cm/3m) for subgrades and subbases and $\frac{1}{8}$ in./10 ft (0.3 cm/3m) for bases. Typical roadway components are illustrated in Figure 14.

Finishing is seldom a pay item in a construction contract because the quantity of earthwork involved is difficult to measure. As a result, the planning of finishing operations is usually rudimentary. However, studies have shown that the careful planning and execution of finishing operations can pay large dividends.

Motor Grader

The *motor grader* is one of the most versatile items of earthmoving equipment. It can be used for light stripping, grading, finishing, trimming, bank sloping, ditching, backfilling, and scarifying. It is also capable of mixing and spreading soil and asphaltic mixtures. It is used on building construction projects as well as in heavy and highway construction. It is frequently used for the maintenance of highways and haul roads.

The blade of a motor grader is referred to as a *moldboard* and is equipped with replaceable cutting edges and end pieces (end bits). The wide range of possible blade positions is illustrated in Figure 15. The pitch of the blade may be changed in a manner similar to dozer blades. Pitching the blade forward results in a rolling action of the excavated material and is used for finishing work and for blending materials. Pitching the blade backward increases cutting action but may allow material to spill over the top of the blade. Blade cutting edges are available in flat, curved, or serrated styles. Flat edges produce the least edge wear, but curved edges are recommended for cutting hard materials and for fine grading. Serrated edges are used for breaking up packed gravel, frozen soil, and ice.

Motor graders are available with articulated frames that increase grader maneuverability. The three possible modes of operation for an articulated grader are

FIGURE 15. Blade positions for the motor grader. (U.S. Department of the Army)

FIGURE 16. Articulated grader positions.

illustrated in Figure 16. The machine may operate in the conventional manner when in the straight mode (Figure 16A). The articulated mode (Figure 16B) allows the machine to turn in a short radius. Use of the crab mode (Figure 16C) permits the rear driving wheels to be offset so that they remain on firm ground while the machine cuts banks, side slopes, or ditches. The front wheels of both conventional and articulated graders may be leaned from side to side. Wheels are leaned away from the cut to offset the side thrust produced by soil pressure against the angled blade. Wheel lean may also be used to assist in turning the grader.

Graders are available with automatic blade control systems that permit precise grade control. Such graders utilize a sensing system that follows an existing surface, string line, or laser beam to automatically raise or lower the blade as required to achieve the desired grade. Scarifiers are used to loosen hard soils before grading and to break up asphalt pavements and frozen soil. Their operation is similar to that of the ripper. However, scarifiers are not intended for heavy-duty use as are rippers. While rippers are available for graders, their ripping ability is limited by the weight and power of the grader. Grader rippers are usually mounted on the rear of the machine.

Grade Excavators and Trimmers

Grade excavators or *trimmers* are machines that are capable of finishing roadway and airfield subgrades and bases faster and more accurately than can motor graders. Many of these machines also act as reclaimers. That is, they are capable of scarifying and removing soil and old asphalt pavement. Trimmers and reclaimers are usually equipped with integral belt conveyors that are used for loading excavated material into haul units or depositing it in windrows outside the excavated area. The large grade trimmer/reclaimer shown in Figure 17 is also capable of compacting base material, laying asphalt, or acting as a slipform paver.

While grade trimmers lack the versatility of motor graders, their accuracy and high speed make them very useful on large roadway and airfield projects. Their large size often requires that they be partially disassembled and transported between job sites on heavy equipment trailers.

FIGURE 17. Large-grade trimmer/reclaimer/paver. (Courtesy of Terex Roadbuilding)

Estimating Grader Production

Grader production is usually calculated on a linear basis (miles or kilometers completed per hour) for roadway projects and on an area basis (square yards or square meters per hour) for general construction projects. The time required to complete a roadway project may be estimated as follows:

$$\text{Time (h)} = \left[\sum \frac{\text{Number of passes} \times \text{Section length (mi or km)}}{\text{Average speed for section (mi/h or mi/h)}} \right] \times \frac{1}{\text{Efficiency}} \quad (2)$$

Average speed will depend on operator skill, machine characteristics, and job conditions. Typical grader speeds for various types of operations are given in Table 6.

Table 6. Typical grader operating speed

Operation	Speed mi/h	Speed km/h
Bank sloping	2.5	4.0
Ditching	2.5–4.0	4.0–6.4
Finishing	4.0–9.0	6.5–14.5
Grading and road maintenance	4.2–6.0	6.4–9.7
Mixing	9.0–20.0	14.5–32.2
Snow removal	12.0–20.0	19.3–32.3
Spreading	6.0–9.0	9.7–14.5

Example 1 Fifteen miles (24.1 km) of gravel road require reshaping and leveling. You estimate that six passes of a motor grader will be required. Based on operator skill, machine characteristics, and job conditions, you estimate two passes at 4 mi/h (6.4 km/h), two passes at 5 mi/h (8.0 km/h), and two passes at 6 mi/h (9.7 km/h). If job efficiency is 0.80, how many grader hours will be required for this job?

Solution

$$\text{Time (h)} = \left(\frac{2 \times 15}{4.0} + \frac{2 \times 15}{5.0} + \frac{2 \times 15}{6.0} \right)$$
$$\times \frac{1}{0.80} = 23.1 \text{ h} \quad \text{(Eq 2)}$$
$$\left[= \left(\frac{2 \times 24.1}{6.4} + \frac{2 \times 24.1}{8.9} + \frac{2 \times 24.1}{9.7} \right) \right.$$
$$\left. \times \frac{1}{0.80} = 23.1 \text{ h} \right]$$

Job Management

Careful job planning, the use of skilled operators, and competent supervision are required to maximize grader production efficiency. Use the minimum possible number of grader passes to accomplish the work. Eliminate as many turns as possible. For working distances less than 1000 ft (305 m), have the grader back up rather than turn around. Grading in reverse may be used for longer distances when turning is difficult or impossible. Several graders may work side by side if sufficient working room is available. This technique is especially useful for grading large areas.

Problems

1. Why might the laboratory and field optimum moisture contents vary for a particular soil?

2. List the types of compactors which are available for compaction in confined areas.

3. a. What is a compaction wheel?
   b. What is the typical lift thickness for an excavator-mounted compaction wheel?
   c. State the minimum pipe cover which should be used when compacting with an excavator-mounted compaction wheel.

4. What type of compactor would you expect to be most suitable for compacting a clean sand?

5. Estimate the production in compacted cubic yards (meters) per hour of a self-propelled tamping foot roller under the following conditions: average speed = 5 mph (8.0 km/h), compacted lift thickness = 6 in. (15.2 cm), effective roller width = 10 ft (3.05 m), job efficiency = 0.75, and number of passes = 8.

6. Twenty miles (32 km) of gravel road require reshaping and leveling. You estimate that a motor grader will require two passes at 3 mph (4.8 km/h), two passes at 4 mph (6.4 km/h), and two pass at 5.5 mph (8.9 km/h) to accomplish the work. How many grader hours will be required for this work if the job efficiency factor is 0.75?

7. A highway embankment is being constructed of low-plasticity clay (CL) whose natural moisture content is slightly below the standard AASHTO optimum. Specifications require the use of a tamping foot roller for compaction. However, the roller being used does not always "walk out" as compaction proceeds, and even when it does, it often fails to produce the required soil density. The contractor and the project engineer disagree over appropriate corrective measures. The contractor wants to increase the weight of the roller by adding more ballast, thus increasing the contact pressure of the roller feet. The project engineer disagrees and suggests that the weight of the roller is adequate and that the foot size should be increased. Which recommendation is more nearly correct? Why?

8. The data in the accompanying table resulted from performing Standard Proctor Tests on a soil. Plot the

Dry Density		Moisture Content (%)
lb/cu ft	g/cm³	
100	1.602	14
103	1.650	16
106	1.698	18
108	1.730	20
105	1.682	22
102	1.631	24

data and determine the soil's laboratory optimum moisture content.

9. List the four principal methods for achieving ground modification or soil stabilization. Provide one example of each.

10. Develop a computer program to calculate the time required (hours) for a motor grader to perform a finishing operation. Input should include section length, number of passes at each expected speed, and job efficiency. Solve Problem 6 using your computer program.

References

1. *Compaction Industry Vibratory Roller Handbook*. Association of Equipment Manufacturers, Milwaukee, WI.

2. *Fundamentals of Compaction*. Caterpillar Inc., Peoria, IL.

3. *Handbook of Soil Compactionology*. Bros, Inc., Brooklyn Park, MN.

4. Hausmann, Manfred R. *Engineering Principles of Ground Modification*. New York: McGraw-Hill, 1990.

5. Nunnally, S. W. *Managing Construction Equipment*, 2nd ed. Upper Saddle River, NJ: Prentice Hall, 2000.

6. Townsend, D. L. *The Performance and Efficiency of Standard Compacting Equipment* (Engineering Report No. 6). Kingston, Ontario: Queens University, 1959.

7. Wahls, H. E., C. P. Fisher, and L. J. Langfelder. *The Compaction of Soil and Rock Materials for Highway Purposes* (Report No. FHWA-RD-73-8). Washington, D.C.: U.S. Department of Transportation, 1966.

ROCK EXCAVATION

From Chapter 6 of *Construction Methods and Management*, Eighth Edition. S. W. Nunnally. Copyright © 2011 by Pearson Education, Inc. Published by Pearson Prentice Hall.

ROCK EXCAVATION

1 INTRODUCTION

Rock Characteristics

Rock may be classified as igneous, sedimentary, or metamorphic, according to its origin. *Igneous rock* formed when the Earth's molten material cooled. Because of its origin, it is quite homogeneous and is therefore the most difficult type of rock to excavate. Examples of igneous rock are granite and basalt. *Sedimentary rock* was formed by the precipitation of material from water or air. As a result, it is highly stratified and has many planes of weakness. Thus, it is the most easily excavated type of rock. Examples include sandstone, shale, and limestone. *Metamorphic rock* originated as igneous or sedimentary rock but has been changed by heat, pressure, or chemical action into a different type of rock. Metamorphic rock is intermediate between igneous rock and sedimentary rock in its difficulty of excavation. Examples of metamorphic rock include slate, marble, and schist.

The difficulty involved in excavating rock depends on a number of factors in addition to the rock type. Some of these factors include the extent of fractures and other planes of weakness, the amount of weathering that has occurred, the predominant grain size, whether the rock has a crystalline structure, rock brittleness, and rock hardness.

Rock Investigation

Relative hardness is measured on *Moh's scale* from 1 (talc) to 10 (diamond). As a rule, any rock that can be scratched by a knife blade (hardness about 5) can be easily excavated by ripping or other mechanical methods. For harder rock, additional investigation is required to evaluate the rock characteristics described above. The principal methods for investigating subsurface conditions include drilling, excavating test pits, and making seismic measurements. Drilling may be used to remove core samples from the rock or to permit visual observation of rock conditions. Core samples may be visually inspected as well as tested in the laboratory. Observation in a test pit or inspection by TV cameras placed into drilled holes will reveal layer thickness, the extent of fracturing and weathering, and the presence of water. Use of the refraction seismograph permits a rapid determination of rock soundness by measuring the velocity at which sound travels through the rock.

In performing a seismic refraction test, a sound source and a number of receivers (geophones) are set up, as illustrated in Figure 1. The time required for a sound wave to travel from the sound source to each receiver is measured and plotted against the distance from the sound source, as illustrated in Figure 2. In this plot the slope of each segment of the curve represents the sound velocity in the corresponding subsurface layer. This velocity has been found to range from about 1000 ft/s (305 m/s) in loose soil to about 20,000 ft/s (6100 m/s) in sound rock. Since the relationship between the angle of incidence and the angle of refraction of a sound wave crossing the interface of two rock layers is a function of their respective sound velocities, the seismic refraction test method may also be used to determine the thickness of rock layers. Equation 1 may be used to determine the thickness of the upper layer when the sound velocity increases with layer depth, that is, when the velocity in the top layer is less than the velocity in the second layer, which is the usual case in the field.

$$H_1 = \frac{D_1}{2} \left[\frac{V_2 - V_2}{V_s + V_1} \right]^{1/2} \tag{1}$$

where
H_1 = thickness of upper layer (ft or m)

D_1 = distance from sound source to first intersection of lines on time-distance graph (ft or m) (point A, Figure 2)

V_1 = velocity in upper layer (ft/s or m/s)

V_2 = velocity in second layer (ft/s or m/s)

FIGURE 1. Schematic representation of seismic refraction test.

FIGURE 2. Graph of refraction test data.

V_1 = 1000 ft/s (305 m/s)
V_2 = 3000 ft/s (915 m/s)
V_3 = 5000 ft/s (1525 m/s)

Example 1 Find the seismic wave velocity and depth of the upper soil layer based on the following refraction seismograph data:

Distance from Sound Source to Geophone		Time (ms)
ft	m	
10	3.05	5
20	6.10	10
30	9.15	15
40	12.20	20
50	15.25	22
60	18.30	24
70	21.35	26
80	24.40	28

FIGURE 3. Graph of refraction test data, Example 1.

Solution

Plot time of travel against distance from sound source to geophone as shown in Figure 3.

$$V_1 = \frac{40 - 0}{0.020 - 0} = 2000 \text{ ft/s}$$

$$\left[= \frac{12.2 - 0}{0.020 - 0} = 610 \text{ m/s} \right]$$

$$V_2 = \frac{80 - 40}{0.028 - 0.020} = 5000 \text{ ft/s}$$

$$\left[= \frac{24.4 - 12.2}{0.028 - 0.020} = 1525 \text{ m/s} \right]$$

$$H_1 = \frac{40}{2} \left(\frac{5000 - 2000}{5000 + 2000} \right)^{\frac{1}{2}} = 13.1 \text{ ft}$$

$$\left[= \frac{12.2}{2} \left(\frac{1525 - 610}{1525 + 610} \right)^{\frac{1}{2}} = 4.0 \text{ m} \right]$$

Rock-Handling Systems

The process of rock moving may be considered in four phases: loosening, loading, hauling, and compacting. Therefore, this discussion of rock-handling systems will be limited to the phases of loosening, loading, and hauling. The principal methods and equipment available for accomplishing each of these phases are listed in Table 1.

The traditional method for excavating rock involves drilling blastholes in the rock, loading the holes with explosives, detonating the explosives, loading the fractured rock into haul units with power shovels, and hauling the rock away in trucks or wagons. Newer alternatives include the use of tractor-mounted rippers to loosen rock, the use of wheel loaders to load fractured rock into haul units, and the use of reinforced (or "special application") scrapers to both load and haul fractured rock. The equipment and procedures utilized are explained in Sections 2 to 4. The selection of the rock-handling system to be employed in a particular situation should be based on maximizing the contractor's profit from the operation.

Tunneling

Tunneling in rock is a specialized form of rock excavation that has traditionally been accomplished by drilling and blasting. Recently, however, *tunneling machines* or mechanical *moles* equipped with multiple cutter heads and capable of excavating to full tunnel diameter have come into increasing use. The tunneling machine shown in Figure 4 weighs 285 tons (258 t), produces a thrust of 1,850,000 lb (8229 kN), and drills a 19-ft (5.8-m)–diameter hole.

Some of the specialized terms used in tunneling include jumbos, hydraulic jumbos, and mucking machines. A *jumbo* is a large mobile frame equipped with platforms at several elevations to enable drills and workers to work on the full tunnel face at one time. The *hydraulic jumbo* illustrated in Figure 5 is a self-propelled machine equipped with a number of hydraulic drills, each mounted on its own hydraulic boom. Such a machine is capable of drilling blastholes across the full tunnel face at one time. A *mucking machine* is a form of shovel especially designed for loading fractured rock into haul units during tunnel excavation.

2 DRILLING

Drilling Equipment

Common types of drilling equipment include percussion drills, rotary drills, and rotary-percussion drills, as listed in Table 2. *Percussion drills* penetrate rock by impact action alone. While the bits of these drills rotate to assist in cleaning the hole and to provide a fresh surface for each

Table 1. Principal rock-handling systems

Operation	Equipment and Process
Loosen	Drill and blast
	Rip
Load	Shovel
	Wheel loader
Haul	Truck
	Wagon
Load and haul	Reinforced scraper

FIGURE 4. Large tunneling machine. (Courtesy of The Robbins Company)

FIGURE 5. Hydraulic jumbo. (Courtesy of Atlas Copco)

Table 2. Typical characteristics of rock drilling equipment

Type of Drill	Maximum Drill Diameter		Maximum Depth	
	in.	cm	ft	m
Percussion drill				
Jackhammer	2.5	6.3	20	6.1
Drifter	4.5	11.4	15	4.6
Wagon drill	6.0	15.2	50	15.3
Track drill	6.0	15.2	50	15.3
Rotary drill	72	183	1000+	305+
Rotary–percussion	6.0	15.2	150	46

impact, rotation takes place on the upstroke. Thus, no cutting is accomplished during rotation. Common types of percussion drills include the hand-held rock drill (or jackhammer); the drifter, which is mounted on a frame or column; the wheel-mounted wagon drill; and the crawler-mounted track drill. Wagon drills are basically large drifter drills mounted on wheels for mobility. They have been used extensively for construction and quarry drilling but are largely being displaced by track drills. Track drills (Figure 6) are large, self-propelled, crawler-mounted drills usually equipped with a hydraulically powered boom for positioning the drill feed.

Rotary drills (Figure 7) cut by turning a bit under pressure against the rock face. *Rotary-percussion drills* combine rotary and percussion cutting action to penetrate rock several times as fast as a comparable percussion drill. *Downhole drills* (Figure 8) utilize a percussion drilling device mounted directly above the drill bit at the bottom of the hole. Downhole drills have several advantages over conventional percussion drills: Drill rod life is longer, because drill rods are not subjected to impact; less air is required for cleaning the hole, because drill exhaust may be used for this purpose; noise level is lower, for the same reason; and there is little loss of energy between the drill and the bit. Although downhole drills are available for track drills, they are usually mounted on rotary drilling machines, since relatively large diameter holes are necessary to provide sufficient space for the downhole drill body. The combination of a rotary drill mechanism and a downhole drill permits such a machine to function as a rotary drill, a percussion drill, or a rotary–percussion drill.

Drilling rate (rate of penetration) depends on rock hardness, drill type and energy, and the type of drill bit used. Table 3 provides representative drilling rates for common drilling equipment.

Increased air pressure at the drill will result in increased drill production (penetration/h) as shown in Figure 9. However, for safety, pressure at the drill must not exceed the maximum safe operating pressure specified by the drill manufacturer. In addition, the use of increased air pressure will also shorten the life of drills, drill steel, and bits, as well as increase drill maintenance and repair costs. Thus, field tests should be run to determine the drilling pressure that results in minimum cost per unit of rock excavation.

FIGURE 6. Hydraulic track drill. (Courtesy of Atlas Copco)

Increasingly, large-diameter vertical and inclined holes are being drilled for rescue of miners, to create blast-holes for spherical charges in mining operations, and for constructing penstocks and other shafts. In addition to the use of large-diameter downhole and rotary drills, raise boring machines have been used to drill vertical shafts over 20 ft (6 m) in diameter. *Raise boring* is a drilling technique in which the large-diameter hole is drilled upward from the bottom. The procedure is as follows. First, a pilot hole is drilled from the surface into a mine or other underground cavity. Next, a large reaming head is attached to the lower end of a raise boring machine drill string which has been lowered into the mine. The large-diameter hole is then created as the reaming head is rotated and raised by the raise boring machine sitting on the surface. Raise boring machines are capable of creating an upward thrust of 1 million pounds (44.5 MN) or more and a torque exceeding 400,000 ft-lb (542 kN m).

FIGURE 7. Rotary blast hole drill. (Courtesy of Ingersoll-Rand Company)

FIGURE 8. Downhole drill mounted on a rotary drill. (Courtesy of Ingersoll-Rand Company)

Rock drills have traditionally been powered by compressed air. However, the current trend is toward the use of hydraulically powered drills (Figure 6). Hydraulic drills penetrate faster and consume less energy than do comparable compressed air drills. Hydraulic drills also produce less noise and dust than do compressed air drills.

Drill Bits and Steel

Major types of rock drill bits are illustrated in Figure 10. Principal percussion drill bits include cross-type bits (Figure 10a), X-type bits, and button bits (Figure 10b). *X-type bits* differ from *cross-type bits* only in that the points of the X-type bits are not spaced at 90° angles but rather form the shape of an X. X-type bits tend to drill straighter holes than do cross-type bits. Both types of bits are available with either solid steel or tungsten carbide cutting edges. Since tungsten carbide bits cut faster and last longer than do solid steel bits, carbide bits are more widely used. *Button-type bits* have a higher penetration rate than X or cross-type bits and are less likely to jam in the hole. Button bits do not normally require grinding or sharpening. Bits used with rotary–percussion drills are similar to X-type percussion drill bits but utilize special designs for the cutting edges.

Common types of bits for rotary drills include coring bits (Figure 10c) and rolling cutter or cone bits (Figure 10d). *Coring bits* are available as diamond drill bits and shot drill bits. Diamond drill bits utilize small diamonds set in a matrix on the bit body as the cutting agent to achieve rapid rock penetration. Diamond bits are also available in other shapes, such as concave bits, to drill conventional holes. The shape of a shot drill coring bit is similar to that of the diamond coring bit. However, chilled steel shot fed into the hole around the bit replaces diamond as the cutting agent. The lower end of the shot drill bit is slotted to assist in retaining the shot between the bit and rock as the bit rotates. *Rolling cutter bits* use several cutters (usually three) shaped like gears to penetrate the rock as the drill bit rotates.

Table 3. Representative drilling rates (carbide bit)

Bit Size		Hand Drill		Wagon Drill		Crawler Drill		Hydraulic Drill	
in.	cm	ft/h	m/h	ft/h	m/h	ft/h	m/h	ft/h	m/h
1⅝	4.1	14–24	4.3–7.3						
1¾	4.4	11–21	3.4–6.4						
2	5.1	10–19	3.1–5.8	25–50	7.6–15.3	125–290	38.1–88.5	185–425	56.4–129.6
2½	6.4			19–48	5.8–14.9	80–180	24.4–54.9	120–280	36.6–85.4
3	7.6			18–46	5.5–14.0	75–160	22.9–48.8	100–240	30.5–73.2
4	10.2			10–35	3.1–10.7	50–125	15.3–31.1	80–180	24.4–54.9
6	15.2					20–50	6.1–15.3	30–75	9.2–22.9

FIGURE 9. Drill penetration versus air pressure.

The steel rod connecting a percussion drill and its bit is referred to as *drill steel* or simply *steel*. Drill steel is available in sections $\frac{7}{8}$ in (2.2 cm) to 2 in. (5.1 cm) in diameter and 2 ft (0.61 m) to 20 ft (6.1 m) in length. Drill steel sections are fitted with threaded ends so that sections may be added as the bit penetrates. Sections are hollow to allow air flow to the bit for hole cleaning. The drill rod used for

FIGURE 10. Major types of rock drill bits.

a. 4-point cross-type bit

b. Button bit

c. Diamond core bit

d. Roller bit

rotary drilling is called a *drill pipe*. It is available in length increments of 5 ft (1.5 m) starting with 10 ft (3.1 m) and threaded on each end. Drill pipe is also hollow to permit the flow of compressed air or drilling fluid to the bottom of the hole.

Drilling Patterns and Rock Yield

The choice of hole size, depth, and spacing, as well as the amount of explosive used for each hole, depends on the degree of rock break desired, rock type and soundness, and the type of explosive utilized. In general, small holes closely spaced will yield small rock particles while large holes widely spaced will yield large rock particles. Although equations have been developed for estimating hole spacing based on rock strength and explosive pressure, test blasts are usually necessary to determine optimum hole spacing and quantity of explosive per hole. Table 4 indicates typical drill hole spacing.

The two principal drilling patterns used for rock excavation are illustrated in Figure 11. While the rectangular pattern is most widely used, the staggered pattern reduces the amount of oversized rock produced. For a rectangular pattern the volume of blasted rock produced per hole may be computed by the use of Equation 2. The effective depth of a blast hole is the average depth of the excavation area after the blast, not the original hole depth.

$$\text{Volume/hole (cu yd)} = \frac{S^2 \times H}{27} \qquad \textbf{(2A)}$$

$$\text{Volume/hole (m}^3) = S^2 \times H \qquad \textbf{(2B)}$$

Table 4. Typical drill hole spacing (rectangular pattern) [ft (m)]

Rock Type	Hole Diameter [in. (cm)]							
	$2\frac{1}{4}$ (5.7)	$2\frac{1}{2}$ (6.4)	3 (7.6)	$3\frac{1}{2}$ (8.9)	4 (10.2)	$4\frac{1}{2}$ (11.4)	5 (12.7)	$5\frac{1}{2}$ (14.0)
Strong rock (granite, basalt)	4.5 (1.4)	5.0 (1.5)	6.0 (1.8)	7.0 (2.1)	8.5 (2.6)	9.0 (2.7)	10.0 (3.0)	11.0 (3.4)
Medium rock (limestone)	5.0 (1.5)	6.0 (1.8)	7.0 (2.1)	8.0 (2.4)	9.0 (2.7)	10.0 (3.0)	11.5 (3.5)	12.5 (3.8)
Weak rock (sandstone, shale)	6.0 (1.8)	6.5 (2.0)	8.0 (2.4)	10.0 (3.0)	11.0 (3.4)	12.0 (3.7)	13.5 (4.1)	15.5 (4.7)

a. Rectangular pattern

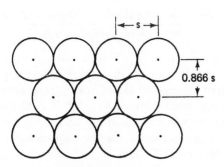

b. Staggered pattern

FIGURE 11. Principal drilling patterns.

where S = pattern spacing (ft or m)
   H = effective hole depth (ft or m)

Effective hole depth should be determined by trial blasting. However, effective depth has been found to average about 90% of original hole depth.

The rock produced per hole may be divided by the original hole depth to yield rock volume per unit of hole drilled:

$$\text{Volume/ft of hole} = \frac{\text{Volume per hole (cu yd)}}{\text{Drilled hole depth (ft)}} \quad (3A)$$

$$\text{Volume/m of hole} = \frac{\text{Volume per hole (m}^3)}{\text{Drilled hole depth (m)}} \quad (3B)$$

The amount of drilling required to produce a unit volume of blasted rock may then be calculated as the reciprocal of the volume per unit of drilled depth.

Example 2   Trial blasting indicates that a rectangular pattern of drilling using 3-in. (7.6-cm) holes spaced on 9-ft (2.75-m) centers and 20 ft (6.1 m) deep will produce a satisfactory rock break with a particular explosive loading. The effective hole depth resulting from the blast is 18 ft (5.5 m). Determine the rock volume produced per foot (meter) of drilling.

Solution

$$\text{Volume/hole} = \frac{9^2 \times 18}{27} = 54 \text{ cu yd} \quad (\text{Eq 2A})$$

$$[= 2.75^2 \times 5.5 = 41.6 \text{ m}^3] \quad (\text{Eq 2B})$$

$$\text{Volume/unit depth} = \frac{54}{20} = 2.7 \text{ cu yd/ft} \quad (\text{Eq 3A})$$

$$\left[= \frac{41.6}{6.1} = 6.8 \text{ m}^3/\text{m} \right] \quad (\text{Eq 3B})$$

3 BLASTING

Explosives

The principal explosives used for rock excavation include dynamite, ammonium nitrate, ammonium nitrate in fuel oil (ANFO), and slurries. For construction use, dynamite has largely been replaced by ammonium nitrate, ANFO, and slurries because these explosives are lower in cost and easier to handle than dynamite. Ammonium nitrate and ANFO are the least expensive of the explosives listed. ANFO is particularly easy to handle because it is a liquid that may simply be poured into the blasthole. However, ammonium nitrate explosives are not water resistant, and they require an auxiliary explosive (primer) for detonation. *Slurries* are mixtures of gels, explosives, and water. They may also contain powdered metals (metalized slurries) to increase blast energy. Slurries are cheaper than dynamite but are more expensive than the ammonium nitrate explosives. Water resistance and greater power are their principal advantages over ammonium nitrate explosives. Slurries are available as liquids or packaged in plastic bags. Slurries also require a primer for detonation.

Detonators used to initiate an explosion include both electric and nonelectric caps. Electric blasting (EB) caps are most widely used and are available as instantaneous caps or with delay times from a few milliseconds up to several seconds. For less-sensitive explosives such as ammonium nitrates and slurries, caps are used to initiate *primers,* which in turn initiate the main explosive. Primers may be small charges of high explosives or *primacord,* which is a high explosive in cord form.

The amount of explosive required to produce the desired rock fracture is usually expressed as a *powder factor.* The powder factor represents the weight of explosive used per unit volume of rock produced (lb/BCY or kg/BCM). Except in specialized applications, blastholes are usually loaded with a continuous column of explosive to within a few feet of the surface. *Stemming* (an inert material used to confine and increase the effectiveness of the blast) is placed in the top portion of the hole above the explosive. A primed charge is placed near the bottom of the hole for blast initiation.

Electric Blasting Circuits

Electric blasting caps may be connected in series, parallel, or parallel–series circuits, as illustrated in Figure 12. The types of insulated wires used to make up these circuits include legwires, buswires, connecting wires, and firing lines. *Legwires* are the two wires that form an integral part of each electric blasting cap. *Buswires* are wires used to connect the legwires of caps into parallel or parallel–series circuits. *Connecting wires,* when used, are wires that connect legwires or buswires to the firing line. The *firing line* consists of two parallel conductors that connect the power source to the remainder of the blasting circuit. Note the use of a "reverse hookup" for the buswires shown in Figure 12. In the reverse hookup, the firing lines are connected to opposite ends of the two buswires. Such a hookup has been found to provide a more equal distribution of current to all caps in the circuit than would be the case if the firing lines were connected to the same ends of the two buswires. Power sources include AC and DC power lines and blasting machines. *Blasting machines* are small DC generators or capacitive discharge (CD) units designed especially for firing electric cap circuits.

When designing or analyzing an electric blasting circuit, it is necessary to determine the total circuit resistance and the current required to safely fire all caps. Recall that in a series circuit the same current flows through all elements of the circuit, whereas in a parallel circuit the current in the main (firing) line is the sum of the currents in all the parallel branches. Ohm's law (Equation 4) may then be used to find the power source voltage required to safely detonate all caps.

$$\text{Voltage (volts)} = \text{Current (amperes)} \times \text{Resistance (ohms)} \quad (4)$$

or

$$E = IR$$

Conversely, if the power source voltage and circuit resistance are known, Equation 4 may be used to determine whether sufficient current will be produced to fire the blast. Representative current requirements for firing electric blasting caps are given in Table 5. Notice that a maximum current per cap is specified to prevent arcing of parallel circuits. Arcing results when excessive heat is produced in a cap by high current. Arcing may result in misfires or erratic timing of delay caps and, therefore, must be avoided.

If the same number and type of caps are used in each series, the resistance of the cap circuit may be calculated as follows:

$$R_c = \frac{\text{Number of caps/series} \times \text{Resistance/cap}}{\text{Number of parallel branches}} \quad (5)$$

Representative values of individual cap resistance are presented in Table 6. Note that cap resistance depends on the length of cap legwire used. Caps are normally available with legwires ranging from 4 to 100 ft (1.2–30.5 m). Caps with longer legwires are available on special order. Each legwire of a cap in a series must be long enough to extend from the bottom of the hole to the surface and then half the distance to the adjacent hole. Minimum legwire length may be calculated on this basis. Buswire, connecting wire,

FIGURE 12. Types of electric blasting circuits.

a. Series circuit

b. Parallel circuit

c. Parallel series circuit

Table 5. Representative current requirements for firing electric blasting caps

| Type of Circuit | Minimum Current (A) | | | | Maximum Current |
| | Normal | | Leakage | | |
	dc	ac	dc	ac	
Single cap	0.5	0.5	—	—	—
Series	1.5	2.0	3.0	4.0	—
Parallel	1.0/cap	1.0/cap	—	—	10/cap
Parallel-series	1.5/series	2.0/series	3.0/series	4.0/series	—

Table 6. Representative resistance of electric blasting caps

| Legwire | Length | |
ft	m	Nominal Resistance (Ω)
4	1.2	1.5
6	1.8	1.6
8	2.4	1.7
10	3.1	1.8
12	3.7	1.8
16	4.9	1.9
20	6.1	2.1
24	7.3	2.3
28	8.5	2.4
30	9.2	2.2
40	12.2	2.3
50	15.3	2.6
60	18.3	2.8
80	24.4	3.3
100	30.5	3.8

and firing-line resistance may be calculated using the resistance factors of Table 7. The effective length of buswire to be used in resistance calculations may be taken as the distance along the wire from the firing-line end of one buswire to the center of the cap pattern and from there to the firing-line end of the other buswire.

Table 7. Resistance of solid copper wire

American Wire Gauge Number	Ohms/1000 ft (305 m)
6	0.395
8	0.628
10	0.999
12	1.59
14	2.53
16	4.02
18	6.38
20	10.15

The steps in performing a blasting circuit analysis are listed below. This procedure is illustrated by Example 3.

1. Determine the resistance of the cap circuit.
2. Determine the resistance of buswires and connecting wires.
3. Determine the resistance of the firing line.
4. Compute the total circuit resistance as the sum of cap, buswire, connecting wire, and firing-line resistance.
5. Determine the minimum total current requirement (and maximum, if applicable).
6. Solve Equation 4 for required power voltage. If the power source voltage is known, solve Equation 4 for the circuit current and compare with the values in step 5.

Example 3 Analyze the cap circuit shown in Figure 13 to determine circuit resistance and the minimum power source current and voltage necessary to fire the blasts. Caps are equipped with 30-ft (9.2-m) legwires. Assume normal firing conditions.

Solution

$$R_{cap} = \frac{3 \times 2.22}{3} = 2.20\Omega \quad (Eq\ 5)$$

Effective length of buswire $= 80$ ft (24.4 m)
$(A - B) + (C - D)$

$$R_{bus} = \frac{80 \times 6.38}{1000} = 0.51\Omega$$

$$R_{firing\ line} = \frac{2 \times 1000 \times 1.59}{1000} = 3.18\Omega$$

$$R_{total} = 2.20 + 0.51 + 3.18$$
$$= 5.89\Omega$$

Minimum current per cap $= 1.5$ A   (Table 5)

Minimum current per series $= 1.5$ A

Required current in firing line $= 3 \times 1.5 = 4.5$ A

Minimum voltage for power source $= 4.5 \times 5.89$
$$= 26.5\ V \quad (Eq\ 4)$$

FIGURE 13. Circuit for Example 3.

s = 10 ft (3.1 m)
AE = CF = 20 ft (6.1 m)

The current leakage conditions indicated in Table 5 may exist when legwire insulation is damaged or bare connections are allowed to touch wet ground. To test for current leakage conditions, use a blasting ohmmeter to measure the resistance from one end of the circuit to a good ground (metal rod driven into wet earth). If resistance is less than 10,000Ω, use the current-leakage conditions values of Table 5.

Nonelectric Blasting Circuits

There has long been an interest in developing a blasting system which combines the safety of nonelectric explosives with the precise timing and flexibility of electric blasting systems. Several such nonelectric systems have been put on the market in recent years. Although a number of proprietary systems exist, most of these fall into one of the three categories to be described next. With all of these systems, two firing paths are normally used to ensure firing of all charges in the event of a break in the firing circuit.

The first and most conventional type of system utilizes detonating cord, either conventional or low energy, for the trunkline (main firing line), branch lines, and downlines (lines extending into individual blast holes). When using conventional detonating cord downlines, special primer assemblies that accept variable-delay detonator inserts are placed on the downline at one or several depths. Thus, several charges having differing delays may be placed at different depths into a single blast hole. However, in this case, cap-insensitive explosives must be used to avoid premature detonation of charges by the detonating cord itself. When low-energy detonating cord is used for downlines, a separate downline with an in-hole delay detonator is used for each charge. Due to the low sensitivity of low-energy detonating cord, special starter detonators must be used to fire the cord and propagate the explosion between trunklines and downlines. Although detonating cord firing circuits are easy to check visually, no positive circuit check can be made prior to firing. In addition, such systems may not be compatible with all types of explosives.

A second type of system uses a special shock/signal tube in lieu of detonating cord to initiate in-hole delay detonators. The hollow plastic shock/signal tube used may be uncharged or may contain a small thread of explosive. The tubes permit sharp bends and kinks without misfiring. The trunkline may consist of conventional detonating cord or shock/signal tubes. Shock/signal tubes that incorporate delay detonators are used for downlines. Special connectors are required to connect shock/signal tubes to each other or to conventional detonating cord. The use of shock/signal tubes for both trunklines and downlines results in a noiseless initiation system but leaves a residue (plastic tubing) that must be removed after the blast. Again, no positive circuit check is possible prior to firing.

The third type of system utilizes a firing circuit (trunklines and downlines) made up of inert plastic tubing, manifolds, tees, and connectors. Immediately prior to use, the system is charged with an explosive gas mixture. The gas mixture is then ignited to initiate in-hole delay detonators or conventional detonating cord. The firing circuit may be checked prior to firing using a pressure meter in a manner similar to the blasting galvanometer check of an electric blasting circuit. This is the only nonelectric blasting system that permits such a positive circuit check prior to firing. However, the requirement for specialized tubing, fittings, and test equipment, together with the use of hazardous gases makes the system more complex than other nonelectric blasting systems. Plastic tubing residue must be removed after the blast.

Controlled and Secondary Blasting

Secondary blasting is blasting used to break up boulders and oversized fragments resulting from primary blasting. The two principal methods of secondary blasting are block holing and mud capping. *Block holing* utilizes conventional drilling and blasting techniques to further fragment the rock. A hole is drilled to the center of the rock, an explosive charge is inserted, the hole is stemmed, and the charge is detonated. *Mud capping* utilizes an explosive charge placed on the surface of the rock and tamped with an inert material such as mud (wet clay). While mud capping requires 10–15 times as much explosive as block holing, the time and expense of drilling are eliminated.

Nonexplosive techniques for breaking up boulders and oversized rock fragments include rock splitting and the use of percussion hammers. *Rock splitters* are hydraulically powered devices which are expanded inside a drilled hole to shatter the rock. *Percussion hammers* available for fragmenting rock include pneumatic handheld paving breakers and

FIGURE 14. Hydraulic demolition hammer. (Courtesy of Allied Construction Products, Inc.)

larger hydraulically powered units that may be attached to backhoes or other machines. *Hydraulic hammers* such as that shown in Figure 14 are increasingly popular for use in all types of demolition. Mechanical methods of rock breaking eliminate the safety hazards and liability problems associated with blasting.

Controlled blasting is utilized to reduce disturbance to nearby structures, to reduce rock throw, to obtain a desired fracture line, or to reduce the cost of overbreak (fracture of rock beyond the line required for excavation). The principal controlled blasting technique is called *presplitting*. Presplitting involves drilling a line of closely spaced holes, loading the holes with light charges evenly distributed along the hole depth, and exploding these charges before loading and shooting the main blast. Typical presplitting procedures involve 2½- to 3-in. (5.4- to 7.6-cm)—diameter holes spaced 18–30 in. (45.7–76.2 cm) apart. Detonation of the presplitting charges results in a narrow fracture line that serves to reflect shock waves from the main blast and leaves a relatively smooth surface for the final excavation.

A related technique for producing a smooth fracture line is called *line drilling*. In this technique, a single row of closely spaced unloaded holes [4–12 in. (10–30 cm) on center] is drilled along the desired fracture line. In preparing the main blast, blastholes adjacent to the line drilling holes are moved close together and loaded lighter than usual. The line drilling technique normally produces less disturbance to adjacent structures than does presplitting. However, drilling costs for line drilling are high and the results can be unpredictable except in very homogeneous rock formations.

Blasting Safety

Blasting is a dangerous procedure that is controlled by a number of governmental regulations. Following are a few of the major safety precautions that should be observed:

- Storage magazines for explosives should be located in isolated areas, properly marked, sturdily constructed, and resistant to theft. Detonators (caps) must be stored in separate containers and magazines from other explosives.
- Electrical blasting circuits should not be connected to the power source and should be kept short-circuited (except for testing) until ready to fire.
- Permit no radio transmission in the vicinity of electric blasting circuits, and discontinue work if there is evidence of an approaching electrical storm.
- Protect detonators and primed charges in the work area from all physical harm.
- Check blastholes before loading, because hot rock or a piece of hot drill steel in the hole can cause an explosion.
- Do not drop or tamp primed charges or drop other charges directly on them.
- Use only nonmetallic tools for tamping.
- Employ simple, clear signals for blasting, and ensure that all persons in the work area are familiar with the signals.
- Make sure that the blasting area is clear before a blast is fired.
- Misfires are particularly dangerous. Wait at least 1 h before investigating a misfire. Allow only well-trained personnel to investigate and dispose of misfires.

4 ROCK RIPPING

Employment of Rippers

Rippers have been utilized since ancient times to break up hard soils. However, only since the advent of the heavy-duty tractor-mounted ripper has it become feasible to rip rock. The availability of powerful heavy tractors such as the one shown in Figure 15 now makes it possible to rip all but the toughest rock. Where ripping can be satisfactorily employed, it is usually cheaper than drilling and blasting. Additional advantages of ripping over drilling and blasting include increased production, fewer safety hazards, and reduced insurance cost.

Ripping Equipment

Although other types of rippers are available, most modern rippers are of the adjustable parallelogram type, shown in Figure 16. This type of ripper maintains a constant angle

FIGURE 15. Heavy-duty crawler-mounted ripper. (Reprinted Courtesy of Caterpillar Inc.)

FIGURE 16. Adjustable parallelogram ripper.

with the ground as it is raised and lowered. However, the upper hydraulic cylinder permits the tip angle to be varied as desired to obtain optimum results. The tip angle that produces the best surface penetration is usually different from the tip angle that produces optimum rock breakage after penetration. Automatic ripper control systems are available that control ripping depth and automatically vary tip angle as the ripper is raised or lowered.

Impact rippers utilize a hydraulic mechanism to impart a hammering action to a single shank ripper. As a result, impact rippers are able to effectively rip tougher rock than can conventional rippers and usually produce a significant increase in ripper production. Some typical values for the increased performance provided by impact rippers include a 5–15% increase in the maximum seismic velocity for rippability and a 10–45% increase in hourly ripper production.

Ripper shanks and tips are available in several different styles and in a variety of lengths for use in different types of material. Shank protectors, which fit on the front of the ripper shank immediately above the tip, are used to reduce wear on the shank itself. Both tips and shank protectors are designed to be easily replaced when necessary.

Ripper Production

The seismic velocity of a rock formation (Section 1) provides a good indication of the rock's rippability. Charts such as the one shown in Figure 17 have been prepared to provide a guide to the ripping ability of a particular tractor/ripper combination in various types of rock over a range of seismic velocities. When ripping conditions are marginal, the use of two tractors to power the ripper (tandem ripping) will often produce a substantial increase in production and reduce unit excavation cost.

Equation 6 may be used to predict ripper production when effective ripping width, depth, and speed can be established. Trial operations are usually required to accurately estimate these values unless such data are available from previous operations under similar conditions.

$$\text{Production (BCY/h)} = \frac{2.22 \times D \times W \times L \times E}{T} \quad \textbf{(6A)}$$

$$\text{Production (BCM/h)} = \frac{60 \times D \times W \times L \times E}{T} \quad \textbf{(6B)}$$

where D = average penetration (ft or m)

W = average width loosened (ft or m)

FIGURE 17. Ripper performance vs. seismic velocity. (Reprinted Courtesy of Caterpillar Inc.)

L = length of pass (ft or m)

E = job efficiency factor

T = time for one ripper pass, including turn (min)

Considerations in Ripping

Ripping speed and depth, spacing of ripper passes, and the number of shanks to be used for maximum ripper production depend on rock type and soundness, and tractor power. The presence and inclination of laminations will also affect ripping procedures. In general, rip downhill to take advantage of gravity. However, when ripping laminated material, it may be necessary to rip uphill to enable the ripper teeth to penetrate under the layers. The number of shanks to be used in a ripper should be the number that yields the desired penetration without straining the tractor. Depth of ripping will depend on the number of shanks used and the tractor power. In stratified material, try to match ripping depth to layer thickness. Ripping speed should be kept low to reduce wear on ripper teeth and shanks. First gear is usually used when ripping tough materials. The spacing of ripper passes will depend on rock hardness and the degree of fracture desired.

When loading ripped material, always leave a thin layer of material on the surface to provide a good working surface for the tractor. When ripping extremely hard rock, production may be increased and unit cost lowered if the rock is loosened by light blasting before ripping.

5 ESTIMATING PRODUCTION AND COST

The procedure for estimating rock excavation production and cost for a typical project is illustrated by Examples 4 and 5. Example 4 employs conventional drilling and blasting procedures for rock loosening, while Example 5 employs a tractor-mounted ripper.

Example 4 Estimate the hourly production and the unit cost of the rock excavation involved in preparing an industrial building site by drilling and blasting. The site is 300 ft (91.4 m) by 400 ft (121.9 m) and must be excavated to an average depth of 12 ft (3.658 m). The material to be excavated is a thinly laminated shale with a sonic velocity of 4000 ft/s (1220 m/s). The drilling equipment to be used will consist of an air-powered track drill and air compressor. The average drilling rate, including steel changes, moves, and delays, is estimated at 100 ft/h (30.5 m/h).

Trial blasting indicates that 3-in. (7.6-cm) holes drilled in a 12-ft (3.658-m) rectangular pattern will provide adequate fracturing. A hole depth of 13.5 ft (4.115 m) must be drilled to yield a 12-ft (3.658-m) effective depth. The blasting agent is ANFO. One-half pound (0.23 kg) of primer with an electric blasting cap will be used in each hole. The powder factor is 0.5 lb/BCY (0.297 kg/BCM).

A labor force of one drill operator and one compressor operator will be used for drilling. One blaster and one helper will be employed in blasting.

Cost information:

Labor:	Blaster	= $18.00/h
	Helper	= $15.00/h
	Drill operator	= $17.50/h
	Compressor operator	= $18.00/h
Equipment:	Track drill and compressor	= $63.00/h
Material:	ANFO	= $0.32/lb ($0.705/kg)
	Primer, cap, and stemming	= $3.00/hole

Solution

(a) Production

$$\text{Total volume} = \frac{300 \times 400 \times 12}{27} = 53{,}333 \text{ BCY}$$

$$[= 91.4 \times 121.9 \times 3.66 = 40{,}778 \text{ BCM}]$$

$$\text{Yield} = \frac{12^2 \times 12}{27} = 64.0 \text{ BCY/hole}$$

$$[= (3.658)^2 \times 3.658 = 48.9 \text{ BCM/hole}]$$

$$\text{Drilling yield} = \frac{64.0}{13.5} = 4.74 \text{ BCY/ft}$$

$$\left[= \frac{48.9}{4.115} = 11.88 \text{ BCM/m} \right]$$

$$\text{Production} = 4.74 \text{ BCY/ft} \times 100 \text{ ft/h} = 474 \text{ BCY/h}$$

$$[= 11.88 \times 30.5 = 362.3 \text{ BCM/h}]$$

$$\text{Time required} = \frac{53{,}333 \text{ BCY}}{474 \text{ BCY/h}} = 112.5 \text{ h}$$

$$\left[= \frac{40{,}778}{362.3} = 112.5 \text{ h} \right]$$

(b) Drilling cost

$$\text{Labor} = \$35.50/h$$

$$\text{Equipment} = \$63.00/h$$

$$\frac{\text{Drilling cost}}{\text{volume}} = \frac{\$98.50/h}{474 \text{ BCY/h}} = \$0.208/\text{BCY}$$

$$\left[= \frac{\$98.50}{362.3} = \$0.272/\text{BCM} \right]$$

(c) Blasting cost Material:

$$\text{ANFO} = 0.5 \text{ lb/BCY} \times 64 \text{ BCY} \times \$0.32/\text{lb}$$

$$= \$10.24/\text{hole}$$

$$[= 0.297 \times 48.9 \times 0.705 = \$10.24/\text{hole}]$$

$$\frac{\text{Prime, cap,}}{\text{and stemming}} = \$3.00/\text{hole}$$

$$\frac{\$13.24}{64 \text{ BCY}} = \$0.207/\text{BCY}$$

$$\left[\frac{\$13.24}{48.9} = \$0.271/\text{BCM} \right]$$

Labor:

$$\text{Unit cost} = \frac{\$33.00/h}{474 \text{ BCY/h}} = \$0.070/\text{BCY}$$

$$\left[= \frac{\$33.00}{362.3} = \$0.091/\text{BCM} \right]$$

$$\text{Total blasting} = \$0.207 + \$0.070 = \$0.277/\text{BCY}$$

$$[= \$0.271 + \$0.091 = \$0.362/\text{BCM}]$$

(d) Total cost = $0.208 + $0.277 = $0.485/BCY

$$[= \$0.272 + \$0.362 = \$0.634/\text{BCM}]$$

Example 5 Estimate the hourly production and the unit cost of rock excavation by ripping for the problem of Example 4. Field tests indicate that a D7G dozer with ripper can obtain satisfactory rock fracturing to a depth of 27 in. (0.686 m) with two passes of a single ripper shank at 3-ft (0.914-m) intervals. Average speed, including turns, is estimated at 82 ft/min (25 m/min).

Cost information:

$$\text{Labor (operator)} = \$20.00/h$$

Equipment (D7G with ripper, including ripper tips, shanks, and shank protectors) = $75.00/h

Solution

(a) Production

$$\text{Volume} = 53{,}333 \text{ BCY} (40{,}778 \text{ BCM})$$

$$\text{Production} = \frac{2.22 \times 2.25 \times 3 \times L \times 50/60}{2 \times L/82} \quad \text{(Eq 6)}$$

$$= 512 \text{ BCY/h}$$

$$\left[= \frac{60 \times 0.686 \times 0.914 \times L \times 50/60}{2 \times L/25} \right.$$
$$\left. = 392 \text{ BCM/h} \right]$$

$$\text{Time required} = \frac{53{,}333 \text{ BCY}}{512 \text{ BCY/h}} = 104 \text{ h}$$

$$\left[= \frac{40{,}778}{392} = 104 \text{ h} \right]$$

(b) Cost

$$\text{Labor} = 20.00/h$$

$$\text{Equipment} = 75.00/h$$

$$\text{Unit cost} = \frac{95.00/h}{512 \text{ BCY/h}} = 0.186/\text{BCY}$$

$$\left[= \frac{95.00}{392} = 0.242/\text{BCM} \right]$$

Problems

1. A parallel series electric blasting circuit consists of five branches of six caps each. Holes are spaced 10 ft (3.1 m) apart in a rectangular pattern. Cap legwire length is 24 ft (7.3 m). Each side of the cap circuit is connected by a No. 16 gauge buswire 40 ft (12.2 m) long. The lead wires are No. 12 gauge 1200 ft (336 m) long. Find the minimum current and voltage required to safely fire this blast under normal conditions.

2. List five safety precautions that should be observed in storing and handling blasting agents.

3. You measure a seismic velocity of 9000 ft/s (2743 m/s) in limestone. Would you expect this rock to be rippable by a D9H tractor equipped with a ripper (Figure 17)? If so, would you recommend using a single or tandem ripper in this situation? Why?

4. Estimate the hourly production and unit cost of rock excavation by drilling and blasting. The rock is a limestone having a seismic velocity of 6000 ft/s (1830 m/s). Trial blasting indicates that $3\frac{1}{2}$-in. (8.9-cm) holes drilled in an 8-ft (2.44-m) rectangular pattern will provide the desired fracturing. A hole depth of 20 ft (6.1 m) yields an effective depth of 18 ft (5.5 m). The average drilling rate is estimated to be 70 ft/h (21.4 m/h). A powder factor of 1 lb/BCY (0.59 kg/BCM) of ANFO will be used.

Cost Information:

Labor:	Drilling crew	$40.00/h
	Blasting crew	$42.00/h
Drilling equipment		$70.00/h
Material:	ANFO	$0.40/lb
		($0.88/kg)
	Primer, caps, & stemming	$4.00/hole

5. A tractor-mounted ripper will be used for excavating a limestone having a seismic velocity of 6000 ft/s (1830 m/s). Field tests indicate that the ripper can obtain satisfactory rock fracturing to a depth of 2 ft (0.61 m) with one pass of a single ripper shank at 3-ft (0.91-m) intervals. Average ripping speed for each 400-ft (122-m) pass is 1.5 mph (2.4 km/h). Maneuver and turn time at the end of each pass averages 0.3 min. Job efficiency is estimated at 0.70. Machine cost including the operator is $130/h. Estimate the hourly production and unit cost of excavation.

6. What effect does increased air pressure at the drill have on drill production? What limitations must be observed in using increased air pressure and what are the disadvantages of using increased air pressure?

7. A parallel series electric blasting circuit consists of six branches of eight caps each. Holes are spaced 10 ft (3.1 m) apart in a rectangular pattern. Cap legwire length is 28 ft (8.5 m). Each side of the cap circuit is connected by a No. 16 gauge buswire 50 ft (15.3 m) long. The lead wires are No. 14 gauge 1000 ft (305 m) long one-way. Find the minimum dc current and voltage required to safely fire this blast under current leakage conditions.

8. Using the seismograph test data in the table, find the seismic wave velocity in each layer and the depth of the upper layer.

Distance		
(ft)	(m)	Time (ms)
10	3.05	5.0
20	6.10	10.0
30	9.15	15.0
40	12.20	20.0
50	15.25	21.0
60	18.3	22.0
70	21.25	23.0
80	24.4	24.0

9. Trial blasting operations indicate that a rectangular pattern with holes 21-ft (6.4-m) deep spaced on 10-ft (3.05-m) centers will yield a satisfactory rock break with an effective depth of 19 ft (5.8 m). Determine the rock volume produced per foot (meter) of drilling.

10. Develop a computer program to estimate hourly production and unit cost of rock excavation by ripping. Input should include length of each pass, average ripper speed, effective depth of ripping, spacing of passes, turning time at the end of each pass, job efficiency, hourly operator cost, and hourly machine cost including ripper tips, shanks, and shank protectors. Solve Problem 5 using your computer program.

References

1. *Blasters Handbook.* E.I. du Pont de Nemours and Co. (Inc.), Wilmington, DE.

2. Church, Horace K. *Excavation Planning Reference Guide.* Jeremy Robison, project ed. New York: McGraw-Hill, 1988.

3. *Crawlair Drill Production Calculator.* Ingersoll-Rand Company, Phillipsburg, NJ.

4. *Handbook of Electric Blasting.* Atlas Powder Company, Dallas, TX.

5. *Handbook of Ripping.* Caterpillar Inc., Peoria, IL.

6. Pugliese, J. M. *Designing Blast Patterns Using Empirical Formulas* (Bureau of Mines Information Circular No. 8550). U.S. Government Printing Office, Washington, D.C., 1972.

7. Rollins, John P., ed. *Compressed Air and Gas,* 5th ed. Upper Saddle River, NJ: Prentice Hall, 1988.

PRODUCTION OF AGGREGATE, CONCRETE, AND ASPHALT MIXES

The production of high-quality concrete and asphalt mixes requires a supply of aggregate (gravel, sand, and mineral filler) meeting the specified gradation and other requirements. Most commonly, such aggregate is produced by crushing rock or gravel and blending it with sand and other minerals as required. Other construction operations which require crushed stone include highway and airfield base courses, drainage facilities, asphalt surface treatments, bedding for pipelines, and railroad ballast. The following sections describe the major steps in the production of aggregate, concrete mixes, and asphalt mixes.

1 PRODUCTION OF AGGREGATE

To produce quality aggregate, rock or gravel must be excavated, loaded, and transported to an aggregate processing plant (crushing plant) such as that shown in Figure 1. Here the raw material is washed if necessary, crushed, screened, sorted, and blended if necessary, and stored or loaded into haul units. Sands are not crushed but often require washing and dewatering before use.

Rock Crushers

Rock crushers such as the one shown in Figure 2 utilize mechanical action to reduce rock or gravel to a smaller size. The principal types of rock crushers and their characteristics are shown in Table 1 and include jaw crushers, impact crushers, cone or gyratory crushers, and roll crushers.

Jaw crushers (Figure 3a) utilize a fixed plate and a moving plate to crush stone between the two jaws. Jaw crushers are principally used as primary crushers. *Impact crushers* (Figure 3b) use breakers or hammers rotating at high speed to fracture the input stone. There are various types of impact crushers including impact breakers, horizontal and vertical shaft impactors, hammermills, and limemills. *Cone or gyratory*

crushers (Figure 3c) use an eccentrically rotating head to crush stone between the rotating head and the crusher body. *Roll crushers* (Figure 3d) produce fracturing of stone by passing the material between two or more closely spaced rollers. *Limemills* are similar to hammermills but are designed to produce a fine product from limestone.

The gradation of crusher output depends on crusher type and size, crusher setting, feed size, crusher speed, and other operating conditions. The best estimate of the gradation of a particular crusher output will be obtained from the crusher manufacturer's data or previous experience. However, Tables 2 and 3 present representative output gradations for jaw and roller crushers, respectively. These tables will be used in the examples and problems which follow. Notice that a significant fraction of crusher output is larger than the selected crusher closed side setting.

The crusher which first receives raw stone is known as the *primary crusher*. If the product is passed to another crusher, this crusher is known as a *secondary crusher*. Similarly, if yet another stage of crushing is required, the third crusher in line is known as a *tertiary crusher*. Screens are used to sort crusher output and feed oversize material back for recrushing. If the material makes a single pass through the crusher and none is fed back to the crusher, this is classified as *open circuit* crushing. When some material is fed back to the crusher for recrushing, the crusher is operating in *closed circuit*.

Feeders and Screens

Feeders (Figure 4) are used to supply gravel or stone to a crusher. Types of feeders include apron feeders, reciprocating plate feeders, vibrating feeders, and belt feeders. An *apron feeder* consists of a hopper box mounted above a plate feeder which operates like a conveyor to feed stone into a crusher. Apron feeders often incorporate a grizzly to remove oversize stone from the crusher input. A *grizzly* is simply a set of widely spaced bars or rods which serve to remove oversized material which might jam the crusher. A *reciprocating plate feeder* is

FIGURE 1. Aggregate processing plant. (Courtesy of Cedarapids, Inc.)

somewhat similar to an apron feeder but is smaller and used mainly to feed secondary or tertiary crushers. A reciprocating motion rather than the conveyor action of the apron feeder is used to move material into the crusher. A *vibrating feeder* uses vibratory action to move material from the receiving hopper into the crusher. *Belt feeders* combine a receiving hopper with a conveyor belt to move material to the crusher.

Screens (Figure 5) are used at a number of points in the aggregate processing cycle to separate aggregate by size for storage, blending, or recrushing. There are a number of types of screens including horizontal and inclined vibrating screens and rotating screens. Screens are often placed into a *deck* consisting of two or more screens placed one above the other. A *scalping screen* is simply a screen used to remove oversized particles from the aggregate stream.

The capacity of a screen is determined by a number of factors including screen size and screen opening size; slope of the

FIGURE 2. Portable cone crusher. (Courtesy of Kolberg-Pioneer, Inc., and Johnson Crushers International)

Table 1. Principal types of rock crushers and their characteristics

Crusher Type	Maximum Feed Size	Reduction Ratio	Product Size [in. (mm)]	Crushing Stage
Jaw crusher	50″ (1270 mm)	6 to 1	3″–20″ (76–508 mm)	Primary
Impact breakers	60″ (1524 mm)	20 to 1	2–16 (51–406 mm)	Primary
Horizontal secondary impactor	16″ (406 mm)	6–8 to 1	¾–4 (19–102 mm)	Secondary/Tertiary
Standard head cone	14″ (356 mm)	12 to 1	¾–4 (19–102 mm)	Secondary/Tertiary
Hammermill	8″ (203 mm)	20 to 1	#4–1½ (4.8–38 mm)	Secondary/Tertiary
Fine head cone	8″ (203 mm)	4–6 to 1	¼–2 (6.4–51 mm)	Secondary/Tertiary
Triple roll	8″ (203 mm)	4–5 to 1	¼–2 (6.4–51 mm)	Secondary/Tertiary
Dual roll	6″ (152 mm)	2–2.5 to 1	¼–3 (6.4–76 mm)	Secondary/Tertiary
Limemill	4″ (101 mm)	20 to 1	#10–#4 (1.7–4.8 mm)	Secondary/Tertiary
Vertical shaft impactor	3″ (76 mm)	4–8 to 1	⅜–1½ (9.5–38mm)	Secondary/Tertiary

Jaw crusher

Impact crusher

Cone or gyratory crusher

Roll crusher

FIGURE 3. Major types of rock crushers.

Table 2. Gradation of jaw crusher output (percent passing—open circuit)

Screen Size		in.	¾	1	1¼	1½	2	2½	3	4	5	6	7	8
in.	mm	mm	19	25	32	38	51	64	76	102	127	152	178	203
10	254										100	97	87	84
8	203										96	88	81	73
7	178									100	90	82	74	65
6	152								100	94	83	69	64	55
5	127							100	98	86	75	63	55	47
4	102							97	90	75	62	51	43	36
3	76						100	86	78	58	47	37	32	27
2½	64				100	100	93	78	66	48	38	31	25	23
2	51			100	98	96	82	64	52	39	29	25	21	18
1½	38		100	96	90	84	65	47	39	29	22	20	17	14
1¼	32		99	91	83	74	55	40	33	25	20	17	15	12
1	25		94	79	68	58	43	31	26	19	16	14	11	10
¾	19		80	61	55	43	31	23	20	15	13	11	9	7
½	13		58	41	33	30	22	16	14	11	9	8	7	6
⅜	10		41	29	25	22	17	13	11	8	7	6	6	5
¼	6		27	20	18	16	12	9	8	6	5	5	4	3
#4	4.8		20	15	13	12	9	7	6	5	4	4	3	2
#8	2.4		10	8	8	7	6	4	4	3	2	2	2	1
#16	1.2		7	5	5	5	3	3	3	3	2	2	2	1
#30	0.6		4	3	3	3	2	2	1	1	1	0.8	0.6	0.6
#50	0.3		2	2	2	1	1	1	1	1	0.6	0.5	0.4	0.4
#100	0.2		1	1	1	1	1	0.5	0.5	0.4	0.3	0.3	0.2	0.2

screen; position in the deck; amount of oversize and half-size material; and material condition, shape, and weight factors. Due to the complexity of the problem of estimating screen capacity, the methods used are largely empirical. One method for estimating both permissible total feed (oversize plus undersize) to the screen and the passing capacity of the screen is presented in Figure 6 and illustrated in Example 1.

Example 1 A jaw crusher is producing 250 tons/h (227 t/h) of crushed gravel and discharging it onto a three-screen deck. The top screen in the deck is a 1½ in. (38-mm) screen. The gradation of crusher output shows 100% passing 3 in. (76 mm), 92% passing 1½ in. (38 mm), and 80% passing ½ in. (19 mm). Material weight is 115 lb/cu ft (1842 kg/m³). Find the minimum size of the 1½ in. (38-mm) screen to be used. Check both total screen load and screen passing capacity.

Solution

Basic capacity (Figure 6):

$$\text{Total feed} = 6.5 \text{ tons/h/sq ft } (62 \text{ t/h/m}^2)$$

$$\text{Passing screen} = 3.5 \text{ tons/h/sq ft } (34 \text{ t/h/m}^2)$$

Deck position factor (top) = 1.0

Halfsize factor (80%) = 1.8

Oversize factor (8%):

$$\text{Total feed} = 0.96 \text{ Passing screen} = 1.04$$

$$\text{Weight factor} = \frac{115}{100} = 1.15$$

$$\left[= \frac{1842}{1600} = 1.15 \right]$$

$$\text{Total feed} = 250 \text{ tons/h } (227 \text{ t/h})$$

$$\text{Passing screen} = 250 \times 0.92$$

$$= 230 \text{ tons/h } (209 \text{ t/h})$$

$$\text{Total feed capacity} = 6.5 \times 1.0 \times 1.8 \times 0.96 \times 1.15$$

$$= 12.9 \text{ tons/h/sq ft}$$

$$[= 62 \times 1.0 \times 1.8 \times 0.96 \times 1.15$$

$$= 123 \text{ t/h/m}^2]$$

$$\left[= \frac{227}{123} = 1.85 \text{ m}^2 \right]$$

$$\text{Passing capacity} = 3.5 \times 1.0 \times 1.8 \times 1.04 \times 1.15$$

$$= 7.5 \text{ tons/h/sq ft}$$

$$[= 34 \times 1.0 \times 1.8 \times 1.04 \times 1.15$$

$$= 73 \text{ h/t/m}^2]$$

Table 3. Gradation of roll crusher output (percent passing—open circuit)

| Screen Size | | Crusher Closed Side Setting | | | | | | | | | | | |
in.	mm	in. mm	¼ 6	⅜ 10	½ 13	¾ 19	1 25	1¼ 32	1½ 38	2 51	2½ 64	3 76	4 102
6	152											100	100
5	127										100	96	78
4	102									100	95	84	75
3	76								100	93	78	76	58
2½	64							100	96	82	72	64	48
2	51						100	95	87	77	63	52	37
1½	38						92	82	78	58	48	38	28
1¼	32					100	86	80	66	49	40	33	25
1	25				100	90	79	66	52	39	32	27	20
¾	19			100	92	80	60	49	38	29	25	21	16
½	13		100	90	81	58	41	32	27	22	18	16	12
⅜	10		97	82	62	41	29	25	21	16	14	12	9
¼	6		82	60	42	28	21	18	16	12	10	9	7
#4	4.8		59	43	31	21	16	14	12	10	8	7	5
#8	2.4		32	23	17	13	10	8	7	6	5	4	3
#16	1.2		16	13	9	7	6	5	4	3	2	2	2
#30	0.6		9	7	5	4	3	3	3	2	1	1	1
#50	0.3		6	4	3	3	2	2	2	1	0.8	0.7	0.6
#100	0.2		4	3	2	2	1	1	1	0.5	0.3	0.3	0.2

$$\text{Required screen area for passing} = \frac{230}{7.5} = 30.7 \text{ sq ft}$$

$$\left[= \frac{209}{73} = 2.9 \text{ m}^2 \right]$$

Therefore, the minimum screen area required for this screen is determined by the screen passing capacity and is equal to 30.7 sq ft (2.9 m²).

The Crushing Cycle

A typical flow of stone through a primary jaw crusher and a secondary roll crusher is illustrated in Figure 7. Notice that the output of the primary crusher is separated by screening

FIGURE 5. Three-deck vibrating screen.

FIGURE 4. Apron feeder.

and the larger stone is sent to the roll crusher. The output of both crushers is further screened to divide the stone into the desired size ranges.

Estimating the production of an aggregate plant for a specific output is complex since it depends on many factors. Estimates are usually based on manufacturer's data and previous experience. However, computer programs, such as that

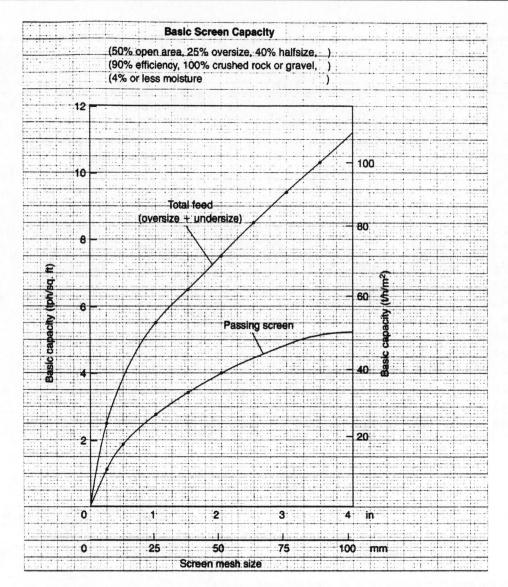

Modifying Factors

Deck factor		Halfsize factor		Oversize factor		
					Factor	
Position	Factor	% Feed less than halfsize	Factor	% Feed larger than opening	Passing screen	Total feed
Top	1.0	0	0.4	0	1.05	0.95
Second	0.9	20	0.6	20	1.02	0.97
Third	0.8	40	1.0	40	0.95	1.10
Fourth	0.7	60	1.4	60	0.85	1.30
		80	1.8	80	0.70	2.00

Weight Factor

$$W = \frac{\text{Weight (lb/cu ft)}}{100}$$

$$\left[W = \frac{\text{Weight (kg/m}^3)}{1600} \right]$$

FIGURE 6. Estimating screen capacity.

FIGURE 7. Aggregate flow through crushers.

presented in reference 5, have been developed to assist in making production estimates.

Example 2 A primary jaw crusher with a closed setting of 4 in. (102 mm) is producing 200 tons/h (181 t/h). The crusher output is to be screened into the following sizes: 2 in. (51 mm) and over, 1¼ in. (32 mm) to 2 in. (51 mm), ½ in. (13 mm) to 1¼ in. (32 mm), and under ½ in. (13 mm). A three-deck vibrating screen will be used to separate the stone. Jaw crusher output which does not pass the 2-in. (51-mm) screen will go to a roll crusher set at 2 in. (51 mm). The output from the roll crusher will be fed back over the 2-in. (51-mm) screen. Determine the output of this plant in tons per hour (t/h) for each of the following sizes:

$$1¼ \text{ to } 2 \text{ in. (32–51 mm)}$$

$$½ \text{ to } 1¼ \text{ in. (13–32 mm)}$$

$$\text{under } ½ \text{ in. (<13 mm)}$$

Solution

Distribution of primary crusher output (Table 2):

Size		Output
inches	mm	tons per hour[t/h]
>2	>51	$(100 - 0.39) \times 200 = 122.0$ [111.0] to roll
1¼–2	32–51	$(0.39 - 0.25) \times 200 = 28.0$ [25.0]
½–1¼	13–32	$(0.25 - 0.11) \times 200 = 28.0$ [25.0]
<½	<13	$(0.11) \times 200 = 22.0$ [20.0]

Distribution of roll crusher output (Table 3):

Crusher load required to yield 122 tons/h (111 t/h) passing 2-in. (51-mm)

$$\text{screen} = \frac{122}{0.77} = 158.4 \text{ tons/h (143.7 t/h)}$$

Size		Output
inches	mm	tons per hour[t/h]
>2	>51	$(1.00 - 0.77) \times 158.4 = 36.4$ [33.1] recycle
1¼–2	32–51	$(0.77 - 0.49) \times 158.4 = 44.4$ [40.2]
½–1¼	13–32	$(0.49 - 0.22) \times 158.4 = 42.8$ [38.8]
<½	<13	$(0.22) \times 158.4 = 34.8$ [31.6]

Combined output:

Size		Output
inches	mm	tons per hour[t/h]
>2	>51	0
1¼–2	32–51	$28.0 + 44.4 = 72.4$ [65.7]
½–1¼	13–32	$28.0 + 42.8 = 70.8$ [64.2]
<½	<13	$22.0 + 34.8 = 56.8$ [51.5]
		Total = 200.0 [181.4]

Notice that the total feed to the roll crusher is the sum of the jaw crusher output larger than 2 in. (51 mm) plus the oversized stone from the roll crusher which is fed back to the roll crusher. Thus, the total roll crusher feed is 122.0 tons/h (111.0 t/h) plus 36.4 tons/h (33.1 t/h) or 158.4 tons/h (144.1 t/h). Initially the plant output will be somewhat less than 200 tons/h (181.4 t/h) but will soon reach a steady-state output of 200 tons/h (181.4 t/h).

Washers and Other Equipment

Aggregates often require washing to remove silt, clay, or organic material prior to processing and sorting. Common types of washing equipment include scrubber drums, wet screens, log washers, sand dehydrators, and classifying tanks. *Scrubber drums* consist of an inclined revolving drum equipped with agitator fins and water spray nozzles. Undesirable material is removed as the aggregate is mixed with water and agitated while moving down the drum. *Wet screens* are essentially vibrating screens equipped with water spray bars to remove undesirable material as the aggregate is screened. *Log washers* utilize revolving auger paddles immersed in a tub of water to wash off undesirable material as the aggregate is moved through the tub by the auger blades. *Sand dehydrators* consist of rotating auger screws mounted in an inclined trough. Water and material to be cleaned are piped into the bottom of the trough. As the aggregate is moved up through the trough by the screw conveyors, the lighter undesirable material overflows into a flume and is drained off. *Classifying tanks* are essentially settling tanks which float off undesirable material while allowing clean aggregate to settle to the tank bottom where it can be removed.

The other major piece of aggregate processing equipment is the *belt conveyor*. Portable or stationary belt conveyors are used to move aggregate between crushers, screens, washers, and stockpiles, and to load the processed material into haul units. A *radial stacker* is a form of belt conveyor which pivots about a base point so that the conveyor discharges its output to form a semicircular stockpile.

2 PRODUCTION OF CONCRETE

Concrete is produced by mixing portland cement, aggregate, and water. In addition, a fourth component, an additive, may be added to improve the workability or other properties of the concrete mix. The construction operations involved in the production of concrete include batching, mixing, transporting, placing, consolidating, finishing, and curing. The production and transporting of plastic concrete are described in this section.

To meet design requirements while facilitating construction, it is important that concrete possess certain properties. Hardened concrete must meet design strength requirements and be uniform, watertight, durable, and wear-resistant. Desirable properties of plastic concrete include workability and economy. All of these properties are influenced by the concrete components and mix design used as well as by the construction techniques employed.

Types of Concrete

Concrete is classified into several categories according to its application and density. *Normal-weight concrete* usually weighs from 140 to 160 lb/cu ft (2243–2563 kg/m^3), depending on the mix design and type of aggregate used. A unit weight of 150 lb/cu ft (2403 kg/m^3) is usually assumed for design

purposes. Typical 28-day compressive strength ranges from 2000 to 4000 psi (13,790–27,580 kPa). *Structural lightweight concrete* has a unit weight less than 120 lb/cu ft (1922 kg/m^3) with a 28-day compressive strength greater than 2500 lb/sq in. (17,237 kPa). Its light weight is obtained by using lightweight aggregates such as expanded shale, clay, slate, and slag. *Lightweight insulating concrete* may weigh from 15 to 90 lb/cu ft (240–1442 kg/m^3) and have a 28-day compressive strength from about 100 to 1000 lb/sq in. (690–6895 kPa). As the name implies, such concrete is primarily utilized for its thermal insulating properties. Aggregates frequently used for such concrete include perlite and vermiculite. In some cases, air voids introduced into the concrete mix in foam replace some or all of the aggregate particles.

Mass concrete is concrete used in a structure such as a dam in which the weight of the concrete provides most of the strength of the structure. Thus, little or no reinforcing steel is used. Its unit weight is usually similar to that of regular concrete. *Heavyweight* is concrete made with heavy aggregates such as barite, magnetite, and steel punchings; it is used primarily for nuclear radiation shielding. Unit weights may range from 180 to about 400 lb/cu ft (2884–6408 kg/m^3). *No-slump concrete* is concrete having a slump of 1 in. (2.5 cm) or less. Slump is a measure of concrete consistency obtained by placing concrete into a test cone following a standard test procedure (ASTM C143) and measuring the decrease in height (slump) of the sample when the cone is removed. Applications of no-slump concrete include bedding for pipelines and concrete placed on inclined surfaces.

Refractory concrete is concrete that is suitable for high-temperature applications such as boilers and furnaces. The maximum allowable temperature for refractory concrete depends on the type of refractory aggregate used. *Precast concrete* is concrete that has been cast into the desired shape prior to placement in a structure. *Architectural concrete* is concrete that will be exposed to view and therefore utilizes special shapes, designs, or surface finishes to achieve the desired architectural effect. White or colored cement may be used in these applications. Surface textures may include exposed aggregates, raised patterns produced by form liners, sandblasted surfaces, and hammered surfaces. Architectural concrete panels are often precast and used for curtain walls and screens.

Concrete Components

The essential components of concrete are portland cement, aggregate, and water. Another component, an admixture or additive, is often added to impart certain desirable properties to the concrete mix. The characteristics and effects of each of these components on the concrete are discussed in the following paragraphs.

Cement   There are five principal types of portland cement, classified by the American Society for Testing and Materials (ASTM) as Types I–V, used in construction.

Type I (normal) portland cement is a general-purpose cement suitable for all normal applications. Type II (modified) portland cement provides better resistance to alkali attack and produces less heat of hydration than does Type I cement. It is suitable for use in structures such as large piers and drainage systems, where groundwater contains a moderate level of sulfate. Type III (high early strength) cement provides 190% of Type I strength after 1 day of curing. It also produces about 150% of the heat of hydration of normal cement during the first 7 days. It is used to permit early removal of forms and in cold-weather concreting. Type IV (low heat) cement produces only 40–60% of the heat produced by Type I cement during the first 7 days. However, its strength is only 55% of that of normal cement after 7 days. It is produced for use in massive structures such as dams. Type V (sulfate-resistant) cement provides maximum resistance to alkali attack. However, its 7-day strength is only 75% of normal cement. It should be used where the concrete will be in contact with soil or water that contains a high sulfate concentration.

In addition to these five major types of cement, ASTM has established standards for a number of special cement types. Types IA, IIA, and IIIA are the same as Types I, II, and III, with the addition of an air-entraining agent. Type IS is similar to Type I except that it is produced from a mixture of blast-furnace slag and portland cement. Type IS-A contains an air-entraining agent. Types IP, IP-A, P, and P-A contain a pozzolan in addition to portland cement. Because of their reduced heat of hydration, pozzolan cements are often used in large hydraulic structures such as dams. Types IP-A and P-A cements also contain an air-entraining agent. White portland cement (ASTM C150 and C175) is also available and is used primarily for architectural purposes.

Aggregates   Aggregate is used in concrete to reduce the cost of the mix and to reduce shrinkage. Because aggregates make up 60–80% of concrete volume, their properties strongly influence the properties of the finished concrete. To produce quality concrete, each aggregate particle must be completely coated with cement paste and paste must fill all void spaces between aggregate particles. The quantity of cement paste required is reduced if the aggregate particle sizes are well distributed and the aggregate particles are rounded or cubical. Aggregates must be strong, resistant to freezing and thawing, chemically stable, and free of fine material that would affect the bonding of the cement paste to the aggregate.

Water   Water is required in the concrete mix for several purposes. Principal among these is to provide the moisture required for hydration of the cement to take place. Hydration is the chemical reaction between cement and water which produces hardened cement. The heat that is produced by this reaction is referred to as *heat of hydration*. If aggregates are not in a saturated, surface-dry (SSD) condition when added to a concrete mix, they will either add or subtract water from the mix. Methods for correcting the amount of water added to a concrete batch to compensate for aggregate moisture are covered in this chapter. The amount of water in a mix also affects the plasticity or workability of the plastic concrete.

It has been found that the strength, watertightness, durability, and wear resistance of concrete are related to the water/cement ratio of the concrete mix. The lower the water/cement ratio, the higher the concrete strength and durability, provided that the mix has adequate workability. Thus, the water/cement ratio is selected by the mix designer to meet the requirements of the hardened concrete. Water/cement ratios normally used range from about 0.40 to 0.70 by weight. In terms of water quality, almost any water suitable for drinking will be satisfactory as mix water. However, organic material in mix water tends to prevent the cement paste from bonding properly to aggregate surfaces. Alkalies or acids in mix water may react with the cement and interfere with hydration. Seawater may be used for mixing concrete, but its use will usually result in concrete compressive strengths 10–20% lower than normal. The use of a lower water/cement ratio can compensate for this strength reduction. However, seawater should not be used for prestressed concrete where the prestressing steel will be in contact with the concrete. When water quality is in doubt, it is recommended that trial mixes be tested for setting time and 28-day strength.

Additives   A number of types of additives or admixtures are used in concrete. Some of the principal types of additives used are air-entraining agents, water-reducing agents, retarders, accelerators, pozzolans, and workability agents. *Air-entrained concrete* has significantly increased resistance to freezing and thawing as well as to scaling caused by the use of deicing chemicals. Entrained air also increases the workability of plastic concrete and the watertightness of hardened concrete. For these reasons, air-entrained concrete is widely used for pavements and other structures exposed to freezing and thawing.

Water-reducing agents increase the slump or workability of a concrete mix. Thus, with a water-reducing agent the amount of water in the mix may be reduced without changing the concrete's consistency. However, note that some water-reducing agents also act as retarders. *Retarders* slow the rate of hardening of concrete. Retarders are often used to offset the effect of high temperatures on setting time. They are also used to delay the setting of concrete when pumping concrete over long distances. *Accelerators* act in the opposite manner to retarders. That is, they decrease setting time and increase the early strength of concrete. Since the most common accelerator, calcium chloride, is corrosive to metal, it should not be used in concrete with embedded prestressing steel, aluminum, or galvanized steel.

Pozzolans are finely divided materials, such as fly ash, diatomaceous earth, volcanic ash, and calcined shale, which are used to replace some of the cement in a concrete mix. Pozzolans are used to reduce the heat of hydration, increase the workability, and reduce the segregation of a mix. *Workability agents* or plasticizers increase the workability of a mix. However, air-entraining agents, water-reducing agents, pozzolans, and retarders will also increase the workability of a mix.

Mix Design

The concrete mix designer is faced with the problem of selecting the most economical concrete mix that meets the requirements of the hardened concrete while providing acceptable workability. The most economical mix will usually be the mix that uses the highest ratio of aggregate to cement while providing acceptable workability at the required water/cement ratio.

A suggested mix design procedure is to first select a water/cement ratio that satisfies requirements for concrete strength, durability, and watertightness. (Table 4 gives maximum water/cement ratios recommended by the American Concrete Institute for various applications.) Next, select the workability or slump required (see Table 5). The third step is to mix a trial batch using a convenient quantity of cement at the selected water/cement ratio. Quantities of saturated, surface-dry fine, and coarse aggregate are then added until the desired slump is obtained. After weighing each trial mix component, the yield of the mix and the amount of each component required for a full-scale batch may be calculated by the method to be described.

Batching and Mixing

The process of proportioning cement, water, aggregates, and additives prior to mixing concrete is called *batching*.

Table 5. Recommended slumps for various types of construction (Courtesy of Portland Cement Association)

| Concrete construction | Slump, mm (in.) | |
	Maximum[a]	Minimum
Reinforced foundation walls and footings	75 (3)	25 (1)
Plain footings, caissons, and substructure walls	75 (3)	25 (1)
Beams and reinforced walls	100 (4)	25 (1)
Building columns	100 (4)	25 (1)
Pavements and slabs	75 (3)	25 (1)
Mass concrete	75 (3)	25 (1)

[a]Many be increased 25 mm (1 in.) for consolidation by hand methods, such as rodding and spading.

Plasticizers can safely provide higher slumps.

Adapted from ACI 211.1

Since concrete specifications commonly require a batching accuracy of 1–3%, depending on the mix component, materials should be carefully proportioned by weight. Central batching plants that consist of separate aggregate and cement batching units are often used for servicing truck mixers and for feeding central mixing plants. In such batching plants cement is usually handled in bulk. The addition of water to the mix may be controlled by the batching plant or it may be accomplished by the mixer operator. Batching for small construction mixers is accomplished by loading the required quantity of cement and aggregate directly into the skip (hopper) of the mixer. Water is added by the mixer operator. Cement for such mixers is usually measured by the sack (94 lb or 42.6 kg).

Table 4. Maximum water-cementitious material ratios and minimum design strengths for various exposure conditions (Courtesy of Portland Cement Association)

Exposure Condition	Maximum Water-Cementitious Material Ratio by Mass for Concrete	Minimum Design compressive strength f_c', MPa (psi)
Concrete protected from exposure to freezing and thawing, application of deicing chemicals, or aggressive substances	Select water-cementitious material ratio on basis of strength, workability, and finishing needs	Select strength based on structural requirements
Concrete intended to have low permeability when exposed to water	0.50	28 (4000)
Concrete exposed to freezing and thawing in a moist condition or deicers	0.45	31 (4500)
For corrosion protection for reinforced concrete exposed to chlorides from deicing salts, salt water, brackish water, seawater, or spray from these sources	0.40	35 (5000)

Adapted from ACI 318 (1999).

A standard classification system consisting of a number followed by a letter is used in the United States to identify mixer type and capacity. In this system, the number indicates the rated capacity of the mixer in cubic feet (0.028 m^3) of plastic concrete. Satisfactory mixing should be obtained as long as the volume of the mix does not exceed the mixer's rated capacity by more than 10%. The letter in the rating symbol indicates the mixer type: S is a construction mixer, E is a paving mixer, and M is a mortar mixer. Thus, the symbol "34E" indicates a 34-cu ft (0.96-m^3) paving mixer, "16S" indicates a 16-cu ft (0.45-m^3) construction mixer, and so on.

Construction mixers are available as wheel-mounted units, trailer-mounted units, portable plants, and stationary plants. Mixer drums may be single or double, tilting or nontilting. Mixer capacities range from 3½ cu ft (0.1 m^3) to over 12 cu yd (9.2 m^3). The wheel-mounted 16-cu ft (type 16S) construction mixer is often used on small construction projects where ready-mixed concrete is not available. Large central mix plants are used to supply concrete for projects such as dams, which require large quantities of concrete.

Truck mixers or *transit mix* trucks (Figure 8) are truck-mounted concrete mixers capable of mixing and transporting concrete. The product they deliver is referred to as *ready-mixed concrete*. The usual procedure is to charge the truck mixer with aggregate, additives, and cement at a central batch plant, then add water to the mix when ready to begin mixing. Truck mixers are also capable of operating as *agitator trucks* for transporting plastic concrete from a central mix plant. A truck mixer used as an agitator truck can haul a larger quantity of concrete than it is capable of mixing. While a unit's capacity when used as an agitator truck is established by the equipment manufacturer, agitating capacity is generally about one-third greater than mixer capacity. Standard truck mixer capacity ranges from 6 cu yd (4.6 m^3) to over 15 cu yd (11.5 m^3).

Paving mixers are self-propelled concrete mixers especially designed for concrete paving operations. They are equipped with a boom and bucket which enable them to place concrete at any desired point within the roadway. With the increasing use of slipform pavers, paving mixers are now most often used to supply slipform pavers or to operate as stationary mixers. Dual-drum paving mixer production is almost double that of a single-drum mixer. When operated as a stationary plant, a type 34E dual-drum paving mixer is capable of producing about 100 cu yd (76.5 m^3) of concrete per hour.

A minimum mixing time of 1 min plus ¼ min for each cubic yard (0.76 m^3) over 1 cu yd (0.76 m^3) is often specified for concrete mixers. However, the time required for a complete mixer cycle has been found to average 2–3 min. A mixing procedure that has been found to help clean the mixer drum and provide uniform mixing is to add 10% of the mix water before charging the drum, 80% during charging, and the remaining 10% when charging is completed. Timing of the mixing cycle should not begin until all solid materials are placed into the drum. All water should be added before one-fourth of the mixing time has passed. Standards of the Truck Mixer Manufacturers

FIGURE 8. Truck mixer. (Courtesy of Kenworth Truck Company)

Bureau require truck mixers to mix concrete for 70–100 revolutions at mixing speed after all ingredients, including water, have been added. Any additional rotation must be at agitating speed. Concrete in truck mixers should be discharged within $1\frac{1}{2}$ h after the start of mixing and before the drum has revolved 300 times.

Estimating Mixer Production

After a concrete mix design has been established, the volume of plastic concrete produced by the mix may be calculated by the *absolute-volume method*. In this method the volume of one batch is calculated by summing up the absolute volume of all mix components. The absolute volume of each component may be found as follows:

$$\text{Volume (cu ft)} = \frac{\text{Weight (lb)}}{62.4 \times \text{specific gravity}} \quad (1A)$$

$$\text{Volume (m}^3) = \frac{\text{Weight (kg)}}{1000 \times \text{specific gravity}} \quad (1B)$$

When calculating the absolute volume of aggregate using Equation 1, aggregate weight must be based on the saturated, surface-dry (SSD) condition. Such aggregate will neither add nor subtract water from the mix. If aggregate contains free water, a correction must be made in the quantity of water to be added to the mix. Example 3 illustrates these procedures.

Example 3

(a) Calculate the volume of plastic concrete that will be produced by the mix design given in the table.

Component	Specific Gravity	Quantity	
		lb	*kg*
Cement	3.15	340	154
Sand (SSD)	2.65	940	426
Gravel (SSD)	2.66	1210	549
Water	1.00	210	95

(b) Determine the actual weight of each component to be added if the sand contains 5% excess moisture and the gravel contains 2% excess moisture.

(c) Determine the weight of each component required to make a three-bag mix and the mix volume.

Solution

(a) $\text{Cement volume} = \dfrac{340}{3.15 \times 62.4} = 1.7 \text{ cu ft}$

$$\left[= \frac{154}{3.15 \times 1000} = 0.05 \text{ m}^3 \right]$$

$\text{Sand volume} = \dfrac{940}{2.65 \times 62.4} = 5.7 \text{ cu ft}$

$$\left[= \frac{426}{2.65 \times 1000} \; 0.16 \text{ m}^3 \right]$$

$\text{Gravel volume} = \dfrac{1210}{2.66 \times 62.4} = 7.3$

$$\left[= \frac{549}{2.66 \times 1000} = 0.21 \text{ m}^3 \right]$$

$\text{Water volume} = \dfrac{210}{1.00 \times 62.4} = 3.4 \text{ cu ft}$

$$\left[= \frac{95}{1.00 \times 1000} = 0.09 \text{ m}^3 \right]$$

$\text{Mix volume} = 1.7 + 5.7 + 7.3 + 3.4 = 18.1 \text{ cu ft}$

$$[= 0.05 + 0.16 + 0.21 + 0.09 = 0.51 \text{ m}^3]$$

(b) $\text{Excess water in sand} = 940 \times 0.05 = 47 \text{ lb}$

$$[= 426 \times 0.05 = 21 \text{ kg}]$$

$\text{Excess water in gravel} = 1210 \times 0.02 = 24 \text{ lb}$

$$[= 549 \times 0.02 = 11 \text{ kg}]$$

$\text{Total excess water} = 47 + 24 = 71 \text{ lb}$

$$[= 21 + 11 = 32 \text{ kg}]$$

Field mix quantities:

$$\text{Water} = 210 - 71 = 139 \text{ lb}$$

$$[= 95 - 32 = 63 \text{ kg}]$$

$$\text{Sand} = 940 + 47 = 987 \text{ lb}$$

$$[= 426 + 21 = 447 \text{ kg}]$$

$$\text{Gravel} = 1210 + 24 = 1234 \text{ lb}$$

$$[= 549 + 11 = 560 \text{ kg}]$$

(c)   Adjusting to a three-bag mix:

$$\text{Cement} = 3 \times 94 = 282 \text{ lb}$$

$$[= 3 \times 42.6 = 127.8 \text{ kg}]$$

$$\text{Sand} = \frac{282}{340} \times 987 = 819 \text{ lb}$$

$$\left[= \frac{127.8}{154} \times 447 = 370 \text{ kg} \right]$$

$$\text{Gravel} = \frac{282}{340} \times 1234 = 1023 \text{ lb}$$

$$\left[= \frac{127.8}{154} \times 560 = 464 \text{ kg} \right]$$

$$\text{Water} = \frac{282}{340} \times 139 = 115 \text{ lb}$$

$$\left[= \frac{127.8}{154} \times 63 = 52 \text{ kg} \right]$$

$$\text{Mix volume} = \frac{282}{340} \times 18.1 = 15.0 \text{ cu ft}$$

$$\left[= \frac{127.8}{154} \times 0.51 = 0.42 \text{ m}^3 \right]$$

After the batch volume has been calculated, mixer production may be estimated as follows:

$$\text{Mixer production} \atop (\text{cu yd/h}) = \frac{2.22 \times V \times E}{T} \qquad (2A)$$

$$\text{Mixer production} \atop (\text{m}^3/\text{h}) = \frac{90 \times V \times E}{T} \qquad (2B)$$

where V = batch volume (cu ft or m^3)
   T = cycle time (min)
   E = job efficiency

Transporting and Handling Concrete

A number of different items of equipment are available for transporting concrete from the mixer to its place of use. Some equipment commonly used includes transit mixer trucks, agitator trucks, dump trucks, conveyors, pumps, and cranes with concrete buckets. Special rail cars designed for transporting plastic concrete are also available, but seldom used except on mass concrete projects such as concrete dams.

Regardless of the equipment used, care must be taken to avoid segregation when handling plastic concrete. The height of any free fall should be limited to 5 ft (1.5 m) unless downpipes or ladders are used. Downpipes having a length of at least 2 ft (0.6 m) should be used at the end of concrete conveyors. When using nonagitator trucks for hauling concrete, specifications may limit the truck speed and maximum haul distance that may be used. Temperature, road condition, truck body type, and mix design are the major factors that influence the maximum safe hauling distance that may be used.

3   PRODUCTION OF ASPHALT MIXES

Asphalt and Other Bituminous Materials

Bituminous materials include both asphalt and tar. Although asphalt is the type of bituminous material most frequently used in surfacing roads and airfields, road tars are sometimes used. Most properties of asphalt and tar are similar, except that tars are not soluble in petroleum products. As a result, tar surface treatments and tar seal coats are often used when the pavement is likely to be subjected to spills of petroleum fuels—for example, on airfield aprons and taxiways and in gasoline stations. A major disadvantage of tar is its tendency to change consistency with small variations in temperature. Tar also has a different coefficient of expansion than does asphalt. Thus, when a tar seal coat is applied to protect an asphalt pavement from petroleum spills, the difference in their coefficients of expansion can result in severe cracking of the seal coat within a few years. Such cracking will allow fuel spills to penetrate into the asphalt pavement, with resulting damage to the asphalt pavement. However, there are also fuel-resistant

asphalts available as described next. Since asphalt predominates in construction, the words bituminous and asphalt are often used interchangeably in construction practice.

Bituminous surfaces (pavements and surface treatments) are used to provide a roadway wearing surface and to protect the underlying material from moisture. Because of their plastic nature, bituminous surfaces are often referred to as flexible pavements, in contrast to concrete pavements, which are identified as rigid pavements. Bituminous surfaces are produced by mixing solid particles (aggregates) and a bituminous material. Since the bituminous material serves to bond the aggregate particles together, it is referred to as *binder*.

The aggregate in a bituminous surface actually provides the load-carrying ability of the surface. The aggregate also resists the abrasion of traffic and provides skid resistance to the travel surface. In addition to the coarse aggregate (gravel) and fine aggregate (sand) used in concrete mixes, asphalt mixes often contain a third size of aggregate called *fines*. Fines, also called *mineral filler* or mineral dust, consist of any inert, nonplastic material passing the No. 200 sieve. Material used as fines includes rock dust, portland cement, and hydrated lime. Aggregates used in asphalt mixes should be angular, hard, durable, well graded, clean, and dry, in order to provide the required strength to the mix and to bond with the binder.

Asphalt cement, the solid form of asphalt, must be heated to a liquid state for use in bituminous mixes. Asphalt cements have traditionally been viscosity-graded based on their absolute viscosity measured at 60°C and 135°C and range from AC-2.5 (soft) to AC-40 (hard). A grading system based on a penetration test is also sometimes used. In this system, the penetration (in hundredths of a centimeter) which occurs in 5 s is measured for a standard needle under a 100-g load with the asphalt temperature at 25°C. Penetration grades range from soft (penetration numbers 200–300) to hard (penetration numbers 40–50). More recently, in order to implement the *Superpave*[TM] asphalt pavement design and construction system, a *Performance Graded Asphalt Binder* classification system has been developed. Under this classification system, asphalt binder Performance Grades range from PG 46-46 to PG 82-34. Note that this is classified as an "asphalt binder" specification since it is intended to apply to both modified and unmodified asphalts. In this system, the first two digits indicate the average 7-day maximum pavement design temperature (in degrees Celsius), and the last two digits indicate the minimum pavement design temperature (in minus degrees Celsius). Some of the laboratory tests and procedures which are required to classify asphalt binder under the Performance Graded (PG) system include the following:

The Rotational Viscometer, which indicates asphalt binder handling and pumping properties at high temperatures.

The Dynamic Shear Rheometer, which provides a measure of the permanent deformation and fatigue cracking of asphalt binder at high and intermediate temperatures.

The Bending Beam Rheometer and the Direct Tension Tester, which provide a measure of low temperature asphalt binder cracking.

The Rolling Thin Film Oven and the Pressure Aging Vessel, which measure asphalt binder aging and hardening characteristics.

Fuel-resistant asphalt, often based on a polymer-modified asphalt (PMA), is available and has demonstrated high resistance to rutting and cracking as well as to petroleum fuels. Some such asphalts can sustain less than 1% material loss after 24 h of immersion in jet fuel.

An asphalt *cutback*, which is liquid at room temperature, is created when petroleum distillates are mixed with asphalt cement. Asphalt cutbacks are classified as medium curing (MC) or rapid curing (RC), depending on the type of solvent used in their production. Road oils or slow-curing (SC) asphalt may be residual asphalt oils or may be produced by blending asphalt cement with residual oils. The classification symbol used for cutbacks and road oils includes a number that indicates the viscosity of the mixture. Viscosity grades range from 30 (viscosity similar to water) to 3000 (barely deforms under its own weight).

Asphalt *emulsions* contain particles of asphalt dispersed in water by means of emulsifying agents. Asphalt emulsions have several important advantages: They can be applied to wet aggregates and they are not flammable or toxic. Asphalt emulsions are classified as rapid setting (RS), medium setting (MS), or slow setting (SS).

Road tars are designated by the symbol RT plus a number indicating viscosity. Twelve grades are available, ranging from RT-1 (low viscosity) to RT-12 (solid at room temperature). Two tar cutback grades, RTCB-5 and RTCB-6, are also available.

Handling Bituminous Materials

When cutbacks are heated for mixing or spraying, they are usually above their flash point. The *flash point* of a liquid is the temperature at which it produces sufficient vapor to ignite in the presence of air and an open flame. Since the flash point is reached at a temperature below that at which the liquid would normally burn, extreme care must be taken when heating cutbacks or when handling the heated material. No open flame or spark-producing equipment should be allowed near the hot liquid. Use only equipment specifically designed for the purpose when heating, storing, mixing, or spraying cutbacks. Adequate fire-extinguishing equipment must be readily available together with personnel properly trained in its use. Proper precautions must also be taken to prevent burns when working with hot materials. Hot surfaces must be conspicuously marked or guarded to protect workers against contacting them. Gloves and other protective clothing must be used by workers handling hot equipment.

Asphalt Plants

While cold asphalt mixes may be produced using asphalt cutbacks or emulsions, asphalt plants are primarily used to produce *hot-mix asphalt* (HMA) from asphalt cement. The principal types of asphalt plants are batch plants and drum-mix plants. The *batch plant* illustrated in Figure 9 uses a cold feed hopper and cold feed belt conveyor to feed aggregate into the dryer. From the dryer, hot aggregate is moved by a hot elevator into an aggregate batcher. Here the hot

FIGURE 9. Asphalt batch plant.

FIGURE 10. Components of a drum-mix asphalt plant.

aggregate is separated by screening and placed into bins by size. Calibrated feeders provide a supply of aggregate and mineral filler in the required quantities to the pugmill (mixer). Asphalt is injected into the pugmill and the mixture is mixed for the required time. The batch of hot-mix asphalt is then deposited into a haul unit.

In recent years the *drum-mix plant* illustrated in Figure 10 has become quite popular and has largely replaced the older continuous-flow plant. As you see, both drying and mixing take place in the drum. The process eliminates the separate aggregate batcher, hot elevator, and pugmill of the batch plant. The dust emitted by the dryer is also less than that emitted by the batch plant dryer because the liquid asphalt tends to trap fines inside the drum. This reduces the amount of pollution control equipment needed. Some recent innovations such as dual-drum mixers and counterflow air systems have further increased these plants' efficiencies. The high production capability, efficiency, economy, and portability of these plants make them attractive to asphalt producers.

Frequent sampling and testing of asphalt plant mixes is required to ensure adequate quality control. Insulated storage bins such as that shown in Figure 11 are available to store plant output when hauling capacity is limited or uncertain. Loading and hauling must be carefully conducted to prevent degradation of the mix. Trucks should be clean and dry before loading. Insulated or heated trucks may be required to ensure that the mix is delivered to the job site at the specified temperature.

Estimating Asphalt Plant Production

An asphalt mix is composed of asphalt, coarse aggregate (gravel), fine aggregate (sand), and mineral filler (or fines). The amount of asphalt in a mix is expressed as a percentage

of total mix weight. Aggregate is heated in the dryer to permit bonding with the hot asphalt. Since fines are largely lost as the aggregate passes through the dryer, mineral filler is usually added directly to the pugmill along with the asphalt and hot aggregate.

Dryer capacity, which depends on aggregate moisture content, is normally the controlling factor in asphalt plant capacity. Thus, the maximum hourly plant capacity may be calculated from the dryer capacity and the percentage of asphalt and fines in the mix. The procedure is illustrated in

FIGURE 11. Insulated hot-mix asphalt storage bin with skip hoist. (Courtesy of Terex Road Building)

Example 4. Notice that the calculations are based on dry aggregate weights. The weight of coarse aggregate and sand must be corrected for moisture to obtain the actual field weight of these materials required to feed the dryer. Additional information on asphalt plant calibration is contained in reference 2.

Example 4

(a) Calculate the maximum hourly production of an asphalt plant based on the data in the following list.

(b) Find the required feed rate (ton/h) for each mix component to achieve this production.

Mix composition:

Asphalt	= 6%
Aggregate composition:	
Coarse A	= 42%
Coarse B	= 35%
Sand	= 18%
Mineral filler	= 5%
Aggregate moisture	= 8%
Dryer capacity at 8% moisture removal	= 110 ton/h

Solution

(a)
$$\text{Plant capacity} = \frac{\text{Dryer capacity} \times 10^4}{(100 - \text{asphalt \%})(100 - \text{fines \%})} \quad (3)$$

$$= \frac{110 \times 10^4}{(100 - 6)(100 - 5)} = 123 \text{ ton/h}$$

(b) Feed rate (ton/h):

Component	Fraction	Total	Rate
Asphalt	0.06	123.0	7.4
Aggregate (dry)	0.94	123.0	115.6
	1.00	123.0	123.0
Aggregate components (dry weight)			
Coarse A	0.42	115.6	48.5
Coarse B	0.35	115.6	40.5
Sand	0.18	115.6	20.8
Mineral filler	0.05	115.6	5.8
	1.00	115.6	115.6

Problems

1. **a.** Determine the water–cement ratio of the mix of Problem 6.
    b. What difficulties might result from lowering the water–cement ratio of the mix and how might these be overcome?

2. Using the data of Example 2, determine the minimum size screen required for the 2-in. (51-mm) screen. The stone weighs 100 lb/cu ft (1602 kg/m³).

3. Select the crusher settings for a primary jaw crusher and a secondary roll crusher to produce 150 tons per hour (136 t/h) of aggregate meeting the following specifications. Indicate the output in tons per hour (t/h) and in percentage for each of the specified size ranges.

Screen Size in. (mm)	Percent Passing
2–½ (6, 4)	100
1 (25)	50–60
¼ (6)	15–30

4. Calculate the feed rate in tons per hour (tph) for a drum-mix asphalt plant under the following conditions:

Asphalt content	= 5%
Aggregate composition:	
Coarse A	= 45%
Coarse B	= 30%
Sand	= 20%
Mineral filler	= 5%

Field moisture content of gravel and sand = 6%
Drum capacity at required moisture removal = 138 tph (125 t/h)

5. Calculate the hot feed required per batch for an asphalt batch plant producing 3 tons (2.7 t) per batch under the following conditions:

Asphalt content	= 5%
Aggregate composition:	
Coarse A	= 45%
Coarse B	= 35%
Sand	= 15%
Mineral filler	= 5%

6. A one-sack trial mix that meets specification requirements has the proportions shown below. Determine the quantity of each ingredient by weight required to batch a 16S mixer with no overload using an integer number of sacks of cement. The field excess moisture of the sand is 4%. The gravel is saturated, surface-dry.

Component	Weight lb	Weight Kg	Specific Gravity
Cement	94	42.6	3.15
Gravel	400	181.4	2.66
Sand	200	90.7	2.65
Water	50	22.7	1.00

7. What are the characteristics of a Performance Grade PG 58-10 asphalt binder?

8. Determine the actual field weight (lb or kg) required to charge a 34E mixer with a 10% overload using the mix proportions given below. The field excess moisture content of the sand is 6% and that of the gravel is 2%.

| Component | Weight | | Specific Gravity |
	lb	kg	
Cement	94	42.6	3.15
Gravel	415	188.2	2.66
Sand	235	106.6	2.65
Water	54	24.5	1.00

9. Develop a computer program to calculate the feed rate for an asphalt plant. For drum-mix plants, output the cold feed rate in tons per hour (t/h) of coarse and fine aggregate, mineral filler, and asphalt cement. For batch plants, output the dry weight in tons (t) per batch for aggregates, mineral filler, and asphalt cement. Input should include the type of plant, the aggregate composition, asphalt content, field aggregate moisture, and drum capacity at the required moisture removal. Solve Problem 4 using your program.

10. Develop a computer program to calculate the field batch weight of each component for a specified concrete mix and mixer capacity. Input should include the rated mixer capacity, percent overload to be used, and mix proportions. For each mix component, input the SSD weight for the component, the specific gravity, and the field excess moisture. Solve Problem 8 using your computer program.

References

1. *The Asphalt Handbook* (MS-4). The Asphalt Institute, Lexington, KY.

2. *Asphalt Plant Manual* (MS-3). The Asphalt Institute, Lexington, KY.

3. *Design and Control of Concrete Mixtures,* 14th ed. Portland Cement Association, Skokie, IL, 2002.

4. *Facts and Figures.* Pioneer Division, PORTEC Inc., Minneapolis, MN, 1980.

5. Hancher, Donn E., and John A. Havers. *Mathematical Model of Aggregate Plant Production.* New York: American Society of Civil Engineers, 1974.

6. Nunnally, S. W. *Managing Construction Equipment*, 2nd ed. Upper Saddle River, NJ: Prentice Hall, 2000.

7. *Pocket Reference Book.* Cedarapids Inc., Cedar Rapids, IA 52402, 1993.

8. *Principles of Construction of Hot-Mix Asphalt Pavements* (MS-22). The Asphalt Institute, Lexington, KY.

9. *Superpave Performance Graded Asphalt Binder Specification and Testing* (SP-1). The Asphalt Institute, Lexington, KY.

PAVING AND SURFACE TREATMENTS

From Chapter 8 of *Construction Methods and Management*, Eighth Edition. S. W. Nunnally. Copyright © 2011 by Pearson Education, Inc.
Published by Pearson Prentice Hall. All rights reserved.

PAVING AND SURFACE TREATMENTS

Pavements and surface treatments are used to provide a roadway wearing surface and to protect the underlying material from moisture. Both concrete and asphalt mixes are used to construct pavements. Because of their plastic nature, asphalt pavements are often referred to as flexible pavements in contrast to concrete pavements, which are identified as rigid pavements. Surface treatments, on the other hand, are produced by applying liquid asphalt or some other bituminous material to a roadway surface, with or without the addition of aggregate. The construction of concrete and asphalt pavements and asphalt surface treatments is described in the following sections.

1 CONCRETE PAVING

Form-Riding Equipment

The frequent use of concrete for paving highways and airfields has led to the development of specialized concrete paving equipment. While slipform pavers that do not require the use of forms are becoming increasingly popular, paving is still accomplished using metal forms to retain the plastic concrete while it is placed and finished. Since much of this equipment is designed to ride on the concrete forms, the equipment is often referred to as *form-riding equipment*. The pieces of equipment used to perform the operations of mixing, placing, finishing, and curing are often referred to as a *paving train*, because they travel together in series along the roadway.

Standard metal paving forms are 10 ft (3 m) long and 8–12 in. (20–30 cm) in height. Metal pins are driven into the ground through holes in the form, and the form ends are locked together to hold them in alignment. Form-riding subgraders similar to the grade excavator are available to bring the pavement subgrade or base to precise elevation before concrete is poured. Concrete is placed within the forms by a paving mixer or by truck mixers. A form-riding concrete spreader is used to spread, strike off, and consoli-

date the concrete. Combination placer/spreader units equipped with conveyor belts are available which are capable of operating with either form-riding or slipform paving equipment.

Finishing follows concrete placing and spreading. Form-riding equipment often includes both a transverse and a longitudinal finisher. The transverse finisher is used to bring the surface to final elevation and provide initial finishing. The longitudinal finisher provides final machine finishing. Hand finishing may follow, employing a form-riding finishing bridge to permit workers to reach the entire surface of the pavement. Finishers may be followed by an automatic curing machine equipped with a power spray that applies curing compound.

When constructing large slabs and decks, concrete may be placed by chutes, buckets, or side discharge conveyors. Mechanical finishing may be supplied by roller finishers, oscillating strike-off finishers, large power floats, or other types of finishers.

Slipform Paving

A *slipform paver* is capable of spreading, consolidating, and finishing a concrete slab without the use of conventional forms. The concrete develops sufficient strength to be self-supporting by the time it leaves the paver, as shown in Figure 1. Since the paver's tracks completely span the pavement slab, reinforcing steel may be placed ahead of the paver. Typical slipform pavers are capable of placing slabs up to 10 in. (25.4 cm) thick and 24 ft (7.3 m) wide at speeds up to 20 ft/min (6 m/min). Other paving equipment, such as tube finishers and curing machines, may be used in conjunction with a slipform paver.

Small slipform pavers such as the one shown in Figure 2 are widely used for pouring curbs and gutters. Some machines are combination grade trimmers and pavers, capable of both preparing the subgrade and placing the curb and gutter. Slipform pavers have placed over 1 mi (1.6 km) of curb and gutter

FIGURE 1. Large slipform paver in operation. (Courtesy of Terex Roadbuilding)

FIGURE 2. Slipform paver for curbs and gutters. (Courtesy of GOMACO Corporation)

per day, although typical production is about one-half of that amount. Small slipform pavers are also capable of constructing sidewalks, highway median barriers (Figure 3), and similar structures.

Concrete saws equipped with diamond or abrasive blades are often used to cut joints in concrete slabs to control shrinkage cracking. The depth of control joints should be about one-fourth of the slab thickness, but not less than the maximum size of the aggregate used. Sawing should be done when the concrete is still green but has hardened sufficiently to produce a clean cut. This is usually 6–30 h after the concrete has been placed.

Roller Compacted Concrete

Roller compacted concrete (RCC) is a relatively new form of concrete construction. First used in the early 1970s for the construction of concrete dams, its use has spread to pavements and other structures. Basically the process involves dumping and spreading zero-slump concrete onto a prepared base and then compacting the mixture with vibratory or rubber-tired rollers. The construction technique has the advantages of speed, economy, and simplicity. In one case of dam construction, it has been reported that the cost using RCC construction was only about one-third that of conventional concrete construction.

In pavement construction, modified asphalt pavers or concrete placer-spreader units can be used to place the RCC in the desired thickness. Compaction of the RCC should take place as soon as possible but not more than 10 min after placing. Vibratory rollers are commonly used for primary compaction. This is often followed by a heavy pneumatic roller to help seal surface cracks and joints. A light smooth-wheel static roller may be employed for final rolling to provide surface smoothing. The rolling pattern commonly used for RCC is similar to that described in Section 2 for asphalt pavements.

FIGURE 3. Slipform paver placing median barrier. (Reprinted Courtesy of Caterpillar Inc.)

However, when an adjacent lane is to be placed before the first lane has hardened, it is suggested that an uncompacted strip about 1 ft (300 mm) wide be left on the adjoining side until the adjacent lane is placed. After the adjacent lane is placed, the strip and joint between the lanes is compacted. Before placing a cold joint, the edge of the existing pavement should be cut off to form a vertical surface. Continuous moist curing by ponding, water spray, or a wet mat is suggested for the first 24 h, followed by a curing membrane spray.

2 ASPHALT PAVING AND SURFACE TREATMENTS

The Bituminous Distributor

The bituminous or asphalt distributor illustrated in Figure 4 is used to apply liquid bituminous materials. It is utilized in almost all types of bituminous construction. The rate of liquid

bituminous application is expressed in gallons per square yard (liters per square meter). The rate at which the bituminous material is applied by a distributor depends on spray bar length, travel speed, and pump output. Spray bar length may range from 4 ft (1.2 m) to 24 ft (7.3 m). Travel speed is measured by a bitumeter calibrated in feet per minute (meters per minute). Pump output is measured by a pump tachometer calibrated in gallons per minute (liter per minute). Since standard asphalt volume is measured at a temperature of 60°F (15.5°C), a volumetric correction factor must be applied to convert asphalt volume at other temperatures to the standard volume (see Table 1).

FIGURE 4. Bituminous distributor components. (Courtesy of The Asphalt Institute Inc.)

Table 1. Volumetric correction factor for asphalt[*]

| Temperature | | To Obtain Standard Volume, Multiply Measured Volume by: |
°F	°C	
60	16	1.0000
80	27	0.9931
100	38	0.9862
120	49	0.9792
140	60	0.9724
160	71	0.9657
180	82	0.9590
200	93	0.9523
220	104	0.9458
240	116	0.9392
260	127	0.9328
280	138	0.9264
300	149	0.9201
320	160	0.9138
340	171	0.9076

[*]Specific gravity above 0.966. Applicable to all grades of asphalt cement and liquid asphalt grades 250, 800, and 3000.

For a particular spray bar length, the road speed (bitumeter reading) and pump output (tachometer reading) needed to obtain a specified application rate can be found in the tachometer chart supplied by the distributor manufacturer. If a tachometer chart is not available, the necessary road speed can be found by using Equation 1.

$$S = \frac{9 \times P}{W \times R} \text{ ft/min} \qquad (1A)$$

$$S = \frac{P}{W \times R} \text{ m/min} \qquad (1B)$$

where S = road speed (ft/min or m/min)
P = pump output (gal/min or ℓ/min)
W = spray bar width (ft or m)
R = application rate (gal/sq yd or ℓ/m²)

Bituminous Surface Treatments

Bituminous surface treatments are used to bond old and new surfaces, to seal and rejuvenate old pavements, or to provide a fresh waterproofing and wearing surface. A wide variety of bituminous surface treatments are available, including prime coats, tack coats, dust palliatives, seal coats, single-pass surface treatments, and multiple-pass surface treatments.

A *prime coat* is a coating of light bituminous material applied to a porous unpaved surface. The purpose of the prime coat is to seal the existing surface and to provide a bond between the existing surface and the new bituminous surface. Bituminous materials commonly used for prime coats include RT-1, RT-2, RT-3, RC-70, RC-250, MC-30, MC-70, MC-250, SC-20, and SC-250. The usual rate of bituminous application varies from 0.25 to 0.50 gal/sq yd (1.1–2.3 ℓ/m²). All liquid bituminous should be absorbed within 24 h and it should cure in about 48 h.

A *tack coat* is a thin coating of light bituminous material applied to a previously paved surface to act as a bonding agent. Bituminous materials commonly used for tack coats include RC-70, RC-250, RS-1, RS-2, RT-7, RT-8, and RT-9. The usual rate of application is 0.1 gal/yd (0.45 ℓ/m²) or less. The tack coat must be allowed to cure to a tacky condition before the new surfacing layer is placed.

A *dust palliative* is a substance applied to an unpaved surface to reduce the amount of dust produced by vehicular traffic and wind. Bituminous dust palliatives are designed to penetrate and bond particles in the unpaved surface and provide some waterproofing. Bituminous materials commonly employed include MC-30, MC-70, and diluted slow-setting emulsions. Other agents used as dust palliatives include water, acrylic copolymer, pine resin, magnesium chloride, calcium chloridem, lignosulfonate, and petroleum resins. While water is effective in reducing dust, under very dry conditions it must be applied almost continuously. The other agents previously named are usually effective for 30 days or more.

A *fog seal* is a light application of a slow-setting asphalt emulsion diluted by one to three parts of water. It is used to seal small cracks and voids and to rejuvenate old asphalt surfaces. The usual application rate is 0.1–0.2 gal/sq yd (0.4–0.9 ℓ/m²).

An *emulsion slurry seal* is composed of a mixture of slow-setting asphalt emulsion, fine aggregate, mineral filler, and water. Usual mixtures contain by weight 20–25% asphalt emulsion, 50–65% fine aggregate, 3–10% mineral filler, and 10–15% water. The slurry is placed in a layer 1/4 in. (0.6 cm) or less in thickness using hand-operated squeegees, spreader boxes, or slurry seal machines.

A *sand seal* is composed of a light application of a medium-viscosity liquid asphalt covered with fine aggregates. Bituminous materials commonly used include RT-7, RT-8, RT-9, RC-250, RC-800, MC-250, MC-800, RS-1, and SS-1. The rate of application varies from 0.10 to 0.15 gal/sq yd (0.45–0.68 ℓ/m²). Fine aggregate is applied at a rate of 10–15 lb/sq yd (5.4–8.1 kg/m²).

Single- and Multiple-Pass Surface Treatments

Single-pass and multiple-pass surface treatments, sometimes called *aggregate surface treatments,* are made up of alternate applications of asphalt and aggregate. Aggregate surface treatments are used to waterproof a roadway and to provide an improved wearing surface. Such surface treatments are widely used because they require a minimum of time, equipment, and material. They also lend themselves to stage construction; that is, successive applications are repeated over a period of time to produce a higher level of roadway surface.

A *single-pass surface treatment* is constructed by spraying on a layer of asphalt and covering it with a layer of aggregate approximately one stone in depth. Hence the thickness of the finished surface is approximately equal to the maximum diameter of the aggregate used. A typical single surface treatment consists of 25–30 lb/sq yd (13–16 kg/m^2) of $\frac{1}{2}$-in. (1.3-cm) or smaller aggregate covering 0.25–0.30 gal/sq yd (1.1–1.4 ℓ/m^2) of binder. The type and quantity of binder selected will depend on ambient temperature, aggregate absorbency, and aggregate size.

The sequence of operations involved in placing a single surface treatment is as follows:

1. Sweep the existing surface.
2. Apply prime coat and cure, if required.
3. Apply binder at the specified rate.
4. Apply aggregate at the specified rate.
5. Roll the surface.
6. Sweep again to remove loose stone.

Rotary power brooms are most often used for cleaning the existing surface, but blowers or water sprays may be used. The prime coat and binder are applied with an asphalt distributor. Spreading of aggregate must follow immediately after binder application. Since binder temperature has been found to drop to ambient surface temperature in about 2 min, every effort must be made to apply aggregate within 2 min after binder application. Major types of aggregate spreaders, including whirl spreaders, vane spreaders, hopper spreaders, and self-propelled spreaders, operate in conjunction with dump trucks. Spreaders must apply aggregate uniformly and at the specified rate. After the application of aggregate, the surface is rolled to embed the aggregate in the binder and to interlock aggregate particles. Either pneumatic or steel wheel rollers may be used for compaction, but pneumatic rollers are preferred because they produce less bridging action and their contact pressure can be easily varied to prevent aggregate crushing. After compaction, the surface is again swept to remove loose stone that might cause damage when thrown by fast vehicles.

Multiple-pass surface treatments consist of two or more single surface treatments placed on top of each other. The construction sequence is the same as that shown above except that steps 3–5 are repeated as required. Thus, a double surface treatment consists of two binder/aggregate layers, a triple surface treatment consists of three binder/aggregate layers, and so on. The maximum size of aggregate used in each layer should be about one-half the size used in the underlying layer.

Asphalt Paving

The principal types of asphalt pavements include penetration macadam and pavements constructed from road mixes and plant mixes. Paving mixes may be either hot mixes or cold mixes. Hot mixes are used in producing high-type pavements for major highways and airfields. Cold mixes are employed primarily for roadway patching but may also be used for paving secondary roads.

Penetration macadam, while usually classified as a pavement, is constructed using equipment and procedures very similar to those employed for constructing aggregate surface treatments. Penetration macadam may be used as a base as well as a pavement. To construct penetration macadam, a single layer of coarse aggregate, which may be 4 in. (10 cm) or more in thickness, is placed. This layer is then compacted and interlocked by rolling with a pneumatic or steel wheel roller. Binder is then applied followed immediately by an application of an intermediate size aggregate ("key" aggregate). The pavement is then rolled again to compact the key stone and force it into the binder. Another application of binder and smaller key stone may follow. The surface is swept after completion of rolling.

Road mixes or mixed-in-place construction are produced by mixing binder with aggregate directly on the roadway. This mix is then spread and compacted to form a pavement. Road mixes may be produced by motor graders, rotary mixers, or travel plants. To produce a road mix using the motor grader, aggregate is spread along the roadway and binder is applied by a distributor. The materials are then mixed by moving them laterally grader, spread to the required depth, and compacted. Rotary mixers use a pulverizing rotor and a spray bar to mix aggregate and binder in one operation. Travel plants pick up aggregate from a windrow on the roadway, mix it with binder, and deposit the mix back on the roadway or into a finishing machine. Problems often encountered in mixed-in-place construction include difficulty in obtaining aggregate moisture control, lack of uniformity in the mix, and difficulty in obtaining uniform spreading of the mix. As a result, the quality of road mixes is generally substantially inferior to that of plant mixes.

Hot-, Warm-, and Cold-Mix Asphalt Paving

Hot-mix asphalt (HMA) pavement is considered the highest form of asphalt pavement. It is suitable for use on airport runways, as well as highways and streets. Since they require no curing, hot-mix asphalt pavements may be put in use as soon as the pavement has cooled to the ambient temperature. After compaction and cooling, such pavements are very stable and resist damage caused by moisture or frost. Cold-mix pavements are constructed in generally the same way as are hot-mix pavements. Cold mixes have certain advantages in that they can be transported long distances, stockpiled if necessary, and used only in the quantity needed. However, they have the disadvantages of requiring curing, having low initial stability, and being difficult to compact adequately in cold weather. Since hot mixes predominate in flexible pavement construction, only their construction will be described here.

Warm-mix asphalt is produced at a temperature 50–100°F (10–38°C) lower than usual hot-mix temperatures of 300–350°F (149–177°C). This reduction in mix temperature greatly reduces the environmental impact of mix production by significantly reducing the odor, fumes, smoke, and stack gas emission associated with mix production. As an added bonus, fuel costs of production are reduced by as much as 10–30%. To produce a workable mix and achieve the required compaction, an additive is usually added during mix production. While the addition of an additive slightly increases the cost of production, savings are realized in increased plant production, lower fuel cost, an increase in the allowable amount of reclaimed asphalt pavement (RAP) in the mix, longer permissible haul distances, and lengthened paving season.

Hot-mix and warm-mix paving operations involve the delivery of the asphalt mix, spreading of the mix, and compacting the mix. Spreading and initial compaction of the mix is accomplished by the asphalt paver or finishing machine shown in Figure 5. In operation, the paver engages the material supply truck, couples the two units together, and pushes the truck as the mix is unloaded and the pavement placed. The two principal parts of an asphalt paver are the tractor unit and the screed unit. The tractor unit propels the paver, pushes the dump truck delivering the mix, and pulls the screed unit. The screed unit strikes off the mix at the proper elevation and provides initial compaction to the mix. Pavers can be fed by a material transfer vehicle as shown in Figure 6. The mobile transfer vehicle serves as a transfer bin, which separates the delivery truck from the paver. The transfer vehicle permits continuous paving by providing an uninterrupted delivery of mix to the paver. Most pavers provide an automatic control system which uses a laser, fixed stringline, ski, shoe, or traveling stringline as an elevation reference to automatically control the screed elevation.

Towed pavers are also available for use on small paving jobs. Another type of paver is the shoulder paver. This is a small paver with a maximum paving width of about 10 ft (3.1 m), which is used for paving highway shoulders or for widening existing pavements. These machines are available as attachments for motor graders or self-propelled machines. Items to be checked during paver operation include grade and tolerance of the finished surface, appearance and temperature of the mix, weight of mix applied per square yard (meter), and average thickness of mix actually obtained.

Hot mix asphalt paving requires large quantities of asphalt mix per hour. For example, an asphalt paver laying a 3-in. (76-mm)-thick pavement 12 ft (3.6 m) wide at a speed of 50 ft/min (15.2 m/min) requires 600 ton/h (544 t/h) of hot mix. Thus, storage, handling, and hauling of the plant mix must be carefully planned and controlled. The use of insulated tanks such as shown in Figure 7 for storing the hot mix at the job site may be necessary when hauling capacity is limited or uncertain because of traffic conditions or other uncertainties. Insulated and heated trucks are also available for hot-mix hauling.

Compacting or rolling of the mix should begin immediately after it is placed by the paver. The usual sequence of rolling involves breakdown rolling, intermediate rolling, and final or finish rolling. Vibratory steel wheel rollers are now frequently used for rolling asphalt pavements as shown in Figure 8. Joints (transverse and longitudinal) and the outside pavement edge should be rolled before the remainder of the pavement is rolled. Static steel wheel or vibratory rollers are commonly used for breakdown rolling. Steel wheel rollers having a single-drive wheel should roll with the drive wheel forward, particularly during initial rolling, to prevent displacement of the mix. Pneumatic-tired rollers are often used for intermediate rolling because they provide a more uniform

FIGURE 5. Asphalt paving machine in operation. (Courtesy of Cedarapids, Inc.)

FIGURE 6. Material transfer vehicle feeding an asphalt paver. (Courtesy of Roadtec, Inc.)

contact pressure than do steel wheel rollers, and they improve the amount of surface sealing obtained during rolling. Two-axle or three-axle tandem steel wheel rollers are commonly used for finish rolling. However, two-drum vibratory rollers are increasingly being employed for all phases of rolling.

The temperature of the asphalt mat can be critical with some asphalt mixes. Rutting or shoving may result from rolling a mix that is too hot, whereas rolling a mix that is too cool may result in ineffective compaction.

It is important to determine whether the required density has been obtained in the compacted pavement. Rapid measurement of pavement density can be made with a nuclear density device, nonnuclear density gauge, or an equipment-mounted measuring system. Many of these devices also measure the temperature of the asphalt pavement to ensure that rolling is taking place at the optimum temperature.

Before rolling operations are begun, carefully check the condition of the rollers. Items to be checked during rolling include the adequacy of compaction, surface smoothness, the use of proper rolling patterns and procedures, and the condition of joints and edges.

Superpave™

Concerned about accelerated failure of asphalt pavements under growing traffic loads on the interstate highway system, the U.S. Congress authorized a Strategic Highway Research Program (SHRP). Research and tests under this program have led to a new asphalt pavement design and construction system known as *Superpave™*. This system differs from conventional hot mix asphalt pavement construction in that it employs stiffer asphalt mixes with lower asphalt content, uses smaller, less rounded crushed aggregate, and utilizes asphalt optimized for local climatic conditions.

Contractors have experienced problems in achieving the specified compaction of Superpave™ mixes because of the stiffness of the mix, particularly when employing a polymer-modified binder. Three surface temperature zones have been identified in an HMA pavement mat: an upper temperature zone between laydown temperature and 240°F (116°C), an intermediate zone between 240 and 90°F (116–88°C), and a lower zone between 190 and 160°F (88–71°C). A "tender mix" which displaces or shoves under compaction has been found to exist at

FIGURE 7. Hot mix asphalt storage bins. (Courtesy of Terex Roadbuilding)

certain mix temperatures. This temperature is usually in the intermediate temperature zone. The mix is usually stable under compaction in either the upper or lower temperature zones. Thus, breakdown rolling should be completed before the surface temperature of the mat falls below 250°F (121°C), intermediate rolling should be completed before the surface temperature reaches 210°F (99°C), and finish rolling should be completed before the surface temperature falls below 175°F (79°C). Using a lift thickness of four times the maximum nominal aggregate size will make it easier to achieve the required density without employing an excessively high mix temperature.

Several different roller compaction schemes have been successfully employed on Superpave™ pavements. Two double-drum vibratory rollers operating in echelon (almost side-by-side) in the upper temperature zone have sometimes been sufficient to provide the required compaction. Another scheme uses one double-drum vibratory roller operating in the upper temperature zone, followed by a rubber-tired roller operating in the middle temperature zone, and a static steel-wheeled roller operating in the lower temperature zone. For very stiff mixes containing high levels of polymer, pneumatic rollers have been used for breakdown rolling, followed closely by a double-drum vibratory roller. No finish rolling was required with this combination.

3 PAVEMENT REPAIR AND REHABILITATION

Concern over the declining condition of the U.S. highway system has caused the U.S. Federal-Aid Highway Act to expand the definition of highway construction to include resurfacing, restoration, rehabilitation, and reconstruction. Within the transportation industry, these categories of work are often identified as *4R construction*. The use of *pavement management systems* to maintain pavements in satisfactory condition at the lowest possible cost is becoming widespread. Such computer-based systems require continuing data collection and evaluation to permit a timely decision on the maintenance strategy to be employed.

Resurfacing may involve surface treatments or overlays of asphalt or concrete. *Restoration* and *rehabilitation* are broad terms that include any of the work required to return the highway to an acceptable condition. One technique that has grown in popularity is the mechanical removal of the upper portion of the pavement by *planing* or *milling* followed by a new pavement overlay. Often, the material removed is recycled and used as a portion of the aggregate for the new overlay. In

FIGURE 8. Rolling an asphalt pavement with vibratory roller. (Courtesy of BOMAG [USA])

addition to reducing cost, recycling reduces the demand for new aggregate sources as well as the problems associated with disposal of the old material. Restoration or rehabilitation may also require that subgrades or base courses be strengthened by soil stabilization or drainage improvements. *Reconstruction* refers to complete removal of the old pavement structure and construction of a new pavement.

Bridge management systems are also being developed to improve bridge life and lower costs by optimum bridge maintenance. Bridge decks often require resurfacing or reconstruction as a result of the corrosion of the concrete reinforcing steel due to salt penetration into the concrete. The use of epoxy-coated reinforcing steel, chemical sealing of the pavement surface, and the use of chemical additives in the concrete mix all show promise in reducing deterioration of bridge decks.

The need to repair concrete highway pavements usually requires the closure of one or more traffic lanes. Since the cost of traffic delays often exceeds the actual cost of repair, increased interest is being paid to the use of rapid-hardening materials which permit the pavement to be reopened to traffic within a few hours instead of several days. To meet this demand, a number of material manufacturers are producing prepackaged, rapid-hardening concrete. Some of these materials can produce a concrete compressive strength as great as 3000 psi (20,685 kPa) within 1 h. Asphalt pavements repaired with hot-mix materials can be reopened as soon as the mix has cooled sufficiently so that it is not rutted by traffic.

Work zone safety, or the prevention of accidents while traffic is maintained during highway repair, is receiving increasing attention from contractors, highway officials, and the Occupational Safety and Health Administration (OSHA).

Recycling of Pavements

In recent years there has been a significant increase in the recycling of pavements. *Recycling* consists of the demolition of old pavement, recrushing of the pavement material, and reusing it in new asphalt or concrete mixes. In addition to saving energy and sometimes scarce aggregate, recycling reduces the volume of waste which must go into landfills or other disposal areas.

Old concrete pavements are commonly broken up by hydraulic hammers and loaded into haul units for transporting to a recycling plant. Here reinforcing steel is removed and the concrete recrushed for reuse as aggregate.

Asphalt pavements are most often removed by milling, cold planing, or profiling as shown in Figure 9 and loaded into haul units for processing in a recycling plant. A portable recycled asphalt crushing plant is shown in Figure 10.

The specifications for the use of reclaimed asphalt pavement (RAP) in hot-mix asphalt (HMA) paving show a wide variation among the various U.S. states as indicated in the following list.

FIGURE 9. Pavement profiler removing old asphalt pavement. (Courtesy of CMI Terex Corporation)

FIGURE 10. Portable recycled asphalt crushing plant. (Courtesy of Kolberg Pioneer, Inc., and Johnson Crushers International)

Maximum allowable RAP content:

Base course:	15–100%
Binder course:	None to 100%
Surface course:	None to 70%
Maximum size of RAP:	1–2 in. (25–51 mm)
Allow blended stockpile of RAP:	some states
Recycling agent allowed:	
Asphalt concrete only:	all states
A/C plus additives:	some states

Another way in which old asphalt pavements are recycled is illustrated in Figure 11. Here old asphalt is removed by a planer, resized, mixed with a rejuvenating agent, and deposited in a windrow ready for placing as a cold-mix pavement.

Milling, cold planing, or profiling can also be used to remove only the upper portion of an existing asphalt or concrete pavement. This provides a smooth, sound base for the placement of a new surface course.

FIGURE 11. Traveling asphalt recycling plant. (Reprinted Courtesy of Caterpillar Inc.)

Problems

1. Identify the three surface temperature zones encountered when compacting an HMA pavement. In which of these zones are compaction problems likely to occur?

2. What methods are available for rapidly determining the density of a compacted HMA pavement?

3. Briefly explain the process of constructing a pavement using roller compacted concrete (RCC). What are the advantages and disadvantages of this method of construction?

4. Calculate the asphalt application rate (standard volume) actually achieved by a bituminous distributor under the following conditions: tank gauge reading before spread, 2200 gal (8327 ℓ); tank gauge reading after spread, 200 gal (757 ℓ); temperature 200°F (93°C); width of spray bar, 20 ft (6.1 m); length of spread, 4500 ft (1373 m).

5. Describe the major steps in the recycling of an asphalt pavement. What are the principal advantages and disadvantages of recycling such pavements?

6. Find the asphalt application rate obtained if the volume of asphalt used (standard conditions) was 700 gal (2650 ℓ), asphalt temperature was 200°F (93°C), the spray bar length was 18 ft (5.5 m), and the length of road section sprayed was 1000 ft (305 m).

7. List the sequence of activities involved in constructing a single-pass bituminous surface treatment and identify the item(s) of equipment used for each step.

8. Find the bituminous distributor pump output required to obtain an application rate of 0.2 gal/sq yd (0.91 ℓ/m^2), when the spray bar length is 20 ft (6.1 m) and road speed is 450 ft/min (137.3 m/min).

9. Briefly explain the rolling sequence for a hot-mix asphalt (HMA) pavement.

10. Develop a computer program to determine the actual rate of application (standard conditions) of a bituminous distributor. Input should include tank readings before and after application, the asphalt temperature, the length of the spray bar, and the length of roadway treated.

References

1. *AASHTO Maintenance Manual: The Maintenance and Management of Roadways and Bridges,* 4th ed. American Association of State Highway and Transportation Officials, Washington, DC, 2007.

2. *The Asphalt Handbook* (MS-4). The Asphalt Institute, Lexington, KY.

3. *Asphalt Cold Mix Manual* (MS-14). The Asphalt Institute, Lexington, KY.

4. *Asphalt Cold Mix Recycling* (MS-21). The Asphalt Institute, Lexington, KY.

5. *Asphalt Overlays for Highway and Street Rehabilitation* (MS-17). The Asphalt Institute, Lexington, KY.

6. *Asphalt Surface Treatments-Construction Techniques* (ES-12). The Asphalt Institute, Lexington, KY.

7. *Basic Asphalt Emulsion Manual* (MS-19). The Asphalt Institute, Lexington, KY.

8. *Construction of Hot-Mix Asphalt Pavements* (MS-22). The Asphalt Institute, Lexington, KY.

9. *Design and Control of Concrete Mixtures,* 14th ed. Portland Cement Association, Skokie, IL, 2002.

10. *A General Overview of Hot Mix Asphalt Paving, Compaction and Milling.* Ingersoll-Rand Co., Woodcliff Lake, NJ, 1994.

11. Hansen, Kenneth D., and William G. Reinhart. *Roller Compacted Concrete Dams.* New York: McGraw-Hill, 1991.

12. *Hot-Mix Asphalt Fundamentals.* Compaction America, Kewanee, IL, 1996.

13. Nunnally, S. W. *Managing Construction Equipment,* 2nd ed. Upper Saddle River, NJ: Prendee Hall, 2000.

14. *Roller-Compacted Concrete.* American Society of Civil Engineers, New York, 1994.

15. *Segregation Causes and Cures for Hot Mix Asphalt.* National Asphalt Pavement Association, Lanham, MD.

16. *Superpave Mix Design* (SP-2). The Asphalt Institute, Lexington, KY.

COMPRESSED AIR
AND WATER SYSTEMS

1 INTRODUCTION

Construction Applications

Compressed air is widely used as a power source for construction tools and equipment. While hydraulic power is gradually replacing compressed air as the power source for rock drills, compressed air is still required for cleaning out the drill hole produced by a hydraulic drill. Some of the other uses for compressed air in construction include paint spraying, the pneumatic application of concrete (shotcrete), conveying cement, pumping water, and operating pneumatic tools. Common pneumatic construction tools include spaders (or trench diggers), concrete vibrators, drills (steel and wood), grinders, hammers, paving breakers, sandblasting guns, saws (circular, chain, and reciprocating), staple guns, nailers, tampers, and wrenches.

Pumps and water supply systems are utilized in construction to dewater excavations and to supply water for cleaning equipment and aggregates, for mixing and curing concrete, for aiding soil compaction, and for jetting piles into place.

Construction Manager's Responsibilities

The construction manager must be able to select the appropriate type and size of air compressor or pump for a construction operation and to design the associated air or water supply system. Sections 2 and 3 provide guidance in performing these tasks.

2 COMPRESSED AIR SYSTEMS

Types of Compressors

Air compressors may be classified as positive displacement compressors or dynamic compressors according to the method by which they compress air. *Positive displacement compressors* achieve compression by reducing the air volume within a confined space. Positive displacement compressor types include reciprocating compressors, rotary vane compressors, and rotary screw compressors. *Dynamic compressors* achieve compression by using fans or impellers to increase air velocity and pressure. The principal type of dynamic compressor used in construction is the centrifugal compressor. Rotary compressors, both positive displacement and dynamic, are smaller, lighter, and quieter than are reciprocating compressors of similar capacity. As a result, most compressors used in construction are rotary compressors.

A schematic diagram of a rotary vane air compressor system is shown in Figure 1. This compressor is classified as a two-stage, oil-flooded, sliding-vane rotary compressor. Oil is injected into each compressor stage for lubrication and cooling. An *oil separator* removes the oil from the output air. The oil is then cooled and returned for reuse. The output of the compressor's first stage is cooled by an *intercooler* to increase the efficiency of the second-stage compressor. The *receiver* serves as a compressed air reservoir, provides additional cooling of the air leaving the compressor, reduces pressure fluctuations in the output, and permits water to settle out of the compressed air. Compressors can sometimes operate satisfactorily without a receiver in the system.

The principle of operation of a sliding-vane rotary compressor is as follows (refer to Figure 1). As the compressor rotor turns, centrifugal force causes the vanes to maintain contact with the cylinder. Air intake occurs while the volume of air trapped between two adjacent vanes is increasing, creating a partial vacuum. As rotation continues, the volume of air trapped between adjacent vanes decreases, compressing the trapped air. The compressed air is exhausted on the opposite side of the cylinder as the volume trapped between vanes approaches a minimum.

Compressors are available as portable units (skid- or wheel-mounted) or stationary units. Although portable units are most often used in construction work, stationary compressors may be employed in quarries and similar permanent installations. Portable units are available in capacities from

From Chapter 9 of *Construction Methods and Management*, Eighth Edition. S. W. Nunnally. Copyright © 2011 by Pearson Education, Inc. Published by Pearson Prentice Hall. All rights reserved.

FIGURE 1. Schematic of sliding-vane rotary air compressor.

75 to over 2000 cu ft/min (2.1–56.6 m³/min). Figure 2 shows a small portable air compressor being used to power two pneumatic paving breakers. Since pneumatic tools normally require air at 90 psig (lb/sq in. gauge) (621 kPa) to deliver rated performance, compressors usually operate in the pressure range of 90–125 psig (621–862 kPa).

A rotary screw or helical screw air compressor utilizes two mating rotating helical rotors to achieve compression (see Figure 3). The main or male rotor is driven by the power source. The mating gate or female rotor is usually driven by timing gears attached to the main rotor but may be driven directly by the main rotor in an oil-flooded unit. The principle of operation is as follows. Air enters at the inlet end, where the volume between mating lobes is large. As the rotors turn, the trapped volume becomes smaller and moves

FIGURE 3. Rotary screw air compressor.

toward the discharge end. The trapped volume reaches a minimum as it lines up with the discharge port and the compressed air is exhausted. The advantages of rotary screw compressors include high efficiency, few moving parts, low maintenance, and long life.

Required Compressor Capacity

Air compressor ratings indicate capacity as the volume of "standard" air or "free" air at standard conditions which the compressor will deliver at a specified discharge pressure. Standard air is defined as air at a temperature of 68°F (20°C), a pressure of 14.7 psia (lb/sq in. absolute) (100 kPa absolute), and 36% relative humidity. Since atmospheric conditions at a construction site rarely correspond exactly to standard air conditions, it may be necessary to adjust the rated compressor capacity to correspond to actual conditions. Since air is less dense at altitudes above sea level, altitude has the most pronounced effect on compressor capacity. A method for adjusting actual air demand at an altitude above sea level to standard conditions is explained later.

The quantity of compressed air required to supply a construction site is found by summing up the air demand of all individual tools and equipment. Representative air consumption values for common pneumatic construction equipment are given in Table 1. However, since all tools of a particular

FIGURE 2. Small portable air compressor powering pneumatic tools. (Courtesy of Ingersoll-Rand Company)

Table 1. Representative air consumption values of pneumatic construction equipment

Type of Equipment	Size	Air Consumption	
		cu ft/min	m³/min
Drills, rock			
Hand-held	35-lb class	55–75	1.6–2.1
	45-lb class	50–100	1.4–2.8
	55-lb class	90–110	2.5–3.1
Drifter and wagon	Light (3½-in. bore)	190–250	5.1–7.1
	Medium (4–4½-in. bore)	225–300	6.4–8.5
	Heavy (5-in. bore)	350–500	9.9–14.2
Track	Medium weight	600–1000	17.0–28.3
	Heavy weight	900–1300	25.5–36.8
Paint sprayers		8–15	0.2–0.4
Paving breakers		40–60	1.1–1.7
Pumps, submersible	Low head	75–100	2.1–2.8
	High head	150–300	4.2–8.5
Shotcrete guns		200–300	5.7–8.5
Spaders/trench diggers		30–50	0.8–1.4
Tampers, backfill		35–50	1.0–1.4

type will seldom operate simultaneously, a tool load factor or diversity factor should be applied to the total theoretical air requirement for each type of tool. Table 2 provides suggested values of the tool load factor to be used for various numbers of tools of the same type. Where a system is being designed to operate several different types of tools or equipment simultaneously, it may be appropriate to apply a second or job load factor to the sum of the adjusted air demand for the different types of tools. If used, the job load factor should be based on the probability that the various types of tools will operate simultaneously. Finally, an allowance should be made for leakage in the air supply system. It is customary to add 5–10% to the estimated air demand as a leakage loss.

After the total air consumption including leakage has been determined, total air demand must be adjusted for altitude before selecting the nominal or rated size of air compressor required to supply the system. The altitude adjustment factor may be calculated as the ratio of the

Table 2. Suggested values of tool load factor for pneumatic construction tools

Number of Tools of Same Type	Diversity Factor
1–6	1.00
7–9	0.94
10–14	0.89
15–19	0.84
20–29	0.80
30 or more	0.77

Table 3. Air compressor altitude-adjustment factors

Altitude		Adjustment Factor
ft	m	
1000	305	1.03
2000	610	1.06
3000	915	1.10
4000	1220	1.14
5000	1525	1.17
6000	1830	1.21
7000	2135	1.25
8000	2440	1.30
9000	2745	1.34
10,000	3050	1.39
11,000	3355	1.44
12,000	3660	1.49
13,000	3965	1.55
14,000	4270	1.61
15,000	4575	1.67

compression ratio at the specified altitude to the compression ratio at sea level. These adjustment factors are listed in Table 3.

The procedure for determining the rated capacity of the air compressor required for a project is illustrated in Example 1.

Example 1 Determine the rated size of air compressor required to operate the following tools at an altitude of

6000 ft (1830 m). Assume a 10% leakage loss and a job load factor of 0.80.

Solution

Use the tool diversity factors from Table 2.

Item	Rated Consumption		
	cu ft/min	m³/min	Number
Drifter drills	215	6.1	2
Hand-held drills	90	2.5	8
Trench diggers	30	0.8	4
Tampers	40	1.1	6
Submersible pumps	80	2.3	2

Item		Tool Consumption	
		cu ft/min	m³/min
Drifter	$= 2 \times 215 \times 1.00 =$	430	12.2
Hand-held drills	$= 8 \times 90 \times 0.94 =$	677	19.2
Trench diggers	$= 4 \times 30 \times 1.00 =$	120	3.4
Tampers	$= 6 \times 40 \times 1.00 =$	240	6.8
Pumps	$= 2 \times 80 \times 1.00 =$	160	4.5
		1627	46.1

Table 4. Pressure drop caused by pipe friction.* (Data from Table 10.23, *Compressed Air and Gas Handbook,* 4th ed., John P. Rollins, ed. Courtesy of Compressed Air and Gas Institute)

Flow		Nominal Diameter [in. (cm)]					
cu ft/min	m³/min	½ (1.3)	¾ (1.9)	1 (2.5)	1¼ (3.2)	1½ (3.8)	2 (5.1)
10	0.3	5.5 (38)	1.0 (6.9)	0.3 (2.1)	0.1 (0.7)		
20	0.6	25.9 (178)	3.9 (27)	1.1 (7.6)	0.3 (2.1)	0.1 (0.7)	
30	0.8	58.5 (403)	9.0 (62)	2.5 (17)	0.6 (4.1)	0.3 (2.1)	
40	1.1		16.1 (111)	4.5 (31)	1.0 (6.9)	0.5 (3.4)	
50	1.4		25.1 (173)	7.0 (48)	1.6 (11)	0.7 (4.8)	0.2 (1.4)
60	1.7		36.2 (250)	10.0 (69)	2.3 (16)	1.0 (6.9)	0.3 (2.1)
70	2.0		49.4 (341)	13.7 (94)	3.2 (22)	1.4 (9.7)	0.4 (2.8)
80	2.3		64.5 (445)	17.8 (123)	4.1 (28)	1.8 (12)	0.5 (3.4)
90	2.5			22.6 (159)	5.2 (36)	2.3 (16)	0.6 (4.1)
100	2.8			27.9 (192)	6.4 (45)	2.9 (20)	0.8 (5.5)
125	3.5			48.6 (335)	10.2 (70)	4.5 (31)	1.2 (8.3)
150	4.2			62.8 (433)	14.6 (101)	6.4 (44)	1.7 (12)
175	5.0				19.8 (137)	8.7 (60)	2.4 (17)
200	5.7				25.9 (179)	11.5 (79)	3.1 (21)
250	7.1				40.4 (279)	17.9 (123)	4.8 (33)
300	8.5				58.2 (401)	25.9 (178)	6.9 (48)
350	9.9					35.1 (242)	9.4 (64)
400	11.3					45.8 (316)	12.1 (83)
450	12.7					58.0 (400)	15.4 (106)
500	14.2						19.2 (132)
600	17.0						27.6 (397)
700	19.8						37.7 (260)
800	22.6						49.0 (338)
900	25.5						60.0 (414)
1000	28.3						
1500	42.5						
2000	56.6						
2500	70.8						
3000	84.9						
4000	113						
5000	141						
10,000	283						
15,000	425						
20,000	566						
30,000	849						

*Psi (kPa) for 1000 ft (305 m) of pipe at 100 psig (690 kPa) initial pressure.

Applying the job diversity factor:

$$\text{Expected consumption} = 1627 \times 0.80$$
$$= 1302 \text{ cu ft/min } (36.9 \text{ m}^3/\text{min})$$
$$\text{Leakage} = 1302 \times 0.10$$
$$= 130 \text{ cu ft/min } (3.7 \text{ m}^3/\text{min})$$
$$\text{Total consumption} = 1302 + 130$$
$$= 1432 \text{ cu ft/min } (40.6 \text{ m}^3/\text{min})$$
$$\text{Altitude adjustment factor} = 1.21 \quad \text{(Table 3)}$$
$$\text{Minimum rated capacity} = 1432 \times 1.21$$
$$= 1733 \text{ cu ft/min } (49.1 \text{ m}^3/\text{min})$$

Friction Losses in Supply Systems

As compressed air travels through a supply system, the pressure of the air gradually drops as a result of friction between the air and the pipe, hose, and fittings. The pressure drop in a pipe is a function of air flow, pipe size, initial pressure, and pipe length. Table 4 indicates the pressure drop per 1000 ft (305 m) of clean, smooth pipe for various flows at an initial pressure of 100 psig (690 kPa). If the initial pressure is greater or less than 100 psig (690 kPa), multiply the value from Table 4 by the appropriate correction factor from Table 5. Notice that the pressure loss due to friction decreases as initial pressure increases.

The pressure drop caused by pipe fittings is most conveniently calculated by converting each fitting to an equivalent length of straight pipe of the same nominal diameter.

Table 4. Continued

			Nominal Diameter [in. (cm)]				
2½ (6.4)	3 (7.6)	4 (10.2)	5 (12.7)	6 (15.2)	8 (20.3)	10 (25.4)	12 (30.5)
0.1 (0.7)							
0.2 (1.4)							
0.2 (1.4)							
0.3 (2.1)							
0.5 (3.4)							
0.7 (4.8)	0.2 (1.4)						
0.9 (6.2)	0.3 (2.1)						
1.2 (8.3)	0.4 (2.8)						
1.8 (12)	0.6 (4.1)						
2.7 (18)	0.8 (5.5)						
3.6 (24)	1.1 (7.6)	0.3 (2.1)					
4.8 (33)	1.5 (10.3)	0.4 (2.8)					
6.0 (41)	1.9 (13)	0.5 (3.4)					
7.4 (51)	2.3 (16)	0.6 (4.1)					
10.7 (74)	3.4 (23)	0.8 (5.5)					
14.6 (101)	4.6 (32)	1.1 (7.6)	0.3 (2.1)				
19.0 (131)	6.0 (41)	1.4 (9.6)	0.4 (2.8)				
24.1 (166)	7.6 (52)	1.8 (12)	0.5 (3.4)				
29.7 (205)	9.4 (65)	2.2 (15)	0.7 (4.8)	0.2 (1.4)			
67.0 (462)	21.0 (145)	5.0 (34)	1.5 (10)	0.6 (4.1)			
	37.4 (258)	8.9 (61)	2.7 (19)	1.0 (6.9)	0.2 (1.4)		
	58.4 (403)	13.9 (96)	4.2 (29)	1.6 (11)	0.4 (2.8)		
		20.0 (138)	6.0 (41)	2.3 (16)	0.5 (3.4)		
		35.5 (245)	10.7 (74)	4.0 (28)	0.9 (6.2)	0.3 (2.1)	
		55.5 (383)	16.8 (116)	6.3 (43)	1.5 (10)	0.4 (2.8)	
		67.1 (463)	25.1 (173)	5.9 (41)	1.8 (12)	0.7 (4.8)	
			56.7 (391)	13.2 (91)	4.0 (28)	1.5 (10)	
				23.6 (163)	7.1 (49)	2.7 (19)	
				52.1 (359)	15.9 (110)	6.2 (43)	

Table 5. Correction factors for friction losses

Inlet Pressure		
psig	kPa (gauge)	Correction Factor
80	552	1.211
90	621	1.096
100	690	1.000
110	758	0.920
120	827	0.852
130	896	0.793

Figure 4 provides a nomograph for finding the equivalent length of common pipe fittings. The equivalent length of all fittings is added to the actual length of straight pipe to obtain the total effective length of pipe. This pipe length is then used to calculate pressure drop in the pipe and fittings.

Pressure drop in hoses is calculated in the same manner as pressure drop in pipe except that values from Table 6 are used. Table 6 indicates the pressure drop per 50-ft (15.3-m) length of hose at an initial pressure of 100 psig (690 kPa). The pressure drop in manifolds or other special

A simple way to account for the resistance offered to flow by valves and fittings is to add to the length of pipe in the line a length which will give a pressure drop equal to that which occurs in the valves and fittings in the line. The chart on this page can be used to find the additional length which must be added for each resistance.

Example: The dotted line shows that the resistance of a 6-inch standard elbow is equivalent to approximately 16 feet of 6-inch standard pipe.

Note: For sudden enlargements or sudden contractions, use the smaller diameter, d, on the pipe size scale.

FIGURE 4. Resistance of valves and fittings to fluid flow. (Adapted from a nomograph appearing in *Contractor's Pump Manual*, 1976. Copyright © Crane Company, by permission)

Table 6. Pressure drop caused by hose friction.* [psi (kPa) per 50 ft (15.3 m) of hose]. (Data from Table 10.27, *Compressed Air and Gas Handbook,* 4th ed., John P. Rollins, ed. Courtesy of Compressed Air and Gas Institute, New York, 1973)

Flow		Hose Size [in. (cm)]				
cu ft/min	m³/min	½ (1.3)	¾ (1.9)	1 (2.5)	1¼ (3.2)	1½ (3.8)
20	0.6	1.8 (12)				
30	0.8	4.0 (28)				
40	1.1	6.8 (47)	1.0 (6.9)			
50	1.4	10.4 (72)	1.4 (9.7)			
60	1.7		2.0 (14)			
80	2.3		3.5 (24)			
100	2.8		5.2 (36)	1.2 (8.3)		
120	3.4		7.4 (51)	1.8 (12)		
140	4.0		9.9 (68)	2.4 (17)		
160	4.5		12.7 (88)	3.1 (21)		
180	5.1			3.8 (26)		
200	5.7			4.6 (32)	1.6 (11)	
220	6.2			5.5 (38)	1.9 (13)	
240	6.8			6.5 (45)	2.2 (15)	
250	7.1			7.0 (48)	2.4 (17)	
300	8.5			9.9 (68)	3.4 (23)	1.4 (9.7)
350	9.9			13.3 (92)	4.5 (31)	1.9 (13)
400	11.3				5.8 (40)	2.4 (17)
450	12.7				7.3 (50)	3.0 (21)
500	14.2				8.9 (61)	3.7 (26)
550	15.6				10.7 (74)	4.4 (30)
600	17.0				12.6 (87)	5.2 (36)

*Clean, dry air (no line lubricator), hose inlet pressure of 100 psig (690 kPa).

fittings should be based on manufacturers' data or actual measurements.

The procedure for calculating total pressure drop from receiver to individual tool is illustrated in Example 2.

Example 2 The compressed air system illustrated in Figure 5 is being operated with a receiver pressure of 110 psig (758 kPa). Pressure drop in the manifold is determined to be 2 psig (13.8 kPa). If all three drills are operated simultaneously, what is the pressure at the tools? Assume no line leakage.

Solution
Equivalent length of fittings (Figure 4):

2 globe valves at 85 ft = 170 ft (51.8 m)

1 standard ell at 8 ft = $\dfrac{8 \text{ ft (2.4 m)}}{178 \text{ ft (54.2 m)}}$

Length of pipe plus fittings = 1000 + 178 = 1178 ft

[= 304.8 + 54.2 = 359 m]

Total flow = 3 ×150
= 450 cu ft/min (12.7 m³/min)

Pressure loss per 1000 ft (305 m) = 1.9 psig (13.1 kPa) (Table 4)

Correction factor = 0.92 (Table 5)

Pressure loss in pipe and fittings (P_f):

$$P_f = \frac{1178}{1000} \times 1.9 \times 0.92 = 2.1 \text{ psig}$$

$$\left[= \frac{359}{305} \times 13.1 \times 0.92 = 14.2 \text{ kPa} \right]$$

Pressure at hose inlet (P_h):

$$P_h = 110 - (2.1 + 2) = 105.9 \text{ psig}$$
$$[= 758 - (14.2 + 13.8) = 730 \text{ kPa}]$$

Hose pressure correction factor = 0.95 (interpolate in Table 5)

Drill consumption = 150 cfm each
(4.2 m³/min)

FIGURE 5. Compressed air system, Example 2.

Pressure loss in 60-ft (18.3-m) hose (P'_f):

$$P'_f = \frac{60}{50} \times 2.7 \times 0.95 = 3.1 \text{ psig}$$

$$\left[= \frac{18.3}{15.3} \times 18.6 \times 0.95 = 21.1 \text{ kPa} \right]$$

Pressure at tool (P_t):

$$P_t = 105.9 - 3.1 = 102.8 \text{ psig}$$

$$[= 730 - 21.1 = 708.9 \text{ kPa (gauge)}]$$

Compressed Air Costs

Air cost is usually expressed in dollars per 1000 cu ft (or per cubic meter). Typical production and distribution costs range from $0.10 to $0.25/1000 cu ft($0.0036–$0.0088/m³).

Leaks in the air system can be costly. For example, a ½-in. (0.3-cm) hole in a 100-psig (690-kPa) supply line would waste about 740,000 cu ft (20,942 m³) of air per month. At a cost of $0.20/1000 cu ft ($0.0071/m³), this amounts to almost $150 per month.

Compressed Air Safety

Compressed air systems present several unique safety hazards. A sudden release of pressure caused by rupture of a hose, pipe, or storage tank can produce an effect similar to that of an explosive detonation. An accidentally disconnected hose can inflict severe damage caused by its whipping action.

Some major precautions which should be observed in the operation of compressed air systems are the following.

- Compressed air storage tanks and receivers must meet American Society of Mechanical Engineers (ASME) code standards.
- Before performing maintenance on a compressor, cut off power by pulling fuses or disconnects and tagging the cutoff.
- Test safety valves at least once a week.
- Compressed air used for cleaning purposes must be reduced to less than 30 psi (207 kPa) and used with effective chip guarding and personal protective equipment.
- Do not exceed the manufacturer's safe operating pressure for hoses, pipes, valves, filters, and other fittings.
- Hoses exceeding ½-in. (13 mm) in inside diameter must have a safety device installed at the supply source to reduce pressure in the event of hose failure.
- Pneumatic power tools must be secured to the hose in such a manner as to prevent the tool from becoming accidentally disconnected.

3 WATER SUPPLY SYSTEMS

Principal Types of Pumps

The principal types of pumps by method of operation include displacement pumps and centrifugal (or dynamic) pumps. *Displacement pumps* include reciprocating pumps and diaphragm pumps. Although *reciprocating pumps* are not often used in construction operations, it is well to understand the terminology used for such pumps. Double-acting reciprocating pumps have a chamber on each end of the piston so that water is pumped as the piston moves in either direction; single-acting pumps move water only when the piston travels in one direction. A simplex pump has one cylinder, a duplex pump has two cylinders, and a triplex pump has three cylinders. Thus, a single-acting duplex pump is a two-cylinder reciprocating pump in which pumping occurs during only one-half of the piston travel.

Diaphragm pumps utilize flexible circular disks or diaphragms and appropriate valves to pump water. As the diaphragm is pushed back and forth, the size of the pump chamber increases and decreases to produce the pumping action. Diaphragm pumps are self-priming, capable of pumping water containing a high percentage of sand or trash, and can handle large volumes of air along with water. Hence diaphragm pumps are widely used for dewatering excavations that contain large quantities of mud or trash or have an unsteady influx of water. Standard sizes of diaphragm pump include 2 in. (5.1 cm), 3 in. (7.6 cm), 4 in. (10.2 cm), and double 4 in. (10.2 cm). Pump size designates the nominal diameter of the intake and discharge openings. A gasoline-engine-powered diaphragm pump is shown in Figure 6.

Centrifugal pumps are available in a number of models and types. Conventional centrifugal pumps must have the impeller surrounded by water before they will operate. Self-priming centrifugal pumps utilize a water reservoir built into the pump housing to create sufficient pumping action to remove air from the suction line and fully prime the pump. Most centrifugal pumps utilized in construction are of the self-priming variety.

In the United States, the Contractors Pump Bureau (CPB) has developed standards for self-priming centrifugal pumps, submersible pumps, and diaphragm pumps designed for construction service. Self-priming centrifugal pumps certified by the Contractors Pump Bureau include M-, MT-, and MTC-rated pumps. M-rated pumps are available in sizes of (3.8 cm)

to 10 in. (25.4 cm), with capacities of 5000–200,000 gal (18,925–757,000 ℓ) per hour. A contractor's 3-in. self-priming centrifugal pump is shown in Figure 7. M-rated pumps are required to pass spherical solids having a diameter equal to 25% of the nominal pump size and to handle up to 10% solids by volume. MT-rated or trash pumps are designed to handle up to 40% solids by volume. The maximum diameter of spherical solids that they can handle ranges from 1 in. (2.5 cm) for a (3.8-cm) pump to 2½ in. (6.4 cm) for a 6-in. (15.2-cm) pump. MTC-rated pumps are compact light-weight trash pumps designed for easy portability. Sizes range from (3.8 cm) to 4 in. (10.2 cm) with capacities of 5000–23,000 gal/h (18,925–83,220 (ℓ/h). The maximum diameter of spherical particles which they must pass is 50% of the nominal pump size. A compact 2-in. centrifugal trash pump is shown in Figure 8.

Submersible pumps are centrifugal pumps designed to operate within the body of the fluid which they are pumping. Submersible pumps may be powered by electricity, hydraulic fluid, or compressed air. Of these, electric and hydraulic models are most common. Electric pumps are simpler to set up and use since they do not require any hydraulic power source. However, hydraulic pumps are small and powerful and can run dry. Submersible pumps are available in both low-head and high-head models, as well as trash models. Since submersible pumps operate submerged, suction lines and priming problems are eliminated, and pump noise is reduced.

Determining Required Head

In water supply systems, pressure is expressed as the equivalent height of a column of water (feet or meters). This unit of measure is called *head*. The total head that a pump must overcome is the sum of the static head (difference in elevation between two points) and the friction head (loss of pressure due to friction). For the usual pumping system, *static head* is the elevation distance between the inlet and the point of free discharge. If the outlet pipe is below the discharge surface,

FIGURE 6. Gas-powered diaphragm pump. (Courtesy of Crane Pumps & Systems)

FIGURE 7. Self-priming centrifugal pump at dam construction site. (Reproduced with permission from the Association of Equipment Manufacturers)

static head is the difference in elevation between the surface of the source and the surface of the discharge water.

Friction head is calculated in a manner similar to pressure loss in a compressed air system. That is, all fittings are converted to an equivalent pipe length using Figure 4. The length of pipe plus the equivalent length of fittings is then multiplied by the appropriate friction factor from Table 7. The friction loss for any hose in the system must be calculated separately by multiplying its length by the appropriate factor from Table 8. Total friction head is then found as the sum of pipe friction and hose friction. Static head is then added to obtain total head. The procedure is illustrated in Example 3.

Example 3 Water must be pumped from a pond to an open discharge 40 ft (12.2 m) above the pump. The line from the pump to discharge consists of 340 ft (103.7 m) of 4-in. (10.2-cm) pipe equipped with a check valve and three standard elbows. The pump is located 10 ft (3.1 m) above the pond water level. The intake line consists of a 20-ft (6.1-m) hose 4 in. (10.2 cm) in diameter equipped with a foot valve. Find the total head that the pump must produce for a flow of 280 gal/min (1060 ℓ/min). The equivalent length of the foot valve is 70 ft (21.4 m).

Solution

Equivalent length of fittings (Figure 4):

$$3 \text{ elbows at } 11 \text{ ft } (3.4 \text{ m}) = 33 \text{ ft } (10.1 \text{ m})$$
$$1 \text{ foot valve at } 70 \text{ ft } (21.4 \text{ m}) = 70 \text{ ft } (21.4 \text{ m})$$
$$1 \text{ check valve at } 25 \text{ ft } (7.6 \text{ m}) = \underline{25 \text{ ft } (7.6 \text{ m})}$$
$$\text{Total} = 128 \text{ ft } (39.1 \text{ m})$$
$$\text{Length of straight pipe} = \underline{340 \text{ ft } (103.7 \text{ m})}$$
$$\text{Total equivalent pipe length} = 468 \text{ ft } (142.8 \text{ m})$$

$$h_f \text{ (pipe)} = \frac{468}{100} \times 5.4 = 25.3 \text{ ft}$$
$$\left[= \frac{142.8}{100} \times 5.4 = 7.7 \text{ m} \right]$$

FIGURE 8. Stow's CP-20H 2-in. centrifugal trash pump. (Reproduced with permission from the Association of Equipment Manufacturers)

152

Table 7. Water friction (head) in pipe.* (Courtesy of Contractors Pump Bureau, Association of Equipment Manufacturers (AEM))

Flow		Pipe Size [in. (cm)]													
gal/min	ℓ/min	½ (1.3)	¾ (1.9)	1 (2.5)	1¼ (3.2)	1½ (3.8)	2 (5.1)	2½ (6.4)	3 (7.6)	4 (10.2)	5 (12.7)	6 (15.2)	8 (20.3)	10 (25.4)	12 (30.5)
2	8	4.8	1.2												
3	11	10.2	2.7	0.82											
4	15	17.4	4.5	1.39	0.37										
5	19	26.5	6.8	2.11	0.55										
10	38	95.0	24.7	7.61	1.98	0.93	0.31	0.11							
15	57		52.0	16.3	4.22	1.95	0.70	0.23							
20	76		88.0	27.3	7.21	3.38	1.18	0.40							
25	95			41.6	10.8	5.07	1.75	0.60	0.25						
30	114			57.8	15.3	7.15	2.45	0.84	0.35						
35	132			77.4	20.3	9.55	3.31	1.1	0.46						
40	151				26.0	12.2	4.29	1.4	0.59	0.14					
45	170				32.5	15.1	5.33	1.8	0.75	0.18					
50	189				39.0	18.5	6.43	2.2	0.90	0.22					
60	227				56.8	26.6	9.05	3.0	1.3	0.32					
70	265				73.5	35.1	11.9	4.0	1.7	0.41	0.14				
75	284					39.0	13.6	4.6	2.0	0.48	0.16				
80	303					44.8	15.4	5.0	2.3	0.58	0.18				
90	341					55.5	18.9	6.3	2.7	0.68	0.22				
100	379					66.3	23.3	7.8	3.2	0.79	0.27	0.09			
125	473						35.1	11.8	4.9	1.2	0.42	0.18			
150	578						49.4	16.6	6.8	1.7	0.57	0.21			
175	662						66.3	22.0	9.1	2.2	0.77	0.31			
200	757							28.0	11.6	2.9	0.96	0.40			
225	852							35.5	14.5	3.5	1.2	0.48			
250	946							43.0	17.7	4.4	1.5	0.60	0.15		
275	1041								21.2	5.2	1.8	0.75	0.18		
300	1136								24.7	6.1	2.0	0.84	0.21		
325	1230								29.1	7.0	2.3	0.92	0.24		
350	1325								33.8	8.0	2.7	1.0	0.27		
375	1419									9.2	3.1	1.2	0.31		
400	1514									10.4	3.5	1.4	0.35		
450	1703									12.9	4.4	1.7	0.45	0.14	
500	1893									15.6	5.3	2.2	0.53	0.18	0.08
600	2271									22.4	6.2	3.1	0.74	0.25	0.10
700	2650									30.4	9.9	4.1	1.0	0.34	0.14
800	3028											5.2	1.3	0.44	0.18
900	3407											6.6	1.6	0.54	0.22
1000	3785											7.8	2.0	0.65	0.27
1100	4164											9.3	2.3	0.78	0.32
1200	4542											10.8	2.7	0.95	0.37
1300	4921											12.7	3.1	1.1	0.42
1400	5299											14.7	3.6	1.2	0.48

(Continued)

Table 7. Continued

Flow		Pipe Size [in. (cm)]													
gal/min	ℓ/min	1/2 (1.3)	3/4 (1.9)	1 (2.5)	1¼ (3.2)	1½ (3.8)	2 (5.1)	2½ (6.4)	3 (7.6)	4 (10.2)	5 (12.7)	6 (15.2)	8 (20.3)	10 (25.4)	12 (30.5)
1500	5678											16.8	4.1	1.4	0.55
1600	6056												4.7	1.6	0.65
1800	6813												5.6	2.0	0.78
2000	7570												7.0	2.4	0.93
2500	9463													3.5	1.5
3000	11,355													5.1	2.1
3500	13,248													6.5	2.7
4000	15,140														3.5
4500	17,033														4.5
5000	18,925														5.5

*Values are ft/100 ft or m/100 m.

Table 8. Water friction (head) in hose.* (Courtesy of Contractors Pump Bureau, Association of Equipment Manufacturers (AEM))

Flow		Hose Size [in. (cm)]											
gal/min	ℓ/min	3/8 (1.0)	3/4 (1.9)	1 (2.5)	1¼ (3.2)	1½ (3.8)	2 (5.1)	2½ (6.4)	3 (7.6)	4 (10.2)	5 (12.7)	6 (15.2)	8 (20.3)
1.5	5.7	2.3	0.97										
2.5	9.5	6.0	2.5										
5	19	21.4	8.9	2.2	0.74	0.3							
10	38	76.8	31.8	7.8	2.64	1.0	0.2						
15	57		68.5	16.8	5.7	2.3	0.5						
20	76			28.7	9.6	3.9	0.9	0.32					
25	95			43.2	14.7	6.0	1.4	0.51					
30	114			61.2	20.7	8.5	2.0	0.70	0.3				
35	132			80.5	27.6	11.2	2.7	0.93	0.4				
40	151				35.0	14.3	3.5	1.2	0.5				
45	170				43.0	17.7	4.3	1.5	0.6				
50	189				52.7	21.8	5.2	1.8	0.7				
60	227				73.5	30.2	7.3	2.5	1.0				
70	265					40.4	9.8	3.3	1.3				
80	303					52.0	12.6	4.3	1.7				
90	341					64.2	15.7	5.3	2.1	0.5			
100	379					77.4	18.9	6.5	2.6	0.6			
125	473						28.6	9.8	4.0	0.9			
150	568						40.7	13.8	5.6	1.3			
175	662						53.4	18.1	7.4	1.8			

Table 8. Continued

Flow		3/8 (1.0)	3/4 (1.9)	1 (2.5)	1¼ (3.2)	1½ (3.8)	2 (5.1)	2½ (6.4)	3 (7.6)	4 (10.2)	5 (12.7)	6 (15.2)	8 (20.3)
gal/min	ℓ/min												
200	757						68.5	23.4	9.6	2.3	0.8	0.32	
225	852							29.0	11.9	2.9	1.0	0.40	
250	946							35.0	14.8	3.5	1.2	0.49	
275	1041							42.0	17.2	4.2	1.4	0.58	
300	1136							49.0	20.3	4.9	1.7	0.69	
325	1230								23.5	5.7	2.0	0.80	
350	1325								27.0	6.6	2.3	0.90	
375	1419								30.7	7.4	2.6	1.0	
400	1514									8.4	2.9	1.1	0.28
450	1703									10.5	3.6	1.4	0.35
500	1893									12.7	4.3	1.7	0.43
600	2271									17.8	6.1	2.4	0.60
700	2650									23.7	8.1	3.3	0.80
800	3028										10.3	4.2	1.1
900	3407										12.8	5.2	1.3
1000	3785										15.6	6.4	1.6
1100	4164										18.5	7.6	1.9
1200	4542											9.2	2.3
1300	4921											10.0	2.6
1400	5299											11.9	3.0
1500	5678											13.6	3.3
1600	6056												3.7
1800	6813												4.7
2000	7570												5.7
2500	9463												8.6
3000	11,355												12.2

*Values are ft/100 ft or m/100 m.

$$h_f \text{(hose)} = \frac{20}{100} \times 4.3 = 0.9 \text{ ft}$$

$$\left[= \frac{6.1}{100} \times 4.3 = 0.3 \text{ m} \right]$$

$$\text{Static head} = 40 + 10 = 50 \text{ ft } (15.3 \text{ m})$$

$$\text{Total head} = 50 + 25.3 + 0.9 = 76.2 \text{ ft}$$

$$[= 15.3 + 7.7 + 0.3 = 23.3 \text{ m}]$$

Pump Selection

The capacity of a centrifugal pump depends on the pump size and horsepower, the resistance of the system (total head), and the elevation of the pump above the source water level. After the total head and the height of the pump above water have been established, the minimum size of rated self-priming centrifugal pump that will provide the required capacity may be selected from the minimum capacity tables published by the Contractors Pump Bureau. The capacity table for M-rated pumps is reproduced in Table 9. Linear interpolation may be used to estimate capacity for values of total head and height of pump not shown in the table. The procedure for pump selection is illustrated in Example 4.

Example 4 Determine the minimum size of M-rated centrifugal pump required to pump 280 gal/min (1060 ℓ/min) through the system of Example 3.

Table 9. Minimum capacity [gal (ℓ/min] of M-rated centrifugal pumps (Courtesy of Contractors Pump Bureau)

Model 5-M (1$^1/_2$-in.)

Total Head Including Friction	Height of Pump Above Water [ft (m)]			
	10 (3.0)	15 (4.6)	20 (6.1)	25 (7.6)
15 (4.6)	85 (321.7)	—	—	—
20 (6.1)	84 (317.9)	68 (257.4)	—	—
25 (7.6)	82 (310.4)	67 (253.6)	—	—
30 (9.1)	79 (299.0)	66 (249.8)	49 (185.5)	35 (132.5)
40 (12.2)	71 (268.7)	60 (227.1)	46 (174.1)	33 (124.9)
50 (15.2)	59 (223.3)	52 (196.8)	41 (155.2)	28 (106.0)
60 (18.3)	42 (159.0)	40 (151.4)	32 (121.1)	22 (83.3)
70 (21.3)	22 (83.3)	22 (83.3)	20 (75.0)	12 (45.4)

Model 7-M (1$^1/_2$-in.)

Total Head Including Friction	Height of Pump Above Water [ft (m)]			
	10 (3.0)	15 (4.6)	20 (6.1)	25 (7.6)
20 (6.1)	117 (442.8)	—	—	—
30 (9.1)	116 (439.1)	102 (386.1)	82 (310.4)	—
40 (12.2)	105 (397.4)	100 (378.5)	80 (302.8)	58 (219.5)
50 (15.2)	92 (348.2)	90 (340.7)	76 (287.7)	55 (208.2)
60 (18.3)	70 (265.0)	70 (265.0)	70 (265.0)	55 (208.2)
70 (21.3)	40 (151.4)	40 (151.4)	40 (151.4)	40 (151.4)

Model 8-M (2-in.)

Total Head Including Friction	Height of Pump Above Water [ft (m)]			
	10 (3.0)	15 (4.6)	20 (6.1)	25 (7.6)
20 (6.1)	135 (511.0)	—	—	—
25 (7.6)	134 (507.2)	117 (442.8)	—	—
30 (9.1)	132 (499.6)	115 (435.3)	93 (352.0)	65 (246.0)
40 (12.2)	123 (465.6)	109 (412.6)	88 (333.1)	63 (238.5)
50 (15.2)	109 (412.6)	99 (374.7)	81 (306.6)	59 (223.3)
60 (18.3)	90 (340.7)	84 (317.9)	70 (265.0)	51 (193.0)
70 (21.3)	66 (249.8)	65 (246.0)	57 (215.7)	41 (155.2)
80 (24.4)	40 (151.4)	40 (151.4)	40 (151.4)	28 (106.0)

Model 10-M (2-in.)

Total Head Including Friction	Height of Pump Above Water [ft (m)]			
	10 (3.0)	15 (4.6)	20 (6.1)	25 (7.6)
25 (7.6)	166 (628.3)	—	—	—
30 (9.1)	165 (624.5)	140 (529.9)	110 (416.4)	—
40 (12.2)	158 (598.0)	140 (529.9)	110 (416.4)	75 (283.9)
50 (15.2)	145 (548.8)	130 (492.1)	106 (401.2)	70 (265.0)
60 (18.3)	126 (476.9)	117 (442.8)	97 (367.1)	68 (257.4)
70 (21.3)	102 (386.1)	100 (378.5)	85 (321.7)	60 (227.1)
80 (24.4)	74 (280.1)	74 (280.1)	68 (257.4)	48 (181.7)
90 (27.4)	40 (151.4)	40 (151.4)	40 (151.4)	32 (121.1)

(Continued)

Table 9. Continued

Model 15-M (3-in.)

Total Head Including Friction	Height of Pump Above Water [ft (m)]			
	10 (3.0)	15 (4.6)	20 (6.1)	25 (7.6)
20 (6.1)	259 (980.3)	—	—	—
30 (9.1)	250 (946.3)	210 (794.9)	200 (757.0)	—
40 (12.2)	241 (912.2)	207 (783.5)	177 (669.9)	160 (605.6)
50 (15.2)	225 (851.6)	202 (764.6)	172 (651.0)	140 (529.9)
60 (18.3)	197 (745.6)	197 (745.6)	169 (639.7)	140 (529.9)
70 (21.3)	160 (605.6)	160 (605.6)	160 (605.6)	138 (522.3)
80 (24.4)	125 (473.1)	125 (473.1)	125 (473.1)	125 (473.1)
90 (27.4)	96 (363.4)	96 (363.4)	96 (363.4)	96 (363.4)

Model 18-M (3-in.)

Total Head Including Friction	Height of Pump Above Water [ft (m)]			
	10 (3.0)	15 (4.6)	20 (6.1)	25 (7.6)
25 (7.6)	301 (1139.3)	—	—	—
30 (9.1)	295 (1116.6)	255 (965.2)	200 (757.0)	—
40 (12.2)	276 (1044.7)	250 (946.3)	200 (757.0)	162 (613.2)
50 (15.2)	250 (946.3)	237 (897.0)	198 (749.4)	159 (601.8)
60 (18.3)	216 (817.6)	212 (802.4)	182 (688.9)	146 (552.6)
70 (21.3)	174 (658.6)	174 (658.6)	158 (598.0)	127 (480.7)
80 (24.4)	129 (488.3)	129 (488.3)	125 (473.1)	104 (393.6)
90 (27.4)	82 (310.4)	82 (310.4)	82 (310.4)	74 (280.1)
95 (29.0)	57 (215.7)	57 (215.7)	57 (215.7)	57 (215.7)

Model 20-M (3-in.)

Total Head Including Friction	Height of Pump Above Water [ft (m)]			
	10 (3.0)	15 (4.6)	20 (6.1)	25 (7.6)
30 (9.1)	333 (1260.0)	280 (1059.8)	235 (889.5)	165 (624.5)
40 (12.2)	315 (1192.3)	270 (1022.0)	230 (870.6)	162 (613.2)
50 (15.2)	290 (1097.7)	255 (965.2)	220 (832.7)	154 (582.9)
60 (18.3)	255 (965.2)	235 (889.5)	205 (775.9)	143 (541.3)
70 (21.3)	212 (802.4)	209 (791.1)	184 (696.4)	130 (492.1)
80 (24.4)	165 (624.5)	165 (624.5)	157 (594.2)	114 (431.5)
90 (27.4)	116 (439.1)	116 (439.1)	116 (439.1)	94 (355.8)
100 (30.5)	60 (227.1)	60 (227.1)	60 (227.1)	60 (227.1)

Model 40-M (4-in.)

Total Head Including Friction	Height of Pump Above Water [ft (m)]			
	10 (3.0)	15 (4.6)	20 (6.1)	25 (7.6)
25 (7.6)	665 (2517.0)	575 (2176.4)	475 (1797.9)	355 (1343.7)
30 (9.1)	660 (2498.1)	565 (2138.5)	465 (1760.0)	350 (1324.8)
40 (12.2)	645 (2441.3)	545 (2062.8)	455 (1722.2)	345 (1305.8)
50 (15.2)	620 (2346.7)	510 (1930.3)	435 (1646.5)	335 (1268.0)
60 (18.3)	585 (2214.2)	475 (1797.9)	410 (1551.9)	315 (1192.3)
70 (21.3)	535 (2025.0)	410 (1551.9)	365 (1381.5)	280 (975.8)
80 (24.4)	465 (1760.0)	325 (1230.1)	300 (1135.5)	220 (832.7)
90 (27.4)	375 (1419.4)	215 (813.8)	195 (738.1)	145 (548.8)
100 (30.5)	250 (946.3)	60 (227.1)	50 (189.2)	40 (151.4)
110 (33.5)	65 (246.0)			

(Continued)

Table 9. Continued

Model 90-M (6-in.)

Total Head Including Friction	Height of Pump Above Water [ft (m)]			
	10 (3.0)	15 (4.6)	20 (6.1)	25 (7.6)
25 (7.6)	1500 (5677.5)	—	—	—
30 (9.1)	1480 (5601.8)	1280 (4844.8)	1050 (3974.3)	790 (2990.1)
40 (12.2)	1430 (5412.6)	1230 (4655.6)	1020 (3860.7)	780 (2952.3)
50 (15.2)	1350 (5109.8)	1160 (4390.6)	970 (3671.5)	735 (2782.0)
60 (18.3)	1225 (4636.6)	1050 (3974.2)	900 (3406.5)	690 (2611.7)
70 (21.3)	1050 (3974.2)	900 (3406.5)	775 (2933.4)	610 (2308.9)
80 (24.4)	800 (3028.0)	680 (2573.8)	600 (2271.0)	490 (1854.7)
90 (27.4)	450 (1703.3)	400 (1514.0)	365 (1381.5)	300 (1135.5)
100 (30.5)	100 (378.5)	100 (378.5)	100 (378.5)	100 (378.5)

Model 125-M (8-in.)

Total Head Including Friction	Height of Pump Above Water [ft (m)]			
	10 (3.0)	15 (4.6)	20 (6.1)	25 (7.6)
25 (7.6)	2100 (7948.5)	1850 (7002.3)	1570 (5942.5)	—
30 (9.1)	2060 (7797.1)	1820 (6888.7)	1560 (5904.6)	1200 (4542.0)
40 (12.2)	1960 (7418.6)	1740 (6585.9)	1520 (5753.2)	1170 (4428.5)
50 (15.2)	1800 (6813.0)	1620 (6131.7)	1450 (5488.3)	1140 (4314.9)
60 (18.3)	1640 (6207.4)	1500 (5677.5)	1360 (5147.6)	1090 (4125.7)
70 (21.3)	1460 (5526.1)	1340 (5071.9)	1250 (4731.3)	1015 (3840.8)
80 (24.4)	1250 (4731.3)	1170 (4428.5)	1110 (4201.4)	950 (3595.8)
90 (27.4)	1020 (3860.7)	980 (3709.3)	940 (3557.9)	840 (3179.4)
100 (30.5)	800 (3028.0)	760 (2876.6)	710 (2687.4)	680 (2573.8)
110 (33.5)	570 (2157.5)	540 (2043.9)	500 (1892.5)	470 (1779.0)
120 (36.6)	275 (1040.9)	245 (927.3)	240 (908.4)	240 (908.4)

Model 200-M (10-in.)

Total Head Including Friction	Height of Pump Above Water [ft (m)]			
	10 (3.0)	15 (4.6)	20 (6.1)	25 (7.6)
20 (6.1)	3350 (12,679.8)	3000 (11,355.0)	—	—
30 (9.1)	3000 (11,355.0)	2800 (10,598.0)	2500 (9462.5)	1550 (5866.8)
40 (12.2)	2500 (9462.5)	2500 (9462.5)	2250 (8516.3)	1500 (5677.5)
50 (15.2)	2000 (7570.0)	2000 (7570.0)	2000 (7570.0)	1350 (5109.8)
60 (18.3)	1300 (4920.5)	1300 (4920.5)	1300 (4920.5)	1150 (4352.8)
70 (21.3)	500 (1892.5)	500 (1892.5)	500 (1892.5)	500 (1892.5)

Solution

Height of
pump above = 10 ft (3.1m)
source water

Required
total head = 76.2 ft (23.3 m)

Capacity of
40-M pump $= 535 - \left(\dfrac{76.2 - 70.0}{80 - 70}\right)(535 - 465)$

$= 535 - 43 = 492 \text{ gal/min}$

$\left[= 2025 - \left(\dfrac{23.3 - 21.3}{24.4 - 21.3}\right)(2025 - 1760) \right.$

$\left. = 2025 - 171 = 1854 \; \ell/\text{min} \right]$

The 40-M pump is satisfactory.

Effect of Altitude and Temperature

The maximum lift (height of pump above the source water level) at which a centrifugal pump will theoretically operate is equal to the atmospheric pressure minus the vapor pressure of water at the prevailing temperature. At a temperature of 68°F (20°C), for example, the maximum theoretical lift at sea level is 33.1 ft (10.1 m). The maximum practical lift is somewhat less: about 23 ft (7.0 m) at sea level at a temperature at 68°F (20°C). Figure 9 illustrates the effect of temperature and altitude on the maximum practical suction lift.

Special Types of Pumps

It is sometimes necessary to pump water in situations where the vertical distance between the source water level and the ground surface exceeds the maximum practical lift for conventional pumps. In such a situation submersible pumps are a logical choice. When construction-type submersible pumps cannot be used, deep-well submersible pumps capable of operating in wells up to 500 ft (152.5 m) deep are available.

Jet pumps and air-lift pumps are two other types of pumps capable of lifting water more than 33 ft (10 m). *Jet pumps* recirculate a portion of the pump output to a venturi tube located below the source water level and then back to the pump inlet. Low pressure in the venturi tube draws water from the source into the recirculating line, where it flows to the pump inlet. While jet pumps are relatively inefficient, they are capable of lifting water 100 ft (30.5 m) or more. Other advantages of jet pumps include simplicity, ease of maintenance, the ability to operate in wells having diameters as small as 2 in. (5.1 cm), and the ability to locate the pump mechanism on the surface or even at some distance from the well. *Airlift pumps* discharge compressed air below the source water level inside a discharge line. The air bubbles formed within the discharge line lower the specific gravity of the water and air mixture enough to cause the mixture to flow up through the discharge line. The pump discharge must be fed into an open tank for deaeration if the water is to be repumped by a conventional pump. Air-lift pumps have low efficiency and a limited lift capability. They are principally used for testing new wells and for cleaning and dewatering drilled pier excavations.

FIGURE 9. Maximum practical suction lift for centrifugal pumps. (Reproduced with permission from the Association of Equipment Manufacturers)

Problems

1. Explain the method by which air compressor capacity is rated.

2. A compressed air system consists of a compressor and receiver, 1500 ft (458 m) of 4-in. (10.2-cm) pipe, two gate valves, six standard elbows, and a manifold. Four rock drills requiring 200 cu ft/min (5.7 m³/min) each are connected to the manifold by 1-¼-in. (3.2-cm) hoses 100 ft (30.5 m) long. Pressure drop in the manifold is 3 psig (20 kPa) and line leakage is 5%. Determine the pressure at the drill when all four drills are operating simultaneously and receiver pressure is 100 psig (690 kPa).

3. An M-rated self-priming centrifugal pump will be used to dewater an excavation during construction. The required pumping volume is estimated at 250 gal/min (946 ℓ/min). The pump will be located 10 ft (3.1 m) above the bottom of the excavation. The suction line will consist of 20 ft (6.1 m) of 3-in. (7.6-cm) hose, and the discharge line will consist of 80 ft (24.4 m) of 3-in. (7.6-cm) hose. Water will be discharged 30 ft (9.2 m) above pump level. What is the total head developed? What is the minimum size pump required?

4. Estimate the air consumption of the following equipment to be used on a rock excavation project. Assume an 8% leakage loss, a job load factor of 0.90, and average values of tool air consumption from Table 1. What is the minimum rated size of air compressor required if the project is located at an altitude of 6000 ft (1830 m)?

Equipment	Number
Medium-weight track drill	2
Heavy-weight track drill	1
55-lb hand-held drill	5

5. Water must be pumped from a stream to a water tank 500 ft (153 m) away. The discharge point will be 30 ft (9.2 m) above the stream. The pipeline from the pump to the tank will consist of 550 ft (168 m) of 4-in. (10.2-cm) straight pipe, four standard elbows, two 45° elbows, and a gate valve. The pump will be located 10 ft (3.1 m) above the stream. The suction line will consist of 25 ft (7.5 m) of 4-in. (10.2-cm) hose equipped with a strainer [equivalent straight pipe length = 5 ft (1.5 m)]. If the required flow is 300 gal/m (1136 (ℓ/min), find the total head that the pump must overcome. What is the minimum-size M-rated pump required for this system?

6. What is the maximum practical suction lift for a centrifugal pump located at an altitude of 6000 ft (1830 m) when the temperature is 95°F (35°C)?

7. You are designing an air delivery system to supply air from a receiver operated at 100 psig (690 kPa) through 1600 ft (488 m) of pipe and a manifold to three hand-held rock drills. Each drill requires 100 cfm (2.18 m³/min) of compressed air and is connected to the manifold by 75 ft (22.8 m) of 1-in (2.5 cm) hose. Manifold pressure loss is rated at 2 psig (14 kPa). Determine the minimum size of pipe required to maintain a pressure of at least 90 psig (621 kPa) at the drills when all drills are operating simultaneously. Assume a 5% line leakage.

8. What types of pumps might be used to dewater an excavation in a situation where the suction lift for a conventional centrifugal pump would exceed 32 ft (9.8 m)?

9. How does the friction loss in a compressed air pipeline vary with pressure?

10. Develop a computer program which will determine the minimum rated size of air compressor required to service a compressed air system. Input should include (for each tool type) the type of tool, the number of tools, and the expected air consumption per tool. Additional input should include the job load factor, the leakage allowance, and the altitude adjustment factor. Solve Problem 4 using your program.

References

1. *Selection Guidebook for Portable Dewatering Pumps.* Contractors Pump Bureau of Association of Equipment Manufacturers, Milwaukee, WI.

2. Loomis, A. W., ed. *Compressed Air and Gas Data,* 3rd ed. Woodcliff, NJ: Ingersoll-Rand Company, 1982.

3. Nayyar, Mohinder L., ed. *Piping Handbook,* 7th ed. New York: McGraw-Hill, 2000.

4. Rollins, John P., ed. *Compressed Air and Gas Handbook,* 5th ed. Upper Saddle River, NJ: Prentice, 1988.

FOUNDATIONS

From Chapter 10 of *Construction Methods and Management*, Eighth Edition. S. W. Nunnally. Copyright © 2011 by Pearson Education, Inc. Published by Pearson Prentice Hall. All rights reserved.

FOUNDATIONS

1 FOUNDATION SYSTEMS

The *foundation* of a structure supports the weight of the structure and its applied loads. In a broad sense, the term *foundation* includes the soil or rock upon which a structure rests, as well as the structural system designed to transmit building loads to the supporting soil or rock. Hence the term *foundation failure* usually refers to collapse or excessive settlement of a building's supporting structure resulting from soil movement or consolidation rather than from a failure of the foundation structure itself. In this chapter the term *foundation* will be used in its more limited sense to designate those structural components that transfer loads to the supporting soil or rock.

A foundation is a part of a building's substructure—that portion of the building which is located below the surrounding ground surface. The principal types of foundation systems include spread footings, piles, and piers. These are illustrated in Figure 1 and described in the following sections.

One method of describing a building's construction is based on the location of the lowest building floor. In this method, the types of construction include slab-on-grade construction, crawl space construction, and basement construction. In *slab-on-grade* construction, the lowest floor of the building rests directly on the ground. In *crawl space* construction, the lowest floor of the building is suspended a short distance (less than a full floor height) above the ground. The crawl space provides convenient access to utility lines and simplifies the installation of below-the-floor utilities. *Basement* construction provides one or more full stories below ground level. The use of basements provides storage space or additional living space at relatively low cost. Unless carefully constructed, however, basements are often troubled by water leakage or dampness.

2 SPREAD FOOTINGS

A *spread footing* is the simplest and probably the most common type of building foundation. It usually consists of a square or rectangular reinforced concrete pad that serves to distribute building loads over an area large enough so that the resulting pressure on the supporting soil does not exceed the soil's allowable bearing strength. The principal types of spread footings are illustrated in Figure 2. They include individual footings, combined footings, and mat foundations. *Individual footings* include isolated (or single) footings, which support a single column (Figure 2a), and wall footings (Figure 2b), which support a wall. *Combined footings* support a wall and one or more columns, or several columns (Figure 2c).

Mat or *raft foundations* (Figure 2d) consist of a heavily reinforced concrete slab extending under the entire structure, in order to spread the structure's load over a large area. Because such foundations are usually employed for large buildings, they generally involve deep excavation and large-scale concrete pours. A *floating foundation* is a type of mat foundation in which the weight of the soil excavated approximately equals the weight of the structure being erected. Thus, in theory, the erection of the building would not result in any change in the load applied to the soil and hence there would be no settlement of the structure. In practice, however, some soil movement does occur, because the soil swells (or rebounds) during excavation and then recompresses as the building is erected.

If the underlying soil can be strengthened, the allowable bearing pressure on the soil surface will be increased. As a result, it may be possible to use spread footings for foundation loads that normally would require piles or other deep foundation methods. The process of improving soils in place is called *ground modification* or *soil stabilization*. In addi-

FIGURE 1. Foundation systems.

Spread footing

Piles   Pier or caisson

FIGURE 2. Types of spread footings.

a. Isolated footing

b. Wall footing

c. Combined footing

d. Mat foundation

tion to improving bearing capacity, ground modification may also reduce foundation settlement, groundwater flow, and the subsidence resulting from seismic action. An example of soil densification resulting from vibratory compaction under a footing is illustrated in Figure 3.

Densified cohesionless soil

FIGURE 3. Soil densification under footing.

3 PILES

A *pile* is nothing more than a column driven into the soil to support a structure by transferring building loads to a deeper and stronger layer of soil or rock. Piles may be classified as either end-bearing or friction piles, according to the manner in which the pile loads are resisted. However, in actual practice, virtually all piles are supported by a combination of skin friction and end bearing.

Pile Types

The principal types of piles include timber, precast concrete, cast-in-place concrete, steel, composite, and bulb piles. *Timber piles* are inexpensive, easy to cut and splice, and require no special handling. However, maximum pile length is limited to about 100 ft, load-carrying ability is limited, and pile ends may splinter under driving loads. Timber piles are also subject to insect attack and decay. However, the availability of pressure-treated wood has greatly reduced the vulnerability of timber piles to such damage.

Precast concrete piles may be manufactured in almost any desired size or shape. Commonly used section shapes include round, square, and octagonal shapes. Advantages of concrete piles include high strength and resistance to decay. However, a precast concrete pile is usually the heaviest type of pile available for a given pile size. Because of their brittleness and lack of tensile strength, they require care in handling and driving to prevent pile damage. Since they have little strength in bending, they may be broken by improper lifting procedures. Cutting requires the use of pneumatic hammers and cutting torches or special saws. Splicing is relatively difficult and requires the use of special cements.

Cast-in-place concrete piles (or shell piles) are constructed by driving a steel shell into the ground and then filling it with concrete. Usually, a steel mandrel or core attached to the pile driver is placed inside the shell to reduce shell damage during driving. Although straight shells may be pulled as they are filled with concrete, shells are usually left in place and serve as additional reinforcement for the concrete. The principal types of shell pile include uniform taper, step-taper, and straight (or monotube) piles. The shells for cast-in-place piles are light, easy to handle, and easy to cut and splice. Since shells may be damaged during driving, they should be visually inspected before filling with concrete. Shells driven into expansive soils should be filled with concrete as soon as possible after driving to reduce the possibility of shell damage due to lateral soil pressure.

Steel piles are capable of supporting heavy loads, can be driven to great depth without damage, and are easily cut and spliced. Common types of steel piles include H-piles and pipe piles, where the name indicates the shape of the pile section.

Pipe piles are usually filled with concrete after driving to obtain additional strength. The principal disadvantage of steel pile is its high cost.

Composite piles are piles made up of two or more different materials. For example, the lower section of pile might be timber while the upper section might be a shell pile. This would be an economical pile for use where the lower section would be continuously submerged (hence not subject to decay) while the upper section would be exposed to decay.

Bulb piles are also known as *compacted concrete piles, Franki piles,* and *pressure-injected footings.* They are a special form of cast-in-place concrete pile in which an enlarged base (or bulb) is formed during driving. The enlarged base increases the effectiveness of the pile as an end-bearing pile. The driving procedure is illustrated in Figure 4. A drive tube is first driven to the desired depth of the base either by a powered hammer operating on the top of the drive tube (called *top driving*) or by placing a plug of zero-slump concrete [concrete having a slump of 1 in. (25 mm) or less] into the drive tube and driving both the concrete plug and the drive tube simultaneously using a drop hammer operating inside the drive tube (called *bottom driving*). The drive tube is then held in place and more zero-slump concrete added and hammered out of the end of the drive tube to form the base. Finally, the body or shaft of the pile is constructed by either of two methods. A compacted concrete shaft is formed by hammering zero-slump concrete into the ground as the drive tube is raised. A cased shaft is constructed by placing a steel shell inside the drive tube and then hammering a plug of zero-slump concrete into place to form a bond between the base and the shell. The shell is then filled in the same manner as a conventional cast-in-place concrete pile. Compacted shaft piles usually have a higher load capacity than do

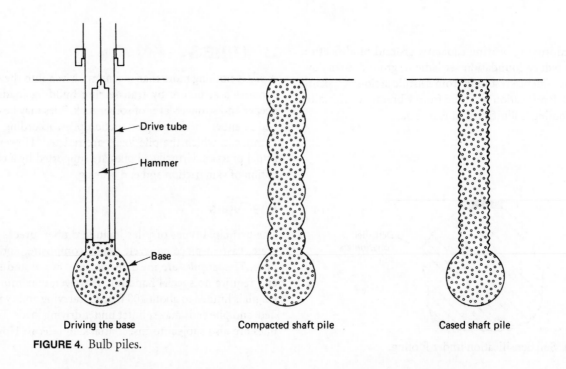

FIGURE 4. Bulb piles.

cased shaft piles due to the increased pressure between the shaft and the surrounding soil.

Minipiles or *micro piles* are small-diameter [2–8 in. (5–20 cm)], high-capacity [to 60 tons (54 t)] piles. They are most often employed in areas with restricted access or limited headroom to underpin (provide temporary or additional support to) building foundations. Some other applications include strengthening bridge piers and abutments, anchoring or supporting retaining walls, and stabilizing slopes. While they may be driven in place, minipiles are often installed by drilling a steelcased hole 2–8 in. (5–20 cm) in diameter, placing reinforcing in the casing, and then bonding the soil, casing, and reinforcement together by grouting.

Pile Driving

In ancient times, piles were driven by raising and dropping a weight such as a large stone onto the pile. The drop hammer, the modern version of this type of pile driver, is illustrated in Figure 5. As you see, the pile-driving assembly is attached to a mobile crane, which provides the support and the power for the pile driver. The *leads* act as guides for the drop weight and the pile. Driving operations consist of lifting the pile, placing it into the leads, lowering the pile until it no longer penetrates the soil under its own weight, and then operating the drop hammer until the pile is driven to the required

resistance. Safety requirements for drop hammers include the use of stop blocks to prevent the hammer from being raised against the head block (which could result in collapse of the boom), the use of a guard across the head block to prevent the drop cable from jumping out of the sheaves, and placing a blocking device under the hammer whenever workers are under the hammer.

The remaining types of pile drivers are all powered hammers. That is, they use a working fluid rather than a cable to propel the ram (driving weight). Early powered hammers used steam as a working fluid. Steam power has now been largely replaced by compressed air power. Hydraulic power is replacing compressed air in many newer units. Single-acting hammers use fluid power to lift the ram, which then falls under the force of gravity. Double-acting and differential hammers use fluid power to both lift the ram and then drive the ram down against the pile. Thus, double-acting and differential hammers can be lighter than a single-acting hammer of equal capacity. Typical operating frequencies are about 60 blows/min for single-acting hammers and 120 blows/min for double-acting hammers. Differential hammers usually operate at frequencies between these two values.

A diesel hammer contains a free-floating ram-piston that operates in a manner similar to that of a one-cylinder diesel engine. The principle of operation is illustrated in Figure 6. The hammer is started by lifting the ram

FIGURE 5. Drop hammer pile driver.

FIGURE 6. Operation of a diesel pile hammer. (Courtesy of MKT Manufacturing, Inc.)

(B) with the crane hoist line (A). The trip mechanism (C) automatically releases the ram at the top of the cylinder. As the ram falls, it actuates the fuel pump cam (D), causing fuel to be injected into the fuel cup in the anvil (E) at the bottom of the cylinder. As the ram continues to fall, it blocks the exhaust ports (F), compressing the fuel–air mixture. When the ram strikes the anvil, it imparts an impact blow to the pile top and also fires the fuel–air mixture. As the cylinder fires, it forces the body of the hammer down against the pile top and drives the ram upward to start a new cycle. Operation of the hammer is stopped by pulling the rope (G),

which disengages the fuel pump cam (D). Diesel hammers are compact, light, and economical and can operate in freezing weather. However, they may fail to operate in soft soil, where hammer impact may be too weak to fire the fuel–air mixture.

Vibratory hammers drive piles by a combination of vibration and static weight. As you might expect, they are most effective in driving piles into clean granular soils. Sonic hammers are vibratory hammers that operate at very high frequencies. Figure 7 shows a hydraulically powered vibratory driver/extractor in operation.

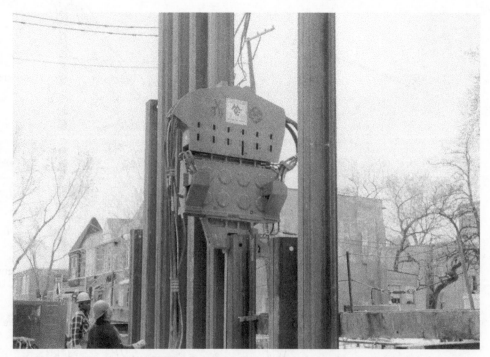

FIGURE 7. Hydraulically powered vibratory driver/extractor. (Courtesy of MKT Manufacturing, Inc.)

Pile-Driving Procedures A typical pile-driving operation for a straight shell pile is illustrated in Figure 8. Figure 8a shows the piles stockpiled at the job site. Notice the depth marks that have been painted on the pile. These will be used during driving to facilitate counting the number of blows required to obtain a foot of penetration. In Figure 8b, the pile has been hooked to the hoist cable and is being swung into position for lowering into a hollow casing previously driven into the ground. After the shell has been lowered into the casing, the pile driver's mandrel (Figure 8c) is lowered into the shell. The shell and mandrel are then raised from the casing and swung into position for driving. The hammer (in this case a single-acting compressed air hammer) then drives the pile (Figure 8d) until the required depth or driving resistance is obtained. After the mandrel is raised, the shell is cut off at the required elevation with a cutting torch (Figure 8e). When the reinforcing steel for the pile cap has been placed (Figure 8f), the shell is ready to be filled with concrete.

For driving piles with an impact-type pile driver, it is recommended that a hammer be selected that will yield the required driving resistance at a final penetration of 8–12 blows/in. (reference 6). For fluid-powered hammers, it is also recommended that the weight of the ram be at least one-half the pile weight. For diesel hammers, ram weight should be at least one-fourth of the pile weight. When selecting a vibratory driver/extractor, a machine should be used that will yield a driving amplitude of $\frac{1}{4}$ to $\frac{1}{2}$-in. (0.6–1.2 cm).

(a) (b) (c)

(d) (e) (f)

FIGURE 8. Driving a shell pile.

$$\text{Driving amplitude (in.)} = 2 \times \frac{\text{Eccentric moment (in.-lb)}}{\text{Vibrating mass (lb)}} \quad (1)$$

In solving Equation 1 for driving amplitude, pile weight should be added to the weight of the driver's vibrating mass to obtain the value of the vibrating mass.

Powered hammers with leads should be used for driving piles at an angle (batter piles), because drop hammers lose significant energy to friction when the leads are inclined. Powered hammers without leads may be used in vertical driving, but the use of leads assists in maintaining pile alignment during driving. Double-acting, differential, and vibratory hammers may be used to extract piles as well as to drive them.

Determining Pile Load Capacity

The problem of determining pile load capacity is a complex one since it involves pile–soil–hammer interaction during driving, pile–soil interaction after the pile is in place, and the structural strength of the pile itself. The geotechnical engineer who designs the foundation must provide a pile design that is adequate to withstand driving stresses as well as to support the design load of the structure without excessive settlement. The best measure of in-place pile capacity is obtained by performing pile load tests as described later in this section.

A number of dynamic driving equations have been developed in attempting to predict the safe load capacity of piles based on behavior during driving. The traditional basis for such equations is to equate resisting energy to driving energy with adjustments for energy lost during driving. These equations treat the pile as a rigid body. A number of modifications to basic driving equations have been proposed in an attempt to provide better agreement with measured pile capacity. Equation 2, for determining the safe capacity of piles driven by powered hammers, has been incorporated in some U.S. building codes. Minimum hammer energy may also be specified by the building code.

$$R = \left(\frac{2E}{S + 0.1} \right)\left(\frac{W_r + KW_p}{W_r + W_p} \right) \quad (2)$$

where

R = safe load (lb)

S = average penetration per blow, last six blows (in.)

E = energy of hammer (ft-lb)

$K = \begin{cases} \text{coefficient} \\ \text{of restitution} \end{cases} \begin{cases} 0.2 \text{ for piles weighing 50 lb/ft or less} \\ 0.4 \text{ for piles weighing } 50-100 \text{ lb/ft} \\ 0.6 \text{ for piles weighing over 100 lb/ft} \end{cases}$

W_r = weight of hammer ram (lb)

W_p = weight of pile, including driving appurtenances (lb)

Example 1 Using Equation 2 and the driving data below, determine the safe load capacity of a 6-in.-square concrete pile 60 ft long. Assume that the unit weight of the pile is 150 lb/cu ft.

$$\text{Pile driver energy} = 14,000 \text{ ft-lb}$$
$$\text{Ram weight} = 4000 \text{ lb}$$
$$\text{Weight of driving appurtenances} = 1000 \text{ lb}$$
$$\text{Average penetration last six blows} = \frac{1}{5} \text{ in./blow}$$

Solution

$$\text{Weight of pile} = \frac{6 \times 6}{144} \times 60 \times 150 = 2250 \text{ lb}$$

$$W_p = 2250 + 1000 = 3250 \text{ lb}$$

$$\text{Weight per foot of pile} = \frac{2250}{60} = 37.5 \text{ lb/ft}$$

$$K = 0.2$$
$$S = 0.2 \text{ in./blow}$$

$$R = \left(\frac{2E}{S + 0.1} \right)\left(\frac{W_r + KW_p}{W_r + W_p} \right)$$

$$= \left(\frac{(2)(14,000)}{0.2 + 0.1} \right)\left(\frac{4000 + (0.2)(3250)}{4000 + 3250} \right)$$

$$= \frac{(28,000)(4650)}{(0.3)(7250)} = 59,862 \text{ lb}$$

Equation 3 is used in several building codes and construction agency specifications for predicting the safe load capacity of bulb piles.

$$L = \frac{W \times H \times B \times V^{2/3}}{K} \quad (3)$$

where L = safe load capacity (tons)

W = weight of hammer (tons)

H = height of drop (ft)

B = number of blows per cubic foot of concrete used in driving final batch into base

V = uncompacted volume of concrete in base and plug (cu ft)

K = dimensionless constant depending on soil type and type of pile shaft

Nordlund (reference 11) has presented recommended K values which range from 9 for a compacted shaft pile in gravel to 40 for a cased shaft pile in very fine sand.

Example 2 Calculate the safe load capacity of a bulb pile based on the following driving data.

$$\text{Hammer weight} = 3 \text{ tons}$$
$$\text{Height of drop} = 20 \text{ ft}$$
$$\text{Volume in last batch driven} = 5 \text{ cu ft}$$
$$\text{Number of blows to drive last batch} = 40$$
$$\text{Volume of base and plug} = 25 \text{ cu ft}$$
$$\text{Selected } K \text{ value} = 25$$

Solution

$$B = \frac{40}{5} = 8 \text{ blows/cu ft}$$

$$R = \frac{W \times H \times B \times V^{2/3}}{K}$$

$$= \frac{(3)(20)(8)(25)^{2/3}}{25} = 164 \text{ tons}$$

A newer and better approach to predicting pile capacity is provided by the use of wave equation analysis which analyzes the force and velocity waves developed in a pile as a result of driving. For pile design, the analysis is based on a specific type and length of pile, a specific driving system, and the expected soil conditions. Computer wave equation analysis programs, such as the WEAP (Wave Equation Analysis of Pile Driving) program, are available for analyzing wave data to predict pile behavior during driving and to confirm pile performance during construction. Pile driving analyzers which measure and analyze the force and velocity waves actually developed during driving are also available. They are particularly useful for establishing pile driving criteria and for quality control during driving. They can be used to measure hammer efficiency, driving energy delivered to the pile, and to indicate pile breakage during driving. The pile driving analyzer may be successfully employed to predict the capacity of production piles when results are correlated with pile load tests and good driving records.

Pile capacity may be determined by performing pile load tests. One such test procedure (ASTM D-1143) involves loading the pile to 200% of design load at increments of 25% of the design load. Each load increment is maintained until the rate of settlement is not greater than 0.01 in./h (0.25 mm/h) or until 2 h have elapsed. The final load (200% of design load) is maintained for 24 h. Quick load tests utilizing a constant rate of penetration test or a maintained load test are also used. Quick load tests can usually be performed in 3 h or less.

With all of the methods of load testing, pile settlement is plotted against load to determine pile capacity. A number of methods have been proposed for identifying the failure load on a load-settlement curve (references 7 and 8). One procedure for interpreting the load-settlement curve to determine ultimate pile capacity, often called the tangent method, involves drawing tangents to the initial and final segments of the curve as illustrated in Figure 9. The load (A) corresponding to the intersection of these two tangents is designated the ultimate pile capacity. A procedure used by the U.S. Army Corps of Engineers determines ultimate pile capacity as the average of the following three values:

1. A settlement of 0.25 in. (6.35 mm) on the net settlement vs. load curve.
2. The load determined by the tangent method previously described.
3. The load that corresponds to the point on the net settlement vs. load curve where the slope equals 0.01 in. per ton (0.28 mm/t).

To determine safe pile load capacity, an appropriate factor of safety must be applied to the ultimate pile capacity. The factor of safety to be used will depend on soil–pile properties and the loading conditions to be encountered. However, a minimum factor of safety of 2.0 is usually employed.

Pile capacity usually increases after a period of time following driving. This increase in capacity is referred to as *soil setup* or *soil freeze*. However, in some cases pile capacity decreases with time. This decrease in capacity is referred to as *soil relaxation*. Soil setup or soil relaxation can be measured by performing load tests or by restriking the pile several days after pile driving. Building codes may specify a minimum waiting period between driving and loading a test pile.

FIGURE 9. Determination of pile capacity from load test.

4 PIERS AND CAISSONS

A *pier* is simply a column, usually of reinforced concrete, constructed below the ground surface. It performs much the same function as a pile. That is, it transfers the load of a structure down to a stronger rock or soil layer. Piers may be constructed in an open excavation, a lined excavation (caisson), or a drilled excavation. Since piers are often constructed by filling a caisson with concrete, the terms *pier foundation, caisson foundation,* and *drilled pier foundation* are often used interchangeably.

A *caisson* is a structure used to provide all-around lateral support to an excavation. Caissons may be either open or pneumatic. Pneumatic caissons are air- and watertight structures open on the bottom to permit the excavation of soil beneath the caisson. The caisson is filled with air under pressure to prevent water and soil from flowing in as excavation proceeds. To prevent workers from suffering from the bends upon leaving pneumatic caissons, they must go through a decompression procedure like that employed for divers. Because of the health hazards and expense of this procedure, pneumatic caissons are rarely used today.

Drilled piers are piers placed in holes drilled into the soil. Holes drilled into cohesive soils are not usually lined. If necessary, the holes may be filled with a slurry of clay and water (such as bentonite slurry) during drilling to prevent caving of the sides. Concrete is then placed in the hole through a tremie, displacing the slurry. This procedure is similar to the slurry trench excavation method described in Section 6.

Holes drilled in cohesionless soils must be lined to prevent caving. Metal or fiber tubes are commonly used as liners. Linings may be left in place or they may be pulled as the concrete is placed. Holes for drilled piers placed in cohesive soil are often widened (or belled) at the bottom, as shown in

Figure 1, to increase the bearing area of the pier on the supporting soil. Although this increases allowable pier load, such holes are more difficult to drill, inspect, and properly fill with concrete than are straight pier holes.

5 STABILITY OF EXCAVATIONS

Slope Stability

To understand the principal modes of slope failure, it is necessary to understand the basic concepts of soil strength. The soil identification procedures include the classification of soil into cohesionless and cohesive types. As you recall, cohesionless soil is one whose grains do not show any tendency to stick together. The shear strength of a cohesionless soil is thus due solely to the friction developed between soil grains. A normal force (or force perpendicular to the sliding surface) is required to develop this strength. When an embankment composed of a cohesionless soil fails, it fails as shown in Figure 10. That is, material from the upper part of the slope breaks away and falls to the toe of the slope until the face of the embankment reaches the natural angle of repose for the soil.

In a cohesive soil, on the other hand, shear strength is provided primarily by the attraction between soil grains (which we call *cohesion*). Theoretically, a completely cohesive soil would exhibit no friction between soil grains. Failure of a highly cohesive soil typically occurs as shown in Figure 11. Notice that a large mass of soil has moved along a surface, which we call a *slip plane*. The natural shape of this failure surface resembles the arc of an ellipse but is usually considered to be circular in soil stability analyses.

FIGURE 10. Slope failure of cohesionless soil.

FIGURE 11. Slope failure of cohesive soil.

Embankment Failure During Construction

Most soils encountered in construction exhibit a combination of the two soil extremes just described. That is, their shear strength is from a combination of intergranular friction and cohesion. However, the behavior of a highly plastic clay will closely approximate that of a completely cohesive soil.

Theoretically, a vertical excavation in a cohesive soil can be safely made to a depth that is a function of the soil's cohesive strength and its angle of internal friction. This depth can range from under 5 ft (1.5 m) for a soft clay to 18 ft (5.5 m) or so for a medium clay. The safe depth is actually less for a stiff clay than for a medium clay, because stiff clays commonly contain weakening cracks or fissures. In practice, however, the theoretically safe depth of unsupported excavation in clay can be sustained for only a limited time. As the clay is excavated, the weight of the soil on the sides of the cut causes the sides of the cut to bulge (or move inward at the bottom) with an accompanying settlement (or subsidence) of the soil at the top of the cut, as shown in Figure 12. Subsidence of the soil at the top of the cut usually results in the formation of tension cracks on the ground surface, as shown in Figure 13. Such cracks usually occur at a distance from the face of the cut equal to $\frac{1}{2}$–$\frac{2}{3}$ of the depth of the cut. If lateral support is not provided, tension cracks will continue to deepen until failure of the embankment occurs. Failure may occur by sliding of the soil face into the cut (Figure 14a) or by toppling of the upper part of the face into the cut (Figure 14b).

The stability of an embankment or excavation is also affected by external factors. These include weather conditions,

FIGURE 12. Subsidence and bulging.

FIGURE 13. Formation of tension crack.

a. Face sliding into excavation

b. Face toppling into excavation

FIGURE 14. Modes of embankment failure.

ground water level, the presence of loads such as material and equipment near the top of the embankment/excavation, and the presence of vibration from equipment or other sources.

Stability of Cut Bottom

Whenever cohesive soil is excavated, heaving (or rising) of the bottom of the cut will occur due to the weight of the soil on the sides of the cut. Heaving is most noticeable when the sides of the cut have been restrained, as shown in Figure 15. A more serious case of bottom instability may occur in cohesionless soils when a supply of water is present. If the sides of the cut are restrained and the bottom of the cut is below the groundwater level, water will flow up through the bottom of the excavation, as shown in Figure 16. The upward flow of water reduces the effective pressure between the soil grains in the bottom of the

cut. This may result in one of several different conditions. If the water pressure exactly equals soil weight, the soil will behave like a liquid and we have a condition called *liquefaction* (or quicksand). Such a soil is unable to support any applied load. If the water pressure is strong enough to move subsurface soil up through the bottom of the cut, this condition is called *boiling* or *piping*. Such a movement of soil often leads to failure of the surrounding soil. This has been the cause of the failure of some dams and levees.

Preventing Embankment Failure

An analysis of the causes of excavation slope failure described above will indicate methods that can be used to prevent such failures. Side slopes may be stabilized by cutting them back to an angle equal to or less than the angle of repose of the soil, or by providing lateral support for the excavation as discussed in Section 6. Both side and bottom stability may be increased

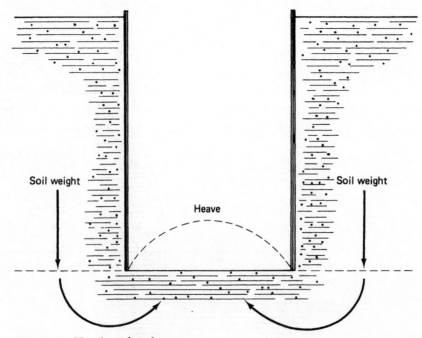

FIGURE 15. Heaving of cut bottom.

FIGURE 16. Boiling and piping of cut bottom.

by dewatering the soil surrounding the excavation. Methods for dewatering and protecting excavations are described in the following sections.

To protect more permanent slopes, such as highway cuts, retaining walls are often used. Slopes of cohesive soil may be strengthened by increasing the shearing resistance along the potential slip plane. This may be done by driving piles or inserting stone columns into the soil across the potential slip plane. Another technique for reinforcing slopes is called *soil* (or earth) *reinforcement*. One form of this process is known under the trademark name Reinforced Earth. As shown in Figure 17, soil reinforcement involves embedding high-tensile-strength nonbiodegradable elements in a compacted soil mass. The embedded tensile elements are attached to

facing material, usually of concrete or timber, to prevent erosion or raveling of soil at the cut surface. Soil reinforcement is often a less expensive method for stabilizing slopes than is the construction of conventional retaining walls.

6 PROTECTING EXCAVATIONS AND WORKERS

Excavation cave-ins are responsible for the greatest number of U.S. construction fatalities, accounting for over 300 deaths during a recent year. Because of the frequency and severity of cave-in accidents, OSHA has established a number of safety regulations affecting excavation operations. While it may be

FIGURE 17. Soil reinforcement.

Table 1. OSHA soil and rock classification system

Stable Rock	Type A	Type B	Type C
Stable rock means natural solid mineral matter that can be excavated with vertical sides and remain intact while exposed.	Type A means cohesive soil with an unconfined compressive strength of 1.5 tsf (144 kPa) or greater. Examples of cohesive soils are clay, silty clay, sandy clay, clay loam and, in some cases, silty clay loam and sandy clay loam. Cemented soils such as caliche and hardpan are also considered Type A if i. The soil is fissured; or ii. The soil is subject to vibration from heavy traffic, pile driving, or similar effects; or iii. The soil has been previously disturbed; or iv. The soil is part of a sloped, layered system where the layers dip into the excavation on a slope of four horizontal to one vertical (4H:1V) or greater; or v. The material is subject to other factors that would require it to be classified as a less stable material.	Type B means: i. Cohesive soil with an unconfined compressive strength greater than 0.5 tsf (48 kPa) but less than 1.5 tsf (144 kPa); or ii. Granular cohesionless soils including angular gravel (similar to crushed rock), silt, silt loam, sandy loam and, in some cases, silty clay loam and sandy clay loam. iii. Previously disturbed soils except those which would otherwise be classed as Type C soil. iv. Soil that meets the unconfined compressive strength or cementation requirements for Type A, but is fissured or subject to vibration; or v. Dry rock that is not stable; or vi. Material that is part of a sloped, layered system where the layers dip into the excavation on a slope less steep than four horizontal to one vertical (4H:1V), but only if the material would otherwise be classified as Type B.	Type C means: i. Cohesive soil with an unconfined compressive strength of 0.5 tsf (48 kPa) or less; or ii. Granular soils including gravel, sand, and loamy sand; or iii. Submerged soil or soil from which water is freely seeping; or iv. Submerged rock that is not stable; or v. Material in a sloped, layered system where the layers dip into the excavation on a slope of four horizontal to one vertical (4H:1V) or steeper.

possible to avoid placing workers into an excavation through the use of remote-controlled equipment or robots, in most cases workers must enter the excavation and OSHA regulations will apply. These regulations require, among other things, that workers in an excavation be protected from cave-ins by one of the following methods:

- Sloping or benching of the sides of the excavation.
- Supporting the sides of the excavation by shoring.
- Placing a shield between workers and the sides of the excavation.

The only exceptions to these requirements are when the excavation is made entirely in stable rock, or the excavation is less than 5 ft (1.524 m) in depth and examination of the ground by a competent person provides no indication of a potential cave-in. As defined by OSHA, *competent person* means one who is capable of identifying existing and predictable hazards in the surroundings, or working conditions which are unsanitary, hazardous, or dangerous to employees, and who has authorization to take prompt corrective measures to eliminate them.

To comply with OSHA rules on sloping, shoring, and shielding, it is necessary to be familiar with the OSHA Soil and Rock Classification System shown in Table 1. In this system, soil and rock are classified as Stable Rock, Type A, Type B, or Type C.

Sloping and Benching

Under OSHA rules, when workers are required to be in an excavation the maximum allowable steepness of the sides of excavations less than 20 ft (6.1 m) deep when employing a simple uniform slope is given in Table 2. However, note the exceptions shown in the footnote to the table.

The requirements for benching (stepping) of excavation sides and for sloping when layered soils of different types are involved are given in reference 5. Sloping or benching for excavations greater than 20 ft (6.1 m) deep must be designed by a registered professional engineer. The major disadvantage of sloping or benching of excavation sides is the space required for the excavation plus side slopes.

Table 2. OSHA maximum allowable slopes for excavation sides. (From *Code of Federal Regulations*, Part 1926, Title 29, Chapter XVII)

Soil or Rock Type	Maximum Allowable Slope (H:V) for Excavations Less Than 20 ft (6.1 m) Deep
Stable Rock	Vertical (90°)
Type A*	¾:1 (53°)
Type B	1:1 (45°)
Type C	1½:1 (34°)

*A short-term (24 h or less) maximum allowable slope of ½H:1V (63°) is allowed in excavations in Type A soil that are 12 ft (3.67 m) or less in depth. Short-term maximum allowable slopes for excavations greater than 12 ft (3.67 m) in depth shall be ¾H:1V (53°).

Shoring and Shielding

Lateral support for the sides of an excavation is usually provided by *shoring*. A shoring system that completely encloses an excavation is essentially a cofferdam, which is a structure designed to keep water and/or soil out of an excavation area. A caisson is also a form of cofferdam, as we have seen. Common types of shoring systems include timber shoring, aluminum hydraulic shoring, lagging, and sheet piling. Shoring and shielding systems must be installed in compliance with OSHA tables, manufacturer's tabulated data, or as designed by a registered professional engineer.

Timber shoring (Figure 18) employs vertical timber uprights placed against the sides of the excavation, either in a continuous fashion or at intervals. Uprights are supported by horizontal beams called wales or stringers. Wales, in turn, are supported by horizontal timber crossbraces or trench jacks. When continuous uprights are used, this shoring system is often called timber sheeting.

Aluminum hydraulic shoring (Figure 19) employs prefabricated vertical rails as uprights with attached hydraulic cylinder crossbraces. Plywood sheets may be placed under the vertical uprights as shown to increase the area of support for the excavation sides. Another arrangement uses timber sheeting supported by prefabricated aluminum wales with attached hydraulic cylinder crossbraces. In this case, the shoring system looks very much like the timber shoring system of Figure 18.

Lagging is nothing more than sheeting placed horizontally. However, in this case vertical supports (called soldier beams) are required between the lagging and wales. Another lagging system uses soldier piles (such as H-piles) with the lagging placed between the open sides of the piling. Wales and struts or tiebacks are used to provide lateral support.

Sheet piling is sheeting of concrete, steel, or timber that is designed to be driven by a pile driver. Sheet piling is used for constructing retaining walls, shoring, and cofferdams. Two sheet pile walls may be constructed parallel to each other, crossbraced, and filled with earth to form a cofferdam. When tight sheeting or sheet piling is used, the shoring system must be designed to withstand the full hydrostatic pressure of the groundwater level unless weep holes or other drains are provided in the shoring system.

FIGURE 18. Timber shoring system.

FIGURE 19. Aluminum hydraulic shoring system.

Labels on figure: Horizontal spacing, Vertical rail, Hydraulic cylinder, 18" max., Vertical spacing, Plywood, 4' max., 2' max.

Trench shields or trench boxes are used in place of shoring to protect workers during trenching operations. Figure 20 illustrates such a movable trench shield. The top of the shield should extend above the sides of the trench to provide protection for workers against objects falling from the sides of the trench. The trench shield is pulled ahead by the excavator as work progresses.

Slurry Trenches

A relatively new development in excavating and trenching is the construction of *slurry trenches*. In this technique, illustrated in Figure 21, a slurry (such as clay and water) is used to fill the excavation as soil is removed. The slurry serves to keep the sides of the trench from collapsing during excavation. No lowering of the water table is required with this method. After completion of the trench, the slurry is displaced by concrete placed through the slurry by use of a tremie. The slurry is pumped away as it is displaced. The slurry trench technique eliminates the necessity for shoring and dewatering excavations. The soil between two rows of completed slurry trenches may be excavated to form a large opening such as a subway tunnel.

FIGURE 20. Trench shield.

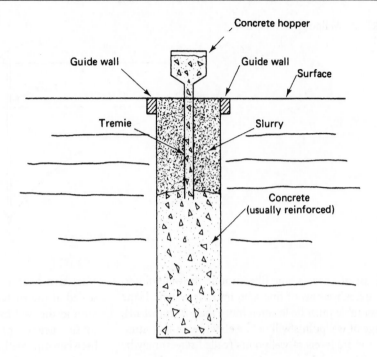

FIGURE 21. Slurry trench construction.

7 DEWATERING EXCAVATIONS

Dewatering is the process of removing water from an excavation. Dewatering may be accomplished by lowering the groundwater table before the excavation is begun. This method is often used for placing pipelines in areas with high groundwater levels. Alternatively, excavation may be accomplished first and the water simply pumped out of the excavation as work proceeds. With either procedure, the result is a lowering of the groundwater level in the excavation area. Hence all dewatering methods involve pumping of water from the ground. Keep in mind that lowering of the water table may cause settlement of the soil in the surrounding area. This, in turn, may cause foundation settlement or even foundation failure in buildings near the excavation area.

The selection of an appropriate dewatering method depends on the nature of the excavation and the permeability of the soil. *Soil permeability,* or the ease with which water flows through the soil, is primarily a function of a soil's grain size distribution. It has been found that the diameter of the soil particle which is smaller than 90% of the soil's grains (i.e., 10% of total soil grains are smaller than the designated grain size) is an effective measure of soil permeability. This soil grain size is referred to as the soil's *effective grain size* and is represented by the symbol D_{10}. Table 3

Table 3. Appropriate dewatering methods

Effective Grain Size (D_{10})	Dewatering Method
Larger than 0.1 mm*	Sumps, ordinary wellpoints
0.1–0.004 mm	Vacuum wells or wellpoints
0.004–0.0017 mm	Electroosmosis

*No. 150 sieve size corresponds to an opening of 0.1 mm.

indicates appropriate dewatering methods as a function of effective soil grain size. Note that gravity drainage (use of pumps and wellpoints) is effective for soils whose effective grain size is about 0.1 mm (corresponding to a No. 150 sieve size) or larger.

Wellpoint Systems

Figure 22 illustrates the use of a standard wellpoint system to dewater an area prior to excavation. Technically, a *wellpoint* is the perforated assembly placed on the bottom of the inlet pipe for a well. It derives its name from the point on its bottom used to facilitate driving the inlet pipe for a well. In practice, the term wellpoint is commonly used to identify each well in a dewatering system, consisting of a number of closely spaced wells. In sandy soils, the usual procedure is to jet the well point and riser into position. This is accomplished by pumping water down through the riser and wellpoint to loosen and liquefy the sand around the wellpoint. Under these conditions, the wellpoint sinks under its own weight to the desired depth. Additional wellpoints are sunk in a line surrounding the excavation area, and then connected to a header pipe. Header pipes used for such systems are essentially manifolds consisting of a series of connection points with valves. After all wellpoints are in place and connected to the header, the header pipes are connected to a self-priming centrifugal pump equipped with an air ejector. Since water from the wellpoints is drawn off by creating a partial vacuum at the pump inlet, the maximum height that water can be lifted by the pump is something less than 32 ft (9.8 m). In practice, the maximum effective dewatering depth is about 20 ft (6.1 m) below the ground surface. Wellpoints are typically spaced 2–10 ft (0.6–3.1 m) apart and yield flows ranging from 3 to 30 gal/min (11–114 ℓ/min) per wellpoint. Wellpoints placed in very fine sands may

FIGURE 22. Wellpoint dewatering system.

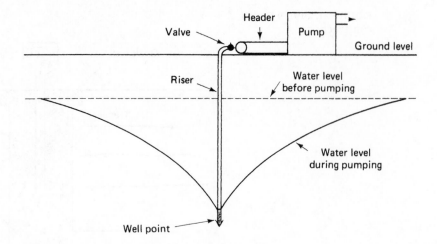

require the use of a coarse sand filter around the wellpoint to prevent an excessive flow of fine sand into the system. If the groundwater table must be lowered more than 20 ft (6.1 m), a single stage of wellpoints will not be effective. In this situation, two or more levels of wellpoints (called *stages*) may be used. The major disadvantage of such a system is the large area required for terracing the stages. For example, to lower the water table 36 ft (11 m) using two stages with embankment side slopes of 1 on 2 and allowing a 5-ft-wide (1.5-m-wide) bench for each pump requires a total width of 82 ft (25 m) on each side of the excavation. Alternatives to the use of staged wellpoints include the use of jet pumps and submersible pumps to lift water from the wells. Figure 23 shows an electrically powered submersible pump being placed into a dewatering well.

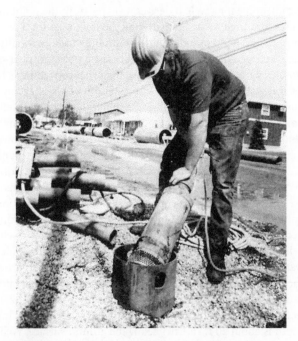

FIGURE 23. Electrically powered submersible pump being placed into dewatering well. (Courtesy of Crane Pumps and Systems)

Vacuum Wells *Vacuum wells* are wellpoints that are sealed at the surface by placing a ring of bentonite or clay around the well casing. A vacuum pump is then connected to the header pipe. The resulting differential pressure between the well and the surrounding groundwater will accelerate the flow of water into the well. In fine-grained soils, it may also be necessary to place a sand filter around the wellpoint and riser pipe.

Electroosmosis *Electroosmosis* is the process of accelerating the flow of water through a soil by the application of a direct current. Although the phenomenon of electroosmosis was discovered in the laboratory early in the nineteenth century, it was not applied to construction dewatering until 1939. As shown in Table 3, the method is applicable to relatively impervious soils such as silts and clays having an effective grain size as small as 0.0017 mm.

The usual procedure for employing electroosmosis in dewatering is to space wells at intervals of about 35 ft (10.7 m) and drive grounding rods between each pair of wells. Each well is then connected to the negative terminal of a dc voltage source and each ground rod is connected to a positive terminal. A voltage of 1.5–4 V/ft (4.9–13 V/m) of distance between the well and anode is then applied, resulting in an increased flow of water to the well (cathode). The applied voltage should not exceed 12 V/ft (39 V/m) of distance between the well and anode to avoid excessive power loss due to heating. Typical current requirements of 15–30 A per well result in power demands of 0.5–2.5 kW per well.

A measure of the effectiveness of electroosmosis can be gained by comparing the flow developed by an electrical voltage with the flow produced by conventional hydraulic forces. Such a calculation for a clay of average permeability indicates that an electrical potential of 3 V/ft (10 V/m) is equivalent to a hydraulic gradient of 50 ft/ft (50 m/m). To obtain a hydraulic gradient of 50 ft/ft by the use of vacuum wells would require wells to be spaced about 1 ft (0.3 m) apart. This calculation provides a measure of the tremendous increase in water flow that electroosmosis provides in soils of low permeability over the flow produced by conventional hydraulic methods.

8 PRESSURE GROUTING

Grouting or *pressure grouting* is the process of injecting a grouting agent into soil or rock to increase its strength or stability, protect foundations, or reduce groundwater flow. Grouting of rock is widely employed in dam construction and tunneling. The need for such grouting is determined by exploratory methods such as core drilling and visual observation in test holes. Pressure tests that measure the flow of water through injector pipes which have been placed and sealed into test holes may also be employed as a measure of the need for grouting and for measuring the effectiveness of grouting. Recent developments in grouting agents and injection methods have led to an increasing use of grouting in soils.

Common grouting patterns include blanket grouting, curtain grouting, and special grouting. *Blanket grouting* covers a large horizontal area, usually to a depth of 50 ft (15 m) or less. *Curtain grouting* produces a linear deep, narrow zone of grout that may extend to a depth of 100 ft (30 m) or more. It is commonly employed to form a deep barrier to water flow under a dam. *Special grouting* is grouting employed for a specific purpose, such as to consolidate rock or soil around a tunnel, fill individual rock cavities, or provide additional foundation support.

Grouting Methods

Major types of grouting include slurry grouting, chemical grouting, compaction grouting, and jet grouting (Figure 24).

Slurry grouting involves the injection of a slurry consisting of water and a grouting agent into soil or rock. Common grouting materials include portland cement, clay (bentonite), fly ash, sand, lime, and additives. In soil, regular portland cement grouts are able to effectively penetrate only gravel and coarse sand. Newer *microfine cement* (or fine-grind cement) grouts are able to penetrate medium and fine sands. Injection of *lime slurry* grout can be used to control the swelling of expansive clays. It can also be used to stabilize low-strength soils such as silts, dredge spoil, and saturated soils.

Chemical grouting involves the injection of a chemical into soil. It is used primarily in sands and fine gravel to cement the soil particles together for structural support or to control water flow. The proper selection of a chemical grout and additives permit rather precise control of grout hardening (setting) time.

Compaction grouting is the process of injecting a very stiff mortar grout into a soil to compact and strengthen the soil. Grouting materials include silty sand, cement, fly ash, additives, and water. Compaction grouting is able to create grout bulbs or grout piles in the soil which serve to densify the soil and provide foundation support. Compaction grouting can also be used to raise (jack) foundations that have settled back to their original elevation.

Jet grouting employs a rotating jet pipe to remove soil around the grout pipe and replace the soil with grout. As a result, the technique is effective over a wide range of soil types to include silts and some clays. The unconfined compressive strength of the grouted soil structure may run as high as 2500 lb/in.² (17 MPa).

FIGURE 24. Types of grouting. (Courtesy of Hayward Baker Inc., A Keller Company)

Slurry grout
(Intrusion)

Compaction grout
(Displacement)

Chemical grout
(Permeation)

Jet grout
(Replacement)

Injection Methods

The principal method for injecting grout into rock involves drilling a hole and then inserting an injector pipe equipped with expandable seals (*packers*) into the hole. Grout is then injected at the desired depths. Methods for injecting grout into soil include driving an injector pipe into the soil, placing a sleeve port tube into the soil, and jet grouting. Grouting utilizing a sleeve port pipe is illustrated in Figure 25. Notice that the grout pipe is equipped with sleeves that cover ports spaced at intervals along the pipe. The sleeves serve as check valves to allow grout to flow out of the ports but prevent return flow. Packers serve to direct the flow of grout through the desired ports.

Selection of an optimum grouting agent and grouting system should be accomplished by experienced grouting specialists. Trial grouting and testing will usually be required before selecting the grouting system to be employed. Care must be taken to avoid the use of injection pressures that lift the ground surface, unless a jacking action is desired.

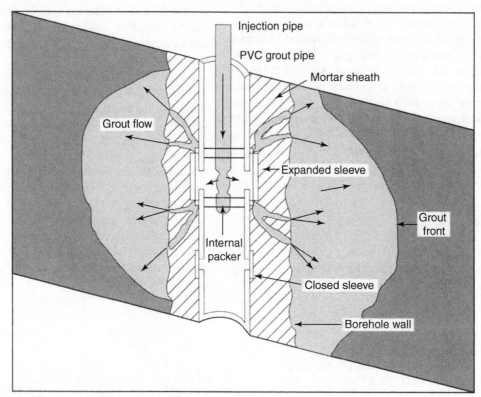

FIGURE 25. Grouting utilizing a sleeve port pipe. (Courtesy of Hayward Baker, Inc., A Keller Company)

Problems

1. When sloping the sides of an excavation in type A soil, what maximum slope may be used if the excavation will be 15 ft (4.6 m) deep and will be open less than 24 h?

2. Explain the significance of a soil's effective grain size (D_{10}) to the process of dewatering the soil.

3. Briefly describe the four major types of pressure grouting.

4. How does a pile support its applied load?

5. Briefly explain the process of vibratory compaction as used in soil improvement.

6. Using Equation 3 and the driving data below, determine the safe load of this bulb pile.

Hammer weight = 2.5 tons

Height of hammer drop = 22 ft

Volume in last batch driven = 4 cu ft

Number of blows to drive last batch = 36

Volume of base and plug = 27 cu ft

Soil K value = 28

7. Briefly describe the process of installing a shell pile.

8. List the three major types of foundation systems and briefly describe their advantages and disadvantages.

9. What three methods meet OSHA requirements for protecting workers in an excavation when worker protection against cave-in is required?

10. Write a computer program to predict the safe capacity of a bulb pile using Equation 3. Solve Problem 6 above using your computer program.

References

1. Ahlvin, Robert G., and Vernon A. Smoots. *Construction Guide for Soils and Foundations,* 2nd ed. New York: Wiley, 1988.

2. Baker, W. H. "Grouting in Geotechnical Engineering," *Proceedings of ASCE Specialty Conference, New Orleans.* American Society of Civil Engineers, New York, 1982.

3. Bowles, Joseph E. *Foundation Analysis and Design,* 5th ed. New York: McGraw-Hill, 1996.

4. Butler, H. D., and Horace E. Hoy. *Users Manual for the Texas Quick-Load Method for Foundation Load Testing.* Federal Highway Administration, Washington, D.C., 1977.

5. *Code of Federal Regulations,* Title 29, Chapter XVII, Part 1926. Office of the Federal Register, National Archives and Records Administration, Washington, D.C.

6. Compton, G. Robert, Jr. *Selecting Pile Installation Equipment,* 3rd ed. Dover, NJ: MKT Geotechnical Systems, 1982.

7. *Design of Pile Foundations.* Reston, VA: American Society of Civil Engineers, 1993.

8. Fellenius, B. H. "The Analysis of Results from Routine Pile Load Tests," *Ground Engineering,* vol 13, no. 6 (1980), pp. 19–31.

9. Hausmann, Manfred R. *Engineering Principles of Ground Modification.* New York: McGraw-Hill, 1990.

10. *Manual on Design and Construction of Driven Pile Foundations.* Demonstration Projects Division and Construction and Maintenance Division, Federal Highway Administration, Washington, DC, 1985.

11. Nordlund, Reymond L. "Dynamic Formula for Pressure Injected Footings," *Journal of the Geotechnical Engineering Division,* ASCE, vol. 108, no. GT3 (1982), pp. 419–437.

12. Welsh, J. P. "Soil Improvement-A Ten Year Update," *ASCE Geotechnical Special Publication No. 12.* American Society of Civil Engineers, New York, 1987.

WOOD CONSTRUCTION

WOOD CONSTRUCTION

1 INTRODUCTION

Wood is one of humankind's oldest construction materials. Today it is still widely used to construct residential, commercial, and industrial buildings, as well as such varied structures as piers, bridges, retaining walls, and power transmission towers. In the United States, for example, 90% of all houses are constructed of wood. In this chapter, we will consider the properties of wood that influence its use in construction, together with the principles and practices of both frame and timber construction.

2 WOOD MATERIALS AND PROPERTIES

Types

Wood is divided into two major classes, hardwood and softwood, according to its origin. *Hardwood* is produced from deciduous (leaf-shedding) trees. *Softwood* comes from conifers (trees having needlelike or scalelike leaves), which are primarily evergreens. The terms *hardwood* and *softwood* indicate only the wood species and may be misleading, because some softwoods are actually harder than some hardwoods. In the United States, lumber is grouped into several grading types, which have similar properties. Most of the lumber used in the United States for structural purposes is softwood.

Moisture Content

The moisture content of lumber (which is defined as the weight of moisture in the wood divided by the oven-dry weight of the wood and then expressed as a percentage) has a great influence on its strength properties. At moisture contents above 30%, wood is essentially in its natural state, and no changes in size or strength properties occur. At moisture contents below 30%, wood shrinks and its strength properties increase. For example, the bending strength of common softwood at moisture contents below 19% is approximately $2\frac{1}{2}$ times its bending strength at moisture contents above 30%. Warping of lumber often occurs as it shrinks.

Structural Wood

Lumber is any wood that is cut into a size and shape suitable for use as a building material. *Timber* is broadly classified as lumber having a smallest dimension of at least 5 in. (12.7 cm). Structural lumber is further divided into *board, dimension, beam and stringer,* and *post and timber* classifications. The board classification applies to lumber less than 2 in. (5 cm) thick and at least 2 in. (5 cm) wide. Dimension applies to lumber at least 2 in. (5 cm) but less than 5 in. (12.7 cm) thick and 2 in. (5 cm) or more wide. The beam and stringer classification applies to lumber at least 5 in. (12.7 cm) thick and 8 in. (20 cm) wide, graded for its strength in bending with the load applied to the narrow face (thickness). The post and beam classification applies to lumber that is approximately square in cross section, at least 5 in. (12.7 cm) in thickness and width, and intended for use where bending strength is not important. Lumber may be either rough or dressed. *Rough lumber* has been sawn on all four sides but not surfaced (planed smooth or dressed). *Dressed lumber* has been surfaced on one or more sides. Possible classifications include surfaced one side (S1S), surfaced two sides (S2S), surfaced one edge (S1E), surfaced two edges (S2E), and combinations of sides and edges (S1S1E, S1S2E, and S4S).

Structural lumber is usually available in lengths from 10 ft (3 m) to 20 ft (6 m) in 2-ft (0.6-m) increments. Studs are available in 8-ft (2.4-m) lengths. Longer lengths may be available on special order. Section dimensions and properties for common sizes of dimension lumber are given in Table 7. Warping can be minimized by shaping lumber after it has been dried to within a few percent of the moisture content at which it will be used. Grading rules define *green lumber* as having a moisture content greater than 19%, *dry lumber* as having a moisture content of 19% or less, and *kiln-dried lumber* as having a moisture content of 15% or less.

Strength

In the United States, lumber grading rules are set by a national Grading Rule Committee established by the U.S. Department of Commerce. The allowable stresses for dimensioned lumber are determined by the wood species, moisture content, and grade. Allowable stresses for common species are set forth in reference 8. Allowable stresses should be adjusted for duration of load and wet conditions as explained in the notes to that table. Some typical values of allowable stress are shown in Table 8 of this text.

Wood Preservation

Wood is subject to damage by decay and by wood-boring insects. Mechanical shields of solid metal or stainless steel mesh may be used to reduce exposure to insect damage. However, wood preservation by chemical treatment is the principal method used today to provide protection against decay and insect damage. Surface treatment of wood has largely been replaced by pressure treatment, which forces the preservatives deep into wood cells. The principal wood preservatives now used for below-ground applications include creosote and chromated copper arsenate (CCA). Common treatments for above-ground applications include copper azole (CA), alkaline copper quaternary (ACQ), sodium borates (SBX), and newer nonmetallic preservatives. These preservatives leave a paintable, nonstaining surface. The nonmetallic preservatives also serve to repel water. However, borates should be used only for above-ground applications that are continuously protected from liquid water. Chromated copper arsenate (CCA) treatment was formerly widely used but is now being replaced by CA, ACQ, and SBX because of concerns over possible harmful health effects of CCA. Cuts and borings on treated wood made at the job site should be field-treated with copper naphthenate having a minimum of 2% metallic solution in accordance with American Wood Preservers' Association (AWPA) Standard M4.

Fire-Retardant and Mold-Resistant Treated Wood

Wood impregnated under pressure with a fire-retardant chemical is classified as fire-retardant treated wood (FRTW). After treatment, the fire-retardant chemical remains in the wood indefinitely. When the wood temperature reaches that of a fire, a chemical reaction occurs. In this reaction, the fire-retardant chemical reacts with the combustible gases and tars normally generated by a wood fire and converts them to carbon char, carbon dioxide, and water. The use of fire-retardant wood often reduces the cost of wood structures due to reduced fire insurance rates. The use of FRTW may also eliminate the need for fire sprinklers in concealed spaces of wood structures, thus further reducing construction costs. The FRTW treatment also provides additional termite and decay resistance to the wood.

Mold-resistant treatment of structural wood minimizes the growth of mold which has been cited as a health hazard to building occupants. Mold-resistant coatings are usually applied by brush or spray in an industrial facility. Such coatings usually contain a coloring agent to identify the treatment applied.

Glued Laminated Timber

Glulam, glued laminated timber (Figure 1), is composed of layers of wood 2 in. (5 cm) or less in thickness which are glued together to form a solid structural member. Glued

FIGURE 1. Glued laminated timber beam. (Courtesy of American Institute of Timber Construction)

laminated timber has several advantages over sawn timber. It provides a way to manufacture wood structural members of great size, curved as well as straight. Since the individual wood pieces used for lamination are rather thin, they can be readily dried to a moisture content that produces a dimensionally stable member of high strength. The strength of a glued laminated timber member can be closely controlled by placing high-strength lumber in areas of high stress and lower-strength lumber in areas of lower stress. This practice reduces the cost of the structural member. The production of glued laminated timber under carefully controlled conditions results in precisely dimensioned structural members of high strength at a minimum cost.

Glued laminated members are widely used in large buildings such as churches, auditoriums, shopping centers, and sports arenas, as well as in industrial plants. The radial arch structure shown in Figure 2 has a clear span of 240 ft (73 m). Other structural applications range from bridge beams to power transmission towers. Reference 1 provides data on standard sizes and allowable stresses for glued laminated timber.

Plywood

Plywood is a wood structural material formed by gluing three or more thin layers of wood (veneers) together with the grain of alternate layers running perpendicular to each other. This process results in a material having a high strength/weight ratio which can be produced in a wide range of strength and appearance grades. Grading rules established by APA—The Engineered Wood Association divide wood veneers into groups 1 through 5, based on strength and stiffness, with group 1 having the highest strength characteristics. In addition to the basic Exterior and Interior type classification, Engineered Grades and an Identification Index indicating the maximum allowable span of the member under standard loads are incorporated in the grading rules. Exterior-type plywood is manufactured with waterproof glue and veneers with higher grade than those used for Interior-type plywood.

Surface appearance grades of N, A, B, C, and D are available, with grade N being of the highest appearance quality. Plyform, a grade of plywood intended for use in concrete formwork, can be manufactured in two grades, class I and class II. Class II is most readily available. High-Density Overlay (HDO) and Medium-Density Overlay (MDO) plywoods have an abrasion-resistant resin-fiber overlay on one or both faces. Plywood with rough-sawn, grooved, or other special faces is available for siding and other uses where appearance is a major consideration. The usual size of plywood sheets in the United States is 4 ft by 8 ft (1.2 m by 2.4 m). Thicknesses of $\frac{3}{8}$ in. (1.0 cm) to $1\frac{1}{8}$ in. (2.9 cm) are available. Plywood is available with tongue-and-groove edges for use in floor construction. Plywood design specifications are given in reference 11. Plywood applications and construction guidelines are described in reference 3.

Other Wood Products

Faced with a declining supply of large old growth timber, the U.S. forest products industry has developed a number of wood products to replace conventional lumber. These products combine selected portions of lower quality wood with adhesives to produce a higher quality wood product. Such products are often referred to as *Engineered Wood*. In addition to plywood and glued laminated timber, these products include laminated veneer lumber (LVL), I-joists, parallel strand lumber (PSL), laminated strand lumber (LSL), particleboard, waferboard, and oriented strand board.

Laminated veneer lumber is similar to plywood but consists of thin veneer about $\frac{1}{16}$ to $\frac{1}{10}$ in. (1.6–2.5 mm) thick with all plies and grains parallel to the length. It is produced in billets as large as 2 ft (610 mm) wide, 80 ft (24 m) long, and up to 4 in. (100 mm) thick. Billets are then cut to form lumber of the desired width and length.

I-joists or *wood I-beams* consist of plywood or oriented strand board webs bonded to sawn wood or laminated veneer lumber flanges. They are lighter but stronger than conventional sawn joists or beams. They can be manufactured in lengths exceeding 60 ft (18.3 m).

Parallel strand lumber (PSL) is produced by cutting logs into long strands, drying them, and treating them with a resin adhesive. The strands are then aligned parallel to each other, microwave heated, and pressed into solid billets. The process uses virtually the entire tree so there is little wood waste in the process.

FIGURE 2. Erecting large glued laminated timber arches. (Courtesy of American Institute of Timber Construction)

Laminated strand lumber is produced by a process similar to that used for parallel strand lumber but uses wood strands about 12 in. (305 mm) long. After being treated with adhesive, the strands are pressed together using a steam-injection pressing process.

Particleboard is produced in sheets by bonding wood chips together with resin. The usual panel size is 4 ft × 8 ft (1.2 m × 2.4 m). Usual thicknesses are $\frac{1}{4}$–$1\frac{1}{2}$ in. (6–38 mm).

Waferboard is similar to particleboard except that it is manufactured from larger wood chips.

Oriented strand board is built up in layers like plywood. However, each layer consists of wood strands bonded together by a resin.

Rim board is an engineered wood product designed to fill the space between the sill plate and the bottom wall plate or between the top plate and the bottom plate of multistory construction.

Mixing Sawn Lumber and Engineered Wood

There is usually a significant difference in moisture content between sawn lumber and engineered wood. The moisture content of sawn lumber is often near the upper limit of 19% allowed for classification as dry lumber. Engineered wood is much drier, often around 5%. When these materials are placed in direct contact, their moisture content will attempt to reach equilibrium between the two materials. As a result, the sawn lumber will shrink as it dries while the engineered wood will expand. Therefore, these materials should not be used in direct contact without a careful design analysis.

3 FRAME CONSTRUCTION

Frame construction utilizes studs [typically spaced 16 or 24 in. (0.4 or 0.6 m) on center], joists, and rafters to form the building frame. Framing members are usually of 2 in. (5 cm) nominal thickness. This frame is then covered with siding and roof sheathing of plywood or lumber. Frame construction is widely used in the United States for single-family residences, as well as for small multiple-family residences, offices, and shops. Building codes frequently specify procedures or minimum dimensions to be used in frame construction. The procedures described in this section are those widely recommended in the absence of specific code requirements. The two principal forms of frame construction, platform frame construction and balloon frame construction, are described next.

Platform Frame Construction

Platform frame construction is illustrated in Figure 3. In this type of construction, the subfloor of each story extends to the outside of the building and provides a platform for the construction of the building walls. This method of framing is widely used because it provides a good working platform at each level during construction and also permits preassembled wall sections to be quickly set in place once the subfloor is completed.

The principal framing members are identified in Figure 3. In this example, the first floor joists are supported by sills (placed on top of foundation walls) and ledger strips attached to the girder. Wall panels are composed of sole plates (or soles), studs, and top plates. Double top plates are used for bearing walls (walls that support a load from an upper level).

Balloon Frame Construction

In *balloon frame construction*, exterior wall studs extend all the way from the sill to the top of the second floor wall, as shown in Figure 4. The outside ends of second-floor joists are supported by ribbon strips notched (or let-in) into the studs. Balloon framing is especially well suited for use in two-story buildings that have exterior walls covered with masonry veneer, since this method of framing reduces the possibility of movement between the building frame and the exterior veneer.

Foundation and Floor Construction

Platform frame construction supported by foundation walls is illustrated in Figure 5. In this illustration the floor joists are lapped and rest on top of the girder rather than on the ledger strip used in Figure 3. Notice also the use of a header joist (or band) to close off the exterior end of joists. Lateral bracing (bridging or cross bracing) between joists may be either solid bridging or diagonal bridging as shown. Board or plywood subflooring may be used as shown in Figure 5. Notice that board subflooring should be placed at an angle of 45° to the joists to provide additional stiffness to the floor structure and to permit the finish flooring to be laid either parallel or perpendicular to the joists. When carpeting or other nonstructural flooring is used, subflooring may be eliminated by using a combined subfloor-underlayment of plywood. The APA Glued Floor System, in which plywood is glued to the joists, has been developed by APA—The Engineered Wood Association—to reduce subfloor cost and to increase the stiffness of the floor system.

Floor (flat) trusses and wood I-beams (Figure 6) are increasingly being used for floor support in place of floor joists due to their light weight and high load capacity. Although solid timber or glulam beams may be used to replace joists, built-up wood I-beams are more often used due to their lighter weight. Wood I-beams commonly use nominal 2 × 2 in. (50 × 50 mm), 2 × 3 in. (50 × 75 mm), or 2 × 4 in. (50 × 100 mm) top and bottom flanges with $\frac{3}{8}$ in. (9.5-mm) plywood webs. The characteristics of floor trusses are similar to those of other trusses described later in this section. Floor trusses commonly use nominal 2 × 4 in. (50 × 100 mm) chords and webs to produce a truss $3\frac{1}{2}$ in. (89 mm) wide. The openings between truss webs facilitate the installation of utility lines and ducts.

Most safety precautions applying to the erection of floor trusses are similar to those described later for roof trusses. However, as floors supported by floor trusses provide a

FIGURE 3. Platform frame construction. (Courtesy of American Forest and Paper Association)

convenient surface for storage of materials during construction, the following additional precautions should be observed. *Never stack materials on unbraced trusses.* Even after trusses have been braced and decked, be careful to stack materials against or directly over load-bearing walls and distribute the load over as many trusses as possible. See reference 4 for additional information.

Figure 7 illustrates slab-on-grade construction using a separate foundation wall. Notice the use of rigid insulation on the interior face of the foundation wall and under the edge of the floor slab to provide a thermal barrier. Figure 8 illustrates slab-on-grade construction using a foundation beam poured integrally with the floor slab. Such construction is also referred to as *thickened-edge slab construction.* Finish flooring of wood, carpeting, vinyl, or other material may be applied directly to the top of the slab or it may be supported on *sleepers,* as illustrated in Figure 7. Notice the use of a vapor barrier to prevent ground moisture from rising through the slab.

FIGURE 4. Balloon frame construction. (Courtesy of American Forest and Paper Association)

Framing Details

Two methods of supporting joists are illustrated in Figures 3 and 5. A minimum bearing length of 1½ in. (38 mm) along the joist should be provided when joists rest on wood or metal beams. The bearing length should be increased to 3 in. (76 mm) for bearing on masonry. Framing anchors or joist hangers may be used in place of a ledger strip to support joists, as shown in Figure 9.

The use of both solid and diagonal bridging to provide lateral bracing of joists is illustrated in Figure 5. Prefabricated metal diagonal bridging with integral fastening devices is also available for standard joist spacings. Bridging between joists is not required when the Glued Floor System is used.

Typical platform frame construction of an exterior wall including a window opening is illustrated in Figure 10. The load on the top of the window opening is carried by a

FIGURE 5. Floor framing for platform frame construction. (U.S. Department of Agriculture)

Floor Truss

Wood I-beam

FIGURE 6. Floor truss and wood I-beam.

FIGURE 7. Slab on grade with foundation wall. (U.S. Department of Agriculture)

WALL STUDS
ANCHORED SLEEPERS
WOOD STRIP FLOORING
HOT TAR SEAL
SILL CALK
8" MINIMUM
CONCRETE SLAB
VAPOR BARRIER
RIGID INSULATION
FOUNDATION WALL
GRAVEL FILL
FOOTING

FIGURE 8. Combined slab and foundation. (U.S. Department of Agriculture)

SHEATHING
STUD
WOOD-BLOCK OR RESILIENT TILE
SILL CALK
ADHESIVE
8" MINIMUM
WIRE MESH
CONCRETE SLAB
VAPOR BARRIER
GRAVEL
REINFORCING RODS

FIGURE 9. Joists supported by joist hangers and framing anchors. (Courtesy of Cleveland Steel Specialty, Bedford Hts., Ohio 44146)

All-purpose framing anchors.

Joist hangers.

header, which is in turn supported by double studs at the sides of the opening. Note the use of *let-in braces* (braces notched into the studs) to reinforce the wall at building corners. Plywood panels may be used as sheathing at building corners to replace corner braces. Corner braces are not required when full plywood wall sheathing is used.

Roof Construction

One method of roof construction, called *joist and rafter framing,* is illustrated in Figure 11. Rafters are notched where they rest on wall plates and are held in place by nailing them to the wall plates or by the use of metal framing

anchors. The *collar beam* shown is used to assist in resisting wind loads on the roof.

Roof trusses are now widely used in wood frame construction in place of rafter framing. The use of roof trusses permits interior walls to be nonbearing because all roof loads are supported by the exterior walls. Additional advantages of prefabricated roof trusses over rafters include high strength, economy, controlled quality, less skilled labor required on-site, and an open web design which facilitates installation of plumbing, electrical, and HVAC systems. Components of common roof trusses are illustrated in Figure 12. While there are many types of trusses, some of the more common types of roof trusses are illustrated in Figure 13.

FIGURE 10. Exterior wall framing, platform construction. (U.S. Department of Agriculture)

FIGURE 11. Roof framed with rafters and ceiling joists. (Courtesy of American Forest and Paper Association)

FIGURE 12. Truss components. (Courtesy of ITW Building Components Group Inc., Alpine)

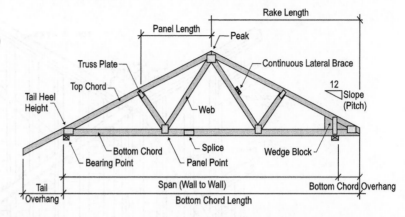

FIGURE 13. Common types of roof truss. (Courtesy of ITW Building Components Group Inc., Alpine)

Roof sheathing normally consists of plywood or nominal 1-in. (25-mm) boards applied perpendicular to the rafters or trusses. Roofing is applied over the roof sheathing to provide a watertight enclosure.

Handling and Erecting Roof Trusses

Care must be taken to avoid damage to trusses while transporting, storing, or erecting them. They are particularly vulnerable to damage by excessive lateral bending which can damage joints and truss members. Since trusses are commonly delivered to the erection site in bundles, they should be left bundled until needed. When stored horizontally, trusses should be placed on blocking placed at intervals of not more than 10 ft (3.1 m) on a level surface and covered if possible to minimize weather damage. When trusses are stored vertically, truss bundles should be braced to prevent overturning, which could result in truss damage or injury to workers.

Short trusses (under 40 ft or 12 m) can usually be erected satisfactorily by hand. A recommended procedure for erecting trusses manually is to lift them into place in a peak down position, rotate them into place with the peak up, and fasten them into place. The amount of lifting required can be minimized by installing a board ramp from the ground to the top of the wall and shoving the truss up the ramp. Longer trusses should be lifted into place using a crane or forklift together with appropriate slings or spreader bars. Suggested procedures for lifting a truss with a crane are illustrated in Figure 14. Do not use a plain hook hooked directly onto the top chord of the truss. Such a

procedure applies a twist to the truss which may damage the truss. In addition, the hook may slide laterally and any slack in the lifting line will release the hook. The crane operator should swing loads slowly and smoothly and avoid jerks when starting or stopping. A tag line should always be used when lifting a truss by crane. This will help control the swing and guide the truss into place while reducing the chance of injury to workers. Reference 4 provides additional guidance on handling and erecting wood trusses.

Proper lateral bracing of trusses during erection is critical to safety and the structural integrity of the roof. Although the truss designer will specify the permanent bracing required, the builder must provide temporary bracing until the permanent bracing is installed. Proper bracing of the first end truss is particularly important to obtain the correct alignment of the truss system. After bracing the end truss, the remaining trusses must be braced in the following three planes: top chord (sheathing) plane, web (vertical) plane, and bottom chord (ceiling) plane. Some suggestions for the proper bracing of trusses are provided in Figure 15 and reference 4. A suggested checklist for truss installation is shown in Figure 16. Common truss installation errors identified by the Wood Truss Council of America are shown in Figure 17.

Truss Damage and Repair

Banded trusses shipped from the truss fabrication plant make up a rigid assembly which is not easily damaged. However, damage may occur when the assembly is struck by

FIGURE 14. Lifting trusses by crane. (Reproduced from HIB-91, courtesy of Truss Plate Institute, Inc.)

FIGURE 15. Bracing roof trusses. (Reproduced from HIB-91, courtesy of Truss Plate Institute.)

a forklift or when carelessly unloaded. More often, damage occurs when unbanded trusses are handled carelessly during repositioning, erection, or installation. Trusses may also be damaged when they roll over or "domino" by falling against each other during erection before being properly braced. Any damaged truss should be inspected by an engineer to determine repair needed. Dominoed trusses should not be repaired because hairline cracks which are difficult to detect often occur. Web and chord members should never be drilled or notched without approval of the truss design engineer. Truss web members should never be removed.

Siding

Exterior frame walls are most often covered with wood or plywood siding or a masonry veneer applied over sheathing. Sheathing may consist of nominal 1-in. (2.5-cm) boards placed diagonally, plywood, or nonstructural sheathing.

FIGURE 15. (Continued)

Sheathing may be omitted when plywood siding is applied in accordance with the recommendations of APA—The Engineered Wood Association. Such construction is referred to as *single-wall construction*. To make a watertight enclosure, joints in the siding of single-wall construction must be caulked, lapped, battened, or backed with building paper.

Brick veneer siding over plywood sheathing is shown in Figure 18. Note that building paper is not required over plywood sheathing when an air space and weep holes are provided. However, building paper should be used over wood sheathing. A stucco exterior wall finish over plywood sheathing is illustrated in Figure 19.

BE SURE TO BRING COPY OF TRUSS DESIGN DRAWINGS FOR READY REFERENCE

		OK	REJECT
A.	**JOBSITE STORAGE (if applicable)**		
1.	Are trusses protected against foul weather?	☐	○
2.	Truss bundles intact?	☐	○
3.	Trusses supported out of mud, dirt and standing water?	☐	○
B.	**BRACING & ERECTION**		
1.	Truss handling techniques proper? (See HET-80)	☐	○
2.	Adequate temporary bracing installed during erection? (See BWT-76)	☐	○
3.	Are loads being applied to trusses prematurely?	☐	○
4.	Is permanent bracing installed as shown on Architect or Engineer's framing plan? ..	☐	○
C.	**CONFIGURATION**		
	Does truss match design drawing?	☐	○
		☐	○
		☐	○
		☐	○
		☐	○
	If sealed drawings are required has seal been affixed?	☐	○
D.	**SOURCE**		
	Is truss manufacturer same as supplier of design drawings?	☐	○
	Where code requires approved third-party quality control inspection, does inspector's stamp appear on trusses?	☐	○

		GRADE		SIZE	
		OK	REJECT	OK	REJECT
E.	**LUMBER SIZES & GRADES**				
	Do they match or better design drawing requirements in:				
1.	Top chord?	☐	○	☐	○
2.	Bottom chord?	☐	○	☐	○
3.	Web members?	☐	○	☐	○
4.	Special webs (if required)?	☐	○	☐	○

		OK	REJECT
F.	**TRUSS CONNECTORS**		
1.	Is connector plate manufacturer the same as specified on drawing?	☐	○
2.	Is connector plate size and gauge as specified on all joints?	☐	○
3.	Are any joints missing plates?	☐	○
4.	Plate position on joint and slotted hole direction in accordance with design?	☐	○
G.	**INSTALLATION**		
1.	Cantilevered trusses positioned in correct direction?	☐	○
2.	Interior bearing trusses properly positioned?	☐	○
3.	Flat trusses right-side up?	☐	○
4.	Are all the end walls straight enough to ensure safe and proper bearing?	☐	○
5.	Have any of the wall dimensions (thickness of walls) or placement of walls changed to something other than the dimensions called for on the drawing?	☐	○
6.	Are trusses being properly nailed to bearing plates, or are the correct type of hangers and fastenings called out in shop drawings being properly applied?	☐	○
7.	Are any holes being drilled into the webs or chords?	☐	○
8.	Verify location and details of extra trusses required (if any) to handle concentrated loads, stair headers, etc.	☐	○
9.	Is truss camber oriented in correct direction (see truss drawings)?	☐	○
10.	Is on-center spacing correct?	☐	○
H.	**MISHANDLING & ALTERATION**		
1.	Damage due to mishandling?	☐	○
2.	Connector plates buckled?	☐	○
3.	Missing or broken members?	☐	○
4.	Cut, notched, or altered members?	☐	○

Wood Truss Jobsite Inspection Check List is only a guide and cannot cover all points and conditions. All points and conditions should comply with sound engineering judgment and construction procedures.

FIGURE 16. Checklist for truss installation. (Courtesy of Alpine Engineered Products, Inc.)

Typical types of wood siding are shown in Figure 20. Note the nailing methods used. Plywood siding over sheathing is shown in Figure 21.

Plank-and-Beam Construction

Plank-and-beam construction (or post-and-beam construction) is a method of framing in which flooring and roof planks (usually nominal 2-in. lumber) are supported by posts and beams spaced up to 8 ft apart. This is essentially a lighter version of the heavy timber construction described in Section 4. Plank-and-beam framing is contrasted with conventional framing in Figure 22. In plank-and-beam construction, supplementary framing (not shown) is provided in exterior walls to support siding, doors, and windows.

Several advantages are claimed for this method of framing, the principal one being the reduction in framing labor

---

Common Installation Errors

1. Cantilever trusses installed backward.
2. Parallel chord trusses installed upside down.
3. Trusses, designed for interior bearing walls, installed backward.
4. Large concentrated loads that do not land on panel points.
5. Girder trusses not fastened together.
6. Girder trusses incorrectly fastened together. (Truss ply-to-ply connections are specified in the truss design drawing.)
7. Use of incorrect girder hangers.
8. Common trusses incorrectly fastened to truss girders. (Truss-to-truss connections are specified in the truss design drawing.)
9. Trusses installed in the wrong location.
10. Gable end trusses installed without continuous bottom chord support or web member bracing.
11. Un-braced and unsheathed truss top chords beneath over framing.
12. Conventionally framed hip ends of the building supported on common trusses not designed for hip framing. This condition requires a girder truss or special truss design for the specific load condition.
13. Trusses spaced wider than the design specifications.
14. Using two standard floor trusses at locations that required specially designed floor truss girders.
15. Cutting of trusses at the roof fireplace opening instead of installing the fireplace girder trusses designed for such openings.
16. Trusses with web members or chords drilled for the use of lag screws to support sprinkler loads that have not been included in the design of the truss.
17. Trusses with webs removed by plumbers and mechanical trades.
18. Trusses repaired without following the truss repair drawings provided by the truss designer.
19. Truss chord or web members drilled or notched for the passage of electrical wires, plumbing lines and/or mechanical duct work.

FIGURE 17. Common truss installation errors. (Information provided courtesy of the Wood Truss Council of America [WTCA]. This information is from WTCA's *Metal Plate Connected Wood Truss Handbook,* 3rd ed., 2002. For more information, contact WTCA at 608/274-4849 or visit www.woodtruss.com)

FIGURE 18. Brick veneer wall. (Courtesy of APA)

BRICK VENEER OVER APA PANEL SHEATHING

- APA RATED SHEATHING
- Building paper or other code-approved weather-resistive barrier required
- Brick veneer or masonry
- 1" air space
- "Weep holes" in bottom course every 24"
- Hold panel edge 1/2" above base flashing
- Extend flashing up behind sheathing at least 6"

FIGURE 19. Stucco over sheathing. (Courtesy of APA)

STUCCO OVER APA PANEL SHEATHING

Building paper is required*

Stucco

Self-furring metal lath

Metal bead

Building paper

APA RATED SHEATHING

Note:
International Residential Code requires two layers of grade D paper for stucco over wood-based sheathing.

*Check local building code and applicator for specific requirements.

Bevel siding

Drop siding

Board and batten siding

Tongue and groove siding

FIGURE 20. Common types of wood siding. (Courtesy of American Forest and Paper Association)

APA RATED SIDING (PANEL SIDING) OVER NAILABLE SHEATHING

1/8" spacing is recommended at all edge and end joints unless otherwise indicated by panel manufacturer

Building paper or other code-approved weather-resistive barrier required

Panel siding or APA Rated Sheathing meets code requirement for wall bracing

APA RATED SIDING panels applied over sheathing

6" minimum clearance, siding to grade

FIGURE 21. Plywood siding over sheathing. (Courtesy of American Forest and Paper Association)

FIGURE 22. Comparison of plank-and-beam and conventional framing. (Courtesy of American Forest and Paper Association)

Plank-and-beam framing.

Conventional framing.

cost due to the smaller number of framing members required. The system also produces a distinctive architectural effect that many people find attractive. Some construction details for plank-and-beam framing of a one-story residence are shown in Figure 23.

4 TIMBER CONSTRUCTION

Buildings

The term *heavy timber construction* originally identified a multistory structure whose structural members (except for exterior walls) were primarily composed of timber. Such structures were widely used for industrial and storage purposes. Today heavy timber construction indicates the type of wood building construction that carries the highest fire-resistance classification. Such high fire resistance is obtained by specifying construction details, the minimum sizes of wood structural members, the composition and minimum thickness of floors and roofs, the types of fasteners and adhesives used, and the fire resistance of walls, as well as by prohibiting concealed spaces under floors and roofs.

Both glued laminated and sawn timber are used in modern heavy timber construction. Modern structures are often only one story in height. Such construction is widely used for schools, churches, auditoriums, sports arenas, and stores, as well as for industrial and storage buildings.

FIGURE 23. Plank-and-beam framing for one-story house. (Courtesy of American Forest and Paper Association)

A typical multistory building of traditional heavy timber construction is illustrated in Figure 24. Some construction details recommended by the National Forest Products Association for roof beam and column connections are shown in Figure 25. Such details are typical of the practices that are specified to attain the high fire resistance of heavy timber construction. Some typical varieties of modern heavy timber buildings are illustrated in Figures 26 to 28. Figure 26 shows a rigid arch structure using glued laminated timber arches that are supported at ground level. A barrel arch roof using curved glued laminated timber arches supported by exterior piers is depicted in Figure 27. A bowstring roof truss supported by wood columns is used in the building of Figure 28. The knee brace shown in Figure 28 may be eliminated when plywood roof sheathing is used and the building's perimeter frame is designed to carry lateral loads.

FIGURE 24. Traditional heavy timber construction. (Courtesy of American Forest and Paper Association)

Bridges

Timber bridges have been used throughout recorded history to span streams and valleys. Major types of timber bridge structures include trestle bridges, truss bridges, and arch bridges. *Trestle bridges* consist of stringers whose ends are supported by timber or pile bents, as illustrated in Figure 29. Loads are transferred to the stringer by decking laid across the stringers. Note the use of sway bracing (or cross bracing) on the bents of Figure 30. Tower bents consisting of several parallel bent frames and connected by bent caps and longitudinal bracing may also be used. Stringers may be fabricated of sawn or glued

laminated timber or other materials. Girder, truss, and arch bridges are capable of spanning greater distances than can trestle bridges. Wood girders are usually fabricated of glued laminated timber. The trusses used in timber *truss bridges* are similar in design to those used for roof trusses. Truss designs frequently used include parallel chord trusses, triangular trusses, and bowstring trusses.

Timber *arch bridges* utilize arches built up from wood members. Arches are usually fabricated of glued laminated timber. A highway overpass whose glued laminated timber arches span 155 ft (47 m) is shown in Figure 31. Note

FIGURE 25. Typical roof beam and column connection details. (Courtesy of American Forest and Paper Association)

the smaller bridge, which utilizes a curved continuous-span glued laminated timber girder 170 ft (52 m) long.

Other Structures

Timber construction is often used for many other types of structures, such as tanks, water towers, observation towers, and power transmission towers. Timber crossarms are sometimes used on metal power transmission towers because of wood's good dielectric properties.

5 FASTENINGS, CONNECTIONS, AND NOTCHING

Fastenings

As in any mechanical system, a wood structure cannot develop the full strength of its members unless connections between members are at least as strong as the members themselves. There are a number of types of fasteners used to join wood members, the most common being nails and

FLOOR CONNECTION

CONCEALED PURLIN HANGER

FIGURE 26. Rigid arch frame supported at floor. (Courtesy of American Forest and Paper Association)

wood screws. Sizes of common wire nails are presented in Table 1. Other major types of fasteners include bolts, lagscrews, spikes, dowels, and drift-bolts (or drift-pins). Major factors controlling the allowable strength of mechanical fasteners include the lumber species, the angle of the load with respect to the wood grain, the size of the member perpendicular to the load, the distance of the fastener from the edge of the wood, and the spacing of fasteners. Methods for determining the allowable load on common wood fasteners are given in references 1 and 7.

Connectors

To provide the most efficient use of materials and labor while providing the required strength, a number of special timber connectors have been developed. Major types of

FIGURE 27. Barrel arch frame supported by exterior pier. (Courtesy of American Forest and Paper Association)

COLUMN AND TRUSS CONNECTION

FIGURE 28. Bowstring roof truss supported by wood column. (Courtesy of American Forest and Paper Association)

1 – Tread
2 – Open-laminated deck
3 – Curb
4 – Curb riser block
5 – Handrail
6 – Handrail post
7 – Handrail brace

8 – End dam
9 – Timber stringers
10 – Steel stringers
14 – Longitudinal bracing
18 – Abutment sill
19 – Abutment footing

FIGURE 29. Timber trestle bridge with frame bent. (U.S. Department of the Army)

timber connectors include split-ring connectors, toothed-ring connectors, and shear plates. These are illustrated in Figure 32. These connectors use a bolt or lag screw to join the wood members and place the connector under compression. Split-ring connectors and shear plates fit into grooves precut into the wood members. Toothed-ring connectors are forced into the wood under the pressure of the bolt joining the members.

Light-metal framing devices are available in a wide range of types and sizes, some of which are illustrated in Figure 33. Light-metal connector plates may incorporate integral teeth or may use nails for load transfer. All-purpose framing anchors may be used for a variety of connections, such as rafters to wall plates and studs to top and sole plates.

Notching and Boring of Beams

Notching the top or bottom of a beam will seriously reduce its bending strength. In short, heavily loaded beams, horizontal shear stress may be critical. The safe vertical reaction on an end-notched beam (such as a joist) which is notched on the tension side (as shown in Figure 34) may be calculated as follows:

$$R_v = \frac{2F_v b d_e^2}{3d} \tag{1}$$

where
R_v = safe vertical end reaction (lb)
F_v = allowable shear stress (psi)
b = width of beam (in.)
d = depth of beam (in.)
d_e = depth of beam above notch (in.)

When the notch is curved, or is beveled over a distance greater than d_e, Equation 2 may be used in lieu of Equation 1 to calculate the maximum allowable end reaction for the beam.

$$R_v = \frac{2F_v b d_e}{3} \tag{2}$$

When it is necessary to notch joists to provide passage for piping or electrical cables, the following limits should not be exceeded without a design analysis of the joist. Notches in the top or bottom of joists should not exceed one-sixth of the joist depth and should be located less than one-third of the joist length from either end of the joist. The diameter of holes bored in joists should not exceed one-third of the depth of the joist and should not extend closer than 2 in. to the top or bottom edge of the joist.

Some suggested guidelines for cutting openings in wood I-beams are presented in Figure 35.

FIGURE 30. Typical timber trestle and pile bridge bent.

Timber trestle bent

Pile bent

FIGURE 31. Highway bridges supported by glued laminated timber beams. (Courtesy of American Institute of Timber Construction)

Table 1. Common wire nail sizes

Size: Penny (d)	Wire Gauge	Length	
		in.	cm
4	12½	1.50	3.8
6	11½	2.00	5.1
8	10¼	2.50	6.4
10	9	3.00	7.6
12	9	3.25	8.3
16	8	3.50	8.9
20	6	4.00	10.2
30	5	4.50	11.4
40	4	5.00	12.7
50	3	5.50	14.0
60	2	6.00	15.2

Split ring   Toothed ring

Shear plates

FIGURE 32. Typical timber connectors. (Courtesy of American Forest and Paper Association)

Connector or truss plate

All purpose framing anchors

FIGURE 33. Typical light-metal framing devices. (Courtesy of Cleveland Steel Specialty, Bedford Hts., Ohio 44146)

FIGURE 34. End notching of beam.

Figure 1. Round hole maximum size and minimum spacing.
Maximum round hole size is 0.9 times the web depth. Any round hole must be located at least 4 diameters from inside face of bearing. Adjacent round holes must be at least 7 diameters of the larger hole apart, center-to-center. A 2" hole may be cut anywhere in the web (pre-punched knockouts are provided 24" o.c.).

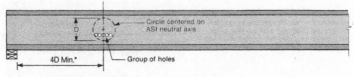

Figure 2. Group of small holes.
A group of small holes must fit inside a circle meeting the limitations for round holes (see Figure 1).

Figure 3. Square hole maximum size and minimum spacing.
Maximum square hole size is 0.7 times the web depth. Any square hole must be located at least four times the length of a side from inside face bearing. Adjacent square holes must be at least six times the length of a side of the larger hole apart.

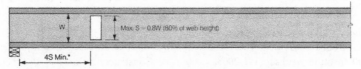

Figure 4. Vertical rectangular hole maximum size and minimum spacing.
Vertical rectangular holes follow the rules for square holes using the longer side for all calculations.

Figure 5. Rectangular hole maximum size and minimum spacing.
Maximum rectangular hole size is 0.7 times the web depth for the shorter side, with the longer side 1.5 times the web depth or 18" at most. Any rectangular hole must be located at least four times the length of the longer side from the inside face of a bearing. Adjacent rectangular holes must be at least six times the length of the longer long side apart.

Legend

W = Inside flange dimension.

D = Diameter of round opening.

S = Vertical dimension of square or rectangular opening.

L = Horizontal dimension of rectangular opening.

Notes: If adjacent holes have different shapes, the spacing between them is the greater of the two obtained by following the rules for the shapes involved.

Recommendations in figures 1 thru 5 apply only to simple support, uniform load situations. Exceptions to the criteria shown in figures 1 thru 5 may be possible. Make special inquiry to your ASI distributor.

FIGURE 35. Cutting openings in wood I-beams. (Courtesy of Alpine Engineered Products, Inc.)

Problems

1. The vertical reaction at the end of a 2 × 6 in. (50 × 150 cm) floor joist is 524 pounds (2.33 kN). If the allowable shear stress in the joist is 180 psi (1241 kPa), what is the maximum depth that the joist can be safely end-notched? Assume that the notch is a square notch on the tension side of the joist.

2. Briefly explain the meaning of the term "glulam" and identify the characteristics of this material.

3. What is FRTW wood? What advantages does it have over conventional lumber?

4. Sketch and briefly explain the construction of a *thickened-edge slab*.

5. Explain the limitations which should be observed when notching joists for the passage of pipe or electrical conduit.

6. What purpose does a *collar beam* serve in a roof framed with rafters and ceiling joists?

7. Explain the major safety hazards involved in erecting the roof trusses for a two-story frame building.

8. What precautions should be observed in storing roof trusses at the construction site?

9. Briefly describe the following wood products and their uses.
   a. Laminated veneer lumber
   b. Wood I-beam
   c. Particleboard

10. Develop a computer program to calculate the safe vertical end reaction of an end-notched beam (Equations 1 and 2). The program input should include the allowable shear stress, depth of notch, and distance over which the notch is beveled. Using your program, solve Problem 1.

References

1. American Institute of Timber Construction. *Timber Construction Manual*, 5th ed. Hoboken, NJ: Wiley, 2005.

2. Anderson, L. O. *Wood-Frame House Construction* (Agriculture Handbook No. 73). U.S. Department of Agriculture, Washington, D.C., 1975.

3. *APA Design/Construction Guide: Residential & Commercial*. APA—The Engineered Wood Association, Tacoma, WA.

4. *Guide to Good Practice for Handling, Installing & Bracing Metal Plate Connected Wood Trusses* (BCSI 1-03). Wood Truss Council of America and Truss Plate Institute, Madison, WI, 2003.

5. *Heavy Timber Construction Details* (Wood Construction Data No. 5). American Forest and Paper Association, Washington, D.C., 1971.

6. *I-Joists for Residential Floors*. APA—The Engineered Wood Association, Tacoma, WA.

7. *Manual for Wood Frame Construction* (Wood Construction Data No. 1). American Forest and Paper Association, Washington, D.C., 1988.

8. *National Design Specification for Wood Construction*. American Forest and Paper Association, Washington, D.C.

9. Nunnally, Stephens W., and Joan A. Nunnally. *Residential and Light Building Construction*. Upper Saddle River, NJ: Prentice Hall, 1990.

10. *Plank-and-Beam Framing for Residential Buildings* (Wood Construction Data No. 4). American Forest and Paper Association, Washington, D.C., 1970.

11. *Plywood Design Specification*. APA—The Engineered Wood Association, Tacoma, WA.

12. *Wood Handbook: Wood as an Engineering Material*. Forest Products Society, Madison, WI, 1999.

CONCRETE CONSTRUCTION

1 CONSTRUCTION APPLICATIONS OF CONCRETE

Concrete, or more properly portland cement concrete, is one of the world's most versatile and widely used construction materials. Other construction applications, which range from its use in foundations for small structures, through structural components such as beams, columns, and wall panels, to massive concrete dams, are discussed in this chapter.

Because concrete has little strength in tension, virtually all concrete used for structural purposes contains reinforcing material embedded in the concrete to increase the concrete member's tensile strength. Such concrete is called *reinforced concrete*. While the steel reinforcing *(rebar)* described in Section 4 is most commonly used, metal and plastic fibers dispersed in the concrete mix are also available.

A typical distribution of concrete construction costs for a reinforced concrete building is shown in Figure 1. The objective of the construction manager should be to develop a construction plan which minimizes construction costs while meeting all safety and quality requirements. Major elements of a concrete construction cost analysis include the following:

Formwork costs including labor, equipment, and materials.

Cost of reinforcing steel and its placement.

Concrete materials, equipment, and labor for placing, curing, and finishing the concrete.

Since formwork cost may make up as much as 60% of total concrete construction cost, every effort must be made to reduce formwork cost using the methods suggested in Section 3.

Cast-in-Place Concrete

Concrete structural members have traditionally been built in-place by placing the plastic concrete into forms and allowing it to harden. The forms are removed after the concrete has developed sufficient strength to support its own weight and the weight of any construction loads. Typical shapes and types of concrete structural members are described in the following paragraphs. The construction and use of concrete forms are described in Section 3.

Walls and Wall Footings Although almost any type of concrete wall may be cast in-place, this method of construction is now used primarily for foundation walls, retaining walls, tank walls, and walls for special-purpose structures such as nuclear reactor containment structures. High-rise concrete structures often use a concrete column and beam framework with curtain wall panels inserted between these members to form the exterior walls. Columns are normally of either circular or rectangular cross section. Some typical cast-in-place wall and column shapes are illustrated in Figure 2. In placing concrete into wall and column forms, care must be taken to avoid segregation of aggregate and paste that may result from excessive freefall distances. Another problem frequently encountered in wall construction is the formation of void spaces in the concrete under blockouts for windows, pipe chases, and so on. This can be prevented by using concrete with adequate workability accompanied by careful tamping or vibration of the concrete in these areas during placing.

The relatively new technique of pumping concrete into vertical forms through the bottom of the form may also be used to eliminate the formation of voids in the concrete. Figure 3 shows a 2-ft (0.6-m)-square column form 18 ft (5.5 m) high being prepared for pumping. Notice the method of attachment of the pumping hose to the form shown in Figure 3b. When the form is filled to the

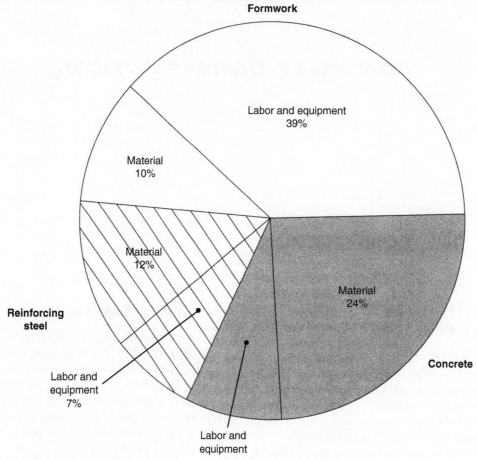

FIGURE 1. Typical distribution of concrete construction costs.

Rectangular column   Circular column

Foundation wall and footing   Circular tank wall

FIGURE 2. Typical cast-in-place column and wall shapes.

required height, the gate on the form fixture is closed and the pumping hose is removed.

Floors and Roofs   There are a number of different types of structural systems used for concrete floors and roofs. Such systems may be classified as one-way or two-way slabs. When the floor slab is principally supported in one direction (i.e., at each end), this is referred to as a *one-way slab. Two-way slabs* provide support in two perpendicular directions. Flat slabs are supported directly by columns without edge support.

One-Way Slabs.   Supporting beams, girders, and slabs may be cast at one time (monolithically), as illustrated in Figure 4a. However, columns are usually constructed prior to casting the girders, beams, and slabs to eliminate the effect of shrinkage of column concrete on the other members. This type of construction is referred to as *beam-and-slab* or as slab-beam-and-girder construction. Notice that the outside beam is referred to as a *spandrel beam.* When beams are replaced by more closely spaced joists, the type of construction illustrated in Figure 4b results. Joists may be either straight or tapered, as shown. The double joist in the

a. Preparation of form

b. Pumping hose in place on fixture at bottom of form

FIGURE 3. Pumping concrete into bottom of column form. (Courtesy of Gates & Sons, Inc.)

a. Slab-beam-and-girder floor

b. Concrete joist floor

FIGURE 4. Floor slab construction. (Courtesy of Concrete Reinforcing Steel Institute [CRSI])

illustration is used to carry the additional load imposed by the partition above it. Slabs may also be supported by nonintegral beams. Such supporting beams may be made of precast or cast-in-place concrete, timber, steel, or other materials. This type of construction is referred to as *solid slab construction*.

Two-Way Slabs. The principal type of two-way slab is the *waffle slab*, illustrated in Figure 5. Notice that this is basically a joist slab with joists running in two perpendicular directions.

Flat Slabs. Slabs may be supported directly by columns without the use of beams or joists. Such slabs are referred to as *flat slabs* or *flat plate slabs*. A flat plate slab is illustrated in Figure 6a. A flat slab is illustrated in Figure 6b. Note that the flat slab uses column capitals to distribute the column reaction over a larger area of slab, while the drop panels serve to strengthen the slab in this area of increased stress. Both of these measures reduce the danger of the column punching through the slab when the slab is loaded.

Precast Concrete

Precast concrete is concrete that has been cast into the desired shape prior to placement in a structure. There are a number of advantages obtained by removing the concrete forming, placing, finishing, and curing operations from the construction environment. Precasting operations usually

FIGURE 5. Waffle slab. (Courtesy of Concrete Reinforcing Steel Institute [CRSI])

FIGURE 6. Flat slab and flat plate slab. (Courtesy of Concrete Reinforcing Steel Institute [CRSI])

take place in a central plant where industrial production techniques may be used. Since standard shapes are commonly used, the repetitive use of formwork permits forms to be of high quality at a low cost per unit. These forms and plant finishing procedures provide better surface quality than is usually obtained in the field. Because of controlled environment and procedures, concrete quality control is also usually superior to that of cast-in-place concrete. Forming procedures used make it relatively simple to incorporate prestressing in structural members. Many of the common members described next are prestressed. Upon arrival at the job site, precast structural members may be erected much more rapidly than conventional cast-in-place components.

There are a number of standard shapes commonly used for precast concrete structural members. Figure 7 illustrates some common beam and girder sections. The inverted

tee shape is normally used with a cast-in-place concrete slab which forms the upper flange of the section.

Precast concrete joists and purlins (roof supports spanning between trusses or arches) are most often of the I- or T-section shape. Sizes commonly available provide depths of 8–12 in. (20–30 cm) and lengths of 10–20 ft (3–6 m). Precast roof and floor panels (often integral slabs and beams) include flat, hollow-core, tee, double-tee, and channel slabs. These shapes are illustrated in Figure 8. Concrete planks are commonly available in thicknesses of 1–4 in. (2.5–10.1 cm), widths of 15–32 in. (38–81 cm), and lengths of 4–10 ft (1.2–3 m). Hollow-core planks range from 4 to 12 in. (10–30 cm) in thickness, are usually 4–8 ft (1.2–2.4 m) wide, and range from 15 to 50 ft (4.6–15.3 m) in length. Channel slabs range from 2 to 5 ft (0.6–1.5 m) wide and from 15 to 50 ft (4.6–15.3 m) in length. Tee and double-tee slabs are available in widths of 4–12 ft (1.2–3.7 m) and spans of 12 ft (3.7 m) up to 100 ft (30.5 m).

Wall panels may also be precast, hauled to the site, and erected. However, the major use of precast wall panels (excluding tilt-up construction) is for curtain-wall construction, in which the panels fit between the structural framework to form exterior walls. In this type of construction, the walls serve to provide a weatherproof enclosure and transmit any wind loads to the frame. The building frame actually supports all loads.

Tilt-up construction is a special form of precast wall construction in which wall panels are cast horizontally at the job site and then erected. The wall panels are usually cast on the previously placed building floor slab using only edge forms to provide the panel shape. The floor slab thus serves as the bottom form for the panel. Panels may also be cast one on top of another where slab space is limited. A bond-breaker compound is applied to the slab to prevent the tilt-up panel from sticking to the slab. Figure 9 illustrates the major steps in a tilt-up construction project.

FIGURE 7. Precast beam and girder shapes.

FIGURE 8. Precast slab shapes.

Single tee

Double tee

Channel

Flat slab

Hollow-core slab

Some suggestions for obtaining the best results with tilt-up construction procedures include:

Do

- Pour a high-quality slab.
- Keep all plumbing and electrical conduits at least 1 in. under floor surface.
- Vibrate the slab thoroughly.
- Let cranes operate on the floor slab.
- Pour wall panels with their exterior face down.
- Use load-spreading frames when lifting panels that have been weakened by windows and other cutouts.

Don't

- Erect steel framework before raising wall panels.
- Fail to cure floor slab properly.
- Move crane farther than necessary when raising wall panels.
- Lay wall panels down after lifting.

Prestressed Concrete

Prestressed concrete is concrete to which an initial compression load has been applied. Since concrete is quite strong in compression but weak in tension, prestressing serves to increase the load that a beam or other flexural member can carry before allowable tensile stresses are reached. Figure 10 illustrates the stress pattern across a beam section resulting from external loads and prestressing. The use of prestressing in a concrete structural member permits a smaller, lighter member to be used in supporting a given load. Prestressing also reduces the amount of deflection in a beam. Since the member is always kept under compression, any cracking that does occur will remain closed up and not be apparent. These advantages of prestressing are offset somewhat by the higher

material, equipment, and labor cost involved in the production of prestressed components. Nevertheless, the use of prestressing, particularly in precast structural members, has become widespread.

There are two methods for producing prestress in concrete members: pretensioning and posttensioning. *Pretensioning* places the prestressing material (reinforcing steel or prestressing cables) under tension in the concrete form before the member is poured. After the concrete has hardened, the external tensioning devices are removed. Bonding between the concrete and the prestressing steel holds the prestressing in place and places the concrete under compression. *Posttensioning* places the prestressing steel (usually placed inside a metal or plastic tube cast into the member) under tension after the concrete member has been erected. The prestressing is then tensioned by jacks placed at each end of the member. After the prestressing load has been applied, the prestressing steel is anchored to the concrete member by mechanical devices at each end or by filling the prestressing tubes with a cementing agent. After the steel has been anchored to the member, jacks are removed and the prestressing steel is cut off flush with the ends of the member.

Caution must be observed in handling and transporting pretensioned prestressed members, particularly if they are asymmetrically stressed. In the beam of Figure 11, the prestressing has been placed off center in the lower portion of the beam. This placement better offsets the tension that would normally occur in the lower chord when the beam is loaded. If this beam were to be lifted at the top center, it would tend to bend as shown, resulting in tension along the top chord. The presence of the off-center compression load provided by the prestressing would serve to increase the tension in the top chord and may cause failure of the member prior to erection. Hence this type of beam should not be raised using a center lift. It should be lifted by the ends or by using multiple lift points along the beam.

217

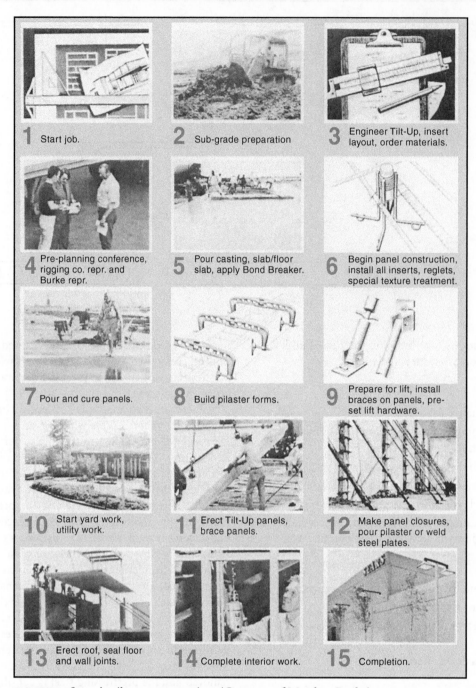

FIGURE 9. Steps in tilt-up construction. (Courtesy of Meadow Burke)

FIGURE 10. Stresses in a prestressed simple beam.

FIGURE 11. Lifting prestressed beam at the center.

FIGURE 12. Application of architectural concrete. (Courtesy of Portland Cement Association)

Architectural Concrete

The architectural use of concrete to provide appearance effects has greatly increased in recent years. Architectural effects are achieved by the shape, size, texture, and color used. An example of the use of shape and texture in a wall treatment is given in Figure 12. Here precast panels made from a mix of white quartz aggregate and white cement were applied to the exterior of the building frame to achieve the desired color and three-dimensional surface. The availability of plastic forms and form liners has made it possible to impart special shapes to concrete at a relatively low cost.

Some of the major methods used for obtaining architectural concrete effects include exposed aggregate surfaces (Figure 13a), special surface designs and textures achieved by the use of form liners (Figure 13b), and mechanically produced surfaces (Figure 14). Exposed aggregate surfaces are produced by removing the cement paste from the exterior surface, exposing the underlying aggregate. A method frequently used is to coat the interior surface of the form with a retarder. After the concrete has cured enough to permit the removal of the forms, the cement paste near the surface (whose curing has been retarded) is removed by brushing and washing or by sandblasting. In the case of horizontal surfaces, a retarder may be applied to the surface after final troweling. Surface textures and designs such as those illustrated in Figure 13b may be achieved by using form liners of plastic, rubber, or wood. Sandblasting or mechanical hammering may also be used to produce special surface effects. To achieve the surface texture of the building shown in Figure 14, a form liner was used to produce triangular surface ridges, which were then chipped with a hammer.

2 CONCRETE CONSTRUCTION PRACTICES

Concrete construction involves concrete batching, mixing, transporting, placing, consolidating, finishing, and curing. In this section, we will discuss the equipment and methods involved in placing, consolidating, finishing, and curing concrete used for structural purposes. Special considerations for pouring concrete during extremely hot or cold weather are also described.

Transporting and Handling

A number of different items of equipment are available for moving concrete from the mixer to its final position. Equipment commonly used includes wheelbarrows, buggies, chutes, conveyors, pumps, buckets, and trucks. Regardless of the equipment used, care must be taken to avoid segregation when handling plastic concrete. The height of free fall should be limited to about 5 ft (1.5 m) unless downpipes or ladders are used to prevent segregation. Downpipes having a length of at least 2 ft (0.6 m) should be used at the end of concrete conveyors.

Wheelbarrows have a very limited capacity (about $1\frac{1}{2}$ cu ft or 0.04 m³) but are often used for transporting and placing small amounts of concrete. Push buggies that carry 6–11 cu ft (0.17–0.31 m³) and powered buggies carrying up to ½ cu yd (0.38 m³) are often employed on building construction projects. However, these items of equipment are gradually being replaced by concrete pumps capable of

a. Exposed aggregate   b. Pattern produced by a form liner

FIGURE 13. Architectural concrete surfaces. (Courtesy of Portland Cement Association)

FIGURE 14. Mechanically produced concrete surface texture. (Courtesy of Portland Cement Association)

moving concrete from a truck directly into final position up to heights of 500 ft (152 m) or more. Truck-mounted concrete pumps equipped with placement booms such as that shown in Figure 15 are widely used in building construction.

Concrete conveyors are available to move concrete either horizontally or vertically. Chutes are widely used for moving concrete from the mixer to haul units and for placing concrete into forms. Truck mixers are equipped with integral retracting chutes that may be used for discharging concrete directly into forms within the radius of the chute. When chuting concrete, the slope of the chute must be high enough to keep the chute clean but not high enough to produce segregation of the concrete. Concrete buckets attached to cranes

FIGURE 15. Concrete pump and truck mixer. (Courtesy of Morgen Manufacturing Co.)

are capable of lifting concrete to the top of high-rise buildings and of moving concrete over a wide area. Concrete buckets are equipped with a bottom gate and a release mechanism for unloading concrete at the desired location. The unloading mechanism may be powered or may be operated manually. The use of remotely controlled power-operated bucket gates reduces the safety hazard involved in placing concrete above ground level.

Although truck mixers are most often employed for hauling plastic concrete to the job site, dump trucks equipped with special concrete bodies are also available for hauling concrete. The bodies of such trucks are designed to reduce segregation during hauling and provide easy cleaning and dumping. When using nonagitator trucks for hauling concrete, specifications may limit the truck speed and maximum haul distance that may be used. Temperature, road condition, truck body type, and mix design are the major factors that influence the maximum safe hauling distance. Railway cars designed for hauling concrete are also available but are not widely used.

Placing and Consolidating

The movement of plastic concrete into its final position (usually within forms) is called *placing*. Before placing concrete, the underlying surface and the interior of all concrete forms must be properly prepared. Concrete forms must be clean and tight and their interior surfaces coated with form oil or a parting agent to allow removal of the form from the hardened concrete without damaging the surface of the concrete.

When concrete is poured directly onto a subgrade, the subgrade should be moistened or sealed by a moisture barrier to prevent the subgrade from absorbing water from the plastic concrete. When placing fresh concrete on top of hardened concrete, the surface of the hardened concrete should be roughened to provide an adequate bond between the two concrete layers. To improve bonding between the layers, the surface of the hardened concrete should also be coated with grout or a layer of mortar before the fresh concrete is placed. Concrete is usually placed in layers 6–24 in. (15–61 cm) thick except when pumping into the bottom of forms. When placing concrete in layers, care must be taken to ensure that the lower layer does not take its initial set before the next layer is poured.

The strength, watertightness, durability, and wear resistance of concrete are largely determined by the water/cement ratio of the concrete mix. Therefore, do not allow construction crews or transit mix operators to add additional water to the mix for the purpose of increasing the workability of the plastic concrete. If a more workable mix is needed, the mix design should be modified accordingly. The addition of one of the workability agents should provide plastic concrete with acceptable workability.

Concrete may also be pneumatically placed by spraying it onto a surface. Concrete placed by this process is designated *shotcrete* by the American Concrete Institute but is also called *pneumatically applied concrete, gunned concrete,* or *gunite.* Since a relatively dry mix is used, shotcrete may be applied to overhead and vertical surfaces. As a result, shotcrete is often used for constructing tanks, swimming pools, and tunnel liners, as well as for repairing damaged concrete structures.

Concrete may be placed underwater by the use of a tremie or by pumping. A *tremie* is nothing more than a vertical tube with a gate at the bottom and a hopper on top. In operation the tremie tube must be long enough to permit the concrete hopper to remain above water when the lower end of the tremie is placed at the desired location. With the gate closed, the tremie is filled with concrete and lowered into position. The gate is then opened, allowing concrete to flow into place. The pressure of the plastic concrete inside the tremie prevents water from flowing into the tremie. The tremie is raised as concrete is poured, but care must be taken to keep the bottom end of the tremie immersed in the plastic concrete.

Consolidation is the process of removing air voids in concrete as it is placed. Concrete vibrators are normally used for consolidating concrete, but hand rodding or spading may be employed. Immersion-type electric, pneumatic, or hydraulic concrete vibrators are widely used. However, form vibrators or vibrators attached to the outside of the concrete forms are sometimes employed. Vibrators should not be used to move concrete horizontally, as this practice may produce segregation of the concrete mix. Vibrators should be inserted into the concrete vertically and allowed to penetrate several inches into the previously placed layer of concrete. The vibrator should be withdrawn and moved to another location when cement paste becomes visible at the top of the vibrator.

Finishing and Curing

Finishing is the process of bringing the surface of concrete to its final position and imparting the desired surface texture. Finishing operations include screeding, floating, troweling, and brooming. *Screeding* is the process of striking off the concrete in order to bring the concrete surface to the required grade. When the concrete has hardened sufficiently so that a worker's foot makes only a small impression in the surface, the concrete is floated with a wood or metal float. *Floating* smooths and compacts the surface while embedding aggregate particles. *Troweling* with a steel trowel follows floating when a smooth dense surface is desired. A three-unit riding-type power trowel is shown in Figure 16. Finally, the concrete may be *broomed* by drawing a stiff broom across the surface. This technique is used when a textured skid-resistant surface is desired.

The completion of cement hydration requires that adequate moisture and favorable temperatures be maintained after concrete is placed. The process of providing the required water and maintaining a favorable temperature for a period of time after placing concrete is referred to as *curing*. Methods for maintaining proper concrete temperatures in hot-weather and cold-weather concreting are described in this chapter. Methods used to retain adequate curing moisture include covering the concrete surface with wet straw or burlap, ponding water on the surface, covering the surface with paper or plastic sheets, and applying curing compounds. The use of sprayed-on curing compounds applied immediately after finishing has become widespread in recent years.

Vacuum dewatering may be employed to reduce the amount of free water present in plastic concrete after the

FIGURE 16. Ride-on power trowel. (Courtesy of Wacker Corporation)

concrete has been placed and screeded. The dewatering process involves placing a mat having a porous lower surface on top of the concrete and applying a vacuum to the mat. Vacuum within the mat causes excess water from the mix to flow into the mat and eventually to the vacuum source. Removal of excess water results in a lower water/cement ratio and a denser mix. Floating and troweling then follow as usual. In concept, vacuum dewatering permits placing concrete with a high water content (for good workability) while obtaining the strength and durability of concrete with a low water/cement ratio. Other advantages claimed for concrete placed by this method include high early strength, increased ultimate strength and wear resistance, reduced shrinkage, reduced permeability, and increased resistance to freeze/thaw damage. While the vacuum dewatering process was invented and patented in the United States in 1935, it has not been widely used in this country. Recent improvements in the equipment used for the process have led to increased use of the process in both Europe and the United States.

When constructing large slabs and decks, concrete may be placed by chutes, buckets, or side discharge conveyors. Mechanical finishing may be supplied by roller finishers, oscillating strike-off finishers, large power floats, or other types of finishers. Figure 17 shows a large slab being poured directly from a truck mixer and finished by a roller finisher.

Hot-Weather Concreting

The rate of hardening of concrete is greatly accelerated when concrete temperature is appreciably higher than the optimum temperature of 50–60°F (10–15.5°C). Ninety degrees

FIGURE 17. Roller finisher being used on large slab pour. (Courtesy of Terex Roadbuilding)

Fahrenheit (32°C) is considered a reasonable upper limit for concreting operations. In addition to reducing setting time, higher temperatures reduce the amount of slump for a given mix. If additional water is added to obtain the desired slump, additional cement must also be added or the water–cement ratio will be increased with corresponding strength reduction. High temperatures, especially when accompanied by winds and low humidity, greatly increase the shrinkage of concrete and often lead to surface cracking of the concrete. Several steps may be taken to reduce the effect of high temperatures on concreting operation. The temperature of the plastic concrete may be lowered by cooling the mixing water and/or aggregates before mixing. Heat gain during hydration may be reduced by using Type IV (low-heat) cement or by adding a retarder. Air-entraining agents, water-reducing agents, or workability agents may be used to increase the workability of the mix without changing water/cement ratios. It is also advisable to reduce the maximum time before discharge of ready-mixed concrete from the normal $1\frac{1}{2}$ to 1 h or less. The use of shades or covers will be helpful in controlling the temperature of concrete after placement. Moist curing should start immediately after finishing and continue for at least 24 h.

Cold-Weather Concreting

The problems of cold-weather concreting are essentially opposite to those of hot-weather concreting. Concrete should not be placed on a frozen surface and must not be allowed to freeze during the first 24 h after placing to avoid permanent damage and loss of strength. Concrete forms and reinforcing steel should be free of frost, ice, and snow and at a temperature above freezing. Specifications often require that, when air temperature is 40°F (5°C) or less, concrete be placed at a minimum temperature of 50°F (10°C) and that this temperature be maintained for at least 3 days after placing. However, the American Concrete Institute (ACI) recommends that a temperature of 70°F (21°C) be maintained for 3 days or 50°F (10°C) be maintained for 5 days after pouring to ensure that the concrete will attain its design strength. Type III (high early strength) cement or an accelerator may be used to reduce concrete setting time during low temperatures. The air content of the concrete mix should be checked to ensure that the air content does not exceed mix design specifications. Mix water and/or aggregates may be heated prior to mixing to raise the temperature of the plastic concrete. However, cement should not be allowed to contact hot water. Therefore, the aggregate should be mixed with the heated water prior to adding cement to the mix. The use of unvented heaters inside an enclosure during the first 36 h after placing may cause the concrete surface to dust after hardening. To avoid this problem, any fuel-burning heaters used during this period must be properly vented. When heat is used for curing, the concrete must be allowed to cool gradually at the end of the heating period or cracking may result.

3 CONCRETE FORMWORK

General Requirements for Formwork

The principal requirements for concrete formwork are that it be safe, produce the desired shape and surface texture, and be economical. Construction procedures relating to

FIGURE 18. Typical wall form.

formwork safety are discussed later in this section. Requirements for the shape (including deflection limitations) and surface texture of the finished concrete are normally contained in the construction plans and specifications. Since the cost of concrete formwork often exceeds the cost of the concrete itself, the necessity for economy in formwork is readily apparent.

Typical Formwork

A typical *wall form* with its components is illustrated in Figure 18. Sheathing may be either plywood or lumber. Double wales are often used as illustrated so that form ties may be inserted between the two wales. With a single wale, it would be necessary to drill the wales for tie insertion. While the pressure of the plastic concrete is resisted by form ties, bracing must be used to prevent form movement and to provide support against wind loads or other lateral loads. Typical form ties are illustrated in Figure 19. Form ties may incorporate a spreader device to maintain proper spacing between form walls until the concrete is placed. Otherwise, a removable spreader bar

must be used for this purpose. Ties are of two principal types, continuous single-member and internally disconnecting. *Continuous single-member ties* may be pulled out after the concrete has hardened or they may be broken off at a weakened point just below the surface after the forms are removed. Common types of *internally disconnecting ties* include the coil tie and stud rod (or she-bolt) tie. With internally disconnecting ties, the ends are unscrewed to permit form removal with the internal section left embedded in the concrete. The holes remaining in the concrete surface after the ends of the ties are removed are later plugged or grouted.

Column forms are similar to wall forms except that studs and wales are replaced by column clamps or yokes that resist the internal concrete pressure. A typical column form is shown in Figure 20. Yokes may be fabricated of wood, wood and bolts (as shown), or of metal. Commercial column clamps (usually of metal) are available in a wide range of sizes (Figure 3). Round columns are formed with ready-made fiber tubes or steel reinforced fiberglass forms. Openings or "windows" may be provided at several elevations in high, narrow forms to facilitate placement of concrete. Special fittings may also be inserted near the bottom of vertical forms to permit pumping concrete into the form from the bottom.

FIGURE 19. Typical form ties.

Snap point Spreader Wedge

Snap tie with washer spreader

Coil Cone Bolt

Washer

Coil tie with cone spreader

Tie rod Stud rod Nut washer

Stud rod (she-bolt) tie

Sheathing

Bolts

Wedge

FIGURE 20. Typical column form. (U.S. Department of the Army)

Figure 21 illustrates a typical elevated floor or desk slab form with its components identified. Forming for a slab with an integral beam is illustrated in Figure 22. Forming for the one-way and two-way slabs described in Section 1 is usually accomplished using commercial pan forms. Figure 23 illustrates the use of long pans for a one-way joist slab. Figure 24 shows a waffle slab formed with dome pans. Such pan forms may be made of metal or plastic. Wooden stairway forms suitable for constructing stairways up to 3 ft wide are illustrated in Figure 25.

Minimizing Cost of Formwork

Since formwork may account for 40–60% of the cost of concrete construction, it is essential that the formwork plan be carefully developed and thoroughly evaluated. A cost comparison should be made of all feasible forming systems and methods of operation. Such an analysis must include the cost of equipment and labor required to install reinforcing steel and to place and finish the concrete, as well as the cost of formwork, its erection, and removal. The formwork plan that provides the required safety and construction quality at the minimum overall cost should be selected for implementation.

FIGURE 21. Form for elevated slab. (Courtesy of American Concrete Institute)

In general, lower formwork cost will result from repetitive use of forms. Multipleuse forms may be either standard commercial types or custom-made by the contractor. Contractor-fabricated forms should be constructed using assembly-line techniques whenever possible. *Flying forms,* large sections of formwork moved by crane from one position to another, are often economical in repetitive types of concrete construction. Where appropriate, the use of slip forms and the tilt-up construction techniques described earlier can greatly reduce forming costs. A flying form is pictured in Figure 26.

Construction Practices

Forms must be constructed with tight joints to prevent the loss of cement paste, which may result in honeycombing. Before concrete is placed, forms must be aligned both horizontally and vertically and braced to remain in alignment. Form alignment should be continuously monitored during concrete placement, and adjustments made if necessary. When a vertical form is wider at the bottom than at the top, an uplift force will be created as the form is filled. Such

forms must be anchored against uplift. Inspect the interior of all forms and remove any debris before placing concrete. Use drop chutes or rubber elephant trunks to avoid segregation of aggregate and paste when placing concrete into high vertical forms. Free-fall distance should be limited to 5 ft or less. When vibrating concrete in vertical forms, allow the vibrator head to penetrate through the freshly placed concrete about 1 in. (2.5 cm) [but not more than 8 in. (20 cm)] into the previously placed layer of concrete. It is possible to bulge or rupture any wall or column form by inserting a large vibrator deep into previously placed, partially set concrete. However, revibration of previously compacted concrete is not harmful to the concrete as long as it becomes plastic when vibrated. When pumping forms from the bottom, it is important to fill the forms rapidly so that the concrete does not start to set up before filling is completed. If the pump rate is so low that setting begins, excessive pressure will be produced inside the form, resulting in bulging or rupturing of the form.

Concrete forms are removed after the concrete has developed the required strength. When removing (or *stripping*) concrete forms, care must be taken to minimize

FIGURE 22. Beam and slab form. (Courtesy of American Concrete Institute)

FIGURE 23. One-way slab form. (Courtesy of American Concrete Institute)

damage to the surface of the concrete during the removal process.

Expansion and Control Joints

Expansion and control joints are used to permit differential movement of wall sections, columns, and slabs caused by concrete shrinkage, temperature and moisture changes, and foundation settlement. Interior columns should be isolated from floor slabs by either providing a blockout in the floor slab around the column before placing the slab or forming a pinwheel isolation joint at the column. To construct a pinwheel isolation joint, contraction or construction joints are placed around the column at 90? angles to each other in line with the column sides. In either method, the column is wrapped with a preformed joint filler before placing concrete around the column.

227

FIGURE 24. Two-way slab form. (Courtesy of American Concrete Institute)

Formwork Safety

The frequency and serious consequences of formwork failure require that special attention be paid to this aspect of construction safety. The following are some safety precautions that should be observed in constructing formwork:

1. Provide adequate foundations for all formwork. Place mudsills under all shoring that rests on the ground. Typical mudsills are illustrated in Figure 27. Check surrounding excavations to ensure that formwork does not fail due to embankment failure.

2. Provide adequate bracing of forms, being particularly careful of shores and other vertical supports. Ensure that all connections are properly secured, especially nailed connections. Vibration from power buggies or concrete vibrators may cause connections to loosen or supports to move.

3. Control the rate and location of concrete placement so that design loads are not exceeded.

4. Ensure that forms and supports are not removed before the concrete has developed the required strength. The process of placing temporary shores under slabs or structural members after forms have been stripped is called *reshoring*. Reshoring is a critical operation that must be carried out exactly as specified by the designer. Only a limited area should be stripped and reshored at one time. No construction loads should be allowed on the partially hardened concrete while reshoring is under way. Adequate bracing must be provided for reshoring.

5. When placing prefabricated form sections in windy weather, care must be taken to avoid injury caused by swinging of the form caused by wind forces.

6. Protruding nails are a major source of injury on concrete construction sites. As forms are stripped, form lumber must be promptly removed to a safe location and nails pulled.

4 REINFORCING STEEL

Concrete Reinforcing Steel

Concrete reinforcing steel is available as standard reinforcing bars, spirals (for column reinforcing), and welded wire fabric (WWF).

FIGURE 25. Wood form for stairway. (U.S. Department of the Army)

FIGURE 26. Repositioning flying form. (Courtesy of CMI Terex Corporation)

Reinforcing Bars *Reinforcing bars* are usually deformed; that is, they are manufactured with ridges that provide an interlocking bond with the surrounding concrete. Deformed bars are available in the 11 American Society for Testing and Materials (ASTM) standard sizes listed in Table 1. Note that the size number of the bar indicates the approximate diameter of the bar in eighths of an inch (millimeters for metric sizes).

Marking systems used to identify standard reinforcing bars are illustrated in Figure 28. The top letter or symbol identifies the producing mill. The second symbol represent the bar size (in conventional units for Grade 60 or 75, in metric units for Grades 420 or 520). The third symbol indicates the steel type: S for carbon steel (ASTM A615) or W for low-alloy steel (ASTM A706). Next, the steel grade is indicated in conventional units by a number or by one or two lines running the length of the bar. Grade 60 (60 ksi yield strength) is indicated by the number 60 or by one line running the length of the bar, Grade 75 (75 ksi yield strength) is indicated by the number 75 or by two lines running the length of the bar. The metric equivalent for Grade 60 is Grade 420 (420 MPa yield strength) and for Grade 75 is Grade 520 (520 MPa yield strength). Grade 420 may be indicated by the bar marking 4 or by one line running the length of the bar, while Grade 520 is indicated by the bar marking 5 or by two lines running the length of the bar.

Welded Wire Fabric *Welded wire fabric,* commonly used for slab reinforcement, is available with smooth wire or deformed wire. Fabric is made from bright wire unless galvanized wire is specified.

Welded wire fabric is identified by the letters WWF followed by the spacing of longitudinal wires [in. (mm)], the spacing of transverse wires [in. (mm)], the size of longitudinal wires [sq in. 100 (mm²)], and the size of transverse wires

FIGURE 27. Mudsills. (Courtesy of American Concrete Institute)

Table 1. ASTM standard reinforcing bar sizes

Size Number	Metric Size Number	Weight		Diameter		Section Area	
		lb/ft	kg/m	in.	mm	sq in.	mm²
3	10	0.376	0.560	0.375	9.52	0.11	71
4	13	0.668	0.994	0.500	12.70	0.20	129
5	16	1.043	1.552	0.625	15.88	0.31	200
6	19	1.502	2.235	0.750	19.05	0.44	284
7	22	2.044	3.042	0.875	22.22	0.60	387
8	25	2.670	3.973	1.000	25.40	0.79	510
9	29	3.400	5.059	1.128	28.65	1.00	645
10	32	4.303	6.403	1.270	32.26	1.27	819
11	36	5.313	7.906	1.410	35.81	1.56	1006
14	43	7.650	11.384	1.693	43.00	2.25	1452
18	57	13.600	20.238	2.257	57.33	4.00	2581

FIGURE 28. Reinforcing bar identification marks. (Courtesy of Concrete Reinforcing Steel Institute [CRSI])

[sq in. × 100 (mm²)]. Metric sizes are identified by the letter M preceding the wire sizes. Standard wire sizes are given in Table 2. Deformed wire is indicated by the letter D preceding the wire size. For example, "WWF 6 × 6 − 4.0 × 4.0 [152 × 152 MW 25.8 × MW 25.8]" denotes a square wire pattern with both transverse and longitudinal wires spaced 6 in. (152 mm) on center. Both wires are size W4 [0.04-sq in.

(25.8-mm²) section area]. Requirements for welded wire fabric are given in ASTM A185 and A497.

Spirals Spirals are available in three standard rod sizes: ³⁄₈ in. (0.95 cm), ¹⁄₂ in. (1.27 cm), and ⁵⁄₈ in. (1.59 cm) in diameter. Standard spiral diameters (outside to outside) range from 12 in. (30 cm) to 33 in. (84 cm). Pitch (distance

Table 2. Steel wire data for welded wire fabric

Wire Size Number		Diameter		Area		Weight	
Smooth	Deformed	in.	mm	sq in.	mm²	lb/ft	kg/m
W31	D31	0.628	16.0	0.31	200	1.054	1.568
W28	D28	0.597	15.2	0.28	181	0.952	1.417
W26	D26	0.575	14.6	0.26	168	0.934	1.390
W24	D24	0.553	14.1	0.24	155	0.816	1.214
W22	D22	0.529	13.4	0.22	142	0.748	1.113
W20	D20	0.505	12.8	0.20	129	0.680	1.012
W18	D18	0.479	12.2	0.18	116	0.612	0.911
W16	D16	0.451	11.5	0.16	103	0.544	0.810
W14	D14	0.422	10.7	0.14	90	0.476	0.708
W12	D12	0.391	9.9	0.12	77	0.408	0.607
W11	D11	0.374	9.5	0.11	71	0.374	0.557
W10	D10	0.357	9.1	0.10	65	0.340	0.506
W9.5		0.348	8.8	0.095	61	0.323	0.481
W9	D9	0.338	8.6	0.09	58	0.306	0.455
W8.5		0.329	8.4	0.085	55	0.289	0.430
W8	D8	0.319	8.1	0.08	52	0.272	0.405
W7.5		0.309	7.8	0.075	48	0.255	0.379
W7	D7	0.299	7.6	0.07	45	0.238	0.354
W6.5		0.288	7.3	0.065	42	0.221	0.329
W6	D6	0.276	7.0	0.06	39	0.204	0.304
W5.5		0.265	6.7	0.055	35	0.187	0.278
W5	D5	0.252	6.4	0.05	32	0.170	0.253
W4.5		0.239	6.1	0.045	29	0.153	0.228
W4	D4	0.226	5.7	0.04	26	0.136	0.202
W3.5		0.211	5.4	0.035	23	0.119	0.177
W2.9		0.192	4.9	0.029	19	0.099	0.147
W2.5		0.178	4.5	0.025	16	0.085	0.126
W2		0.160	4.1	0.02	13	0.068	0.101
W1.4		0.134	3.4	0.014	9	0.048	0.071

between centers of adjacent spirals) ranges from 1¾ in. (4.4 cm) to 3¼ in. (8.3 cm) by ¼-in. (0.64-cm) increments. Steel grades available include grades 40, 60, and 70.

Placement of Reinforcing

Since concrete is weak in resistance to tensile forces, reinforcing steel is used primarily to resist tension and thus prevent cracking or failure of the concrete member under tension. Tension may be induced by shrinkage of concrete as it hardens and by temperature changes as well as by bending and shear forces. Typical placement of reinforcing steel in concrete structural members is illustrated in Figure 29.

To provide protection of reinforcing steel against corrosion and fire, a minimum cover of concrete must be furnished. Building codes usually specify minimum cover requirements. The American Concrete Institute (ACI) recommends the following minimum cover when not otherwise specified:

- Slabs, joists, and walls not exposed to weather or ground: ¾ in. (1.9 cm).
- Beams, girders, and columns not exposed to weather or ground: 1½ in. (3.8 cm).
- Concrete placed in forms but exposed to weather or ground: 1½ in. (3.8 cm) for No. 5 bars or smaller; 2 in. (5.1 cm) for bars larger than No. 5.
- Concrete placed without forms directly on the ground: 3 in. (7.6 cm).
- At least one bar diameter of cover should be used in any case.

Reinforcing steel must be placed within the tolerances specified by the designer. General placement tolerances suggested

FIGURE 29. Placement of reinforcing steel. (Courtesy of Concrete Reinforcing Steel Institute [CSRI])

by the Concrete Reinforcing Steel Institute (CRSI) include the following:

- Spacing of outside top, bottom, and side bars in beams, joists, and slabs: $\pm\frac{1}{4}$ in. (0.64 cm).

- Lengthwise position of bar ends:
  Sheared bars ±2 in. (5.1 cm).
  Bars with hooked ends $\pm\frac{1}{2}$ in. (1.3 cm).

- Horizontal spacing of bars in slabs and walls: ±1 in. (2.5 cm).

- Stirrup spacing (distance between adjacent stirrups): ±1 in. (2.5 cm).

The minimum clear distance between parallel bars in columns should be the greater of $1\frac{1}{2}$ bar diameters, $1\frac{1}{2}$ in. (3.8 cm), or $1\frac{1}{2}$ times the maximum aggregate size. For other than columns, the minimum clear distance between parallel bars should be the greater of one bar diameter, 1 in. (2.5 cm), or $1\frac{1}{3}$ times the maximum aggregate size. Bars are maintained in their specified position by tying to adjacent bars or by the use of bar supports. Standard types and

Typical types and sizes of wire bar supports

SYMBOL	BAR SUPPORT ILLUSTRATION	BAR SUPPORT ILLUSTRATION PLASTIC TIPPED	TYPE OF SUPPORT	TYPICAL SIZES
SB	5"	TIPPED 5"	Slab Bolster	¾, 1, 1½, 2, and 3 in. heights in 5 ft and 10 ft lengths
SBU*	5"		Slab Bolster Upper	Same as SB
BB	2½" 2½"	TIPPED 2½" 2½"	Beam Bolster	1, 1½, 2 to 5 in. heights in increments of 1/4 in. in lengths of 5 ft
BBU*	2½" 2½"		Beam Bolster Upper	Same as BB
BC		TIPPED	Individual Bar Chair	¾, 1, 1½, 1¾ and 2 in. heights
JC		TIPPED TIPPED	Joist Chair	4, 5, and 6 in. widths and ¾, 1 and 1½ in. heights
HC		TIPPED	Individual High Chair	2 to 15 in. heights in increments of ¼ in.
HCM*			High Chair for Metal Deck	2 to 15 in. heights in increments of ¼ in.
CHC	7½"	TIPPED 7½"	Continuous High Chair	Same as HC in 5 ft and 10 ft lengths
CHCU*	7½"		Continuous High Chair Upper	Same as CHC
CHCM*			Continuous High Chair for Metal Deck	Up to 5 in. heights in increments of ¼ in.
JCU**	Top of slab #4 [13] or ½"φ ¾" min. Height 14"	TIPPED Top of slab #4 [13] or ½"φ ¾" min. Height 14"	Joist Chair Upper	14 in. span; heights -1 in. thru + 3½ in. vary in ¼ in. increments
CS			Continuous Support	1½ to 12 in. in increments of ¼ in. in lengths of 6'-8"
SBC			Single Bar Centralizer (Friction)	6in. to 24 in. diameter

* Usually available in Class 3 only, except on special order.
** Usually available in Class 3 only, with upturned or end-bearing legs.

1 in. = 25.4 mm
1 ft = 304.8 mm

FIGURE 30. Wire bar supports. (Courtesy of Concrete Reinforcing Steel Institute [CSRI])

sizes of wire bar supports are illustrated in Figure 30. Figure 31 illustrates the CRSI-suggested sequence for placing reinforcing steel in a deep, heavily reinforced concrete beam when a preassembled reinforcing cage cannot be used.

5 QUALITY CONTROL

Common Deficiencies in Concrete Construction

Adequate quality control must be exercised over concrete operations if concrete of the required strength, durability, and appearance is to be obtained. Quality control measures specifically applicable to formwork are described in Section 3. Deficiencies in concrete construction practice may usually be traced to inadequate supervision of construction operations. A review by the U.S. Army Corps of Engineers has produced the following ist of repetitive deficiencies observed in concrete construction:

Structural Concrete

1. Unstable form bracing and poor form alignment evidenced by form bulging, spreading, or inaccurately aligned members.

2. Poor alignment of reinforcing steel and exceeding prescribed tolerances.

3. Obvious cold joints in walls.

Typical types and sizes of all-plastic bar supports

SYMBOL	BAR SUPPORT ILLUSTRATION	TYPE OF SUPPORT	TYPICAL SIZES, IN.	DESCRIPTION
BS		Bottom Support	Heights, ¾ to 6	Generally for horizontal work. Not recommended for ground or exposed aggregate finish.
BS-CL		Bottom Support	Heights, ¾ to 2	Generally for horizontal work, provides bar clamping action. Not recommended for ground or exposed aggregate finish.
HC		High Chair	Heights, ¾ to 6	For use in slabs or panels.
HC-V		High Chair, Variable	Heights, 2½ to 7¾	For horizontal and vertical work. Provides for different heights.
WS		Wheel Side-Form Spacer	Concrete cover, ¾ to 3	Generally for vertical work. Bar clamping action and minimum contact with forms. Applicable for column reinforcing bars.
DSWS		Side-Form Spacer for drilled shaft applications	Concrete cover, 2½ to 6	Generally used to align reinforcing bars in a drilled shaft.* Two-piece wheel that closes and locks on to the tie or spiral assuring proper clearance from the shaft wall surface.
VLWS		Locking Wheel Side-Form Spacer for all vertical applications	Concrete cover, ¾ to 6	Generally used in both drilled shaft and vertical applications where heavy loading occurs. Surface spines provide minimal contact while maintaining required tolerance.
DSBB		Bottom Bolster (Gripping)	Concrete cover, 3; Height, 6	Used to keep the reinforcing bar cage off of the bottom of a drilled shaft.* Fits #6 through #14 [#19 through #43] reinforcing bars.
SB		Slab Bolster	Heights ¾ to 3; Lengths up to 30**	Commonly used in horizontal and vertical applications. When used as a side-form spacer in vertical work, slab bolster must be tied to the reinforcement.
HDHC		Heavy Duty High Chair	Heights, 2¾ to 14	For use in slabs, or on grade with plate.
OGC		On Grade Chair	Heights, 1½ to 6¼	Used primarily on grade.
SBU		Slab Bolster Upper	Heights, 1 to 3¼; Lengths up to 30	Commonly used in supporting the upper mat in a double mat application.

* Also known as a pier, caisson or cast-in drilled hole.
** Pieces can be locked together to form longer lengths.

1 inch = 25.4 mm

FIGURE 30. Continued

4. Excessively honeycombed wall areas.
5. Belated form tie removal, form stripping, and patching.
6. Inadequate compaction (mechanical vibration, rodding, or spading).

Concrete Slabs on Grade

1. Poor compaction of subgrade evidenced by slab settlement.
2. Saturation and damage to subgrade caused by water standing around foundation walls and/or inadequate storm drainage.
3. Uneven floor slab finishes.
4. Inadequate curing of floor slabs.

Inspection and Testing

The inspection and testing associated with concrete quality control may be grouped into five phases. These include mix design; concrete materials quality; batching, mixing, and transporting concrete; concrete placing, vibrating, finishing, and curing; and testing of fresh and hardened concrete at the job site. Mix design includes the quantity of each component in the mix, the type and gradation of aggregates, the type of cement, and so on. Aggregate testing includes tests for organic impurities and excessive fines, gradation, resistance to abrasion, and aggregate moisture. Control of concrete production includes accuracy of batching and the mixing procedures used. With modern

FIGURE 31. Placing reinforcing steel in a beam. (Courtesy of Concrete Reinforcing Steel Institute [CRSI])

concrete production equipment, the producer's quality control procedures and certification that specifications have been met may be all that is required in the way of production quality control. Transporting, placing, finishing, and curing procedures should be checked for compliance with specifications and with the general principles explained earlier.

Testing of concrete delivered to the job site involves testing of plastic concrete and performing strength tests on hardened concrete. The principal tests performed on plastic concrete include the slump test and tests for air and cement content. The temperature of plastic concrete should be checked for hot- or cold-weather concreting. The strength of hardened concrete is determined by compression tests on cylinder samples, by tensile splitting tests, or by flexure tests. Such tests are usually made after 7 and 28 days of curing. Standard cylinders used for compression tests are 6 in. (15.2 cm) in diameter by 12 in. (30.5 cm) high. Beam samples for flexure tests are usually 6 in. (15.2 cm) square by 20 in. (50.8 cm) long.

A procedure for evaluating compression tests results, which is recommended by the American Concrete Institute, is contained in ACI 214.

Recent developments in concrete testing technology have greatly reduced the time required to obtain results from on-site testing of plastic concrete. For example, a nuclear water/cement gauge is now available which measures the cement content, water content, and water/cement ratio of plastic concrete within 15 min. When the relationship between the water/cement ratio and 28-day compressive strength of a concrete has been previously established, the ultimate compressive strength of a concrete being placed can be quickly predicted using the on-site reading from the nuclear water/cement gauge.

Problems

1. When placing parallel No. 8 (metric no. 25) reinforcing bars in a column form, what minimum clear distance between bars should be obtained if the maximum concrete aggregate size is 2 in. (51 mm)?

2. What purpose do form ties serve in a concrete wall form?

3. Give at least three major safety precautions which should be observed in constructing and utilizing concrete formwork.

4. What component usually accounts for the largest portion of concrete construction cost for a reinforced concrete building?

5. What tests may be performed on plastic concrete delivered to the job site to ensure that it meets specification requirements? How might a rapid strength test be performed on plastic concrete?

6. Explain the importance of the water/cement ratio of a concrete mix in determining the properties of the resulting concrete.

7. Why should interior columns be isolated from floor slabs? How is this usually accomplished?

8. What are the principal requirements that concrete formwork must satisfy?

9. A steel reinforcing bar contains the markings "B 8 N 60." What is the size and strength of the bar?

10. Develop a computer program to determine the minimum concrete cover over reinforcing bars, the minimum clear distance between parallel reinforcing bars, and the placement tolerances for a specified reinforced concrete design.

References

1. Collins, Michael P., and Denis Mitchell. *Prestressed Concrete Structures.* Upper Saddle River, NJ: Prentice Hall, 1991.

2. *Color and Texture in Architectural Concrete* (SP021AC). Portland Cement Association, Skokie, IL.

3. *Concrete Construction* (Compilation No. 2). American Concrete Institute, Detroit, MI, 1968.

4. *Concrete Forming.* APA-The Engineered Wood Association, Tacoma, WA.

5. *CRSI Handbook,* 8th ed. Concrete Reinforcing Steel Institute, Schaumburg, IL, 1996.

6. *Design and Control of Concrete Mixtures,* 14th ed. Portland Cement Association, Skokie, IL, 2002.

7. "Guide to Troubleshooting Concrete Forming and Shoring Problems," *Concrete Construction,* vol. 24, no. 8 (1979).

8. Hurd, M. K. *Formwork for Concrete* (ACI SP-4), 7th ed. American Concrete Institute, Farmington, MI, 2005.

9. *Manual of Standard Practice,* 26th ed. Concrete Reinforcing Steel Institute, Schaumburg, IL, 1996.

10. McCormac, Jack. *Design of Reinforced Concrete,* 6th ed. Hoboken, NJ: Wiley, 2005.

11. *Placing Reinforcing Bars,* 8th ed. Concrete Reinforcing Steel Institute, Schaumburg, IL, 2005.

12. *Roller-Compacted Concrete.* Reston, VA: American Society of Civil Engineers, 1994.

CONCRETE FORM DESIGN

1 DESIGN PRINCIPLES

The design of concrete formwork that has adequate strength to resist failure and will not deflect excessively when the forms are filled is a problem in structural design. Unless commercial forms are used, this will usually involve the design of wall, column, or slab forms constructed of wood or plywood. In such cases, after the design loads have been established, each of the primary form components may be analyzed as a beam to determine the maximum bending and shear stresses and the maximum deflection that will occur. Vertical supports and lateral bracing are then analyzed for compression and tension loads. The procedures and applicable equations are presented in this chapter.

2 DESIGN LOADS

Wall and Column Forms

For vertical forms (wall and column forms), design load consists of the lateral pressure of the concrete against the forms. The maximum lateral pressure that the concrete exerts against a form has been found to be a function of the unit weight of the concrete, cement type or blend, temperature of the concrete, vertical rate of placing, and the height of the form. For ordinary internally vibrated concrete, the American Concrete Institute (ACI) recommends the use of the following formulas to determine the design lateral concrete pressure.

For all columns and for walls with a vertical rate of placement less than 7 ft/h (2.1 m/h) and a placement height of 14 ft (4.3 m) or less:

$$p = C_w C_c \left(150 + \frac{9000 R}{T} \right) \text{ lb/sq ft} \qquad (1)$$

$$\left[p = C_w C_c \left(7.2 + \frac{785 R}{T + 18} \right) \text{kPa} \right]$$

where: C_w = unit weight coefficient (Table 1)
C_c = chemistry coefficient (Table 2)
p = lateral pressure (lb/sq ft or kPa)
R = rate of vertical placement (ft/h or m/h)
T = concrete temperature (°F or °C)
h = height of form (ft or m)
w = unit weight of concrete (lb/cu ft or kg/m³)

Minimum pressure = $600 \, C_w$ lb/sq ft ($28.7 \, C_w$ kPa)

Maximum pressure = wh lb/sq ft

$$[p = 0.0049 \, wh \text{ kPa}]$$

For walls with a vertical rate of placement of 7–15 ft/h (2.1–4.6 m/h) and walls with a rate of placement less than 7 ft/h (2.1 m/h) whose placement height exceeds 14 ft (4.3 m):

$$p = C_w C_c \left(150 + \frac{43,400}{T} + \frac{2800 R}{T} \right) \text{ lb/sq ft} \qquad (2A)$$

$$\left[p = C_w C_c \left(7.2 + \frac{1154}{T + 18} + \frac{244 R}{T + 18} \right) \text{kPa} \right] \qquad (2B)$$

Table 13-1. Concrete unit weight coefficient (Courtesy of American Concrete Institute)

Unit Weight of Concrete	C_w
Under 140 lb/cu ft	$0.5 \left(1 + \frac{w}{145} \right)$ but at least 0.80
[Under 2243 kg/m³	$0.5 \left(1 + \frac{w}{2323} \right)$ but at least 0.80]
140–150 lb/cu ft	1.0
[2243–2403 kg/m³	1.0]
Over 150 lb/cu ft	$\left(\frac{w}{145} \right)$
[Over 2403 kg/m³	$\left(\frac{w}{2323} \right)$]

Table 2. Concrete chemistry coefficient
(Courtesy of American Concrete Institute)

Cement Type or Blend	C_c
Type I, II, or III without retarders	1.0
Type I, II, or III with a retarder	1.2
Other blends containing less than 70% slag or 40% fly ash without retarders	1.2
Other blends containing less than 70% slag or 40% fly ash with a retarder	1.4
Blends containing more than 70% slag or 40% fly ash	1.4

Table 3. Recommended minimum lateral design load for wall forms

Wall Height, h (ft) [m]	Design Lateral Force Applied at Top of Form (lb/ft) [kN/m]
less than 8 [2.4]	$\dfrac{h \times wf^*}{2}$
8 [2.4] or over but less than 22 [6.7]	100 [1.46] but at least $\dfrac{h \times wf^*}{2}$
22 [6.7] or over	7.5 h [0.358 h] but at least $\dfrac{h \times wf^*}{2}$

*wf = wind force prescribed by local code (lb/sq ft) [kPa] but minimum of 15 lb/sq ft [0.72 kPa]

Minimum pressure $= 600\, C_w$ lb/sq ft $(28.7\, C_w$ kPa)

Maximum pressure $= wh$

For walls with a vertical rate of placement greater than 15 ft/h (4.6 m/h) or when the forms will be filled before the concrete stiffens:

$$p = wh \ lb/sq \, ft \qquad (3)$$

$$[\mathbf{p = 0.0049\ wh\ kPa}]$$

When forms are vibrated externally, it is recommended that a design load twice that given by Equations 1 and 2 be used. When concrete is pumped into vertical forms from the bottom (both column and wall forms), Equation 3 should be used and a minimum additional pressure of 25% should be added to allow for pump surge pressure.

Floor and Roof Slab Forms

The design load to be used for elevated slabs consists of the weight of concrete and reinforcing steel, the weight of the forms themselves, and any live loads (equipment, workers, material, etc.). For normal reinforced concrete, the design load for concrete and steel is based on a unit weight of 150 lb/cu ft (2403 kg/m^3). The American Concrete Institute (ACI) recommends that a minimum live load of 50 lb/sq ft (2.4 kPa) be used for the weight of equipment, materials, and workers. When motorized concrete buggies are utilized, the live load should be increased to at least 75 lb/sq ft (3.6 kPa). Any unusual loads would be in addition to these values. ACI also recommends that a minimum design load (dead load plus live load) of 100 lb/sq ft (4.8 kPa) be used. This should be increased to 125 lb/sq ft (6.0 kPa) when motorized buggies are used. (Note: 1 kg/m^2 = 0.0098 kPa)

Lateral Loads

Formwork must be designed to resist lateral loads such as those imposed by wind, the movement of equipment on the forms, and the placing of concrete into the forms. Such forces are usually resisted by lateral bracing whose design is covered in Section 6. The minimum lateral design loads recommended for tied wall forms are given in Table 3.

When form ties are not used, bracing must be designed to resist the internal concrete pressure as well as external loads.

For slab forms, the minimum lateral design load is expressed as follows:

$$H = 0.02 \times dl \times ws \qquad (4)$$

where H = lateral force applied along the edge of the slab (lb/ft) [kN/m]; minimum value = 100 lb/ft [1.46 kN/m]

dl = design dead load (lb/sq ft) [kPa]

ws = width of slab perpendicular to form edge (ft) [m]

In using Equation 4, design dead load includes the weight of concrete plus formwork. In determining the value of ws, consider only that part of the slab being placed at one time.

3 METHOD OF ANALYSIS
Basis of Analysis

After appropriate design loads have been selected, the sheathing, joists or studs, and stringers or wales are analyzed in turn, considering each member to be a uniformly loaded beam supported in one of three conditions (single-span, two-span, or three-span or larger) and analyzed for bending, shear, and deflection. Vertical supports and lateral bracing must be checked for compression and tension stresses. Except for sheathing, bearing stresses must be checked at supports to ensure against crushing.

Using the methods of engineering mechanics, the maximum values expressed in customary units of bending moment, shear, and deflection developed in a uniformly loaded, simply supported beam of uniform cross section are given in Table 4.

The maximum fiber stresses (expressed in conventional units) developed in bending, shear, and compression

Table 13-4. Maximum bending, shear, and deflection in a uniformly loaded beam

Type	Support Conditions		
	1 Span	2 Spans	3 Spans
Bending moment (in.-lb)	$M = \dfrac{wl^2}{96}$	$M = \dfrac{wl^2}{96}$	$M = \dfrac{wl^2}{120}$
Shear (lb)	$V = \dfrac{wl}{24}$	$V = \dfrac{5wl}{96}$	$V = \dfrac{wl}{20}$
Deflection (in.)	$\Delta = \dfrac{5wl^4}{4608\,EI}$	$\Delta = \dfrac{wl^4}{2220\,EI}$	$\Delta = \dfrac{wl^4}{1740\,EI}$

Notation:
l = length of span (in.)
w = uniform load per foot of span (lb/ft)
E = modulus of elasticity (psi)
I = moment of inertia (in.^{4})

resulting from a specified load may be determined from the following equations:

Bending

$$f_b = \frac{M}{S} \qquad (5)$$

Shear

$$f_v = \frac{1.5V}{A} \text{ for rectangular wood members} \qquad (6)$$

$$f_v = \frac{V}{Ib/Q} \text{ for plywood} \qquad (7)$$

Compression

$$f_c \text{ or } f_{c\perp} = \frac{P}{A} \qquad (8)$$

Tension

$$f_t = \frac{P}{A} \qquad (9)$$

where f_b = actual unit stress for extreme fiber in bending (psi)

f_c = actual unit stress in compression parallel to grain (psi)

$f_{c\perp}$ = actual unit stress in compression perpendicular to grain (psi)

f_t = actual unit stress in tension (psi)

f_v = actual unit stress in horizontal shear (psi)

A = section area (sq in.)

M = maximum moment (in.-lb)

P = concentrated load (lb)

S = section modulus (cu in.)

V = maximum shear (lb)

Ib/Q = rolling shear constant (sq in./ft)

Since the grain of a piece of timber runs parallel to its length, axial compressive forces result in unit compressive stresses parallel to the grain. Thus, a compression force in a formwork brace (Figure 4) will result in unit compressive stresses parallel to the grain (f_c) in the member. Loads applied to the top or sides of a beam, such as a joist resting on a stringer (Figure 1b), will result in unit compressive stresses perpendicular to the grain ($f_{c\perp}$) in the beam. Equating allowable unit stresses in bending and shear to the maximum unit stresses developed in a beam subjected to a uniform load of w pounds per linear foot [kN/m] yields the bending and shear equations of Tables 5 and 5A.

When design load and beam section properties have been specified, these equations may be solved directly for the maximum allowable span. Given a design load and span length, the equations may be solved for the required size of the member. Design properties for Plyform® (plywood especially engineered for use in concrete formwork) are given in Table 6 and section properties for dimensioned lumber and timber are given in Table 7. However, typical allowable stress values for lumber are given in Table 8. The allowable unit stress values in Table 8 (but not modulus of elasticity values) may be multiplied by a load duration factor of 1.25 (7-day load) when designing formwork for light construction and single use or very limited reuse of forms. However, allowable stresses for lumber sheathing (not Plyform®) should be reduced by the factors given in Table 8 for wet conditions. The values for Plyform® properties presented in Table 6 are based on wet strength and 7-day load duration, so no further adjustment in these values is required.

It should be noted that the deflection of plywood sheathing is precisely computed as the sum of bending deflection and shear deflection. While the deflection equations of Tables 5 and 5A consider only bending deflection, the modulus of elasticity values of Table 6 include an allowance for shear deflection. Thus, the deflection computed using these tables is sufficiently accurate in most cases. However, for very short spans (l/d ratio of less than 15), it is recommended that shear deflection be computed separately and added to bending deflection. See reference 3 for a recommended procedure.

Section   Elevation

w = design load (lb/sq ft) [kN/m²]
w_1 = 1 × w = w (lb/ft) [kN/m]

a. Sheathing

s_2 = spacing of joists (ft) [m]
w_2 = w × s_2 (lb/ft) [kN/m]

b. Joists

s_3 = spacing of stringers (ft) [m]
w_3 = w × s_3 (lb/ft) [kN/m]

c. Stringers

FIGURE 1. Design analysis of form members.

4 SLAB FORM DESIGN

Method of Analysis

The procedure for applying the equations of Tables 5 and 5A to the design of a deck or slab form is first to consider a strip of sheathing of the specified thickness and 1 ft (or 1 m) wide (see Figure 1a). Determine in turn the maximum allowable span based on the allowable values of bending stress, shear stress, and deflection. The lower of these values will, of course, determine the maximum spacing of the supports (joists). For simplicity and economy of design, this maximum span value is usually rounded down to the next lower integer or modular value when selecting joist spacing.

Based on the selected joist spacing, the joist itself is analyzed to determine its maximum allowable span. The load conditions for the joist are illustrated in Figure 1b. The joist span selected will be the spacing of the stringers. Again, an integer or modular value is selected for stringer spacing.

Based on the selected stringer spacing, the process is repeated to determine the maximum stringer span (distance between vertical supports or shores). Notice in the design of stringers that the joist loads are actually applied to the stringer as a series of concentrated loads at the points where the joists rest on the stringer. However, it is simpler and sufficiently accurate to treat the load on the stringer as a uniform load. The width of the uniform design load applied to the stringer is equal to the stringer spacing as shown in Figure 1c. The calculated stringer span must next be checked against the capacity of the shores used to support the stringers. The load on each shore is equal to the shore spacing multiplied by the load per unit length of stringer. Thus, the maximum shore spacing (or stringer span) is limited to the lower of these two maximum values.

Although the effect of intermediate form members was ignored in determining allowable stringer span, it is necessary to check for crushing at the point where each joist rests on the stringer. This is done by dividing the load at this point by the bearing area and comparing the resulting stress to the

Table 5. Concrete form design equations

Design Condition	Support Conditions		
	1 Span	2 Spans	3 or More Spans
Bending			
Wood	$\ell = 4.0d\left(\dfrac{F_b b}{w}\right)^{1/2}$	$\ell = 4.0d\left(\dfrac{F_b b}{w}\right)^{1/2}$	$\ell = 4.46d\left(\dfrac{F_b b}{w}\right)^{1/2}$
	$\ell = 9.8\left(\dfrac{F_b S}{w}\right)^{1/2}$	$\ell = 9.8\left(\dfrac{F_b S}{w}\right)^{1/2}$	$\ell = 10.95\left(\dfrac{F_b S}{w}\right)^{1/2}$
Plywood	$\ell = 9.8\left(\dfrac{F_b KS}{w}\right)^{1/2}$	$\ell = 9.8\left(\dfrac{F_b KS}{w}\right)^{1/2}$	$\ell = 10.95\left(\dfrac{F_b KS}{w}\right)^{1/2}$
Shear			
Wood	$\ell = 16\dfrac{F_v A}{w} + 2d$	$\ell = 12.8\dfrac{F_v A}{w} + 2d$	$\ell = 13.3\dfrac{F_v A}{w} + 2d$
Plywood	$\ell = 24\dfrac{F_s Ib/Q}{w} + 2d$	$\ell = 19.2\dfrac{F_s Ib/Q}{w} + 2d$	$\ell = 20\dfrac{F_s Ib/Q}{w} + 2d$
Deflection	$\ell = 5.51\left(\dfrac{EI\Delta}{w}\right)^{1/4}$	$\ell = 6.86\left(\dfrac{EI\Delta}{w}\right)^{1/4}$	$\ell = 6.46\left(\dfrac{EI\Delta}{w}\right)^{1/4}$
If $\Delta = 1/180$	$\ell = 1.72\left(\dfrac{EI}{w}\right)^{1/3}$	$\ell = 2.31\left(\dfrac{EI}{w}\right)^{1/3}$	$\ell = 2.13\left(\dfrac{EI}{w}\right)^{1/3}$
If $\Delta = 1/240$	$\ell = 1.57\left(\dfrac{EI}{w}\right)^{1/3}$	$\ell = 2.10\left(\dfrac{EI}{w}\right)^{1/3}$	$\ell = 1.94\left(\dfrac{EI}{w}\right)^{1/3}$
If $\Delta = 1/360$	$\ell = 1.37\left(\dfrac{EI}{w}\right)^{1/3}$	$\ell = 1.83\left(\dfrac{EI}{w}\right)^{1/3}$	$\ell = 1.69\left(\dfrac{EI}{w}\right)^{1/3}$
Compression	f_c or $f_{c\perp} = \dfrac{P}{A}$		
Tension	$f_t = \dfrac{P}{A}$		

Notation:

ℓ = length of span, center to center of supports (in.)
F_b = allowable unit stress in bending (psi)
$F_b KS$ = plywood section capacity in bending (lb × in./ft)
F_c = allowable unit stress in compression parallel to grain (psi)
$F_{c\perp}$ = allowable unit stress in compression perpendicular to grain (psi)
$F_s Ib/Q$ = plywood section capacity in rolling shear (lb/ft)
F_v = allowable unit stress in horizontal shear (psi)
f_c = actual unit stress in compression parallel to grain (psi)
$f_{c\perp}$ = actual unit stress in compression perpendicular to grain (psi)
f_t = actual unit stress in tension (psi)
A = area of section (in.^{2})*
E = modulus of elasticity (psi)
I = moment of inertia (in.^{4})*
EI = plywood stiffness capacity (kPamm^4/m)
P = applied force (compression or tension) (lb)
S = section modulus (in.^{3})*
Δ = deflection (in.)
b = width of member (in.)
d = depth of member (in.)
w = uniform load per foot of span (lb/ft)
*For a rectangular member: $A = bd$, $S = bd^2/6$, $I = bd^3/12$

Table 5A. Metric (SI) concrete form design equations

Design Conditions	Support Conditions		
	1 Span	2 Spans	3 or More Spans
Bending			
Wood	$\ell = \dfrac{36.5}{1000}\,d\left(\dfrac{F_b b}{w}\right)^{1/2}$	$\ell = \dfrac{36.5}{1000}\,d\left(\dfrac{F_b b}{w}\right)^{1/2}$	$\ell = \dfrac{40.7}{1000}\,d\left(\dfrac{F_b b}{w}\right)^{1/2}$
	$\ell = \dfrac{89.9}{1000}\left(\dfrac{F_b S}{w}\right)^{1/2}$	$\ell = \dfrac{89.9}{1000}\left(\dfrac{F_b S}{w}\right)^{1/2}$	$\ell = \dfrac{100}{1000}\left(\dfrac{F_b S}{w}\right)^{1/2}$
Plywood	$\ell = 2.83\left(\dfrac{F_b KS}{w}\right)^{1/2}$	$\ell = 2.83\left(\dfrac{F_b KS}{w}\right)^{1/2}$	$\ell = 3.16\left(\dfrac{F_b KS}{w}\right)^{1/2}$
Shear			
Wood	$\ell = \dfrac{1.34}{1000}\dfrac{F_v A}{w} + 2d$	$\ell = \dfrac{1.07}{1000}\dfrac{F_v A}{w} + 2d$	$\ell = \dfrac{1.11}{1000}\dfrac{F_v A}{w} + 2d$
Plywood	$\ell = 2.00\dfrac{F_s Ib/Q}{w} + 2d$	$\ell = 1.60\dfrac{F_s Ib/Q}{w} + 2d$	$\ell = 1.67\dfrac{F_s Ib/Q}{w} + 2d$
Deflection	$\ell = \dfrac{526}{1000}\left(\dfrac{EI\Delta}{w}\right)^{1/4}$	$\ell = \dfrac{655}{1000}\left(\dfrac{EI\Delta}{w}\right)^{1/4}$	$\ell = \dfrac{617}{1000}\left(\dfrac{EI\Delta}{w}\right)^{1/4}$
If $\Delta = 1/180$	$\ell = \dfrac{75.1}{1000}\left(\dfrac{EI}{w}\right)^{1/3}$	$\ell = \dfrac{101}{1000}\left(\dfrac{EI}{w}\right)^{1/3}$	$\ell = \dfrac{93.0}{1000}\left(\dfrac{EI}{w}\right)^{1/3}$
If $\Delta = 1/240$	$\ell = \dfrac{68.5}{1000}\left(\dfrac{EI}{w}\right)^{1/3}$	$\ell = \dfrac{91.7}{1000}\left(\dfrac{EI}{w}\right)^{1/3}$	$\ell = \dfrac{84.7}{1000}\left(\dfrac{EI}{w}\right)^{1/3}$
If $\Delta = 1/360$	$\ell = \dfrac{59.8}{1000}\left(\dfrac{EI}{w}\right)^{1/3}$	$\ell = \dfrac{79.9}{1000}\left(\dfrac{EI}{w}\right)^{1/3}$	$\ell = \dfrac{73.8}{1000}\left(\dfrac{EI}{w}\right)^{1/3}$
Compression	$f_c \text{ or } f_{c\perp} = \dfrac{P}{A}$		
Tension	$f_t = \dfrac{P}{A}$		

Notation:

ℓ = length of span, center to center of supports (mm)

F_b = allowable unit stress in bending (kPa)

$F_b KS$ = plywood section capacity in bending (Nmm/m)

F_c = allowable unit stress in compression parallel to grain (kPa)

$F_{c\perp}$ = allowable unit stress in compression perpendicular to grain (kPa)

$F_s Ib/Q$ = plywood section capacity in rolling shear (N/m)

f_v = allowable unit stress in horizontal shear (kPa)

f_c = actual unit stress in compression parallel to grain (kPa)

$f_{c\perp}$ = actual unit stress in compression perpendicular to grain (kPa)

f_t = actual unit stress in tension (kPa)

A = area of section (mm²)*

E = modulus of elasticity (kPa)

I = moment of inertia (mm⁴)*

EI = plywood stiffness capacity (kPamm⁴/m)

P = applied force (compression or tension) (N)

S = section modulus (mm³)*

Δ = deflection (mm)

b = width of member (mm)

d = depth of member (mm)

w = uniform load per meter of span (kPa/m)

*For a rectangular member: $A = bd$, $S = bd^2/6$, $I = bd^3/12$

Table 6. Section properties of plywood.* (Created by author with data from APA—the Engineered Wood Association)

Thickness in. (mm)	Approximate Weight psf (kg/m²)	Face Grain Across Supports			Face Grain Parallel to Supports		
		EI $10^6 \frac{lbin.^2}{ft}$ $10^9 \frac{kPamm^4}{m}$	F_bKS $10^3 \frac{lbin.}{ft}$ $10^3 \frac{Nmm}{m}$	F_slb/Q $10^3 \frac{lb}{ft}$ $10^3 \frac{N}{m}$	EI $10^4 \frac{lbin.^2}{ft}$ $10^9 \frac{kPamm^4}{m}$	F_bKS $10^3 \frac{lbin.}{ft}$ $10^3 \frac{Nmm}{m}$	F_slb/Q $10^3 \frac{lb}{ft}$ $10^3 \frac{N}{m}$
Plyform Class I							
½ (12.7)	1.5 (7.3)	0.116 (1087)	0.517 (191)	0.371 (5.41)	0.036 (339)	0.251 (93)	0.197 (2.88)
⅝ (15.9)	1.8 (8.8)	0.195 (1836)	0.691 (256)	0.412 (6.01)	0.057 (537)	0.338 (125)	0.223 (3.25)
¾ (19.1)	2.2 (10.7)	0.298 (2810)	0.878 (326)	0.517 (7.55)	0.138 (1299)	0.591 (219)	0.293 (4.27)
⅞ (22.2)	2.6 (12.7)	0.444 (4180)	1.127 (418)	0.616 (8.99)	0.226 (2132)	0.814 (302)	0.434 (6.33)
1 (25.4)	3.0 (14.6)	0.641 (6030)	1.422 (527)	0.675 (9.85)	0.405 (3813)	1.224 (454)	0.505 (7.37)
1⅛ (28.6)	3.3 (16.1)	0.831 (7824)	1.639 (607)	0.751 (10.96)	0.597 (5621)	1.542 (572)	0.606 (8.85)
Plyform Class II							
½ (12.7)	1.5 (7.3)	0.097 (918)	0.355 (132)	0.352 (5.14)	0.026 (245)	0.222 (82.3)	0.196 (2.87)
⅝ (15.9)	1.8 (8.8)	0.169 (1591)	0.475 (176)	0.403 (5.88)	0.042 (392)	0.299 (111)	0.221 (3.23)
¾ (19.1)	2.2 (10.7)	0.257 (2423)	0.604 (224)	0.477 (6.97)	0.097 (918)	0.521 (193)	0.292 (4.25)
⅞ (22.2)	2.6 (12.7)	0.390 (3672)	0.786 (291)	0.575 (8.40)	0.160 (1505)	0.721 (267)	0.432 (6.30)
1 (25.4)	3.0 (14.6)	0.547 (5153)	1.003 (372)	0.620 (9.05)	0.286 (2693)	1.080 (400)	0.503 (7.34)
1⅛ (28.6)	3.3 (16.1)	0.736 (6928)	1.156 (428)	0.689 (10.06)	0.420 (3953)	1.361 (504)	0.604 (8.81)
Plyform Structural I							
½ (12.7)	1.5 (7.3)	0.117 (1102)	0.523 (194)	0.501 (7.31)	0.043 (410)	0.344 (127)	0.278 (4.06)
⅝ (15.9)	1.8 (8.8)	0.196 (1850)	0.697 (258)	0.536 (7.83)	0.067 (636)	0.459 (170)	0.313 (4.57)
¾ (19.1)	2.2 (10.7)	0.303 (2853)	0.896 (332)	0.631 (9.21)	0.162 (1525)	0.807 (299)	0.413 (6.02)
⅞ (22.2)	2.6 (12.7)	0.475 (4477)	1.208 (448)	0.769 (11.22)	0.268 (2528)	1.117 (414)	0.611 (8.92)
1 (25.4)	3.0 (14.6)	0.718 (6765)	1.596 (592)	0.814 (11.88)	0.481 (4533)	1.679 (622)	0.712 (10.39)
1⅛ (28.6)	3.3 (16.1)	0.934 (8798)	1.843 (683)	0.902 (13.16)	0.711 (6694)	2.119 (785)	0.854 (12.47)

*All properties adjusted to account for reduced effectiveness of plies with grain perpendicular to applied stress. Stresses adjusted for wet conditions, load duration, and experience factors.

Table 7. Section properties of U.S. standard lumber and timber (*b* = width, *d* = depth) (Copyright 1974 by John Wiley & sons, Inc. By Permission)

Nominal Size (b × d)	Actual Size (S4S)		Area of Section A		Section Modulus S		Moment of Inertia I	
in.	in.	mm	in.²	10³ mm²	in.³	10⁵ mm³	in.⁴	10⁶ mm⁴
1 × 3	0.75 × 2.5	19 × 64	1.875	1.210	0.7812	0.1280	0.9766	0.4065
1 × 4	0.75 × 3.5	19 × 89	2.625	1.694	1.531	0.2509	2.680	1.115
1 × 6	0.75 × 5.5	19 × 140	4.125	2.661	3.781	0.6196	10.40	4.328
1 × 8	0.75 × 7.25	19 × 184	5.438	3.508	6.570	1.077	23.82	9.913
1 × 10	0.75 × 9.25	19 × 235	6.938	4.476	10.70	1.753	49.47	20.59
1 × 12	0.75 × 11.25	19 × 286	8.438	5.444	15.82	2.592	88.99	37.04
2 × 3	1.5 × 2.5	38 × 64	3.750	2.419	1.563	0.2561	1.953	0.8129
2 × 4	1.5 × 3.5	38 × 89	5.250	3.387	3.063	0.5019	5.359	2.231
2 × 6	1.5 × 5.5	38 × 140	8.250	5.323	7.563	1.239	20.80	8.656
2 × 8	1.5 × 7.25	38 × 184	10.88	7.016	13.14	2.153	47.63	19.83
2 × 10	1.5 × 9.25	38 × 235	13.88	8.952	21.39	3.505	98.93	41.18
2 × 12	1.5 × 11.25	38 × 286	16.88	10.89	31.64	5.185	178.0	74.08
2 × 14	1.5 × 13.25	38 × 337	19.88	12.82	43.89	7.192	290.8	121.0
3 × 4	2.5 × 3.5	64 × 89	8.750	5.645	5.104	0.8364	8.932	3.718
3 × 6	2.5 × 5.5	64 × 140	13.75	8.871	12.60	2.065	34.66	14.43
3 × 8	2.5 × 7.25	64 × 184	18.12	11.69	21.90	3.589	79.39	33.04
3 × 10	2.5 × 9.25	64 × 235	23.12	14.91	35.65	5.842	164.9	68.63
3 × 12	2.5 × 11.25	64 × 286	28.12	18.14	52.73	8.642	296.6	123.5
3 × 14	2.5 × 13.25	64 × 337	33.12	21.37	73.15	11.99	484.6	201.7
3 × 16	2.5 × 15.25	64 × 387	38.12	24.60	96.90	15.88	738.9	307.5
4 × 4	3.5 × 3.5	89 × 89	12.25	7.903	7.146	1.171	12.50	5.205
4 × 6	3.5 × 5.5	89 × 140	19.25	12.42	17.65	2.892	48.53	20.20
4 × 8	3.5 × 7.25	89 × 184	25.38	16.37	30.66	5.024	111.1	46.26
4 × 10	3.5 × 9.25	89 × 235	32.38	20.89	49.91	8.179	230.8	96.08
4 × 12	3.5 × 11.25	89 × 286	39.38	25.40	73.83	12.10	415.3	172.8
4 × 14	3.5 × 13.25	89 × 337	46.38	29.92	102.4	16.78	678.5	282.4
4 × 16	3.5 × 15.25	89 × 387	53.38	34.43	135.7	22.23	1034	430.6
6 × 6	5.5 × 5.5	140 × 140	30.25	19.52	27.73	4.543	76.25	19.52
6 × 8	5.5 × 7.5	140 × 191	41.25	26.61	51.56	8.450	193.4	80.48
6 × 10	5.5 × 9.5	140 × 241	52.25	33.71	82.73	13.56	393.0	163.6
6 × 12	5.5 × 11.5	140 × 292	63.25	40.81	121.2	19.87	697.1	290.1
6 × 14	5.5 × 13.5	140 × 343	74.25	47.90	167.1	27.38	1128	469.4
6 × 16	5.5 × 15.5	140 × 394	85.25	55.00	220.2	36.09	1707	710.4
6 × 18	5.5 × 17.5	140 × 445	96.25	62.10	280.7	46.00	2456	1022
6 × 20	5.5 × 19.5	140 × 495	107.2	69.19	348.6	57.12	3398	1415
6 × 22	5.5 × 21.5	140 × 546	118.2	76.29	423.7	69.44	4555	1896
6 × 24	5.5 × 23.5	140 × 597	129.2	83.39	506.2	82.96	5948	2476
8 × 8	7.5 × 7.5	191 × 191	56.25	36.29	70.31	11.52	263.7	109.8
8 × 10	7.5 × 9.5	191 × 241	71.25	45.97	112.8	18.49	535.9	223.0
8 × 12	7.5 × 11.5	191 × 292	86.25	55.65	165.3	27.09	950.5	395.7
8 × 14	7.5 × 13.5	191 × 343	101.2	65.32	227.8	37.33	1538	640.1
8 × 16	7.5 × 15.5	191 × 394	116.2	75.00	300.3	49.21	2327	968.8
8 × 18	7.5 × 17.5	191 × 445	131.2	84.68	382.8	62.73	3350	1394
8 × 20	7.5 × 19.5	191 × 495	146.2	94.36	475.3	77.89	4634	1929
8 × 22	7.5 × 21.5	191 × 546	161.2	104.0	577.8	94.69	6211	2585

Table 7. Continued

Nominal Size $(b \times d)$	Actual Size (S4S)		Area of Section A		Section Modulus S		Moment of Inertia I	
in.	in.	mm	in.^{2}	10^3 mm^2	in.^{3}	10^5 mm^3	in.^{4}	10^6 mm^4
8 × 24	7.5 × 23.5	191 × 597	176.2	113.7	690.3	113.1	8111	3376
10 × 10	9.5 × 9.5	241 × 241	90.25	58.23	142.9	23.42	678.8	282.5
10 × 12	9.5 × 11.5	241 × 292	109.2	70.48	209.4	34.31	1204	501.2
10 × 14	9.5 × 13.5	241 × 343	128.2	82.74	288.6	47.29	1948	810.7
10 × 16	9.5 × 15.5	241 × 394	147.2	95.00	380.4	62.34	2948	1227
10 × 18	9.5 × 17.5	241 × 445	166.2	107.3	484.9	79.46	4243	1766
10 × 20	9.5 × 19.5	241 × 495	185.2	119.5	602.1	98.66	5870	2443
10 × 22	9.5 × 21.5	241 × 546	204.2	131.8	731.9	119.9	7868	3275
10 × 24	9.5 × 23.5	241 × 597	223.2	144.0	874.4	143.3	10,274	4276
12 × 12	11.5 × 11.5	292 × 292	132.2	85.32	253.5	41.54	1458	594.2
12 × 14	11.5 × 13.5	292 × 343	155.2	100.2	349.3	57.24	2358	981.4
12 × 16	11.5 × 15.5	292 × 394	178.2	115.0	460.5	75.46	3569	1485
12 × 18	11.5 × 17.5	292 × 445	201.2	129.8	587.0	96.19	5136	2138
12 × 20	11.5 × 19.5	292 × 495	224.2	144.7	728.8	119.4	7106	2958
12 × 22	11.5 × 21.5	292 × 546	247.2	159.5	886.0	145.2	9524	3964
12 × 24	11.5 × 23.5	292 × 597	270.2	174.4	1058	173.4	12,437	4276
14 × 14	13.5 × 13.5	343 × 343	182.2	117.5	410.1	67.20	2768	1152
14 × 16	13.5 × 15.5	343 × 394	209.2	135.0	540.6	88.58	4189	1744
14 × 18	13.5 × 17.5	343 × 445	236.2	152.4	689.1	112.9	6029	2510
14 × 20	13.5 × 19.5	343 × 495	263.2	169.8	855.6	140.2	8342	3472
14 × 22	13.5 × 21.5	343 × 546	290.2	187.3	1040	170.4	11,181	4654
14 × 24	13.5 × 23.5	343 × 597	317.2	204.7	1243	203.6	14,600	6077

Table 8. Typical values of allowable stress for lumber

Species (No. 2 Grade, 4 × 4 [100 × 100 mm] or smaller)	Allowable Unit Stress (lb/sq in.)[kPa] (Moisture Content = 19%)					
	F_b	F_v	$F_{c\perp}$	F_c	F_t	E
Douglas fir—larch	1450 [9998]	185 [1276]	385 [2655]	1000 [6895]	850 [5861]	1.7 × 10^6 [11.7 × 10^6]
Hemlock—fir	1150 [7929]	150 [1034]	245 [1689]	800 [5516]	675 [4654]	1.4 × 10^6 [9.7 × 10^6]
Southern pine	1400 [9653]	180 [1241]	405 [2792]	975 [6723]	825 [5688]	1.6 × 10^6 [11.0 × 10^6]
California redwood	1400 [9653]	160 [1103]	425 [2930]	1000 [6895]	800 [5516]	1.3 × 10^6 [9.0 × 10^6]
Eastern spruce	1050 [7240]	140 [965]	255 [1758]	700 [4827]	625 [4309]	1.2 × 10^6 [8.3 × 10^6]
Reduction factor for wet conditions	0.86	0.97	0.67	0.70	0.84	0.97
Load duration factor (7-day load)	1.25	1.25	1.25	1.25	1.25	1.00

allowable unit stress in compression perpendicular to the grain. A similar procedure is applied at the point where each stringer rests on a vertical support.

To preclude buckling, the maximum allowable load on a rectangular wood column is a function of its unsupported length and least dimension (or l/d ratio). The l/d ratio must not exceed 50 for a simple solid wood column. For l/d ratios less than 50, the following equation applies:

$$F_c' = \frac{0.3E}{(l/d)^2} \le F_c \qquad (10)$$

where F_c = allowable unit stress in compression parallel to the grain (lb/sq in.) [kPa]

F_c' = allowable unit stress in compression parallel to the grain, adjusted for l/d ratio (lb/sq in.) [kPa]

E = modulus of elasticity (lb/sq in.) [kPa]

l/d = ratio of member length to least dimension

In using this equation, note that the maximum value used for F_c' may not exceed the value of F_c.

These design procedures are illustrated in the following example. Sheathing design employing plywood is illustrated in Example 2.

Example 1   Design the formwork (Figure 2) for an elevated concrete floor slab 6 in. (152 mm) thick. Sheathing will be

Plan

FIGURE 2. Slab form, Example 1.

nominal 1-in. (25-mm) lumber while 2 × 8 in. (50 × 200 mm) lumber will be used for joists. Stringers will be 4 × 8 in. (100 × 200 mm) lumber. Assume that all members are continuous over three or more spans. Commercial 4000-lb (17.8-kN) shores will be used. It is estimated that the weight of the formwork will be 5 lb/sq ft (0.24 kPa). The adjusted allowable stresses for the lumber being used are as follows:

	Sheathing psi [kPa]	Other Members psi [kPa]
F_b	1075 [7412]	1250 [8619]
F_v	174 [1200]	180 [1241]
$F_{c\perp}$		405 [2792]
F_c		850 [5861]
E	1.36×10^6	1.40×10^6
	$[9.4 \times 10^6]$	$[9.7 \times 10^6]$

Maximum deflection of form members will be limited to $\frac{\ell}{360}$. Use the minimum value of live load permitted by ACI. Determine joist spacing, stringer spacing, and shore spacing.

Solution

Design Load

Assume concrete density is 150 lb/cu ft (2403 kg/m³)

$$\text{Concrete} = 1 \text{ sq ft} \times 6/12 \text{ ft} \times 150 \text{ lb/cu ft} = 75 \text{ lb/sq ft}$$
$$\text{Formwork} = 5 \text{ lb/sq ft}$$
$$\text{Live load} = 50 \text{ lb/sq ft}$$
$$\text{Design load} = 130 \text{ lb/sq ft}$$

$$\begin{bmatrix} \text{Pressure per m}^2: \\ \text{Concrete} = 1 \times 1 \times 0.152 \times 2403 \times 0.0098 = 3.58 \text{ kPa} \\ \text{Formwork} = 0.24 \text{ kPa} \\ \text{Live load} = 2.40 \text{ kPa} \\ \text{Design load} = 6.22 \text{ kPa} \end{bmatrix}$$

Deck Design

Consider a uniformly loaded strip of decking (sheathing) 12 in. (or 1 m) wide placed perpendicular to the joists (Figure 13-1a) and analyze it as a beam. Assume that the strip is continuous over three or more spans and use the appropriate equations of Tables 13-5 and 13-5A.

$$w = (1 \text{ sq ft/lin ft}) \times (130 \text{ lb/sq ft}) = 130 \text{ lb/ft}$$
$$[w = (1 \text{ m}^2/\text{m}) \times (6.22 \text{ kN/m}^2) = 6.22 \text{ kN/m}]$$

(a) Bending:

$$l = 4.46d\left(\frac{F_b b}{w}\right)^{1/2}$$
$$= (4.46)(0.75)\left(\frac{(1075)(12)}{130}\right)^{1/2} = 33.3 \text{ in.}$$

$$\left[\begin{array}{l} l = \dfrac{40.7}{1000} d\left(\dfrac{F_b b}{w}\right)^{1/2} \\[2mm] = \dfrac{(40.7)(19)}{1000}\left(\dfrac{(7412)(1000)}{6.22}\right)^{1/2} = 844 \text{ mm} \end{array} \right]$$

(b) Shear:

$$l = 13.3\frac{F_v A}{w} + 2d$$

$$= \frac{(13.3)(174)(12)(0.75)}{130} + (2)(0.75) = 161.7 \text{ in.}$$

$$\left[\begin{array}{l} l = \dfrac{1.11}{1000}\dfrac{F_v A}{w} + 2d \\[2mm] = \dfrac{(1.11)(1200)(1000)(19)}{(1000)(6.22)} + (2)(19) = 4107 \text{ mm} \end{array} \right]$$

(c) Deflection:

$$l = 1.69\left(\frac{EI}{w}\right)^{1/3} = 1.69\left(\frac{Ebd^3}{w12}\right)^{1/3}$$

$$= 1.69\left(\frac{(1.36 \times 10^6)(12)(0.75)^3}{(130)(12)}\right)^{1/3} = 27.7 \text{ in.}$$

$$\left[\begin{array}{l} l = \dfrac{73.8}{1000}\left(\dfrac{EI}{w}\right)^{1/3} = \dfrac{73.8}{1000}\left(\dfrac{Ebd^3}{w12}\right)^{1/3} \\[2mm] = \dfrac{73.8}{1000}\left(\dfrac{(9.4 \times 10^6)(1000)(19)^3}{(12)(6.22)}\right)^{1/3} = 703 \text{ mm} \end{array} \right]$$

Deflection governs in this case and the maximum allowable span is 27.7 in. (703 mm). We will select a 24-in. (610-mm) joist spacing as a modular value for the design.

Joist Design

Consider the joist as a uniformly loaded beam supporting a strip of design load 24 in. (610 mm) wide (same as joist spacing; see Figure 1b). Joists are 2 × 8 in. (50 × 200 mm) lumber. Assume that the joists are continuous over three spans.

$$w = (2 \text{ ft}) \times (1) \times (130 \text{ lb/sq ft}) = 260 \text{ lb/ft}$$
$$[w = (0.610 \text{ m}) \times (1) \times (6.22 \text{ kPa}) = 3.79 \text{ kN/m}]$$

(a) Bending:

$$l = 10.95\left(\frac{F_b S}{w}\right)^{1/2}$$

$$= 10.95\left(\frac{(1250)(13.14)}{260}\right)^{1/2} = 87.0 \text{ in.}$$

$$\left[\begin{array}{l} l = \dfrac{100}{1000}\left(\dfrac{F_b S}{w}\right)^{1/2} \\[2mm] = \dfrac{100}{1000}\left(\dfrac{(8619)(2.153 \times 10^5)}{3.79}\right)^{1/2} = 2213 \text{ mm} \end{array} \right]$$

(b) Shear:

$$l = 13.3\frac{F_v A}{w} + 2d$$

$$= \frac{(13.3)(180)(10.88)}{260} + (2)(7.25) = 114.7 \text{ in.}$$

$$\left[\begin{array}{l} l = \dfrac{1.11}{1000}\dfrac{F_v A}{w} + 2d \\[2mm] = \dfrac{(1.11)}{(1000)}\dfrac{(1241)(7016)}{(3.79)} + (2)(184) = 2918 \text{ mm} \end{array} \right]$$

(c) Deflection:

$$l = 1.69\left(\frac{EI}{w}\right)^{1/3}$$

$$= 1.69\left(\frac{(1.4 \times 10^6)(47.63)}{(260)}\right)^{1/3} = 107.4 \text{ in.}$$

$$\left[\begin{array}{l} l = \dfrac{73.8}{1000}\left(\dfrac{EI}{w}\right)^{1/3} \\[2mm] = \dfrac{73.8}{1000}\left(\dfrac{(9.7 \times 10^6)(19.83 \times 10^6)}{3.79}\right)^{1/3} = 2732 \text{ mm} \end{array} \right]$$

Thus, bending governs and the maximum joist span is 87 in. (2213 mm). We will select a stringer spacing (joist span) of 84 in. (2134 mm).

Stringer Design

To analyze stringer design, consider a strip of design load 7 ft (2.13 m) wide (equal to stringer spacing) as resting directly on the stringer (Figure 1c). Assume the stringer to be continuous over three spans. Stringers are 4 × 8 (100 × 200 mm) lumber. Now analyze the stringer as a beam and determine the maximum allowable span.

$$w = (7)(130) = 910 \text{ lb/ft}$$
$$[w = (2.13)(1)(6.22) = 13.25 \text{ kN/m}]$$

(a) Bending:

$$l = 10.95\left(\frac{F_b S}{w}\right)^{1/2}$$

$$= 10.95\left(\frac{(1250)(30.66)}{910}\right)^{1/2} = 71.1 \text{ in.}$$

$$\left[\begin{array}{l} l = \dfrac{100}{1000}\left(\dfrac{F_b S}{w}\right)^{1/2} \\[2mm] = \dfrac{100}{1000}\left(\dfrac{(8619)(5.024 \times 10^5)}{13.25}\right)^{1/2} = 1808 \text{ mm} \end{array} \right]$$

(b) Shear:

$$l = \frac{13.3\,F_v A}{w} + 2d$$

$$= \frac{(13.3)(180)(25.38)}{910} + (2)(7.25) = 81.3 \text{ in.}$$

$$\left[\begin{array}{l} l = \dfrac{1.11}{1000}\dfrac{F_v A}{w} + 2d \\[2mm] = \dfrac{1.11}{1000}\dfrac{(1241)(16.37 \times 10^3)}{13.25} + (2)(184) = 2070 \text{ mm} \end{array} \right]$$

(c) Deflection:

$$l = 1.69\left(\frac{EI}{w}\right)^{1/3}$$

$$= 1.69\left(\frac{(1.4 \times 10^6)(111.1)^3}{910}\right)^{1/3} = 93.8 \text{ in.}$$

$$\left[\begin{array}{l} I = \dfrac{73.8}{1000}\left(\dfrac{EI}{w}\right)^{1/3} \\[2mm] = \dfrac{73.8}{1000}\left(\dfrac{(9.7 \times 10^6)(46.26 \times 10^6)}{13.25}\right)^{1/3} = 2388 \text{ mm} \end{array}\right]$$

Bending governs and the maximum span is 71.1 in. (1808 mm).

Now we must check shore strength before selecting the stringer span (shore spacing). The maximum stringer span based on shore strength is equal to the shore strength divided by the load per unit length of stringer.

$$I = \frac{4000}{910} \times 12 = 52.7 \text{ in.}$$

$$\left[I = \frac{17.8}{13.25} = 1.343 \text{ m}\right]$$

Thus, the maximum stringer span is limited by shore strength to 52.7 in. (1.343 m). We select a shore spacing of 4 ft (1.22 m) as a modular value.

Before completing our design, we should check for crushing at the point where each joist rests on a stringer. The load at this point is the load per unit length of joist multiplied by the joist span.

$$P = (260)(84/12) = 1820 \text{ lb}$$
$$[P = (3.79)(2.134) = 8.09 \text{ kN}]$$

$$\text{Bearing area } (A) = (1.5)(3.5) = 5.25 \text{ sq in.}$$
$$[A = (38)(89) = 3382 \text{ mm}^2]$$

$$f_{c\perp} = \frac{P}{A} = \frac{1820}{5.25} = 347 \text{ psi} < 405 \text{ psi} (F_{c\perp}) \quad OK$$

$$\left[f_{c\perp} = \frac{809 \times 10^6}{3382} = 2392 \text{ kPa} < 2792 \text{ kPa} (f_{c\perp})\right]$$

Final Design

Decking: nominal 1-in. (25-mm) lumber

Joists: 2 × 8's (50 × 200-mm) at 24-in. (610-mm) spacing

Stringers: 4 × 8's (100 × 200-mm) at 84-in. (2.13-m) spacing

Shore: 4000-lb (17.8-kN) commercial shores at 48-in. (1.22-m) intervals

5 WALL AND COLUMN FORM DESIGN

Design Procedures

The design procedure for wall and column forms is similar to that used for slab forms substituting studs for joists, wales for stringers, and ties for shores. First, the maximum lateral pressure against the sheathing is determined from the appropriate equation (Equation 1, 2, or 3). If the sheathing thickness has been specified, the maximum

allowable span for the sheathing based on bending, shear, and deflection is the maximum stud spacing. If the stud spacing is fixed, calculate the required thickness of sheathing.

Next, calculate the maximum allowable stud span (wale spacing) based on stud size and design load, again considering bending, shear, and deflection. If the stud span has already been determined, calculate the required size of the stud. After stud size and wale spacing have been determined, determine the maximum allowable spacing of wale supports (tie spacing) based on wale size and load. If tie spacing has been preselected, determine the minimum wale size. Double wales are commonly used (see Figure 3) to avoid the necessity of drilling wales for tie insertion.

Next, check the tie's ability to carry the load imposed by wale and tie spacing. The load (lb) [kN] on each tie is calculated as the design load (lb/sq ft) [kPa] multiplied by the product of tie spacing (ft) [m] and wale spacing (ft) [m]. If the load exceeds tie strength, a stronger tie must be used or the tie spacing must be reduced.

The next step is to check bearing stresses (or compression perpendicular to the grain) where the studs rest on wales and where tie ends bear on wales. Maximum bearing stress must not exceed the allowable compression stress perpendicular to the grain or crushing will result. Finally, design lateral bracing to resist any expected lateral loads, such as wind loads.

Example 2 Forms are being designed for an 8-ft (2.44-m)-high concrete wall to be poured at a rate of 4 ft/h (1.219 m/h), internally vibrated, at a temperature of 90°F (32°C). The concrete mixture will use Type I cement without retarders and is estimated to weigh 150 lb/cu ft (2403 kg/m³). Sheathing will be 4 × 8–ft (1.2 × 2.4–m) sheets of ¾-in. (19-mm)-thick Class I Plyform with face grain perpendicular to studs (see Figure 3). Studs and double wales will be 2 × 4-in. (50 × 100–mm) lumber. Snap ties are 3000-lb (13.34-kN) capacity with 1½-in. (38-mm)-wide wedges bearing on wales. Deflection must not exceed $\frac{\ell}{}$. Determine stud, wale, and tie spacing. Use Plyform section properties and allowable stress from Table 6 and lumber section properties from Table 7. Allowable stresses for the lumber being used for studs and wales are as follows:

$$F_b = 1810 \text{ lb/sq in. (12 480 kPa)}$$
$$F_v = 120 \text{ lb/sq in. (827 kPa)}$$
$$F_{c\perp} = 485 \text{ lb/sq in. (3340 kPa)}$$
$$E = 1.7 \times 10^6 \text{ lb/sq in. (11.7} \times 10^6 \text{ kPa)}$$

Solution

Design Load

$$C_w = 1.0$$
$$C_c = 1.0$$
$$p = C_w C_c\left(150 + \frac{9000\,R}{T}\right) = (1)(1)\left\{150 + \frac{(9000)(4)}{90}\right\}$$
$$= 550 \text{ lb/sq ft}$$

FIGURE 3. Wall form, Example 2.

Section

$$\left[p = C_w C_c\left(7.2 + \frac{785\,R}{T + 18}\right) = (1)(1)\left\{7.2 + \frac{(785)(1.219)}{32 + 18}\right\}\right.$$

$$\left. = 26.3 \text{ kN/m}^2\right]$$

Use 600 lb/sq ft [28.7 kN/m²].

Select Stud Spacing (Three or More Spans)

Material: ¾-in. (19-mm) Class I Plyform® (Table 4)

Consider a strip 12-in. wide (or 1-m wide):

$$w = 1 \times 1 \times 600 = 600 \text{ lb/ft}$$

$$[w = 1 \times 1 \times 28.7 = 28.7 \text{ kN/m}]$$

(a) Bending:

$$l = 10.95\left(\frac{F_b KS}{w}\right)^{1/2}$$

$$= 10.95\left(\frac{0.878 \times 10^3}{550}\right)^{1/2} = 13.2 \text{ in.}$$

$$\left[l = 3.16\left(\frac{F_b KS}{w}\right)^{1/2}\right.$$

$$\left. = 3.16\left(\frac{326 \times 10^3}{28.7}\right)^{1/2} = 337 \text{ mm}\right]$$

(b) Shear:

$$l = 20\,\frac{F_s lb/O}{w} + 2d$$

$$= \frac{(20)(0.517 \times 10^3)}{600} + (2)(\tfrac{3}{4})$$

$$= 17.2 + 1.5 = 18.7 \text{ in.}$$

$$\left[l = 1.67\,\frac{F_s lb/O}{w} + 2d\right.$$

$$= \frac{(1.67)(7.55 \times 10^3)}{28.7} + (2)(.19)$$

$$\left. = 439 + 38 = 477 \text{ mm}\right]$$

(c) Deflection:

$$l = 1.69\left(\frac{EI}{w}\right)^{1/3}$$

$$= (1.69)\left(\frac{0.298 \times 10^6}{600}\right)^{1/3} = 13.4 \text{ in.}$$

$$\left[l = \frac{73.8}{1000}\left(\frac{EI}{w}\right)^{1/3}\right.$$

$$= \frac{73.8}{1000}\left(\frac{2810 \times 10^9}{28.7}\right)^{1/3} = 340 \text{ mm}$$

Bending governs. Maximum span = 13.2 in. (337 mm). Use a 12-in. (304-mm) stud spacing.

Select Wale Spacing (Three or More Spans)

Since the stud spacing is 12 in. (304 mm), consider a uniform design load 1-ft (304-mm) wide resting on each stud.

$$w = 1 \times 1 \times 600 = 600 \text{ lb/ft}$$

$$\left[w = \frac{304}{1000} \times 1 \times 28.7 = 8.7 \text{ kN/m}\right]$$

(a) Bending:

$$I = 10.95\left(\frac{F_bS}{2}\right)^{1/2}$$

$$= (10.95)\left(\frac{(1810)(3.063)}{600}\right)^{1/2} = 33.3 \text{ in.}$$

$$\left[\begin{array}{l} I = \dfrac{100}{1000}\left(\dfrac{F_bS}{w}\right)^{1/2} \\[2mm] I = \dfrac{100}{1000}\left(\dfrac{(12{,}480)(0.5019 \times 10^5)}{8.7}\right)^{1/2} = 849 \text{ mm} \end{array}\right]$$

(b) Shear:

$$I = 13.3\frac{F_vA}{w} + 2d$$

$$= \frac{(13.3)(120)(5.25)}{600} + (2)(3.5) = 21.0 \text{ in.}$$

$$\left[\begin{array}{l} I = \dfrac{1.11}{1000}\dfrac{F_vA}{w} + 2d \\[2mm] = \dfrac{(1.11)(827)(3.387 \times 10^3)}{(1000)(8.7)} + (2)(88.9) = 535 \text{ mm} \end{array}\right]$$

(c) Deflection:

$$I = 1.69\left(\frac{EI}{w}\right)^{1/3}$$

$$= 1.69\left(\frac{1.7 \times 10^6)(5.359)}{600}\right)^{1/3} = 41.8 \text{ in.}$$

$$\left[\begin{array}{l} I = \dfrac{73.8}{1000}\left(\dfrac{EI}{w}\right)^{1/3} \\[2mm] = \dfrac{73.8}{1000}\left(\dfrac{(11.7 \times 10^6)(2.231 \times 10^6)}{8.7}\right) = 1064 \text{ mm} \end{array}\right]$$

Shear governs, so maximum span (wale spacing) is 22.23 in. (566 mm). Use a 16-in. (406-mm) wale spacing for modular units.

Select Tie Spacing (Three or More Spans, Double Wales)

Based on a wale spacing of 16 in. (406 mm),

$$w = \frac{16}{12} \times 600 = 800.0 \text{ lb/ft}$$

$$\left[w = \frac{406}{304} \times 8.7 = 11.6 \text{ kN/m}\right]$$

(a) Bending:

$$I = 10.95\left(\frac{F_bS}{w}\right)^{1/2}$$

$$= 10.95\left(\frac{(1810)(2 \times 3.063)}{800}\right)^{1/2} = 40.8 \text{ in.}$$

$$\left[\begin{array}{l} I = \dfrac{100}{1000}\left(\dfrac{F_bS}{w}\right)^{1/2} \\[2mm] = \dfrac{100}{1000}\left(\dfrac{(12{,}480)(2 \times 0.5019 \times 10^5)}{11.6}\right)^{1/2} = 1039 \text{ mm} \end{array}\right]$$

(b) Shear:

$$I = 13.3\frac{F_vA}{w} + 2d$$

$$= \frac{(13.3)(120)(2 \times 5.25)}{800} + (2)(3.5) = 27.9 \text{ in.}$$

$$\left[\begin{array}{l} I = \dfrac{1.11}{1000}\dfrac{F_vA}{w} + 2d \\[2mm] = \dfrac{(1.11)(827)(2 \times 3.387 \times 10^3)}{(1000)(11.6)} + (2)(88.9) = 714 \text{ mm} \end{array}\right]$$

(c) Deflection:

$$I = 1.69\left(\frac{EI}{w}\right)^{1/3}$$

$$= 1.69\left(\frac{(1.7 \times 10^6)(2 \times 5.359)}{800}\right)^{1/3} = 47.9 \text{ in.}$$

$$\left[\begin{array}{l} I = \dfrac{73.8}{1000}\left(\dfrac{EI}{w}\right) \\[2mm] = \dfrac{73.8}{1000}\left(\dfrac{(11.7 \times 10^6)(2 \times 21 \times 10^6)}{11.6}\right)^{1/3} = 1218 \text{ mm} \end{array}\right]$$

Shear governs. Maximum span is 27.9 in. (714 mm). Select a 24-in. (610-mm) tie spacing for a modular value.

(d) Check tie load:

$$P = \text{Wale spacing} \times \text{Tie spacing} \times p$$

$$= \frac{16}{12} \times \frac{24}{12} \times (600) = 1600 \text{ lb/tie} < 3000 \text{ lb} \quad OK$$

$$\left[P = \frac{(406)(610)}{(1000)(1000)} \times 28.7 = 7.11 \text{ kN} < 13.34 \text{ kN}\right]$$

Check Bearing

(a) Stud on wales:

Bearing area (A) (double wales) $= (2)(1.5)(1.5) = 4.5$ sq in.

$$[A = (2)(38)(38) = 2888 \text{ mm}^2]$$

Load at each panel point (P) $=$ Load/ft(m) of stud $\times$ Wale spacing (ft/m)

$$P = (600)\frac{16}{12} = 800 \text{ lb}$$

$$\left[P = (8.7)\frac{406}{1000} = 3.53 \text{ kN}\right]$$

$$f_c = \frac{P}{A} = \frac{800}{4.5} = 178 \text{ lb/sq in.} < 485 \text{ lb/sq in.} (F_c) \quad OK$$

$$\left[f_c = \frac{3.53 \times 10^6}{2888} = 1222 \text{ kPa} < 3340 \text{ kpa} (F_c)\right]$$

(b) Tie wedges on wales:

Tie load (P) $= 1600$ lb [7.11 kN]

Bearing area (A) $= (1.5)(1.5)(2) = 4.5$ sq in.

$$[A = (38)(38)(2) = 2888 \text{ mm}^2]$$

$$f_{c\perp} = \frac{P}{A} = \frac{1600}{4.5} = 356 \text{ lb/sq in.} < 485 \text{ lb/sq in.} \ (F_{c\perp})\perp \ OK$$

$$\left[f_{c\perp} = \frac{7.11 \times 10^6}{2888} = 2462 \text{ kPa} < 3340 \text{ kPa} \ (F_{c\perp}) \right]$$

Final Design

Sheathing: 4 × 8 ft (1.2 × 2.4 m) sheets of ³/₄-in. (19-mm) Class I Plyform placed with the long axis horizontal.

> Studs: 2 × 4's (50 × 100 mm) at 12 in. (304 mm) on center.
> Wales: Double 2 × 4's (50 × 100 mm) at 16 in. (406 mm) on center.
> Ties: 3000-lb (13.34-kN) snap ties at 24 in. (610 mm) on center.

6 DESIGN OF LATERAL BRACING

Many failures of formwork have been traced to omitted or inadequately designed lateral bracing. Minimum lateral design load values were given in Section 2. Design procedures for lateral bracing are described and illustrated in the following paragraphs.

Lateral Braces for Wall and Column Forms

For wall and column forms, lateral bracing is usually provided by inclined rigid braces or guy-wire bracing. Since wind loads, and lateral loads in general, may be applied in either direction perpendicular to the face of the form, guy-wire bracing must be placed on both sides of the forms. When rigid braces are used, they may be placed on only one side of the form if designed to resist both tension and compression forces. When forms are placed on only one side of a wall with the excavation serving as the second form, lateral bracing must be designed to resist the lateral pressure of the concrete as well as other lateral forces.

Inclined bracing will usually resist any wind uplift forces on vertical forms. However, uplift forces on inclined forms may require additional consideration and the use of special anchors or tiedowns. The strut load per foot of form developed by the design lateral load can be calculated by the use of Equation 11. The total load per strut is then P' multiplied by strut spacing.

$$P' = \frac{H \times h \times l}{h' \times l'} \tag{11}$$

$$l = (h'^2 + l'^2)^{1/2} \tag{12}$$

where P' = strut load per foot of form (lb/ft) [kN/m]

H = lateral load at top of form (lb/ft) [kN/m]

h = height of form (ft) [m]

h' = height of top of strut (ft) [m]

l = length of strut (ft) [m]

l' = horizontal distance from form to bottom of strut (ft) [m]

If struts are used on only one side of the form, the allowable unit stress for strut design will be the lowest of the three possible allowable stress values (F_c, F'_c, or F_t).

Example 3 Determine the maximum spacing of nominal 2 × 4–in. (50 × 100–mm) lateral braces for the wall form of Example 2 placed as shown in Figure 4. Assume that local code wind requirements are less stringent than Table 3. Allowable stress values for the braces are as follows.

	Allowable Stress	
	lb/sq in.	kPa
F_c	850	5861
F_t	725	4999
E	1.4×10^6	9.7×10^6

FIGURE 4. Wall form bracing, Example 3.

Solution

Determine the design lateral force per unit length of form.

$$H = 100 \text{ lb/ft} \quad \text{(Table 3)}$$

$$[H = 1.46 \text{ kN/m}] \quad \text{(Table 3)}$$

Determine the length of the strut using Equation 12.

$$l = \left(h'^2 + l'^2\right)^{1/2}$$

$$= \left(6^2 + 5^2\right)^{1/2} = 7.81 \text{ ft}$$

$$\left[l = \left(1.83^2 + 1.53^2\right)^{1/2} = 2.38 \text{ m}\right]$$

The axial concentrated load on the strut produced by a unit length of form may now be determined from Equation 1.

$$P' = \frac{H \times h \times l}{h' \times l'} = \frac{(100)(8)(7.81)}{(6)(5)} = 208.3 \text{ lb/ft of form}$$

$$\left[P' = \frac{(1.46)(2.44)(2.38)}{(1.83)(1.53)} = 3.03 \text{ kN/m}\right]$$

Next, we determine the allowable compressive stress for each strut using Equation 10. To do this, we must determine the l/d ratio of the strut.

$$l/d = \frac{(7.81)(12)}{1.5} = 62.5 > 50$$

$$\left[l/d = \frac{(2.38)(1000)}{(38.1)} = 62.5 > 50\right]$$

Since the l/d ratio exceeds 50, each strut must be provided lateral bracing to reduce its unsupported length. Try a single lateral support located at the midpoint of each strut, reducing ℓ to 46.9 in. (1.19 m).

$$Fc' = \frac{0.3E}{(l/d)^2} = \frac{(0.3)(1.4 \times 10^6)}{(46.9/1.5)^2} = 430 \text{ psi}$$

$$\left[Fc' = \frac{(0.3)(9.7 \times 10^6)}{(1190/38)^2} = 2.97 \text{ kPa}\right]$$

As $Fc' < Ft < Fc$, the value of Fc' governs.

The maximum allowable compressive force per strut is as follows:

$$P = (1.5)(3.5)(430) = 2257 \text{ lb}$$

$$\left[P = \frac{(38)(89)(2967)}{10^6} = 10.03 \text{ kN}\right]$$

Thus maximum strut spacing is as follows:

$$s = \frac{P}{P'} = \frac{2257}{208.3} = 10.8 \text{ ft}$$

$$\left[s = \frac{10.03}{3.03} = 3.31 \text{ m}\right]$$

Keep in mind that this design is based on providing lateral support to each strut at the midpoint of its length.

Lateral Braces for Slab Forms

For elevated floor or roof slab forms, lateral bracing may consist of cross braces between shores or inclined bracing along the outside edge of the form similar to that used for wall forms. The following example illustrates the method of determining the design lateral load for slab forms.

Example 4 Determine the design lateral force for the slab form 6 in. (152 mm) thick, 20 ft (6.1 m) wide, and 100 ft (30.5 m) long shown in Figure 5. The slab is to be poured in one pour. Assume concrete density is 150 lb/cu ft (2403 kg/m^3) and that the formwork weighs 15 lb/sq ft (0.72 kPa).

Solution

Dead load $= (^1/_2)(1)(150) + 15 = 90 \text{ lb/sq ft}$

$$\left[dl = \frac{(0.152)(1)(2403)(9.8)}{1000} + 0.72 = 4.30 \text{ kPa}\right]$$

$$H = 0.02 \times dl \times ws$$

For the 20-ft (6.1-m) face, the width of the slab is 100 ft (30.5 m).

$$H_{20} = (0.02)(90)(100) = 180 \text{ lb/lin ft}$$

$$[H = (0.02)(4.30)(30.5) = 2.62 \text{ kN/m}]$$

For the 100-ft (30.5-m) face, the width of the slab is 20 ft (6.1 m).

$$H_{100} = (0.02)(90)(20) = 36 \text{ lb/ft} < 100 \text{ lb/ft (minimum value)}$$

$$[H = (0.02)(4.29)(6.1) = 0.52 \text{ kN/m} < 1.46 \text{ kN/m}]$$

Therefore, use $H_{100} = 100 \text{ lb/ft}$ (1.46 kN/m) = minimum load.

FIGURE 5. Slab form bracing design, Example 4.

Problems

1. Determine the maximum allowable spacing of joists used with nominal 1-in. (25-mm) lumber decking if the design load is 200 lb/sq ft (9.6 kPa). Assume the decking is continuous over three or more spans and is Hem-Fir. Limit deflection to I/360.

2. What loads must formwork for elevated slabs be designed to resist?

3. Determine the maximum allowable span of nominal 2 × 4 in. (50 × 100 mm) wall form studs carrying a design load of 1000 lb/sq ft (47.9 kPa). Tie stud spacing is 16 in. (406 mm) on center. Use the allowable stresses for Douglas Fir from Table 8 and 7-day load duration. Assume that studs are continuous over three or more spans. Limit deflection to 1/360 of span length. Based on the maximum allowable span, check for crushing of studs on double 2 × 4 in. (50 × 100 mm) wales.

4. Derive the equations for bending given in Table 5 using the relationships of Table 4 and Equation 5.

5. Design the formwork for a concrete slab 8-in. (203-mm) thick whose net width between beam faces is 15 ft (4.58 m). Concrete will be placed using a crane and bucket. The formwork is estimated to weigh 5 lb/sq ft (24.4 kg/m²). Decking will be ³/₄ in. (19 mm) Class I Plyform with face grain across supports. All lumber will be Southern Pine. Joists will be nominal 2-in. (50-mm) wide lumber. One 4-in. (100-mm) wide stringer will be placed between the beam faces. Limit deflection to ¹/₃₆₀ of span length. Commercial shores of 4500 lb (20 kN) capacity will be used. Lateral support will be provided by the beam forms.

6. Calculate the appropriate design load due to concrete pressure for a wall form 9-ft (2.75-m) high to be poured at a rate of 6.5 ft (2.0 m) per hour at a temperature of 68°F (20°C). Type I cement without a retarder will be used. The concrete weighs 150 lb/cu ft (2403 kg/m³).

7. Design the formwork for a wall 8-ft (2.44-m) high to be poured at the rate of 5 ft/h (1.53 m/h) at a temperature of 77°F (25°C). The concrete mixture will use Type I cement without retarders and is estimated to weigh 150 lb/cu ft (2403 kg/m³). All lumber is Southern Pine. Sheathing will be ³/₄-in. (19-mm) Class I Plyform with face grain across supports. All lumber is Southern Pine. Use nominal 2 × 4-in. (50 × 100–mm) studs, double 2 × 4-in. (50 × 100–mm) wales, and 3000-lb (13.3 kN) snap ties. Lateral wood bracing of 2 × 4 in. (50 × 200 mm) will be attached at a height of 5 ft (1.5 m) above the form bottom and anchored 4 ft (1.22 m) away from the base of the form. Use the allowable stresses of Table 8 adjusted for a 7-day load. Limit deflection to ¹/₃₆₀ of the span length. Design wind load is 25 lb/sq ft (1.2 kPa).

8. Calculate the maximum allowable span for ³/₄-in. (19-mm) Class I Plyform decking with face grain across supports carrying a design load of 150 lb/sq ft (7.2 kPa). Assume that the decking is continuous over three or more spans and limit deflection to 1/240 of span length.

9. Calculate the design load for the form of a floor slab 8-in. (203-mm) thick if the hand buggies are to be used and the formwork weighs 10 lb/sq ft (48.8 kg/m²).

10. Develop a computer program to calculate the maximum span of a plywood deck used as an elevated slab form based on the equations of Table 5 and the Plyform properties given in Table 6. Input should include design load, support conditions, allowable deflection, Plyform type, and thickness, and the data whether face grain is across supports or parallel to supports.

References

1. American Institute of Timber Construction. *Timber Construction Manual,* 5th ed. Hoboken, NJ: Wiley, 2005.

2. *American Plywood for Concrete Forms.* APA-The Engineered Wood Association, Tacoma, WA.

3. *Concrete Forming.* APA-The Engineered Wood Association, Tacoma, WA.

4. *Guide to Formwork for Concrete* (ACI 347R-94). American Concrete Institute, Detroit, MI, 1994.

5. Hurd, M.K. *Formwork for Concrete,* 7th ed. American Concrete Institute, Farmington Hills, MI, 2005.

6. Hurst, Michael P. *Formwork.* New York: Construction Press, 1983.

7. *Minimum Design Loads for Buildings and Other Structures* (ASCE 7). ASCE, Reston, VA.

8. *National Design Specification for Wood Construction.* American Forest and Paper Products Association, Washington, DC.

9. Peurifoy, Robert L., and Garold D. Oberlender. *Formwork for Concrete Structures,* 3rd ed. New York: McGraw-Hill, 1996.

10. *Plywood Design Specifications.* APA-The Engineered Wood Association, Tacoma, WA.

MASONRY CONSTRUCTION

From Chapter 14 of *Construction Methods and Management*, Eighth Edition. S. W. Nunnally. Copyright © 2011 by Pearson Education, Inc.
Published by Pearson Prentice Hall. All rights reserved.

MASONRY CONSTRUCTION

1 BRICK MASONRY

Masonry Terms

A number of specialized terms are commonly used in brick masonry construction. The reader should be familiar with these terms in order to understand the construction practices described in this section and observed in the field. Many of these terms and procedures described in this section are also applicable to concrete masonry construction, which is presented in Section 2. Figure 1 illustrates the terms applied to the six possible positions in which an individual brick may be placed. The six surfaces of a brick are identified as the face, the end, the side, the cull, and the beds, as shown in Figure 2. Brick frequently must be cut to fit into corners and other places where a whole brick cannot be used. Several common shapes are shown in Figure 3.

Figure 4 illustrates the terms applied to the components of a brick wall. A *course* is a horizontal layer of brick in the plane of the wall. In this illustration the individual bricks in each course, except the top course, are in the *stretcher* position. A *wythe* is a vertical section one brick thick. A *header* is a brick placed with its long axis perpendicular to the direction of the wall. Headers are used to bond two wythes together. The bricks in the top course of Figure 4 are in the header position. A *bed joint* is a horizontal layer of mortar (or bed) on which bricks are laid. *Headjoints* are vertical mortar joints between brick ends. A *collar joint* is a vertical joint between brick wythes. The usual thickness of mortar joints is $\frac{1}{4}$ in. (6 mm) for glazed brick and tile and either $\frac{3}{8}$ in. (10 mm) or $\frac{1}{2}$ in. (13 mm) for unglazed brick and tile. The exposed surfaces of mortar joints may be finished by troweling, tooling, or raking, as shown in Figure 5. A *troweled joint* is formed by cutting off excess mortar with the trowel and then compacting the joint with the tip of the trowel. Troweled joints include the flush joint, the struck joint, and the weather joint. A *tooled joint* is formed by using a special tool to compact and shape the mortar in the joint. The two most common tooled joints are the concave joint and the V-joint. Tooled joints form the most watertight joints. Raked joints are formed by removing a layer of mortar from the joint with a special tool. *Raked joints* are often used for appearance but are difficult to make completely watertight.

Materials

Brick is manufactured in a number of sizes and shapes. Typical brick shapes are illustrated in Figure 6. The actual size ($W \times H \times L$) of standard nonmodular brick is $3\frac{3}{4} \times 2\frac{1}{4} \times 8$ in. ($95 \times 57 \times 203$ mm). Oversized nonmodular brick is $3\frac{3}{4} \times 2\frac{3}{4} \times 8$ in. ($95 \times 70 \times 203$ mm). The other bricks shown are a few of the modular shapes available. The actual sizes of these bricks are as follows: Standard Modular, $3\frac{5}{8} \times 2\frac{1}{4} \times 7\frac{5}{8}$ in. ($92 \times 57 \times 194$ mm); Economy, $3\frac{5}{8} \times 3\frac{5}{8} \times 7\frac{5}{8}$ in. ($92 \times 92 \times 194$ mm); Utility, $3\frac{5}{8} \times 3\frac{5}{8} \times 11\frac{5}{8}$ in. ($92 \times 92 \times 295$ mm); and SCR, $5\frac{5}{8} \times 2\frac{1}{4} \times 11\frac{5}{8}$ in. ($143 \times 57 \times 295$ mm).

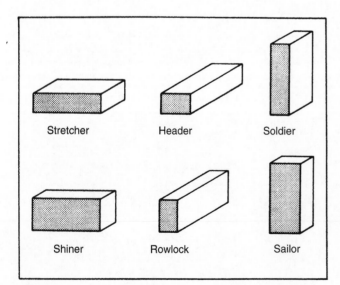

FIGURE 1. Terms applied to brick positions. (Courtesy of Brick Industry Association)

FIGURE 2. Identification of brick surfaces.

FIGURE 3. Names of cut brick.

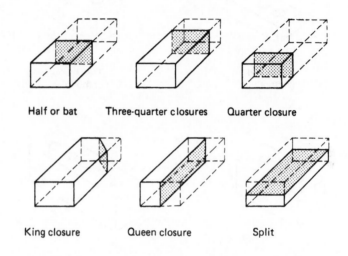

Half or bat   Three-quarter closures   Quarter closure

King closure   Queen closure   Split

FIGURE 4. Elements of a brick wall.

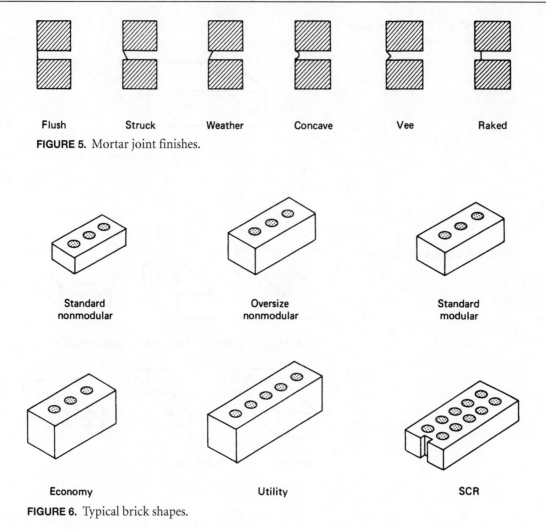

| Flush | Struck | Weather | Concave | Vee | Raked |

FIGURE 5. Mortar joint finishes.

Standard nonmodular   Oversize nonmodular   Standard modular

Economy   Utility   SCR

FIGURE 6. Typical brick shapes.

The compressive strength of individual bricks produced in the United States ranges from about 2500 lb/sq in. (17.2 MPa) to over 22,000 lb/sq in. (151.7 MPa). The overall compressive strength of brick assemblies is a function of both the compressive strength of the individual brick and the type of mortar used. Reference 5 describes procedures for determining the design strength of brick structural units by either performing tests on masonry assemblies or by using assumed strength values based on brick strength and mortar type. Assumed 28-day compressive strength values for masonry range from 530 lb/sq in. (3.7 MPa) for 2000 lb/sq in. (13.8 MPa) brick with Type N mortar and no inspection to 4600 lb/sq in. (31.7 MPa) for 14,000 lb/sq in. (96.5 MPa) brick with Type M mortar and construction inspection by an architect or engineer.

Mortars for unit masonry are covered by ASTM Standard C270 (Standard Specification for Mortar for Unit Masonry) and ASTM Standard C476 (Standard Specification for Mortar and Grout for Reinforced Masonry). The principal mortar types include types M, S, N, O, PM, and PL. Type M mortar is a high-strength mortar for use whenever high compressive strength and durability are required. Type S mortar is a medium-high-strength mortar for general-purpose use. Type N mortar is a medium-strength mortar for general use except that it should not be used below grade in contact with the earth. Type O is a low-strength mortar principally used for non-load-bearing partitions and for fireproofing. Types PM and PL are used for reinforced masonry. Mortar properties may be specified by strength or by proportions, but not both, as shown in Table 1.

Pattern Bonds

Structural bonding of masonry units is accomplished by the adhesion of mortar to masonry and by interlocking the masonry units or by embedding ties in the mortar joints. The manner in which the masonry units are assembled produces a distinctive pattern referred to as *pattern bond*. The five most common pattern bonds are the running bond, common bond, Flemish bond, English bond, and stack bond, shown in Figure 7. *Running bond* uses only stretcher courses with head joints centered over stretchers in the course below. *Common bond* uses a header course repeated at regular intervals; usually every fifth, sixth, or seventh course. Headers provide structural bonding between wythes. *Flemish bond* alternates stretchers and headers in each course

Table 1. Mortar specifications

Mortar Type	By Strength	By Proportion*		
	28-day Compressive Strength-lb/sq in. (MPa)	Portland Cement	Masonry Cement	Hydrated Lime
M	2500 (17.2)	1	None	1/4
		1	1	None
S	1800 (12.4)	1	None	1/4–1/2
		1/2	1	None
N	750 (5.2)	1	None	1/2–1
		None	1	None
O	350 (2.4)	None	1	1–2
PM	2500 (17.2)	1	1	None
PL	2500 (17.2)	1	None	1/4–1/2

*Aggregate volume should be 2¼–3 times the sum of the volumes of cement and lime used.

with headers centered over stretchers in the course below. *English bond* is made up of alternate courses of headers and stretchers, with headers centered on stretchers. *Stack bond* provides no interlocking between adjacent masonry units and is used for its architectural effect. Horizontal reinforcement should be used with stack bond to provide lateral bonding.

Hollow Masonry Walls

Masonry *cavity walls* are made up of two masonry wythes separated by an air space 2 in. (50 mm) or more in width and tied together by metal ties. Brick cavity walls combine an exterior wythe of brick with an interior wythe of brick, structural clay tile, or concrete masonry. Cavity walls have a number of advantages over a single solid masonry wall. These advantages include greater resistance to moisture penetration, better thermal and acoustical insulation, and excellent fire resistance. A hollow masonry-bonded wall constructed of utility brick, called a *utility wall,* is shown in Figure 8. While masonry-bonded walls are not as water resistant as cavity walls, they can resist water penetration when properly constructed. Recommended practice for construction of the utility wall includes bonding every sixth course (with alternating headers and stretchers), installing flashing at the bottom of the wall, providing weep holes

FIGURE 7. Principal brick pattern bonds.

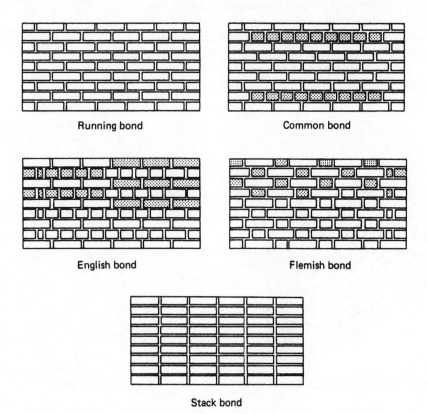

Running bond

Common bond

English bond

Flemish bond

Stack bond

Masonry bonded hollow wall

Brick cavity wall

FIGURE 8. Brick cavity and masonry-bonded hollow walls.

along the bottom exterior brick course on 24-in. (610-mm) centers, using type S mortar, and providing concave tooled joints on the exterior surface. The cavity between wythes may be filled with insulation if desired.

Reinforced Brick Masonry

The term *reinforced brick masonry* (or RBM) is applied to brick masonry in which reinforcing steel has been embedded to provide additional strength. Typical reinforced brick masonry wall construction is illustrated in Figure 9. Notice the construction is basically the same as that of a cavity wall except that reinforcing steel has been placed in the cavity and the cavity was then filled with portland cement grout. Design requirements for reinforced brick masonry are presented in reference 1. A 17-story apartment building constructed with 11-in.-thick (280-mm) reinforced brick masonry bearing walls is

FIGURE 9. Reinforced brick masonry wall.

Table 2. Protection for masonry reinforcement

Application	Minimum Cover (Exposed Face)
Bottom of footings	3 in. (76 mm)
Columns, beams, or girders not exposed to weather or soil	1½ in. (38 mm)
Horizontal joint reinforcement bars ¼ in. (6 mm) or less in diameter	⅝ in. (16 mm)
All other	
Not exposed to weather or soil	1 bar diameter but at least ¾ in. (19 mm)
Exposed to weather or soil	2 in. (51 mm)

shown in Figure 10. Prefabricated reinforced brick panels are now being used to provide special shapes in wall construction. Such panels may be rapidly erected in the field, even during inclement weather. The minimum suggested amount of mortar protection for masonry reinforcement is shown in Table 2.

Bond Beams and Lintels

A *bond beam* is a continuously reinforced horizontal beam of concrete or masonry designed to provide additional strength and to prevent cracking in a masonry wall. Bond beams are frequently placed at foundations and roof levels but may be used at any vertical interval specified by the designer. Support over openings in masonry walls may be provided by lintels or by masonry arches, as shown in Figure 11. *Lintels* are short beams of wood, steel, stone, or reinforced brick masonry used to span openings in masonry walls.

FIGURE 10. Seventeen-story building constructed with reinforced brick masonry bearing walls. (Courtesy of Brick Industry Association)

Control Joints and Flashings

Expansion or *control joints* in masonry walls are used to permit differential movement of wall sections caused by shrinkage of concrete foundations and floor slabs, temperature and moisture changes, and foundation settlement. Control joints are grooves placed in masonry to control shrinkage cracking. The usual procedure is to separate walls into sections with vertical expansion joints where differential movement may occur. Long, straight walls should be divided into sections.

Other expansion joints are placed at window and door openings, at columns and pilasters, at wall offsets, at cross walls, and under shelf angles in multistory buildings. Structural bonding across the expansion joint may be provided by interlocking construction or by flexible ties extending across the joint. Some typical expansion joints used for brick walls are shown in Figure 12. The exterior of expansion joints must be sealed with a flexible sealant to prevent moisture penetration.

Jack arch

Segmental arch

Precast concrete lintel

Reinforced brick masonry lintel

FIGURE 11. Support over openings in brick walls.

FIGURE 12. Expansion joints in brick masonry. (Courtesy of Brick Industry Association)

Expansion joints in straight walls

Expansion joints at pilasters

Expansion joints at concealed column

Expansion joints at offsets

Expansion joints at junctures

Flashing consists of layers of impervious material used to seal out moisture or to direct any moisture that does penetrate back to the outside. Flashing is used above vertical joints in parapet walls, at the junction of roofs and walls, at window sills and other projections, around chimney openings, and at the base of exterior walls. Typical flashings used with brick masonry are illustrated in Figure 13. Flashings used where roofs intersect walls or chimneys are frequently composed of two parts, a base flashing and a counterflashing. The base flashing covers the joint between intersecting surfaces while the counterflashing seals the joint between the base flashing and the vertical surface, as shown in the chimney of Figure 13.

2 CONCRETE MASONRY
Materials

Concrete masonry units are classified as concrete brick, concrete tile, solid load-bearing concrete block, hollow load-bearing concrete block, and hollow non-load-bearing concrete block. Concrete block that is glazed on one or more surfaces is available. Such units are used for their appearance, ease of cleaning, and low cost. *Solid concrete block* must have at least 75% of its cross section made up of concrete. Block having over 25% of its cross-sectional area empty is classified as *hollow block*. The usual hollow concrete block has a core area

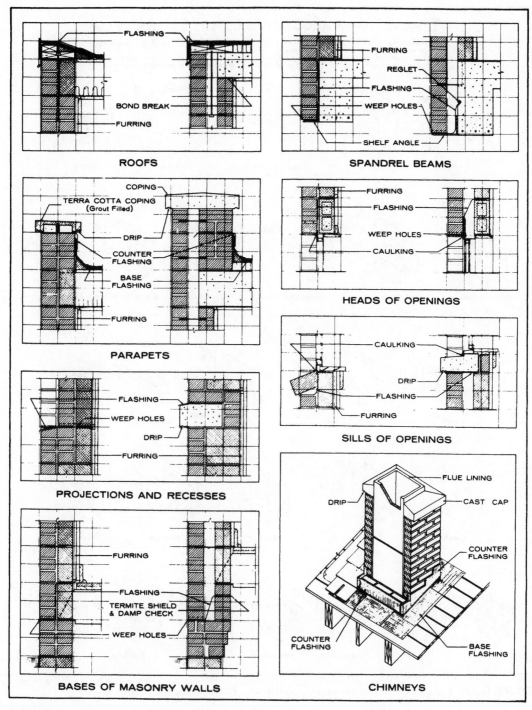

FIGURE 13. Flashing used in brick masonry construction. (Courtesy of Brick Industry Association)

making up 40–50% of its cross section. Typical shapes and sizes of concrete masonry units are shown in Figure 14. The most common nominal size of standard block is 8 × 8 × 16 in. (203 × 203 × 406 mm) [actual size $7\frac{5}{8} \times 7\frac{5}{8} \times 15\frac{5}{8}$ in. (194 × 194 × 397 mm)]. Half-thick (4-in. or 100-mm) and half-length (8-in. or 203-mm) blocks are also available. Concrete block is available as either heavyweight or lightweight block, depending on the type of aggregate used. Heavyweight load-bearing block typically weighs 40–50 lb (18.1–22.7 kg)

per unit, while a similar lightweight unit might weigh 25–35 lb (11.3–15.9 kg). Mortars used for concrete masonry units are the same as those used for brick masonry (Section 1). Mortar joints are usually $\frac{3}{8}$ in. (9.5 mm) thick. Joints in exterior walls should be tooled for maximum watertightness.

Concrete block may also be laid without mortar joints. Either standard or ground block may be stacked without mortar and then bonded by the application of a special bonding material to the outside surfaces. In this case, the

FIGURE 14. Typical concrete masonry units. (Courtesy of Portland Cement Association)

bonding agent provides structural bonding as well as water-proofing for the wall. The time required to construct a concrete block wall using this method may be as low as one-half the time required for conventional methods. In addition, the flexural and compressive strength of a surface-bonded wall may be greater than that of a conventional block wall. There are also special types of concrete block made with interlocking edges to provide structural bonding as the units are stacked without mortar.

Lintels spanning openings in concrete block usually consist of precast concrete shapes, cast-in-place concrete beams, or reinforced concrete masonry.

Reinforced Concrete Masonry

Reinforced concrete masonry construction is used to provide additional structural strength and to prevent cracking. Figure 15 illustrates several methods of reinforcing a one-story concrete block wall. At the top of the wall a concrete bond beam (A) is created by filling U-shaped block (called lintel block or beam block) with reinforced concrete. Vertical reinforcement is provided by placing reinforcing steel in some of the block cores and filling these cores with concrete (B). Additional horizontal reinforcement is obtained from reinforcing steel placed in the mortar joints (D). This type of

FIGURE 15. Some methods for reinforcing concrete masonry walls. (Courtesy of Portland Cement Association)

A- Continuous reinforced concrete bond beam. Lap bars at corners
B- Reinforced concrete studs tied to footing
C- Reinforced concrete footing
D- Reinforcement in horizontal mortar joints

construction is appropriate for areas of high design loads, such as earthquake and hurricane zones.

Additional applications of horizontal joint reinforcement illustrated in Figure 16 include tying face units to backup units, bonding the two wythes of cavity walls, and reinforcing single wythe walls. Reinforced concrete masonry construction is also used in high-rise building construction. Depending on wall height and design load, some or all of the concrete block cores may be filled with reinforced concrete. A high-rise motel using reinforced concrete masonry walls is shown under construction in Figure 17. Details of the placement of reinforcement in a reinforced concrete masonry wall are shown in Figure 18. Figure 19 shows grout being pumped into the block cores of a reinforced concrete masonry wall. The minimum suggested amount of mortar protection for masonry reinforcement is shown in Table 2.

Pattern Bonds

The running bond is probably the most common pattern bond used in concrete masonry as it is in brick masonry. However, a number of other pattern bonds have been developed to provide architectural effect. Several of these patterns are illustrated in Figure 20. The term *ashlar masonry* is carried over from stone masonry and is now commonly used to identify masonry of any material which uses rectangular units larger than brick laid in a pattern resembling stone.

3 OTHER MASONRY MATERIALS

In addition to brick and concrete, masonry units of stone and clay tile are also available. Load-bearing structural clay tile is used in a manner similar to concrete block. However, structural clay tile is seldom used in the United States today, and only a small quantity of glazed structural clay tile is currently being manufactured in this country. Stone and architectural terra-cotta are used primarily as wall veneers. Stone veneer is held in place by ties embedded in the mortar joints or by mechanical anchors fastened to the supporting structure, as shown in Figure 21. Shaped stone is also used for window sills, lintels, parapet coping (caps), and wall panels. Construction details for use of large architectural stone panels on a multistory building are shown in Figure 22.

4 ESTIMATING QUANTITY OF MASONRY

Number of Bricks Required

Although tables are available for estimating the quantity of brick required for standard walls, the estimating procedure is not difficult. Estimating the number of bricks required for a masonry wall involves five steps: (1) calculating the net surface area of the wall, (2) calculating the surface area of one brick as positioned (including the mortar joint),

FIGURE 16. Horizontal joint reinforcement. (With permission Dayton Superior Corporation)

Tied wall

Cavity wall

Stack bond wall

Running bond wall

FIGURE 17. Construction of a high-rise motel using reinforced concrete masonry walls. (Courtesy of Portland Cement Association)

FIGURE 18. Placement of reinforcing steel in reinforced concrete masonry wall. (Courtesy of Portland Cement Association)

(3) dividing the wall area by the surface area of one brick, (4) multiplying this number by the number of wythes of wall thickness, and (5) adding an amount for waste.

First, the gross surface area of the wall is calculated in square feet (m²) and the area of openings is subtracted to give the net surface area of the wall. Do not double count the area of corners where two walls intersect. Next, the surface area of the brick as positioned (including the mortar joint) is calculated. Dividing the wall net surface area by the surface area of one brick (including the mortar joint) yields the number of bricks per wythe for the wall. The number of bricks per wythe is then multiplied by the wall thickness (number of wythes). Finally, a factor (usually 2–10%) must be added for waste. The method is illustrated in Example 1.

Example 1 Calculate the number of bricks $3\frac{3}{4} \times 2\frac{1}{4} \times 8$ in. ($95 \times 57 \times 203$ mm) laid in running bond required for a double wythe wall 8-ft high by 14-ft wide (2.44×4.27 m) having one opening 48×72 in. (1.22×1.83 m) and one opening 32×48 in. (0.81×1.22 m). Mortar joints are $\frac{1}{2}$ in. (13 mm). Allow 3% for brick waste.

FIGURE 19. Pumping grout into reinforced concrete masonry wall. (Courtesy of Portland Cement Association)

Solution

$$\text{Net wall area} = (8 \times 14) - \frac{(48 \times 72)}{144} - \frac{(32 \times 48)}{144}$$

$$= 77.33 \text{ sq ft}$$

$$[= (2.44 \times 4.27) - (1.22 \times 1.83)$$
$$- (0.81 \times 1.22) = 7.2 \text{ m}^2]$$

$$\text{Area of 1 brick} = \frac{(2.25 + 0.5)(8.0 + 0.5)}{144} = 0.1623 \text{ sq ft}$$

$$[= (0.057 + 0.013)(0.203 + 0.013)$$
$$= 0.01512 \text{ m}^2]$$

$$\begin{array}{c}\text{Number of}\\\text{bricks required}\end{array} = \frac{77.33}{0.1623} \times 2 \times 1.03 = 982$$

$$\left[= \frac{7.2}{0.01512} \times 2 \times 1.03 = 981\right]$$

Quantity of Mortar Required

A similar procedure can be used to calculate the quantity of mortar required for a particular wall. First, the volume of mortar required for a single brick is calculated. Equation 1 may be used for this purpose.

$$\begin{array}{c}\text{Volume per brick}\\\text{(cu in. or m}^3\text{)}\end{array} = (t)(W)(L + H + t) \qquad (1)$$

where t = joint thickness (in. or m)

W = brick width/depth (in. or m)

L = brick length (in. or m)

H = brick height (in. or m)

Multiplying the mortar required per brick by the number of bricks and adding a waste factor (usually about 25%) yields the mortar required per wythe. When the wall is more than one wythe thick, we must multiply by the number of wythes and add the volume of mortar needed to fill the gap between wythes. The volume of mortar between wythes is simply the product of the joint thickness times the net area of the wall. Again a waste factor must be added. A sample calculation is given in Example 2.

Example 2 Estimate the quantity of mortar required for the problem of Example 1. The joint thickness between wythes is $\frac{1}{2}$ in. (13 mm). Assume a 25% waste factor.

Solution

$$\text{Volume per brick} = \frac{(0.5)(3.75)(8.0 + 2.25 + 0.5)}{1728}$$

$$= 0.01166 \text{ cu ft}$$

$$[= (0.013)(0.095)(0.203 + 0.057 + 0.013)]$$

$$= 0.00033716 \text{ m}^3$$

$$\begin{array}{c}\text{Volume per}\\\text{wythe}\end{array} = 0.01166 \times \frac{982}{2} = 5.7 \text{ cu ft}$$

$$\left[= 0.00033716 \times \frac{981}{2} = 0.165 \text{ m}^3\right]$$

FIGURE 20. Concrete masonry pattern bonds. (Courtesy of Portland Cement Association)

$$\text{Volume between wythes} = \frac{(0.5)}{12}(77.33) = 3.2 \text{ cu ft}$$

$$[= (0.013)(7.2) = 0.094 \text{ m}^3]$$

$$\text{Mortar required} = 1.25(2 \times 5.7 + 3.2) = 18.3 \text{ cu ft}$$

$$[= 1.25(2 \times 0.165 + 0.094] = 0.53 \text{ m}^3]$$

5 CONSTRUCTION PRACTICE

Wind Load on Fresh Masonry

Masonry walls must be designed to safely resist all expected loads, including dead loads, live loads, and wind loads. While the designer must provide a safe structural design, the builder must erect the structure as designed and must also be able to determine the support requirements during construction. Many failures of masonry walls under construction have occurred as the result of inadequate bracing against wind load.

The maximum safe height of an unbraced masonry wall under construction may be calculated by setting the overturning moment produced by wind force equal to the resisting moment produced by the weight of the wall. Referring to Figure 23, we will analyze moments about the toe of the wall (A) for a unit length of wall. The design wind load in lb/sq ft (kPa) obtained from the local building code may be used to compute bracing requirements. Alternatively, the maximum anticipated wind velocity can be estimated from local weather records and converted to wind load using Table 3. The method of analysis is as follows:

$$\text{Overturning moment } (M_o) = P \cdot \frac{h}{2} = qh \cdot \frac{h}{2} = \frac{qh^2}{2}$$

$$\text{Resisting moment } (M_r) = W \cdot \frac{t}{2} = d \cdot h \cdot \frac{t}{2} = \frac{dht}{2}$$

Free equilibrium $\qquad \Sigma M_A = 0$

Hence $\qquad M_o - M_r = 0$

and $\qquad M_o = M_r$

Substitution yields $\qquad \dfrac{qh^2}{2} = \dfrac{dht}{2}$

$$h_s = \frac{dt}{q} \qquad (2)$$

Stone Veneer with Bond Stone Anchored to Brick Backing

Stone Veneer Anchored to Wood Frame Backing

N.C. = noncorrosive

FIGURE 21. Stone veneer. (Courtesy of Indiana Limestone Institute of America, Inc.)

where q = wind force (lb/sq ft or kPa)

H = wall height (ft or m)

h_s = safe unbraced height (ft or m)

t = wall thickness (ft or m)

d = weight of wall per unit of surface (lb/sq ft or kN/m^2)

P = resultant wind force (lb or kPa)

W = resultant weight force (lb or kN)

Typical values for the weight of masonry walls per unit of height are given in Table 4. Notice that this analysis does not include any specific factor of safety. However, it does neglect all bonding provided by the partially set mortar. In practice, this should provide an adequate factor of safety except in unusual cases.

The proper bracing of a concrete masonry wall under construction is illustrated in Figure 24. Shores, forms, and braces must not be removed until the mortar has developed sufficient strength to carry all construction loads. Concentrated loads should not be applied to a masonry wall or column until 3 days after construction.

Example 3 Find the maximum safe unsupported height in feet and meters for an 8-in. (20-cm) heavyweight concrete block wall if the maximum expected wind velocity is 50 mi/h (80 km/h).

Solution

$$h_s = \frac{d \times t}{q} \quad \text{(Eq 2)}$$

d = 56 lb/ft^2 (2.68 kN/m^2)   (Table 4)

t = $^8/_{12}$ ft (0.20 m)

q = 6 lb/sq ft (0.29 kPa)   (Table 3)

$$h_s = \frac{(56)(^8/_{12})}{6} = 6.2 \text{ ft}$$

$$\left[= \frac{(2.68)(0.20)}{0.29} = 1.9 \text{ m} \right]$$

Masonry Materials

Masonry mortar must meet the requirements of ASTM C270. Sand should be clean and well graded in accordance with ASTM C144. The best mortar workability is obtained when the sand contains particles of all sizes from very fine to coarse. Harsh mortars are produced by sand having insufficient fines while excess fines will result in mortar having good workability but lower strength and high porosity. Machine mixing is recommended but in any case, mixing should continue for at least 3 min. Mortar that has stiffened from evaporation may be retempered by adding additional water and remixing. However, to avoid the possibility of using mortar that has stiffened due to hydration, mortar should be discarded $2\frac{1}{2}$ h after initial mixing.

Placing Masonry and Reinforcement

Concrete masonry units should be stored and laid in a dry condition. Brick having adsorption rates greater than 20 g of water per minute should be wetted before being placed to reduce its absorption rate. However, such brick should be allowed to dry after wetting so that it is in a saturated, surface-dry condition when laid.

Masonry units should be placed with joints of the specified width. Brick should be laid with full bed and head joints. In general, concrete block may be laid with either full mortar bedding or face-shell bedding (illustrated in Figure 25). However, full mortar bedding should be used for the bottom or starting course of block and for high-load-bearing units. Tooled mortar joints should be carefully compacted with a finishing tool after the mortar has partially stiffened to provide maximum watertightness. Maximum construction tolerances for brick masonry specified by the Brick Institute of America include vertical or plumb variations of $\frac{1}{4}$ in. (6 mm) in 10 ft (3 m) and $\frac{1}{2}$ in. (13 mm) in 40 ft (12 m); horizontal or grade variation of $\frac{1}{4}$ in. (6 mm) in 20 ft (6 m) and $\frac{1}{2}$ in. (13 mm) in 40 ft (12 m) or more; variation from the plan position of $\frac{1}{2}$ in. (13 mm) in 20 ft (6 m) and $\frac{3}{4}$ in.

In multi-story construction limestone panels should be structurally supported at vertical intervals not to exceed the floor spacings. The preferred method of doing this is to attach a structural member (angle, plate) to the building frame and projecting out from it, as shown on this sheet. This method allows for all panels to be of the same thickness thus giving a uniformity to both fabrication and setting methods. A second method is to actually rest the stone on the building frame.

elevation

Recommended No. & Spacing of Anchors

- For panels up to 4'-6" wide
  panels 2' to 4' high—2 anchors each top & bottom beds
  panels over 4' high, add one side anchor for each 4' of height
- For panels over 4'-6" wide, add additional anchors at approx. 4' o.c. in both top & bottom beds.

FIGURE 22. Anchorage of stone panels to multistory building. (Courtesy of Indiana Limestone Institute of America, Inc.)

(19 mm) in 40 ft (12 m) or more; and variation in section thickness of $-\frac{1}{4}$ in. (6 mm) to $+\frac{1}{2}$ in. (13 mm). Reinforcing steel must be protected by the minimum thickness of cover described in Table 2. Masonry reinforcement not exceeding $\frac{1}{4}$ in. (6 mm) in diameter should have a minimum mortar cover of $\frac{5}{8}$ in. (16 mm) on exterior faces and $\frac{1}{2}$ in. (13 mm) on interior faces. This type of reinforcement should be lapped at least 6 in. (152 mm) at splices to provide adequate bonding at the splice.

Bonding Masonry

Adequate bonding must be provided where masonry walls intersect, between the wythes of cavity walls or multiple-wythe walls, and between units in stack bond construction. Bonding may be provided by masonry bonding units, by corrosion-resistant metal ties, or by truss or ladder-type masonry reinforcement. The size and spacing of bonding specified by the designer must be used. Care must also be

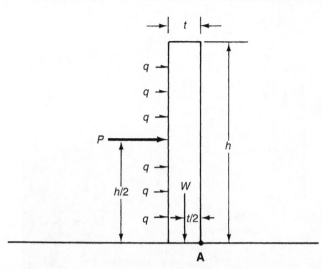

FIGURE 23. Analysis of loads on fresh masonry wall.

Table 4. Typical unit weight for masonry walls

Type of Wall	Weight per Unit of Wall Surface	
	lb/ft²	kN/m²
Heavyweight concrete block		
4-in. (10-cm)	29	1.39
6-in. (15-cm)	44	2.11
8-in. (20-cm)	56	2.68
12-in. (30-cm)	80	3.83
Lightweight concrete block		
4-in. (10-cm)	21	1.01
6-in. (15-cm)	30	1.44
8-in. (20-cm)	36	1.72
12-in. (30-cm)	49	2.35
Brick (solid)		
4-in. (10-cm)	40	1.92
6-in. (15-cm)	60	2.87
8-in. (20-cm)	80	3.83
12-in. (30-cm)	120	5.75

exercised to ensure that expansion joints are properly filled with elastic material and kept clean of mortar and other rigid materials.

Masonry grout is a fluid mixture of cement, sand, and water or cement and water. It may also contain various admixtures. Grout may be used to fill reinforced bond beams, bond together adjacent masonry wythes and their reinforcement, and bond together masonry units and steel reinforcement placed in the hollow cores of masonry units. *Self-consolidating grouts* use a superplasticizing admixture to produce an extremely fluid grout capable of easily filling small spaces within masonry units. The procedures for protecting grout in hot or cold weather conditions are similar to those described next for masonry construction. However, for air temperatures of 25°F (−4°C) or below, grout should be protected by insulating blankets or heated enclosures for 48 h after it is placed unless only Type III cement is used in the grout.

Weather Protection

Concrete masonry units must be dried to the specified moisture content before use. After drying, they should be stored off the ground and protected from rain. The top of exposed concrete and brick masonry under construction should be protected from rain by covering with a waterproof material whenever work is stopped. Masonry walls that are saturated by rain during construction may require months to completely dry out and will undergo increased shrinkage during drying. Efflorescence, or staining of brick surfaces by dissolved salts, often results when brick walls are saturated during construction.

Hot- and Cold-Weather Masonry Construction

Hot-weather masonry construction is defined in reference 1 as masonry construction occurring when ambient temperature exceeds 100°F (38°C), or 90°F (32°C) with wind velocity greater than 8 mph (13 km/h). High temperature of mortar and masonry units serve to reduce mortar workability, increase evaporation, increase moisture absorption by masonry units, reduce the amount of air entrained by air-entraining agents, and speed the set of the mortar. Under these conditions, reference 1 requires the contractor to take steps to minimize the effect of high temperature. Some of these include:

- Maintain sand piles in a loose, damp condition.
- Avoid hot midday hours when scheduling masonry construction.
- Utilize cool water to mix and retemper mortar.

Table 3. Design wind load pressure

Wind Velocity		Design Wind Load*	
mi/h	km/h	lb/sq ft	kPa
50	80	6	0.29
60	96	7	0.34
70	112	11	0.53
80	128	15	0.72
90	144	20	0.96
100	161	26	1.24
110	177	32	1.53
120	193	39	1.87
130	209	45	2.15

*Effective wind pressure on ordinary structures less than 30 ft (9.1 m) high in flat, open country (ANSI A58.1-1972).

FIGURE 24. Bracing of a concrete masonry wall under construction. (Courtesy of Portland Cement Association)

- Use mortar within 2 h of initial mixing.
- Flush the mixer, mortar boards, and transport containers with cool water before adding mortar.
- Maintain mortar temperature below 120°F (49°C).
- Spray newly constructed masonry with a fog spray of water at least three times per day for at least 3 days.

When ambient temperature is above 115°F (46°C), shading of mixing equipment and masonry units from direct sunlight is also required. If necessary, wind breaks and covering of completed masonry construction to prevent loss of moisture during curing may also be required.

The precautions for placing masonry units during cold weather are similar to those for placing concrete in cold weather. The requirements for cold-weather masonry construction are also contained in reference 1. Some requirements include the following:

- Do not place masonry on a frozen base or bed since proper bond will not be developed between the mortar bed and the frozen surface. If necessary, thaw the supporting surface by careful use of heat.

Full mortar bedding

Face-shell mortar bedding

FIGURE 25. Mortar bedding of concrete block. (Courtesy of Portland Cement Association)

- Do not lay wet or frozen masonry units.
- For ambient temperatures below 40°F (60°C), do not lay glass masonry units. Since the units absorb little water, the mortar may be damaged by freezing.
- For temperatures between 25°F (−4°C) and 40°F (4°C), heat mixing water and/or sand to obtain a mortar temperature between 40°F (4°C) and 120°F (89°C). Keep mortar above freezing until placed.
- For temperatures below 25°F (−4°C), heat masonry units to 40°F (4°C). If wind speed exceeds 15 mph (24 km/h) or ambient temperature is below 20°F (−7°C), use enclosures and auxiliary heat to keep air temperature above 32°F (0°C).
- Protect newly laid masonry by covering it with a weather-resistant membrane or insulating blanket for 24 h after placing.

The use of an admixture to lower the mortar freezing point is not recommended. However, a nonchloride-based accelerator may be used to shorten the time required for the mortar to develop sufficient strength to resist freezing. The use of an accelerator does not eliminate the requirement of protecting masonry from freezing but does reduce the time required for protection.

The durability of completed masonry panels during freeze–thaw cycles has been evaluated in laboratory tests sponsored by the Portland Cement Association. It was found that masonry panels constructed from durable brick and air-entrained ASTM C270 Type S mortar and air-entrained Type S masonry cement could withstand prolonged exposure to severe freeze–thaw conditions without damage. However, masonry panels constructed with the same brick and Type S mortar with low air content suffered frost damage ranging from slight to severe.

Problems

1. What is the minimum mortar cover required for a No. 3 rebar located near the exterior face of a reinforced concrete masonry wall exposed to weather?

2. What is the nominal size and typical weight of a standard concrete block?

3. Find the maximum safe unsupported height of a 6-in. (150-mm) lightweight concrete block wall if the design wind load is 15 lb/sq ft (0.72 kPa).

4. How many $3\frac{3}{4} \times 2\frac{1}{4} \times 8$ in. ($95 \times 57 \times 203$ mm) bricks are required for a double wythe wall 8 ft (2.44 m) high × 30 ft (9.14 m) wide having one opening 48×72 in. (1220×1830 mm) and three openings 26×48 in. (660×1219 mm). Mortar joints are $\frac{1}{2}$ in. (13mm). Allow 3% for brick waste.

5. Estimate the amount of mortar required for the brick wall of Problem 4 if the joint between wythes is $\frac{5}{8}$ in. (16 mm). Assume 25% mortar waste.

6. Describe the use and method of construction of reinforced concrete masonry.

7. What are the limitations on the use of Type N mortar?

8. How long after initial mixing may mortar be used before discarding?

9. If the cost of brick construction in place is $880 per 1000 bricks, estimate the cost of the brick exterior wall for the following building. The building is rectangular with a perimeter of 100 ft (30.5 m). The wall is 8 ft (2.44 m) high with one opening 36×80 in. (914×2032 mm) and 10 openings 30×48 in. (762×1220 mm). The brick is $3\frac{3}{4} \times 2\frac{1}{4} \times 8$ in. ($95 \times 57 \times 203$ mm) laid in running bond, double wythe.

10. Develop a computer program to calculate the maximum safe height of an unbraced masonry wall under construction using Equation 2. Solve Problem 3 using your program.

References

1. *All-Weather Concrete Masonry Construction,* NCMA TEK3-1C, National Concrete Masonry Association, Herndon, VA, 2002.

2. *Cold and Hot Weather Construction,* BIA Technical Notes 1, Brick Industry Association, Reston, VA, June 2006.

3. *Concrete Masonry Handbook,* 6th ed. Portland Cement Association, Skokie, IL, 2008.

4. *Hot & Cold Weather Masonry Construction,* Masonry Industry Council, Lombard, IL, 1999.

5. *Masonry Structures: Behavior and Design.* Brick Institute of America, Reston, VA.

6. *Principles of Brick Masonry.* Brick Industry Association, Reston, VA.

7. *Recommended Practice for Engineered Brick Masonry.* Brick Industry Association, Reston, VA, 1975.

8. *Recommended Practices and Guide Specifications for Cold Weather Masonry Construction.* International Masonry Industry All-Weather Council, International Masonry Institute, Washington, DC, 1993.

9. *Specification for Masonry Structures and Commentaries (ACI 530.1-08/ASCE 6-08/TMS 602-08).* Reston, VA: ASCE, 2008.

10. *Technical Notes on Brick Construction,* Series. Brick Industry Association, Reston, VA, various dates.

STEEL CONSTRUCTION

From Chapter 15 of *Construction Methods and Management*, Eighth Edition. S. W. Nunnally. Copyright © 2011 by Pearson Education, Inc.
Published by Pearson Prentice Hall. All rights reserved.

STEEL CONSTRUCTION

1 INTRODUCTION

Elements of Steel Construction

Structural steel construction is a specialized task that is usually performed by specialty subcontractors. However, construction managers and inspectors must understand the principles and procedures involved. The process of steel construction can be broken down into the three major elements of advanced planning, steel fabrication and delivery to the job site, and field operations. Each of these elements involves a number of operations which are described in this chapter.

For large or complex projects, advanced planning includes divisioning the steel and planning shipping and erection procedures. *Divisioning* is the process of dividing a structure into units (called *divisions*) which are used to schedule the fabrication and delivery of structural steel members to the job site. Since divisioning is determined by the order in which the structure will be erected, it must be performed as a joint effort of the steel fabricator and the erection manager. When planning shop fabrications procedures, the size and weight of large members must be checked against plant capacity, transportation size and weight limits, and the capacity of erection equipment. In planning erection procedures, the type of equipment to be utilized and the procedures to be followed are determined by the type of structure being erected and the anticipated site conditions. Lifting equipment, alignment requirements, and field connections are described in succeeding sections of this chapter.

The erection of the structural steel frame for a shopping center is shown in Figure 1.

Field Operations

Field operations include receiving and unloading, sorting (or "shaking out"), inspecting, storing, and erecting the steel. The process of unloading steel to a temporary storage area and then moving it from storage to the point of erection is called *yarding*. Structural steel members are often carelessly handled during unloading at the job site. They may be thrown off the truck or railcar and stacked up in a manner that will cause distortion in the member and damage to its paint. Such practices must be avoided. In unloading long flexible members and trusses, double slings should be used to avoid bending the member. If the steel has not been inspected at the fabrication shop, it must be inspected after unloading for conformance to the shop drawings and the tolerances specified in Table 1. Camber and sweep of beams are illustrated in Figure 2. In any case, members must be checked at the job site for possible shipping and unloading damage.

Shaking out steel is the process of sorting it out by identifying each member and storing it in such a manner that it can be easily obtained during erection. Code numbers are often painted on the members to facilitate identification during erection. Steel should be stored off the ground on platforms, skids, or other supports and protected from dirt, grease, and corrosion. Erection, the final element of field operations, is described in Section 3.

2 STRUCTURAL STEEL

Types of Steel

The type of steel contained in a structural steel member is designated by the letter A followed by the American Society for Testing and Materials (ASTM) designation number. The principal types of structural steel include the following:

- A36 Carbon Structural Steel.
- A572 High-Strength Low-Alloy Structural Steel.
- A588 Corrosion-Resistant High-Strength Low-Alloy Structural Steel.

FIGURE 1. Erection of the structural steel frame for a shopping center.

Steel strength is designated by the symbol F_y, which indicates the minimum yield point of the steel expressed in thousands of pounds per square inch (ksi), pounds per square inch (psi), or megapascals (MPa). Type A36 steel has a yield strength of 36 ksi (36,000 lb/sq in. or 248.2 MPa). The high-strength steels (types A572 and A588) are available in yield strengths of 42 ksi (289.6 MPa) to 65 ksi (448.2 MPa).

Weathering steel is a type of steel that develops a protective oxide coat on its surface upon exposure to the elements so that painting is not required for protection against most atmospheric corrosion. That natural brown color that develops with exposure blends well with natural settings. However, care must be taken to prevent staining of structural elements composed of other materials which are located in the vicinity

Table 1. Fabrication and mill tolerance for steel members

Dimensions	Tolerance
Depth	$\pm\frac{1}{8}$ in. (0.32 cm)
Width	$+\frac{1}{4}$ in. (0.64 cm), $-\frac{3}{16}$ in. (0.48 cm)
Flanges out-of-square	
Depth 12 in. (30 cm) or less	$\frac{1}{4}$ in. (0.64 cm)
Depth over 12 in. (30 cm)	$\frac{5}{16}$ in. (0.79 cm)
Area and weight	$\pm2.5\%$
Length	
End contact bearing	$\pm\frac{1}{32}$ in. (0.08 cm)
Other members	
Length 30 ft (9.2 m) or less	$\pm\frac{1}{16}$ in. (0.16 cm)
Length over 30 ft (9.2 m)	$\pm\frac{1}{8}$ in. (0.32 cm)
Ends out-of-square	$\frac{1}{64}$ in./in. (cm/cm) of depth or flange width, whichever is greater
Straightness	
General	$\pm\frac{1}{8}$ in./10 ft (0.1 cm/m) of length
Compression members	Deviation from straightness of $\frac{1}{1000}$ of axial length between points of lateral support

FIGURE 2. Camber and sweep of beams.

of the weathering steel and thus exposed to the runoff or windblown water from the weathering steel.

Standard Rolled Shapes

There are a number of rolled steel shapes produced for construction which have been standardized by the American Society for Testing and Materials. Figure 3 illustrates five major section shapes. A list of standard shapes and their AISC designations is given in Table 2. Note that the usual designation code includes a letter symbol (identifying the section shape) followed by two numbers (indicating the section depth in inches and the weight per foot). Designations for angles, bars, and tubes are slightly different, in that the numbers used identify principal section dimensions in inches rather than the section depth and weight. Detailed section properties as well as the weight of pipe, plates, and crane rails are given in reference 3.

Built-Up Members

Girders are used when regular rolled shapes are not deep enough or wide enough to provide the required section properties. Plate girders (Figure 4a) normally consist of a

Table 2. Rolled-steel shape designations

Type of Shape	Example Designation
W shape	W27 × 114
S shape	S20 × 95
M shape	M8 × 25
American Standard Channel	C12 × 30
Miscellaneous Channel	MC12 × 50
HP (bearing pile) shape	HP14 × 89
Equal leg angle	L6 × 6 × ½
Unequal leg angle	L8 × 4 × ½
Structural tee cut from:	
W shape	WT8 × 18
S shape	ST6 × 25
M shape	MT4 × 16.3
Plate	PL½ × 12
Square bar	Bar 2 ⊡
Round bar	Bar 2 φ
Flat bar	Bar 2 × ½
Pipe	Pipe 6 std.
Structural tubing	
Square	TS6 × 6 × 0.250
Rectangular	TS6 × 4 × 0.250
Circular	TS4 OD × 0.250

web and top and bottom flanges. Stiffeners may be added if needed to prevent buckling of the web. Box girders are constructed using two webs as shown in Figure 4b.

Open-web steel joists (Figure 5) and joist girders are other forms of built-up steel members. These are lightweight open trusses that are strong and economical. They are widely used for supporting floors and roofs of buildings. *Bar joists* are steel joists whose diagonal members consist of steel bars. Standard *open-web steel joist* designations include K, LH, and DLH series. All are designed to support uniform loads. K series are parallel chord joists that span up to 60 ft (18.3 m) with a maximum depth of 30 in. (76 cm). Series K uses steel with a yield strength of 50 ksi (345 MPa) for chords and either 36 ksi (248 MPa) or 50 ksi (345 MPa) for webs. Series LH (longspan joists) and DLH (deep longspan joists) joists

FIGURE 3. Rolled-steel section shapes.

278

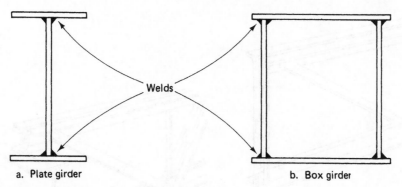

FIGURE 4. Built-up steel members.

FIGURE 5. Open-web steel joist.

are available with parallel chords or with the top chord pitched one way or two ways (Figure 6). The standard pitch is ⅛ in./ft (1 cm/m) to provide drainage. Longspan and deep longspan joists are normally cambered to offset the deflection of the joist due to its own weight. They use steel with a yield strength of either 36 or 50 ksi (248 or 345 MPa). Series LH joists span up to 96 ft (29.3 m) with a maximum depth of 48 in. (122 cm). Series DLH joists span up to 144 ft (43.9 m) with depths to 72 in. (183 cm).

Joist girders, Series G, are similar to open-web steel joists except that they are designed to support panel point loads.

Series G girders use steel with a yield strength of 36–50 ksi (248–345 MPa), span up to 60 ft (18.3 m), and have a maximum depth of 72 in. (183 cm). Joist girders and open-web steel joists are available with square ends, underslung ends, or extended ends, as shown in Figure 7.

Castellated steel beams are created from standard rolled shapes by shearing one side and then joining two sections together to create the shape shown in Figure 8. Beams such as these are deeper and have a higher strength/weight ratio than do standard rolled sections. The open portions of the web also facilitate the installation of building utilities.

Parallel chords, underslung

Parallel chords, square ends

Top chord pitched one way, underslung

Top chord pitched one way, square ends

Top chord pitched two ways, underslung

FIGURE 6. Steel joist types.

Top chord pitched two ways, square ends

Square end

Underslung end

Extended end

FIGURE 7. Types of joist ends.

FIGURE 8. Castellated steel beams. (Copyright © American Institute of Steel Construction, Inc. Reprinted with permission. All rights reserved)

3 STEEL ERECTION

Erection Procedure

The usual steel erection procedure employs three crews (a raising crew, a fitting crew, and a fastening crew) which operate in sequence as erection proceeds. The raising crew lifts the steel member into position and makes temporary bolted connections that will hold the member safely in place until the fitting crew takes over. OSHA safety regulations use the term *structural integrity* to indicate the ability of a structure to safely stand up during erection and have prescribed specific safety measures to ensure *structural integrity*. For example, the erection deck cannot be more than eight stories above the highest completed permanent floor. Neither can there be more than four floors or 48 ft (14.6 m) of unfinished bolting or welding above the highest permanently secured floor (not necessarily completed floor). The fitting crew brings the member into proper alignment and tightens enough bolts to hold the structure in alignment until final connections are made. The fastening crew makes the final connections (bolted or welded) to meet specification requirements.

Lifting Equipment

The mobile crane and tower crane are often used for handling steel and lifting it into final position. Figure 9 shows a tower crane erecting steel. There are also a number of other lifting devices which are often used in steel construction. The *gin pole* shown in Figure 10a is one of the simplest types of powered lifting device. Two or more of these may be used together to lift large pieces of equipment such as boilers or tanks. A *guy derrick* is shown in Figure 10b. This is probably the most widely used lifting device in high-rise building construction. An advantage of the guy derrick is that it can easily be moved (or jumped) from one floor to the next as construction proceeds. Figure 10c illustrates a heavy-duty lifting device called a *stiffleg derrick*. Stiffleg derricks may be mounted on tracks to facilitate movement within a work area.

Alignment of Steel

Alignment of steel members must be accomplished within the tolerances of the AISC Code of Standard Practice (see reference 3). Under AISC standards, the vertical (or plumb) error cannot exceed 1 unit in 500 units of height and the

FIGURE 9. Tower crane erecting steel. (Courtesy of FMC Corporation)

centerline of exterior columns cannot be more than 1 in. (2.5 cm) toward or 2 in. (5 cm) away from the building line in 20 stories.

The minimum clearance between steel members is also specified in reference 3. *Coping* or *blocking* is the name applied to notching beams to provide the necessary clearance when beams connect to columns or other beams. Electrical, plumbing, and other trades often find it convenient to make attachments to steel or to cut openings (inserts) in the steel to facilitate installation of their equipment. No attachments or inserting, including blocking and coping, should be permitted without the approval of the structural designer.

Guy ropes and supports are often used in the process of bringing steel into alignment, as illustrated in Figure 11. Erection planning should include the number, type, and location of all guys and supports to be used. Guys should be placed so as to minimize interference with travel ways and erection equipment, and must be kept taut. Care must be taken not to overstress guys during alignment.

Erection of Steel Joists

The requirements for the lateral bracing of steel joists by bridging have been established by the Steel Joist Institute (SJI) (reference 5). The lateral bracing of longspan and deep longspan joists during erection is especially critical. For these joists, the SJI requires that hoisting cables not be released until a minimum number of lines of bridging have been installed: one line for spans to 60 ft (18.3 m), two lines for spans of 60–100 ft (18.3–30.5 m), and all lines for spans over 100 ft (30.5 m). Joists should be completely braced before any loads are applied.

4 FIELD CONNECTIONS

Fastening Systems

The three principal systems used for connecting steel members are bolting, riveting, and welding. Riveting is now seldom used for making field connections or for shop fabrications. Riveting procedures will not be described here.

Bolted Connections   While unfinished (ASTM A307) bolts are still available for low stress applications, high-strength bolts are used in most of today's steel construction. To prevent confusion in identification, ASTM has prescribed special markings for high-strength bolts, which are illustrated in Figure 12. Bolts that are driven into place and use oversize shanks to prevent turning during tightening are referred to as *interference-body* or *interference-fit bolts*. Bolts that incorporate a torque control groove so that the stem breaks off under a specified torque are referred to as *tension control bolts* or *tension set bolts*.

The Specifications for Structural Joists Using ASTM A325 or A490 Bolts, approved by the Research Council on Riveted

a. Gin pole

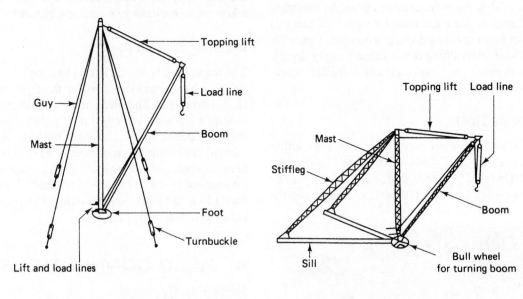

b. Guy derrick

c. Stiffleg derrick

FIGURE 10. Steel-lifting equipment.

and Bolted Structural Joints and endorsed by the AISC, has prescribed acceptable procedures for assembling steel using high-strength bolts (reference 3). These procedures are described briefly in the remainder of this section. Two of the methods used for tightening standard high-strength bolts to the specified tension are the turn-of-nut method and the calibrated wrench method.

Quality control procedures may require the use of a torque wrench to verify that the required bolt tension is being obtained. When used, torque wrenches should be calibrated with a bolt-tension calibrator at least once a day by tightening at least three bolts of each diameter being used. A *bolt-tension calibrator* is a device that can be used to calibrate both impact wrenches (used for bolt tightening)

and hand indicator torque wrenches (used by inspectors for checking the tension of bolts that have been tightened by either method). Torque-control devices on impact wrenches should be set to produce a bolt tension 5–10% greater than the specified minimum bolt tension. Air pressure at the impact wrench used for bolt tightening should be at least 100 lb/sq in. (690 kPa), and the wrench should be capable of producing the required bolt tightening in about 10 s.

When tightening a high-strength bolt by either the turn-of-nut method or the calibrated wrench method, the bolt is first brought to a snug condition. (The snug condition is reached when an impact wrench begins to impact solidly or when a worker uses his full strength on an

Guy

Turnbuckle

FIGURE 11. Plumbing a steel structure.

ordinary spud wrench.) Except for interference-body bolts, final bolt tightening may be accomplished by turning either the nut or the bolt head. Residual preservative oil on bolts may be left in place during tightening. When the surface to be bolted is inclined at a slope greater than 1 in 20 to an axis perpendicular to the bolt, a beveled washer must be used to provide full bearing for the nut or head. Both A325 and A490 bolts tightened by the calibrated wrench tightening method and A490 bolts installed by the turn-of-nut method must have a hardened washer under the element being turned (head or nut). Hardened washers must be used under both the head and the nut of A490 bolts used to connect material having a yield strength of less than 40 ksi (276 MPa). For final tightening by the calibrated wrench method, the bolt is impacted until the torque-control device cuts off. Using the turn-of-nut method, the specified rotation must be obtained from the snug condition while the stationary end (bolt head or nut) is held by hand wrench to prevent rotation. The tightening requirement for a bolt not more than 8 diameters or 8 in. (20 cm) in length, having both faces perpendicular to the bolt axis, is one-half turn from the snug condition.

The procedure for tightening tension control or tension set bolts is illustrated in Figure 13. After bolts have been installed finger-tight, the installation tool is placed over the bolt end so that it engages both the bolt spline and nut. The installation tool holds the bolt spline to prevent the bolt from rotating while torque is applied to the nut. When the torque on the nut reaches the required value, the bolt spline will shear off at the torque control groove. Visual inspection will indicate whether bolts have been properly tightened by determining that the spline end of the bolt has sheared off. If desired, bolt tension may be verified by the use of

a calibrated torque wrench, as described in the previous paragraph.

Welded Connections

Welding (Figure 14) is another specialized procedure that must be accomplished properly if adequate connection strength is to be provided. Welding requirements for steel construction are contained in reference 3 and the publications of the American Welding Society (AWS). A few of the principal welding requirements are described in this section. In the United States, all welders responsible for making connections in steel construction should be certified by the American Welding Society. All supervisors and inspectors must be able to interpret the standard welding symbols shown in Figure 15. The major types of structural welds include fillet welds, groove (or butt or vee) welds, and plug or rivet welds. These are illustrated in Figure 16.

In addition to the use of qualified welders, requirements for producing satisfactory electric welds include the proper preparation of the base metal, the use of proper electrodes, and the use of the correct current, voltage, and polarity settings.

There are a number of inspection methods available for determining the quality of welds. Test methods include visual inspection, destructive testing, radiographic inspection, ultrasonic inspection, magnetic-particle inspection, and liquid-penetrant inspection. Visual inspection is the quickest, easiest, and most widely used method of inspection. However, to be effective it requires the use of highly trained and experienced inspection personnel. It is also the least reliable method for ensuring adequate weld strength. Destructive testing is used primarily in welder

FIGURE 12. High-strength steel bolts.

qualification procedures. Its use may also be necessary to determine the actual strength of welds when nondestructive test methods indicate questionable weld quality. Radiographic inspection involves producing an X-ray picture of the weld. When properly employed, it can detect defects as small as 2% of the joint thickness. Ultrasonic inspection uses high-frequency vibration to detect defects. The nature of the signals that are reflected back from the weld gives an indication of the type, size, and location of any defect. Magnetic-particle inspection utilizes magnetic particles spread on a weld to indicate defects on or near the weld surface. However, it cannot be used on nonmagnetic metals such as aluminum. Liquid-penetrant inspection involves spraying the weld with a liquid penetrant, drying the surface, and then applying a developing fluid which shows the location where penetrant has entered the weld. The method is inexpensive and easy to use but can detect only those flaws that are open to the surface.

5 SAFETY

As stated earlier, steel erection is a very hazardous construction task. As a result, a number of safety requirements have been developed and many of these are contained in OSHA safety regulations (reference 2). Some of these requirements have been described earlier in the chapter. Two additional safety areas that deserve comment are the use of protective equipment and the hazards presented by site conditions.

Bolt installed finger tight.   Installation tool tightens nut while holding spline.

Sheared spline drops off.

FIGURE 13. Installation of tension control bolts.

FIGURE 14. Welded steel construction. (Copyright © American Institute of Steel Construction, Inc. Reprinted with permission. All rights reserved)

Protective Equipment

OSHA regulations contain a number of requirements for the use of personal protective equipment. Hardhats and gloves are standard requirements for steel erection. Eye protection must be provided for workers engaged in welding, cutting, and chipping operations, as well as for those working nearby. Employees working above ground level require protective measures against falls. Temporary floors and scaffolds with guard rails should be provided whenever possible. If these are not feasible, lifelines and safety belts must be used. Where the potential fall exceeds 25 ft (7.6 m) or two stories, safety nets should also be used. When used, safety nets should be placed as close under the work surface as practical and extend at least 8 ft (2.4 m) beyond the sides of the work surface.

Site Hazards

Weather is responsible for many of the hazards at the steel erection site. High and gusty winds may throw workers off balance and cause steel being lifted to swing dangerously.

FIGURE 15. Standard welding symbols. (Copyright © American Institute of Steel Construction, Inc. Reprinted with permission. All rights reserved)

Tag lines must be used for all hoisting operations. Since steel workers will be walking on members shortly after they are lifted, care must be taken to prevent the surfaces of members from becoming slippery. Wet and icy surfaces are obvious hazards. Structural members should be checked to ensure that they are free of hazards such as dirt, oil, loose debris, ice, and wet paint before being hoisted into place.

FIGURE 16. Weld types.

Problems

1. Explain the meaning of the term *blocking* as used in steel construction.

2. Identify at least six safety precautions which should be observed in structural steel construction.

3. Identify the following steel sections:

   a. W36 × 260
   b. S24 × 90
   c. HP14 × 89
   d. L8 × 4 × ½

4. When erecting a steel building structure, what is the maximum height that the erection deck can be above the highest completed permanent floor?

5. Describe how high-strength steel bolts may be identified.

6. Describe the principal characteristics of Series LH open-web steel joists.

7. Describe the procedure for tightening tension control or tension set bolts.

8. What is the yield strength of type A36 steel?

9. Identify the maximum fabrication tolerance of a steel column in terms of depth, width, length, and squareness.

10. Develop a computer program to provide an inventory of structural steel required for a building project. Provide for all shapes listed in Table 2. Input should include shape and size, length, quantity, and unit weight. Output should include a summary by steel shape as well as the total weight of steel for the project. Using your program, provide an inventory example.

References

1. *Code of Federal Regulations,* Title 29, Chapter XVII, Part 1926. Office of the Federal Register, National Archives and Records Administration, Washington, D.C.

2. *Construction Industry Digest* (OSHA 2202). U.S. Department of Labor, Washington, D.C.

3. *Manual of Steel Construction,* 13th ed. American Institute of Steel Construction, Inc., Chicago, IL, 2005.

4. Oppenheimer, Samuel P. *Erecting Structural Steel.* New York: McGraw-Hill, 1960.

5. *Standard Specifications, Load Tables, and Weight Tables for Steel Joists and Joist Girders.* Steel Joist Institute, Myrte Beach, SC, 1995.

PLANNING AND SCHEDULING

PLANNING AND SCHEDULING

1 INTRODUCTION

Planning and Scheduling

As you already know, some planning must be done in order to perform any function with a minimum of wasted time and effort. This is true whether the function is getting to work on time or constructing a multimillion dollar building. A schedule is nothing more than a time-phased plan. Schedules are used as guides during the performance of an operation in order to control the pace of activities and to permit completion of the operation at the desired or required time.

Scheduling is utilized for many different phases of the construction process, from master planning through facility construction to facility operation and maintenance. In the construction phase itself, schedules are useful for a number of purposes before starting a project and after completion of the project as well as during the actual conduct of construction work. Some of the principal uses for schedules during each of these phases of construction are listed below.

Before Starting

1. Provides an estimate of the time required for each portion of the project as well as for the total project.
2. Establishes the planned rate of progress.
3. Forms the basis for managers to issue instructions to subordinates.
4. Establishes the planned sequence for the use of personnel, materials, machines, and money.

During Construction

1. Enables the manager to prepare a checklist of key dates, activities, resources, and so on.
2. Provides a means for evaluating the effect of changes and delays.

3. Serves as the basis for evaluating progress.
4. Aids in the coordination of resources.

After Completion of Construction

1. Permits a review and analysis of the project as actually carried out.
2. Provides historical data for improving future planning and estimating.

Scheduling Principles

There are a number of different forms of schedules that may be used, including written schedules, bar graph schedules, network schedules, and others. In this chapter, we will consider only bar graph, network, and linear scheduling methods. Regardless of the scheduling method employed, the following general principles of scheduling should be observed.

1. Establish a logical sequence of operations.
2. Do not exceed the capabilities of the resources that are available.
3. Provide for continuity of operations.
4. Start project controlling (or critical) activities early.

It must be recognized that the accuracy or validity of scheduling depends on the validity of the work quantity and productivity estimates used. The accuracy of an estimate of the time it will take to perform a construction operation is a function of the kind of work involved and prior experience in doing that sort of work. For example, one expects a more accurate estimate of the time required to install a wastewater line in a residential structure than of the time required to install a cooling line in a nuclear power plant. Methods for dealing with the uncertainty associated with activity-time estimates will be discussed later in this chapter.

In addition to valid time estimates for activities, the planner must have a thorough understanding of the nature of the work to be performed and the relationships between the various work items making up the project. One of the major deficiencies of the bar graph schedule described in the following section is the fact that the bar graph fails to show relationships between work items. That is, what activities must be started or completed before other activities can be started or completed?

2 BAR GRAPH METHOD

The Bar Graph Schedule

The *bar graph* or *bar chart schedule* is a graphical schedule relating progress of items of work to a time schedule. The bar schedule traces its origin to a chart developed by Henry L. Gantt, a pioneer in the application of scientific management methods to industrial production. These charts, referred to as *Gantt charts*, took several different forms, depending on their application. Because of their origin, all forms of bar graph schedules are sometimes called Gantt charts. In spite of the advent of network planning methods, the bar graph schedule is still the most widely used schedule form found in construction work. Its continued popularity in the face of the significant deficiencies that are described in the next section is undoubtedly due to its very graphic and easily understood format. A simple bar graph schedule for a construction project is shown in Figure 1. The major work items, or activities, making up the project are listed on the left side of the schedule with a time scale across the top. The column headed "Hours" indicates the estimated number of labor-hours required for each activity. The column headed "Weight" indicates the portion of the total project effort accounted for by each activity. For example, "Clearing and Stripping" requires 750 labor-hours of work, which represents 4.7% of the 15,900 labor-hours required for the entire project. While a weighting column is not always present on a bar chart, its presence is very useful when calculating cumulative project progress. Activities may be weighted on any desired basis. However, dollar value and labor-hours are most frequently used as a weighting basis.

Construction Progress Chart

Project Construct Runway xyz

Date 4/10/09

Operation	Hours	Weight (%)		Weeks										
				1	2	3	4	5	6	7	8	9	10
1. Clear and Strip	750	4.7	SCH	▓▓20	70								
			ACT	▨▨45		90							
2. Drainage	150	0.9	SCH		60								
			ACT		▨30	100							
3. Subgrade	4200	26.4	SCH		15	40	65	85					
			ACT		▨5	25							
4. Base Course	4000	25.2	SCH				10	30	60	85			
			ACT										
5. Pave	6800	42.8	SCH					20	45	65	80	95	
			ACT										
			SCH										
			ACT										
			SCH										
			ACT										
			SCH										
			ACT										
			SCH										
			ACT										

FIGURE 1. Bar graph schedule for construction project.

Notice that two horizontal blocks are provided opposite each activity. The upper block (SCH) represents scheduled progress and the lower block (ACT) is used to record actual progress as work proceeds. For each block, a bar extends from starting to ending times. The numbers above each bar indicate percentage of activity completion at each major time division. Again such a system greatly simplifies calculation of scheduled cumulative progress and its comparison with actual progress. To aid in the evaluation of progress, it is suggested that the actual progress of each activity be inserted at the end of each major time period, as shown in Figure 1.

Cumulative Project Progress

Figure 2 shows a cumulative progress-versus-time curve for the bar graph of Figure 1. The vertical scale represents cumulative project progress in percent and the horizontal scale indicates time. Once the bar graph schedule has been prepared and weighting factors calculated for each activity, scheduled cumulative progress can be calculated and plotted as shown on the figure. Actual cumulative progress is calculated and plotted as work progresses. To construct the scheduled cumulative progress curve, scheduled cumulative progress must be calculated and plotted for a sufficient number of points to enable a smooth curve to be drawn. In Figure 2 scheduled cumulative progress for the bar graph schedule of Figure 1 has been calculated and plotted at the end of each week. Cumulative progress may be calculated as follows:

$$\text{Cumulative progress} = \sum_{i=1}^{n} (\text{Activity progress})_i \times (\text{Weight})_i \qquad (1)$$

Example calculations for the scheduled cumulative progress for the first 3 weeks of the project whose bar graph schedule appears in Figure 1 follow.

End of First Week

[Activity 1]
Progress $= (0.20 \times 4.7) = 0.9\%$

End of Second Week

[Activity 1] [Activity 2] [Activity 3]
Progress $= (0.70 \times 4.7) + (0.60 \times 0.9)$
$+ (0.15 \times 26.4) = 7.8\%$

End of Third Week

[Activity 1] [Activity 2] [Activity 3]
Progress $= (1.00 \times 4.7) + (1.00 \times 0.9)$
$+ (0.40 \times 26.4) = 16.2\%$

Frequently, cumulative progress curves for a project are superimposed on the project's bar graph schedule as illustrated in Figure 3.

The Normal Progress Curve

At this point, let us consider the probable shape of a cumulative progress-versus-time curve. Observation of a large number of projects indicates that the usual shape of the curve is that shown in Figure 4. As the curve indicates, progress is slow at the beginning of a project as work is organized and

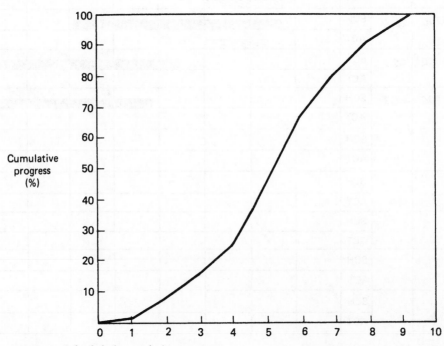

FIGURE 2. Scheduled cumulative progress.

FIGURE 3. Bar graph with cumulative progress curve.

293

workers become familiar with work assignments and procedures. Thus, only about 15% of the project is completed in the first 25% of project time. After that, progress is made at a rather constant rate until 85% of the work is completed at the end of 75% of project time. Progress again slows as finishing work and project demobilization take place. The progress curve illustrated in Figure 4 is referred to as a *normal progress curve* or *S-curve* and will generally apply to any type of nonrepetitive work. If you find that the shape of a scheduled cumulative progress curve deviates substantially from the curve of Figure 4, you should carefully investigate the reason for this deviation. If progress is based on dollar value, the presence of a few high-dollar-value items may cause the curve to assume an abnormal shape. Otherwise, it is likely that a mistake has been made and that the planned rate of progress is unrealistic.

3 CPM—THE CRITICAL PATH METHOD

Deficiencies in Bar Graph Schedules

As indicated earlier, a major deficiency of the bar graph schedule is its failure to show relationships between project activities. Thus there is no way to determine from a bar graph schedule whether the person preparing the schedule was, in fact, aware of these relationships. A related weakness of the bar graph schedule is its failure to identify those activities which actually control the project duration. We will refer to such duration-controlling activities as *critical activities*. As a result of its failure to identify activity relationships and critical activities, the bar graph schedule also fails to show the effect of delay or change in one activity on the entire project. Recognizing these weaknesses in bar graph

schedules, planners have for a number of years attempted to devise improved planning and scheduling methods.

However, it was not until the development of network planning methods in 1957–1958 that a major improvement in planning and scheduling methods took place. During this period the *Critical Path Method (CPM)* was developed jointly by the DuPont and Remington Rand Companies as a method for planning and scheduling plant maintenance and construction projects utilizing computers. At almost the same time, the Special Projects Office of the U.S. Navy, with Booz, Hamilton, and Allen as consultants, was developing the *Program Evaluation and Review Technique (PERT)* for planning and controlling weapons systems development. Successful application of both CPM and PERT by their developers soon led to widespread use of the techniques on both governmental and industry projects.

Both CPM and PERT use a network diagram to graphically represent the major activities of a project and to show the relationships between activities. The major difference between CPM and PERT is that PERT utilizes probability concepts to deal with the uncertainty associated with activity-time estimates, whereas CPM assigns each activity a single fixed duration.

The Network Diagram

As indicated, a network graphically portrays major project activities and their relationships. There are basically two methods of drawing such networks: the *activity-on-arrow diagram* and the *activity-on-node diagram*. Special forms of activity-on-node diagram, such as *precedence diagrams,* will be discussed later in the chapter. While activity-on-node diagrams have certain advantages, activity-on-arrow format will be utilized to illustrate network construction and time calculations.

FIGURE 4. Normal progress curve.

In the activity-on-arrow format, each activity is represented by an arrow that has an associated description and expected duration. Each *activity*, as illustrated in Figure 5, must start and terminate at an *event* (represented by a circle). Events are numbered for identification purposes and event numbers are also utilized to identify activities on the diagram. That is, activities are identified by citing the event number at the tail of the arrow (I number) followed by the event number at the head of the arrow (J number). Thus activity 10–11 refers to the activity starting at event 10 and ending at event 11, as seen in Figure 5. This activity numbering system is referred to as the *I–J numbering system*. An event is simply a point in time and, as used in network diagramming, is assumed to occur instantaneously when all activities leading into the event have been completed. Similarly, all activities leading out of an event *may* start immediately upon the occurrence of an event. Figure 6 shows a simple network diagram for a construction project. As mentioned earlier, the diagram graphically indicates the relationships between activities. These relationships are *precedence* (what activities must precede the activity?), *concurrence* (what activities can go on at the same time?), and *succession* (what activities must follow the activity?). In Figure 6, activity 1–2 must precede activity 2–5, activities 1–2 and 1–3 are concurrent, and activity 2–5 succeeds activity 1–2. Activities progress in the direction shown by the arrows. Good diagramming practice requires that diagrams present a clear picture of the project logic and generally flow from left to right. Arrows should not point backward, although they may point straight up or down.

Notice the dashed arrow in Figure 6. This is called a *dummy activity* or simply a *dummy*. Dummies are used to impose logic constraints and prevent duplication of activity I–J numbers. They do not represent any work and, hence, always have a duration of zero.

Event-Time Calculations

Once a network diagram has been drawn that represents the required relationships between activities, network time calculations may be made. The first step is to calculate the earliest time at which each event may occur based on an arbitrary starting time of zero. This earliest event occurrence is referred to as *early event time*, commonly abbreviated (*EET*). It is usually placed above the event circle as shown in Figure 7. Calculations then proceed from left to right, starting with 0 at the first event. This calculation is referred to as the forward pass through the network. At each event the early event time is found as the early event time of the previous event plus the duration of the activity connecting the two events. Thus the early event time of event 2 is found as the sum of the early event time at event 1 plus the duration of activity 1–2 (0 + 4 = 4). When two or more activity arrows meet at an event, the largest value of possible early event times is chosen as the early event time because, by definition, the event cannot occur until all activities leading into the event have been completed. In Figure 7, note the activity early completion times of 3, 5, and 7 at event 5, leading to the proper early event-time value of 7. The early event time at the last event is, of course, the minimum time required to complete the project.

FIGURE 5. Activity-on-arrow notation.

FIGURE 6. Example network diagram.

FIGURE 7. Example network—
early event times.

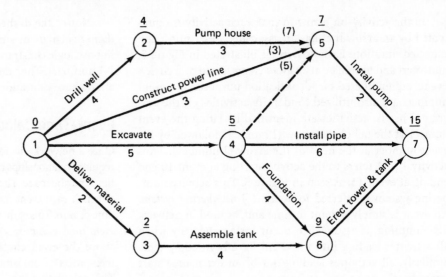

When all early event-time values have been calculated and entered on the network, a backward pass is made to compute the latest possible time at which each event may occur without changing the project duration. As a starting point, the *late event time (LET)* of the last event is set equal to the early event time of the event. Starting with the assigned late event time at the last event, work backward through the network, calculating each late event time as the late event time of the previous event minus the duration of the activity connecting the events. The results are illustrated in Figure 8. The late event time of event 6 is found as the late event time of event 7 minus the duration of activity 6–7 ($15 - 6 = 9$). When two or more activities meet at an event, the lower of possible times is chosen as the late event time because, by definition, the event must occur before any activity leading out of the event may start. In order for all activities to be completed within the allotted time, the event must occur at the earliest of the possible time values. In Figure 8, note the possible late times at event 4 of 5, 9, and 13, leading to a late event time of 5.

The Critical Path

That path through the network which establishes the minimum project duration is referred to as the *critical path*. This path is the series of activities and events that was used to determine the project duration (or early event time of the final event) in the forward pass. However, it is usual to wait until all early and late event times have been calculated to mark the critical path. Notice in Figure 9 that the critical path passes through all events whose early event times are equal to their late event times. Critical activities are those which make up the critical path and, of course, connect critical events. Where parallel activities connect critical events, however, only the activities whose duration equals the difference between event times at the ends of the arrow are critical. Thus in Figure 9, activities 4–7, as well as activities 4–6 and 6–7, connect the critical events 4 and 7. However, the time difference between event times at event 7 and event 4 is 10 units, while the duration of activity 4–7 is only 6 units. Hence activity 4–7 is *not* critical. When the critical

FIGURE 8. Example network—
late event times.

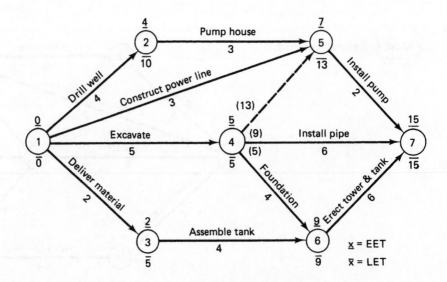

FIGURE 9. Example network—critical path.

path has been identified, it should be clearly indicated on the network by color, double arrow (as used in Figure 9), or similar means.

Activity Times

Up to this point, we have determined the minimum duration of our project and identified the critical path. The next step is to calculate the earliest and latest starting and finishing time and the total float (scheduling leeway) for each activity based on the event times already calculated. These time values are used as the basis for scheduling and resource allocation. Two of these values, early start and late finish, may be read directly off the network while the remaining values must be calculated. The following relations may be used to determine activity times

$$\text{Early start (ES)} = \frac{\text{Early event time of preceding}}{\text{(I) event}} \quad (2)$$

$$\text{Early finish (EF)} = \text{Early start} + \text{Activity duration} \quad (3)$$

$$\text{Late finish (LF)} = \frac{\text{Late event time of following}}{\text{(J) event}} \quad (4)$$

$$\text{Late start (LS)} = \text{Late finish} - \text{Activity duration} \quad (5)$$

$$\text{Total float (TF)} = \text{Late finish} - \text{Early finish} \quad (6)$$

or

$$\text{Total float (TF)} = \text{Late start} - \text{Early start} \quad (7)$$

Activity-time values for the example network are given in Figure 10. Note that activity times are not usually calculated for dummy activities. *Float* (*slack* in PERT terminology) is the amount of scheduling leeway available to an activity. While several different types of float have been defined, *total float* is the most useful of these values and is the only type of float that will be used here. Application of float to the scheduling process is covered in the following section.

FIGURE 10. Activity-time data for example network.

Act no.	Description	Duration	Early start	Early finish	Late start	Late finish	Total float
1–2	Drill well	4	0	4	6	10	6
1–3	Deliver material	2	0	2	3	5	3
* 1–4	Excavate	5	0	5	0	5	0
1–5	Power line	3	0	3	10	13	10
2–5	Pump house	3	4	7	10	13	6
3–6	Assemble tank	4	2	6	5	9	3
* 4–6	Foundation	4	5	9	5	9	0
4–7	Install pipe	6	5	11	9	15	4
5–7	Install pump	2	7	9	13	15	6
* 6–7	Erect tower and tk	6	9	15	9	15	0

* = critical activity

Activity-on-Node Diagrams

As stated earlier, there are two principal formats used in drawing network diagrams. The activity-on-arrow format has been used up to this point. The second format is the activity-on-node format. This technique uses the same general principles of network logic and time calculations as does the activity-on-arrow technique. However, the activity-on-node network diagram looks somewhat different from the activity-on-arrow diagram because the node (which represented an event in the activity-on-arrow method) is now used to represent an activity. A simple form of the activity-on-node diagram is the *circle diagram* or *circle notation,* in which each activity is represented by a circle containing the activity description, an identifying number, and the activity duration.

Figure 11 illustrates a circle diagram for a five-activity construction project. In the activity-on-node technique, notice that arrows are used to represent logic constraints only. Thus all arrows act in the same manner as do dummies in the activity-on-arrow format. This feature has been found to make activity-on-node diagramming somewhat easier for beginners to understand. The principal disadvantage of activity-on-node diagramming has been the limited availability of computer programs for performing network time calculations. However, there are now a number of such programs available, and the use of the activity-on-node techniques is expected to increase.

Another form of activity-on-node diagram is illustrated in Figure 12. Here an enlarged node is used to provide space for entering activity time values directly on the node. This format is particularly well suited to manual network calculation, because activity times may be entered directly on the network as they are calculated. When time calculations are performed in this manner, it is suggested that calculations be performed independently by two individuals and the results compared as an error check.

The third form of activity-on-node diagram is the *precedence diagram.* Because of its special characteristics, it is described in greater detail in the following paragraphs.

Precedence Diagrams

The precedence diagram is an extension of the activity-on-node format that provides for incorporation of lag-time factors as well as permitting additional precedence relationships. The use of lag time is very useful when diagramming construction project relationships, where activities can often start as soon as a portion of a preceding activity is completed. In addition to the usual finish-to-start precedence relationship,

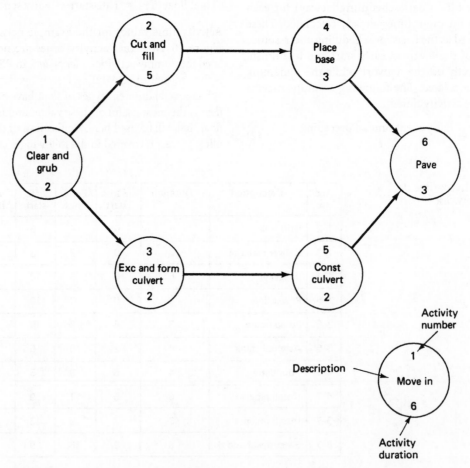

FIGURE 11. Circle diagram for a project.

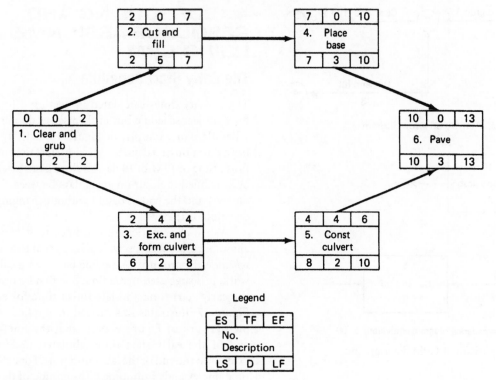

FIGURE 12. Expanded node diagram.

this technique permits start-to-start and finish-to-finish relationships. These relationships and the use of lag times are illustrated in Figure 13.

To appreciate the value of incorporating lag-time relationships, it is useful to consider how such relationships could be represented in the usual network diagramming techniques. For example, consider the network of Figure 12. The planner decides that activity 2, cut and fill, can start when activity 1, clear and grub, is 50% complete (equivalent to 1 day's work). Figure 14 illustrates how this situation

FIGURE 13. Precedence diagram relationships.

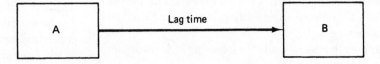

a. Finish-to-start: start of B depends on finish of A plus lag time.

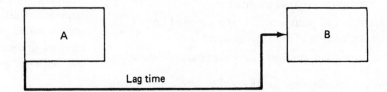

b. Start-to-start: start of B depends on start of A plus lag time.

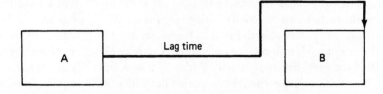

c. Finish-to-finish: finish of B depends on finish of A plus lag time.

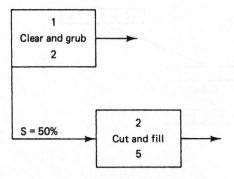

a. Activity-on-arrow diagram

b. Precedence diagram equivalent to (a)

FIGURE 14. Comparison of CPM diagram and precedence diagram.

would be represented in both conventional CPM and in a precedence diagram. To represent this situation in conventional CPM, it is necessary to split activity 1 into two activities, each having a duration of 1 day (Figure 14a). Using precedence diagram procedures, a 1-day lag time is simply inserted in a start-to-start relationship from activity 1 to activity 2 (Figure 14b).

The precedence diagram for the example project is shown in Figure 15. Notice that this diagram is essentially the same as any other activity-on-node diagram for the project since only finish-to-start relationships are employed and no lag times are used.

Suppose that we now add the following logic constraints to the example project:

1. Erection of the tower and tank cannot begin until 3 days after completion of the foundation.

2. Installation of pump cannot be completed until 1 day after completion of pipe installation.

3. The foundation can start 3 days after start of excavation.

The precedence diagram for the revised project is shown in Figure 16. Notice that the early start of activity 8 (day 3) is the early start of activity 4 (day 0) plus a 3-day lag time. The early finish of activity 10 (day 12) is determined by the early finish of activity 7 (day 11) plus a 1-day lag time. The early start of activity 10 is, therefore, day 10 (early finish minus duration). The early start of activity 11 (day 10) is the early finish of activity 8 (day 7) plus a lag time of 3 days. As noted earlier, the increased flexibility of the precedence diagram comes at the cost of increased computational complexity.

4 SCHEDULING AND RESOURCE ASSIGNMENT USING CPM

The Early Start Schedule

The activity times calculated in Section 3 form the basis for a project schedule but in themselves do *not* constitute a schedule. For example, in Figure 10, activity 1–5, which has a duration of 3 days, has an early start time of 0 and a late finish time of 13 with 10 days of float. Thus activity 1–5 may be scheduled to occur on any 3 days between the beginning of day 1 and the end of day 13 without changing the project duration of 15 days.

When all activities are scheduled to start at the earliest allowable time, such a schedule is referred to as an *early start schedule.* To produce a schedule based on a calculated network, it is suggested that a time line first be drawn between the early start time and late finish time for each activity. Figure 17 illustrates this procedure applied to the example network of Figure 9. Note that the line starts at the end of the early start time tabulated in Figure 10 and extends to the end of the late finish time. For activity 1–2, the time line extends from time 0 (beginning of day 1) through time 10 (end of day 10). Notice also that the time has been filled in solid for activities on the critical path (activities 1–4, 4–6, and 6–7). This serves to warn the scheduler that these activities can be scheduled only at the time indicated unless the project duration is to be changed.

Each activity may now be scheduled at any position desired on the time line. If all activities are started at the beginning of their time line, the early start schedule of Figure 18 is produced. Here each workday is indicated by an asterisk while each day of float is represented by the letter F. Float may be used to rearrange the schedule as desired by the scheduler without changing project duration.

Some of the uses for float in scheduling are to incorporate preferential logic, to satisfy resource constraints, and to allow weather-sensitive activities to be scheduled when weather conditions are expected to be most favorable. *Preferential logic* is that network logic which is imposed by the planner solely because the planner prefers to conduct the operation in that sequence. In other words, it is not logic imposed by the fundamental nature of the process. An example would be the scheduling of all concreting activities in sequence so that only one concrete crew would be required for the project.

Late Start and Other Schedules

When all activities are started at their latest allowable starting time, a *late start schedule* is produced, as shown in Figure 19. Note that all float is used before the activity starts. An obvious disadvantage to the use of such a schedule is that it leaves no time cushion in the event that an activity requires longer than its estimated duration. In practice, the usual schedule is neither an early start nor a late start schedule. Rather, it is an intermediate schedule produced by

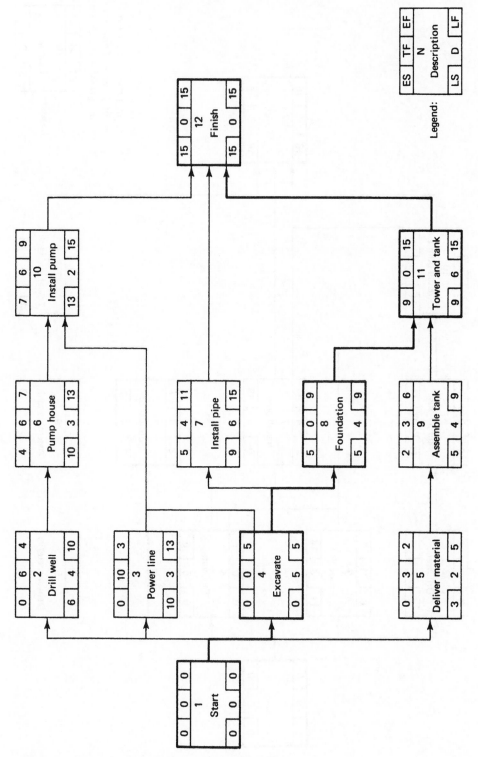

FIGURE 15. Precedence diagram for example project.

delaying some activities to permit resource leveling or the incorporation of preferential logic while retaining as much float as possible.

When producing a schedule other than an early start schedule, care must be taken to ensure that no activity is scheduled to start before its predecessor event has occurred. This, of course, would be a violation of network logic. Such an error may be prevented by referring to the network diagram each time an activity is scheduled. However, a simple technique makes use of the activity numbers on the schedule to check logic constraints. Referring to Figures 17 and 9, we see activity 2–5 may be started as soon as all activities ending with event 2 (*J* number = 2) have been completed. In this case, this is only activity 1–2. In using this technique, some

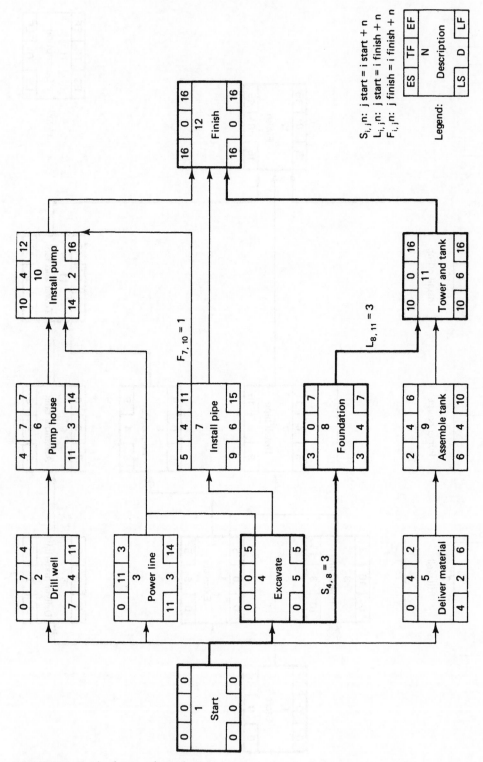

FIGURE 16. Revised example project.

provision must be made for incorporating the logic constraints imposed by dummies. This may be done by putting a third number in parentheses after the usual activity *I–J* number. The number in parentheses represents the event number at the end of the dummy. For example, in Figure 19, note that activity 1–4 has been identified as activity 1–4 (5). Here

the number 5 indicates that activities starting with number 5 (*I* number = 5) cannot begin until activity 1–4 is completed. Reference to the network diagram of Figure 9 shows that this is the correct logic and is the result of the presence of dummy 4–5. Thus the real predecessors of activity 5–7 are activities 1–4, 1–5, and 2–5.

Act No.	Description	D	1	2	3	4	5	6	7	8	9	10	11	12	13	14	15
1 – 2	Drill well	4	─	─	─	─	─	─	─	─	─	─					
1 – 3	Deliver matl	2	─	─	─	─	─										
1 – 4	Excavate	5	█	█	█	█	█										
1 – 5	Power line	3	─	─	─	─	─	─	─	─	─	─	─	─	─		
2 – 5	Pump house	3					─	─	─	─	─	─	─	─	─		
3 – 6	Assemble tank	4			─	─	─	─	─	─	─						
4 – 6	Foundation	4						█	█	█	█						
4 – 7	Install pipe	6						─	─	─	─	─	─	─	─	─	─
5 – 7	Install pump	2								─	─	─	─	─	─	─	─
6 – 7	Erect tower & tank	6										█	█	█	█	█	█

FIGURE 17. Allowable activity time span for example network.

Act No.	Description	D	1	2	3	4	5	6	7	8	9	10	11	12	13	14	15
1 – 2	Drill well	4	*	*	*	*	F	F	F	F	F	F					
1 – 3	Deliver matl	2	*	*	F	F	F										
1 – 4	Excavate	5	*	*	*	*	*										
1 – 5	Power line	3	*	*	*	F	F	F	F	F	F	F	F	F	F		
2 – 5	Pump house	3					*	*	*	F	F	F	F	F	F		
3 – 6	Assemble tank	4			*	*	*	*	F	F	F						
4 – 6	Foundation	4						*	*	*	*						
4 – 7	Install pipe	6						*	*	*	*	*	*	F	F	F	F
5 – 7	Install pump	2								*	*	F	F	F	F	F	F
6 – 7	Erect tower & tank	6										*	*	*	*	*	*

* = work day   F = float

FIGURE 18. Early start schedule for example network.

Act no.	Description		1	2	3	4	5	6	7	8	9	10	11	12	13	14	15
1 – 2	Drill well	4	F	F	F	F	F	F	*	*	*	*					
1 – 3	Deliver matl	2	F	F	F	*	*										
1 – 4(5)	Excavate	5	*	*	*	*	*										
1 – 5	Power line	3	F	F	F	F	F	F	F	F	F	F	*	*	*		
2 – 5	Pump house	3						F	F	F	F	F	*	*	*		
3 – 6	Assemble tank	4			F	F	F	*	*	*	*						
4 – 6	Foundation	4						*	*	*	*						
4 – 7	Install pipe	6						F	F	F	F	*	*	*	*	*	*
5 – 7	Install pump	2								F	F	F	F	F	F	*	*
6 – 7	Erect tower & tank	6										*	*	*	*	*	*

* = work day   F = float

FIGURE 19. Late start schedule for example network.

Resource Assignment

In planning the assignment of resources to a project, the planner is usually faced with two major considerations. For each type of resource, these are (1) the maximum number of resources available during each time period, and (2) the desire to eliminate peaks and valleys in resource requirements (i.e., resource leveling).

If the asterisk designating a workday in Figures 18 and 19 is simply replaced by a number representing the quantity of the resource required for the activity during that time period, it is a simple matter to determine the total quantity of the resource required for each time period for any particular schedule. Thus Figure 20 illustrates the number of workers needed on each day for the early start schedule (Figure 18) of the example network. The daily labor requirements are rather uneven, varying from 19 workers on the first 2 days to 8 workers on the twelfth day. Unless the contractor has other nearby projects that can utilize the excess labor produced by these fluctuations, labor problems would soon develop. A far better policy would be to attempt to level out the daily labor requirements. This can often be done by simply utilizing float to reschedule activities.

A quick calculation will indicate that the total resource requirement for the example network indicated in Figure 20 is 195 worker days. This yields an average requirement of about 13 workers per day. By utilizing float to reschedule activities, the revised schedule of Figure 21

may be obtained. The daily requirements of this schedule only vary between 12 and 15 workers. Similar procedures may be applied when maximum resource limits are established. However, it will often be necessary to extend the project duration to satisfy limited resource constraints. The daily requirements for each resource must be calculated separately, although several resources may be tabulated on the same schedule sheet by utilizing different colors or symbols for each resource. While the manual technique suggested above will be satisfactory for small networks, it is apparent that the procedure would become very cumbersome for large networks. Thus computer programs have been developed for both resource leveling and limited resource problems. Reference 1 identifies a number of such computer programs.

5 PRACTICAL CONSIDERATIONS IN NETWORK USE

When to Use Network Methods

The methodology involved in drawing a network diagram forces the planner to consider in some detail and to put down on paper the manner in which the project is to be carried out. In addition, the network diagram is an excellent communications device for transmitting this information

Act No.	Description	D	Time														
			1	2	3	4	5	6	7	8	9	10	11	12	13	14	15
1 – 2	Drill well	4	4	4	4	4											
1 – 3	Deliver matl	2	4	4													
1 – 4(5)	Excavate	5	5	5	5	5	5										
1 – 5	Power line	3	6	6	6												
2 – 5	Pump house	3						2	2	2							
3 – 6	Assemble tank	4			3	3	3	3									
4 – 6	Foundation	4						7	7	7	7						
4 – 7	Install pipe	6						4	4	4	4	4	4				
5 – 7	Install pump	2									5	5					
6 – 7	Erect tower & tank	6										8	8	8	8	8	8
	Total		19	19	18	12	10	16	13	16	16	12	12	8	8	8	8

Resources (Workers) Required by Activity

Activity	Number required
1 – 2	4
1 – 3	4
1 – 4	5
1 – 5	6
2 – 5	2
3 – 6	3
4 – 6	7
4 – 7	4
5 – 7	5
6 – 7	8

FIGURE 20. Resource assignment—early start schedule.

Act No.	Description	D	1	2	3	4	5	6	7	8	9	10	11	12	13	14	15
1 – 2	Drill well	4	4	4	4	4											
1 – 3	Deliver matl	2	4	4													
1 – 4(5)	Excavate	5	5	5	5	5	5										
1 – 5	Power line	3			6	6	6										
2 – 5	Pump house	3						2	2	2							
3 – 6	Assemble tank	4						3	3	3	3						
4 – 6	Foundation	4						7	7	7	7						
4 – 7	Install pipe	6								4	4	4	4	4	4		
5 – 7	Install pump	2														5	5
6 – 7	Erect tower & tank	6										8	8	8	8	8	8
	Total		13	13	15	15	13	12	12	14	14	12	12	12	12	13	13

FIGURE 21. Improved level of resource assignment.

to everyone involved in a project. For these reasons, preparation of a network diagram is useful for any project, regardless of size. The size of the network used will, of course, depend on the size and complexity of the project. Rules of thumb on network size and the need for a network diagram proposed by some experts are based on a particular method of operation and do not necessarily apply to your situation. Projects as large as a $3.5 million 25-story building have been successfully managed with a CPM network consisting of less than 90 activities. Where repetitive operations are involved, it may be worthwhile to draw a subnetwork to show each operation in some detail while using only a single activity to represent the operation on the major network.

Even prior to bid submittal, a summary or outline network can be very useful. For example, the network diagram can be used to determine whether the project can reasonably be completed within the time specified on the bid documents. Thus a decision can be made at this point whether a bid should even be submitted. If the decision is to proceed, the network diagram can then be used as a framework for developing the project's cost estimate for the bid. Upon award of the construction contract, a full network should be prepared to the level of detail considered necessary for carrying out the project. Some of the factors to be considered in determining the level of detail to be used include the dollar value, size, complexity, and duration of the project.

Preparing the Network

Regardless of the size of the planning group (which may be as small as the project manager alone) chosen to develop the network, it is important that input be obtained from the field personnel most familiar with the construction techniques to be applied. If specialty subcontractors are not represented in the planning group, it is important that they review the plan prior to its finalization to ensure that they can carry out their work in the manner contemplated.

Manual or Computer Techniques

One of the major factors that has sometimes led to dissatisfaction with network methods has been the excessive or inappropriate use of computers. Manual techniques have much to recommend them, particularly for personnel not well versed in network procedures. The manual preparation and calculation of a network is one of the best ways for a manager to really understand a project and to visualize potential problems and payoffs.

When it is necessary to utilize a network of more than several hundred activities, the use of computers for performing time calculations is advantageous. However, do not let yourself or your subordinates become inundated with unnecessary computer output. Output should be carefully selected to provide all levels of management with only the information they can effectively utilize.

An obvious advantage of the computer is its ability to rapidly update network calculations and to provide reports in any format and quantity desired. However, the preparation of reports too frequently or in an excessive quantity is simply a waste of paper and computer time. While the network diagram at the project site should always be kept current, computer reports should be produced on a more limited basis. For projects of average duration and importance an updating interval of 2–4 weeks should be satisfactory. As with all computer operations, the output is only as good as the input, so care must be taken to ensure that data are correctly entered before running a network program.

Advanced Network Techniques

There are a number of more sophisticated network-based management techniques that have been developed. Among these are selection of an optimum (lowest total cost) project duration based on project time-cost relations, minimizing project cost through financial planning and cost control techniques, and resource leveling over multiple projects. Although beyond the scope of this chapter, many of these techniques are described in the end-of-chapter references.

6   LINEAR SCHEDULING METHODS

Scheduling Repetitive Projects

Many in the construction industry feel that conventional network methods such as CPM are not well suited to highly repetitive work. Such projects include highways, airfields, pipelines, multiple housing units, and high-rise buildings. Highway projects whose activities progress linearly from one end of the project to the other are particularly difficult to adequately represent in CPM. As a result, linear scheduling techniques are increasingly being employed on such projects.

The *Linear Scheduling Method (LSM)* is similar to the Line of Balance (LOB) scheduling technique developed in the early 1950s for industrial and aerospace projects and is sometimes identified by the same name. The objective of the LOB technique is to ensure that components or sub-assemblies are available at the time they are required to meet the production schedule of the final assembly. The objective of the LSM technique is to display and prevent interference between repetitive activities that progress linearly from one end of a project to the other. A brief explanation of the LSM applied to a highway construction project is provided below.

A Linear Scheduling Method Diagram

An LSM diagram of the highway construction project of Figure 1 is shown in Figure 22. The five activities involved are Clear and Strip, Drainage, Subgrade, Base Course, and Pave. Notice that activities are represented by a line or band representing time versus location.

The height (A) of an activity at a specific time represents the distance over which that activity is being carried out at that instant. Thus, Subgrade work extends from station 13 to station 21 at the start of week 3. The width (B) of an activity indicates the time from start to finish of that activity at a specific location. Hence, at station 40 Subgrade work starts at week 4.4 and continues to week 5.0. The horizontal distance between activities (C) represents the time lag or interval between the finish of one activity and the start of the succeeding activity at a specific location. Thus, the start of Base work at station 10 lags the completion of Subgrade work at that location by 1.4 weeks.

Notice that the Drainage activity follows Clear and Strip but extends only to station 30. That is, no drainage work is required from station 30 to station 50. The Drainage activity could also overlap the Clear and Strip activity if it were determined that the two activities could be carried out concurrently at the same location without interference between the two.

FIGURE 22. LSM diagram for project of Figure 1.

Problems

1. Redraw the accompanying network diagram, adding early and late event times to the diagram. Mark the critical path. Prepare an activity-time tabulation showing early start, late start, early finish, late finish, and total float.

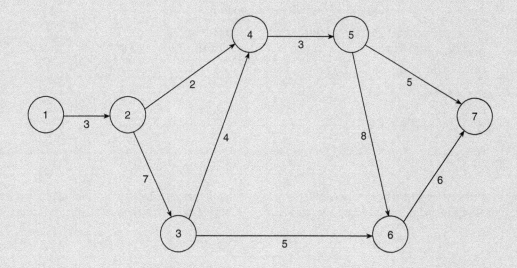

2. Prepare an Early Start schedule for the network shown. Indicate the allowable time span for each activity. Activity durations are in days.

3. What advantages do CPM diagrams have over conventional bar graph schedules?

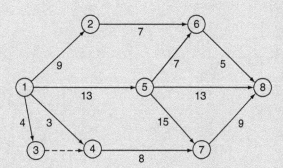

4. For the LSM diagram of Figure 22, how long does it take to complete the Base activity at a specified location?

5. Compare the actual progress with the scheduled progress at the end of the third week in Figure 1. Express your answer as the percentage by which the project is ahead or behind schedule at the end of the third week.

6. For the network of Problem 1, assign resources based on an early start schedule. Indicate the total resource requirements for each time period. Level the resource requirements as much as possible utilizing float. The resource requirements for each activity are as follows.

Activity	Workers Required
1–2	6
2–3	4
2–4	15
3–4	10
3–6	5
4–5	6
5–6	5
5–7	8
6–7	4

7. Redraw the precedence diagram of Figure 15 adding the relationships given below. Enter the early start, late start, early finish, late finish, and total float times on the diagram. Mark the critical path.

Activity Relationships			
Start to Start	Finish to Start	Finish to Finish	Lag Time
8–7			3
	7–10		2
		8–11	4

8. Redraw the accompanying network diagram adding early and late event times to the diagram. Mark the critical path. Prepare an activity-time tabulation showing early start, late start, early finish, late finish, and total float.

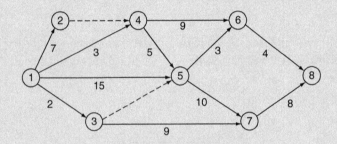

9. Draw an activity-on-arrow network diagram representing the following logical relationships.

10. Utilizing a personal computer program, solve Problem 1.

Activity	Depends on Completion of Activity
A	—
B	—
C	—
D	A
E	B
F	C
G	B
H	D and G
I	B
J	—
K	I and F

References

1. Ahuja, Hira N. *Project Management,* 2nd ed. New York: Wiley, 1994.

2. Arditi, David, and M. Zeki Albulak. "Line-of-Balance Scheduling in Pavement Construction," *ASCE Journal of Construction Engineering and Management,* vol. 112, no. 3 (1986), pp. 411–424.

3. Clough, Richard, Glenn A. Sears, and Keoki Sears. *Construction Project Management,* 4th ed. New York: Wiley, 2000.

4. Harris, Robert B. *Precedence and Arrow Networking Techniques for Construction.* New York: Wiley, 1978.

5. Johnston, David W. "Linear Scheduling Method for Highway Construction," *ASCE Journal of the Construction Division,* vol. 107, no. C02 (1981), pp. 247–261.

6. Moder, Joseph J., Cecil R. Phillips, and Edward W. Davis. *Project Management with CPM, PERT and PRECEDENCE Diagramming,* 3rd ed. New York: Van Nostrand Reinhold, 1983.

7. O'Brien, James J., and Frederic L. Plotnick. *CPM in Construction Management,* 6th ed. Boston, MA: McGraw-Hill, 2005.

8. Pinnell, Steven S. "Critical Path Scheduling: An Overview and a Practical Alternative," *Civil Engineering-ASCE* (May 1981).

9. Vorster, M. C., Y. J. Beliveau, and T. Bafna. "Linear Scheduling and Visualization," *Transp. Res. Rec. 1351* (1992). Transportation Research Board, Washington, D.C., pp. 32–39.

10. Whitehouse, Gary E. "Critical Path Program for a Microcomputer," *Civil Engineering-ASCE* (May 1991), pp. 54–56.

11. Yamin, Rene A., and David J. Harmelink. "Comparison of Linear Scheduling Model (LSM) and Critical Path Method (CPM)," *ASCE Journal of Construction Engineering and Management,* vol.127, no. 5 (2001), pp.374–381.

CONSTRUCTION ECONOMICS

From Chapter 17 of *Construction Methods and Management*, Eighth Edition. S. W. Nunnally. Copyright © 2011 by Pearson Education, Inc. Published by Pearson Prentice Hall. All rights reserved.

CONSTRUCTION ECONOMICS

1 INTRODUCTION

As has been noted on a number of occasions, construction contracting is a highly competitive business. Therefore, the financial management of a construction company is equally as important to company success as is its technical management. As a matter of fact, many successful constructors have evolved from a background of business and finance rather than from construction itself. However, there is little doubt that a strong technical base supported by business skills and management ability provides the best foundation for success as a construction professional.

A complete discussion of the many facets of construction economics is beyond the scope of this book. Rather, the purpose of this chapter is to introduce the reader to the terminology and basic principles involved in determining the owning and operating costs of construction plant and equipment, analyzing the feasibility of renting or leasing rather than purchasing equipment, and the financial management of construction projects.

2 TIME VALUE OF MONEY

Everyone is aware that the amount of money held in a savings account will increase with time if interest payments are allowed to remain on deposit (compound) in the account. The value of a sum of money left on deposit after any period of time may be calculated using Equation 1.

$$F = P(1 + i)^n \tag{1}$$

where F = value at end of n periods (future value)
  P = present value
  i = interest rate per period
  n = number of periods

The expression $(1 + i)^n$ is often called the *single-payment compound interest factor*. Equation 1 can be solved to find the present value (present worth) of some future amount, resulting in Equation 2.

$$P = \frac{F}{(1 + i)^n} \tag{2}$$

The expression $1/(1 + i)^n$ is called the *single-payment present worth factor*. Expressions have also been developed that yield the value of a series of equal periodic payments at the end of any number of periods *(uniform series compound amount factor)*, the present worth of such a series *(uniform series present worth factor)*, the periodic payment required to accumulate a desired amount at some future date *(sinking fund factor)*, and the annual cost to recover an investment, including the payment of interest, over a given period of time *(capital recovery factor)*. Other expressions have been developed to find the present and future worth of gradient (nonuniform) series of payments.

These equations form the basis of a type of economic analysis commonly called *engineering economy*. The methods of engineering economy are widely used to analyze the economic feasibility of proposed projects, to compare alternative investments, and to determine the rate of return on an investment. However, because of their complexity and the difficulty of accounting for the effects of inflation and taxes, these techniques have not been widely used within the construction industry. Construction equipment owning costs, for example, are usually determined by the methods described in the following section rather than by employing engineering economy techniques. A present worth analysis, however, is very helpful when comparing the cost of different alternatives. This is illustrated by the rent–lease–buy analysis described in Section 4.

3 EQUIPMENT COST

Elements of Equipment Cost

In earlier chapters, we have discussed the proper application of the major items of construction equipment and some methods for estimating equipment's hourly production. We then divided the equipment's hourly cost by its hourly production to obtain the cost per unit of production. However, up to this point we have simply assumed that we knew the hourly cost of operation of the equipment. In this section, we consider methods for determining the hourly cost of operation of an item of equipment. Although the procedures explained in this section are those commonly employed in the construction industry, they are not the only possible methods.

In following the procedures of this section, you will note that it is necessary to estimate many factors, such as fuel consumption, tire life, and so on. The best basis for estimating such factors is the use of historical data, preferably those recorded by your construction company operating similar equipment under similar conditions. If such data are not available, consult the equipment manufacturer for recommendations.

Equipment *owning and operating costs* (frequently referred to as *O & O costs*), as the name implies, are composed of owning costs and operating costs. Owning costs are fixed costs that are incurred each year whether the equipment is operated or not. Operating costs, however, are incurred only when the equipment is used.

Owning Costs

Owning costs are made up of the following principal elements:

- Depreciation.
- Investment (or interest) cost.
- Insurance cost.
- Taxes.
- Storage cost.

Methods for calculating each of these items are described next.

Depreciation *Depreciation* represents the decline in market value of an item of equipment due to age, wear, deterioration, and obsolescence. In accounting for equipment costs, however, depreciation is used for two separate purposes: (1) evaluating tax liability, and (2) determining the depreciation component of the hourly equipment cost. Note that it is possible (and legal) to use different depreciation schedules for these two purposes. For tax purposes many equipment owners depreciate equipment as rapidly as possible to obtain the maximum reduction in tax liability during the first few years of equipment life. However, the result is simply the shifting of tax liability between tax years, because current tax rules of the U.S. Internal Revenue Service (IRS) treat any gain (amount received in excess of

the equipment's depreciated or book value) on the sale of equipment as ordinary income. The depreciation methods explained in the following pages are those commonly used in the construction equipment industry. Readers familiar with the subject of engineering economics should recognize that the methods of engineering economy may also be employed. When the methods of engineering economics are used, the depreciation and investment components of equipment owning costs will be calculated together as a single cost factor.

In calculating depreciation, the initial cost of an item of equipment should be the full delivered price, including transportation, taxes, and initial assembly and servicing. For rubber-tired equipment, the value of tires should be subtracted from the amount to be depreciated because tire cost will be computed separately as an element of operating cost. Equipment salvage value should be estimated as realistically as possible based on historical data.

The equipment life used in calculating depreciation should correspond to the equipment's expected economic or useful life. The IRS guideline life for general construction equipment is currently 5 years, so this depreciation period is widely used by the construction industry.

The most commonly used depreciation methods are the straight-line method, the sum-of-the-years'-digits method, the double-declining balance method, and IRS-prescribed methods. Procedures for applying each of these methods are explained below.

Straight-Line Method. The *straight-line method* of depreciation produces a uniform depreciation for each year of equipment life. Annual depreciation is thus calculated as the amount to be depreciated divided by the equipment life in years (Equation 3). The amount to be depreciated consists of the equipment's initial cost less salvage value (and less tire cost for rubber-tired equipment).

$$D_n = \frac{\text{Cost} - \text{Salvage} \, (-\text{tires})}{N} \tag{3}$$

where N = equipment life (years)
n = year of life (1, 2, 3, etc.)

Example 1 Using the straight-line method of depreciation, find the annual depreciation and book value at the end of each year for a track loader having an initial cost of $50,000, a salvage value of $5000, and an expected life of 5 years.

Solution

$$D_{1,2,3,4,5} = \frac{50,000 - 5000}{5} = \$9000$$

Sum-of-the-Years'-Digits Method. The *sum-of-the-years'-digits method* of depreciation produces a nonuniform depreciation which is the highest in the first year of life and gradually decreases thereafter. The amount to be depreciated is the same as that used in the straight-line method. The depreciation for

Year	Depreciation	Book Value (End of Period)
0	0	$50,000
1	$9000	41,000
2	9000	32,000
3	9000	23,000
4	9000	14,000
5	9000	5000

a particular year is calculated by multiplying the amount to be depreciated by a depreciation factor (Equation 4). The denominator of the depreciation factor is the sum of the years' digits for the depreciation period (or $1 + 2 + 3 + 4 + 5 = 15$ for a 5-year life). The numerator of the depreciation factor is simply the particular year digit taken in *inverse* order (i.e., $5 - 4 - 3 - 2 - 1$). Thus for the first year of a 5-year life, 5 would be used as the numerator.

$$D_n = \frac{\text{Year digit}}{\text{Sum of years' digits}} \times \frac{\text{Amount to be}}{\text{depreciated}} \quad (4)$$

The procedure is illustrated in Example 2.

Example 2 For the loader of Example 1, find the annual depreciation and book value at the end of each year using the sum-of-the-years'-digits method.

Solution

Using Equation 4:

$$D_1 = \frac{5}{15} \times (50,000 - 5000) = 15,000$$

$$D_2 = \frac{4}{15} \times (50,000 - 5000) = 12,000$$

$$D_3 = \frac{3}{15} \times (50,000 - 5000) = 9000$$

$$D_4 = \frac{2}{15} \times (50,000 - 5000) = 6000$$

$$D_5 = \frac{1}{15} \times (50,000 - 5000) = 3000$$

Year	Depreciation	Book Value (End of Period)
0	0	$50,000
1	$15,000	35,000
2	12,000	23,000
3	9000	14,000
4	6000	8000
5	3000	5000

Double-Declining-Balance Method. The *double-declining-balance method* of depreciation, like the sum-of-the-years'-digits method, produces its maximum depreciation in the

first year of life. However, in using the double-declining-balance method, the depreciation for a particular year is found by multiplying a depreciation factor by the equipment's *book value at the beginning of the year* (Equation 5). The annual depreciation factor is found by dividing 2 (or 200%) by the equipment life in years. Thus for a 5-year life, the annual depreciation factor is 0.40 (or 40%). Unlike the other two depreciation methods, the double-declining-balance method does not automatically reduce the equipment's book value to its salvage value at the end of the depreciation period. Since the book value of equipment is not permitted to go below the equipment's salvage value, care must be taken when performing the depreciation calculations to stop depreciation when the salvage value is reached. The correct procedure is as follows:

$$D_n = \frac{2}{N} \times \text{Book value at beginning of year} \quad (5)$$

Example 3 For the loader of Example 1, find the annual depreciation and book value at the end of each year using the double-declining-balance method.

Solution

Using Equation 5:

$$\text{Annual depreciation factor} = \frac{2.00}{5} = 0.40$$

$$D_1 = 0.40 \times 50,000 = 20,000$$

$$D_2 = 0.40 \times 30,000 = 12,000$$

$$D_3 = 0.40 \times 18,000 = 7200$$

$$D_4 = 0.40 \times 10,800 = 4320$$

$$D_5 = 0.40 \times \quad 6480 = 2592 \text{ use } \$1480^*$$

Year	Depreciation	Book Value (End of Period)
0	0	$50,000
1	$20,000	30,000
2	12,000	18,000
3	7200	10,800
4	4320	6480
5	1480*	5000

*Because a depreciation of $2592 in the fifth year would reduce the book value to less than $5000, only $1480 ($6480 − $5000) may be taken as depreciation.

IRS-Prescribed Methods. Since the Internal Revenue Service tax rules change frequently, always consult the latest IRS regulations for the current method of calculating depreciation for tax purposes. The Modified Accelerated Cost Recovery System (MACRS) has been adopted by the Internal Revenue Service for the depreciation of most equipment placed in service after 1986. Although several different depreciation methods are permitted under MACRS, the depreciation method most commonly used is the General Depreciation System (GDS) with a modified double-declining-balance schedule (200% DB) and the half-year convention.

Under the MACRS system, depreciation for all property except real property is spread over a 3-year, 5-year, 7-year, or 10-year period. Most vehicles and equipment, including automobiles, trucks, and general construction equipment, are classified as 5-year property. The yearly deduction for depreciation is calculated as a prescribed percentage of initial cost (cost basis) for each year of tax life without considering salvage value. The "half-year convention" considers all property placed in service or disposed of during a year as having been acquired or disposed of at midyear. Using the 200% DB method and the half-year convention, the annual depreciation percentages are 20%, 32%, 19.2%, 11.52%, 11.52%, and 5.76% of years 1 through 6, respectively. Notice that regardless of the month of purchase, only one-half of the normal double-declining-balance depreciation is taken in the year of purchase. The remaining cost basis is spread over a period extending through the year following the recovery life. Thus, depreciation for 5-year property actually extends over a 6-year period as illustrated in Example 4.

Example 4 For the loader of Example 1, find the annual depreciation and book value at the end of each year using the MACRS method.

Solution

$$D_1 = \quad 0.20 \times 50{,}000 = 10{,}000$$
$$D_2 = \quad 0.32 \times 50{,}000 = 16{,}000$$
$$D_3 = \quad 0.192 \times 50{,}000 = 9600$$
$$D_4 = 0.1152 \times 50{,}000 = 5760$$
$$D_5 = 0.1152 \times 50{,}000 = 5760$$
$$D_6 = 0.0576 \times 50{,}000 = 2880$$

Year	Depreciation	Book Value (End of Period)
0	0	$50,000
1	10,000	40,000
2	16,000	24,000
3	9600	14,400
4	5760	8640
5	5760	2880
6	2880	0

Investment Cost *Investment cost* (or interest) represents the annual cost (converted to an hourly cost) of the capital invested in a machine. If borrowed funds are utilized, it is simply the interest charge on these funds. However, if the item of equipment is purchased from company assets, an interest rate should be charged equal to the rate of return on company investments. Thus investment cost is computed as the product of an interest rate multiplied by the value of the equipment,

then converted to cost per hour. The true investment cost for a specific year of ownership is properly calculated using the average value of the equipment during that year. However, the average hourly investment cost may be more easily calculated using the value of the average investment over the life of the equipment given by Equation 6.

$$\text{Average investment} = \frac{\text{Initial cost} + \text{Salvage}}{2} \qquad (6)$$

The results obtained using Equation 6 should be sufficiently accurate for calculating average hourly owning costs over the life of the equipment. However, the reader is cautioned that the investment cost calculated in this manner is not the actual cost for a specific year. It will be too low in the early years of equipment life and too high in later years. Thus this method should not be used for making replacement decisions or for other purposes requiring precise investment cost for a particular year.

Insurance, Tax, and Storage *Insurance cost* represents the cost of fire, theft, accident, and liability insurance for the equipment. *Tax cost* represents the cost of property tax and licenses for the equipment. *Storage cost* represents the cost of rent and maintenance for equipment storage yards and facilities, the wages of guards and employees involved in handling equipment in and out of storage, and associated direct overhead.

The cost of insurance and taxes for each item of equipment may be known on an annual basis. In this case, these costs are simply divided by the hours of operation during the year to yield the cost per hour for these items. Storage costs are usually obtained on an annual basis for the entire equipment fleet. Insurance and tax cost may also be known on a fleet basis. It is then necessary to prorate these costs to each item. This is usually done by converting total annual cost to a percentage rate by dividing these costs by the total value of the equipment fleet. When this is done, the rate for insurance, tax, and storage may simply be added to the investment cost rate to calculate the annual cost of investment, tax, insurance, and storage.

Total Owning Cost Total equipment owning cost is found as the sum of depreciation, investment, insurance, tax, and storage. As mentioned earlier, the elements of owning cost are often known on an annual cost basis. However, whether the individual elements of owning cost are calculated on an annual-cost basis or on an hourly basis, total owning cost should be expressed as an hourly cost.

Depreciation Bonus and Investment Credit In order to stimulate the economy and encourage businesses to purchase new equipment, the U.S. government has sometimes created a *depreciation bonus* for equipment purchases. When in effect, such laws provide an immediate depreciation equal to a designated percentage of the cost of new equipment for the year in which the equipment is placed in service. The remaining portion of equipment cost is then depreciated according to normal depreciation procedures.

There are two major tax implications of equipment ownership. The first, depreciation, including the depreciation bonus, has already been discussed. The second is investment credit. *Investment credit* is another mechanism sometimes used by the U.S. government to encourage industry to modernize production facilities by providing a tax credit for the purchase of new equipment. When in effect, investment credit provides a direct credit against tax due, not merely a reduction in taxable income. The investment credit last authorized allowed a tax credit equal to 10% of the investment for the purchase of equipment classified as 5-year property and 6% for equipment classified as 3-year property. However, when investment credit is taken, the cost basis (amount used for cost recovery calculations) must be reduced or a smaller investment credit used. Current IRS regulations should always be consulted for up-to-date tax information, including investment credit procedures.

Operating Costs

Operating costs are incurred only when equipment is operated. Therefore, costs vary with the amount of equipment use and job operating conditions. Operating costs include operators' wages, which are usually added as a separate item after other operating costs have been calculated.

The major elements of operating cost include:

- Fuel cost.
- Service cost.
- Repair cost.
- Tire cost.
- Cost of special items.
- Operators' wages.

Fuel Cost   The *hourly cost of fuel* is simply fuel consumption per hour multiplied by the cost per unit of fuel (gallon or liter). Actual measurement of fuel consumption under similar job conditions provides the best estimate of fuel consumption. However, when historical data are not available, fuel consumption may be estimated from manufacturer's data or by the use of Table 1. Table 1 provides approximate fuel consumption factors in gallons per hour per horsepower for major types of equipment under light, average, and severe load conditions.

Service Cost   *Service cost* represents the cost of oil, hydraulic fluids, grease, and filters as well as the labor required to perform routine maintenance service. Equipment manufacturers publish consumption data or average cost factors for oil, lubricants, and filters for their equipment under average conditions. Using such consumption data, multiply hourly consumption (adjusted for operating conditions) by

Table 1. Fuel consumption factors (gal/h/hp)

Type of Equipment	Load Conditions*		
	Low	Average	Severe
Clamshell and dragline	0.024	0.030	0.036
Compactor, self-propelled	0.038	0.052	0.060
Crane	0.018	0.024	0.030
Excavator, hoe, or shovel	0.035	0.040	0.048
Loader			
Track	0.030	0.042	0.051
Wheel	0.024	0.036	0.047
Motor grader	0.025	0.035	0.047
Scraper	0.026	0.035	0.044
Tractor			
Crawler	0.028	0.037	0.046
Wheel	0.028	0.038	0.052
Truck, off-highway	0.014	0.020	0.029
Wagon	0.029	0.037	0.046

*Low, light work or considerable idling; average, normal load and operating conditions; severe, heavy work, little idling.

cost per unit to obtain the hourly cost of consumable items. Service labor cost may be estimated based on prevailing wage rates and the planned maintenance program.

Since service cost is related to equipment size and severity of operating conditions, a rough estimate of service cost may be made based on the equipment's fuel cost (Table 2). For example, using Table 2 the hourly service cost of a scraper operated under severe conditions would be estimated at 50% of the hourly fuel cost.

Repair Cost   *Repair cost* represents the cost of all equipment repair and maintenance except for tire repair and replacement, routine service, and the replacement of high-wear items, such as ripper teeth. It should be noted that repair cost usually constitutes the largest item of operating expense for construction equipment.

Lifetime repair cost is usually estimated as a percentage of the equipment's initial cost less tires (Table 3). It is then necessary to convert lifetime repair cost to an hourly repair cost. This may be done simply by dividing lifetime repair cost by the expected equipment life in hours to yield an average

Table 2. Service cost factors (% of hourly fuel cost)

Operating Conditions	Service Cost Factor
Favorable	20
Average	33
Severe	50

Table 3. Typical lifetime repair cost (% of initial cost less tires)

Type of Equipment	Operating Conditions		
	Favorable	Average	Severe
Clamshell and dragline	40	60	80
Compactor, self-propelled	60	70	90
Crane	40	50	60
Excavator, hoe, or shovel	50	70	90
Loader			
Track	85	90	105
Wheel	50	60	75
Motor grader	45	50	55
Scraper	85	90	105
Tractor			
Crawler	85	90	95
Wheel	50	60	75
Truck, off-highway	70	80	90
Wagon	45	50	55

Table 4. Typical tire life (hours)

Type of Equipment	Operating Conditions		
	Favorable	Average	Severe
Dozers and loaders	3200	2100	1300
Motor graders	5000	3200	1900
Scrapers			
Conventional	4600	3300	2500
Twin engine	4000	3000	2300
Push-pull and elevating	3600	2700	2100
Trucks and wagons	3,500	2100	1100

similar operating conditions provide the best basis for estimating tire life. However, Table 4 may be used as a guide to approximate tire life. Tire repair will add about 15% to tire replacement cost. Thus, Equation 8 may be used to estimate tire repair and replacement cost.

$$\text{Tire cost} = 1.15 \times \frac{\text{Cost of a set of tires (\$)}}{\text{Expected tire life (h)}} \quad (8)$$

Special Items   The cost of replacing high-wear items such as dozer, grader, and scraper blade cutting edges and end bits, as well as ripper tips, shanks, and shank protectors, should be calculated as a separate item of operating expense. As usual, unit cost is divided by expected life to yield cost per hour.

Operator   The final item making up equipment operating cost is the operator's wage. Care must be taken to include all costs, such as worker's compensation insurance, Social Security taxes, overtime or premium pay, and fringe benefits, in the hourly wage figure.

Total Owning and Operating Costs

After owning cost and operating cost have been calculated, these are totaled to yield total owning and operating cost per hour of operation. Although this cost may be used for estimating and for charging equipment costs to projects, notice that it does not include overhead or profit. Hence overhead and profit must be added to obtain an hourly rental rate if the equipment is to be rented to others.

Example 6   Calculate the expected hourly owning and operating cost for the second year of operation of the twin-engine scraper described below.

Cost delivered	= $152,000
Tire cost	= $12,000
Estimated life	= 5 years
Salvage value	= $16,000
Depreciation method	= sum-of-the-years'-digits
Investment (interest) rate	= 10%
Tax, insurance, and storage rate	= 8%

hourly repair cost. Although this method is adequate for lifetime cost estimates, it is *not* valid for a particular year of equipment life. As you might expect, repair costs are typically low for new machines and rise as the equipment ages. Thus, it is suggested that Equation 7 be used to obtain a more accurate estimate of repair cost during a particular year of equipment life.

$$\begin{array}{l}\text{Hourly} \\ \text{repair} \\ \text{cost}\end{array} = \frac{\text{Year digit}}{\text{Sum of years' digits}} \times \frac{\begin{array}{c}\text{Lifetime} \\ \text{repair cost}\end{array}}{\text{Hours operated}} \quad (7)$$

This method of prorating repair costs is essentially the reverse of the sum-of-the-years'-digits method of depreciation explained earlier, because the year digit used in the numerator of the equation is now used in a normal sequence (i.e., 1 for the first year, 2 for the second year, etc.).

Example 5   Estimate the hourly repair cost for the first year of operation of a crawler tractor costing $136,000 and having a 5-year life. Assume average operating conditions and 2000 h of operation during the year.

Solution

Lifetime repair cost factor = 0.90   (Table 3)

Lifetime repair cost = 0.90 × 136,000 = $122,400

$$\text{Hourly repair cost} = \frac{1}{15} \times \frac{122,400}{2000} = \$4.08$$

Tire Cost   Tire cost represents the cost of tire repair and replacement. Among operating costs for rubber-tired equipment, tire cost is usually exceeded only by repair cost. Tire cost is difficult to estimate because of the difficulty in estimating tire life. As always, historical data obtained under

Operating conditions = average

Rated power = 465 hp

Fuel price = $1.30/gal

Operator's wages = $32.00/h

Solution

Owning Cost

Depreciation cost:

$$D_2 = \frac{4}{15} \times (152{,}000 - 16{,}000 - 12{,}000)$$

$$= \$33{,}067 \quad \text{(Eq. 4)}$$

$$\text{Depreciation} = \frac{33{,}067}{2000} = \$16.53/h$$

Investment, tax, insurance, and storage cost:

$$\text{Cost rate} = \text{Investment} + \begin{array}{l} \text{tax, insurance,} \\ \text{and storage} \end{array}$$

$$= 10 + 8 = 18\%$$

$$\text{Average investment} = \frac{152{,}000 + 16{,}000}{2}$$

$$= \$84{,}000 \quad \text{(Eq. 6)}$$

$$\begin{array}{l} \text{Investment, tax,} \\ \text{insurance, and storage} \end{array} = \frac{84{,}000 \times 0.18}{2000} = \$7.56/h$$

$$\text{Total owning cost} = 16.53 + 7.56 = \$24.09/h$$

Operating Cost

Fuel cost:

$$\begin{array}{l} \text{Estimated} \\ \text{consumption} \end{array} = 0.035 \times 465 = 16.3 \text{ gal/h} \quad \text{(Table 1)}$$

$$\text{Fuel cost} = 16.3 \times 1.30 = \$21.19/h$$

Service cost:

$$\text{Service cost} = 0.33 \times 21.19 = \$7.06/h \quad \text{(Table2)}$$

Repair cost:

$$\text{Lifetime repair cost} = 0.90 \times (152{,}000 - 12{,}000)$$

$$= \$126{,}000 \quad \text{(Table 3)}$$

$$\text{Repaircost} = \frac{2}{15} \times \frac{126{,}000}{2000} = \$8.40/h \quad \text{(Eq. 7)}$$

Tire cost:

$$\text{Estimated tire life} = 3000h \quad \text{(Table 4)}$$

$$\text{Tirecost} = 1.15 \times \frac{12{,}000}{3000} = \$4.60/h$$

Special item cost: None

$$\text{Operator wages} = \$32.00/h$$

$$\text{Total operating cost} = 21.19 + 7.06 + 8.40$$

$$+ 4.60 + 32.00 = \$73.25/h$$

Total O & O Cost

$$\text{Owning and operating cost} = 24.09 + 73.25 = \$97.34/h$$

4 EQUIPMENT RENTAL

Historically there has been a growing use of rental equipment by contractors and subcontractors. For example, in a recent year the value of new equipment purchases totaled some $20–25 billion while a like amount was spent on equipment rental. Over the same period, the value of used equipment purchases amounted to about $15 billion. With the growing demand for rental equipment, several national equipment rental chains have been formed along with increased rental of equipment by major equipment manufacturers.

Since a rental agreement is a short-term arrangement (usually having a duration of less than 1 year) and no advance payment is normally required, rental equipment provides the contractor with great flexibility in meeting project requirements. In addition, the rental dealer commonly provides all equipment maintenance except for high-wear items. A rental-purchase option (RPO), which credits a portion of the rental payments to the purchase price if the option is exercised, may also be available.

A discussion of the rent-lease-buy decision process is contained in the following section.

5 THE RENT-LEASE-BUY DECISION

The question of whether it is better to purchase a piece of construction equipment rather than renting or leasing the item is difficult to answer. Leasing involves a commitment for a fixed period and may include a purchase option in which a portion of the lease payments is credited toward the purchase price if the option is exercised. In recent years, there has been a trend toward increased leasing and renting of construction equipment. Some of the reasons for this trend include the rising cost of equipment, rapid changes in equipment technology, and the wide fluctuation in the rate of demand for construction services. Some construction companies make it a policy to rent or lease all major items of equipment.

Advantages of equipment ownership include governmental tax incentives (investment credit and depreciation), full control of equipment resources, and availability of equipment when needed. However, leasing and renting require little initial capital (usually none for renting) and equipment costs are fully tax deductible as project expenses. A rational analysis of these alternatives for obtaining equipment is complex and must include cost under the expected conditions, as well as equipment availability and productivity. In general, purchasing equipment will result in the lowest hourly equipment cost if the equipment is properly maintained and fully utilized. However, as we noted earlier, equipment owning costs continue whether equipment is being utilized or sitting idle. Therefore, renting is usually least expensive for equipment with low utilization. Leasing is intermediate between the two and may be the best solution when capital is limited and equipment utilization is high. The lease-with-purchase option may provide an attractive opportunity to purchase the equipment at low cost after lease costs have been paid under a cost-type contract.

One approach to comparing the cost of buying, leasing, and renting an item of equipment is illustrated in Example 7. The analysis considers net after-tax cash flow and its present value (present worth). The example is based on a method suggested by David J. Everhart of Caterpillar Inc. In making the calculations for present value, the present worth factors for midyear were used for yearly costs. To ensure that alternatives were compared under equal conditions, maintenance and repair costs were excluded from all calculations, although maintenance and repair is often included in rental rates. Notice that such an analysis depends on the specific tax rules applied (in this case, ACRS depreciation and 10% investment credit).

Under the particular circumstances of Example 7, buying is significantly less expensive than either leasing or renting if the equipment is fully utilized for the planned 5 years or 10,000 h. However, notice that the cost difference is considerably smaller when considered on a present worth basis. Figure 1 illustrates the effect on hourly cost (present value) when equipment utilization declines. Since total capital cost is constant over the 5-year period for both leasing and buying, hourly capital cost increases as utilization declines for both of these alternatives. Since the 5-year cost of leasing is fixed, leasing is always more expensive than owning in these circumstances. Since the hourly cost for renting is constant, the hourly cost for renting and buying become equal at 42% utilization, or 4200 h of use. As utilization continues to decline, renting becomes even more advantageous.

Example 7 Analyze the cost of renting, leasing, and purchasing an item of construction equipment under the conditions described. Evaluate total net after-tax cash flow and its present value.

Basic assumptions:

Company's marginal tax rate = 46%

Company's after-tax rate of return = 8%

Planned equipment use = 2000 h/year for 5 years

Purchase assumptions:

Equipment cost = $150,000

Estimated resale value after 5 years = $60,000

Cost recovery method = 5-year ACRS (yearly depreciation of 15%, 22%, 21%, 21%, and 21%)

Investment credit (10%) = $15,000

Cost basis = $142,500 (cost less 1/2 investment credit)

Down payment (20%) = $30,000

Loan period = 36 months

Loan interest rate = 12%

Monthly payment = $3985.72

Loan amortization:

Year	Payments	To Principal	Interest
1	$47,828.64	$35,329.91	$12,498.73
2	$47,828.64	$39,810.61	$8018.03
3	$47,828.64	$44,859.48	$2969.16

Lease assumptions:

Term of lease = 5 years

Lease payment = $2800 per month

Initial payment = 3 months in advance

Rental assumptions:

Rental period = 5 years, month to month

Rental rate = $5150 per month

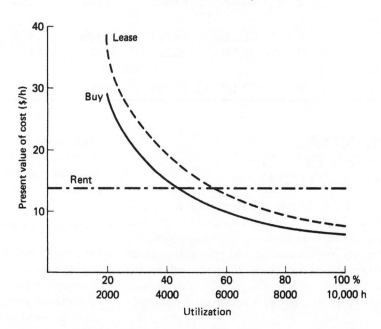

FIGURE 1. Hourly cost of buying, leasing, and renting for Example 7.

Mid-year present worth factors (average of start-of-year and end-of-year values) for $i = 8\%$:

Initial (year 0) = 1.00000

Year 1 = 0.96297

Year 2 = 0.89164

Year 3 = 0.82559

Year 4 = 0.76443

Year 5 = 0.70781

Final (end of Year 5) = 0.68058

Solution

Values are rounded to nearest whole dollar.

Purchase Cost ($)	Initial	Year 1	Year 2	Year 3	Year 4	Year 5	Final	Total
Payments	30,000	47,829	47,829	47,829	0	0	0	173,487
Resale	0	0	0	0	0	0	(60,000)	(60,000)
Tax at resale	0	0	0	0	0	0	27,600	27,600
Tax savings—depreciation	0	(9832)	(14,421)	(13,766)	(13,766)	(13,766)	0	(65,551)
Tax savings—interest	0	(5749)	(3688)	(1366)	0	0	0	(10,803)
Investment credit	0	(15,000)	0	0	0	0	0	(15,000)
Net cost	30,000	17,248	29,720	32,697	(13,766)	(13,766)	(32,400)	49,733
Present value of net cost	30,000	16,609	26,500	26,994	(10,523)	(9744)	(22,051)	57,785

Lease Cost ($)	Initial	Year 1	Year 2	Year 3	Year 4	Year 5	Final	Total
Payments	8400	33,600	33,600	33,600	33,600	25,200	0	168,000
Tax savings—payments	(3864)	(15,456)	(15,456)	(15,456)	(15,456)	(11,592)	0	(77,280)
Net cost	4536	18,144	18,144	18,144	18,144	13,608	0	90,720
Present value of net cost	4536	17,472	16,178	14,980	13,870	9632	0	76,668

Rental Cost ($)	Initial	Year 1	Year 2	Year 3	Year 4	Year 5	Final	Total
Payments	0	61,800	61,800	61,800	61,800	61,800	0	309,000
Tax savings—payments	0	(28,428)	(28,428)	(28,428)	(28,428)	(28,428)	0	(142,140)
Net cost	0	33,372	33,372	33,372	33,372	33,372	0	166,860
Present value of net cost	0	32,136	29,756	27,552	25,511	23,621	0	138,576

6 FINANCIAL MANAGEMENT OF CONSTRUCTION

Statistics compiled by Dun & Bradstreet on construction company failure in the United States indicate that the four major factors of inadequate financing, underestimating costs, inadequate cost accounting, and poor management account for over 80% of all failures. Thus, the basis for the statement earlier in this chapter that "the financial management of a construction company is equally as important to company success as is its technical management" is apparent. In this section, we shall consider the basic principles of financial planning and cost control for construction projects.

Financial Planning

Financial planning for a construction project includes cost estimating prior to bidding or negotiating a contract, forecasting project income and expenditure (or cash flow), and determining the amount of work that a construction firm can safely undertake at one time.

Cost estimating for a project, as the name implies, involves estimating the total cost to carry out a construction project in accordance with the plans and specifications. Costs that must be considered include labor, equipment, materials, subcontracts and services, indirect (or job management) costs, and general overhead (off-site management and administration costs).

A finance schedule or cash flow schedule shows the planned rate of project expenditure and project income. It is common practice in the construction industry for the owner to withhold payment for a percentage of the value of completed work (referred to as "retainage") as a guarantee until acceptance of the entire project. Even when periodic progress payments are made for the value of completed work, such payments (less retainage) are not received until some time after the end of each accounting period. Hence project income will almost always lag behind project expenditure. The difference must be provided in cash from company assets or borrowed funds. The construction industry relies heavily on the use of borrowed funds for this purpose. Therefore, the finance charges associated with the use of such funds, as well as the maximum amount of funds available, are important considerations in the financial planning for a construction project. While a financial schedule may be developed manually from any type of project schedule, the use of CPM methods will facilitate preparation of a financial schedule. The use of CPM procedures also makes it easy to determine the effect on cash flow of different project schedules. Figure 2 shows a graph of project cost versus time for three different schedules: an early start schedule, a late start schedule, and a proposed schedule which is between these limits. Figure 3 illustrates a financial schedule showing project expenditures, value of completed work, and receipts for a particular project schedule.

FIGURE 3. Project financial schedule.

Another important consideration in financial planning is the capacity of a firm to undertake additional projects. It has been found that most construction contracts require a minimum working capital of about 10% of the contract value. This working capital is needed to cover the difference between project income and project expenditures described above. The availability of working capital also affects the type of construction contract that might be appropriate for any additional work to be undertaken. When working capital is marginal, any additional work should be limited to low-risk projects such as cost-reimbursable contracts.

Project Cost Control

Project cost control involves the measurement and recording of project costs and progress and a comparison between actual and planned performance. The principal objective of project cost control is to maximize profit while completing the project on time at a satisfactory level of quality. Proper cost control procedures will also result in the accumulation of historical cost data, which are invaluable in estimating and controlling future project costs.

To carry out project cost control it is necessary to have a method for identifying cost and progress by project work element. The use of CPM procedures greatly simplifies this process, because major work items have already been identified as activities when preparing the project network diagram. A cost code system is usually combined with activity numbering to yield a complete system of project cost accounts. It is essential that the coding system permit charging all labor, material, equipment, and subcontract costs to the appropriate work item. Indirect and overhead costs for the project are usually assigned a separate cost code. Record-keeping requirements for foremen and other supervisors should be kept to a minimum consistent with meeting the objectives of accurate and timely reporting. Labor costs may be easily computed if time sheets are coded to identify the

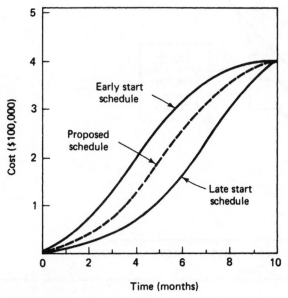

FIGURE 2. Project cost versus time.

activity on which the time is expended. Plant and equipment costs may be similarly computed if a record is kept of the time spent on each activity by each machine. The cost of materials used may be based on priced delivery invoices coded to the appropriate activity. Since subcontract and service work may not be billed at the same interval at which costs are recorded, it may be necessary to apportion such costs to the appropriate activity at each costing interval.

To permit a comparison of project progress versus cost, it is necessary that progress reporting intervals coincide with cost reporting intervals. The interval between reports will depend on the nature and importance of the project. Monthly intervals are commonly used as the basis for requesting progress payments. However, construction management may desire weekly or even daily cost and

performance reports for the control of critical construction projects.

A number of systems have been developed for relating project cost and progress and for forecasting time and cost to project completion. One such system, called PERT/Cost, has been developed by the U.S. government and has been extensively used by government agencies for project control. Figure 4 illustrates a PERT/Cost report for a project. Note that project progress and cost to date are graphed, together with the value of the work completed to date and projections of final completion time and cost. While PERT/Cost itself has not been widely used in the construction industry, systems have been developed within the construction industry which offer similar capabilities tailored to the construction environment.

FIGURE 4. PERT/Cost progress and cost report. (PERT Coordinating Group, U.S. Government)

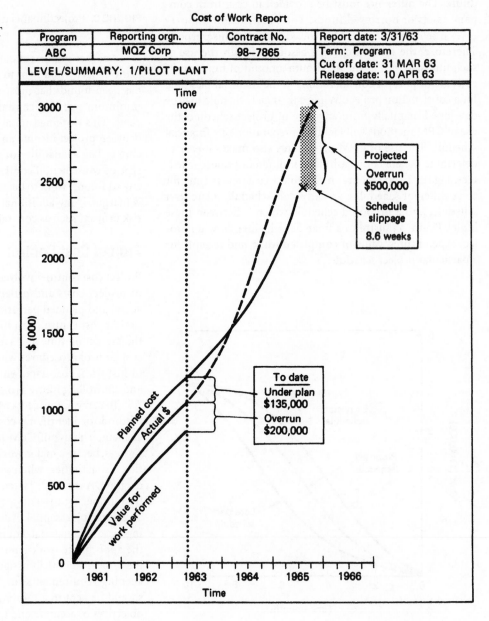

Problems

1. Find the hourly operating cost for the first year of life of the tractor of Problem 3. Use the following additional data.

Rated power	= 300 hp (224 kW)
Fuel price	= $1.50/gal ($0.396/ℓ)
Load conditions	= average
Operating conditions	= average
Hours operated	= 2000 h/year
Operator cost	= $20.00/h

2. Determine the probable average cost per hour over the life of the equipment for owning and operating a bottom-dump wagon under the conditions listed below. Use the straight-line method of depreciation.

Operator cost	= $20.00/h
Operating conditions	= average
Delivered price	= $142,000
Cost of a set of tires	= $12,000
Expected life of wagon	= 5 years
Hours operated	= 2000 h/year
Estimated salvage value	= $42,000
Fuel cost	= $2.00/gal ($0.53/ℓ)
Loader horsepower	= 440 hp (328 kW)
Rate for interest, tax, insurance, and storage	= 15%

3. A crawler tractor costs $250,000 and has an estimated salvage value of $50,000 and a 5-year life. Find the annual depreciation and book value at the end of each year using the double-declining-balance method of depreciation.

4. Analyze the cost of renting, leasing, and purchasing a backhoe loader using the data given below. Evaluate after-tax cash flow and its present value.

Basic assumptions:

Marginal tax rate	= 46%
After-tax rate of return	= 7%
Planned equipment use	= 2000 h/year for 5 years
Present value factors ($i = 7\%$)	

Year	P/F
1	0.967
2	0.904
3	0.845
4	0.790
5	0.738
End of 5	0.713

Purchase assumptions:

Cost	= $100,000
Estimated resale value after 5 years	= $40,000
Cost recovery method	= 5-year MACRS
Down payment	= $20,000
Loan terms	= $80,000, 12%, 36 months
	= $2,657.20/month

Interest payments:

Year	Interest
1	$8333
2	5346
3	1979

Lease assumptions:

Term of lease	= 5 years
Lease payments	= $1850/month
Initial payment	= 3 months in advance

Rental assumptions:

Rental period	= 5 years, month to month
Rental rate	= $3375/month

5. For the project whose data are shown below, plot the cumulative project expenditures, value of work, and progress payments received versus time. What is the contractor's maximum negative cash flow and when does it occur? Progress payments are calculated at the end of each month and received the middle of the following month. Retainage is 10% until project completion. Assume that final project payment, including released retainage, is received the middle of the month following project completion.

Month	End-of-Month Cumulative Expenditures	Value of Work
1	$14,400	$9600
2	28,800	24,000
3	49,200	45,600
4	72,000	69,600
5	102,000	76,800
6	144,000	144,000
7	210,000	216,000
8	276,000	288,000
9	288,000	300,000
10	294,000	312,000
11	295,200	321,600
12	296,400	330,000

6. What are the advantages and disadvantages of equipment rental compared with equipment purchase?

7. For the tractor of Problem 3, find the annual depreciation and book value at the end of each year using the sum-of-the-years'-digits method of depreciation.

8. Find the present value (present worth) of $40,000 when a piece of equipment is sold 5 years from now if the rate of return on investment is 7% per year.

9. Briefly explain the principal elements of financial planning for a construction project.

10. Develop a computer program to determine the probable average hourly owning and operating cost of a piece of construction equipment over the life of the equipment. Use the straight-line method of depreciation. Solve Problem 4 using your program.

References

1. *Caterpillar Performance Handbook*, Caterpillar Inc., Peoria, IL.

2. Collier, Courtland A., and Charles R. Glagola. *Engineering Economic and Cost Analysis*, 3rd ed. Menlo Park, CA: Addison Wesley Longman, 1998.

3. *Contractors' Equipment Cost Guide*. Dataquest Incorporated, San Jose, CA.

4. *Deere Performance Handbook*. Deere & Company, Moline, IL.

5. Humphreys, Kenneth K., ed. *Jelen's Cost and Optimization Engineering*, 3rd ed. New York: Mc-Graw-Hill, 1991.

6. Nunnally, Stephens W. *Managing Construction Equipment*, 2nd ed. Upper Saddle River, NJ: Prentice Hall, 2000.

7. Thuesen, Gerald J., and Wolter J. Fabrycky. *Engineering Economy*, 9th ed. Upper Saddle River, NJ: Prentice Hall, 2001.

CONTRACT CONSTRUCTION

1 INTRODUCTION

The Construction Process

Construction by a general contractor employed under a prime construction contract is only one of these methods. However, since this method of obtaining construction services is widely used, it will form the basis for this chapter's discussion of contract construction, including bidding and contract award, construction contracts, plans and specifications, and contract administration.

Construction Contract Law

Construction professionals are not usually lawyers and therefore should not attempt to act as their own lawyers. However, construction professionals must have a thorough understanding of the customary practices and underlying legal principles involving contract construction. Virtually every action taken by a contractor, construction manager, or architect/engineer at a construction site has legal implications. There is simply not time to consult a lawyer every time a decision must be made. Thus, construction professionals must understand the contractual consequences of their activities and be able to recognize when legal advice should be secured. Hence the purpose of the discussion of contract law in this chapter is to familiarize the reader with the general principles of construction contract law and practice and to provide a basis for further study. A study of the summaries of court decisions pertaining to construction contract disputes found in many professional magazines will also be very helpful in acquiring further knowledge in this area.

2 BIDDING AND CONTRACT AWARD

Bid Preparation

In the United States, as in much of the world, construction contracting is a highly competitive business. To prosper and grow, a construction company must achieve a reputation for quality workmanship and timely completion while achieving a reasonable return on its capital investment. Thus, profit is an obvious and principal motive for bidding on a construction contract. However, there are a number of other reasons why a contractor may choose to bid on a project. During times of low construction activity, contractors may submit bids with little or no profit margin in order to keep their equipment in operation and prevent the loss of skilled workers and managers. Although such a policy may be successful on a short-term basis, it is apparent that it will lead to financial disaster if long continued. Other reasons for bidding on a project include a desire for prestige and the maintenance of goodwill with regular clients. Projects that receive wide publicity because of their national importance or their unusual nature are often bid at low profit margins for the prestige they confer on the builder. In these cases, the loss of potential profit can be justified by the public recognition gained. Likewise, contractors sometimes bid on relatively undesirable projects in order to maintain a relationship with an owner. In such cases, the profit margin used for the bid would be expected to be high.

Regardless of motivation, a contractor who has decided to bid on a project must then prepare a detailed cost estimate for the execution of the project. The first step in preparation of a cost estimate is to take off (or extract) the quantities of material required by the plans and specifications. These quantities are then extended (or multiplied by unit cost estimates) to provide a total estimated material cost for the

From Chapter 18 of *Construction Methods and Management*, Eighth Edition. S. W. Nunnally. Copyright © 2011 by Pearson Education, Inc. Published by Pearson Prentice Hall. All rights reserved.

project. Similar estimates are made for labor, equipment, and subcontract costs. The costs of equipment, labor, and material are often referred to as *direct costs*. Next, estimates are made of the administrative and management expenses that will be incurred at the project site. These costs are often referred to as job overhead or *indirect costs.*

After all project costs have been estimated, it is necessary to add an additional amount (or markup) for general overhead and profit. *General overhead* must cover the cost of all company activities not directly associated with individual construction projects. Major items of general overhead include salaries of headquarters personnel (company officials, estimators, clerks, accountants, etc.), rent and utilities, advertising, insurance, office supplies, and interest on borrowed capital. The usual procedure for prorating general overhead expenses to projects is to estimate total annual overhead expense, divide by the expected dollar volume of construction work for the year, and then multiply by the project bid price. The amount to be added for *profits* is, of course, a management decision. Although some projects may be bid with low profit margins for the reasons discussed earlier in this section, in the long run, construction operations must yield a reasonable return on invested capital. Unless the return on capital is greater than the yield of standard commercial investments, the owner would be better off investing in such items than in operating a construction business.

Bidding strategy, or the selection of a specific bid price for a fixed-price construction contract, is a mixture of art and science that is beyond the scope of this book. Methods used range from statistical analyses and application of game theory to seat-of-the-pants decisions. The bid price actually submitted by a contractor is usually based on an analysis of the expected competition and the state of the construction market in addition to the contractor's estimate of the cost to execute that project.

Bidding Procedure

The principal steps in the bidding procedure for a fixed-price construction contract include solicitation, bid preparation, bid submission, bid opening, selection of the lowest qualified bid, and contract award. Solicitation may range from an invitation sent to a selected few contractors to public advertisement. Except in special circumstances, U.S. governmental agencies are required to solicit bids by public advertising. To ensure adequate competition, at least three bids should be obtained.

Contractors indicating an interest in bidding should be supplied with at least one complete set of contract documents. A deposit may be required to ensure the return of project plans and specifications furnished to unsuccessful bidders. The time allowed for bid preparation should be based on the size and complexity of the project. Three weeks has been suggested as a reasonable minimum time.

The Associated General Contractors of America, in cooperation with other professional organizations, has developed recommended bidding procedures for both building construction and engineered construction which are designed to ensure fairness to both contractors and owners (references 6 and 8). Among these recommendations are the use of standard bid proposal forms, specifying the order of selection of alternates, and suggested minimum times to be allowed for bid preparation. Alternates are optional items beyond the basic project scope. Since alternates may or may not be selected by the owner, their order of selection will affect the determination of the lowest bid price.

Bid openings are frequently open to the public, and in such cases bid prices are announced as the bids are opened. To facilitate communications between contractors and subcontractors immediately prior to bid submission, the deadline for submission of bids should not occur on a holiday or the day immediately following a holiday.

Contract Award

After the bids are opened, they are evaluated by the owner to determine the lowest qualified bid. The *qualification* of a contractor is the determination that the contractor possesses both the technical and financial ability to perform the work required by the contract. The method of qualification used will depend on the owner involved. U.S. government regulations require the *contracting officer* (person empowered to execute contracts binding the government) to make a formal finding that a contractor is qualified to perform before a contract may be awarded.

Another method of bidder qualification is called *prequalification*. Under this procedure only those contractors determined to be capable of performing are invited to submit bids for the project. A more common, although indirect, method of prequalification is to require bonding of the contractor. Bonds used in construction include bid bonds, performance bonds, and payment bonds. A *bid bond* guarantees that a contractor will provide the required performance and payment bonds if awarded the contract. A *performance bond* guarantees completion of the project as described in the contract documents. A *payment bond* guarantees the payment of subcontractors, laborers, and suppliers by the contractor. After identifying of the lowest responsible (i.e., one from a qualified bidder) and responsive (i.e., complying with bid requirements) bid, the winning bidder is notified by a letter of acceptance or notice of award. This document brings into force the actual construction contract between the owner and the contractor.

Subcontracts

Subcontracts are contracts between a prime contractor and secondary contractors or suppliers. Subcontracts are widely used in building construction for the installation of electrical, plumbing, and heating and ventilating systems. The contractual arrangements between the prime contractor and the subcontractors are similar to those between the owner and the prime contractor. However, subcontractors are responsible only to the prime contractor (not to the owner) in the performance of their subcontracts. Subcontracts are included in this section only for the purpose of relating them to the bidding process.

Since subcontract costs often make up a major portion of the cost for a project, it is essential that the prime contractor obtain timely and competitive prices for subcontract services. In fairness, the successful prime contractor should execute contracts with those subcontractors whose prices have been used for preparation of the bid. However, after receiving the contract award, some contractors attempt to obtain lower subcontract prices by negotiating with other subcontractors. This practice is referred to as *bid shopping* and is widely considered an unethical practice which leads to poor subcontractor performance. As a result, bidding procedures often require the bidder to identify subcontractors at the time of bidding and to use only these subcontractors on the project. Some governmental agencies even go so far as to award separate prime contracts for general construction and for each area of specialty work. While protecting the subcontractors, such a procedure greatly complicates project control and coordination.

3 CONSTRUCTION CONTRACTS

Contract Elements

The legally essential elements of a construction contract include an offer, an acceptance, and a consideration (payment for services to be provided). The offer is normally a bid or proposal submitted by a contractor to build a certain facility according to the plans, specifications, and conditions set forth by the owner. Acceptance takes the form of a notice of award, as stated earlier. Consideration usually takes the form of cash payment, but it may legally be anything of value.

Contract Types

Contracts may be classified in several ways. Two principal methods of classification are by method of award and by method of pricing. The types of contract by *method of award* are formally advertised contracts and negotiated contracts. The procedure for the solicitation and award of an advertised construction contract was described in the previous section. A *negotiated contract*, as the name implies, is one negotiated between an owner and a construction firm. All terms and conditions of the final contract are those mutually agreed to by the two parties. While federal procurement regulations establish formally advertised competitive bidding as the normal process, negotiated contracts are permitted under special circumstances. Private owners may, of course, award a contract in whatever manner they choose.

The two types of contract by method of pricing are *fixed-price contracts* and *cost-type contracts*. Each of these types has a number of variations. There are two principal forms of fixed-price contracts: firm fixed-price contracts and fixed price with escalation contracts. Other classifications of fixed-price contracts include *lump-sum contracts* and *unit-price contracts*. A *lump-sum contract* provides a specified payment for completion of the work described in the contract documents. Unit-price contracts specify the amount to be paid for each unit of work but not the total contract amount. Such contracts are used when the quantities of work cannot be accurately estimated in advance. The principal disadvantages of unit-price contracts are the requirement for accurately measuring the work actually performed and the fact that the precise contract cost is not known until the project is completed. A combination of lump-sum and unit-price provisions may be used in a single contract.

Fixed price with escalation contracts contain a provision whereby the contract value is adjusted according to a specified price index. Such contracts reduce the risk to the contractor during periods of rapid inflation. Since the alternative during periods of inflation is for the contractor to add a large contingency amount for protection, the use of an escalation clause may well result in a lower cost to the owner than would a firm fixed-price contract. In spite of this, fixed-price construction contracts with escalation clauses have not been widely used in the United States.

Cost-type (or cost-plus) contracts are available in a number of forms. Some of these include the following:

- Cost plus percentage of cost.
- Cost plus fixed fee.
- Cost plus fixed fee with guaranteed maximum cost.
- Cost plus incentive fee.

A *cost plus percentage of cost contract* pays the contractor a fee that is a percentage of the project's actual cost. This type of contract may not be used by U.S. government agencies because it provides a negative incentive for the contractor to reduce project cost. That is, the higher the project cost, the greater the contractor's fee. The most widely used form of cost reimbursement contract, the *cost plus fixed fee contract*, does not reward the contractor for an increased project cost but still fails to provide any incentive to minimize cost. The *cost plus fixed fee with guaranteed maximum cost contract* adds some of the risk of a fixed-price contract to the cost reimbursement contract because the contractor guarantees that the total contract price will not exceed the specified amount. Hence it is to be expected that the contractor's fee for this type of contract will be increased to compensate for the added risk involved. The *cost plus incentive fee contract* is designed to provide an incentive for reducing project cost. In this type of contract, the contractor's nominal or target fee is adjusted upward or downward in a specified manner according to the final project cost. Thus, the contractor is rewarded by an increased fee if able to complete the project at a cost lower than the original estimate. All cost-type contracts should clearly define the items of cost for which the contractor will be reimbursed and specify the basis for determining the acceptability of costs.

Contract Documents

A construction contract consists of the following documents:

- Agreement.
- Conditions of the Contract (usually General Conditions and Special Conditions).
- Plans.
- Specifications.

The *agreement* describes the work to be performed, the required completion time, contract sum, provisions for progress payments and final payment, and lists the other documents making up the complete contract. The *General Conditions* contain those contract provisions applicable to most construction contracts written by the owner. The *Special Conditions* contain any additional contract provisions applicable to the specific project. The contents of the *plans* and *specifications* are discussed in Section 4.

The Associated General Contractors of America, in cooperation with the American Institute of Architects, the American Society of Civil Engineers, and the other professional organizations, has developed standard construction contract provisions and a number of associated forms. The federal government also utilizes standard contract documents. The use of such standard contract forms will minimize the amount of legal review that the contractor must perform before signing a contract. However, even if the contractor is familiar with the standard contract forms being used, care must be taken to fully evaluate all special conditions as well as the plans and specifications. The principal contract clauses and their interpretation are discussed in Section 5.

Construction contracts may contain a *value engineering (VE) clause*. Value engineering is the analysis of a design with the objective of accomplishing the required function at a lower cost. This objective may also be expressed as eliminating gold plating. When included in a construction contract, a value engineering clause encourages the contractor to propose changes in the project that will reduce project cost without affecting the ability of the facility to perform its intended function. The cost savings resulting from value engineering proposals accepted by the owner are shared between the contractor and owner on the basis specified in the contract. The usual clause prescribes a 50/50 split between the owner and contractor.

Contract Time

The time allowed (expressed as either days allowed or as a required completion date) for completion of a construction project is normally specified in the contract along with the phrase "time is of the essence." If no completion date is specified, a "reasonable time," as interpreted by the courts, is allowed. If the phrase "time is of the essence" is included in a contract and the project is not completed within the specified time, the contractor is liable for any damages (monetary loss) incurred by the owner as the result of late completion. In such a case, the courts will hold the contractor responsible for the actual damages that the owner incurs. A *liquidated damages clause* in the contract may be used to simplify the process of establishing the amount of damages resulting from late completion. Such a clause will specify the amount of damages to be paid by the contractor to the owner for each day of late completion. If challenged in court, the owner must prove that the amount of liquidated damages specified in the contract reasonably represents the owner's actual loss. If the liquidated damages are shown to be reasonable, the courts will sustain their enforcement.

Construction contracts normally contain provisions for time extensions to the contract due to circumstances beyond the control of the contractor, such as owner-directed changes, acts of God (fire, flood, etc.), and strikes. The purpose of such provisions is, of course, to reduce contractors' risk from events beyond their control. If such provisions were not included, the contractor would have to increase the bid price to cover such risks. It should also be pointed out that the owner is financially responsible to the contractor for any owner-caused delays. The subject of changes and delays is discussed further in Section 5.

4 PLANS AND SPECIFICATIONS

Plans

Construction plans are drawings that show the location, dimensions, and details of the work to be performed. Taken together with the specifications, they should provide a complete description of the facility to be constructed. Types of contract drawings include site drawings and detailed working drawings. Contract drawings are usually organized and numbered according to specialty, such as structural, electrical, and mechanical.

Specifications

Construction technical specifications provide the detailed requirements for the materials, equipment, and workmanship to be incorporated into the project. Contract drawings and specifications complement each other and must be used together. An item need not be shown on both the plans and specifications to be required. Frequently, the item may be identified on only one of these documents. However, when the provisions of the plans and specifications conflict, the General Conditions of the contract generally provide that the requirements of the specifications will govern. In the absence of such a provision, the courts have commonly held that the requirements of the specifications will govern. The two basic ways in which the requirements for a particular operation may be specified are by method specification or by performance specification. A *method specification* states the precise equipment and procedure to be used in performing a construction operation. A *performance* (or result or end-result) *specification*, on the other hand, specifies only the result to be achieved and leaves to the contractor the choice of equipment and method. Recent years have seen an increase in the use of performance specifications, particularly by governmental agencies. Specification writers should avoid specifying both method and performance requirements for the same operation. When both requirements are used and satisfactory results are not obtained after utilizing the specified method, a dispute based on impossibility of performance will invariably result.

The format most widely used for construction specifications consists of 16 divisions, organized as shown in Table 1. This format was developed by the Construction Specifications Institute (CSI) and is usually identified as the CSI format or Uniform System for Building Specifications. Although developed for use on building construction projects, it is also widely used for other types of construction.

Shop Drawings and Samples

Shop drawings are drawings, charts, and other data prepared by a contractor or supplier which describe the detailed characteristics of equipment or show how specific structural elements or items of equipment are to be fabricated and installed. Thus, they complement but do not replace the contract drawings. *Samples* are physical examples of materials, equipment, or workmanship which are submitted to the owner for approval prior to their incorporation in a project.

Contract documents should contain the specific requirements for submission of shop drawings and samples. Some suggested provisions include the following:

- Identification of items requiring samples or shop drawings.
- Procedure for submission of shop drawings, including format, marking, and number and distribution of copies.

Table 1. Organization of the uniform system for building specifications

Division	Title
1	General Requirements
2	Site Work
3	Concrete
4	Masonry
5	Metals
6	Wood and Plastics
7	Thermal and Moisture Protection
8	Doors and Windows
9	Finishes
10	Specialties
11	Equipment
12	Furnishings
13	Special Construction
14	Conveying Systems
15	Mechanical
16	Electrical

- Procedure for submission of samples, including size and number required.
- Eliminating the requirement for shop drawings and samples when standard catalog items are to be used.

5 CONTRACT ADMINISTRATION

Progress Reports and Payment

Construction contracts commonly require the contractor to submit a proposed progress schedule to the owner shortly after contract award. Upon approval by the owner or owner's representative, this schedule forms the basis for judging the contractor's progress toward project completion. The contract may require the contractor to submit the plan and schedule in the CPM format and may also require periodic updating of the schedule as work progresses. The owner's representative must continuously evaluate the contractor's progress to keep the owner informed and to provide a basis for the approval of the contractor's requests for progress payments. Failure of the contractor to attain a satisfactory rate of progress may provide the basis for termination of the contract by the owner, as described later in this section.

For projects expected to require more than a few months to complete, it is customary for the owner to make *progress payments* to the contractor. Progress payments are made at the interval specified in the contract, usually monthly or upon completion of certain milestones. Payment is customarily made for the work completed, materials delivered to the work site, and work prefabricated but not yet incorporated into the project. It is customary to withhold a percentage of the value of work completed as a guarantee against defective work and to ensure that the remaining work can be completed within the unpaid amount of the contract. The amount withheld is referred to as *retainage* or *retention*. A retainage of 10% is rather typical.

Changes and Delays

It is rare indeed if a construction project is completed without changes being made. The usual construction contract contains a clause authorizing the owner or owner's representative to order changes to the project within the general scope of the contract. The document directing such a change is referred to as a *change order*. The contract also provides that an equitable adjustment in time and contract value will be made for such changes. The majority of changes are due to design modifications initiated by the owner or designer. However, change orders may also be used to formalize adjustments to the contract required by site conditions differing from those anticipated at the time of contract award (commonly referred to as "changed conditions").

To minimize disputes, all change orders issued should contain an adjustment in contract time and price which is mutually acceptable to the contractor and owner. However, it is frequently not possible to delay issuing a change order until such an agreement has been reached without delaying the work in progress. As a result, many change orders are issued before an agreement has been reached on the corresponding price and time adjustment. Agreement must therefore be reached later as work progresses or the item will end up as a dispute. In estimating the cost associated with a change or owner-caused delay, the contractor must be careful to evaluate its effect on other project activities. Frequently, it will be found that changes or delay in one activity will necessitate changes in resource allocation or progress on other activities that result in additional project cost. These costs are sometimes referred to as *consequential costs*. To obtain reimbursement of consequential costs, the contractor must be able to document their existence. A CPM network is a valuable aid in identifying and justifying consequential costs.

Delays in the orderly progress of a construction project may result from a multitude of causes. The three general categories of delay include those beyond the control of either the contractor or the owner ("acts of God"), those under the control of the owner, and those under the control of the contractor. The general principles established by law and precedent for financial and time adjustments to the contract as a result of such delays are as follows. In the case of fire, flood, earthquake, or other disaster, and strikes, a compensating time extension to the contract will be made. Any financial compensation to the contractor would be provided by the contractor's insurance, not by the owner. If the owner is responsible for the delay (such as by the late delivery of owner-provided equipment), the owner must compensate the contractor for any additional costs incurred as well as provide an appropriate time extension to the contract. If the delay is under the control of the contractor, no compensation or time extension is provided to the contractor. Rather, the contractor is responsible for reimbursing the owner for any damages (actual or liquidated) resulting from the delay.

Acceptance and Final Payment

The acceptance of a completed project is customarily based on a final inspection performed by the owner's representative and conditioned upon the correction of any deficiencies noted. The list of deficiencies to be corrected which is prepared at the final inspection is sometimes referred to as the *punch list of record*. If the facility or a portion thereof is substantially complete, the owner's representative will execute a *certificate of substantial completion* for the work. The contractor may then request and receive a final progress payment for the completed portion of the project. However, sufficient retainage is withheld to ensure the correction of any remaining deficiencies. The certificate of substantial completion should clearly state the responsibilities of the contractor and the owner for maintenance, utility service, and insurance until final acceptance.

Upon correction of all deficiencies on the punch list of record, the contractor should notify the owner's representative of this fact and submit a *request for final payment*, together with any other documents required by the contract (such as releases of liens, an affidavit that all payrolls and bills connected with the project have been paid, consent of surety to final payment, etc.). When inspection confirms the correction of all deficiencies, the owner's representative will issue a final *certificate of payment*. The contract customarily provides a warranty against defective work for some period, usually 1 year. Any deficiencies discovered after preparation of the punch list of record should be handled under the warranty provision of the contract. Final payment and its acceptance by the contractor usually constitute a waiver of all claims by either the owner or the contractor except for unsettled liens and claims and deficiencies falling under warranty provisions.

Claims and Disputes

A *claim* is a request by the contractor for a time extension or for additional payment based on the occurrence of an event beyond the contractor's control that has not been covered by a change order. Examples of such events include unexpected site conditions, delays in delivery of owner-provided property, and changes directed by the owner. The usual construction contract empowers the owner's representative (architect/engineer or government contracting officer) to decide on the validity of such claims. However, if the contractor is not satisfied with the decision, the matter becomes a dispute.

Disputes are disagreements between the contractor and owner over some aspect of contract performance. In addition to unsettled claims, disputes may involve such matters as substitution for specified materials, the responsibility for delays in project completion, and the effect of changes ordered by the owner. In recent years there has been an increase in the use of *alternate dispute resolution (ADR)* methods instead of taking the matter to court. When successful, these nonjudicial techniques greatly reduce the time and expense involved in settling disputes. Some ADR techniques include negotiation, mediation, arbitration, nonbinding minitrials, and neutral fact finding. Probably the most common of these techniques are negotiation and arbitration. In 1966, the American Arbitration Association, together with a number of professional organizations involved in construction, established arbitration procedures for the construction industry, known as the *Construction Industry Arbitration Rules*. Under these procedures, one or more independent professionals are appointed to resolve the dispute. Hearing procedures are less formal than those of a trial, and the arbitrators are not bound by the legal rules of evidence. Because the parties to the dispute must agree to the use of arbitration, no appeal of the arbitration award is usually possible. State laws governing the use of arbitration vary, and some states do not recognize the use of a contract clause requiring arbitration of all disputes arising under the contract.

Contract Termination

Although contract termination is usually envisioned as an adversary process, there are a number of nonadversary methods by which a contract may be terminated. Most construction contracts are terminated by satisfactory performance, one method of contract termination. Other nonadversary methods of contract termination include mutual agreement and impossibility of performance.

The principal adversary basis for contract termination is for breach of contract. Either the owner or the contractor may terminate a contract for breach of contract. The basis for termination by the contractor based on breach of contract is usually the failure of the owner to make the specified progress payments or owner-caused delay of the project for an unreasonable period of time. Termination by the owner for breach of contract is most commonly due to failure of the contractor to make reasonable progress on the project or to default by the contractor. When termination is due to breach of contract by the owner, the contractor is generally held to be entitled to payment for all work performed and the expenses of demobilization and cancellation of orders, plus profit. When termination is due to breach of contract by the contractor, the contract commonly permits the owner to take possession of the work site and all on-site equipment and tools owned by the contractor and to complete the project at the contractor's (or surety's) expense.

Problems

1. Explain the purpose and operation of a value engineering clause in a construction contract.

2. Briefly explain the legal basis for issuing change orders to a construction contract. Who issues the change order and how are the project cost and duration affected?

3. List and briefly describe the documents making up a construction contract.

4. Briefly describe the two principal types of construction specifications.

5. What alternate dispute resolution (ADR) methods are available for resolving construction contract disputes? What advantages do these methods have over court proceedings?

6. What are shop drawings and who prepares them?

7. What type of construction contract provides the greatest incentive for a construction contractor to minimize project cost?

8. What are the legally essential elements of a construction contract?

9. How does a construction company's bonding capacity (bonding limit established by a bonding company) affect the ability of the construction firm to bid on projects?

10. Develop a computer program that can be used to maintain the current status of all active contracts of a construction firm. Input should include contract number and description, contract amount, date of contract award, date work started, required completion date, current work status (percent complete), projected completion date, amount billed to date, payments received to date, payments due but not received, number and value of contract modifications, and number and value of pending modifications and claims. Provide output in a format that can be used by company management as a summary of contract status. Using your computer program, solve an example problem.

References

1. Abdallah, Eli T., ed. *Preparing Specifications for Design-Bid Build Projects.* Reston, VA: ASCE, 2000.

2. Bockrath, Joseph T. *Contracts and the Legal Environment for Engineers and Architects,* 6th ed. Boston, MA: McGraw-Hill, 2000.

3. Clough, Richard H., and Glenn A. Sears. *Construction Contracting,* 7th ed. New York: Wiley, 2005.

4. Collier, Keith. *Construction Contracts,* 3rd ed. Upper Saddle River, NJ: Prentice Hall, 2001.

5. *Deere Performance Handbook.* Deere & Company, Moline, IL.

6. Fisk, Edward R. *Construction Project Administration,* 7th ed. Upper Saddle River, NJ: Prentice Hall, 2003.

7. Kelleher, Thomas J., Jr., ed. *Smith, Currie & Hancock's Common Sense Construction Law,* 3rd ed. Hoboken, NJ: Wiley, 2005.

8. Levin, Paul. *Construction Contract Claims, Changes and Dipute Resolution,* 2nd ed. Reston, VA: American Society of Civil Engineers, 1998.

9. *Recommended Guide for Competitive Bidding Procedures and Contract Awards for Building Construction* (AIA Document A501). The Associated General Contractors of America, Inc., Washington, D.C.

10. Rosen, Harold J., John R. Regener Jr.: M. D. Morris, advisory ed. *Construction Specifications Writing,* 5th ed. Hoboken, NJ: Wiley, 2005.

11. Smith, Robert J. *Recommended Competitive Bidding Procedures for Construction Projects* (EJCDC 1901-9D). Reston, VA: American Society of Civil Engineers, 1987.

12. Thomas, H. Randolph, and Ralph Ellis. *Interpreting Construction Contracts.* Reston, VA: American Society of Civil Engineers, 2008.

CONSTRUCTION SAFETY AND
HEALTH AND EQUIPMENT MAINTENANCE

From Chapter 19 of *Construction Methods and Management*, Eighth Edition. S. W. Nunnally. Copyright © 2011 by Pearson Education, Inc.
Published by Pearson Prentice Hall. All rights reserved.

CONSTRUCTION SAFETY AND HEALTH AND EQUIPMENT MAINTENANCE

1 IMPORTANCE OF SAFETY

It has been reported that construction, which consists of about 5% of the U.S. work force, accounts for some 20% of work fatalities and 12% of disabling injuries. The total annual cost (direct and indirect) of construction accidents has been estimated to exceed $31 billion. In the United States, national concern over the frequency and extent of industrial accidents and health hazards led to the passage of the Occupational Safety and Health Act of 1970, which established specific safety and health requirements for virtually all industries, including construction. The Occupational Safety and Health Administration (OSHA) is responsible for developing and enforcing regulations implementing this act. The extent and nature of OSHA requirements is discussed further in the remainder of this chapter. However, the concern over OSHA regulations and penalties has tended to obscure the fact that there are at least two other major reasons for construction management to be seriously concerned about safety. These reasons are humanitarian and financial.

Everyone is understandably distressed when a fellow employee is killed or disabled, so the humanitarian basis for safety is apparent. However, many managers do not fully appreciate the financial consequences of accidents. Worker's compensation insurance premiums, for example, are based on a firm's accident rate. Public liability, property damage, and equipment insurance rates are also affected by accident rates. It has been shown that a construction firm can lose its competitive bidding position simply because of the effect of high insurance premiums resulting from a poor safety record. In addition to the visible cost of accidents represented by insurance and worker's compensation payments, there are other costs, which are difficult to estimate. Such costs associated with an accident include the monetary value of lost project time while the accident is investigated and damages are repaired, the time required to replace critical materials and equipment and to train replacement workers, as well as the effect on those portions of the project not directly involved in the accident.

2 OSHA

The U.S. Occupational Safety and Health Administration (OSHA) has produced a comprehensive set of safety and health regulations, inspection procedures, and record-keeping requirements. The law has also established both civil and criminal penalties for violations of OSHA regulations. Table 1 indicates the maximum penalty for major categories of violations. As shown in Table 1, civil penalties of $7000 per day may be assessed for failure to correct a cited violation. Under criminal proceedings, a fine of $20,000 and imprisonment for 1 year may be adjudged for a second conviction of a violation resulting in the death of an employee. OSHA officials may also seek a restraining order through a U.S. District Court to stop work or take other action required to alleviate a condition identified as presenting imminent danger of serious injury or death.

Under OSHA regulations, employers are required to keep records of all work-related deaths, injuries, and illnesses. It is not necessary to record minor injuries that require only first-aid treatment. However, all injuries involving medical treatment, loss of consciousness, restrictions on work or body motion, or transfer to another job must be recorded. A special report of serious accidents resulting in one or more deaths or the hospitalization of five or more employees must be made to OSHA officials within 48 h.

One of the major inequities of OSHA is that only management may be penalized for safety violations. Thus, even though an employee willfully violates both OSHA and company safety regulations, only the company and its management can be penalized under OSHA for any safety violation.

Table 1. Maximum penalties under OSHA

Administrative Proceedings	
Violation	Maximum Penalty
Willful or repeated	$70,000/violation
Routine or serious	7000/violation
Failing to correct cited violation	$7000/day
Failing to post citation near the place where violation exists	7000/violation

Criminal Proceedings		
Violation	Maximum Fine	Maximum Imprisonment
Killing, assaulting, or resisting OSHA officials	$10,000	Life
Willful violation resulting in death of employee, first conviction	10,000	6 months
Willful violation resulting in death of employee, second conviction	20,000	1 year
Falsifying required records	10,000	6 months
Unauthorized advanced notice of inspection	1000	6 months

Therefore, the only way in which management may enforce safety regulations is to discipline or fire workers engaging in unsafe acts.

OSHA safety regulations for construction (reference 3) consist largely of safety standards developed by segments of the construction industry. Requirements for equipment safety include rollover protection (ROPS), seat belts, back-up alarms, improved brake systems, and guards for moving parts. Maximum noise levels are also set for equipment operators and other workers. A number of OSHA safety requirements have been mentioned in earlier chapters in connection with specific construction operations. However, supervisors at all levels must be familiar with all applicable OSHA standards.

It should be pointed out that OSHA safety regulations are considered to be the minimum federal safety standards and that the various states may impose more stringent safety standards for construction within the state. The U.S. Department of Labor has also delegated to certain states the authority and responsibility for enforcing OSHA regulations within those states.

3 SAFETY PROGRAMS

All construction firms need a carefully planned and directed safety program to minimize accidents and ensure compliance with OSHA and other safety regulations. However, no safety program will be successful without the active support of top management. Job-site supervisors have traditionally neglected safety in their haste to get the job done on time and within budget. Only when supervisors are convinced by higher management that safety is equally as important as production will the benefits of an effective safety program be achieved. An effective safety program must instill a sense of safety consciousness in every employee.

Although there are many ingredients in a comprehensive safety program, some of the major elements are listed below:

1. A formal safety training program for all new employees. *Note:* OSHA regulations require every employer to "instruct each employee in the recognition and avoidance of unsafe conditions and the regulations applicable to his work environment. . . ."

2. Periodic refresher training for each worker.

3. A formal supervisory safety training program for all supervisors.

4. A program of regular site visits by safety personnel to review and control job hazards.

5. Provision of adequate personal protective equipment, first-aid equipment, and trained emergency personnel.

6. An established procedure for the emergency evacuation of injured workers.

7. Provisions for maintaining safety records and reporting accidents in compliance with OSHA requirements.

The accident prevention manual of the Associated General Contractors of America, Inc. (reference 9) provides many suggestions for an effective construction safety program.

Minimizing Insurance Cost

As noted earlier, a construction contractor's cost of insurance is largely determined by the construction company's accident experience. Some of the factors considered by an insurer in evaluating the risk involved in providing insurance coverage for a construction company include the following:

- The company's record of accidents and safety violations.
- Adequacy of the company's safety program including testing of employees for skill qualification as well as for

drug and alcohol use, training of workers, existence of a company safety plan and evidence of its enforcement, the system for accident reporting, and adequacy of the workers' personal protective equipment.

- Job-site appearance and evidence of proper equipment maintenance.

Some indicators of unsafe and risky construction operations include the following:

- Failure to follow required safety procedures, such as those discussed in Section 4.
- Poor housekeeping at the construction site.
- Failure to use necessary personal protective equipment.
- Evidence of inadequate worker training, particularly on hazardous operations.
- High rate of employee turnover.

4 SAFETY PROCEDURES

It has been found that most serious construction accidents involve construction equipment operations, trench and embankment failure, falls from elevated positions, collapse of temporary structures and formwork, or the failure of structures under construction. OSHA safety regulations (reference 3) are quite specific in many of these areas, and special management attention should be devoted to the safety of these activities.

Reference 2 provides an excellent discussion, along with examples, of construction failure involving both design and construction practice. The safety manuals published by the Association of Equipment Manufacturers, which incorporates the former Construction Industry Manufacturers Association (CIMA) (reference 5), provide safety rules and suggestions for the safe operation of many types of construction equipment.

Many safety precautions for specific construction operations have been discussed in previous chapters. In addition, the following list of major safety precautions should be helpful as a general guide.

General

Good housekeeping on a project site is both a safety measure and an indicator of good project supervision. Lumber, used formwork, and other material lying around a work area increase the likelihood of falls and puncture wounds.

Equipment Operations

- Require operators and mechanics to use steps and hand-holds when mounting equipment.
- Utilize guides or signalpersons when the operator's visibility is limited or when there is danger to nearby workers. Backup alarms or guides must be used when equipment operates in reverse.
- Exercise extreme caution and comply with safety regulations when operating near high-voltage lines. In case of accidental contact with a high-voltage line, the operator should attempt to move the equipment enough to break contact. If unsuccessful, the operator should remain on the equipment until the line can be deenergized.

- Make sure that machines are equipped with required safety features and that operators use seat belts when provided.
- Use care when operating equipment on side slopes to prevent overturning.
- When operating cranes, be extremely careful not to exceed safe load limits for the operating radius and boom position. Electronic load indicators are available.
- Do not allow workers to ride on equipment unless proper seating is provided.
- Haul roads must be properly maintained. Items to check include condition of the road surface (holes, slippery surface, excess dust), visibility (curves, obstacles, intersections, and dust), and adequate width for vehicles to pass (unless one-way).
- Park equipment with the brake set, blade or bowl grounded, and ignition key removed at the end of work.
- Equipment used for land clearing must be equipped with overhead and rear canopy protection. Workers engaged in clearing must be protected from the hazards of irritant and toxic plants and instructed in the first-aid treatment for such hazards.
- When hauling heavy or oversized loads on highways, make sure that loads are properly secured and covered if necessary. Slow-moving and oversized vehicles must use required markings and signals to warn other traffic.
- Take positive action to ensure that equipment under repair cannot be accidentally operated.
- Utilize blocking, cribbing, or other positive support when employees must work under heavy loads supported by cables, jacks, or hydraulic systems.
- Ensure that any guards or safety devices removed during equipment repair are promptly replaced.
- Shut down engines and do not allow smoking during refueling.

Construction Plant

- Set equipment containing hot or flammable fluids on firm foundations to prevent overturning. Clearly mark high-temperature lines and containers to prevent burns. Be especially careful of live steam. Provide fire extinguishers and other required safety equipment.
- Aggregate bins and batching plants should be emptied before performing major repairs.
- When electrical equipment is being repaired, shut off and tag electrical circuits.
- Ensure that wire rope and cable are of the proper size and strength, well maintained, and inspected at least weekly.

Excavations

- The location of underground utilities and other hazards must be determined before starting an excavation. Contact utility companies and property owners to request that they establish the location of such installations. Almost all U.S. states have central One-Call telephone numbers, which coordinate with utility companies to provide prompt service in locating and marking their underground lines when requested. When utility companies or owners cannot provide this information promptly (usually within 24 h), the contractor may cautiously proceed with excavation. However, in this situation, the contractor must employ detection equipment or other acceptable means to locate and avoid underground hazards.

- The sides of excavations must be properly shored or sloped to the angle of repose to prevent cave-ins. OSHA regulations require that banks over 5 ft (1.5 m) must be shored, cut back to a stable slope, or otherwise protected. Regulations also require that protective systems (sloping, benching, shoring, or shielding) for excavations over 20 ft (6.1 m) deep must be designed by a registered professional engineer.

- When workers are required to enter a trench excavation 4 ft (1.2192 m) or more in depth, a stairway, ladder, ramp, or other safe means of egress must be located in such a manner as to require no more than 25 ft (7.62 m) of lateral travel by any worker in the trench.

- Avoid the operation of equipment near the top edge of an excavation because this increases the chance of slope failure. The storage of materials near the top edge of an excavation, vibration, and the presence of water also increase the chance of slope failure. When these conditions cannot be avoided, additional measures must be taken to increase slope stability. If workers are required to enter the excavation, no spoil or other material may be stored within 2 ft (0.6 m) of the edge of the excavation.

- Ensure that workers are not allowed under loads being handled by excavators or hoists.

- Watch out for buried lines and containers when excavating. Possible hazards include toxic and flammable gases, electricity, and collapse of side slopes caused by sudden release of liquids. If a gas line is ruptured and catches fire, get personnel and flammable material away from the fire and have the gas turned off as quickly as possible. Do not attempt to extinguish the fire because an accumulation of unburned gas poses a greater threat than does a fire.

Construction of Structures

- Properly guard all openings above ground level.
- Provide guard rails, safety lines, safety belts, and/or safety nets for workers on scaffolds or steelwork.

- Ensure that temporary structures are properly designed, constructed, and braced.

- Special caution should be exercised in high-rise concrete construction. Forms must be of adequate strength and properly braced. The rate of pour must be maintained at or below design limits. Shoring and reshoring must be adequately braced and not removed until the concrete has developed the required strength.

Marine or Over-Water Construction

Marine or over-water construction operations present all of the usual construction hazards plus additional hazards posed by the marine environment. These additional hazards include drowning, slippery surfaces, increased tripping and height hazards, as well as weather and wave action.

Some of the major safety precautions that should be taken are listed below:

- Unless workers can safely step onto vessels, a ramp or safe walkway must be provided. Access ways must be adequately illuminated, free of obstructions, and located clear of suspended loads.

- Working areas should have nonslip surfaces, be maintained clear of obstructions, and be equipped with adequate handrails.

- Workers on unguarded decks or surfaces over water must wear approved life jackets or buoyant vests. Life rings and a rescue boat must also be available. Workers more than 25 ft (7.6 m) above a water surface must be protected by safety belts, safety nets, or similar protective equipment.

5 ENVIRONMENTAL HEALTH IN CONSTRUCTION

Increased governmental interest in occupational safety has been accompanied by an increased concern for occupational health and environmental controls. The major environmental health problems encountered in construction consist of noise, dust, radiation (ionizing and nonionizing), toxic materials, heat, and cold. These hazards and appropriate control measures are discussed in the following paragraphs.

Noise

OSHA construction safety and health regulations (reference 3) prescribe maximum noise levels to which workers may be exposed. Permissible noise levels are a function of length of exposure and range from 90 dBA (decibels measured on the A-scale of a standard sound meter) for an 8-h exposure to 140 dBA for impulse or impact noise. When a satisfactory noise level cannot be attained by engineering controls, personal ear protection must be provided.

Noise controls have resulted in the increasing use of cab enclosures on construction equipment to protect equipment operators from equipment noise. The use of such enclosures has necessitated improved equipment instrumentation to enable the operator to determine whether the machine is operating properly without depending on the sound of the equipment's operation. Although the use of operator enclosures permits an improved operator environment, it also creates a safety hazard, because it is difficult for workers outside the enclosures to communicate with the equipment operator. As a result, increased attention must be given to the use of guides, backup alarms, and hand signals if accidents are to be avoided.

Dust

In addition to creating a safety hazard due to loss of visibility, dust may be responsible for a number of lung diseases. Silica dust and asbestos dust are particularly dangerous and produce specific lung diseases (asbestosis and silicosis). Asbestos dust has also been found to be a cancer-producing agent. As a result, OSHA safety and health standards limit the concentration of dust to which workers may be exposed. The allowable concentration of asbestos particles is, as would be expected, quite low.

Radiation

Ionizing radiation is produced by X-ray equipment and by radioactive material. Such radiation may be present on the construction site when X-raying welds, measuring soil density, or performing nondestructive materials testing. Any use of such equipment must be accomplished by trained personnel in accordance with regulations of the Nuclear Regulatory Commission.

Nonionizing radiation is produced by laser equipment and electronic microwave equipment. Laser equipment is coming into widespread use for surveying and for alignment of pipelines, tunnels, and structural members. Again, only well-trained employees should be permitted to operate such equipment. OSHA regulations limit the exposure of workers to both laser output and microwave power output. Workers must be provided antilaser eye protection when working in areas having a potential exposure to laser light output greater than 5 mW.

Toxic Materials

Construction workers may accidentally encounter toxic materials at any time, particularly on reconstruction projects. However, the most frequent hazards consist of buried utility lines and underground gases. Every effort must be made to locate and properly protect utility lines during excavation operations. The air in a work area should be tested whenever an oxygen deficiency or toxic gas is likely to be encountered. Emergency rescue equipment such as breathing equipment and lifelines should be provided whenever adverse atmospheric (breathing) conditions may be encountered. Specific safety procedures and protective equipment should be provided if hazardous liquids or solids are likely to be encountered.

Heat

Construction workers are often required to work under high-temperature conditions. Fortunately, the human body will acclimate itself to high-temperature conditions within a period of 7–10 days. However, serious heat illness may result when workers are not properly acclimated and protected. Medical effects range from fatal heat stroke to minor heat fatigue. It is particularly important to health that the body's water and salt levels be maintained. Heat cramps result when the body's salt level drops too low. Factors that have been found to increase the heat strain experienced by workers include drug consumption, fever from an infection, exposure to low-frequency noise, and exposure to environmental gases such as carbon monoxide.

Methods for reducing heat effect on workers include use of mechanical equipment to reduce physical labor requirements, scheduling hot work for the cooler part of the day, use of sun shields, providing cool rest areas [optimum temperatures about 77°F (25°C)], providing a water and salt supply easily accessible to workers, and the use of proper hot-weather clothing.

Cold

Extreme cold-weather conditions, although not encountered as often as heat conditions, pose essentially opposite problems to those of hot-weather operations. The human body will acclimate itself to cold as it will to heat, but the acclimation period for cold is much longer. Medical effects of cold include frostbite, trenchfoot, and general hypothermia (reduction of the core body temperature). General hypothermia is usually fatal when the body core temperature drops below 65°F (18°C).

Military operations have demonstrated that human beings can successfully perform in temperatures much lower than those encountered in the continental United States when they are properly clothed, fed, and acclimated. Thus, the major requirement for successful cold-weather construction appears to be the provision of adequate clothing and warming areas. The use of bulky cold-weather clothing, however, reduces manual dexterity and may increase the possibility of accidents.

6 EQUIPMENT MAINTENANCE

Equipment maintenance is the servicing, adjusting, and repairing of equipment. Construction equipment managers must be aware of the importance of proper equipment maintenance and the effect of equipment breakdowns on job production and costs. Some typical relationships between equipment age, downtime, and downtime costs were explored previously. However, specific factors will vary greatly, depending on job and equipment conditions. All too frequently operators and supervisors in the field attempt to increase production by operating equipment under load conditions greater than the equipment was designed to handle. The result is premature breakdown with accompanying delays and cost increases.

Proper preventive maintenance procedures and an efficient repair system will minimize equipment failures and their consequences. Suggestions for providing effective maintenance procedures are given in the following paragraphs. Maintenance can be divided into several levels or categories. The categories that will be used here are preventive maintenance, minor repair, and major repair.

Preventive Maintenance

Preventive maintenance (sometimes referred to as PM) is routine periodic maintenance and adjustment designed to keep equipment in the best possible operating condition. It consists of a number of elements that may be compared to links in a chain. The primary links in the PM chain are the skill of the operator, the manner in which the equipment is used, proper fuel handling, proper equipment lubrication, and correct periodic adjustment. If any of the links of this chain fails, the result will be premature equipment breakdown.

Equipment manufacturers have developed specific lubrication, servicing, and adjustment procedures for each piece of their equipment. These procedures should be carefully followed. Upon request, major petroleum companies will provide guidance on the proper lubricants to be used under specific operating conditions. While construction equipment managers and operators have long depended on manual equipment lubrication using hand-operated or power grease guns, automatic lubrication systems are now available for most items of construction equipment. Automatic lubrication systems consist of a powered grease pump connected by piping to the equipment's lubrication (lube) points. A controlled amount of lubricant is automatically injected into equipment lube points at intervals determined by a lubrication control unit which has been previously programmed for the desired interval. Some advantages claimed for automated lubrication systems include the following:

Increased productivity from elimininating the time lost for manual lubrication.

Reduced service labor because manual lubrication is no longer needed.

Extended machine component life as a result of optimum lubrication and less opportunity for dirt to enter the machine during servicing.

Reduced grease consumption since there is little waste of grease during lubrication.

Increased safety because mechanics do not have to crawl under or over the equipment to perform lubrication.

Because of the hostile environment in which construction equipment operates, it is important to keep dust, dirt, and water from entering the engine and other mechanical assemblies of the equipment. This requires special precautions to keep fuel clean and to keep the equipment's air and fuel filters operating properly. Some precautions to be observed in fuel handling include the following:

- Avoid using barrels for storing and transferring fuel whenever possible. If barrels must be used, allow time for contaminants to settle and use barrel pumps for removing fuel.

- Whenever possible, store fuel at the job site in tank trucks or storage tanks. Storage tanks should be located away from haul roads and other sources of dust. Storage tanks should be sloped or equipped with sumps and equipped with drains for removing water and sediment from the bottom of the tank.

- Water-sensing compounds may be used to check for the presence of water in tanks. If water is detected, the tank, filters, and water separators should be drained until all traces of water are removed.

- Dispensing equipment should be equipped with filters and water separators to remove any contaminants present. Hose nozzles and filler openings should be equipped with caps and wiped clean before the start of fuel transfer.

- Fill equipment fuel tanks at the end of each day's operation to reduce moisture condensation in the tanks during the night. This is especially important during cold weather operations.

- Fuel samples should be taken upon receipt of fuel from the distributor and again during fueling operations. Samples should be analyzed for cleanliness. The source of any contamination should be located and corrected.

- Avoid refueling equipment in the open when it is raining, snowing, or very dusty.

Clean air is equally as important as clean fuel is to an engine. Air cleaners must be serviced at the interval recommended by the equipment manufacturers or more often under extremely dusty conditions. Filter housings and precleaners must be blown out, vacuumed, or wiped clean when filters are changed. Crankcase breathers should be serviced in the same manner as air filters.

Wipe fittings clean before lubricating. Crankcase oil must also be kept clean. Precautions similar to those used in fueling should be observed when replacing crankcase oil. Filters must be replaced and the filter housing wiped clean at specified intervals. When changing filters, observe the condition of the seals on filter housing caps and check for ruptured filters. If ruptured filters are found, shorten the interval for oil and filter change. After filling the crankcase, run the engine for a few minutes, check for leaks, observe oil pressure, and check dipstick level. Transmissions and hydraulic control systems should be serviced in much the same manner as the engine oil system. Use the specified hydraulic fluids and filters. The system should be checked frequently for leaks. Air entering the hydraulic control system will cause rough operation and a chattering noise.

Oil analysis programs consisting of periodic sampling and laboratory analysis of equipment lubricants are rapidly becoming common. Samples are analyzed by spectrometry and physical tests to determine the presence of metals, suspended and nonsuspended solids, water, or fuel in the lubricants. It has been found that the oil circulating in an engine reflects the condition of the engine by the presence of wear particles and contaminants. Thus, oil analysis provides an excellent guide to the internal condition of an engine. The interpretation of laboratory results is not based primarily on indicator levels obtained for a single test but rather on the deviation from the equipment's historical pattern. Oil analysis programs have often significantly reduced repair and maintenance costs by allowing adjustment of maintenance intervals to fit job conditions and by detecting potential failures prior to a breakdown. The reduction in downtime cost can also be significant.

Many of the bearings on modern construction equipment are sealed to prevent entrance of dirt and water and to reduce the frequency of required lubrication. Except for permanently lubricated sealed bearings, enclosed bearings must be lubricated at the interval specified by the equipment manufacturer. Exposed mechanical parts (gears, cables, etc.), however, require different treatment. They should receive only a light covering of the specified lubricant. A heavy coating of lubricant on exposed parts collects dust and dirt and results in rapid wear of moving parts.

PM Indicators   *Preventive maintenance indicators* (PM indicators) are conditions which may be readily observed by an equipment manager and provide a guide to the maintenance condition of the equipment. Although a number of these indicators have been developed for specific equipment, the following are of general application:

- After the equipment has been standing idle for several hours, check on the ground for grease, oil, or water spots that will indicate leaks.
- Make a visual inspection of the equipment for loose bolts, leaking hoses or seals, and any unusual wear.
- Check blades for holes or dents. Check cutting edges and end bits for excessive wear and loose bolts.
- On crawler-type equipment check the track for correct tension and loose shoe bolts. Loose track bolts are indicated if there is a shiny surface around the bolt head and if dirt is knocked off loose bolt heads by vibration. Modern equipment often uses hydraulic track adjusters which are tensioned with a grease gun. Track adjustments must be made on the job since certain soils tend to tighten the track during operation. The undercarriage should be kept as free as possible of mud and debris to prevent loss of power and unnecessary track wear.
- Make sure that the radiator is free of debris and that the radiator core openings are clean. Fan belts and other drive belts should be in good condition and properly tensioned. Using a belt tension gauge for checking belt tension is strongly recommended.

- Be sure that fuel, oil, hydraulic fluid, and water are in their proper levels. Gauges should be checked for condition and proper operation.
- Ensure that the air cleaner and precleaner are serviced as required.
- Check that cables and sheaves are clean and properly lubricated and that cables are free of kinks and broken strands.
- Be sure that the operator's floor is clear of hazards and loose objects and is free of grease and oil.
- Check that the battery is clean and undamaged. Battery cables should not be frayed and connections should be tight.
- Adjust brakes and clutches properly.
- Check tires for proper inflation and check the condition of treads and sidewalls. Improper inflation is the major maintenance and safety problem for tires.
- Watch for dark smoke coming from the exhaust after the engine has warmed up. Smokey exhaust usually indicates a clogged air intake or fuel problem (damaged fuel injector or wrong fuel).

Equipment Maintenance and Repair

While the subject of specific maintenance and repair procedures is beyond the scope of this section, a relatively recent development in this area is of interest. It has been found that freezing equipment components such as backhoe teeth, blade cutting edges, rock drill bits, brake rotors, and engine blocks to a temperature of −300°F (−184°C) can substantially extend the life of these components. This freezing process is called "deep cryogenic treatment." While the cryogenic treatment increases the cost of treated components, the increased component life often reduces the equipment's overall maintenance and repair cost. Contractors should run tests to compare the overall cost, including labor and downtime, of equipment using treated versus untreated components.

Maintenance Organization

Routine maintenance and servicing may be performed in the open or at a covered job-site facility by either the operator or a service team. Servicing is usually performed in the open except when frequent adverse weather conditions prevail, but service areas should be located away from haul roads and other sources of dust. Both operator maintenance and crew maintenance systems have been successfully employed. However, specialized service teams equipped with mobile power lubrication and fueling equipment have been used most successfully by many contractors. This system allows maintenance to be performed during shift breaks, at the end of the day, or at staggered intervals during equipment operations. Minor repairs may be performed on the job by mobile repair teams or at an on-site repair facility. Equipment requiring major repairs is normally brought to an equipment dealer or company shop for repair. Large projects, particularly at an isolated location, may justify the establishment of a major repair facility near the job site.

Since the supply of repair parts is a frequent problem at all maintenance levels, repair parts stockage policies must be carefully developed based on experience, manufacturer's demand data, and job conditions. Frequently the stockage and repair by replacement of assemblies and subassemblies will result in a lowering of total maintenance costs. The defective assemblies which are removed are later repaired or exchanged for rebuilt assemblies. When computers are available, they may be used advantageously to maintain data on equipment repair and cost history as well as to regulate repair parts stockage.

Problems

1. What construction activities are responsible for the majority of serious construction accidents?

2. What job-site conditions serve to increase the chance of an excavation slope failure?

3. What are PM indicators?

4. When should equipment fuel tanks be filled? Why?

5. Explain the action that should be taken if an excavator ruptures a gas line.

6. Identify the major safety hazards involved in crane operations and describe how these hazards might be minimized.

7. Where may the OSHA regulations pertaining to construction be found?

8. What are the requirements for the design of a protective system for an excavation 25 ft (7.6 m) deep?

9. Briefly describe the major health hazards involved in construction operations under high-temperature conditions and how these hazards might be minimized.

10. Suggest at least two ways in which a personal computer might be employed to improve the equipment maintenance of a construction company.

References

1. *AGC Guidelines for a Basic Safety Program.* The Associated General Contractors of America, Inc., Washington, D.C.

2. Carper, Kenneth L., and Jacob Feld. *Construction Failure,* 2nd ed. New York: Wiley, 1997.

3. *Code of Federal Regulations,* Title 29, Chapter XVII, Part 1926. Office of the Federal Register, National Archives and Records Administration, Washington, D.C.

4. *Construction Industry Digest* (OSHA 2202). U.S. Department of Labor, Washington, D.C.

5. *Construction Machine Operators' Safety Manuals.* Association of Equipment Manufacturers, Milwaukee, WI. Volumes for many construction machines.

6. *Crane Safety on Construction Sites.* Reston, VA: American Society of Civil Engineers, 1998.

7. Culver, C. G. "Construction Site Safety," *Handbook of Temporary Structures in Construction, 2nd* ed., R. T. Ratay, ed. New York: McGraw-Hill, 1996.

8. Lee, D.H.K. *Hear and Cold Effects and Their Control* (Public Health Monograph No. 72). U.S. Department of Health, Education, and Welfare, Washington, D.C., 1964.

9. *Manual of Accident Prevention in Construction.* The Associated General Contractors of America, Inc.,Washington, D.C.

10. Nicastro, David, ed. *Failure Mechanisms in Building Construction.* Reston, VA: ASCE, 1997.

IMPROVING PRODUCTIVITY AND PERFORMANCE

IMPROVING PRODUCTIVITY
AND PERFORMANCE

1 THE BIG PICTURE

State of the Industry

The Business Roundtable Construction Industry Cost Effectiveness (CICE) study found that the U.S. construction industry faced a number of problems in remaining competitive in the international construction market. However, it concluded that the majority of industry problems could be overcome by improved management of the construction effort. At the project management level, the study discovered inadequate management performance in a number of areas. These included construction safety, control of the use of overtime, training and education, worker motivation, and failure to adopt modern management systems. Thus, the purpose of this chapter is to look at ways in which construction managers can improve construction productivity and performance.

What Is Productivity?

There is serious disagreement about the proper definition of the term *productivity* within the construction industry. As usually employed, the term means the output of construction goods and services per unit of labor input. Obviously, such a definition ignores the contribution of technology and capital investment to the measured productivity. The heavy construction element of the industry has demonstrated that the use of larger and more productive earthmoving equipment can increase productivity and lower unit production costs in the face of generally rising labor and materials costs. The continued rapid growth of technology in the world economy makes it likely that new technology such as robotics and industrialized building processes will have a significant impact on construction productivity in the not too distant future.

Probably a better measure of construction industry performance is cost-effectiveness as used by the Business Roundtable CICE study. However, for the purpose of this chapter we will use the traditional definition of productivity as output per unit input of labor and focus our attention on ways in which construction industry productivity and cost-effectiveness can be increased by improved management.

Tools for Better Management

A number of studies, including the CICE study, have shown that most on-site delays and inefficiencies lie within the control of management. Management is responsible for planning, organizing, and controlling the work. If these management responsibilities were properly carried out, there would be few cases of workers standing idle waiting for job assignment, tools, or instructions. As you see, the scope of management responsibility is great and the techniques for efficiently carrying out these responsibilities are varied and complex. Many books have been written on individual topics and techniques in this area. Thus, the purpose of this chapter is simply to introduce the reader to some of these techniques and their potential for improving the management of construction.

One of the major tools for improving construction productivity is *work improvement*: that is, the scientific study and optimization of work methods. Such techniques are also known as *work simplification, motion and time study, work study*, and *methods analysis*. Human factors, often not adequately considered, also play an important part in productivity. Workers' physical capacity, site working conditions, morale, and motivation are important elements in determining the most effective work methods and the resulting productivity for a particular task.

Other techniques available to assist the construction manager in improving construction productivity and cost-effectiveness include network planning methods, economic analyses, safety programs, quantitative management methods, simulation, and the use of computers. Many of these topics have been introduced in previous chapters. Other major topics are discussed in the following sections.

2 WORK IMPROVEMENT

What Is It?

Techniques for improving industrial production by scientific study of work methods can be traced back many centuries. However, only in the twentieth century did such techniques begin to be widely adopted by manufacturing industries. Frederick W. Taylor and Frank Gilbreth were among the early pioneers of what came to be known as *scientific management* and which today forms the basis for the field of industrial engineering. However, it is interesting to note that Frank Gilbreth began his career as a bricklayer and performed his early studies in that field. Another pioneer, D. J. Hauer, published his book *Modern Management Applied to Construction* in 1918. In spite of these early efforts by Gilbreth, Hauer, and others, work improvement methods were never widely adopted by the construction industry. Today there is renewed interest in these techniques by a construction industry faced with declining productivity and cost-effectiveness.

An important but often overlooked component of work improvement is preplanning, that is, detailed planning of work equipment and procedures prior to the start of work. Physical models as well as traditional work improvement charts and diagrams may be used to advantage in the preplanning process. Models are often used for large and complex projects such as power plants, dams, and petrochemical process plants to check physical dimensions, clearance between components, and general layout. Carried to a greater level of detail, they are very useful in planning concrete placement, blockouts for placing equipment, erection of structural components, and the actual procedure for placing equipment into a structure. Computer graphics and computer-aided design (CAD) can perform similar functions faster and at lower cost than can physical models or other manual techniques.

Traditional work improvement techniques, described in more detail in the following pages, include time studies, flow process charts, layout diagrams, and crew balance charts.

Time Studies

Time studies are used to collect time data relating to a construction activity for the purpose of either statistical analysis or of determining the level of work activity. In either case, it is important that the data collected be statistically valid. Hence a random-number procedure is usually employed in selecting the time for making each observation. The number of observations required for statistical validity depends on the type of study being made. For time analysis, the number of observations required depends on sample size, the standard deviation of the sample, and the level of accuracy and confidence desired. For effectiveness ratings, the number of observations required depends on the confidence desired, the acceptable error, and the measured percentage of effectiveness.

Work sampling is the name for a time study conducted for the purpose of determining the level of activity of an operation. A study of a construction equipment operation, for example, may classify work activity into a number of categories, each designated as either active or nonworking. The number of active observations divided by the total number of observations will yield the level of activity. The distribution of observations by category will provide an indication to management of how machine time is being spent.

The types of work sampling performed to determine labor utilization and effectiveness include field ratings and 5-min ratings. *Field ratings* are used to measure the level of activity of a large work force. At the selected random times, each worker is observed and instantaneously classified as either working or nonworking. The number of working observations divided by the total number of observations yields the level of activity. The *5-min rating* is used primarily to measure the level of activity of a crew. Each crew member is observed for a minimum of 1 min (or a minimum of 12 min per crew). If the crew member is working more than 50% of the time observed, the observation is recorded as working.

Sampling for labor effectiveness may also divide observations into categories. Some common categories used include effective work, essential contributory work, ineffective work, and nonworking. Analysis of work by category will again assist management in determining how labor time is being utilized and provide clues to increasing labor effectiveness.

Although time studies are traditionally made using stopwatches and data sheets, there is growing use of time-lapse photography and video time-lapse recording for this purpose. The use of time-lapse equipment for conducting work improvement studies on construction projects provides several advantages over stopwatch studies. A permanent record of the activity is provided which can be studied as long as necessary to obtain necessary time data. In addition, a historical record of the activity is obtained which may be useful in training managers and supervisors as well as providing evidence in event of legal disputes.

Flow Process Charts

A *flow process chart* for a construction operation serves the same purpose as does a flowchart for a computer program. That is, it traces the flow of material or work through a series of processing steps (classified as operations, transportations, inspections, delays, or storages). Depending on the level of detail, it usually indicates the distance and time required for each transportation and the time required for each operation, inspection, or delay. From the chart the manager should be able to visualize the entire process and to tabulate the number of operations, transportations, inspections, delays, and storages involved, and the time required for each category.

In preparing a flow process chart (see Figure 1), list in sequence a brief description of each step as it occurs. Trace the work flow by connecting the appropriate symbol in the second column. Enter the transportation distance and the time involved for each step. Figure 1 illustrates a flow process chart for the assembly of the roof truss shown in Figure 2, employing a crew of two workers and a forklift.

FIGURE 1. Flow process chart.

FLOW PROCESS CHART		NUMBER 101	PAGE NO. 1	NO. OF PAGES 1

PROCESS: **Assemble Truss**
☒ MAN OR ☐ MATERIAL

CHART BEGINS: **Parts stack** CHART ENDS: **Parts stack**
CHARTED BY: **J. Doe** DATE: **7/13**
ORGANIZATION: **E Z Construction**

SUMMARY						
ACTIONS		PRESENT		PROPOSED		DIFFERENCE
		NO.	TIME	NO.	TIME	NO.	TIME
○ OPERATIONS	10	137				
⇨ TRANSPORTATIONS	9	90				
☐ INSPECTIONS	0					
D DELAYS	0					
▽ STORAGES	0					
DISTANCE TRAVELLED (Feet)	300					

#	DETAILS OF ☒ PRESENT / PROPOSED METHOD	SYMBOLS	DISTANCE IN FEET	QUANTITY	TIME (sec)	NOTES
1	Remove chords from stack	○⇨☐D▽		2	3	
2	Transport chord to jig	○⇨☐D▽	25	2	10	
3	Position chords in jig	○⇨☐D▽		2	5	
4	Return to parts stack	○⇨☐D▽	25		6	
5	Remove rafters from stack	○⇨☐D▽		2	3	
6	Transport rafters to jig	○⇨☐D▽	25	2	10	
7	Position rafters in jig	○⇨☐D▽		2	5	
8	Return to parts stack	○⇨☐D▽	25		6	
9	Remove diagonals	○⇨☐D▽		2	3	
10	Transport diagonals	○⇨☐D▽	25	2	10	
11	Position diagonals in jig	○⇨☐D▽		2	5	
12	Return to parts stack	○⇨☐D▽	25		6	
13	Remove hanger from stack	○⇨☐D▽		1	3	
14	Transport hanger to jig	○⇨☐D▽	25	1	10	
15	Position hanger in jig	○⇨☐D▽		1	5	
16	Fasten truss plates	○⇨☐D▽		12	85	
17	Remove truss from jig	○⇨☐D▽		1	20	
18	Trans & stack truss	○⇨☐D▽	50	1	15	Using forklift
19	Return to parts stack	○⇨☐D▽	75		17	
20		○⇨☐D▽				Cycle time
21		○⇨☐D▽				= 227 sec

The production rate for the process is determined by the time required to perform those steps that cannot be performed concurrently. This time is called the *control factor*. The control factor can be reduced only by speeding up these steps or by devising a method that permits some of its activities to be performed concurrently.

After preparing a flow process chart, it should be analyzed and revised to reduce the number of operations, movements, storages, and delays, as well as the control factor, to a minimum. Challenge each step in the process. Ask yourself: Is it necessary? Is it being done at the proper place and in the most efficient manner? How can it be done faster and safer?

FIGURE 2. Roof truss diagram.

Layout Diagrams

A *layout diagram* is a scaled diagram that shows the location of all physical facilities, machines, and material involved in a process. Since the objective of a work improvement study is to minimize processing time and effort, use a layout diagram to assist in reducing the number of material movements and the distance between operations. A *flow diagram* is similar to a layout diagram but also shows the path followed by the worker or material being recorded on a flow process chart. The flow diagram should indicate the direction of movement and the locations where delays occur. Step numbers on a flow diagram should correspond to the sequence numbers used on the corresponding flow process chart.

It should be apparent that flow process charts, flow diagrams, and layout diagrams must be studied together for maximum benefit and must be consistent with each other. Since layout diagrams and flow diagrams help us to visualize the operation described by a flow process chart, these diagrams should suggest jobs that might be combined, storages that might be eliminated, or transportations that might be shortened. The objective is to position the materials and machines so that the shortest possible path can be used without creating traffic conflicts or safety hazards.

Crew Balance Charts

A *crew balance chart* uses a graphical format to document the activities of each member of a group of workers during one complete cycle of an operation. A vertical bar is drawn to represent the time of each crew member during the cycle. The bar is then divided into time blocks showing the time spent by that crew member on each activity which occurs during the cycle. The usual convention utilizes a color code to indicate the level of activity during each time block. The darker the color, the higher the level of activity. Thus, effective work might be shown by a dark block, contributory work by a lighter-colored block, and noneffective work or idle time by a white block. As the name indicates, the crew balance chart enables us easily to compare the level of activity of each worker during an operation cycle. Often its use will suggest ways to reduce crew size or to realign jobs so that work is equalized between crew members.

A crew balance chart for the assembly of the roof truss of Figure 2 is illustrated in Figure 3. However, note that here the crew size has been increased to four members instead of the two members used in the flow process chart of Figure 1.

Crew balance charts are sometimes referred to as *multiman charts*. Charts showing both crew activities and machine utilization are called *man–machine charts* or *multiman-and-machine charts*.

Human Factors

In attempting to improve construction productivity and cost-effectiveness, it is important to remember that people are the essential element in the construction process. Workers who are fatigued, bored, or hostile will never perform at an optimum level of effectiveness. Some major human factors to be considered include environmental conditions, safety conditions, physical effort requirements, work hours, and worker morale and motivation.

There are several considerations involved in assessing the effect of physical exertion on workers. It has been found that the maximum long-term rate of human energy expenditure for the average worker is approximately equal to the energy expended in walking. Attempts at sustained higher levels of effort will only result in physical fatigue and lower performance. Therefore, physical work requirements should be adjusted to match worker capability. For example, Frederick Taylor found in his early studies that the best performance of workers loading material using hand shovels was obtained by matching shovel style, size, and weight to individual worker characteristics. Physical fatigue can be caused by holding an object in a fixed position for an extended period of time as well as by overexertion.

Studies (see reference 11) have shown that worker productivity is seriously reduced by sustained periods of overtime work. In general, a 40-h workweek appears to be the optimum for U.S. construction workers. When construction workers are put on a scheduled overtime basis, productivity usually drops sharply during the first week, recovers somewhat during the following 3 weeks, then continues to decline until it finally levels off after about 9 weeks. When first put on overtime, total worker production per week is initially higher than for a standard 40-h week. However, as productivity continues to decline, the total output for a 50-h or 60-h week falls to that of a 40-h week after about 8 weeks. When the premium cost of overtime is considered, it is apparent that the labor cost per unit of production will always be higher for overtime work than for normal work. As the length of the overtime period increases, the cost differential becomes sizable. For example, if the hourly pay rate for overtime work (work beyond 40 h) is 150% of the standard rate, the labor cost per unit of production for a 60-h week after 8 weeks would be more than 80% higher than for a 40-h week.

Worker morale and motivation have also been found to be important factors in construction worker productivity. In studies of 12 large power-plant construction projects, Borcherding and Garner (reference 4) analyzed the factors inhibiting craft productivity on these projects. Of the factors studied, nonavailability of material was the most significant, followed by nonavailability of tools, and the need to redo work. Interfacing of crews, overcrowded work areas, delays for inspection, craft turnover, absenteeism, changes in foremen, and incompetence of foremen were also found to inhibit productivity. However, these factors were much less significant than were the first three factors cited above. The same study identified a number of circumstances that acted as worker motivators or demotivators on these projects. As might be expected, the most productive projects tended to have the highest number of worker motivators and the

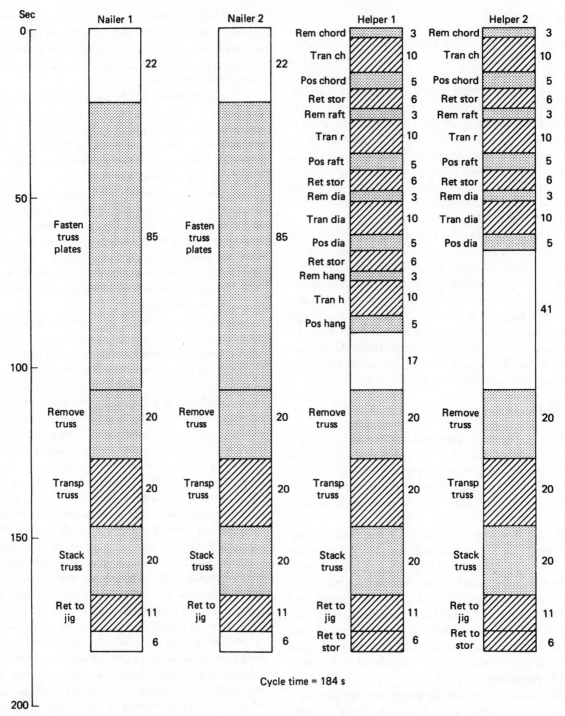

FIGURE 3. Crew balance chart.

lowest number of worker demotivators. It appears from the study that the presence of worker demotivators has more effect on productivity than does the presence of worker motivators. Some of the worker demotivators identified by the study included the following:

- Disrespectful treatment of workers.
- Lack of sense of accomplishment.
- Nonavailability of materials and tools.
- Necessity to redo work.
- Discontinuity in crew makeup.
- Confusion on the project.
- Lack of recognition for accomplishments.
- Failure to utilize worker skills.
- Incompetent personnel.
- Lack of cooperation between crafts.
- Overcrowded work areas.

- Poor inspection programs.
- Inadequate communication between project elements.
- Unsafe working conditions.
- Workers not involved in decision making.

Some of the worker motivators identified in the study include the following:

- Good relations between crafts.
- Good worker orientation programs.
- Good safety programs.
- Enjoyable work.
- Good pay.
- Recognition for accomplishments.
- Well-defined goals.
- Well-planned projects.

3 QUANTITATIVE MANAGEMENT METHODS

The science that uses mathematical methods to solve operational or management problems is called *operations research*. After World War II, operations research techniques began to be employed by industry to provide management with a more logical method for making sound predictions and decisions. Basically, these techniques deal with the allocation of resources to various activities so as to maximize some overall measure of effectiveness. Although a number of mathematical optimization techniques are available, linear programming is by far the most widely used for management purposes. In this section we consider briefly the application of linear programming to construction management.

Linear Programming—Graphical Solution

As the name implies, all relationships considered in linear programming must be linear functions. To apply linear programming, it is necessary to have a set of linear *constraint* (boundary) *equations* and a linear *objective function* which is to be maximized or minimized. We consider first a graphical solution technique that may be employed when only two variables are present. This relatively simple case, which is illustrated by Example 1, should enable us to visualize the nature of the solution procedure. As you recognize, it would be impossible to use a graphical procedure to solve a problem involving more than three variables.

Example 1 A project manager for a large earthmoving project is faced with the task of selecting the dozers to be used on a relatively remote project. The project manager is advised by the equipment division manager that both heavy and medium dozers are available for the project. However, only 10 heavy dozers are available. The supply of medium dozers is relatively unlimited. Because of time and transportation limitations, a maximum of 1080 tons of dozers may be transported to the site. The project manager also has the following information on dozer performance and weight.

Dozer	Weight (tons)	Production Index
Heavy	60	2 units/day
Medium	40	1 unit/day

Solution

We must first formulate the constraint equations defining the limits of the solution. Obviously, the number of each type of dozer must be zero or greater. (This assumption is implicit in all linear programming solution procedures.) If we let X_1 represent the number of heavy dozers and X_2 represent the number of medium dozers, these constraints become

$$X_1 \geq 0 \qquad \qquad (1)$$

$$X_2 \geq 0 \qquad \qquad (2)$$

Another constraint is that the number of heavy dozers cannot exceed 10. Hence

$$X_1 \leq 10 \qquad \qquad (3)$$

Finally, the maximum weight to be transported is 1080 tons. Hence

$$60X_1 + 40X_2 \leq 1080 \qquad \qquad (4)$$

After establishing the constraints, we must define the objective function that is to be maximized or minimized. In this case we want to maximize some measure of production of the dozer fleet. Since each heavy dozer will produce twice as much as each medium dozer, the objective function can be expressed as

$$(\text{maximize}) \ 2X_1 + X_2$$

Summarizing the equations, we have

Constraints:

$$X_1 \geq 0 \qquad (\text{Eq 1})$$

$$X_2 \geq 0 \qquad (\text{Eq 2})$$

$$X_1 \leq 10 \qquad (\text{Eq 3})$$

$$60 \, X_1 + 40 \, X_2 \leq 1080 \qquad (\text{Eq 4})$$

Objective function:

$$(\text{maximize}) \ 2X_1 + X_2$$

The graphical solution procedure is illustrated in Figure 4. The feasible region for a solution as defined by the constraint equations is shown in Figure 4a. In Figure 4b, the objective function has been set equal to 10 and to 20. Notice that the objective function can be represented by a family of lines having a slope of –2. As this line is moved away from the origin, the value of the objective function increases. Since we wish to maximize the value of this function, the optimum value of the objective function will be obtained when this line is as far from the origin as possible while remaining in the feasible region. In this case, the optimum value occurs at the point (10, 12) defined by the intersection of constraints 3 and 4. Following the usual

FIGURE 4. Graphical solution of Example 1.

convention for mathematical optimization procedures, we designate optimum values using an asterisk. Hence for our problem

$$X_1^* = 10$$
$$X_2^* = 12$$
$$OF^* = 32$$

As the reader may recognize, this very simple problem could easily be solved by analytical procedures. However, for more complex problems, linear programming usually provides a much faster and simpler solution procedure than do other techniques.

Computer Solution

Since the graphical solution technique cannot be used for problems involving more than three variables, a more general solution procedure is required. A manual solution algorithm, the simplex method, is available for solving the general linear programming problem. However, the procedure is computationally cumbersome and, therefore, of practical value only for the solution of small problems. Moreover, computerized solution techniques are available which can rapidly solve linear programming problems involving thousands of variables and constraints.

Because of the wide availability of microcomputers and linear programming software, this discussion will be confined to the use of computers for solving the general linear programming problem. As we have learned, the essential elements in the formulation of a linear programming problem are a set of constraint equations and an objective function. Care must be taken to ensure that constraint equations are not mutually exclusive, which would result in there being no feasible region for a solution. In such a case, the computer output will advise you that no feasible solution exists. While linear programming computer programs differ somewhat, the user is normally required to enter the number of variables, the number of constraint equations, and whether the objective function is to be maximized or minimized. Then, for each constraint equation, enter the coefficient for each variable, the equality relationship ($\leq$, $=$, or $\geq$), and the right-hand-side constant. Finally, the coefficient of each variable in the objective function is entered. The program output will indicate whether a feasible solution exists. If it does, the optimum value of each variable and of the objective function will be given. A sensitivity analysis is often provided which indicates the effect on the objective function resulting from a unit change in the right-hand-side constant of each binding constraint. A computer solution produced by a microcomputer for the problem of Example 2 is shown in Figure 5.

FIGURE 5. Computer solution of Example 2.

```
THE FOLLOWING LINEAR OPTIMIZATION MODEL WILL BE MAXIMIZED

THE OBJECTIVE FUNCTION =      +4.000X 1     +3.000X 2

SUBJECT TO THE FOLLOWING CONSTRAINTS

        +0.11X 1      +0.21X 2    <=    80
        +0.81X 1      +1.01X 2    <=   440
        +0.52X 1      +0.22X 2    <=   160


THE FEASIBLE SOLUTION FOUND AFTER     2      ITERATIONS

        ITERATION          3              OBJECTIVE =   0
        ITERATION          4              OBJECTIVE =   1230.77
        ITERATION          5              OBJECTIVE =   1600

VARIABLES IN THE SOLUTION

        VARIABLES        2              AMOUNT =      282.353
        VARIABLE         1              AMOUNT =      188.235

VARIABLES OUT OF THE SOLUTION

BINDING CONSTRAINTS

        CONSTRAINT       3              SHADOW PRICE = 6
        CONSTRAINT       1              SHADOW PRICE = 8

SLACK CONSTRAINTS

        CONSTRAINT       2              SLACK =       2.35294

THE OPTIMUM OBJECTIVE FUNCTION IS        1600
```

Example 2 A paving contractor is planning his work schedule for the following week. He has a choice of either of two types of concrete, plain concrete or concrete with an additive. The use of additive concrete reduces concrete finishing time but increases the time required for placement. Cost records indicate that the contractor can expect a profit of $4 per cubic yard for plain concrete and $3 per cubic yard for additive concrete. Naturally, the objective of the contractor is to maximize his profits. However, he does not want to hire additional workers. Labor requirements [in man-hours per cubic yard (mh/cu yd)] for each type of concrete are given below. Assuming that sufficient demand exists, how many cubic yards of each type of concrete should the contractor place the following week? The contractor works a 40-h week.

| Type | Number | Labor Required | |
		Plain	Additive
Foreperson	2	0.11 mh/cu yd	0.21 mh/cu yd
Laborer	11	0.81 mh/cu yd	1.01 mh/cu yd
Finishers	4	0.52 mh/cu yd	0.22 mh/cu yd

Solution

From the table of labor requirements it is determined that 80 foreperson man-hours, 440 laborer man-hours, and 160 finisher man-hours are available each week. We will let X_1 represent the quantity of plain concrete to be placed and X_2 represent the quantity of additive concrete. Hence the constraint equations and objective function are as follows:

Constraints:

$$0.11X_1 + 0.21X_2 \leq 80$$
$$0.81X_1 + 1.01X_2 \leq 440$$
$$0.52X_1 + 0.22X_2 \leq 160$$

Objective function:

$$(\text{maximize}) \ 4.00X_1 + 3.00X_2$$

The optimum solution, shown in Figure 5, is

$X_1^* = 188.235$ cu yd (plain concrete)
$X_2^* = 282.353$ cu yd (additive concrete)
OF* = $1600.00 (profit)

The shadow prices shown for the binding constraints indicate the amount by which the objective function (profit) would be increased if the respective constraint constant were increased by one unit. That is, profit would be increased by $8 if the number of foreperson man-hours available were increased to 81. Similarly, profit would be increased by $6 if the number of finisher man-hours were increased to 161. Note also that there are slightly over two excess laborer man-hours available at the optimum solution.

4 COMPUTERS AND OTHER TOOLS

Computers in Construction

Perhaps the most exciting development in construction use of computers is the wide availability of electronic mail (e-mail) and the Internet (World Wide Web) with its almost unlimited resources. Electronic communications using computers permit contractors to exchange information and data among projects and between project sites and the main office. Equipment manufacturers are increasingly engaging in electronic communications with dealers and dealers with contractors. Manufacturers are also providing online parts catalogs and service and repair bulletins to dealers as well as processing equipment warranty claims electronically. While some manufacturers' information is available only to dealers and not to contractors, increasingly such data and services will become available to contractors. Electronic sales of new and used equipment and parts are also growing rapidly. Much information of value to contractors is available on the Internet.

A number of the end-of-chapter problems in the preceding chapters have illustrated the use of computers for solving construction engineering and management problems. For the most part, solutions to these problems have been obtained using computer programs written in a traditional computer language. However, a growing library of packaged computer software, as well as special-purpose computer programming languages, is available. Many of these can be profitably employed by the construction manager. Some of the widely used software packages include word processors, electronic spreadsheets, database programs, communications programs, graphics programs, and project and equipment management programs. Integrated software packages that include several of these programs utilizing a common file structure are also available. Some of the software written specifically for the construction industry includes estimating programs, bidding programs, project management programs, and programs for maintaining cost and performance data for equipment and labor. With the increasing power and declining cost of computers, more powerful user-friendly construction software is becoming available almost daily.

Word processors are used for general correspondence, as well as to prepare memos, reports, training manuals, and procedures manuals. They are particularly useful for preparing repetitive documents such as contract specifications, where much of the material is standard (often called "boilerplate") but is modified somewhat for each specific project. Word processors often have associated spelling checkers which identify words not contained in its standard dictionary. The user can correct the word, accept it without adding it to the dictionary, or add it to the dictionary. Mailing-list programs are also available for many word processors. These enable the user to prepare form letters and associated address files.

Address files can be used to prepare mailing labels or envelopes as well as to merge names, addresses, and other data into form letters.

Electronic spreadsheets are a more powerful form of the familiar row-and-column spreadsheet used for tabulating such data as quantity, unit cost, total cost, sales price, and profit. By allowing the user to specify mathematical relationships between cells, results for any input data can be quickly calculated. For example, the value for each row of column 4 may be specified as that obtained by multiplying column 2 by column 3. Many electronic spreadsheet programs also contain built-in functions such as interest calculations, loan amortization, present value, future value, and internal rate of return. The use of such a program will enable the manager quickly to determine the effect produced by any change in the assumed or actual data.

Database programs are used to organize, maintain, and manipulate a collection of data. Special-purpose database programs are written for a specific purpose such as inventory control. Although such specialized programs are relatively easy to learn and put into use, they can be used only for the specific purpose for which they were written. Therefore, general-purpose database programs are much more widely used. General-purpose programs are very flexible but must be customized for each specific application. The two major types of general-purpose database programs are file managers and relational databases. File managers are simpler and usually less expensive than are relational databases. However, they can access only one data file at a time. Relational databases, on the other hand, are capable of using data from a number of files at the same time. For example, they are capable of integrating material, labor, and equipment cost data from many different cost files to produce total project cost.

Communications programs are used for communications between computer and with *Internet Service Providers* (ISPs). They can be used to access such information services as electronic mail, electronic bulletin boards, and the Internet. Used with a computer and modem, they allow wireless communication or communication over an ordinary telephone line.

Internet Service Providers (ISP's) provide access to e-mail and Internet services. Again a computer, modem, and the services of an ISP are all that are required to utilize these resources.

Graphics programs greatly speed up and facilitate the preparation of graphic material. They are widely used for preparing charts and other illustrations for reports and presentations. Computer-aided design and drafting programs are becoming widely used for construction design.

Project management programs are usually built around network planning techniques. They often provide for maintaining and forecasting cost and resource data as well as time data. Some programs also contain functions capable of resource leveling.

Equipment management programs provide many capabilities for managing an equipment fleet. They can maintain equipment cost and maintenance history, schedule preventive maintenance, and inventory, order, and purchase repair parts.

Advanced Techniques

In addition to the quantitative management techniques and computer software described above, there are several more advanced techniques available to the progressive construction manager. For example, there are various optimization techniques available for the solution of optimization problems involving nonlinear functions.

Computer simulation is a powerful tool for analyzing problems not easily solved by analytical methods. The simulation of construction operations may be accomplished by writing a simulation program using a conventional programming language or a simulation language or by utilizing a packaged simulation program. An example of the output of a scraper simulation program is shown in Figure 6. Packaged simulation programs are relatively simple to use but are usually limited in the type of operation and equipment which can be modeled. However, a programmer using a simulation language can quickly model almost any type of construction operation and any combination of equipment. Reference 10 describes several earthmoving simulation programs written in the GPSS simulation program.

In this day of rapid technological advance, one can never predict the exact impact of new technology on construction. As we have seen, the wide availability of the personal computer has placed a powerful tool at the disposal of the construction professional. In addition, computers have already begun to be applied to the control systems of earthmoving equipment and to the construction robots discussed in the following section.

5 ROBOTS IN CONSTRUCTION

Robots or manipulator machines controlled by computer have been employed on industrial production lines for some years. As the technology has improved, robots have found increasing use in a number of industries, including the automobile manufacturing industry. Advantages of robots over human workers include higher speed, greater accuracy, absence of worker fatigue or boredom, and the ability to work under hazardous conditions without endangering worker health. While robots do displace some production workers, they increase the demand for skilled workers to design, manufacture, program, and maintain the robots.

Despite the advantages that robots can offer, robot manufacturers and construction firms have been slow to apply robots to construction tasks. Many argue that the field environment and unique characteristics of each construction project make the use of robots impractical for construction. Despite these obstacles, progress is being made in the application of robots and automated equipment to construction tasks.

Simulation Number 5

Type of Material	Loading Method	Project Conditions	Delay Option	Pushing Method
1-Common earth 2-Rock	1-Single pusher 2-Tandem pushers 3-Push-pull 4-Elevating	Length of haul road- 3000 ft Type of material-1 Total excavation-25000 LCY Total shift time-3.89 hrs Delay option-1	0-No delays used 1-Delays used	1-Single pusher 2-Tandem pushers

Scrapers

Scraper Number	No. Eng	Load Meth	Rated Load (LCY)	Ave. Load (LCY)	No. Loads	Load Time (sec)	Total Exc (LCY)	Travel Time (sec)	Cnst Time (sec)	Prod Time (sec)	Wait Time (sec)	Ext. Delay Time (sec)	Total Cycle Time (sec)	% Util	Prod LCY/ hr
1	2	3	31	26	26	107	676	319	52	478	9	72	559	85.5	168.18
2	2	3	31	26	25	106	650	347	49	502	26	48	576	87.2	161.71
3	2	3	31	26	26	108	676	339	54	501	18	29	548	91.4	168.18
4	2	3	31	26	26	106	676	321	54	481	25	43	549	87.6	168.18
5	2	3	31	26	27	107	702	324	56	487	31	41	559	87.1	174.65
6	2	3	31	26	25	103	650	337	52	492	48	33	573	85.9	161.71
7	2	3	31	26	25	119	650	321	49	489	14	56	559	87.5	161.71
8	2	3	31	26	26	106	676	307	53	466	26	51	543	85.8	168.18

Fleet

Overall production = 1332.52 LCY/HR = 1039.20 BCY/HR

Fleet cost per hour = $699.20

Overall cost per LCY = $0.525 – PER BCY $0.673

Total time of simulation = 4.02 HOURS

Total production = 5356 LCY = 4177 BCY

FIGURE 6. Scraper simulation program output.

Recent Developments

Considerable research and development work on the use of robots in construction is taking place in universities and construction research facilities, particularly in Japan. Some of the construction tasks to which automation and robotics have been successfully applied are described in references 6 and 12. These include the following:

Building Construction

- Finishing of concrete floor slabs.
- Fireproofing of structural steel after erection.
- Positioning steel members for steel erection.
- Spray linings for silos and similar structures.
- Surfacing of walls and other building components.

Heavy Construction

- Automated asphalt and concrete plants.
- Automated excavators.
- Automated tunnel boring machines.

- Concrete demolition in radioactive areas.
- Manufacture of precast concrete beams.

The automatic grade control of a dozer, excavator, and grader using a laser transmitter as a reference plane is illustrated in Figure 7. A pipe manipulator controlled by the excavator operator and using an integrated laser beam for pipe alignment is shown in Figure 8. The use of such a machine removes the hazards involved in having construction workers in the trench during pipe installation. The multipurpose interior robot shown in Figure 9 is capable of constructing block walls, setting tile, plastering, and painting inside buildings.

The availability of the Global Positioning System (GPS) has provided a new tool for surveying and mapping, site layout, and the automated control of earthmoving equipment. The GPS system consists of 24 satellites orbiting the Earth at an altitude of 12,000 mi (19,308 km). By using two GPS receivers operating together in a differential mode, it is possible to obtain a location accuracy within less than 1 in. (25 mm) with GPS.

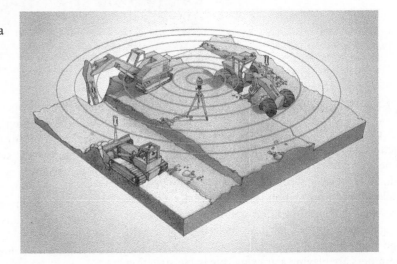

FIGURE 7. Automatic grade control of an excavation using a laser. (Courtesy of Trimble)

FIGURE 8. Remote-controlled pipe manipulator. (Courtesy of the Construction Automation and Robotics Laboratory, North Carolina State University)

FIGURE 9. Robot for interior construction. (Courtesy of Prof. A.Warszawski)

6 THE FUTURE

As has been noted throughout this book, changes in the construction industry are occurring at an ever-increasing rate. Some recent trends in construction include increasing international competition, rapid changes in technology, the wide availability of information via the Internet, increasing ease and speed of communication, and increasing governmental regulation of the industry, particularly in the areas of safety and environmental protection.

Computers are playing a growing role in construction equipment design and operation. Automation has taken over many aspects of construction equipment control. When equipment control systems are integrated with wireless communication systems and GPS (Global Positioning System) systems, remote and even off-site control of construction equipment operations become highly feasible. In addition to requiring highly trained managers and operators, such developments will increasingly demand skilled technicians to maintain and repair the equipment involved.

In light of these developments, tomorrow's construction professional faces an exciting future.

Problems

1. a. The control factor for the process of precutting the rafters of the truss of Figure 2 is 12 s based on the cutting rate of one saw. What is the maximum number of precut rafters that can be produced using one saw in a 40-min hour when labor supply is unlimited?

   b. Using a crew of two workers (one worker carrying material and one saw operator) with one saw, the cycle time for precutting rafters is 54 s. Using this crew, how many 50-min hours would it take to precut the rafters for 200 trusses?

2. What are the advantages of time-lapse recording (photo or video) over traditional stopwatch studies of construction operations?

3. Explain the effect of sustained overtime on the labor cost per unit of construction production.

4. What is an electronic spreadsheet computer program?

5. How could the process of assembling roof trusses described in Figure 3 be made more efficient?

6. Using any Internet source, find the annual value (current dollars) of Total Construction Put in Place in the

United States for the three most recent years as reported by the U.S. Census Bureau. Identify the Internet source used to obtain this data.

7. Solve the problem of Example 2 using the graphical solution technique for linear programming.

8. What is the purpose of work sampling and how is it performed as applied to construction?

9. Construction productivity is often defined as the output of construction goods and services per unit of labor input. Why is this an inadequate measure of construction productivity?

10. Use a linear programming computer program to solve the problem of Example 1.

References

1. Adrian, James J. *Construction Productivity Improvement*. New York: Elsevier, 1987.

2. Alfeld, Louis Edward. *Construction Productivity*. New York: McGraw-Hill, 1988.

3. Borcherding, John D., and Douglas F. Garner. "Work Force Motivation and Productivity on Large Jobs," *ASCE Journal of the Construction Division*, vol. 107, no. C03 (1981), pp. 443–453.

4. *Construction Labor Motivation*, CICE Report A-2. The Business Roundtable, Washington, D.C., August 1982.

5. Cousineau, Leslie, and Nobuyasu Miura. *Construction Robots: The Search for New Building Technology in Japan*. Reston, VA: ASCE, 1998.

6. Drewin, F. J. *Construction Productivity*. New York: Elsevier, 1982.

7. Kangari, Roozbeh, and Tetsuji Yoshida. "Prototype Robotics in Construction Industry," *ASCE Journal of Construction Engineering and Management*, vol. 115, no. 2 (1989), pp. 284–301.

8. Myers, Fred E. *Motion and Time Study*, 2nd ed. Upper Saddle River, NJ: Prentice Hall, 1999.

9. Nunnally, S. W. *Managing Construction Equipment*, 2nd ed. Upper Saddle River, NJ: Prentice Hall, 2000.

10. Oglesby, Clarkson H., Henry W. Parker, and Gregory A. Howell. *Productivity Improvement in Construction*. New York: McGraw-Hill, 1989.

11. Paulson, Boyd C., Jr. "Automation and Robotics for Construction," *ASCE Journal of Construction Engineering and Management*, vol. 111, no. 3 (1985), pp. 190–207.

12. *Scheduled Overtime Effect on Construction Projects*, CICE Report C-2. The Business Roundtable, Washington, D.C., November 1980.

13. Stark, Robert M., and Robert H. Mayer, Jr. *Quantitative Construction Management*. New York: Wiley, 1983.

Index

Page references followed by "f" indicate illustrated figures or photographs; followed by "t" indicates a table.

A

Abrasive sawing machines
  operation, 27-29, 59, 90-92, 98, 133, 290, 317, 347
  safety, 41, 99, 335-337, 347
  selecting, 31
Absenteeism, 347
Accident costs
  estimating, 7-9, 76, 313, 330
Accident/incident theory
  in practice, 162
Accident-prevention program
  development of, 294
Accidents
  cost of, 7-9, 140, 334-335
Accounting
  system, 174, 314
Accounting consistency
  cost control, 7, 320-321
  defined, 1, 174
  services, 1, 321
Accuracy
  GPS, 355-356
Acts of God, 328
Actual damages, 328
Advertising, 326
Agreement
  fixed price, 327
  lease, 318-319
AIA, 331
Air barriers
  exterior, 196-198, 259-260, 281
Air systems, 127, 143
Air-handling equipment and systems
  configurations, 196
  fans, 143
AISC, 278
Allowable stress, 185, 245
Allowable stresses, 185-186, 239
Alpine Engineered Products, 198
Alternates, 258, 326
Altitude adjustment
  air compressor, 143-145
  vehicle performance, 51
Aluminum alloy
  strength of, 120-121, 174, 277
American Institute of Architects, 328
American Institute of Steel Construction, 2, 280
American Society of Mechanical Engineers (ASME), 150
American Wire Gauge, 105
American Wood Preservers' Association (AWPA), 185
Ammonium nitrate, 103
Amortization schedule
  sample, 8
  schedule, 8, 276, 300-301, 315, 329, 352-353
Anchors
  bolt, 208
Angle
  interior, 186
  of repose, 23, 28, 170, 337
  steel, 80-81, 107, 167
Angle of swing
  backhoe, 29-30
  dragline, 28
Angle of swing:
  hydraulic excavator, 27-29
  shovel, 23, 28, 74
APA—The Engineered Wood Association, 186, 243
Arbitration, 330
Arch, 2, 203
Arches
  analysis, 187

Architectural details
  wall, 188-189, 218-219, 259-260
Architectural models
  constructing, 221
Area
  gross, 1, 72, 267
Articulated equipment
  grader, 72, 89-93, 136, 316-317, 355
  hauler, 59
Ashlar masonry, 265
Asphalt
  waterproofing, 135
Asphalt shingles
  patterns, 120, 138
Associated General Contractors, 326, 335
Assumptions, 319
Assurance, 7-8
Atmospheric corrosion, 277
Atmospheric pressure, 159
Axially loaded steel columns
  analysis of, 172, 208, 240, 271

B

Backhoe
  components, 29, 340
  job management, 31, 59
  operation and employment, 28
Backhoes, 27-28, 60, 81, 107
Balloon frame, 187
Balloon frame construction
  bracing, 187, 224, 237-238, 268-269, 281
  floor joists, 187
  posts, 26, 198
  sills, 187, 262
  studs, 184, 224, 238
  subfloor, 187
Band machines
  advantages, 26, 99, 133, 186, 307, 318, 353
Bank cubic yard (meter), 17
Bar
  supports, 228
Bar graph schedule, 291-292
Base
  bid, 305
  wood, 164
Base flashing, 199, 262
Basements
  columns, 162
  walls, 30
Batter piles, 168
Beam
  laminated, 187
  precast, 216-217, 264, 355
Beam columns
  deflection in, 217, 239
  design of, 199, 236, 237
Beams
  box, 278
  camber, 276
  cantilever, 199
Beam(s)
  continuous, 199, 224, 246-247
Beams
  lateral bracing, 187, 281
  longitudinal, 230
  prestressing, 121, 216-217
  reinforced concrete, 122, 213, 264-265
  steel beams, 279-280
  timber beams, 209
  transverse, 230
Beams, reinforced concrete
  rectangular, 162, 211, 213, 239, 265, 278
bearing
  beams, 186-187, 260, 276
  bolts, 282-284
  connections, 199, 228, 276
  platform frame construction, 187-190

  stiffeners, 278
Bearing capacity
  of footings, 260
  ultimate, 169
Bearing capacity equations
  extended, 26, 64, 279
  introduction to, 12
Bearing strength, 77, 162
Bearing stress, 248
Bearing stresses, 238
Bearing walls, 187-188, 260-261
  below grade, 28, 258
Bending strength, 184
Bending stress, 240
Bentonite slurry, 170
Bid
  base, 306
  best, 305
  date, 328
  documents, 305, 327-329
  form, 325
  information, 21, 304-305
  lowest, 21, 305
  lump-sum, 327
  negotiated, 327
  shopping, 327
  time, 304-306, 325
Bid shopping, 327
Bidders, 326
Bidding, 4, 320, 325-327, 334, 352
Bids, 325-326
Bituminous equipment
  aggregate spreaders, 136
  bituminous distributor, 134
  pavers, 123, 132-133
Bituminous surface treatments, 135
Blades
  dozer, 56-58, 90
  motor grader, 89-90
  scraper, 55
Block
  lintels, 264-265
Block holing, 106
Blocks
  management, 46, 71, 291
  title, 341
Boilers, 120, 281
Bolts
  common, 204-205, 224, 340
  machine, 339
  spacing, 205, 224
  unfinished, 281
Bond
  labor, 217
  obtaining, 136, 217, 325
  payment, 326-327
  permit, 219, 261
  subcontractors, 326-327
Bond beams
  in masonry walls, 260-261
Bond patterns:
  brick, 256-257
  concrete masonry, 256
Borings
  number of, 186
Borrow, 21-23, 75
Bottom plate, 187
Braces (bracing)
  diagonal, 187
Bracing
  diagonal bracing, 196
  excavation, 251
Bracing systems description of
  multistory, 187, 270
Breach of contract, 331
Breakers, 106, 113, 143-145
Brick

specifications, 199, 259
Brick masonry
  terms, 256
Brick(s)
  building, 196-197, 260
  clay, 259
  construction of, 259
  efflorescence, 271
Bridge management systems, 140
Bridging
  metal, 189
Brief:
  case, 345
  legal, 345
Bucket
  clamshell, 26
  orange peel, 36-37
Buckling
  compression, 246, 277
Budget
  owner's, 7
Builder, 195, 268, 325
Building
  certification, 6-7, 46, 235
  code, 5, 42, 187, 268, 278, 341
  permits, 6, 108, 187, 216-217, 290, 331
Building case study
  design process, 7
Building codes
  administration, 4, 287, 325, 341
  construction standards, 5
  historical, 290, 340, 345
  objectives of, 7
Building load control
  Burners, 134
  shading, 272
Building paper, 197
Built-up steel members, 278-279
Bulb pile, 168
Business Roundtable CICE study, 344

C

Cable structures
  lengths, 108, 184
Cable suspension systems
  cables, 281, 336
  vertical supports, 175, 228
CAD, 345
Caisson foundation, 170
Camber, 276
Cantilever retaining walls
  toe, 268
Capital gain
  short-term, 318, 325
Capital lease
  amortization, 319
Carbide tools
  new technology, 7, 344
Carbon monoxide, 338
Cash
  account, 8, 320
  need, 328
Cash
  receipts, 321
Cash flow
  after-tax, 319
  complex, 6, 117, 318, 344-345
  developing, 8, 294
  diagrams, 294-295, 345
  monthly, 319
  residential, 6
  updating, 6
Cash flow schedule, 321
Casing, 39, 165
Castellated steel beams, 279-280
Cave-ins
  precautions, 336-337
Ceiling
  joist, 192
Ceiling joists
  placement, 213, 237-238
Centrifugal pump, 152, 177
Certificate of payment, 330
Change
  process of, 12, 77, 162, 328
Change order
  dealing with, 290
  processing, 12, 27, 352
Change orders, 329-331

Changes:
  scope, 8, 329
Chimneys
  flashing, 262-263
Chords, 187, 278-279
CICE study, 344
Circuits
  breakers, 106
  short, 107
Circular curve
  radius, 36
Citation, 335
Civil drafting
  professional organizations, 328
Civil engineering
  companies, 337
Cladding, exterior wall
  stone, 260
  stucco, 197
Clamshell, 26, 64, 316-317
Clamshells, 26-27, 75
Clay(s)
  and water , 170
  black, 14
  loam, 28, 51
Claystone, 109
Cleaning
  service, 151
Cleanup, 30, 58
Clearing, 58, 336
CNC (Computer Numerical Control)
  laser, 91, 338, 355
CNC cutting tools
  coatings, 185
  reaming, 100
Collar joint, 256
Columns
  composite, 163
  spiral, 230
  tied, 238, 259
Combined shear plus tension
  welds, 283-284, 338
Commercial buildings
  details, 201-202
  elevations, 224
commercial plan groups
  civil, 328
  mechanical, 5, 185, 328-329
  structural, 5, 184-186, 213-214, 237, 268, 328-329
Commitment, 318
Common sense, 331
Communication
  electronic, 9, 352-353
  improving, 348-349
  levels of, 8
  maintaining, 352-353
  written, 6, 352-353
Communities, 6
Compact track loader, 60
Compacted cubic yard (meter), 17
Compaction
  laboratory test, 77
  vibroflotation, 88
Compaction equipment
  compaction wheel, 27, 84-85
  grid roller, 81
  pneumatic roller, 86-87, 133
  power required, 87
  sheepsfoot roller, 80-81
  smooth steel drum, 80
  tamping foot roller, 86
Competitive bidding, 327, 334
Composite beams
  shoring, 174-176
Composite piles, 164
Computer analyses
  trusses, 212, 356
Computer-aided design and drafting (CADD)
  and the Internet, 352-353
  national standards, 5
Computer-aided drafting and design (CADD)
  database, 352
Computers, in construction, 352
Concrete
  batching and mixing, 122
  buggies, 219, 238
  building codes and, 168
  cast-in-place, 163-164, 213-216, 264
  cast-in-place concrete, 163-164, 213, 264

  curb, 132
  estimating mixer production, 124
  fire resistance, 259
  footing, 163
  form liners, 120, 219
  modulus of elasticity, 239
  saws, 133, 143, 164
  slipform pavers, 123, 132-133
  steel reinforcement, 271
  transporting and handling, 125, 219
  water quality, 121
  welded wire fabric, 228-231
Concrete equipment:
  curing machines, 132
  mixers, 122-124, 132, 220-221
Concrete floors, beam-supported
  beam and girder, 216
  one-way joist, 225
Concrete joists
  steel and, 143, 213, 278
Concrete masonry, 256, 329
Concrete masonry units (C.M.U.s)
  horizontal reinforcement, 259
  lintel, 264
Concrete masonry units (CMUs)
  shapes, 80, 120, 164, 213-214, 256
Concrete, precast
  curtain walls, 120
Concrete, reinforced
  corrosion protection, 122
  hooks, 46-47, 60
  strands, 186-187
Concrete slab-on-ground
  fibrous, 13-14
Concrete slabs
  flat plate, 215-216
Conditions
  working, 12, 33, 92, 109, 174, 187, 285, 337-338, 344
Conductivity electrical
  hydraulic, 87-88, 107-108, 336
  thermal, 329
Conductors, 104
Cone crusher, 114
Connections
  simple, 107
Connectors, 106, 205
Consolidation
  process, 77, 122, 162, 221-222
Consolidation of soil
  time of, 97, 123
Constraints, 295, 349
Construction:
  company failure, 320
  equipment manager, 340
  industry divisions, 2
  industry productivity, 6, 344
  manager, 5, 21, 143, 213, 276, 290, 325, 340, 344-345
Construction:
  organization for, 8
  platform, 47, 187-190
  safety and health, 6, 46, 334
Construction:
  trends and prospects, 9
Construction documents (CD)
  stage, 113, 135, 143
Construction industry
  overview of, 142
Construction Specifications Institute, 329
Construction Specifications Institute (CSI), 329
Construction surveys
  ditch, 23
  pipeline, 40, 160
  tunnel, 176, 221, 355
Construction type
  fire and, 185, 337
Construction volumes
  mass diagram, 19
Contingency, 327
Contour lines
  finish, 187-188
  slopes, 336
  values, 18-19, 104, 144-145
Contract:
  void, 17
Contract construction
  bidding, 4, 320, 325-327, 334, 352
  termination, 329

Contract documents, 326
Contract formation:
    elements of, 213
Contract law, 325
Contractor (general/prime)
    disadvantage, 298
    excavating, 12-13, 25-27, 58-59, 337
    proposals, 5, 328
    tile, 259
Contribution, 344
Control devices, 282
Control surveys
    networks, 304
Conveyors
    earthmoving, 72-73, 90
Coordination, 5, 13, 68, 290, 327
Coping, 265, 281
Corners, 192, 256
Corrosion protection, of steel
    of reinforced, 98, 236, 273
Cost
    accounting, 312-313
    actual, 48, 140, 149, 163, 263, 315-316, 327-328, 345
    capital, 72, 312, 325-326, 344
    control procedures, 235, 321
    for bidding, 325
    freight, 72
    incurred, 313, 326
    indirect, 321, 326, 334
    maintenance, 4, 13, 31, 75, 99, 139-140, 150, 315-316, 325, 336, 353
    operating, 4, 12, 48, 65, 87, 99, 132, 150, 164-165, 312-313, 326, 336, 355
    opportunity, 319, 339
    ownership, 315-316
    subcontract, 321-322
    to complete, 4, 22, 140, 327
    up-to-date, 316
    variable, 65, 106, 351
    variance, 74
    vehicle, 75, 137-138
Cost code system, 321
Costs
    consequential, 330
    direct, 5, 315-316
Cost-type contracts, 8, 327
Counterflashing, 262
Crane
    crawler, 27, 87, 316-317, 340
    heavy lift, 43
    lifting capacity, 34
    tipping load, 41
    tower, 41, 281
Crane-shovel
    attachments, 26-27, 281
    carrier, 31
Crawler:
    crane-shovel, 26
    excavator, 26-28, 74-75, 316-317, 341
    tractor, 50-54, 87, 109, 316-317
Creosote, 185
Crew, 111, 280-281, 300, 340, 345
Crew balance chart, 348
Critical activities, 294
Critical path, 294
Critical Path Method, 294
Critical Path Method (CPM), 294
Crowding, 31
Curtain walls, glass fiber-reinforced concrete (GFRC)
    anchors, 189, 251, 262
Curtain walls, glass-aluminum
    details of, 265
Curves
    layout, 13
Customer focus
    establishing, 8
Cutting fluids
    drilling machines, 99
    effects, 185, 338
Cutting speeds (CS)
    sawing, 133
Cutting tools
    clearance, 48, 200, 345
Cutting-plane lines
    identification, 170, 186, 230, 257, 281
Cycle time, 23, 26, 49, 125, 356

D

Damages
    costs, 327, 334
Dams
    concrete dams, 125, 133, 213
Data
    analyzing, 8, 169, 312, 353
    display, 306
    formats, 298
    graphic, 291, 353
Databases, 353
Dead load, 238
Decision making
    objective, 306, 328, 349
    scientific, 291, 344-345
Decking
    plywood for, 253
    roof, 202-204, 252
Deep foundations
    caissons, 170
Deep mixing methods, 89
Deformed bars, 229
Delays, 6-7, 106, 140, 290, 328-330, 339, 344-347
Depreciation of equipment
    declining-balance method, 314
    IRS-prescribed methods, 313-314
    straight-line method, 313
Design
    lumber, 185-187, 224, 239, 336
    references, 1, 23, 76, 129, 142, 181, 212, 236, 253, 273, 331, 341, 355
    truss, 195-196, 270
Detail drawings
    sections, 276, 344
Detonators, 103
Developers, 294
Dewatering excavations, 151, 176-177
Diagonal bridging, 187
Diaphragms, 151
Diesel hammer, 165
Diesel pile hammer, 166
Differential settlement, 77
Digging face, 32-33
Dimension lumber, 184
Dimensioning systems, in drawings
    tolerances, 90, 276
Direct current, 178
Dispute resolution
    arbitration, 330
    mediation, 330
Distance measurement
    recording, 80, 321, 345
    slope, 50, 96, 170, 220
Ditching, 26, 56, 90
Dividends, 90
Documents
    contract, 5, 325, 352
    record, 330
Dome, 225
Doors
    panel, 199
Dozer
    blades, 56-57, 90
    pusher tractor, 64
Drafting machines
    track, 31, 59, 99-100, 316-317, 340
Dragline
    bucket, 27-33
    employment, 27-28
Drawbar pull, 51-52
Drawings
    floor, 199
    site, 276, 329
    symbol, 277
Dressed, 184
Dressed lumber, 184
Drift, 205
Drill presses
    cutting tools, 89
    procedures, 170, 223, 339-340
Drilled piers
    reinforcing, 120, 165
Drop hammer, 46, 164-165
Drop panels, 215
Dry lumber, 184
Dummy activity, 295
Dump truck, 72-73, 137

E

Early start schedule, 300-301, 321

Earth pressure
    lateral, 28, 164, 224, 237-238, 259, 281
Earthmoving, 1, 12-13, 26, 54, 80, 344
Earthwork
    calculations, 17
Eccentric connections
    bolted, 280-283
Effective grade, 50
Effective grain size, 177-178
Effective length, 105, 148
Effective stress method
    basic concepts, 170
Efflorescence, 271
Electrical
    conduit, 212
    plans, 4, 89, 325
Electrical design and wiring
    mechanical equipment, 338
    National Electrical Code, 5
    schematic diagram, 143
Electrical hazards
    sources of, 339-340
Electrical resistance systems
    elements, 74, 104, 173, 213, 327, 335, 344
Electricity
    frequency, 338
Electronic distance measurement (EDM)
    precise, 35, 74-75, 106, 179, 315
Electronic mail, 8, 352-353
Electronic spreadsheet, 353
Electroosmosis, 88, 177-178
Elevations
    four, 51, 98
E-mail, 8, 352-353
Emergency action plans (EAPs)
    evacuation, 335
    training, 7, 335-336
Emulsion slurry seal, 135
End mills
    shell, 164
    tapered, 26
Engineered wood, 186-187, 236, 243
English bond, 258-259
Entry, 80
Epoxy-coated reinforcing, 140
Equipment
    allocation, 330, 349
    cleaning, 26, 98-99, 136, 143, 221
    control over, 7
    depreciation, 313-320
    erection, 8, 217, 276-277, 345
    fuel, 125-127, 137, 223, 313, 339
    insurance, 7, 107, 313, 326, 334-335
    lubricants, 316, 339-340
Equipment:
    maintenance and repair, 99, 319, 340
    management programs, 352-353
    operating costs, 312-313
    optional, 326
    overhaul, 75
    owned, 331
    rent, 315, 326
Equipment:
    rental, 317-320
    rental cost, 320
    rented, 317
    return of, 326
    sale of, 313
    technical, 1, 34-35, 273, 312, 326
Equipment
    wear items, 59, 316-318
Equivalent grade, 50
Erection, 8, 162, 187, 217, 276-277, 300, 345
Error
    random, 345
Estimate
    detailed, 325
    sheet, 304
Estimating
    opportunities, 7
Event times, 295-297
Events, 295-296, 328
Excavation(s)
    open, 36, 159, 170, 339-340
    trenches, 26, 176
Excavators
    compact, 29
    loaders, 26, 63
    telescoping boom, 29

track loader, 63
wheel loader, 63
Explosives, 98
Exterior finish materials
plywood, 186-187, 224, 237
Exterior insulation and finish system (EIFS)
categories of, 139, 330, 334
Extracting, 27
Eye protection, 285, 338

F

Factor of safety
of piles, 168
Facts, 129
Failure:
construction company, 8-9, 335
formwork, 8, 216, 237-238, 336
Fall protection
systems, 106, 121, 175, 225, 326, 335-337, 356
Family, 5, 26, 187, 349
Fans, 143
Fast-track construction, 5
Federal
regulations, 41, 174-175, 287, 326-327, 334-336
Fee
Percentage, 327
Felt-tip pens
tips, 108
Field
supervision, 92
Field identification of soil, 14
Fillet welds, 283
Filter fabric, 89
Final payment, 328
Financial
objectives, 7, 321
profit margin, 7, 325
Financing
construction project, 320-321
projects, 320-321
Finish
coat, 136
grade, 55, 137, 188
finishes
level of, 121
radiation, 120
Finishing
earthwork, 77
Fire
extinguishers, 336
protection, 5, 185, 231, 260, 327, 335-338
safety programs, 335
sprinklers, 185
Fire blocking
requirement, 105, 200, 327, 338
Fire hazards
identification of, 329
Fire protection equipment and systems
construction hazards, 337
Fire-prevention strategies
housekeeping, 336
Fireproofing, 258, 355
Fire-rated
roofs, 201
Fixed
fee, 327
with guaranteed maximum cost, 327
Flat plate, 215-216
Flat slab, 215-216
Flat slabs, 214-215
Flemish bond, 258
Flexure, 235
Float
free, 121
Floating foundation, 162
Floor
openings, 199, 224, 260-262, 281, 339-340
Floor plans
traffic flow, 32
Floors
sheathing, 187
slab-on-grade, 188
Flow nets
quicksand, 172
Flow process chart, 345-347
Fluorescent light sources
Fuel handling, 339
Generators, 104
Flying forms, 226

Fog seal, 135
Footing
spread, 162
Footings
combined, 162
individual, 162
settlement of, 162
soil and, 162
steel reinforcing, 213
Forked trucks
operators, 221, 338-339
Forklift, 195-196, 345
Form liners, 120, 219
Form tie, 234
Formulas, 112, 237
Formwork
allowable stresses, 185-186, 239
for walls, 237-238
requirements for, 8, 223-224, 335
Formwork, concrete:
minimizing cost, 225
Forward pass, 295-296
Foundation failure, 162
Foundation walls
brick cavity, 259-260
crawl space, 162
Foundations
drains, 175
flexible, 261-262
floating, 162
live, 336
raft, 162
water pressure, 172
Foundations, deep
piles, 18, 88, 162-169
Framing
floors, 187
Framing plan, 195
Friction losses
compressed air, 145-155, 167
Fringe benefits, 317
Fuel consumption, 313
Fumes, 137

G

Gage blocks
applications, 40, 72, 165
Gantt charts, 291
General
liability insurance, 315
General ledger
accounts, 2, 236, 321, 334
General overhead budget
budget, 7, 335
estimate, 27, 58, 92, 108, 317, 326-327, 334
expense, 316-317, 326
Geographic information system (GIS)
arc, 170
node, 294
Geographic information systems (GIS)
and GPS, 356
history, 341, 353
trends, 9-10, 356
Global positioning system (GPS)
receivers, 355
satellites, 355
Global positioning systems (GPS)
differential, 79, 178, 355
Glued engineered wood products
glulam, 185
Glulam
structural members, 186
Goodwill, 325
Government, 7, 112, 315-316, 327-328
Grade line, 53
Grader, motor
articulated, 73, 90-91
automatic blade control, 91
Graphics programs, 352-353
Green
power, 132
Green lumber, 184
Gross profit defined
margin, 7, 325
Ground modification, 87, 162-163
Grouting
cement, 88, 179
chemical, 179
jet, 89, 178-179

slurry, 179
Guaranteed maximum cost, 327
Gunite, 221
Gunned concrete, 221
Guy derrick, 281

H

Hammers
diesel, 165-167
double-acting, 165
pile-driving, 165
single-acting, 165
soft, 59, 166
Hand and power tools
pneumatic tools, 143-144
power tools, 150
Haul, 12-13, 31, 50, 90-91, 98, 113, 140, 220, 339-340
Hauling equipment
cycle time, 23, 26, 49, 125, 356
load capacity, 41-42
Head:
static, 45, 151-152, 166
Head joints, 258
Header, 177-178, 187, 256
Health, 6, 46, 140, 170, 185, 334, 353
Heating production equipment and systems
air systems, 127, 143
boilers, 120, 281
burners, 134
fuel handling, 339
water treatment, 6
Heating, ventilating, and air-conditioning (HVAC)
protection of, 231
Heavy timber construction, 198
Heavy Timber Construction Details, 212
Heavyweight concrete, 269
Hills, 253
Historical data, 290, 313
Holiday, 326
Hollow masonry walls, 259
Hooks, 46-47, 60, 195
Horizontal drainage
fabric, 89, 231
Horizontal earth boring, 37
Horizontal jib tower crane, 45-46
Horizontal line, 21-22, 52
Horizontal milling machines
cutters, 29, 60, 101
routine maintenance, 316, 340
Horizontal reinforcement, 259
Horizontal scale, 52, 292
Horsepower, 50-51, 155, 316
Housing, 6, 151, 306, 339
Human factors, 344
Hydraulic drill, 101, 143
Hydraulic excavators, 26, 80-81
Hydraulic jumbo, 98-99
Hydrostatic pressure, 175

I

I-joists, 186
Improvement
measuring, 179
Income
net, 319-320
Income
ordinary, 313
taxable, 316
Income tax
credits, 318
different, 8, 312-314
Income tax
general overhead, 321
income, 1, 313
Income tax
marginal, 319
ordinary income, 313
personal, 8
rates, 8, 316
state, 6
Indirect costs, 326
Influence, 12, 121, 184, 221
Information
quantitative, 349
Injuries
notice, 335
Inserts, 106, 218, 281
Inspection(s)

substantial completion, 330
Insulation
    board, 187
    floor slabs, 261
Insurance
    fire, 106, 185, 315, 330, 335-336
    hazard, 185
    health, 6, 185, 333-336
    liability, 107, 313, 334
    life, 313-318, 335
    premiums, 334
    required, 6-7, 106-108, 312, 326, 334-336
    theft, 107, 315
    transportation, 6, 313
Interest
    paid, 140, 319, 327
Interest rate
    nominal, 12, 105, 139, 253, 327
    prime, 110, 135, 325-327
Interference, 72, 281, 306
Internal Revenue Service (IRS), 313
International Code Council (ICC), 5
International Organization for Standardization (ISO)
        9000:2000
    future of, 9
International Residential Code, 5, 200
Interpolating contour lines
    mathematical, 349
Inventory
    purchase, 353
Investment cost, 315
Investment credit, 315-316
IRS, 314

J
Jaw crusher, 115-117
Jet grouting, 179-180
Job cost
    reporting, 321-322, 335-336
Joints
    bed, 256
    ceiling, 195
    component, 234
    head, 226-227, 269, 283
Joist floor
    one-way, 214
Joists
    band, 187
    rim, 187
Joists. See also Beams
    bridging, 136, 187, 281
    cutting openings in, 208
    notching, 204, 281
    tail, 295
Jumbo, 98-99
Jurisdiction, 6
Just-in-time (JIT) manufacturing
    suppliers, 5, 326
    visibility, 336

K
Knee brace, 202

L
labor
    availability, 9, 321, 352-353
Labor
    jobs, 347
    leveling, 304-305, 353
    overtime, 317, 344
labor
    productivity, 9-10, 290, 339, 343-348
Labor
    scheduling, 9, 290-292, 338
    wages, 315-316
Lag screws, 199
Lagging, 175
Laminated timber, 185-186
Laminated veneer lumber, 186
Laminated veneer lumber (LVL), 186
Laser, 91, 137, 338, 355
Late start schedule, 300, 321
Lateral loads, 202, 224, 238
Lateral support
    plate girders, 278
Lathe operations
    parting, 221
Layout

tools for, 344
Leadership in Energy and Environmental Design
        (LEED)
    qualifications, 6
Lease
    present value of, 320
Leasing
    company, 312-313
Let-in braces, 192
Level
    loop, 195
    string, 100
Liability insurance, 315
Licenses, 315
Liens, 330
Lifting equipment, 26, 276
Light construction
    plank-and-beam, 198
    steel frame, 276-277
    wood frame, 192
Light controls
    transmission, 58
Lighting design
    color, and, 14, 236
Lighting equipment and systems
    light output, 338
Lightweight insulating concrete, 120
Line of action
    force and, 31
Line weights
    varying, 78
Linear programming, 349
Lines
    break, 46, 103, 336
    curved, 186
    intersecting, 20
Liquidated damages, 328
Live load, 238
Load factor, 17-18, 28, 145-146
Load growth curve, 69-70
Load-bearing walls, 188
Loader
    skid-steer, 60-61
    travel time, 63
Loads
    anticipated, 268
    ceiling joists, 193
    determining, 67, 80, 238
    hoisting, 45, 281
    intended, 43, 74, 79, 186
    miscellaneous, 278
    rafters, 187
    rated, 42, 58, 199-200
    roof trusses, 187
    wind loads, 192, 216, 248, 268
Loan
    balance, 323
    duration, 318
    present value, 319-320, 353
Local codes, 6
Logic, 295
Losses, 147-148
Lowest bid, 326
Lumber
    dressed, 184
    laminated veneer, 186
    metric sizes, 229
    moisture content, 185-187, 245
    parallel strand, 186-187
    strength and appearance, 186
Lump-sum
    agreement, 328
    price, 65, 313, 326-327
Lump-sum contract, 327

M
Macadam, 136
MACRS, 314-315
Maintenance of equipment
    preventive maintenance, 339-340, 353
    records, 181, 334-335, 352
Management problems, 349
Manual of Steel Construction, 287
Market, 1-2, 106, 313, 326, 344
Marking systems, 229
Markup, 326
Masonry
    ashlar, 265
    coping, 265

course of, 256
    glazed, 262
    grout, 258
    horizontal joint reinforcement, 260
    units, 258-259
    weep holes, 197, 259
    wythe, 259
Masonry arches, 260
Masonry construction
    construction practice, 125, 233, 268, 336
    estimating quantity, 265
Mass diagram, 19
Mat foundations, 162
Material
    prices, 326, 352
Material handler, 61-62
Materials
    cost, 110
    damaged, 65, 164, 195-196, 272
mechanical
    drawings, 199, 328-329
Mechanical equipment, 338
Mechanical stabilization, 88
Metal
    furring, 200
Metal roofing
    aluminum, 121
    cooling, 223
    copper, 105
Metamorphic rock, 96
Metric changes
    structural steel, 8, 355
Metric resources
    building codes, 6, 231
Metric system
    construction applications, 40
    economics, 313-316
Mini-excavator, 29
Minimum flexural tension steel area
    one-way slabs, 214
Minipiles, 88, 165
Mobile cranes, 26
Modified Accelerated Cost Recovery System, 314
Moldboard, 90
Morale, 7, 344
Motion and time study, 344
Motivators, 347
Movement of water through soil
    effect of soil type, 78
Mucking machine, 98
Mud capping, 106
Multistory construction, 187

N
NAHB Research Center home program
    architect, 330
National standards, 5
Net area, 267
Network
    diagram, 298-302, 321
Network diagram, 294-295, 321
Nitrates, 104
Node, 294
Noise and vibration
    receiver, 56, 96, 149
nonbearing, 192
nonstructural, 187
Normal progress curve, 292
Nuclear power, 290

O
Occupational Safety and Health Act (OSH Act)
    coverage, 335
Occupational Safety and Health Administration
        (OSHA)
    establishment of, 341
    occupational health and environmental controls,
        337
Office
    project, 7-9, 112, 287, 294-295, 352-353
    supplies, 7
Offsets, parallel of latitude
    tangent, 31
off-site, 321, 356
Oil analysis, 340
on-site, 27, 192, 236, 331, 340, 344
Open
    shop, 341

Open web steel joists
    load tables, 287
Open-web steel joists, 278-279
Operating costs, 312-313
Operations research, 349
Orange peel bucket, 36-37
Ordinate, 22
Oriented strand board, 186-187
OSHA, 6, 46, 140, 173-175, 280, 334-335
OSHA standards, 335
Overexertion, 347
Overload, 75, 128-129
Overtime, 317, 344
Overturning, 195, 268, 336
Overturning moment, 268
Owners, 4, 313, 326-327, 337
Owning and operating costs
    investment, 12, 312-313, 325, 344
    special items, 316-317

P
Panels, wood
    Parallel strand lumber (PSL), 186
Parallel bars, 232
Partial disability
    permanent, 143
Pavement management systems, 139
Payment
    down, 75, 323
    loan, 323
Payment bond, 326
Penalty, 334-335
Percussion drills, 98-99
Performance bond
    form of, 5, 52, 125, 136, 327, 353
Performance charts, 50
Performance specifications, 79, 329
Personal
    injury, 197, 334
PERT/Cost, 322
Pier
    drilled, 159, 170
    formed, 159
Pier, foundation, 170
Pile cap, 46, 167
Pile capacity, 88, 168-169
Pile driving, 165
Pile foundations, 88, 181
Piles
    efficiency of, 143
    end bearing, 163
    group, 46
    hammers, 143, 164-168
    length of, 169
    load tests, 168-169
    structural strength of, 168
Pipe bursting, 40
Pipe jacking, 37
Piping equipment and systems
    check valves, 180
    gate valve, 160
Placing concrete, 8, 72, 120, 213, 272
Planing, 139-141
Plank-and-beam construction
    limitations, 34, 63, 111, 211-212, 224, 273, 349
Plate structures
    capitals, 215
    waffle slab, 215
Platform frame, 187-190
Platform frame construction
    floor trusses, 187
Plow, 38
Plumbing
    arrangement, 1
    hangers, 192
Plumbing equipment and systems
    fire protection, 5
    sinks, 177
    swimming pools, 221
Plywood
    panels, 187
PM indicators, 340-341
Pneumatic rollers, 80-81, 136
Pneumatic tools, 143-144
Pneumatically applied concrete, 221
Pollution, 127
Positioning, 56, 99, 355-356
Powder factor, 104
Power

capability, 46, 59, 347
    position, 29, 49, 220-222, 347
Power equipment and systems
    conductors, 104
    fuses, 150
    grounding, 178
    wire sizes, 230
Power transmission and distribution, related safety
            practices
    material handling, 60
    underground lines, 337
Precast
    wall panels, 216-217, 265
Precedence, 294-295
Precedence diagrams
    finish-to-finish, 299
    finish-to-start, 298
    start-to-start, 299-300
Precipitation, 6, 96
Preferential logic, 300-301
Presentation drawings
    successful, 327
Pressure loss
    compressed air system, 149
Pressures
    hydrostatic, 56
Pressure-treated wood, 164
Pretensioning, 217
Price
    effect of, 74, 330
    escalation, 327
    unit, 74-76, 313, 325, 352-353
Primacord, 104
Prime contractor, 1, 326-327
Prime contractors, 1
Primer, 103
Process average
    describing, 6, 162
Procurement, 327
Production estimation
    drilling and blasting, 98
    ripper, 26, 58, 107-111, 316-317
Productivity
    factor, 317, 346
Professional construction manager, 5
Professional organizations, 326
Profit
    equation, 12-13, 317, 351
    estimated, 316-318, 325-327
    increasing, 98, 352-353
    potential, 325
    project management, 7, 352-353
    reasonable, 325-326
Program Evaluation and Review Technique (PERT),
            294
Progress payment, 330
Progress payments, 321-323, 328-329
Progress reports, 329
Project
    profitability, 12
Project deliver
    construction phase, 290
Project development, 4
Project duration, 294
Project management, 7, 309, 344
Project management programs, 352-353
Proposal
    submission of, 326
Pull-scraper, 76
Pump
    air-lift, 159
    reciprocating, 143
    submersible, 151
Pumping water, 143, 177
Punch list, 330
Purlins, 196, 216
Pusher tractor:
    number required, 69
    push-loading, 58
PVC, 180

Q
Quantities
    in-place, 136
Quicklime, 88-89
Quicksand, 172

R

Radial tires, 49
Radius
    of earth, 40
Raise boring, 100
Ramping down, 32
Ready-mixed concrete, 123, 223
Rebar, 213, 273
Receiver, 56, 96, 143
Receivers, GPS, 355
Recognition, 325, 335, 348-349
Refractory concrete, 120
Reinforced brick masonry, 260-261
Reinforced concrete
    stirrups, 232
Reinforced concrete masonry, 264-267
Reinforced earth, 173
Reinforcing
    diameter, 165, 229, 260
    splice, 270
Rental
    property, 316
Rental cost, 320
Rental rates, 319
Repair of equipment
    repair parts, 341, 353
Reputation
    professional, 7-9, 325-326
Request for final payment, 330
Reshoring, 228, 337
Residential, 5-6, 184, 290
Resilient flooring
    forms of, 187
Resin, 186-187
Resistance factor, 49-50
Resistance factors, 49, 105
Resisting moment, 268
Resource allocation, 297, 330
Resource leveling, 301, 353
Retainage, 321, 329-330
Retaining walls
    drainage of, 88
    reinforced earth, 173
    shape of, 101, 164
Retention
    withheld, 329-330
Return on
    assets, 315
    sales, 352-353
Rewards, 8-9
Rework, 7-8
Rigid body, 168
Rigid insulation, 188
Rimpull, 51-52
Roadway components, 90
Rock
    crushers, 113-115
    excavation production and cost, 109
    handling systems, 98
    ripping, 29, 64, 96
    tunneling, 72, 98, 179
Rock excavation, 27, 98-99, 160
Rocks
    formation, 108
Rolled shapes, 278-279
Rollers
    sheepsfoot, 80-81
    smooth wheel, 87
Rolling shear, 239
Roof
    pitch, 197
Roof trusses
    prefabricated, 7-8, 189, 260
Roof(s)
    live load, 238
Rotary drill, 99
Rough lumber, 184
Rules
    narrow, 184
Rules of thumb, 305
Runoff, 6, 278

S
Safety
    concrete formwork, 186, 223-224
    crane, 42, 151, 165-166, 195, 226, 281, 341
    factor of, 48, 111, 169, 269
    nets, 285, 337
    steel construction, 279-281
Safety and health professionals

responsibilities of, 330
Safety and health team
    employees, 174, 285, 315, 334-336
    supervisors, 72, 283, 321, 335, 345
Safety committees
    guidelines for, 341
Safety facts and fines
    personal protective equipment, 150, 285, 335-336
    unsafe working conditions, 349
Salaries, 326
Salvage value, 313-315
Sand
    piles in, 179, 271
Scaffolding, 8
Schedule
    critical path, 300
    network, 290, 321, 330, 353
    rate of progress, 290, 329
Schedules
    of payments, 312
Scheduling principles, 290
Schematic diagram, 143
Schist, 96
Schools, 201
Scientific management, 291, 345
Scrapers
    all-wheel drive, 65
    elevating, 64-65, 317
    optimum load time, 69-70
    pull, 65-68, 317
    push loading, 76
    push-pull, 64-65, 317
S-curve, 294
Section modulus, 239
sections
    full, 58, 98
Security, 317
Sedimentary rock, 96
Seismic refraction, 96-97
Seismic refraction test, 96-97
Seismic velocity, 108-109
Seismic wave velocity, 97
Seismograph, 96-97
Septic tanks, 6
Shading, 272
Shallow structural foundation
    spread footings, 162
Shear reinforcement
    design requirements, 260
Shear strength
    of cohesionless soil, 170
    of cohesive soil, 170
Shear stress
    equations, 212, 237-242
Shear stud
    economy, 240
Sheet metal
    connectors, 205
Sheet piling, 175
Shelf angles, 261
Shoring, 174-176, 236
Shovel
    digging action, 28
Shrinkage factor, 18
SI system of units
    loads in, 251
Sieve/sieving
    for coarse-grained soils, 15
Sinks, 177
Six Sigma
    lean, 91
Skid-steer loader, 60-61
Slab
    on grade, 191
Slabs
    cover requirements, 231
Sleepers, 188
Slip plane, 170
Slipform paving, 132
Slopes
    steep, 60
Slopes
    submerged, 164
Slurry grouting, 179
Slurry trench, 170
Smoke, 137
Smoking, 336
Smooth drum rollers, 80
Snow, 51, 92, 223

Social security, 317
Softwood, 184
Soil
    angle of repose, 170, 337
    foundation systems, 162-163
    nailing, 88
    preloading, 88
    stabilization, 88-89, 140, 162
Soil categories
    liquefaction, 172
Soldier piles, 175
Sorting, 119, 276
Southface Energy and Environmental Resource
        Center
    home office, 8
    library, 352
Space
    activity, 297-299
Spandrel beam, 214
Specifications
    alternates, 258, 326
    metals, 329
    projects and, 8, 92, 352
    writing, 331, 353
Spirals, 228
Splices, 270
Spoil banks, 18, 31
Spotting haul units, 75
Spreadsheet
    program, 353-354
Spreadsheets, 352-353
Sprinklers, 185
Standard Building Code, 5
Standard penetration test (SPT)
    cohesive soils and, 13
Steel
    workers, 1, 39, 98, 132, 174, 238, 285-286,
        355-356
Steel construction
    field connections, 276
    field operations, 276
    steel erection, 280, 355
Steel Joist Institute, 281
Steel, light-gauge
    advantages and disadvantages of, 142
    wall framing, 193
Steel, structural
    joists and joist girders, 287
Steels
    alloy, 276
Steep slopes, 60
Stemming, 104
Stirrup design
    notes on, 273
Stirrups, 232
Stone column, 88
Stone columns, 88, 173
Storage space, 162
Straw bale construction
    load-bearing, 188, 258
    moisture and, 124, 222
    non-load-bearing, 258
Strengths, weaknesses, opportunities, and threats
        (SWOT) analysis
    weaknesses in, 294
Stress and strain
    bearing stress, 248
Stresses
    in structural members, 216
Strike, 132, 222
Stringers, 175, 203, 238
Structural clay tile, 259
Structural connections
    welded connections, 283
Structural insulated panels (SIP)
    disadvantages of, 5, 136, 327
Structural members
    plank-and-beam framing, 198
    stresses in, 218, 239
Structural models
    exterior walls, 201, 213, 262-263
Structural steel
    advantages and disadvantages, 180
    manufacture, 1, 355
    yield strength, 229, 278-279
Subcontracts, 1, 321, 326-327
Subfloor
    particleboard, 186-187
Submersible pumps, 146, 178

Substantial completion, 330
Suction, 151
Sumps, 177, 339
Superintendent, 7
Superstructure, 27-28
Supervisors, responsibilities of
    accident prevention, 335
Surveying
    plane, 355
Swimming pools, 221

T
Tapers, cutting of
    measurement of, 58, 316
Targets, 75
Taylor, Frederick W., 347
Telecommunication systems
    control devices, 282
    transmitter, 355
Telephone, 337, 353
Temperature
    zones, 138-139
Temporary
    enclosure, 195
    light, 164, 338
Termination of the contract, 329
Terrain, 55
Third-angle projection
    planes, 96
Tiebacks, 175
Timber, 163-164, 184-187, 215, 239
Timber construction, 184-186, 253
Timber piles, 163-164
Time
    start and finish, 299
Time management
    planning and, 9, 87, 290, 320
Time studies, 345
Top plates
    triple, 115, 136
Topography, 13
Torque wrenches, 282
Total quality
    values and, 297
Tower crane, 44, 281
Tractor
    pusher, 64-65
Traffic flow, 32
Trafficability, 13, 27, 55
Training
    evaluating, 335
    inadequate, 8, 336, 344
    providing, 8, 335, 345
    quality control, 7-8
Transmitter, 355
Transportation departments, 6
Trash pump, 151-152
Travel, 27, 52-56, 80, 96-97, 125, 132, 151, 281, 337
Treads, 340
Trench shield, 176
Trenching, 26-27, 176
Trenchless excavation, 36
Trenchless technology, 36-37
Trimble, 355
Trimming, 90
Truck
    dump, 71-72, 125
Truck
    off-highway, 72
Truss:
    bridge, 204
Trusses
    depths, 216, 279
Trusses, wood
    specifying, 329
Tubing, 106, 278
Tungsten, 101
Tunneling, 39, 72, 98, 179
Turnkey construction, 4
Turn-of-nut method, 282-283
Two-way slab, 215

U
Underground construction
    work areas, 347-348
Underground hazards, 337
Unit masonry, 258
Unit weight

expressing, 50, 79
Useful life
  economic, 312-313, 344
Utilities, 6, 162, 279, 326, 337
Utility tunneling, 39

V

Vacuum dewatering, 222
Value
  schedule of, 292
Value engineering, 328
Vapor barrier, 188
Veneer walls
  air space, 197, 259
  shelf angles, 261
Vertical band saws
  applications of, 135, 213, 265
  welding, 281
Vertical milling machines
  ram, 167-168
Vertical scale, 52-53, 292
Vertical supports, 175, 228, 237-238
Vibrations
  walking, 87
Vibratory compactors, 60, 80
Vibratory hammers, 166
Vibratory replacement, 88
Vibroflotation, 88
Visibility, 336
Visualize, 305, 345
Volvo, 27, 59

W

Waferboard, 186-187
Wage
  prevailing, 316
Wages
  fringe benefits, 317
Wagon, 73, 98-99, 145, 316
Wagons, 52, 98, 317
Wall
  curtain, 179, 213
  openings in, 208, 264
Wall details
  brick veneer, 199
Walls
  barrier, 188
  glass masonry, 272
  tilt-up, 216-217
Walls, masonry bearing
  bond beams, 260
  vertical reinforcement, 264
Warping, 184
Warranty, 8, 330, 352
Water quality, 121
Water supply system, 143
Water treatment, 6
Water-reducing agents, 121-122, 223
Wave equation analysis, 169
Waves
  body, 168
Weather
  adverse, 338
Weathering steel, 277-278
Webs, 186-187, 278
Welded joints
  fillet welds, 283
Welded wire fabric, 228-231
Welding
  inspection, 283-284
Welds
  fillet, 283
  groove, 283
Wellpoint system, 177
Wetlands, 6
Wheel loader, 59-60, 98
Wheel scraper, 53-54
Wheel tractor, 30, 50
Wind loads, 192, 216, 248, 268
Windows
  frame, 216
Wire bar supports, 233
Wire rope, 336
Wire sizes, 230
Wood
  durability of, 222
  engineered, 187, 236, 243
  fire-retardant, 185

girder, 187
nailers, 143
pressure-treated, 164
sleepers, 188
Wood products, manufactured
  laminated veneer lumber (LVL), 186
  parallel strand lumber (PSL), 186
Wood shingles
  material, 188
Work
  in place, 29, 176-177, 217, 280
  in progress, 330
Work improvement, 344-345
Work sampling, 345
Workers
  availability of, 8-9, 12, 164, 351-353
  train, 132
Workers' compensation
  medical treatment, 334
World Wide Web, 8, 352
Wrenches
  torque, 281-283
WWF, 228-229
Wythe, 259

Y

Yield point, 277
Yield strength, 229, 278-279

Z

Zero-slump concrete, 133, 164
Zoning regulations, 4-6